PLOTINUS

IV

PLOTINUS

WITH AN ENGLISH TRANSLATION BY

A. H. ARMSTRONG

EMERITUS PROFESSOR OF GREEK
UNIVERSITY OF LIVERPOOL

IN SEVEN VOLUMES

IV

ENNEADS
IV. 1–9

CAMBRIDGE MASSACHUSETTS
HARVARD UNIVERSITY PRESS

LONDON
WILLIAM HEINEMANN LTD
MCMLXXXIV

American ISBN 0-674-99488-4
British ISBN 0 434 99443 X

Printed in Great Britain

CONTENTS

PREFACE

TO LOEB PLOTINUS IV–V

The text of these volumes, except in a few places, is that of the second volume of the revised *editio minor* of Henry and Schwyzer, *Plotini Opera II* Oxford Classical Texts, 1977. The editors, translator, and publishers have agreed that somewhat fuller critical notes should be appended to the Greek text than in the first three volumes of the Loeb Plotinus. These critical notes show clearly all places where the printed text departs from the manuscripts and all places where the text of these volumes differs from that of the Oxford Plotinus (H-S²): as a result of the extensive critical revision of the text of their first edition which the editors undertook in the preparation of the Oxford text, and in which the translator to a modest degree participated (hence the use of the first person plural in the notes where the changes are agreed by all), these latter are very few (26 in the Fourth Ennead, 7 in the Fifth). A number of them are corrections adopted by the editors after the publication of the Oxford Plotinus II and recorded in *Addenda et Corrigenda ad Textum et Apparatum Lectionum* in III (1982) pp. 304–325.

A word of explanation and apology is due to the reader for the long interval between the publication of the first three volumes and that of these two. The translator's work was completed (except for

vii

PREFACE

minor corrections and revisions) in 1976: but as the result of the agreement between the Oxford University Press and the Loeb Classics the volumes could not have been published with the Greek text before 1979. The subsequent delay was due to the financial stringencies which beset all academic publishing at the present time.

A. H. ARMSTRONG.

SIGLA

A = Laurentianus 87, 3.
A′ = Codicis A primus corrector.
E = Parisinus Gr. 1976.
B = Laurentianus 85, 15.
R = Vaticanus Reginensis Gr. 97.
J = Parisinus Gr. 2082.
U = Vaticanus Urbinas Gr. 62.
S = Berolinensis Gr. 375.
N = Monacensis Gr. 215.
M = Marcianus Gr. 240.
C = Monacensis Gr. 449.
V = Vindobonensis philosophicus Gr. 226.
Q = Marcianus Gr. 242.
L = Ambrosianus Gr. 667.
D = Marcianus Gr. 209.

w = AE
x = BRJ
y = USM
z = QL

Enn.^{a} = wxUC
Enn.^{b} = A^{mg}xUC

mg = in margine
ac = ante correctionem
pc = post correctionem
 * = consensus editorum sequentium cum editore nominato
ital. = cod. vel ed. Eusebii

H-S ^{1} = Henry-Schwyzer, editio maior
H-S ^{2} = Henry-Schwyzer, editio minor (= OCT)
B-T = Beutler-Theiler
Dodds = *CQ* 28 (1934) 47–53

ORDO ENNEADVM COMPARATVR
CVM ORDINE CHRONOLOGICO

Enn.	chron.	Enn.	chron.	Enn.	chron.
I 1	53	II 1	40	III 1	3
I 2	19	II 2	14	III 2	47
I 3	20	II 3	52	III 3	48
I 4	46	II 4	12	III 4	15
I 5	36	II 5	25	III 5	50
I 6	1	II 6	17	III 6	26
I 7	54	II 7	37	III 7	45
I 8	51	II 8	35	III 8	30
I 9	16	II 9	33	III 9	13

Enn.	chron.	Enn.	chron.	Enn.	chron.
IV 1	21	V 1	10	VI 1	42
IV 2	4	V 2	11	VI 2	43
IV 3	27	V 3	49	VI 3	44
IV 4	28	V 4	7	VI 4	22
IV 5	29	V 5	32	VI 5	23
IV 6	41	V 6	24	VI 6	34
IV 7	2	V 7	18	VI 7	38
IV 8	6	V 8	31	VI 8	39
IV 9	8	V 9	5	VI 9	9

ORDO CHRONOLOGICVS COMPARATVR
CVM ORDINE ENNEADVM

chron.	Enn.	chron.	Enn.	chron.	Enn.
1	I 6	19	I 2	37	II 7
2	IV 7	20	I 3	38	VI 7
3	III 1	21	IV 1	39	VI 8
4	IV 2	22	VI 4	40	II 1
5	V 9	23	VI 5	41	IV 6
6	IV 8	24	V 6	42	VI 1
7	V 4	25	II 5	43	VI 2
8	IV 9	26	III 6	44	VI 3
9	VI 9	27	IV 3	45	III 7
10	V 1	28	IV 4	46	I 4
11	V 2	29	IV 5	47	III 2
12	II 4	30	III 8	48	III 3
13	III 9	31	V 8	49	V 3
14	II 2	32	V 5	50	III 5
15	III 4	33	II 9	51	I 8
16	I 9	34	VI 6	52	II 3
17	II 6	35	II 8	53	I 1
18	V 7	36	I 5	54	I 7

PLOTINUS

ENNEAD IV

SVMMARIVM

Πλωτίνου ἐννεάδος τετάρτης

ENNEAD IV. 1 [2]–2 [1]

IV. 1 [2]. ON THE ESSENCE OF THE SOUL I

Introductory Note

THIS little work is placed first in the Fourth Ennead by most MSS, and this order is confirmed by Porphyry in his account of his edition (*Life* ch. 25, see vol. I p. 78 ff.) and by the *Pinax* (table of contents: see p. 3). Ficino and the *editio princeps*, with the later editors, however, place it second, after the little detached note (IV. 2 [1]) which here follows it. Henry and Schwyzer print it first, but continue to number it IV. 2. It seemed to me slightly less illogical to print it first and number it IV. 1, while retaining the original numbering of the printed editions in brackets.

IV. 1 [2]. (4) ΠΕΡΙ ΟΥΣΙΑΣ ΨΥΧΗΣ ΠΡΩΤΟΝ

1. Τὴν τῆς ψυχῆς οὐσίαν τίς ποτέ ἐστι ζητοῦντες
σῶμα οὐδὲν αὐτὴν δείξαντες εἶναι, οὐδ' ἐν ἀσωμάτοις αὖ ἁρμονίαν, τό τε τῆς ἐντελεχείας οὔτε
ἀληθὲς οὕτως, ὡς λέγεται, οὔτε δηλωτικὸν ὂν τοῦ
5 τί ἐστιν ἀφέντες, καὶ μὴν τῆς νοητῆς φύσεως
εἰπόντες καὶ τῆς θείας μοίρας εἶναι τάχα μὲν ἄν τι
σαφὲς εἰρηκότες εἴημεν περὶ τῆς οὐσίας αὐτῆς.
ὅμως γε μὴν προσωτέρω χωρεῖν βέλτιον· τότε
μὲν οὖν διῃροῦμεν αἰσθητῇ καὶ νοητῇ φύσει
διαστελλόμενοι, ἐν τῷ νοητῷ τὴν ψυχὴν τιθέμενοι.
10 νῦν δὲ κείσθω μὲν ἐν τῷ νοητῷ· κατ' ἄλλην δὲ
ὁδὸν τὸ προσεχὲς τῆς φύσεως αὐτῆς μεταδιώκωμεν.
λέγωμεν δὴ τὰ μὲν πρώτως εἶναι μεριστὰ καὶ τῇ
αὑτῶν φύσει σκεδαστά· ταῦτα δὲ εἶναι, ὧν οὐδὲν
μέρος ταὐτόν ἐστιν οὔτε ἄλλῳ μέρει οὔτε τῷ ὅλῳ,
τό τε μέρος αὐτῶν ἔλαττον εἶναι δεῖ τοῦ παντὸς
15 καὶ ὅλου. ταῦτα δέ ἐστι τὰ αἰσθητὰ μεγέθη καὶ
ὄγκοι, ὧν ἕκαστον ἴδιον τόπον ἔχει, καὶ οὐχ οἷόν
τε ἅμα ταὐτὸν ἐν πλείοσι τόποις εἶναι. ἡ δέ ἐστιν

---

[1] The references back are to IV. 7 (2). Chs. 1–8[3] demonstrate that the soul is not a body; ch. 8[4] that it is not a har-

8

IV. 1 [2]. ON THE ESSENCE OF
THE SOUL I

1. In our enquiry into what the soul's essential
being is, we have shown that it is not any body, and,
again, that in the class of bodiless things it is not a
harmony; we have abandoned the concept of entelechy, which is not true in the sense in which it is
stated and does not make clear what the soul is;
and certainly, when we said that the soul belongs to
the intelligible nature and the divine order, we did
perhaps manage to say something exact about its
essential being.[1] But all the same, it would really
be better to go further: for then we were dividing
and defining things by their perceptible or intelligible
nature, and putting the soul in the intelligible class.
But now, let it remain in the intelligible, but we will
follow another route in our attempt to track down the
particularity of its nature. Let us state that there
are some things which are primarily divisible and by
their very nature liable to dispersion: these are the
things no part of which is the same as either another
part or the whole, and the part of which must necessarily be less than the all and whole. These are the
perceptible sizes and masses, which each have their
own place, and it is not possible for the same one to

mony; ch. 8[5] that it is not an Aristotelian entelechy; chs. 9–12
expound Plotinus's own view as stated in the text.

ἀντιτεταγμένη ταύτῃ οὐσία, οὐδαμῇ μερισμὸν
δεχομένη, ἀμερής τε καὶ ἀμέριστος, διάστημά τε
οὐδὲν οὐδὲ δι᾽ ἐπινοίας δεχομένη, οὐ τόπου
20 δεομένη οὐδ᾽ ἔν τινι τῶν ὄντων γιγνομένη οὔτε
κατὰ μέρη οὔτε κατὰ ὅλα, οἷον πᾶσιν ὁμοῦ τοῖς
οὖσιν ἐποχουμένη, οὐχ ἵνα αὐτοῖς ἱδρυθῇ, ἀλλ᾽ ὅτι
μὴ δύναται τὰ ἄλλα ἄνευ αὐτῆς εἶναι μηδὲ θέλει,
ἀεὶ κατὰ τὰ αὐτὰ ἔχουσα οὐσία, κοινὸν ἁπάντων
25 τῶν ἐφεξῆς οἷον κέντρον ἐν κύκλῳ, ἀφ᾽ οὗ πᾶσαι
αἱ πρὸς τὴν περιφέρειαν γραμμαὶ ἐξημμέναι οὐδὲν
ἧττοι ἐῶσιν αὐτὸ ἐφ᾽ ἑαυτοῦ μένειν ἔχουσαι παρ᾽
αὐτοῦ τὴν γένεσιν καὶ τὸ εἶναι, καὶ μετέχουσι μὲν
τοῦ σημείου, καὶ ἀρχὴ τὸ ἀμερὲς αὐταῖς, προῆλθόν
γε μὴν ἐξαψάμεναι αὐτὰς ἐκεῖ. τούτου δὴ τοῦ
30 πρώτως ἀμερίστου ὄντος ἐν τοῖς νοητοῖς καὶ τοῖς
οὖσιν ἀρχηγοῦ καὶ αὖ ἐκείνου τοῦ ἐν αἰσθητοῖς
μεριστοῦ πάντη, πρὸ μὲν τοῦ αἰσθητοῦ καὶ ἐγγύς
τι τούτου καὶ ἐν τούτῳ ἄλλη ἐστὶ φύσις, μεριστὴ
μὲν οὐ πρώτως, ὥσπερ τὰ σώματα, μεριστή γε
μὴν γιγνομένη ἐν τοῖς σώμασιν· ὥστε διαιρουμένων
35 τῶν σωμάτων μερίζεσθαι μὲν καὶ τὸ ἐν αὐτοῖς
εἶδος, ὅλον γε μὴν ἐν ἑκάστῳ τῶν μερισθέντων
εἶναι πολλὰ τὸ αὐτὸ γινόμενον, ὧν ἕκαστον πάντη
ἄλλου ἀπέστη, ἅτε πάντη μεριστὸν γενόμενον· οἷα
χροιαὶ καὶ ποιότητες πᾶσαι καὶ ἑκάστη μορφή,
ἥτις δύναται ὅλη ἐν πολλοῖς ἅμα εἶναι διεστηκόσιν
40 οὐδὲν μέρος ἔχουσα πάσχον τὸ αὐτὸ τῷ ἄλλο
πάσχειν· διὸ δὴ μεριστὸν πάντη καὶ τοῦτο θετέον.

be in several places at once. But there is another
kind of being, opposed to this one, which in no way
admits division, is without parts and cannot be divided
into parts: it does not admit any extension, even in
our thought about it; it has no need of place, and
is not in any other being either part-wise or whole-
wise; it rides, so to speak, on all beings at once, not
so as to make them its basis, but because the other
things cannot exist without it and do not want to;
it is real being always in the same state, common to
all that come after it like the centre in the circle, to
which all the lines which extend to the circumference
are attached but none the less let it remain in itself,
and have from it their origin and their being, and
participate in the point, and their principle is what
is without parts; in proceeding from it they attached
themselves to that central point. There is, then,
this primarily indivisible being which dominates in
the intelligible and among real beings, and there is
also that other in the perceptible world which is
altogether divisible; and, bordering on the perceptible, and rather near it, and in it, there is another
nature which is not primarily divisible, like bodies,
but all the same does become divisible in bodies; so
that when bodies are divided, the form in them is
divided too, but is a whole in each of the divided
parts, becoming many and remaining the same, when
each of the parts is completely separated from another part, since it is completely divisible: like
colours and all qualities and every shape, which can
be at the same time in many separate things, while
having no part which is affected in the same way in
which another part is affected: and therefore this too
must be affirmed to be in every way divisible. But

πρὸς δ' αὖ ἐκείνῃ τῇ ἀμερίστῳ πάντη φύσει ἄλλη
ἑξῆς οὐσία ἀπ' ἐκείνης οὖσα, ἔχουσα μὲν τὸ
ἀμέριστον ἀπ' ἐκείνης, προόδῳ δὲ τῇ ἀπ' αὐτῆς
45 ἐπὶ τὴν ἑτέραν σπεύδουσα φύσιν εἰς μέσον ἀμφοῖν
κατέστη, τοῦ τε ἀμερίστου καὶ πρώτου καὶ τοῦ
περὶ τὰ σώματα μεριστοῦ τοῦ ἐπὶ τοῖς σώμασιν,
οὐχ ὅντινα τρόπον χρόα καὶ ποιότης πᾶσα πολλαχοῦ μέν ἐστιν ἡ αὐτὴ ἐν πολλοῖς σωμάτων ὄγκοις,
50 ἀλλ' ἔστι τὸ ἐν ἑκάστῳ ἀφεστὼς τοῦ ἑτέρου πάντη,
καθόσον καὶ ὁ ὄγκος τοῦ ὄγκου ἀπέστη· κἂν τὸ
μέγεθος δὲ ἓν ᾖ, ἀλλὰ τό γε ἐφ' ἑκάστῳ μέρει
ταὐτὸν κοινωνίαν οὐδεμίαν εἰς ὁμοπάθειαν ἔχει, ὅτι
τὸ ταὐτὸν τοῦτο ἕτερον, τὸ δ' ἕτερόν ἐστι· πάθημα
γὰρ τὸ ταὐτόν, οὐκ οὐσία ἡ αὐτή. ἣν δὲ ἐπὶ
ταύτῃ τῇ φύσει φαμὲν εἶναι τῇ ἀμερίστῳ προσ-
55 χωροῦσαν οὐσίᾳ, οὐσία τέ ἐστι καὶ ἐγγίγνεται
σώμασιν, περὶ ἃ καὶ μερίζεσθαι αὐτῇ συμβαίνει οὐ
πρότερον τοῦτο πασχούσῃ, πρὶν σώμασιν ἑαυτὴν
δοῦναι. ἐν οἷς οὖν γίγνεται σώμασι, κἂν ἐν τῷ
μεγίστῳ γίγνηται καὶ ἐπὶ πάντα διεστηκότι,
δοῦσ' ἑαυτὴν τῷ ὅλῳ οὐκ ἀφίσταται τοῦ εἶναι μία.
60 οὐχ οὕτως, ὡς τὸ σῶμα ἕν· τῷ γὰρ συνεχεῖ τὸ
σῶμα ἕν, ἕκαστον δὲ τῶν μερῶν ἄλλο, τὸ δ' ἄλλο
καὶ ἀλλαχοῦ. οὐδ' ὡς ποιότης μία. ἡ δ' ὁμοῦ
μεριστή τε καὶ ἀμέριστος φύσις, ἣν δὴ ψυχὴν
εἶναί φαμεν, οὐχ οὕτως ὡς τὸ συνεχὲς μία, μέρος
65 ἄλλο, τὸ δ' ἄλλο ἔχουσα· ἀλλὰ μεριστὴ μέν, ὅτι

again, next to that altogether indivisible nature there
is another reality following upon it and deriving from
it, having indivisibility from that other nature, which
pressing eagerly on in its progress from the one to
the other nature, established itself in the middle
between the two, the indivisible and primary and
the " divisible which is in the sphere of bodies ",
which is upon bodies: [it does] not [behave] in the
same way in which every colour and quality is the
same in many places and many bodily masses, but the
quality or colour in one mass is totally separate from
that in the other, just as much as one mass is separate
from the other; and even if the magnitude is one,
yet what is the same in each part has no community
[with any other] leading to a common experience,
because this " same " is one thing here, another
there: for what is the same is an affection, not the
same substance. But the reality which we affirm to
be immediately above this nature [of the forms in
body], and bordering on the indivisible reality, is
substance and becomes present in bodies, and it
happens to become divided in the sphere of bodies,
though it was not affected in this way before it gave
itself to bodies. In any bodies, therefore, which it
enters, even if it enters the largest of all and that
which is universally extended, by giving itself to the
whole it does not abandon its unity. It is not one
in the sense in which body is one; for body is one by
continuity, but its parts are different from each other
and in different places. And it is not one in the way
in which quality is, either. But the nature at once
divisible and indivisible which we affirm to be soul
is not one in the way in which the continuous is,
having different parts; but it is divisible in that it

ἐν πᾶσι μέρεσι τοῦ ἐν ᾧ ἔστιν, ἀμέριστος δέ, ὅτι
ὅλη ἐν πᾶσι καὶ ἐν ὁτῳοῦν αὐτοῦ ὅλη. καὶ ὁ τοῦτο
κατιδὼν τὸ μέγεθος τῆς ψυχῆς καὶ τὴν δύναμιν
αὐτῆς κατιδὼν εἴσεται, ὡς θεῖον τὸ χρῆμα αὐτῆς
καὶ θαυμαστὸν καὶ τῶν ὑπὲρ τὰ χρήματα φύσεων.
70 μέγεθος οὐκ ἔχουσα παντὶ μεγέθει σύνεστι καὶ ὡδὶ
οὖσα ὡδὶ πάλιν αὖ ἐστιν οὐκ ἄλλῳ, ἀλλὰ τῷ
αὐτῷ· ὥστε μεμερίσθαι καὶ μὴ μεμερίσθαι αὖ,
μᾶλλον δὲ μὴ μεμερίσθαι αὐτὴν μηδὲ μεμερισμένην
γεγονέναι· μένει γὰρ μεθ' ἑαυτῆς ὅλη, περὶ δὲ τὰ
σώματά ἐστι μεμερισμένη τῶν σωμάτων τῷ
75 οἰκείῳ μεριστῷ οὐ δυναμένων αὐτὴν ἀμερίστως
δέξασθαι· ὥστε εἶναι τῶν σωμάτων πάθημα τὸν
μερισμόν, οὐκ αὐτῆς.

2. Ὅτι δὲ τοιαύτην ἔδει τὴν ψυχῆς φύσιν εἶναι,
καὶ τὸ παρὰ ταύτην οὐχ οἷόν τε εἶναι ψυχὴν οὔτε
ἀμέριστον οὖσαν μόνον οὔτε μόνον μεριστήν, ἀλλ'
ἀνάγκη ἄμφω τοῦτον τὸν τρόπον εἶναι, ἐκ τῶνδε
5 δῆλον. εἴτε γὰρ οὕτως ἦν, ὡς τὰ σώματα, ἄλλο,
τὸ δὲ ἄλλο ἔχουσα μέρος, οὐκ ἂν τοῦ ἑτέρου
παθόντος τὸ ἕτερον μέρος εἰς αἴσθησιν ἦλθε τοῦ
παθόντος, ἀλλ' ἐκείνη ἂν ἡ ψυχή, οἷον ἡ περὶ τὸν
δάκτυλον, ὡς ἑτέρα καὶ ἐφ' ἑαυτῆς οὖσα ᾔσθετο
τοῦ παθήματος· πολλαί γε ὅλως ἦσαν ψυχαὶ αἱ
10 διοικοῦσαι ἕκαστον ἡμῶν· καὶ δὴ καὶ τὸ πᾶν τόδε
οὐ μία, ἀλλὰ ἄπειροι χωρὶς ἀλλήλων. τὸ γὰρ τῆς
συνεχείας, εἰ μὴ εἰς ἓν συντελοῖ, μάταιον· οὐ γὰρ
δὴ ὅπερ ἀπατῶντες ἑαυτοὺς λέγουσιν, ὡς διαδόσει

is in all the parts of that in which it is, but indivisible in that it is present in all the parts of it as a whole and in any one part as a whole. And anyone who clearly sees the greatness of the soul, and clearly sees its power, will know what a divine and wonderful thing it is and that it is one of the natures which transcend the things of this world. It has no size, but is present with every size, and is here and again there, not with a different part of itself but the same: so that it is divided and not divided, or rather it is not itself divided and has not become divided; for it remains whole with itself, but is divided in the sphere of bodies by the peculiar divisibility of bodies, since they are not able to receive it indivisibly; so that the division is an affection of bodies, not of itself.

2. The following arguments make it clear that the soul had to be a nature of this kind, and that there cannot be a soul different from this one which is neither only indivisible nor only divisible, but must be both in the way we have described. For if it was like bodies, having parts different from each other, then when one part was affected the other would not arrive at any perception of the affected part, but it would be that particular soul, the one in the region of the finger, for instance, which would perceive the affection as a soul distinct from the other and on its own: so, speaking generally, there would be many souls directing each one of us, and further-more it would not be one soul which would direct this universe, but innumerable souls separate from each other. For the talk about continuity, if this does not gather to a unity, is futile: we certainly cannot accept what [the Stoics] say, deceiving themselves,

ἐπὶ τὸ ἡγεμονοῦν ἴασιν αἱ αἰσθήσεις, παραδεκτέον.
πρῶτον μὲν γὰρ ἡγεμονοῦν ψυχῆς μέρος λέγειν
15 ἀνεξετάστως λέγεται· πῶς γὰρ καὶ μεριοῦσι καὶ
τὸ μὲν ἄλλο, τὸ δ' ἄλλο φήσουσι, τὸ δὲ ἡγεμονοῦν;
πηλίκῳ ποσῷ διαιροῦντες ἑκάτερον ἢ τίνι διαφορᾷ
ποιότητος, ἑνὸς καὶ συνεχοῦς ὄγκου ὄντος; καὶ
πότερα μόνον τὸ ἡγεμονοῦν ἢ καὶ τὰ ἄλλα μέρη
20 αἰσθήσεται; καὶ εἰ μὲν μόνον, εἰ μὲν αὐτῷ προσπέσοι τῷ ἡγεμονοῦντι, ἐν τίνι τόπῳ ἱδρυμένον τὸ
αἴσθημα αἰσθήσεται; εἰ δὲ ἄλλῳ μέρει τῆς ψυχῆς,
αἰσθάνεσθαι οὐ πεφυκὸς τόδε τὸ μέρος οὐ διαδώσει
τῷ ἡγεμονοῦντι τὸ αὑτοῦ πάθημα, οὐδ' ὅλως αἴσθησις
ἔσται. καὶ αὐτῷ δὲ τῷ ἡγεμονοῦντι εἰ προσπέσοι,
25 ἢ μέρει αὐτοῦ προσπεσεῖται καὶ αἰσθομένου τοῦδε
τὰ λοιπὰ οὐκέτι· μάταιον γάρ· ἢ πολλαὶ αἰσθήσεις
καὶ ἄπειροι ἔσονται καὶ οὐχ ὅμοιαι πᾶσαι· ἀλλ' ἡ
μέν, ὅτι πρώτως ἔπαθον ἐγώ, ἡ δ' ὅτι τὸ ἄλλης
πάθημα ᾐσθόμην· ποῦ τε ἐγένετο τὸ πάθημα,
ἀγνοήσει ἑκάστη πάρεξ τῆς πρώτης. ἢ καὶ ἕκασ-
30 τον μέρος ψυχῆς ἀπατήσεται δοξάζον, ὅπου ἔστιν,
ἐκεῖ γεγονέναι. εἰ δὲ μὴ μόνον τὸ ἡγεμονοῦν,

that the perceptions reach the ruling principle by
" transmission ".[1] For, first of all, to say that the
ruling principle is a part of the soul is speaking without critical reflection: for how will they divide the
soul, and say that one part is different from another,
and one is the ruling principle? By what amount
of quantity or difference of quality will they distin-
guish each part, when the mass is one and continuous?
And will only the ruling principle perceive, or the
other parts also? And if only the ruling principle
perceives, and the object of perception comes into
contact with the ruling principle itself, in what place
will it perceive the object of perception as situated?
But if the object comes into contact with another
part of the soul, since this part is not naturally
adapted to perceive, it will not transmit its affection
to the ruling principle, and there will be no perception at all. And if the object comes into contact
with the ruling principle itself, it will either come into
contact with a part of it, and this will perceive, but
the other parts will not any more: there would be
no point in their doing so; or there will be many,
indefinitely many, perceptions, and they will not all
be alike; but one will say " I was affected first " and
another, " I perceived another's affection "; but
they will every one of them except the first be ignorant of where the affection occurred. Or even perhaps each part of the soul will deceive itself by
supposing that the affection has occurred there where
it is. But if not only the ruling principle, but any
other part of the soul as well, is going to have per-

[1] For the Stoic doctrine see *Stoicorum Veterum Fragmenta*
II 441 and 854 and Alexander of Aphrodisias *De Anima* 41, 5
Bruns.

ἀλλὰ καὶ ὁτιοῦν μέρος αἰσθήσεται, διὰ τί τὸ μὲν
ἡγεμονοῦν ἔσται, τὸ δὲ οὔ; ἢ τί δεῖ ἐπ' ἐκεῖνο τὴν
αἴσθησιν ἀνιέναι; πῶς δὲ καὶ τὰ ἐκ πολλῶν αἰσ-
35 θήσεων, οἷον ὤτων καὶ ὀμμάτων, ἕν τι γνώσεται; εἰ
δ' αὖ πάντη ἓν ἡ ψυχὴ εἴη, οἷον ἀμέριστον πάντη
καὶ ἐφ' ἑαυτοῦ ἕν, καὶ πάντη πλήθους καὶ μερισμοῦ
ἐκφεύγοι φύσιν, οὐδὲν ὅλον, ὅ τι ἂν ψυχὴ κατα-
λάβοι, ἐψυχωμένον ἔσται· ἀλλ' οἷον περὶ κέντρον
στήσασα ἑαυτὴν ἑκάστου ἄψυχον ἂν εἴασε πάντα
40 τὸν τοῦ ζῴου ὄγκον. δεῖ ἄρα οὕτως ἕν τε καὶ
πολλὰ καὶ μεμερισμένον καὶ ἀμέριστον ψυχὴν εἶναι,
καὶ μὴ ἀπιστεῖν, ὡς ἀδύνατον τὸ αὐτὸ καὶ ἓν
πολλαχοῦ εἶναι. εἰ γὰρ τοῦτο μὴ παραδεχοίμεθα,
ἡ τὰ πάντα συνέχουσα καὶ διοικοῦσα φύσις οὐκ
ἔσται, ἥτις ὁμοῦ τε πάντα περιλαβοῦσα ἔχει καὶ
45 μετὰ φρονήσεως ἄγει, πλῆθος μὲν οὖσα, ἐπείπερ
πολλὰ τὰ ὄντα, μία δέ, ἵν' ᾖ ἓν τὸ συνέχον, τῷ
μὲν πολλῷ αὑτῆς ἑνὶ ζωὴν χορηγοῦσα τοῖς μέρεσι
πᾶσι, τῷ δὲ ἀμερίστῳ ἑνὶ φρονίμως ἄγουσα. ἐν
οἷς δὲ μὴ φρόνησις, τὸ ἓν τὸ ἡγούμενον μιμεῖται
τοῦτο. τοῦτ' ἄρα ἐστὶ τὸ θείως ᾐνιγμένον τῆς
50 ἀμερίστου καὶ ἀεὶ κατὰ τὰ αὐτὰ ἐχούσης
καὶ τῆς περὶ τὰ σώματα γιγνομένης μεριστῆς τρίτον ἐξ ἀμφοῖν συνεκεράσατο οὐσίας
εἶδος. ἔστιν οὖν ψυχὴ ἓν καὶ πολλὰ οὕτως· τὰ
δὲ ἐν τοῖς σώμασιν εἴδη πολλὰ καὶ ἕν· τὰ δὲ
55 σώματα πολλὰ μόνον· τὸ δ' ὑπέρτατον ἓν μόνον.

18

ception, why will one part be the ruling principle
and the other not? Or why is there any need for
the perception to go up to the ruling principle?
And how will it know as one the contents of many
perceptions, of eyes and ears for instance? But on
the other hand, if the soul was altogether one, in the
sense of being altogether indivisible and a self-
contained unity, and altogether escaped from multiplicity and divisibility, then nothing which soul took
hold upon would ever be ensouled as a whole: but
soul would set itself, so to speak, at the centre of each
living being and leave the whole mass of it soulless.
So then the soul must be in this way both one and
many and divided and indivisible, and we must not
disbelieve this on the ground that it is impossible for
something which is one and the same to be in many
places. For if we do not accept this, then the nature
which holds together and directs all things will not
exist, which encompassing all together holds and
directs them with wisdom; it is a multiplicity because
the beings of the universe are many, but one, that
what holds them together may be one; by its manifold oneness it dispenses life to all the parts, and by
its indivisible oneness it directs them wisely. This
is the meaning of the divinely inspired riddling saying. " He mixed a third form of being from both,
from the indivisible which is always in the same state
and that which becomes divisible in the sphere of
bodies."[1] So the soul is one and many in this way:
the forms in body are many and one; bodies are
many only; the Supreme is one only.

[1] The reference is *Timaeus* 35A1–4 (a passage repeatedly
quoted or referred to in Plotinus's works on the soul).

IV. 2 [1]. (21) ΠΕΡΙ ΟΥΣΙΑΣ ΨΥΧΗΣ ΔΕΥΤΕΡΟΝ

Ἐν τῷ κόσμῳ τῷ νοητῷ ἡ ἀληθινὴ οὐσία· νοῦς τὸ
ἄριστον αὐτοῦ· ψυχαὶ δὲ κἀκεῖ· ἐκεῖθεν γὰρ καὶ
ἐνταῦθα. κἀκεῖνος ὁ κόσμος ψυχὰς ἄνευ σωμάτων
ἔχει, οὗτος δὲ τὰς ἐν σώμασι γινομένας καὶ
5 μερισθείσας τοῖς σώμασιν. ἐκεῖ δὲ ὁμοῦ μὲν νοῦς
πᾶς καὶ οὐ διακεκριμένον οὐδὲ μεμερισμένον, ὁμοῦ
δὲ πᾶσαι ψυχαὶ ἐν αἰῶνι τῷ κόσμῳ, οὐκ ἐν διαστάσει
τοπικῇ. νοῦς μὲν οὖν ἀεὶ ἀδιάκριτος καὶ οὐ μερι-
στός, ψυχὴ δὲ ἐκεῖ ἀδιάκριτος καὶ ἀμέριστος· ἔχει
δὲ φύσιν μερίζεσθαι. καὶ γὰρ ὁ μερισμὸς αὐτῆς τὸ
10 ἀποστῆναι καὶ ἐν σώματι γενέσθαι. μεριστὴ
οὖν εἰκότως περὶ τὰ σώματα λέγεται εἶναι,
ὅτι οὕτως ἀφίσταται καὶ μεμέρισται. πῶς οὖν
καὶ ἀμέριστος; οὐ γὰρ ὅλη ἀπέστη, ἀλλ' ἔστι
τι αὐτῆς οὐκ ἐληλυθός, ὃ οὐ πέφυκε μερίζεσθαι. τὸ
οὖν ἐκ τῆς ἀμερίστου καὶ τῆς περὶ τὰ σώματα
15 μεριστῆς ταὐτὸν τῷ ἐκ τῆς ἄνω [καὶ κάτω]¹
οὔσης² καὶ τῆς ἐκεῖθεν ἐξημμένης, ῥυείσης δὲ
μέχρι τῶνδε, οἷον γραμμῆς ἐκ κέντρου. ἐλθοῦσα
δὲ ἐνθάδε τούτῳ τῳ μέρει ὁρᾷ,³ ᾧ⁴ καὶ αὐτῷ τῷ

¹ del. Bréhier.
² Enn.ᵃ: ἰούσης Enn.ᵇ, H–S¹⁻².
³ Igal: ὁρᾷ Enn.
⁴ Enn.ᵃ, H–S¹⁻²: ὡς Enn.ᵇ, Igal.

IV. 2 [1]. ON THE ESSENCE OF THE SOUL II

In the intelligible world is true being; Intellect is the best part of it; but souls are There too; for it is because they have come Thence that they are here too. That world has souls without bodies, but this world has the souls which have come to be in bodies and are divided by bodies. There the whole of Intellect is all together and not separated or divided, and all souls are together in the world which is eternity, not in spatial separation. Intellect, then, is always inseparable and indivisible, but soul is inseparable and indivisible There, but it is in its nature to be divided. For its division is departing from Intellect and coming to be in a body. It is therefore properly said to be " divisible in the sphere of bodies " because it departs and is divided in this way. Then how is it also " indivisible "? Because the whole of it did not depart, but there is something of it which did not come [down here] which is not naturally divisible. So then " from the indivisible and that which is divisible in the sphere of bodies " is equivalent to saying that soul is composed of the part which is above and that which is attached to that higher world but has flowed out as far as these parts, like a line from a centre. But when it has come here in this part, see how in this way it preserves in this very part the nature of the whole.

μέρει σῴζει τὴν φύσιν τοῦ ὅλου. οὐδὲ γὰρ ἐνταῦθα μόνον μεριστή, ἀλλὰ καὶ ἀμέριστος· τὸ γὰρ
20 μεριζόμενον αὐτῆς ἀμερίστως μερίζεται. εἰς ὅλον
γὰρ τὸ σῶμα δοῦσα αὑτὴν καὶ μὴ μερισθεῖσα τῷ
ὅλη εἰς ὅλον τῷ ἐν παντὶ εἶναι μεμέρισται.

For even here it is not only divisible, but also indivisible; for that of it which is divided is indivisibly divided. For it gives itself to the whole body and is not divided in that it gives itself whole to the whole and is divided in that it is present in every part.

ENNEAD IV. 3-5

IV. 3–5. ON DIFFICULTIES ABOUT THE SOUL

Introductory Note

THIS great work (Nos. 27–29 in the chronological order), rather oddly divided by Porphyry into two major parts (see notes on IV. 3. 32 and IV. 4. 29) with an appendix on seeing (and hearing), belongs to Plotinus's middle period. It was written soon after the treatise on omnipresence (VI. 4–5 [22–23]) and in Porphyry's chronological order immediately follows the treatise on impassibility (III. 6 [26]). In all these treatises Plotinus seems to have been particularly inclined to minimise the distinction between Intellect and Soul and to represent souls at their highest as virtually indistinguishable from intellects. In the great work which immediately follows in the chronological order (divided by Porphyry into III. 8 [30], V. 8 [31], V. 5 [32], and II. 9 [33]) the distinction between the hypostases is more strongly emphasised. The work consists of a series of very thorough discussions of what seemed to Plotinus to be the main difficulties in the Platonic doctrine of soul as he understood it. It is helpful to us (whose normal philosophical starting-point is very different) in our efforts to understand both the philosophy of Plotinus and late Greek philosophy in general to see how these difficulties arise. In the first place it is important to remember that for Plotinus, as for his Platonist and Stoic predecessors and his Neoplatonic successors, "soul" does not mean only, or primarily, human soul. The physical universe as a whole is a single ensouled living being, and its great parts, the heavenly bodies and the earth, have divine souls greatly superior in dignity and power to human ones. The problem therefore arises of the relationship of our souls to the World-Soul, and we should notice that the conclusion of the very careful discussion of this at the beginning of IV. 3 is that we are not parts or products of the World-Soul, but it and our souls and all other souls are parts of the hypostasis Soul, beings, that is, on essentially the same level. The World-Soul is our elder sister, not our mother, and we can rise as high as it and become its fellow-contemplatives and collaborators. Problems also arise and have to be carefully considered about the psychology of the universe as a whole, the heavenly bodies and the earth, about whether they have or need sense-perception and memory.

We also need to remember that for Plotinus, as for all Platonists, the presence of souls in bodies is something which raises problems and has to be accounted for. The distinctive characteristic of Platonic thinking about the soul is that its activities of pure thought, which seem to be independent of the body, are not considered in any way problematic; it is the soul's presence, activity and experience in the body and the world of the senses which Platonists find in need of explanation. Hence a large part of IV. 3 is devoted to discussing how the soul gets into the body and in what sense it can ever be said to be " in " the body. It does not seem that there is as much difference as has sometimes been maintained between Plotinus's earlier and later views on the descent of souls into bodies, though, as always with him, there are variations of emphasis in different passages. The doctrine at which he eventually arrives in IV. 8 (6) (after a very pessimistic and dualistic beginning) does not appear to be substantially different from that in this treatise or in later writings, e.g. II. 9 (33), I. 4 (46), III. 2–3 (47–8), I. 1 (53). Consistently with this Platonic attitude, Plotinus takes care in his detailed discussions of sense-perception and emotion to maintain a strict body-soul dualism and does his best to show, here as elsewhere, that body cannot really affect soul (this is particularly stressed in the immediately preceding III. 6 [26]). In the last part of the work (IV. 4. 30–end) and in the appendix (IV. 5) the doctrine, already mentioned, that the physical universe is a single living being, is used to solve two different sorts of problem: first, the characteristically late antique problem of how petitionary prayers to the stars and magic spells work; and then, in IV. 5, the problems, much discussed by both ancient and later psychologists, of how we see (and hear) and whether a medium is necessary for this sort of perception at a distance. Both are solved, to the satisfaction of Plotinus, by appealing to the sympathy which unites the parts of the universal living organism.

Readers of the parts of this work which deal with the problems about soul in body are recommended to make continual use of Dr. H. J. Blumenthal's *Plotinus' Psychology. His Doctrines of the Embodied Soul* (The Hague 1971). Reference has been made to this several times in the notes, but its general helpfulness for understanding this very difficult and complex part of Plotinus's thought cannot be sufficiently indicated by particular references.

Synopsis

IV. 3–4

The investigation of the soul is of central importance: it is an investigation of that which investigates. Let us first consider five arguments of those who consider that our souls are part of the Soul of the All (ch. 1). Detailed discussion and refutation of these arguments (chs. 2–8). The entry of soul into body: how body is made by soul's " going forth " and is contained in soul, which is present to it without being affected (ch. 9). Soul between the two universes, intelligible and sense-perceived (which are not spatially separated), making this world in the image of the other (chs. 10–11). The descent of particular souls into bodies is required by the natural order (and their highest

ON DIFFICULTIES ABOUT THE SOUL

parts remain above): it is the result of an irresistible impulse which draws them to the bodies prepared for them by Universal Soul, and so is at once free and necessary (chs. 12–13). Comparison with the story of Prometheus, Epimetheus and Pandora arbitrarily interpreted (ch. 14). Souls descend first from the intelligible world to heaven and then some of them go to earthly bodies; the reasons for their differences here below are diverse (ch. 15). Punishments, suffering, injustices are part of the universal order (ch. 16). Heaven is closer to the intelligible than earth; the distracting magic of our lower world (ch. 17). In what sense disembodied souls, or souls in heavenly bodies, are reasonable, and why they do not talk (ch. 18). The embodied soul: what Plato means by " divisible " in the sphere of bodies, and what in embodied soul remains " indivisible " (ch. 19). Neither soul as a whole nor its so-called parts are in body as a place. In what sense then can soul be said to be " in body "? Discussion of this question, on more or less Peripatetic lines but rejecting the Peripatetic solution that soul is in body as form is in matter (chs. 20–21). The analogy of light; body is in soul, not soul in body, and the different organic parts of body (brain and nervous system etc.) are illumined and activated by soul according to their capacities and needs (chs. 22–3). What happens to souls when they have left their bodies, and how sinful souls inevitably and naturally wander into the appropriate place of punishment (ch. 24). Discussion of memory (continuing to IV. 4. 12): what has memory? Certainly not eternal beings; but does it belong to soul or the composite living being (ensouled body) (ch. 25)? Sense-perception and memory; memory belongs to the soul, not the composite (ch. 26). But to which soul? The analogy of the shade of Heracles (ch. 27). It is soul's image-making power which is the seat of memory, of desires, perceptions, and the verbal expression of our thoughts (chs. 28–30). Two image-making powers are required, one for the higher and one for the lower soul (ch. 31). What memories pass from one soul to the other,

and how quickly good souls lose their memories in the higher
world; they do not even remember who they are, but are
assimilated to Intellect, grasping the whole of intelligible
reality in a single act of intuition (IV. 3. 32–IV. 4. 2).
How souls again re-actualise their potential memories
when they descend from the intelligible world to heaven
and then to the world below (chs. 3–5). Memory and the
souls in heaven (in the living, divine, heavenly bodies):
they do not exercise memory and do not need to (chs. 6–8).
The memory of " Zeus ": this divine name can be used
either for the World-Soul or for Divine Intellect as Maker
of the physical universe; neither needs memory for its
divine activity in the world (chs. 9–11). Calculation and
memory are only necessary to beings which are not yet
intelligent (ch. 12). The difference between Nature and
Intellect (chs. 13–14). Time and souls, universal and
individual (chs. 15–17). Discussion of the experience and
activities of embodied soul (continuing to ch. 29): body
is not soulless but ensouled, like warmed air (ch. 18). The
nature of pain and pleasure (ch. 19). The part played by
body and soul in desire (chs. 20–21). The psychology of
the earth: does it have perceptions (ch. 22)? Organs are
necessary for sense-perception (ch. 23). The perceptions
of the universe and its great parts (heavenly bodies and
earth), which do not need sense-organs like ours (chs. 24–7).
The part played by body and soul in passions (chs. 28–9).
Prayer, magic and the operations of the stars: difficulties
can be resolved by understanding the interaction of the
parts in the organic unity of the whole (chs. 30–39). The
magic of the universal living organism (chs. 40–5).

IV. 5

How do we see? Discussion and detailed refutation of
theories that a medium is necessary for sight (chs. 1–4).
A medium is not necessary for hearing either: both are
to be explained by the organic unity of the universe (ch. 5).
Light as incorporeal energy or activity of the luminous

body (chs. 6–7).   If there was a body outside the universe, could the universe see it, if it had an eye on its outside? No, because there would not be the organic sympathy which makes perception possible (ch. 8).

IV. 3. (27) ΠΕΡΙ ΨΥΧΗΣ ΑΠΟΡΙΩΝ ΠΡΩΤΟΝ

1. Περὶ ψυχῆς, ὅσα ἀπορήσαντας δεῖ εἰς εὐπο-
ρίαν καταστῆναι, ἢ καὶ ἐν αὐταῖς ταῖς ἀπορίαις
στάντας τοῦτο γοῦν κέρδος ἔχειν, εἰδέναι τὸ ἐν
τούτοις ἄπορον, ὀρθῶς ἂν ἔχοι τὴν πραγματείαν
5 ποιήσασθαι. περὶ τίνος γὰρ ἄν τις μᾶλλον τὸ
πολὺ λέγων καὶ σκοπούμενος εὐλόγως ἂν διατρίβοι
ἢ περὶ ταύτης; διά τε πολλὰ καὶ ἄλλα, καὶ ὅτι ἐπ'
ἄμφω τὴν γνῶσιν δίδωσιν, ὧν τε ἀρχή ἐστι καὶ ἀφ'
ὧν ἐστι. πειθοίμεθα δ' ἂν καὶ τῷ τοῦ θεοῦ παρα-
κελεύσματι αὐτοὺς γινώσκειν παρακελευομένῳ περὶ
10 τούτου τὴν ἐξέτασιν ποιούμενοι. ζητεῖν τε τὰ
ἄλλα καὶ εὑρεῖν βουλόμενοι δικαίως ἂν τὸ ζητοῦν
τί ποτ' ἐστὶ τοῦτο ζητοῖμεν, τό γε ἐραστὸν
ποθοῦντες λαβεῖν θέαμα τοῦ νοῦ.[1] ἦν γὰρ καὶ ἐν
τῷ παντὶ νῷ τὸ διττόν· ὥστε εὐλόγως ἐν τοῖς κατὰ
μέρος τὸ μὲν οὕτως μᾶλλον, τὸ δὲ οὕτω. τὰς δὲ

---

[1] θέαμα τοῦ νοῦ Dodds: θεαμάτων Enn.*, H–S¹: θέαμα
Theiler.

---

[1] It is interesting to compare the beginning of this great
treatise on the soul with the beginning of the commentary of
Alexander of Aphrodisias on Aristotle's work on the same
subject (Alexander De Anima 1–2 Bruns). Plotinus had
probably read Alexander's work and quotes the same Delphic

IV. 3. ON DIFFICULTIES ABOUT
THE SOUL I

1. It would be right to occupy ourselves with the
soul, with all the points at which we find ourselves
in difficulties about it and must arrive at a solution,
or, continuing in just these difficulties, at least gain
this advantage, that we know what the difficult
points are. For what could one more reasonably
spend time in discussing and investigating extensively
than this? There are many other reasons for doing
so, and especially that it gives us knowledge in both
directions, of the things of which the soul is the principle and those from which it is derived. And in
enquiring into this we should be obeying the command of the god who urged us to know ourselves.[1]
And, since we wish to seek and find other things,
and long to grasp the lovely vision of the intellect,
it would be proper for us to seek the real nature of
that which seeks. For in universal Intellect, too,
there was duality; so that it is reasonable that in
partial things one should be more of one kind, and

maxim. But while Alexander firmly announces that his
intention is to commend Aristotle's doctrine, Plotinus (though
remaining convinced throughout that Plato's doctrine as he
understands it is the true one) is much more independent in
tone, and even suggests that the investigation would be worth
making even if all it did was to show us what the difficulties
are. It is the difference between a philosopher and a commen-
tator.

15 ὑποδοχὰς τῶν θεῶν ὅπως, σκεπτέον. ἀλλὰ τοῦτο
μέν, ὅταν πῶς ἐν σώματι ψυχὴ γίγνεται ζητῶμεν·
νῦν δὲ πάλιν ἐπανίωμεν ἐπὶ τοὺς λέγοντας ἐκ τῆς
τοῦ παντὸς ψυχῆς καὶ τὰς ἡμετέρας εἶναι. οὐδὲ
γὰρ ἴσως ἱκανὸν φήσουσιν εἶναι τὸ φθάνειν μέχρι
20 τῶν αὐτῶν καὶ τὰς ἡμετέρας, μέχρις ὧν καὶ ἡ τοῦ
παντὸς ψυχὴ ἔρχεται, μηδὲ τὸ ὁμοίως νοερόν, καὶ
εἰ συγχωροῖεν τὸ ὁμοίως, τῷ [1] μὴ μόρια αὐτῆς
εἶναι· εἶναι γὰρ ὁμοειδῆ καὶ τὰ μέρη τοῖς ὅλοις.
παραθήσονται δὲ καὶ Πλάτωνα τοῦτο δοξάζοντα,
ὅταν πιστούμενος τὸ πᾶν ἔμψυχον εἶναι λέγῃ, ὡς
25 σῶμα μέρος ὂν τοῦ παντὸς τὸ ἡμέτερον, οὕτω καὶ
ψυχὴν τὴν ἡμετέραν μέρος τῆς τοῦ παντὸς ψυχῆς
εἶναι. καὶ τὸ συνέπεσθαι δὲ ἡμᾶς τῇ τοῦ παντὸς
περιφορᾷ καὶ λεγόμενον καὶ δεικνύμενον ἐναργῶς
εἶναι, καὶ τὰ ἤθη καὶ τὰς τύχας ἐκεῖθεν λαμβάνοντας
εἴσω τε γενομένους ἐν αὐτῷ ἐκ τοῦ περιέχοντος
30 ἡμᾶς τὴν ψυχὴν λαμβάνειν. καὶ ὅπερ ἐπὶ ἡμῶν
μέρος ἕκαστον ἡμῶν παρὰ τῆς ἡμετέρας ψυχῆς
λαμβάνει, οὕτω καὶ ἡμᾶς ἀνὰ τὸν αὐτὸν λόγον μέρη
πρὸς τὸ ὅλον ὄντας παρὰ τῆς ὅλης ψυχῆς μεταλαμβάνειν ὡς μέρη. καὶ τὸ ψυχὴ δὲ πᾶσα παντὸς
35 ἐπιμελεῖται τοῦ ἀψύχου τὸ αὐτὸ τοῦτο σημαίνειν
καὶ οὐκ ἄλλο τι ἔξωθεν ψυχῆς καταλείποντος μετὰ
τὴν τοῦ ὅλου· αὕτη γὰρ ἡ τὸ πᾶν ἄψυχον ἐν ἐπι-
μελείᾳ τιθεμένη.

2. Πρὸς δὴ ταῦτα πρῶτον ἐκεῖνο λεκτέον, ὡς
ὁμοειδῆ τιθέμενοι τῷ τῶν αὐτῶν συγχωρεῖν
ἐφάπτεσθαι, τὸ αὐτὸ γένος κοινὸν διδόντες ἔξω

_____

[1] τῷ (coniungendum cum 18 ἱκανὸν) H–S[1]: τοῦ Enn.

34

one of another. And we must consider how the gods are received into the soul. But we shall consider this when we investigate how the soul comes to be in a body; but now let us go back to those who say that our own souls, also, come from the soul of the All. For they will, perhaps, assert that it is not a sufficient argument for our souls not being parts of the Soul of the All that they too reach us far as it does, and are intellectual in the same way (even if they accept that " in the same way "), for parts [they will assert] have the same form as their wholes. And they will bring forward Plato as holding this opinion, when, to confirm that the All is ensouled, he says that, just as our own bodies are part of the All, so our souls are part of the Soul of the All. And [they will assert] that it is said and clearly shown that we follow along with the circuit of the All, and, deriving our characters and fortunes from it, and being inside the All, receive our souls from that which encompasses us. And what in us each part of us receives from our soul, in the same way we too, being on the same pattern parts in relation to the whole, receive as parts from the whole soul. And [they will say that] " all soul cares for all that is soulless " means just this, and that when Plato said it he intended not to leave anything else outside soul, beyond the Soul of the All: for this is the soul put in charge of all that is soulless.

2. The first answer which we have to make to this is the following: that, by agreeing that [the Soul of the All and individual souls] occupy themselves with the same [bodies] they admit that they have the same form, and so by this same admission give them

35

ποιοῦσι τοῦ μέρος εἶναι· ἀλλὰ μᾶλλον ἂν τὴν
5 αὐτὴν καὶ μίαν ἑκάστην πᾶσαν δικαιότερον ἂν
εἴποιεν. μίαν δὲ ποιοῦντες εἰς ἄλλο ἀναρτῶσιν, ὃ
μηκέτι τοῦδε ἢ τοῦδε ἀλλὰ οὐδενὸς ὂν αὐτὸ ἢ
κόσμου ἤ τινος ἄλλου αὐτὸ ποιεῖ, ὃ καὶ κόσμου καὶ
ὁτουοῦν ἐμψύχου. καὶ γὰρ ὀρθῶς ἔχει μὴ πᾶσαν
τὴν ψυχήν τινος εἶναι οὐσίαν γε οὖσαν, ἀλλ' εἶναι,
10 ἢ μή τινός ἐστιν ὅλως, τὰς δέ, ὅσαι τινός, γίγνεσθαί
ποτε κατὰ συμβεβηκός. ἴσως δὲ δεῖ λαβεῖν τὸ
μέρος ἐν τοῖς τοιούτοις πῶς λέγεται σαφέστερον.
τὸ μὲν δὴ ὡς σωμάτων μέρος, εἴτε ὁμοειδὲς τὸ
σῶμα, εἴτε ἀνομοειδές, ἐατέον ἐκεῖνο μόνον ἐπιση-
μηναμένους, ὡς ἐπὶ τῶν ὁμοιομερῶν ὅταν λέγηται
15 μέρος, κατὰ τὸν ὄγκον ἐστὶ τὸ μέρος, οὐ κατὰ τὸ
εἶδος, οἷον τὴν λευκότητα· οὐ γὰρ ἡ ἐν τῷ μορίῳ
τοῦ γάλακτος λευκότης μέρος ἐστὶ τῆς τοῦ παντὸς
γάλακτος λευκότητος, ἀλλὰ μορίου μέν ἐστι
λευκότης, μόριον δὲ οὐκ ἔστι λευκότητος· ἀμέγεθες
20 γὰρ ὅλως καὶ οὐ ποσὸν ἡ λευκότης. ἀλλὰ τοῦτο
μὲν οὕτως. ὅταν δ' ἐπὶ τῶν οὐ σωμάτων λέγωμεν
μέρος, ἤτοι οὕτως ὡς ἐπὶ τῶν ἀριθμῶν λέγοιμεν ἄν,
ὡς τὰ δύο τῶν δέκα· ἔστω δὲ ἐπὶ ψιλῶν μόνων τὸ
λεγόμενον· ἢ ὡς κύκλου καὶ γραμμῆς μέρος, ἢ ὡς
ἐπιστήμης μέρος τὸ θεώρημα. ἐπὶ μὲν δὴ τῶν
25 μονάδων καὶ τῶν σχημάτων ἀνάγκη ὥσπερ ἐπὶ

a common genus and exclude individual souls from being parts; on the contrary, it would be more proper for them to say that they are the same, and one, and each soul is all. But if they make it one they attach it to something else, which is no longer the soul of this or that but is not itself the soul of anything, either of the universe or of anything else, but makes that which is soul both of the universe and of anything ensouled. And it really is correct that not all of soul belongs to anything, since of course it is an essence, but there is a soul which absolutely does not belong to anything, and all those which do belong to anything become souls of things occasionally and incidentally. But perhaps we must get a clearer idea of what " part " means in things of this kind. We can leave out of account " part " as understood of bodies, whether the body is all of the same form or not, noting only this, that when one speaks of " part " in the case of bodies whose parts are alike, the " part " refers to the mass, not to the form, as for instance with whiteness; for the whiteness in the portion of milk is not a part of the whiteness of the whole milk but is the whiteness of a portion, but not a portion of whiteness; for whiteness is totally without magnitude, and not a quantity. But when we speak of " part " in things which are not bodies, we should be using it either as we do in the case of numbers, two part of ten, for instance: what we are saying is to be applied only to numbers by themselves; or as we speak of a part of a circle and a line, or as we say a theorem is part of a science. Now in the case of numerical units and geometrical figures it is necessary that, just as with bodies, the

τῶν σωμάτων ἐλαττοῦσθαί τε τὸ ὅλον τῷ εἰς τὰ
μέρη μερισμῷ, ἐλάττω τε τὰ μέρη ἕκαστα τῶν ὅλων
εἶναι· ποσὰ γὰρ ὄντα καὶ τὸ εἶναι ἐν τῷ ποσῷ ἔχοντα, οὐ τὸ αὐτοποσὸν ὄντα, μείζω καὶ ἐλάττω ἐξ
ἀνάγκης γίνεται. κατὰ δὴ ταῦτα οὐκ ἐνδέχεται
30 ἐπὶ ψυχῆς τὸ μέρος λέγεσθαι. οὔτε γὰρ ποσὸν
οὕτως, ὡς δεκάδα τὴν πᾶσαν, τὴν δὲ μονάδα εἶναι·
ἄλλα τε γὰρ πολλὰ καὶ ἄτοπα συμβήσεται, καὶ
οὐχ ἕν τι τὰ δέκα, καὶ ἑκάστη αὐτῶν τῶν μονάδων
ἢ ψυχὴ ἔσται, ἢ ἐξ ἀψύχων ἁπάντων ἡ ψυχή, καὶ ὅτι
καὶ τὸ μέρος τῆς ὅλης ψυχῆς συγκεχώρηται ὁμοειδὲς
35 εἶναι. τὸ δὲ ἐπὶ τοῦ συνεχοῦς οὐκ ἀνάγκη τὸ μέρος,
οἷον τὸ ὅλον ἐστίν, εἶναι, οἷον κύκλου ἢ τετραγώνου,
ἢ οὐ πάντα γε τὰ μόρια ὅμοια ἐφ᾽ ὧν ἔστι λαβεῖν τὸ
μέρος, οἷον ἐπὶ τῶν τριγώνων τρίγωνα, ἀλλὰ παραλ-
λάσσοντα· τὴν δὲ ψυχὴν ὁμοειδῆ τίθενται εἶναι. καὶ
40 ἐπὶ γραμμῆς δὲ τὸ μὲν μέρος ἔχει τὸ γραμμὴ εἶναι,
ἀλλὰ τῷ μεγέθει διαφέρει καὶ ἐνταῦθα. ἐπὶ δὲ
ψυχῆς ἡ διαφορὰ τῷ μεγέθει εἰ λέγοιτο τῆς μερικῆς
πρὸς τὴν ὅλην, ποσόν τι ἔσται καὶ σῶμα τὴν
διαφορὰν λαμβάνουσα καθὸ ψυχὴ παρὰ τοῦ ποσοῦ·
ἀλλὰ ὑπέκειντο πᾶσαι ὅμοιαι καὶ ὅλαι. φαίνεται δὲ
45 οὐδὲ μεριζομένη οὕτως ὡς τὰ μεγέθη, οὐδ᾽ ἂν
συγχωρήσαιεν δὲ οὐδὲ αὐτοὶ κατατέμνεσθαι τὴν
ὅλην εἰς μέρη· ἀναλώσουσι γὰρ τὴν ὅλην, καὶ ὄνομα

whole should become less by division into parts, and each of the parts should be less than the whole; for since they are quantitative and have their reality in their quantity, but are not absolute quantity, they necessarily become more and less. In this sense it is not admissible to speak of " part " when discussing soul; for it is not quantitative in a sense in which the whole could be the ten and the individual soul the unit; many other absurd consequences will follow [from this supposition] and, in particular, the ten are not one thing, and either each of the actual units will be a soul, or the soul will be entirely composed of soulless things, and, besides, it has been agreed that the part of the total soul has the same form as it. And in the case of a continuous surface it is not necessary for the part to be of the same kind as the whole, [the parts of] a circle or a square, for instance; or at any rate it is not necessary for *all* the parts to be like the whole, in the case of those figures where it is possible to take a part like the whole (as the part of a triangle can be a triangle), but they vary; but they assume that the soul is all of the same form. And in the case of a line, the part has the property of being a line, but there is a difference here too, a difference of size. But in the case of soul, if one were to say that the difference of the partial soul from the whole was one of size, then soul will be some kind of quantity, and a body, which gets its distinctive nature as soul from its quantity; but it was assumed that all souls were of like kind and wholes. But soul is obviously not divided in the way in which sizes are, and [our opponents] themselves would not agree that the whole soul is cut up into parts: if they do, they will use up the whole,

μόνον ἔσται, εἰ μὴ ἀρχή τίς ποτε ἦν πᾶσα, ὡς εἰ
οἴνου μερισθέντος εἰς πολλὰ ἕκαστον τὸ ἐν ἑκάστῳ
50 ἀμφορεῖ λέγοι⟨το⟩[1] μέρος οἴνου τοῦ ὅλου. ἆρ᾽
οὖν οὕτω μέρος ὡς θεώρημα τὸ τῆς ἐπιστήμης
λέγεται τῆς ὅλης ἐπιστήμης, αὐτῆς μὲν μενούσης
οὐδὲν ἧττον, τοῦ δὲ μερισμοῦ οἷον προφορᾶς καὶ
ἐνεργείας ἑκάστου οὔσης; ἐν δὴ τῷ τοιούτῳ ἕκαστον μὲν δυνάμει ἔχει τὴν ὅλην ἐπιστήμην, ἡ δέ ἐστιν
55 οὐδὲν ἧττον ὅλη. εἰ δὴ οὕτως ἐπὶ ψυχῆς τῆς τε
ὅλης καὶ τῶν ἄλλων, οὐκ ἂν ἡ ὅλη, ἧς τὰ τοιαῦτα
μέρη, ἔσται τινός, ἀλλὰ αὐτὴ ἀφ᾽ ἑαυτῆς· οὐ
τοίνυν οὐδὲ τοῦ κόσμου, ἀλλά τις καὶ αὕτη τῶν ἐν
μέρει. μέρη ἄρα πᾶσαι μιᾶς ὁμοειδεῖς οὖσαι.
ἀλλὰ πῶς ἡ μὲν κόσμου, αἱ [2] δὲ μερῶν τοῦ κόσμου;

3. Ἀλλ᾽ ἆρα οὕτω μέρη, ὥσπερ ἂν καὶ ἐφ᾽ ἑνὸς
ζῴου τις εἴποι τὴν ἐν τῷ δακτύλῳ [3] ψυχὴν μέρος
τῆς ἐν τῷ παντὶ ζῴῳ ὅλης; ἀλλ᾽ οὗτός γε ὁ λόγος
ἢ οὐδεμίαν ποιεῖ ψυχὴν ἔξω σώματος γίγνεσθαι, ἢ
5 πᾶσαν οὐκ ἐν σώματι, ἀλλ᾽ ἔξω τοῦ σώματος τοῦ

---

[1] Kirchhoff*: λέγοι wRJUC: λέγει B.
[2] Theiler: ἡ Enn.*
[3] R, Creuzer*: δακτυλίῳ wBJUC, H–S.

---

[1] Here and in IV. 3. 8. 43 practically all the MSS read
δακτυλίῳ, which Henry and Schwyzer wish to retain, supposing
that in these two places alone in Greek the word means
digitulus, a " fingerlet " or " toelet ". But (i) everywhere

and it will be only a name, unless it was once a kind of universal principle [but exists no longer], as if when wine has been divided into many portions, one might call each portion of wine in each jar a part of the whole wine. Well then, is it a part in the way in which a theorem that belongs to a science is said to be a part of the whole science, which continues to exist [as a whole] none the less, and its division is a kind of manifestation and activity of each individual part? In a state of affairs like this each theorem contains the whole science potentially, but the science is none the less a whole. If this is how it is with the whole soul and the others, the whole, of which the parts are parts of this kind, will not be the soul of anything, but an independent reality: so it will not even be the soul of the universe, but this too will be one of the partial souls. So all [both individual souls and the soul of the universe] will be parts of one, since they have the same form. But how then does one come to be the soul of the universe, and the others of parts of the universe?

3. But perhaps individual souls are parts in the way in which in one living thing the soul in the toe[1] might be called a part of the whole soul in all the living being? But this way of thinking about it either allows no soul to exist outside body, or makes all soul disembodied, and puts even the soul called

else in Greek δακτύλιος means a ring or something ring-shaped; (ii) there is no reason for Plotinus to use a diminutive in either passage. So it seems to me more reasonable to assume the recurrence of the same scribal mistake twice (perhaps the scribe of the archetype had some reason for thinking about rings while he was copying the early chapters of IV. 3!) than a use of a fairly common Greek word in an unprecedented sense for no good reason.

κόσμου τὴν τοῦ παντὸς λεγομένην. τοῦτο δέ σκεπ-
τέον· νῦν δὲ ὡς λέγοιτο ἂν κατὰ τὴν εἰκόνα
ἐξεταστέον. εἰ γὰρ τοῦ παντὸς παρέχει αὑτὴν
πᾶσι τοῖς ἐν μέρει ζῴοις, καὶ οὕτω μέρος ἑκάστη,
διαιρεθεῖσα μὲν οὐκ ἂν αὑτὴν ἑκάστῳ παρέχοι, ἡ
10 αὐτὴ δὲ πανταχοῦ ἔσται ἡ ὅλη, μία καὶ ἡ αὐτὴ
ἐν πολλοῖς ἅμα οὖσα. τοῦτο δὲ οὐκέτ᾽ ἂν τὴν
μὲν ὅλην, τὴν δὲ μέρος ἂν εἶναι παράσχοιτο, καὶ
μάλιστα οἷς τὸ αὐτὸ δυνάμεως πάρεστιν· ⟨εἰσὶ
γὰρ ἐν ἀμφοτέραις ἅπασαι⟩.[1] ἐπεὶ καὶ οἷς ἄλλο
ἔργον, τῷ δὲ ἄλλο, οἷον ὀφθαλμοῖς καὶ ὠσίν, οὐ
15 μόριον ἄλλο ψυχῆς ὁράσει, ἄλλο δὲ ὠσὶ λεκτέον
παρεῖναι—ἄλλων δὲ τὸ μερίζειν οὕτως—ἀλλὰ τὸ
αὐτό, κἂν ἄλλη δύναμις ἐν ἑκατέροις ἐνεργῇ
[εἰσὶ γὰρ ἐν ἀμφοτέραις ἅπασαι]·[2] τῷ δὲ τὰ
ὄργανα διάφορα εἶναι διαφόρους τὰς ἀντιλήψεις
γίνεσθαι, πάσας μέντοι εἰδῶν εἶναι εἰς [εἶδος][3]
20 πάντα δυναμένης[4] μορφοῦσθαι. δηλοῖ δὲ καὶ τὸ εἰς
ἓν ἀναγκαῖον εἶναι πάντα ἰέναι. τῶν δὲ ὀργάνων,
δι᾽ ὧν, μὴ ⟨πάντα⟩[5] πάντα δύνασθαι δέξασθαι, καὶ
τὰ μὲν παθήματα διάφορα γίνεσθαι τοῖς ὀργάνοις,
τὴν δὲ κρίσιν παρὰ τοῦ αὐτοῦ οἷον δικαστοῦ καὶ
25 τοὺς λόγους τοὺς λεγομένους καὶ τὰ πραχθέντα
κατανενοηκότος. ἀλλ᾽ ὅτι ἕν γε πανταχοῦ, εἴρηται,
καὶ ἐν τοῖς διαφόροις τῶν ἔργων. εἴ τε ὡς αἱ

---

[1] huc transpos. Theiler; ἀμφοτέραις sc. ταῖς ψυχαῖς, ἅπασαι sc. αἱ δυνάμεις.
[2] transpos. Theiler ad lin. 12–13.
[3] del. Kirchhoff*: † εἰς εἶδος πάντα δυνάμενον μορφοῦσθαι†
H–S.
[4] Theiler: δυνάμενον Enn.
[5] Beutler.

that of the All outside the body of the universe. This we must consider [later]; but now we must enquire in what sense it would be possible to speak of " part " according to this analogy. For if the soul of the All gives itself to all the partial living things, and each individual soul is a part in this sense, then if it was divided it would not give itself to each, but it will be itself everywhere, the complete soul existing simultaneously in many things as one and identical. But this would no longer allow one soul to be the whole and the other a part, especially in the case of things which have the same amount of power: for all the powers are present in both souls. For where organs, too, have different functions, eyes and ears for instance, we must not say that one part of the soul is present in sight, another in the ears— this sort of division belongs to other philosophers— but the same part, even if a different power, is active in each separate organ; but because the organs are different, different perceptions occur—though all are of forms, since the soul can take the shape of all forms (the fact that all perceived forms must go to one centre also makes this clear). And [we must say that] it belongs to the organs through which the forms go that not all of them are able to receive everything, and the affections differ according to the organs, but the judgement on them comes from one and the same principle, which is like a judge and is well informed about the words spoken and the things done. But we have already said that the soul is one thing everywhere, also in its different functions.

αἰσθήσεις, οὐκ ἔνι ἕκαστον αὐτὸν νοεῖν, ἀλλ'
ἐκείνην· εἰ δ' οἰκεία ἦν ἡ νόησις, ἐφ' ἑαυτῆς ἑκάστη. ὅταν δὲ καὶ λογικὴ ᾖ ψυχή, καὶ οὕτω λογικὴ
30 ὡς ⟨ἡ⟩[1] ὅλη λέγεται, τὸ λεγόμενον μέρος ταυτόν,
ἀλλ' οὐ μέρος ἔσται τοῦ ὅλου.

4. Τί οὖν φατέον, εἰ οὕτω μία, ὅταν τις ζητῇ τὸ
ἐντεῦθεν πρῶτον μὲν ἀπορῶν, εἰ οἷόν τε οὕτως
ἓν ἅμα ἐν πᾶσιν, ἔπειτα, ὅταν ἐν σώματι ᾖ, ἡ δὲ μὴ
ἐν σώματι; ἴσως γὰρ ἀκολουθήσει ἀεὶ ἐν σώματι
5 πᾶσαν εἶναι καὶ μάλιστα τὴν τοῦ παντός· οὐ
γὰρ ὥσπερ ἡ ἡμετέρα λέγεται καταλείπειν τὸ
σῶμα· καίτοι τινές φασι τόδε μὲν καταλείψειν, οὐ
πάντη δὲ ἔξω σώματος ἔσεσθαι. ἀλλ' εἰ πάντη
ἔξω σώματος ἔσται, πῶς ἡ μὲν καταλείψει, ἡ δὲ
οὔ, ἡ αὐτὴ οὖσα; ἐπὶ μὲν οὖν τοῦ νοῦ ἑτερότητι
10 χωριζομένου ἑαυτοῦ κατὰ μέρη ἄσχιστα[2] ἀπ'
ἀλλήλων, ὄντος[3] δὲ ὁμοῦ ἀεί—ἀμέριστος γὰρ ἂν
εἴη αὕτη ἡ οὐσία—οὐδεμία τοιαύτη ἂν ἀπορία κατέ-
χοι· ἐπὶ δὲ τῆς ψυχῆς τῆς λεγομένης μεριστῆς
εἶναι κατὰ σώματα τοῦτο τὸ ἕν τι εἶναι πάσας
πολλὰς ἂν ἔχοι ἀπορίας· εἰ μή τις τὸ μὲν ἓν
15 στήσειεν ἐφ' ἑαυτοῦ μὴ πῖπτον εἰς σῶμα, εἶτ' ἐξ
ἐκείνου τὰς πάσας, τήν τε τοῦ ὅλου καὶ τὰς ἄλλας,
μέχρι τινὸς οἷον συνούσας ⟨ἀλλήλαις⟩[4] καὶ μίαν
τῷ μηδενός τινος γίνεσθαι, τοῖς δὲ πέρασιν αὐτῶν
ἐξηρτημένας [καὶ συνούσας ἀλλήλαις][5] πρὸς τὸ

---

[1] Theiler.
[2] Theiler: μάλιστα (vel ἕκαστα C) Enn.
[3] Theiler: ὄντων Enn.
[4] Harder.
[5] del. Harder.

And if our souls were like sense-perceptions, it is not possible for each one of us to think himself, but the soul of the All [would have to do the thinking]; but if our thinking was our own, each soul would be independent. But since the soul is also rational, and rational in the sense in which the universal soul is called rational, that which is called a part will be the same as the whole, not a part of the whole.

4. What then is to be said, if the soul is one in this way, when someone enquires into the consequences, and raises the first difficulty, whether this sort of simultaneous unity in all things is really possible, and the next, if it is possible when some soul is in body, and some not in body? For perhaps it will follow that all soul is always in body, and especially the soul of the All: for it is not said to leave the body, as ours is; and yet some people do say that ours will leave this particular body, but will not be altogether outside body. But if it is going to be altogether outside body, how will one soul leave the body and the other not, when it is the same soul [in both]? Now in the case of Intellect, which separates itself by differentiation into parts which are not cut off from each other, but is all together for ever—for this reality is surely undivided—no difficulty of this kind can arise; but in the case of the soul which is said to be divisible in relation to bodies, this assertion that all souls are one thing has many difficulties; unless of course one made the one stand by itself without falling into body, and then said that all the souls, the Soul of the All and the others, came from that one, living together with each other, so to speak, down to a certain level and being one soul by belonging to no particular thing; and that, being

20 ἄνω ὡδὶ καὶ ὡδὶ ἐπιβάλλειν, οἷον φωτὸς ἤδη πρὸς
τῇ γῇ μεριζομένου κατ' οἴκους καὶ οὐ μεμερισμέ-
νου, ἀλλ' ὄντος ἑνὸς οὐδὲν ἧττον. καὶ τὴν μὲν τοῦ
παντὸς ἀεὶ ὑπερέχειν τῷ μηδὲ εἶναι αὐτῇ τὸ κατελθεῖν μηδὲ τῷ ¹ κάτω μηδὲ ἐπιστροφὴν τῶν ² τῇδε,
τὰς δ' ἡμετέρας τῷ τε εἶναι ἀφωρισμένον αὐταῖς τὸ
25 μέρος ἐν τῷδε καὶ τῇ ἐπιστροφῇ τοῦ προσδεομένου
φροντίσεως, τῆς μὲν οὖν ἐοικυίας τῇ ἐν φυτῷ
μεγάλῳ ψυχῇ, ἣ ἀπόνως τὸ φυτὸν καὶ ἀψόφως
διοικεῖ, τοῦ κατωτάτω τῆς ψυχῆς τοῦ παντός, τοῦ
δὲ ἡμῶν κάτω, οἷον εἰ εὐλαὶ ἐν σαπέντι μέρει τοῦ
30 φυτοῦ γίγνοιντο· οὕτω γὰρ τὸ σῶμα τὸ ἔμψυχον ἐν
τῷ παντί. τῆς δὲ ἄλλης ψυχῆς τῆς ὁμοειδοῦς τῷ ἄνω
τῆς ὅλης, οἷον εἴ τις γεωργὸς ἐν φροντίδι τῶν ἐν
τῷ φυτῷ εὐλῶν γίνοιτο καὶ ταῖς μερίμναις πρὸς τῷ
φυτῷ γίγνοιτο, ἢ εἴ τις ὑγιαίνοντα μὲν καὶ μετὰ
τῶν ἄλλων τῶν ὑγιαινόντων ὄντα πρὸς ἐκείνοις
35 εἶναι λέγοι, πρὸς οἷς ἐστιν ἢ πράττων ἢ θεωρίαις
ἑαυτὸν παρέχων, νοσήσαντος δὲ καὶ πρὸς ταῖς τοῦ
σώματος θεραπείαις ὄντος πρὸς τῷ σώματι εἶναι
καὶ τοῦ σώματος γεγονέναι.

5. Ἀλλὰ πῶς ἔτι ἡ μὲν σή, ἡ δὲ τοῦδε, ἡ δὲ ἄλλου
ἔσται; ἆρ' οὖν τοῦδε μὲν κατὰ τὸ κάτω, οὐ τοῦδε δέ,
ἀλλ' ἐκείνου κατὰ τὸ ἄνω; ἀλλ' οὕτω γε Σωκράτης
μὲν ἔσται ὅταν ἐν σώματι καὶ ἡ Σωκράτους ψυχή·

---

¹ Harder, B–T: τὸ Enn.*
² suspic. H–S¹, scr. B–T: τὰ Enn.

fastened [to the one] by their edges on their upper side, they strike down this way and that, like the light which, just when it reaches the earth, divides itself among houses and is not divided, but is one none the less.[1] And the Soul of the All would always remain transcendent because it would have nothing to do with coming down, even with its lower part, nor with a turning to the things here below, but our souls would come down because they would have their part marked off for them in this sphere, and by the turning to them of that which needs their care. The Soul of the All (that is, its lowest part) would be like the soul in a great growing plant, which directs the plant without effort or noise; our lower part would be as if there were maggots in a rotten part of the plant—for that is what the ensouled body is like in the All. The rest of our soul, which is of the same nature as the higher parts of universal soul, would be like a gardener concerned about the maggots in the plant and anxiously caring for it. Or it is as one might speak of a healthy man living with other healthy men as being at the service of his neighbours either in his action or his contemplation; and of a sick man, concerned with the care of his body, as being at the service of his body and belonging to it.

5. But how will there still be one particular soul which is yours, one which is the soul of this particular man, and one which is another's? Are they the souls of particular individuals in the lower order, but belong in the higher order to that higher unity? But this will mean that Socrates, and the soul of Socrates, will exist as long as he is in the body; but

[1] For this image cp. Marcus Aurelius XII. 30.

5 ἀπολεῖται δέ, ὅταν μάλιστα γένηται ἐν τῷ ἀρίστῳ.
ἢ ἀπολεῖται οὐδὲν τῶν ὄντων· ἐπεὶ κἀκεῖ οἱ νόες
οὐκ ἀπολοῦνται, ὅτι μή εἰσι σωματικῶς μεμερισ-
μένοι, εἰς ἕν, ἀλλὰ μένει ἕκαστον ἐν ἑτερότητι
ἔχον τὸ αὐτὸ ὅ ἐστιν εἶναι. οὕτω τοίνυν καὶ ψυχαὶ
10 ἐφεξῆς καθ᾽ ἕκαστον νοῦν ἐξηρτημέναι, λόγοι νῶν
οὖσαι καὶ ἐξειλιγμέναι μᾶλλον ἢ ἐκεῖνοι, οἷον πολὺ
ἐξ ὀλίγου γενόμεναι, συναφεῖς τῷ ὀλίγῳ οὖσαι
ἀμερεστέρῳ ἐκείνων ἑκάστῳ, μερίζεσθαι ἤδη θελή-
σασαι καὶ οὐ δυνάμεναι εἰς πᾶν μερισμοῦ ἰέναι, τὸ
ταὐτὸν καὶ ἕτερον σῴζουσαι, μένει τε ἑκάστη ἓν καὶ
15 ὁμοῦ ἓν πᾶσαι. εἴρηται δὴ κεφάλαιον τοῦ λόγου, ὅτι
ἐκ μιᾶς, καὶ αἱ ἐκ μιᾶς πολλαὶ κατὰ τὰ αὐτὰ τῷ νῷ,
[κατὰ τὰ αὐτὰ]¹ μερισθεῖσαι καὶ οὐ μερισθεῖσαι,
καὶ λόγος εἷς τοῦ νοῦ ἡ μένουσα, καὶ ἀπ᾽ αὐτῆς
λόγοι μερικοὶ καὶ ἄυλοι, ὥσπερ ἐκεῖ.

6. Διὰ τί δὲ ἡ μὲν τοῦ παντὸς ψυχὴ ὁμοειδὴς
οὖσα πεποίηκε κόσμον, ἡ δὲ ἑκάστου οὔ, ἔχουσα καὶ
αὐτὴ πάντα ἐν ἑαυτῇ; τὸ γὰρ δύνασθαι ἐν πολλοῖς

¹ del. Kirchhoff.

he will cease to be precisely when he attains to the very best. Now no real being ever ceases to be; since the Intellects There too are not dissolved into a unity because they are not corporeally divided, but each remains distinct in otherness, having the same essential being. So too it is with souls, which depend in order on each several intellect, and are expressions of intellects, further unfolded than they are, having passed, we may say, from brevity to multiplicity.[1] They are linked to the brevity of intellect by that in each of them which is least divided. They have already willed to be divided but cannot reach complete division; they keep identity and difference; each soul remains one, and all are one together. So we have given the sum of the discussion, that the souls spring from one, and the souls springing from one are many in the same way as Intellect, divided and not divided; and the soul which abides is a single expression of Intellect, and from it spring partial expressions which are also immaterial, just as in the world of Intellect.

6. But why has the Soul of the All, which has the same form as ours, made the universe, but the soul of each individual has not, though it too has all things in itself? (We have explained that it can

---

[1] For the belief that there are Forms or Ideas of individuals (at least of individual men), which is probably, but not quite certainly, asserted here, cp. V. 7. It also seems to be implied in IV. 3. 12, 1–5. For a careful examination of all the evidence about Forms of individuals in Plotinus see H. J. Blumenthal, " Did Plotinus believe in Ideas of Individuals? " in *Phronesis* 11 (1966), 61–80; A. H. Armstrong, " Form, Individual and Person in Plotinus "; in *Dionysius* 1 (1977), 49–68 (=A. H. Armstrong *Plotinian and Christian Studies* (London 1979), No. XX.

γίνεσθαι ἅμα καὶ εἶναι εἴρηται. νῦν δὲ λεκτέον—
5 τάχα γὰρ καὶ πῶς ταυτὸν ἐν ἄλλῳ καὶ ἄλλῳ τὸ μὲν
τοδί, τὸ δὲ τοδὶ ποιεῖ ἢ πάσχει ἢ ἄμφω, γνωσθήσε-
ται· ἢ καθ’ αὑτό γε τοῦτο ἐπισκεπτέον—πῶς οὖν
καὶ διὰ τί κόσμον πεποίηκεν, αἱ δὲ μέρος τι κόσμου
διοικοῦσιν. ἢ θαυμαστὸν οὐδὲν τοὺς τὴν αὐτὴν
ἐπιστήμην ἔχοντας τοὺς μὲν πλειόνων, τοὺς δὲ
10 ἐλαττόνων ἄρχειν. ἀλλὰ διὰ τί, εἰπεῖν ἂν ἔχοι τις.
ἀλλ’ ἔστιν, εἴποι τις ἄν, καὶ ψυχῶν διαφορά, ἢ
μᾶλλον, καθὸ ἡ μὲν οὐκ ἀπέστη τῆς ὅλης, ἀλλ’ ἔσχεν
ἐκεῖ οὖσα περὶ αὑτὴν τὸ σῶμα, αἱ δὲ ἤδη ὄντος οἷον
ἀδελφῆς ψυχῆς ἀρχούσης μοίρας διέλαχον, οἷον
15 προπαρασκευασάσης ταύτης αὐταῖς οἰκήσεις. ἔστι
δὲ καὶ τὴν μὲν πρὸς τὸν ὅλον νοῦν ἰδεῖν, τὰς δὲ
μᾶλλον πρὸς τοὺς αὑτῶν τοὺς ἐν μέρει. τάχα δ’ ἂν
καὶ αὗται δύναιντο ποιεῖν, τῆς δὲ ποιησάσης οὐκέτι
οἷόν τε καὶ αὐταῖς, πρώτης ἐκείνης ἀρξάσης. τὸ δ’
αὐτὸ ἄν τις ἠπόρησε, καὶ εἰ ἡτισοῦν καὶ ἄλλη πρώτη
20 κατεῖχε. βέλτιον δὲ λέγειν τῷ ἐξηρτῆσθαι μᾶλλον
τῶν ἄνω· τῶν γὰρ ἐκεῖ νενευκότων ἡ δύναμις μείζων.
σῴζουσαι γὰρ αὐτὰς ἐπ’ ἀσφαλοῦς ἐκ τοῦ ῥᾴστου
ποιοῦσι· δυνάμεως γὰρ μείζονος μὴ πάσχειν ἐν οἷς
ποιεῖ· ἡ δὲ δύναμις ἐκ τοῦ ἄνω μένειν. μένουσα

come to be and [continue to] exist in many things at once.) But now we must state—perhaps we shall also come to know how the same thing, when it is now in one body and now in another, does now this and now that, or is affected in this or that way, or both: this however requires a special discussion to itself—how then and why the Soul of the All has made the universe, but the particular souls direct [each] a part of it. There is of course nothing remarkable in some of those who have the same knowledge being in control of more, and some of less. But one could ask the reason why. But there is, one might answer, a difference between souls, and all the more in that the Soul of the All has not separated itself from soul as a whole but remained there and put on the body, but the individual souls, since body exists already, received their allotted parts when their sister soul, as we may say, was already ruling, as if it had already prepared their dwellings for them. There is a difference too, in that the soul of the All looks towards Intellect as a whole, but the individual souls rather to their own partial intellects. But perhaps these too would have been able to make [a world], but as the soul of the All had done so already they were unable to do so as well, since it had begun first. One could raise the same difficulty just as well if any other soul had taken the first place. But it is better to say [that the soul of the All has made the world] because it was more closely dependent on the beings above it: the beings which incline that way have greater power. For they keep themselves in a place of safety, and so make with the greatest ease; for it is a mark of greater power not to be affected in what it makes;

25 οὖν ἐν αὐτῇ ποιεῖ προσιόντων, αἱ δὲ αὐταὶ προσ-
ῆλθον. ἀπέστησαν οὖν εἰς βάθος. ἢ πολὺ αὐτῶν
καθελκυσθὲν συνεφειλκύσατο καὶ αὐτὰς ταῖς γνώ-
μαις εἰς τὸ κάτω εἶναι. τὸ γὰρ δευτέρας καὶ
τρίτας τῷ ἐγγύθεν καὶ τῷ πορρώτερον ὑπονοητέον
εἰρῆσθαι, ὥσπερ καὶ παρ᾽ ἡμῖν οὐχ ὁμοίως πάσαις
30 ψυχαῖς ὑπάρχει τὸ¹ πρὸς τὰ ἐκεῖ, ἀλλ᾽ οἱ μὲν
ἑνοῦντο ἄν, οἱ δὲ βάλλοιεν ἂν ἐγγὺς ἐφιέμενοι, οἷς
δὲ ἧττον ἂν ἔχοι τοῦτο, καθὸ ταῖς δυνάμεσιν οὐ
ταῖς αὐταῖς ἐνεργοῦσιν, ἀλλ᾽ οἱ μὲν τῇ πρώτῃ, οἱ
δὲ τῇ μετ᾽ ἐκείνην, οἱ δὲ τῇ τρίτῃ, ἁπάντων τὰς
πάσας ἐχόντων.

7. Ταῦτα μὲν οὖν ταύτῃ. ἀλλὰ τὸ ἐν Φιλήβῳ
λεχθὲν παρέχον ὑπόνοιαν μοίρας τῆς τοῦ παντὸς τὰς
ἄλλας εἶναι; βούλεται δὲ ὁ λόγος οὐ τοῦτο, ὅ τις
οἴεται, ἀλλ᾽ ὅπερ ἦν χρήσιμον αὐτῷ τότε, καὶ τὸν
5 οὐρανὸν ἔμψυχον εἶναι. τοῦτο οὖν πιστοῦται
λέγων, ὡς ἄτοπον τὸν οὐρανὸν ἄψυχον λέγειν
ἡμῶν, οἳ μέρος σώματος ἔχομεν τοῦ παντός, ψυχὴν
ἐχόντων. πῶς γὰρ ἂν τὸ μέρος ἔσχεν ἀψύχου τοῦ
παντὸς ὄντος; δῆλον δὲ μάλιστα τὸ τῆς γνώμης
αὐτοῦ ἐν Τιμαίῳ ποιεῖ, οὗ γενομένης τῆς ψυχῆς
10 τοῦ παντὸς ὕστερον τὰς ἄλλας ποιεῖ ἐκ τοῦ αὐτοῦ
μιγνύων κρατῆρος, ἀφ᾽ οὗ καὶ ἡ τῶν ὅλων,
ὁμοειδῆ ποιῶν καὶ τὴν ἄλλην, τὴν δὲ διαφορὰν
δευτέροις καὶ τρίτοις διδούς. τὸ δὲ ἐν τῷ Φαίδρῳ

¹ Harder B–T: τὰ Enn.*

---

¹ See *Timaeus* 41D7.
² Cp. *Philebus* 30A–B, where, as Plotinus suggests, Plato is
really mainly concerned to argue that the universe must have
a soul just as we have.

and power comes from abiding above. The Soul of
the All, then, abiding in itself makes, and the things
which it makes come to it, but the particular souls
themselves go to the things. So they have departed
to the depths; or rather, a great part of them has
been dragged down and has dragged them with it
by their thoughts to the lower existence. For we
must understand that souls were called " second "
and " third " [1] according to whether they are nearer
to or farther from [the higher world]; just as among
us too not all souls have the same relationship to the
realities There, but some men may unify themselves,
others nearly reach this point in their striving, and
others attain it in a lesser degree, in so far as they
act by powers which are not the same, but some by
the first, others by that which comes after it, others
by the third, though all of them have all.

7. So much for that. But what about the passage
in the *Philebus* which suggests that the other souls
are parts of the soul of the All [2]? But this is not,
as someone thinks, the intention of what is said, but
what suited Plato's purpose at that stage in the
argument, that the universe is ensouled. He establishes that by saying that it is absurd to say that the
universe is soulless, when we, who possess a part of
the body of the All, have souls. For how could the
part have a soul when the All was soulless? He
makes his own thought especially clear in the *Timaeus*,
where [the Demiurge], when the soul of the All has
come into existence, makes the other souls, mixing
them from the same mixing-bowl from which he
made the soul of the whole, making the other kind
of soul of the same form [as the soul of the All] but
giving it a difference by using second and third class

PLOTINUS: ENNEAD IV. 3.

"ψυχὴ πᾶσα παντὸς ἐπιμελεῖται τοῦ ἀψύχου"; τί
γὰρ ἂν εἴη, ὃ σώματος τὴν φύσιν διοικεῖ καὶ ἢ
15 πλάττει ἢ τάττει ἢ ποιεῖ ἢ ψυχή; καὶ οὐχ ἡ μὲν
πέφυκε τοῦτο δύνασθαι, ἡ δὲ οὔ. ἡ μὲν οὖν
τελεία, φησίν, ἡ τοῦ παντὸς μετεωροποροῦσα
οὐ δῦσα, ἀλλ᾽ οἷον ἐποχουμένη, εἰς τὸν κόσμον
ποιεῖ καὶ ἥτις ἂν τελεία ᾖ, οὕτω διοικεῖ. "ἡ δὲ
20 πτερορρυήσασα" εἰπὼν ἄλλην ταύτην παρ᾽
ἐκείνην ποιεῖ. τὸ δὲ συνέπεσθαι τῇ τοῦ παντὸς
περιφορᾷ καὶ ἤδη ἐκεῖθεν κομίζεσθαι καὶ πάσχειν
παρ᾽ αὐτοῦ οὐδὲν ἂν εἴη σημεῖον τοῦτο τοῦ μέρη
τὰς ἡμετέρας εἶναι. ἱκανὴ γὰρ ψυχὴ καὶ παρὰ
φύσεως τόπων πολλὰ ἀπομάττεσθαι καὶ ὑδάτων
25 καὶ ἀέρος· καὶ πόλεων διάφοροι [1] οἰκήσεις καὶ τῶν
σωμάτων αἱ κράσεις. καί τι ἔφαμεν ἔχειν ἐν τῷ
παντὶ ὄντες τῆς τοῦ ὅλου ψυχῆς, καὶ παρὰ τῆς
περιφορᾶς συνεχωροῦμεν τὸ πάσχειν, ἀλλ᾽
ἀντετίθεμεν ἄλλην ψυχὴν πρὸς ταῦτα καὶ μάλιστα
τῇ ἀντιστάσει δεικνυμένην ἄλλην. τὸ δ᾽ ὅτι εἴσω
30 γεννώμεθα ἐν αὐτῷ, καὶ ἐπὶ τῶν μητρῶν [2] φαμεν
ἑτέραν εἶναι οὐ τὴν τῆς μητρὸς τὴν ἐπεισιοῦσαν.

[1] Theiler: διαφόρων Enn.*
[2] Harder B–T (in alvo materna Ficinus): μητέρων Enn.*

---

[1] Again a reference to *Timaeus* 41D7.
[2] The reference is to *Phaedrus* 246B6. He then goes on to
consider Plato's distinction, which follows immediately, between the perfect soul which is " winged " and " walks on
high " and the soul which " loses its feathers " and falls into
a human body, whose fall and subsequent fate is described in
the rest of the great myth.
[3] Cp. *Timaeus* 90C8–D1. For a fuller statement of Plotinus's own position on the determination of the characters of

ingredients.[1] And what about the passage in the *Phaedrus* " All soul cares for all that is soulless " [2]? What could it be, then, which directs the nature of body, and either shapes it or sets it in order or makes it, except soul? And it is not the case that one soul is naturally able to do this, but the other is not. Plato says, then, that the " perfect " soul, the soul of the All, " walks on high ", and does not come down, but, as we may say, rides upon the universe and works in it; and this is the manner of direction of every soul which is perfect. But when he speaks of the " soul which moults " he makes this another, distinct from the perfect one. But as for our following round the circuit of the All,[3] and deriving our characters from it and being affected by it, this would be no sort of indication that our souls are parts [of the soul of the All]. For the soul is capable of taking many impressions from the nature of places and waters and air; and the situations of cities and the temperaments of bodies are different. And we stated that, since we are in the All, we have something from the soul of the whole, and we agreed that we were affected by the circuit of the universe; but we opposed another soul to this, and one which shows itself other especially by its opposition. As for the fact that we are begotten inside the universe, in the womb too we say that the soul which comes into the child is another one, not that of the mother.

our lower selves, the composites of body and soul, by the physical universe of which they are parts, see II. 3. 9–12. Plotinus was always ready to admit that most of what ordinary people think of as distinctive traits of character and personality are due to physical conditions, heredity and environment.

8. Ταῦτα μὲν οὖν οὕτως ἂν ἔχοι λύσεως καὶ τοῦ
τῆς συμπαθείας μὴ ἐμποδίζοντος τὸν λόγον· ἐκ γὰρ
τῆς αὐτῆς πᾶσαι οὖσαι, ἐξ ἧς καὶ ἡ τοῦ ὅλου,
συμπαθεῖς. καὶ γὰρ εἴρηται, ὅτι καὶ μία καὶ
5 πολλαί. περὶ δὲ τοῦ μέρους πρὸς τὸ ὅλον τῆς
διαφορᾶς ὅπως, εἴρηται. εἴρηται δὲ καὶ ὅλως περὶ
διαφορᾶς ψυχῆς καὶ νῦν συντόμως λεγέσθω, ὅτι καὶ
παρὰ τὰ σώματα μὲν ἂν γίγνοιτο διαφέρειν καὶ ἐν
τοῖς ἤθεσι μάλιστα καὶ ἐν τοῖς τῆς διανοίας ἔργοις
καὶ ἐκ τῶν προβεβιωμένων βίων· κατὰ γὰρ τοὺς
10 προβεβιωμένους φησὶ τὰς αἱρέσεις ταῖς ψυχαῖς
γίγνεσθαι. εἰ δέ τις φύσιν ψυχῆς ὅλως λαμβάνοι,
καὶ ἐν ταύταις εἴρηνται αἱ διαφοραί, ἐν οἷς καὶ
δεύτερα καὶ τρίτα ἐλέγετο, καὶ ὅτι πάντα πᾶσαι,
κατὰ δὲ τὸ ἐνεργῆσαν ἐν αὐτῇ ἑκάστη. τοῦτο
δὲ τῷ τὴν μὲν ἑνοῦσθαι ἐνεργείᾳ, τὴν δὲ ἐν
15 γνώσει ⟨εἶναι⟩,[1] τὴν δὲ ἐν ὀρέξει, καὶ ἐν τῷ ἄλλην
ἄλλα βλέπειν καὶ ἅπερ βλέπει εἶναι καὶ γίγνεσθαι·
καὶ τὸ πλῆρες δὲ ταῖς ψυχαῖς καὶ τέλειον οὐχὶ
ταὐτὸν πάσαις. ἀλλ᾽ εἰ ποικίλον τὸ ὅλον σύνταγμα
αὐταῖς—εἷς γὰρ πᾶς λόγος πολὺς καὶ ποικίλος,
ὥσπερ ζῷον ψυχικὸν πολλὰς μορφὰς ἔχον—εἰ δὴ
20 τοῦτο, καὶ σύνταξίς ἐστι, καὶ οὐ διέσπασται τὰ
ὄντα ὅλως ἀπ᾽ ἀλλήλων, οὐδὲ τὸ εἰκῆ ἐν τοῖς
οὖσιν, ὅπου μηδὲ ἐν τοῖς σώμασι, καὶ ἀριθμόν τινα
ἀκόλουθόν ἐστιν εἶναι. καὶ γὰρ αὖ ἑστάναι δεῖ τὰ

[1] Theiler.

8. This then is how it is with the solution of this problem, and the fact of sympathy does not hinder our arguments: for since all souls derive from the same from which the soul of the Whole derives too, they have a community of feeling. For we have said already that they are both one and many. We have also explained how the part differs from the whole. We have made a general statement about the differences between souls, and now let us add briefly that besides their [different] bodies they can differ very notably in character, and in the activities of discursive reason and as a result of the lives they have lived before; for Plato says that the souls' choices take place according to their previous lives. And if one takes a general view of the nature of soul, the differences in souls have been mentioned in those passages too where there was talk of " seconds " and " thirds ", and it was said that all souls are all things, but each [is differentiated] according to that which is active in it: that is, by one being united in actuality, one being in a state of knowledge, one in a state of desire, and in that different souls look at different things and are and become what they look at; and the fullness and completion for souls is not the same for all. But if the whole structure in which they exist is complex—for every single rational principle is manifold and complex, like a soul-organism containing many forms—if this is really so, there is structural organisation, and the realities are not completely cut off from each other, and there is nothing random among the realities (as there is not even among bodies), and it follows that there must be a [definite] number. For, again, realities must be static, and the intelligible realities must remain

ὄντα, καὶ τὰ αὐτὰ τὰ νοητὰ εἶναι, καὶ ἕκαστον ἐν
25 ἀριθμῷ εἶναι· οὕτω γὰρ τὸ τόδε. τοῖς μὲν γὰρ
τῶν σωμάτων τῇ φύσει τοῦ καθέκαστον ῥέοντος ἅτε
ἐπακτοῦ τοῦ εἴδους ὄντος τὸ εἶναι κατ᾽ εἶδος ἀεὶ
ὑπάρχει μιμήσει τῶν ὄντων, τοῖς δὲ ἅτε οὐκ ἐκ
συνθέσεως οὖσι τὸ εἶναί ἐστιν ἐν τῷ ὅ ἐστιν
ἀριθμῷ ἕν, ὅπερ ἐξ ἀρχῆς ὑπάρχει, καὶ οὔτε
30 γίνεται ὃ μὴ ἦν, οὔτε ὅ ἐστιν οὐκ ἔσται. ἐπεὶ καὶ
εἰ ποιοῦν τι ἔσται αὐτά, ἐκ μὲν ὕλης οὐκ ἄν· εἰ δὲ
καὶ τοῦτο, δεῖ τι καὶ ἐξ αὐτοῦ οὐσιῶδες προσθεῖναι·
ὥστε μεταβολὴ περὶ αὐτὸ ἐκεῖνο ἔσται, εἰ νῦν
πλέον ποιεῖ ἢ ἔλαττον. καὶ διὰ τί νῦν, ἀλλ᾽ οὐκ
ἀεὶ οὕτως; καὶ τὸ γενόμενον δὲ οὐκ ἀίδιον, εἴπερ
35 πλέον καὶ ἔλαττον· κεῖται δὲ ἡ ψυχὴ τοιοῦτον.
πῶς οὖν ἄπειρον, εἰ στήσεται; ἢ τῇ δυνάμει τὸ
ἄπειρον, ὅτι ἡ δύναμις ἄπειρος, οὐχ ὡς μερισθησο-
μένης εἰς ἄπειρον. ἐπεὶ καὶ ὁ θεὸς οὐ πεπερασμένος. καὶ αὗται τοίνυν οὐ πέρατι ἀλλοτρίῳ ἐστὶν

---

¹ This passage is interesting as an example of the sense in
which Plotinus is prepared to speak of the Second and Third
Hypostases as ἄπειρος (infinite in the sense of unlimited or
unbounded). ὁ θεός in line 38 is probably Νοῦς. Any kind
of spatially conceived or numerical infinity is excluded from
his intelligible world (cp. line 37 here and VI. 6. 17–18).

the same, and each must be numerically one: for this is how it is *this* definite reality. For in some things, because of their bodily nature, individuality is fluid because the form comes in from outside and they have continual existence only according to specific form, in imitation of the real beings, but in others, since they are not produced by composition, the existence of each is in that which it is, numerically one, which is there from the beginning, and does not become what it was not and will not cease to be what it is. Since even if there is to be something which makes them it will not make them out of matter; if it does do this it must add something substantial from itself: so that there will be change affecting this making power itself, if it now makes more and now less. And why should it make more or less now, but not go on always in this same way? And that which has come into being will not be everlasting, if it is now more and now less; but it is settled that soul is a thing of this [everlasting] kind. How then will it be infinite, if it is going to remain static? Its infinity lies in its power; it is infinite because its power is infinite, and not as if it was going to be divided to infinity. For God too is not limited.[1] And these souls, too, are not each what

---

" Infinity " there can only mean infinity of power (as here) or unboundedness because there is nothing to bound or measure intelligible reality—intelligible number is the ultimate measure and so not itself measured, bounded or limited (as in VI. 6). The doctrine of " relative ἀπειρία " in Proclus (*Elements of Theology* props. 89–96, pp. 83–7 Dodds) is helpful to the understanding of Plotinus here. The One for him is infinite in the sense of being absolutely beyond any sort of determination or limitation, because it is beyond being and thought, but is hardly ever called ἄπειρος.

40 ἑκάστη ὅ ἐστιν, οἷον τοσαύτη, ἀλλ' αὐτή ἐστιν ὅσον
θέλει, καὶ οὐ μή ποτε γένηται προϊοῦσα ἔξω αὑτῆς,
ἀλλὰ φθάνει μὲν πανταχοῦ, ὃ πέφυκεν αὐτῆς ἐπὶ
τὰ σώματα [εἰς τὰ σώματα] ¹ φθάνειν· οὐ μὴν
διέσπασται ἀφ' ἑαυτῆς, ὅταν ᾖ καὶ ἐν τῷ δακτύλῳ
καὶ ἐν τῷ ποδί. οὕτω δὴ καὶ ἐν τῷ παντί, εἰς ὃ
45 ἂν φθάνῃ, ἐν ἄλλῳ καὶ ἄλλῳ μέρει φυτοῦ καὶ
ἀποτετμημένου, ὥστε εἶναι καὶ ἐν τῷ ἐξ ἀρχῆς
φυτῷ καὶ τῷ ἀπ' αὐτοῦ τετμημένῳ· ἓν γὰρ τὸ
σῶμα τοῦ παντός, καὶ ὡς ἐν ἑνί ἐστιν αὐτοῦ
πανταχοῦ. καὶ σαπέντος δὲ ζῴου εἰ πολλὰ ἐξ
αὐτοῦ, ἐκείνη μὲν οὐκέτι ἐστὶν ἡ τοῦ παντὸς ζῴου
50 ψυχὴ ἐν τῷ σώματι· οὐ γὰρ ἔχει αὖ τὸ δεκτικὸν
αὐτῆς· οὐ γὰρ ἂν ἀπέθανε. τὰ δὲ ἐκ τῆς φθορᾶς
ἐπιτηδείως ἔχοντα πρὸς γενέσεις ζῴων, τὰ μὲν
τῶνδε, τὰ δὲ τῶνδε, ἴσχει ψυχὴν οὐδενὸς ὄντος
ὅτου ἀποστατεῖ, ὄντος δὲ τοῦ μὲν δέχεσθαι, τοῦ δὲ
μὴ δέχεσθαι δυναμένου. καὶ τὰ γιγνόμενα οὕτως
55 ἔμψυχα οὐ πλείους ἐποίησε ψυχάς· ἐξήρτηται γὰρ
τῆς μιᾶς, ᾗ μένει μία· ὥσπερ καὶ ἐν ἡμῖν ἀπο-
τεμνομένων τινῶν, ἄλλων δὲ ἀντ' αὐτῶν φυομένων,
τῶν μὲν ἀπέστη ἡ ψυχή, τοῖς δὲ προσεγένετο, ἕως
ἡ μία μένει. ἐν δὲ τῷ παντὶ μένει ἀεὶ ἡ μία· τὰ
δὲ ἐντὸς τὰ μὲν ἴσχει, τὰ δὲ ἀποτίθεται, τῶν
60 αὐτῶν ψυχικῶν μενόντων.

¹ del. Theiler.

they are by some external limit, as if they were a
definite size, but each is itself as much as it wants
to be, and never goes outside itself as it proceeds,
but that part of it which is naturally adapted to
reach bodies reaches everywhere in them; it is
certainly not torn away from itself when it is in the
finger [1] as in the foot. So it is also in the All, to
whatever it reaches; it is in one part of a plant and
also in another, even if it is cut off; so that it is in
the original plant and the part cut off from it: for
the body of the all is one, and soul is everywhere in
it as in one thing. And when an animal rots, if
many others spring from it, the original soul of the
whole animal is no longer in the body: for the body
on its side does not have the capacity to receive it,
or the animal would not have died. But the products
of the decay which are adapted for the generation of
animals, some for those of one kind and some for
those of another, have soul since there is nothing
from which it is absent, but one thing is able to
receive it and another not to receive it. And things
which become ensouled in this way do not make more
souls: for they depend on the one soul which remains
one; just as in ourselves, when some parts are cut
off and others grow instead of them, soul leaves the
old ones and comes to the new as long as the one
soul remains. But in the All the one soul is always
there; but some of the things within it take soul
and some put it off, but the soul-activities remain the
same.

[1] See ch. **3**, n. 1.

9. Ἀλλὰ ⟨καὶ⟩[1] πῶς ἐγγίγνεται σώματι ψυχή,
ζητητέον. τίς ὁ τρόπος; [καὶ πῶς].[2] οὐχ ἧττον
γὰρ καὶ τοῦτο θαυμάσαι τε καὶ ζητῆσαι ἄξιον.
ἐπεὶ τοίνυν διττὸς ὁ τρόπος τῆς εἰς σῶμα ψυχῆς
5 εἰσόδου—ἡ μὲν γὰρ γίνεται ψυχῇ ἐν σώματι οὔσῃ
τῇ τε μετενσωματουμένῃ καὶ τῇ ἐκ σώματος
ἀερίνου ἢ πυρίνου εἰς γήινον γινομένῃ, ἣν δὴ
μετενσωμάτωσιν οὐ λέγουσιν εἶναι, ὅτι ἄδηλον τὸ
ἀφ' οὗ ἡ εἴσκρισις, ἡ δὲ ἐκ τοῦ ἀσωμάτου εἰς
ὁτιοῦν σῶμα, ἣ δὴ καὶ πρώτη ἂν εἴη ψυχῇ κοινωνία
10 σώματι—ὀρθῶς ἂν ἔχοι ἐπισκέψασθαι περὶ ταύτης,
τί ποτέ ἐστι τὸ γινόμενον πάθος τότε, ὅτε ψυχὴ
καθαρὰ οὖσα σώματος πάντῃ ἴσχει περὶ αὑτὴν
σώματος φύσιν. περὶ μὲν δὴ τῆς τοῦ παντός—
ἐντεῦθεν γὰρ ἴσως ⟨εἰκὸς⟩[1] ἄρξασθαι, μᾶλλον δὲ
ἀναγκαῖον τυγχάνει—δεῖ δὴ τῷ λόγῳ τὴν εἴσοδον
15 καὶ τὴν ἐμψύχωσιν διδασκαλίας καὶ τοῦ σαφοῦς
χάριν γίγνεσθαι νομίζειν. ἐπεὶ οὐκ ἦν ὅτε οὐκ
ἐψύχωτο τόδε τὸ πᾶν, οὐδὲ ἦν[3] ὅτε σῶμα ὑφει-
στήκει ψυχῆς ἀπούσης, οὐδὲ ὕλη ποτὲ ὅτε
ἀκόσμητος ἦν· ἀλλ' ἐπινοῆσαι ταῦτα χωρίζοντας
αὐτὰ ἀπ' ἀλλήλων τῷ λόγῳ οἷόν τε. ἔξεστι γὰρ
20 ἀναλύειν τῷ λόγῳ καὶ τῇ διανοίᾳ πᾶσαν σύνθεσιν.
ἐπεὶ τό γε ἀληθὲς ὧδε ἔχει· σώματος μὲν μὴ ὄντος
οὐδ' ἂν προέλθοι ψυχή, ἐπεὶ οὐδὲ τόπος ἄλλος
ἐστίν, ὅπου πέφυκεν εἶναι. προϊέναι δὲ εἰ μέλλοι,
γεννήσει ἑαυτῇ τόπον, ὥστε καὶ σῶμα. τῆς δὴ
στάσεως αὐτῆς ἐν αὐτῇ τῇ στάσει οἱονεὶ ῥωννυμένης
25 οἷον πολὺ φῶς ἐκλάμψαν ἐπ' ἄκροις τοῖς ἐσχάτοις τοῦ πυρὸς σκότος ἐγίνετο, ὅπερ ἰδοῦσα ἡ ψυχή,

___

[1] Theiler. [2] del. Theiler. [3] Preller: οὐδ' ἐνῆν Enn., H–S[1].

9. But we must also enquire how soul comes to be in body. What is its way of entering? This too is a subject no less worth wondering about and enquiring into. Now there are two ways of soul entering body; one is when a soul is already in a body and changes bodies, or passes from a body of air or fire to one of earth (people do not call this change of body because the body from which entry is made is not apparent); and the other, passage from bodilessness to any kind of body, which would of course be the first communication of soul with body. About this last, then, it will be proper to investigate what it is that happens when a soul which is altogether pure and free from body takes upon itself a bodily nature. It is perhaps suitable, or rather it is necessary, to begin with the Soul of the All. Of course [when talking about the Soul of the All] we must consider that the terms " entry " and " ensoulment " are used in the discussion for the sake of clear explanation. For there never was a time when this universe did not have a soul, or when body existed in the absence of soul, or when matter was not set in order; but in discussing these things one can consider them apart from each other. [When one is reasoning about] any kind of composition, it is always legitimate to analyse it in thought into its parts. For the truth is as follows. If body did not exist, soul would not go forth, since there is no place other than body where it is natural for it to be. But if it intends to go forth, it will produce a place for itself, and so a body. Soul's rest is, we may say, confirmed in absolute rest; a great light shines from it, and at the outermost edge of this firelight there is a darkness. Soul sees this darkness and informs

ἐπείπερ ὑπέστη, ἐμόρφωσεν αὐτό. οὐ γὰρ ἦν
θεμιτὸν γειτονοῦν τι αὐτῇ λόγου ἄμοιρον εἶναι, οἷον
ἐδέχετο τὸ λεγόμενον "ἀμυδρὸν ἐν ἀμυδρῷ" τῷ
γενομένῳ. γενόμενος δὴ οἷον οἰκός τις καλὸς καὶ
30 ποικίλος οὐκ ἀπετμήθη τοῦ πεποιηκότος, οὐδ᾽ αὖ
ἐκοίνωσεν αὐτὸν αὐτῇ, ἀλλὰ πανταχοῦ πᾶς ἄξιος
ἐπιμελείας νομισθεὶς ὠφελίμου μὲν ἑαυτῷ τῷ εἶναι
καὶ τῷ καλῷ, ὅσον δὴ τοῦ εἶναι δυνατὸν ἦν αὐτῷ
μεταλαμβάνειν, ἀβλαβοῦς δὲ τῷ ἐφεστηκότι· ἄνω
35 γὰρ μένων ἐπιστατεῖ· ἔμψυχος τῷ τοιούτῳ τρόπῳ,
ἔχων ψυχὴν οὐχ αὑτοῦ, ἀλλ᾽ αὑτῷ, κρατούμενος
οὐ κρατῶν, καὶ ἐχόμενος ἀλλ᾽ οὐκ ἔχων. κεῖται
γὰρ ἐν τῇ ψυχῇ ἀνεχούσῃ αὐτὸν καὶ οὐδὲν ἄμοιρόν
ἐστιν αὐτῆς, ὡς ἂν ἐν ὕδασι δίκτυον τεγγόμενον
ζώῃ, οὐ δυνάμενον δὲ αὐτοῦ ποιεῖσθαι ἐν ᾧ ἐστιν·
40 ἀλλὰ τὸ μὲν δίκτυον ἐκτεινομένης ἤδη τῆς θαλάσ-
σης συνεκτέταται, ὅσον αὐτὸ δύναται· οὐ γὰρ
δύναται ἀλλαχόθι ἕκαστον τῶν μορίων ἢ ὅπου
κεῖται εἶναι. ἡ δὲ τοσαύτη ἐστὶ τὴν φύσιν, ὅτι μὴ
τοσήδε, ὥστε πᾶν τὸ σῶμα καταλαμβάνειν τῷ
αὐτῷ, καὶ ὅπου ἂν ἐκταθῇ ἐκεῖνο, ἐκεῖ ἐστι· καὶ
45 εἰ μὴ εἴη δὲ ἐκεῖνο, οὐδὲν ἂν αὐτῇ εἰς μέγεθος
μέλοι· ἔστι γὰρ ἥτις ἐστί· τοσοῦτον γάρ ἐστι τὸ
πᾶν, ὅπου ἐστὶν αὐτή, καὶ ὁρίζεται τῷ ὅσον, εἰς
ὅσον προϊὸν σώζουσαν αὐτὴν αὐτὸ ἔχει. καὶ
τοσαύτη ἐστὶν ἡ σκιά, ὅσος ὁ λόγος ὁ παρ᾽ αὐτῆς.
ὁ δὲ λόγος τοιοῦτος ἦν, ὡς μέγεθος τοσοῦτον
50 ἐργάσασθαι, ὅσον τὸ εἶδος αὐτοῦ ἐβούλετο μέγεθος
ἐργάσασθαι.

it, since it is there as a substrate for form. For it was not lawful for that which borders on soul to be without its share of formative principle, as far as that was capable of receiving it of which the phrase was used " dimly in the dimness " which came to be. There came into being something like a beautiful and richly various house which was not cut off from its builder, but he did not give it a share in himself either; he considered it all, everywhere, worth a care which conduces to its very being and excellence (as far as it can participate in being) but does him no harm in his presiding over it, for he rules it while abiding above. It is in this sort of way that it is ensouled; it has a soul which does not belong to it, but is present to it; it is mastered, not the master, possessed, not possessor. The universe lies in soul which bears it up, and nothing is without a share of soul. It is as if a net immersed in the waters was alive, but unable to make its own that in which it is. The sea is already spread out and the net spreads with it, as far as it can; for no one of its parts can be anywhere else than where it lies. And soul's nature is so great, just because it has no size, as to contain the whole of body in one and the same grasp; wherever body extends, there soul is. If body did not exist, it would make no difference to soul as regards size; for it is what it is. The universe extends as far as soul goes; its limit of extension is the point to which in going forth it has soul to keep it in being. The shadow is as large as the rational formative principle which comes from soul; and the formative principle is of such a kind as to make a size as large as the form from which it derives wants to make.

PLOTINUS: ENNEAD IV. 3.

10. Οὕτω δὴ ἀκούσαντας χρὴ πάλιν ἐπὶ τὸ ἀεὶ
οὕτως ἐλθόντας ὁμοῦ λαβεῖν πάντα ὄντα· οἷον τὸν
ἀέρα, τὸ φῶς, τὸν ἥλιον, ἢ τὴν σελήνην καὶ τὸ φῶς
καὶ πάλιν τὸν ἥλιον ὁμοῦ πάντα, τάξιν δὲ πρώτων
5 καὶ δευτέρων καὶ τρίτων ἔχοντα, καὶ ἐνταῦθα ψυχὴν
ἀεὶ ἑστῶσαν ᾗ τὰ ¹ πρῶτα καὶ τὰ ἐφεξῆς ὡς πυρὸς
ἔσχατα, εἰς ὕστερον τοῦ πρώτου ἐκ τοῦ ἐσχάτου
νοουμένου πυρὸς σκιᾶς, εἶτα ἐπιφωτιζομένου ἅμα
καὶ τούτου, ὥστε οἷον εἶδος ἐπιθεῖν τῷ ἐπιβληθέντι
10 πρώτῳ γενομένῳ παντάπασιν ἀμυδρῷ. ἐκοσμεῖτο
δὲ κατὰ λόγον ψυχῆς δυνάμει ἐχούσης ἐν αὑτῇ δι᾽
ὅλης δύναμιν κατὰ λόγους κοσμεῖν· οἷα καὶ οἱ ἐν
σπέρμασι λόγοι πλάττουσι καὶ μορφοῦσι τὰ ζῷα
οἷον μικρούς τινας κόσμους. ὅ τι γὰρ ἂν ἐφάψηται
ψυχῆς, οὕτω ποιεῖται ὡς ἔχει φύσεως ψυχῆς ἡ
15 οὐσία· ἡ δὲ ποιεῖ οὐκ ἐπακτῷ γνώμῃ οὐδὲ βουλὴν ἢ
σκέψιν ἀναμείνασα· οὕτω γὰρ ἂν οὐ κατὰ φύσιν,
ἀλλὰ κατ᾽ ἐπακτὸν τέχνην ἂν ποιοῖ. τέχνη γὰρ
ὑστέρα αὐτῆς καὶ μιμεῖται ἀμυδρὰ καὶ ἀσθενῆ
ποιοῦσα μιμήματα, παίγνια ἄττα καὶ οὐ πολλοῦ
ἄξια, μηχαναῖς πολλαῖς εἰς εἴδωλον φύσεως ²
20 προσχρωμένη. ἡ δὲ οὐσίας δυνάμει κυρία σωμάτων

¹ Igal: εἶτα Enn., H–S¹: ἢ τὰ Theiler, H–S².
² suspic. H–S¹: εἰς εἴδωλον φύσιν Enn., Perna: εἰς εἰδώλων
(Perna^{mg}) φύσιν Creuzer* (ad simulacra pingenda Ficinus), sed
φύσις aliud ac κατὰ φύσιν (lin. 16) significare non potest.

---

¹ The context of this depreciation of art, which follows
Plato's closely, should be noted. It is one of Plotinus's
frequent assertions of the inferiority of planned, rational (in
the ordinary human sense) activity as inferior to the divine,
spontaneous activity which works without planning; cp. V. 8.

10. With this understanding we must go back again to that which is always unchanged and grasp all as existing simultaneously; just as the air, the light, the sun, or the moon, the light and again the sun all exist simultaneously, but hold first, second and third positions, so here there is soul always static, or the first, then the next in order, like the last gleams of the light of a fire; afterwards the first coming from this last gleam is thought of as a shadow of fire, and then this at the same time is thought of as illuminated, so that it is as if a form hovered over what is cast upon soul, which at first was altogether obscure. It was given ordered beauty according to a formative rational principle, since soul has potentially in it, and throughout the whole of it, the power to set in order according to rational principles; just as the formative rational principles in seeds mould and shape living beings like little ordered universes. For whatever comes into contact with soul is made as the essential nature of soul is in a state to make it; and it makes, not according to a purpose brought in from outside, nor waiting upon planning and consideration; for in this way it would not make according to nature, but to an art brought in from outside. For art is later than soul, and imitates it, making dim and weak imitations, toys not worth much, bringing in many devices to help it in producing an image of nature.[1]   But soul is by its essential power in control

---

7 for his fullest critique of the idea of " artisan " creation.   But Plotinus can be much more positive about art, and can even say that sometimes art can improve on nature because the artist's mind has direct access to the Forms in the Intelligible world of which natural things are images too, and sometimes, for various reasons, very imperfect ones; cp. V. 8. 1. 34–40.

εἰς τὸ γενέσθαι τε καὶ οὕτως ἔχειν ὡς αὐτὴ ἄγει,
οὐ δυναμένων τῶν ἐξ ἀρχῆς ἐναντιοῦσθαι τῇ αὐτῆς
βουλήσει. ἐν γὰρ τοῖς ὑστέροις ἄλληλα ἐμποδί-
ζοντα πολλάκις ἀποστερεῖται τοῦ τυχεῖν μορφῆς
25 τῆς οἰκείας, ἣν ὁ λόγος ὁ ἐν σμικρῷ θέλει· ἐκεῖ
δὲ γιγνομένης καὶ τῆς ὅλης μορφῆς ὑπ' αὐτῆς
καὶ τάξιν τῶν γενομένων ἅμα ἐχόντων ἀπόνως τὸ
γενόμενον καὶ ἀνεμποδίστως καλόν ἐστι. κατεσκευ-
άσατο δὲ ἐν αὐτῷ τὰ μὲν θεῶν ἀγάλματα, τὰ δὲ
ἀνθρώπων οἰκήματα, τὰ δὲ ἄλλα ἄλλοις. τί γὰρ
30 ἔδει γίνεσθαι παρὰ ψυχῆς, ἢ ὧν τὴν δύναμιν εἰς τὸ
ποιεῖν ἔχει; πυρὸς μὲν γὰρ θερμὰ ποιεῖν, καὶ τὸ
ψύχειν ἄλλου· ψυχῆς δὲ τὸ μὲν ἐν αὐτῇ τὸ δὲ ἐξ
αὐτῆς εἰς ἄλλο. τοῖς μὲν γὰρ ἀψύχοις τὸ μὲν [ἐξ
αὐτῶν]¹ οἷον εὕδει κείμενον ἐν αὐτοῖς, τὸ δὲ ⟨ἐξ
αὐτῶν⟩¹ εἰς ἄλλο ὁμοιῶσαι πρὸς αὐτὸ τὸ παθεῖν
35 δυνάμενον· καὶ κοινὸν δὴ τοῦτο παντὶ τῷ ὄντι
εἰς ὁμοίωσιν ἑαυτῷ ἄγειν. ψυχῆς δὲ ἔργον καὶ τὸ
ἐν αὐτῇ ἐγρηγορός τι καὶ τὸ εἰς ἄλλο ὡσαύτως.
ζῆν οὖν καὶ τὰ ἄλλα ποιεῖ, ὅσα μὴ ζῇ παρ' αὐτῶν,
καὶ τοιαύτην ζωήν, καθ' ἣν αὐτὴ ζῇ. ζῶσα οὖν
ἐν λόγῳ λόγον δίδωσι τῷ σώματι, εἴδωλον οὗ
40 ἔχει—καὶ γὰρ καὶ εἴδωλον ζωῆς, ὅσον δίδωσι τῷ
σώματι—καὶ μορφὰς σωμάτων, ὧν τοὺς λόγους

---

¹ transpos. Kleist (Studien 40): del. Dodds, B–T.

of bodies, so that they come to be and are in the state to which soul leads them, since their first principles are unable to resist its will. In the things that come after one often hinders another and they are deprived of the attainment of their proper form, that which the formative principle operating on a small scale wishes them to have; but there in the universe as a whole, where the whole form is produced by soul and the things which are produced have all together an order, what has come into being is beautiful without labour or hindrance. But soul has constructed in the world shrines of gods and dwellings for men, and others for other creatures. For what else ought to come from soul except the things which it has the power to make? It belongs to fire to make things hot, and to something else to cool them; but one power belongs to soul which remains within it, and another which goes out to form something else. In soulless things the one power, so to speak, lies asleep in them; and the power from them which goes out to something else consists in making like themselves that which is capable of being affected: and this is of course common to all that exists, to bring things to likeness with themselves. But the work of soul is something awake, both that within it and in the same way that which goes out to something else. Soul therefore makes alive all the other things which do not live of themselves, and makes them live the sort of life by which it lives itself. So since it lives in a rational principle, it gives a rational principle to the body, an image of that which it has—for what it gives to the body is also [only] an image of life—and the shapes of body, of which it has the rational formative prin-

ἔχει· ἔχει δὲ καὶ θεῶν καὶ πάντων. διὸ πάντα καὶ
ὁ κόσμος ἔχει.

11. Καί μοι δοκοῦσιν οἱ πάλαι σοφοί, ὅσοι
ἐβουλήθησαν θεοὺς αὐτοῖς παρεῖναι ἱερὰ καὶ
ἀγάλματα ποιησάμενοι, εἰς τὴν τοῦ παντὸς φύσιν
ἀπιδόντες, ἐν νῷ λαβεῖν ὡς πανταχοῦ μὲν εὐάγωγον
5 ψυχῆς φύσις, δέξασθαί γε μὴν ῥᾷστον ἂν εἴη
ἁπάντων, εἴ τις προσπαθές τι τεκτήναιτο ὑποδέξασ-
θαι δυνάμενον μοῖράν τινα αὐτῆς. προσπαθὲς δὲ
τὸ ὁπωσοῦν μιμηθέν, ὥσπερ κάτοπτρον ἁρπάσαι
εἶδός τι δυνάμενον. καὶ γὰρ ἡ τοῦ παντὸς φύσις
πάντα εὐμηχάνως ποιησαμένη εἰς μίμησιν ὧν
10 εἶχε τοὺς λόγους, ἐπειδὴ ἕκαστον οὕτως ἐγένετο
ἐν ὕλῃ λόγος, ὃς κατὰ τὸν πρὸ ὕλης ἐμεμόρφωτο,
συνῆψατο τῷ θεῷ ἐκείνῳ, καθ᾽ ὃν ἐγίνετο καὶ εἰς
ὃν εἶδεν ἡ ψυχὴ καὶ εἶχε ποιοῦσα. καὶ δὴ οὐχ
οἷόν τε ἦν ἄμοιρον αὐτοῦ γενέσθαι, οὐδὲ ἐκεῖνον
αὖ κατελθεῖν εἰς τοῦτον. ἦν δὴ νοῦς ἐκεῖνος ὁ
15 ἐκεῖ ἥλιος—οὗτος γὰρ ἡμῖν γινέσθω παράδειγμα
τοῦ λόγου—ἐφεξῆς δὲ τούτῳ ψυχὴ ἐξηρτημένη
μένοντος νοῦ μένουσα. δίδωσι δὴ αὕτη τὰ πέρατα

---

[1] The allusion here is to the ancient Egyptian practice of
ritually animating statues: cp. the Hermetic *Asclepius* 37. II
p. 347 Nock-Festugière. It became a regular part of later

ciples: it has these of gods and of everything. This, then, is why the universe too has everything.

11. And I think that the wise men of old, who made temples and statues in the wish that the gods should be present to them,[1] looking to the nature of the All, had in mind that the nature of soul is everywhere easy to attract, but that if someone were to construct something sympathetic to it and able to receive a part of it, it would of all things receive soul most easily. That which is sympathetic to it is what imitates it in some way, like a mirror able to catch [the reflection of] a form. Yes, the nature of the All, too, made all things skilfully in imitation of the [intelligible] realities of which it had the rational principles, and when each thing in this way had become a rational principle in matter, shaped according to that which was before matter, it linked it with that god in conformity with whom it came into being and to whom the soul looked and whom it had in its making.[2] For it was certainly not possible for the thing made to be without a share in the god, nor again for the god to come down to the thing made. So that sun in the divine realm is Intellect—let this serve as an example for our discourse—and next after it is soul, dependent upon it and abiding while Intellect abides. This soul gives the edge of itself

Neoplatonic theurgic practice, though not without objection from the more rational members of the school: cp. Eunapius 475 (Maximus, Eusebius of Myndus, and the Emperor Julian).

[2] For a fuller and more developed account of the making of the forms or rational principles in matter by Nature (the lowest, immanent part of universal Soul) and how the weak, dreamy form-making activity of Nature is linked through Soul with the divine forms in Intellect (here referred to as " the god ") see III. 8. 1–5.

αὐτῆς τὰ πρὸς τοῦτον τὸν ἥλιον τούτῳ τῷ ἡλίῳ,
καὶ ποιεῖ διὰ μέσου αὐτῆς κἀκεῖ συνῆφθαι οἷον
20 ἑρμηνευτικὴ γενομένη τῶν τε ἀπ' ἐκείνου εἰς
τοῦτον καὶ τῶν τούτου εἰς ἐκεῖνον, ὅσον διὰ ψυχῆς
εἰς ἐκεῖνον φθάνει. οὐ γὰρ μακρὰν οὐδὲ πόρρω
οὐδενὸς οὐδὲν καὶ αὖ πόρρω τῇ διαφορᾷ καὶ μὴ[1]
μίξει, ἀλλ' εἶναι ἐφ' ἑαυτοῦ [οὐ τόποις][2] καὶ
συνεῖναι χωρὶς ὄν. θεοὶ δέ εἰσιν οὗτοι τῷ ἀεὶ μὴ
25 ἀποστατεῖν ἐκείνων, καὶ τῇ μὲν ἐξαρχῆς ψυχῇ
προσηρτῆσθαι τῇ οἷον ἀπελθούσῃ ψυχῇ, ταύτῃ δέ,
ᾗπερ καί εἰσι καὶ ὃ λέγονται, πρὸς νοῦν βλέπειν
οὐδαμοῦ ψυχῆς αὐτοῖς ἢ ἐκεῖ βλεπούσης.

12. Ἀνθρώπων δὲ ψυχαὶ εἴδωλα αὑτῶν ἰδοῦσαι
οἷον Διονύσου ἐν κατόπτρῳ ἐκεῖ ἐγένοντο ἄνωθεν
ὁρμηθεῖσαι, οὐκ ἀποτμηθεῖσαι οὐδ' αὗται τῆς
ἑαυτῶν ἀρχῆς τε καὶ νοῦ. οὐ γὰρ μετὰ τοῦ νοῦ

---

[1] Theiler: τῇ Enn.*, H–S[1].
[2] ut glossam post συνεῖναι delevimus.

---

[1] For the connection of the visible sun to the intelligible
sun cp. Julian *Oration* IV (To King Helios) *passim*: though
for Plotinus this relationship of the two suns is just an example
of the way in which everything in the sense-world is linked to
the intelligible, of the intimate presence of the divine in the
whole material world, but in Julian it is a theological doctrine
of central importance.

[2] For the Orphic story to which Plotinus here casually
alludes see W. K. C. Guthrie *Orpheus and Greek Religion* 2nd
ed. (London 1952) 122–3. The mirror was one of the toys
with which the Titans lured away the child Dionysus-Zagreus

which borders on this [visible] sun to this sun, and makes a connection of it to the divine realm through the medium of itself, and acts as an interpreter of what comes from this sun to the intelligible sun and from the intelligible sun to this sun, in so far as this sun does reach the intelligible sun through soul.[1] For nothing is a long way off or far from anything else—distance in another sense is a matter of difference and not being mixed—but [the divine] is by itself, and is with the world while remaining separate. These [heavenly bodies] are gods by for ever not departing from those intelligible gods and by being linked to the original soul by the soul which, so to speak, went away [to the visible world], and by this, by which they are what they are also called, they look towards Intellect, since soul for them never looks elsewhere than There.

12. But the souls of men see their images as if in the mirror of Dionysus[2] and come to be on that level with a leap from above: but even these are not cut off from their own principle and from intellect.

to tear him to pieces and eat him; after they had done so Zeus destroyed them with his thunderbolts and men were made out of their ashes; so we contain a " Titanic ", earthy, evil element and also a divine Dionysiac one which must be released by purification. Plotinus here simply takes the mirror, in which Dionysus enjoyed seeing his own reflection, as a symbol of the attractiveness of the visible world for the souls which must descend into it (all material things for him are reflections of soul). The later Neoplatonists worked out an elaborate allegorical interpretation of the whole story, in which the rending of Dionysus by the Titans symbolises the " division " of the divine power in the material world. The relevant passages are collected in O. Kern *Orphicorum Fragmenta* (Berlin 1963) 209. See further J. Pépin in *Revue Internationale de Philosophie* 24 (1970) 304–20.

5 ἦλθον, ἀλλ' ἔφθασαν μὲν μέχρι γῆς, κάρα δὲ αὐταῖς
ἐστήρικται ὑπεράνω τοῦ οὐρανοῦ. πλέον δὲ αὐταῖς
κατελθεῖν συμβέβηκεν, ὅτι τὸ μέσον αὐταῖς ἠναγκάσθη, φροντίδος δεομένου τοῦ εἰς ὃ ἔφθασαν,
φροντίσαι. Ζεὺς δὲ πατὴρ ἐλεήσας πονουμένας
θνητὰ αὐτῶν τὰ δεσμὰ ποιῶν, περὶ ἃ πονοῦνται,
10 δίδωσιν ἀναπαύλας ἐν χρόνοις ποιῶν σωμάτων
ἐλευθέρας, ἵν' ἔχοιεν ἐκεῖ καὶ αὗται γίνεσθαι,
οὗπερ ἡ τοῦ παντὸς ψυχὴ ἀεὶ οὐδὲν τὰ τῇδε
ἐπιστρεφομένη. ὃ γὰρ ἔχει τὸ πᾶν ἤδη, τοῦτο αὔταρκες αὐτῷ καὶ ἔστι καὶ ἔσται, κατὰ λόγους ἀεὶ
ἑστηκότας ἐν χρόνοις περαινόμενον· καὶ κατὰ
15 χρόνους ἀεὶ εἰς τὸ αὐτὸ καθιστάμενον [1] ἐν μέτροις
βίων ὡρισμένων εἰς συμφωνίαν ἀγομένων τούτων [2]
ἐκείνοις καὶ κατ' ἐκεῖνα, [τῶνδε] [3] περαινομένων
ὑφ' ἕνα λόγον, πάντων τεταγμένων ἔν τε καθόδοις
ψυχῶν καὶ ἀνόδοις καὶ εἰς τὰ ἄλλα σύμπαντα.
μαρτυρεῖ δὲ καὶ τὸ τῆς συμφωνίας τῶν ψυχῶν
20 πρὸς τὴν τοῦδε τοῦ παντὸς τάξιν οὐκ ἀπηρτημένων,
ἀλλὰ συναπτουσῶν ἐν ταῖς καθόδοις ἑαυτὰς καὶ
μίαν συμφωνίαν πρὸς τὴν περιφορὰν ποιουμένων,
ὡς καὶ τὰς τύχας αὐτῶν καὶ τοὺς βίους καὶ τὰς
προαιρέσεις σημαίνεσθαι τοῖς τῶν ἄστρων σχήμασι
25 καὶ οἷον μίαν τινὰ φωνὴν οὐκ ἐκμελῶς ἀφιέναι· καὶ

---

[1] ApcBac, Perna, Creuzer, Müller*: καθιστάμενα AacEBpc
RJUC, Kirchhoff, H–S.
[2] Theiler: ἀγόμενα ταῦτα Enn., H–S.
[3] del. Theiler.

ON DIFFICULTIES ABOUT THE SOUL I

For they did not come down with Intellect, but went on ahead of it down to earth, but their heads are firmly set above in heaven. But they experienced a deeper descent because their middle part was compelled to care for that to which they had gone on, which needed their care. But Father Zeus, pitying them in their troubles, makes the bonds over which they have trouble dissoluble by death and gives them periods of rest, making them at times free of bodies, so that they too may have the opportunity of being there where the soul of the All always is, since it in no way turns to the things of this world. For what it has is the All already complete; this is and will be sufficient to itself: it completes its course periodically according to everlastingly fixed rational principles, and everlastingly returns to the same state, period by period, in a proportionate succession of defined lives, these here being brought into harmony with those there and completed according to them,[1] everything being ordered under one rational principle in the descents of souls and their ascents and with regard to everything else. The harmonious adjustment of the souls to the order of this All of ours witnesses to this; they are not cut off from it, but fit themselves in in their descents and make one harmony with its circuit, so that their fortunes and their lives and their choices are indicated by the figures made by the heavenly bodies and they sing, as it were, with one

---

[1] I adopt Theiler's text here (see critical notes), in spite of the three alterations of the MSS which he makes, because it seems to me to be the only way of giving a satisfactory sense to the passage and because the critical reasons he gives for his alterations seem to me persuasive (see his note ad loc.).

τὸ μουσικῶς καὶ ἐναρμονίως μᾶλλον τοῦτο εἶναι
ᾐνιγμένως. τοῦτο δὲ οὐκ ἂν ἦν μὴ τοῦ παντὸς
κατ' ἐκεῖνα ποιοῦντος καὶ πάσχοντος ἕκαστα ἐν
μέτροις περιόδων καὶ τάξεων καὶ βίων κατὰ γένη
διεξόδων, οὓς αἱ ψυχαὶ διεξοδεύουσιν ὁτὲ μὲν ἐκεῖ,
30 ὁτὲ δὲ ἐν οὐρανῷ, ὁτὲ δὲ εἰς τούσδε τοὺς τόπους
ἐπιστρεφόμεναι. νοῦς δὲ πᾶς ἀεὶ ἄνω καὶ οὐ μή
ποτε ἔξω τῶν αὐτοῦ γένοιτο, ἀλλ' ἱδρυμένος πᾶς
ἄνω πέμπει εἰς τὰ τῇδε διὰ ψυχῆς. ψυχὴ δὲ ἐκ
τοῦ πλησίον μᾶλλον κατὰ τὸ ἐκεῖθεν διάκειται
εἶδος καὶ δίδωσι τοῖς ὑπ' αὐτήν, ἡ μὲν ὡσαύτως,
35 ἡ δὲ ἄλλοτε ἄλλως, ἴσχουσα ἐν τάξει τὴν πλάνην.
κάτεισι δὲ οὐκ ἀεὶ τὸ ἴσον, ἀλλ' ὁτὲ μὲν πλέον, ὁτὲ
δὲ ἔλαττον, κἂν πρὸς τὸ αὐτὸ γένος ἴῃ· κάτεισι δὲ
εἰς ἕτοιμον ἑκάστη καθ' ὁμοίωσιν τῆς διαθέσεως.
ἐκεῖ γάρ, ᾧ ἂν ὁμοιωθεῖσα ᾖ, φέρεται, ἡ μὲν εἰς
ἄνθρωπον, ἡ δὲ εἰς ζῷον ἄλλη ἄλλο.

13. Τὸ γὰρ ἀναπόδραστον καὶ ἡ δίκη οὕτως ἐν
φύσει κρατούσῃ ἰέναι ἕκαστον ἐν τάξει πρὸς ὃ
ἔστιν ἕκαστον γενόμενον εἴδωλον προαιρέσεως
καὶ διαθέσεως ἀρχετύπου, καὶ ἔστιν ἐκεῖνο πᾶν
5 ψυχῆς εἶδος ἐκείνου πλησίον, πρὸς ὃ τὴν διάθεσιν
τὴν ἐν αὐτῇ ἔχει, καὶ τοῦ τότε πέμποντος καὶ
εἰσάγοντος οὐ δεῖ, οὔτε ἵνα ἔλθῃ εἰς σῶμα τότε

---

[1] The "fortunes and lives and choices" come from the
concluding myth of Plato's *Republic* (see 617B). For a fuller
discussion by Plotinus of this passage in Plato see III. 4. 5.
Plotinus here, characteristically, interprets "the music of the
spheres" allegorically to suit his own philosophical purposes.
For the old literal interpretation of this Pythagorean doctrine
see Cicero *Somnium Scipionis* 5. 10; and cf. P.-M. Schuhl
Etudes sur la Fabulation Platonicienne (Paris 1947) 117 ff.

voice and are never out of tune. (And this is more properly the hidden meaning of the doctrine that the heavenly spheres move musically and melodically.) [1] But this could not be if the action and experience of the All was not on all occasions in accordance with the intelligible realities, in its measuring of periods and orders and the living through of the lives according to their kinds which the souls live through, sometimes in the intelligible world, sometimes in heaven, and sometimes turning to these regions. But Intellect as a whole is always above, and could never be outside its own world, but is settled as a whole above and communicates with things here through soul. Soul, because it is nearer, is disposed according to the form which comes to it from Intellect, and gives to the things below it, one kind of soul always in the same way, the other in different ways at different times, having its wanderings arranged in regular order. But [the individual soul] does not always come down the same distance, but sometimes more, sometimes less, even if it comes to the same species [of body]: each soul comes down to a body made ready for it according to its resemblance to the soul's disposition. It is carried there to that to which it is made like, one soul to a human being and others to different kinds of animals.

13. The inescapable rule and the justice [which govern the descent of souls] are thus set in a natural principle which compels each to go in its proper order to that to which it individually tends, the image of its original choice and disposition: each form of soul in that world is close to that to which it has an internal disposition, and there is no need of anyone to send it or bring it into body at a particular time,

οὔτε εἰς τοδί, ἀλλὰ καὶ τοῦ ποτὲ ἐνστάντος οἷον
αὐτομάτως κάτεισι καὶ εἴσεισιν εἰς ὃ δεῖ—καὶ
ἄλλος ἄλλῃ χρόνος, οὗ παραγενομένου οἷον κήρυκος
10 καλοῦντος κατίασι—καὶ εἰσέδυ εἰς τὸ πρόσφορον
σῶμα, ὡς εἰκάσαι τὰ γιγνόμενα οἷον δυνάμεσι
μάγων καὶ ὁλκαῖς τισιν ἰσχυραῖς κινεῖσθαί τε καὶ
φέρεσθαι· οἷον καὶ ἐφ' ἑνὸς ἑκάστου τελεῖται ἡ τοῦ
ζῴου διοίκησις, ἐν χρόνῳ ἕκαστον κινούσης καὶ
γεννώσης, οἷον γενειάσεις καὶ ⟨ἐκ⟩φύσεις [1] κεράτων
15 καὶ νῦν πρὸς τάδε ὁρμὰς καὶ ἐπανθήσεις πρότερον
οὐκ οὔσας καὶ περιττάς,[2] τῶν ⟨τε⟩[3] δένδρων
διοίκησις [4] ἐν προθεσμίαις τακταῖς γινομένη.[5]
ἴασι δὲ οὔτε ἑκοῦσαι οὔτε πεμφθεῖσαι· οὔ γε τὸ
ἑκούσιον τοιοῦτον ὡς προελέσθαι, ἀλλ' ὡς τὸ πηδᾶν
κατὰ φύσιν, ἢ ⟨ὡς⟩[6] πρὸς γάμων φυσικὰς προθυ-
20 μίας ἢ [ὡς πρὸς][6] πράξεις τινὲς καλῶν οὐ λογισμῷ
κινούμενοι· ἀλλ' εἱμαρμένον ἀεὶ τῷ τοιῷδε τὸ τοιόνδε, καὶ τῷ τοιῷδε τὸ νῦν, τῷ δὲ τὸ αὖθις. καὶ ὁ
μὲν πρὸ κόσμου νοῦς εἱμαρμένην ἔχει τὴν τοῦ
μένειν ἐκεῖ ὁπόσον καὶ πέμπει,[7] καὶ τὸ καθέκαστον
25 τῷ καθόλου ὑποπῖπτον νόμῳ πέμπεται· ἔγκειται
γὰρ ἑκάστῳ τὸ καθόλου, καὶ ὁ νόμος οὐκ ἔξωθεν
τὴν ἰσχὺν εἰς τὸ τελεσθῆναι ἴσχει, ἀλλὰ δέδοται ἐν
αὐτοῖς ⟨τοῖς⟩[8] χρησαμένοις εἶναι καὶ περιφέρουσιν

---

[1] Theiler, cf. IV. 4. 11. 19.
[2] Theiler: περὶ τὰς Enn., H–S: περὶ del. Volkmann*.
[3] Theiler.
[4] Theiler: διοικήσεις Enn.* ,H–S.
[5] Theiler: γινομένων R, H–S: γιγνομένας Vitringa, Volkmann.
[6] transposuimus.
[7] Harder B–T: πέμπειν Enn.*
[8] αὐτοῖς τοῖς Kirchhoff: αὐτοῖς Enn.: τοῖς H–S².

or into this or that particular body, but when its
moment comes to it it descends and enters where it
must as if of its own accord. Each has its own time
and when it comes, like a herald summoning it, the
soul comes down and goes into the appropriate body,
so that what happens is like a stirring and carrying
away by magic powers and mighty attractions: it is
like the way in which the ordered development of a
living thing comes to its fulfilment as [its soul] stirs
and produces everything in its time—for instance
sprouting of beards and horns, and at the moment
special impulses, and breaking out into spots in
excessive numbers which were not there before, and
like the ordered development of trees coming about
at its appointed time. The souls go neither willingly
nor because they are sent, nor is the voluntary element in their going like deliberate choice, but like a
natural spontaneous jumping or a passionate natural
desire of sexual union or as some men are moved
unreasoningly to noble deeds. Each special kind
has its special destiny and moment, one now and one
at another time. Intellect which is before the universe has its destiny too, to remain There, however
much it also sends out; and the individual, which is
subordinated to the universal, is sent according to
law. For the universal bears heavily upon the particular, and the law does not derive from outside the
strength for its accomplishment, but is given to be
in those themselves who are subject to it, and they

αὐτόν· κἂν ἐνστῇ καὶ ὁ χρόνος, καὶ ὃ θέλει
γενέσθαι, γίνεται τότε ὑπ' αὐτῶν τῶν ἐχόντων
αὐτόν, ὥστε αὐτοὺς αὐτὸν τελεῖν, ἅτε περιφέροντας
30 ἰσχύσαντα[1] ἐν τῷ ἐν αὐτοῖς αὐτὸν ἱδρῦσθαι, οἷον
βρίθοντα εἰς αὐτοὺς καὶ προθυμίαν ἐμποιοῦντα καὶ
ὠδῖνα ἐκεῖ ἐλθεῖν, οὗ ὁ ἐν αὐτοῖς ὢν οἷον ἐλθεῖν
φθέγγεται.

14. Τούτων δὴ γινομένων φῶτα πολλὰ ὁ κόσμος
οὗτος ἔχων καὶ καταυγαζόμενος ψυχαῖς ἐπικοσμεῖ-
ται ἐπὶ τοῖς προτέροις ἄλλους κόσμους ἄλλον παρ'
ἄλλου κομιζόμενος, παρά τε θεῶν ἐκείνων παρά τε
5 νῶν τῶν ἄλλων ψυχὰς διδόντων· οἷον εἰκὸς καὶ τὸν
μῦθον αἰνίττεσθαι, ὡς πλάσαντος τοῦ Προμηθέως
τὴν γυναῖκα ἐπεκόσμησαν αὐτὴν καὶ οἱ ἄλλοι θεοί·
γαῖαν ὕδει φύρειν, καὶ ἀνθρώπου ἐνθεῖναι φωνήν,
θεαῖς δ' ὁμοίαν τὸ εἶδος, καὶ Ἀφροδίτην τι δοῦναι
καὶ Χάριτας καὶ ἄλλον ἄλλο δῶρον καὶ ὀνομάσαι ἐκ
10 τοῦ δώρου καὶ πάντων τῶν δεδωκότων· πάντες γὰρ
τούτῳ ἔδοσαν τῷ πλάσματι παρὰ προμηθείας τινὸς
γενομένῳ. ὁ δὲ Ἐπιμηθεὺς ἀποποιούμενος τὸ

---

[1] περιφέροντας ἰσχύσαντα Vitringa, Harder, Cilento, B–T:
περιφέροντα καὶ ἰσχύσαντα Enn.: περιφέροντας καὶ ἰσχύσαντας
H–S[1].

---

[1] The teaching of this chapter about the descent of the
human soul should be carefully compared with that in the
early treatise *On the Descent of the Soul* IV. 8. 3–6. In this
treatise one can see particularly clearly the variations of
emphasis and the fluctuations between optimism and pessimism about the material world and our life in it which are
characteristic of Plotinus' discussions of this subject, because

bear it about with them. And if the time comes too, then what it wills to happen is also brought about by beings themselves in whom it is present, so that they accomplish it themselves because they bear it about, strong by its firm establishment in them; it makes itself a sort of weight in them and implants a longing, a birth pang of desire to come there where the law within them as it were calls them to come.[1]

14. Because all this has happened this universal order of ours, which has many lights and is illuminated by souls, is being further set in order and adorned, receiving new ordered beauties over and above its former ones, one from one source and one from another, from the gods of that other world and the other intellects which give souls[2]; it seems likely that this is the hidden meaning of the story that when Prometheus had made the woman the other gods too helped to adorn her; that " he mixed earth with water ", and gave her a human voice, and made her like the goddesses in appearance, and that Aphrodite gave her something and the Graces, and different gods gave her different gifts, and that she took her name from the gift and all the givers: for all gave something to this formation which came into existence as a result of a forethought (or " providence "). But what could Epimetheus rejecting

its purpose is to reconcile the divergent accounts, pessimistic and optimistic, given by Plato in different dialogues. But there does not seem to be any fundamental difference between the thought of IV. 8 and the thought of this chapter. See further my Introductory Note to IV. 3–5, p. 26 ff.

[2] Cp. VI. 4. 14. 18–19 (from a treatise written shortly before this one) where the population of the intelligible world is described as including men (in their pure intelligible state) as well as gods.

δῶρον αὐτοῦ τί ἂν σημαίνοι ἢ τὴν τοῦ ἐν νοητῷ
μᾶλλον αἵρεσιν ἀμείνω εἶναι; δέδεται δὲ καὶ αὐτὸς
15 ὁ ποιήσας, ὅτι πως ἐφάπτεται τοῦ γενομένου ὑπ'
αὐτοῦ, καὶ ὁ τοιοῦτος δεσμὸς ἔξωθεν· καὶ ἡ λύσις
ἡ ὑπὸ Ἡρακλέους, ὅτι δύναμίς ἐστιν αὐτῷ, ὥστε
καὶ ὡς λελύσθαι. ταῦτα μὲν οὖν ὅπῃ τις δοξάζει,
ἀλλ' ὅτι ἐμφαίνει τὰ τῆς εἰς τὸν κόσμον δόσεως, καὶ
προσᾴδει τοῖς λεγομένοις.

15. Ἴασι δὲ ἐκκύψασαι τοῦ νοητοῦ εἰς οὐρανὸν
μὲν πρῶτον καὶ σῶμα ἐκεῖ προσλαβοῦσαι δι' αὐτοῦ
ἤδη χωροῦσι καὶ ἐπὶ τὰ γεωδέστερα σώματα, εἰς
ὅσον ἂν εἰς μῆκος ἐκταθῶσι. καὶ αἱ μὲν ἀπ'
5 οὐρανοῦ εἰς σώματα τὰ κατωτέρω, αἱ δὲ ἀπ'
ἄλλων εἰς ἄλλα εἰσκρινόμεναι, αἷς ἡ δύναμις οὐκ
ἤρκεσεν ἆραι ἐντεῦθεν διὰ βάρυνσιν καὶ λήθην
πολὺ ἐφελκομέναις, ὃ αὐταῖς ἐβαρύνθη. γίνονται δὲ

---

[1] The story of Prometheus, Epimetheus and Pandora here
follows Hesiod, with slight variations: for the making of
Pandora see Hesiod *Op.* 60–89; for the binding and loosing
of Prometheus see Hesiod *Theog.* 521–8. Plotinus' remark
about his own casual allegorical interpretation (line 17) shows
how little seriously he took this sort of thing. The ancient
myths do of course for him, as for other men of his age, express
profound truths in symbolic form. But as long as you recognise what the truths are, it does not matter whether you discover them in any particular myth, or how you interpret the
details of the poets' stories.

[2] Here there appears the " cosmic religiosity " which Plotinus shared with other philosophers of late antiquity: the
belief, that is, that the celestial regions and the heavenly
bodies are divine and far closer to any higher, spiritual or
intelligible, divinities there may be, than the world below the

the gift of what had been formed signify except that the choice of a life lived more in the intelligible world is the better one? And the maker is bound because he is somehow in contact with that which he has made, and a bond of this kind is external; and his freeing by Heracles means that he has power even so to free himself. This interpretation is as anyone likes to think it, except that the story displays the gifts made to the universal order and is in harmony with what we say.[1]

15. The souls when they have peeped out of the intelligible world go first to heaven, and when they have put on a body there go on by its means to earthier bodies, to the limit to which they extend themselves in length.[2] And some souls [only] come from heaven to lower bodies; others pass from one body into another, those whose power is not sufficient to lift them from this region because they are weighed down and forgetful, dragging with them much that weighs upon them. They become different

---

moon, and that consequently the primary and proper material abode of souls is in this higher region from which they descend, assuming progressively inferior sorts of bodies according to the depth of their descent, the earthly body being the last and lowest: cp. chs. 9 and 17 of this treatise and Appendix II, *The Astral Body in Neoplatonism* in Proclus *The Elements of Theology* ed. E. R. Dodds, 2nd ed. (Oxford 1963) 313–21. Philosophical cosmic religion was something which Plotinus took seriously. He defends it vigorously against astrological superstition in II. 3 and against the Gnostic contempt for the divinities of the visible heaven in II. 9. But it occupies a place of moderate importance in his thought, and is not easy to reconcile with other aspects of it; and the idea of " astral " or " pneumatic " bodies superior to our earthly bodies is of much less importance to him than the belief in the divinity of the heavenly bodies.

διάφοροι ἢ σωμάτων εἰς ἃ ἐνεκρίθησαν παραλ-
λαγαῖς ἢ καὶ τύχαις ἢ καὶ τροφαῖς, ἢ αὐταὶ παρ'
10 αὐτῶν τὸ διάφορον κομίζουσιν ἢ πᾶσι τούτοις ἢ
τισιν αὐτῶν. καὶ αἱ μὲν τὰ πάντα ὑποπεπτώκασιν
εἱμαρμένῃ τῇ ἐνταῦθα, αἱ δὲ ὁτὲ μὲν οὕτως, ὁτὲ δὲ
αὐτῶν, αἱ δὲ ὅσα μὲν ἀναγκαῖα ὑπομεῖναι συγχωρ-
οῦσι, δύνανται δὲ ὅσα ἐστὶν αὐτῶν ἔργα αὐτῶν εἶναι,
ζῶσαι κατ' ἄλλην τὴν τῶν συμπάντων τῶν ὄντων
15 νομοθεσίαν ἄλλῳ ἑαυτὰς θεσμῷ δοῦσαι. πέπλεκται
δὲ αὕτη ἔκ τε τῶν τῇδε λόγων τε καὶ αἰτίων
πάντων καὶ ψυχικῶν κινήσεων καὶ νόμων τῶν
ἐκεῖθεν, συμφωνοῦσα ἐκείνοις καὶ ἀρχὰς ἐκεῖθεν
παραλαβοῦσα καὶ συνυφαίνουσα τὰ ἑξῆς ἐκείνοις,
20 ἀσάλευτα μὲν τηροῦσα, ὅσα δύναται σῴζειν ἑαυτὰ
πρὸς τὴν ἐκείνων ἕξιν, τὰ δὲ ἄλλα ᾗ πέφυκε
περιάγουσα, ὡς τὴν αἰτίαν ἐν τοῖς κατελθοῦσιν
εἶναι, ὅτι οὕτως, ὡς τὰ μὲν ὡδὶ τεθῆναι, τὰ δὲ ὡδὶ
κεῖσθαι.

16. Τὰ μὲν οὖν γινόμενα τιμωρήματα εἰς τοὺς
πονηροὺς μετὰ δίκης τῇ τάξει ἀποδιδόναι προσήκει
ὡς κατὰ τὸ δέον ἀγούσῃ· ὅσα δὲ τοῖς ἀγαθοῖς
συμβαίνει ἔξω δίκης, οἷον κολάσεις ἢ πενίαι ἢ
5 νόσοι, ἆρα διὰ προτέρας ἁμαρτίας λεκτέον γίνεσθαι;
συμπέπλεκται γὰρ ταῦτα καὶ προσημαίνεται, ὡς

either because of the variety of the bodies into which they entered or because of their fortunes or their upbringing, or they themselves bring with them a difference coming from themselves, or all these causes, or some of them, operate together to produce the differences. And some of them have altogether become subject to the destiny of this world, but others are sometimes subject to it and sometimes belong to themselves; others again accept all that it is necessary to endure, but are able to be self-possessed in all that is their own work, living according to another code of laws, that which governs the whole of reality, and submitting themselves to [this] other ordinance. This code of laws is woven from all the rational principles and causes here below, and the movement of souls and the laws which come from the intelligible world; it is in harmony with these last, and takes its principles from that world and weaves together what comes after with the intelligible principles, keeping undisturbed all things which can maintain themselves in accordance with the disposition of the intelligibles, and making the others circulate according to their natures, so that the responsibility lies with the souls which have come down for coming down in such a way that some are put in this place and others find themselves in that.

16. It is fitting to attribute the punishments which fall with justice on the wicked to the [universal] order in that it directs the world according to what is right; but as for all that happens without justice to the good, like [unjust] punishments or poverty or sickness, are these to be said to have come upon them because of previous sins? For these are woven in and signified beforehand, so that they too happen

καὶ αὐτὰ κατὰ λόγον γίγνεσθαι. ἢ οὐ κατὰ λόγους
φυσικοὺς ταῦτα, οὐδ' ἦν ἐν τοῖς προηγουμένοις,
ἀλλ' ἑπόμενα ἐκείνοις· οἷον πιπτούσης τινὸς
οἰκοδομίας τὸν ὑποπεσόντα ἀποθανεῖν ὁποῖός ποτ'
10 ἂν ᾖ, ἢ καὶ ἵππων [1] δύο κατὰ τάξιν φερομένων ἢ
καὶ ἑνὸς τὸ ἐμπεσὸν τρωθῆναι ἢ πατηθῆναι. ἢ καὶ
τὸ ἄδικον τοῦτο οὐ κακὸν ὂν τῷ παθόντι πρὸς τὴν
τοῦ ὅλου χρήσιμον πλοκήν. ἢ οὐδὲ ἄδικον ἐκ τῶν
πρόσθεν ἔχον [2] τὴν δικαίωσιν. οὐ γὰρ τὰ μὲν δεῖ
νομίζειν συντετάχθαι, τὰ δὲ κεχαλάσθαι εἰς τὸ
15 αὐτεξούσιον. εἰ γὰρ κατ' αἰτίας γίγνεσθαι δεῖ καὶ
φυσικὰς ἀκολουθίας καὶ κατὰ λόγον ἕνα καὶ τάξιν
μίαν, καὶ τὰ σμικρότερα δεῖ συντετάχθαι καὶ
συνυφάνθαι νομίζειν. καὶ τὸ ἄδικον δὴ τὸ παρ'
ἄλλου εἰς ἄλλον αὐτῷ μὲν τῷ ποιήσαντι ἄδικον,
20 καὶ οὐκ ἀφείθη αἰτίας ὁ δράσας, συντεταγμένον δ'
ἐν τῷ παντὶ οὐκ ἄδικον ἐν ἐκείνῳ οὐδ' εἰς τὸν
παθόντα, ἀλλ' οὕτως ἐχρῆν. εἰ δ' ἀγαθὸς ὁ παθών,
εἰς ἀγαθὸν ἡ τελευτὴ τούτων. δεῖ γὰρ τήνδε τὴν
σύνταξιν οὐκ ἀθεεὶ οὐδὲ ἄδικον, ἀλλ' ἀκριβῆ εἰς
τὴν τοῦ προσήκοντος ἀπόδοσιν νομίζειν, ἀδήλους
25 δὲ ἔχειν τὰς αἰτίας καὶ τοῖς οὐκ εἰδόσι παρέχειν
μέμψεως αἰτίας.

17. Ὅτι δὲ ἐκ τοῦ νοητοῦ εἰς τὴν οὐρανοῦ ἴασιν αἱ
ψυχαὶ τὸ πρῶτον χώραν, λογίσαιτο ἄν τις ἐκ τῶν
τοιούτων. εἰ γὰρ οὐρανὸς ἐν τῷ αἰσθητῷ τόπῳ
ἀμείνων, εἴη ἂν προσεχὴς τῶν νοητῶν τοῖς ἐσχάτοις.

---

[1] Theiler: τινων Enn.*, H–S[1].
[2] Vitringa, Müller*: ἐχόντων Enn., H–S[1].

according to rational principle. No, these things do not occur according to the rational principles of nature and are not given in their premises, but are consequences of them; for instance, if a building falls the man who is underneath it is killed, whatever sort of man he is; or if two horses are moving in an orderly way—or even one—anything which gets in the way is injured or trampled. Or [we should think that] this injustice is not an evil to the sufferer [and contributes] to the interweaving of the whole. Or it is not unjust because it has its justification from former faults. For one must not think that some things are contained in the order, while others are let loose for the operation of free will. For if things have to happen according to causes and rational sequences and according to one rational principle and a single order, one must think that the less important things too are contained in the order and woven in. And the injustice which one man does to another is certainly an injustice from the point of view of the doer, and the man who perpetrates it is not free from guilt, but as contained in the universal order it is not unjust in that order, or in relation to the sufferer, but it was ordained that he should so suffer. But if the sufferer is a good man, this will turn out for his good. For one must not think that the order is godless or unjust, but that it is accurate in the distribution of what is appropriate, but it keeps its reasons hidden and gives grounds for blame to those who do not know them.

17. One could deduce from considerations like the following that the souls when they leave the intelligible first enter the space of heaven. For if heaven is the better part of the region perceived by the

5 ἐκεῖθεν τοίνυν ψυχοῦται ταῦτα πρῶτα καὶ μετα-
λαμβάνει ὡς ἐπιτηδειότερα μεταλαμβάνειν. τὸ δὲ
γεηρὸν ὕστατόν τε καὶ ψυχῆς ἥττονος πεφυκὸς
μεταλαμβάνειν καὶ τῆς ἀσωμάτου φύσεως πόρρω.
πᾶσαι μὲν δὴ καταλάμπουσι τὸν οὐρανὸν καὶ δι-
δόασιν οἷον τὸ πολὺ αὑτῶν καὶ τὸ πρῶτον ἐκείνῳ,
10 τὰ δὲ ἄλλα τοῖς ὑστέροις ἐναυγάζονται, αἱ δ'
ἐπιπλέον κατιοῦσαι ἐναυγάζουσι μᾶλλον κάτω,
αὐταῖς δὲ οὐκ ἄμεινον εἰς πολὺ προϊούσαις. ἔστι
γάρ τι οἷον κέντρον, ἐπὶ δὲ τούτῳ κύκλος ἀπ'
αὐτοῦ ἐκλάμπων, ἐπὶ δὲ τούτοις ἄλλος, φῶς ἐκ
φωτός· ἔξωθεν δὲ τούτων οὐκέτι φωτὸς κύκλος
15 ἄλλος, ἀλλὰ δεόμενος οὗτος οἰκείου φωτὸς ἀπορίᾳ
αὐγῆς ἀλλοτρίας. ἔστω δὲ ῥόμβος οὗτος, μᾶλλον
δὲ σφαῖρα τοιαύτη, ἣ δὴ κομίζεται ἀπὸ τῆς τρίτης—
προσεχὴς γὰρ αὐτῇ—ὅσον ἐκείνη ἐναυγάζεται. τὸ
μὲν οὖν μέγα φῶς μένον ἐλλάμπει, καὶ διήκει κατὰ
20 λόγον ἐξ αὐτοῦ αὐγή, τὰ δ' ἄλλα συνεπιλάμπει, τὰ
μὲν μένοντα, τὰ δ' ἐπιπλέον ἐπισπᾶται τῇ τοῦ
ἐλλαμπομένου ἀγλαΐᾳ. εἶτα δεομένων τῶν ἐλ-
λαμπομένων πλείονος φροντίδος, ὥσπερ χειμαζο-
μένων πλοίων κυβερνῆται ἐναπερείδονται πρὸς τὸ
πλέον τῇ τῶν νεῶν φροντίδι καὶ ἀμελήσαντες αὑτῶν

---

[1] See note on ch. 15. There is here a certain " creeping
spatiality ". Plotinus does not really think that any part of
the material universe, even the highest heaven, can be nearer
to the intelligible than any other, because the intelligible is
not in space at all. But here his language is influenced, perhaps not only by the " cosmic religiosity " of his time, but by
his favourite myth in Plato's *Phaedrus* (cp. 246D6–247E6).

[2] Cp. VI. 4. 9. 25–6 and the Nicene creed. It is interesting

senses, it borders on the last and lowest parts of the intelligible.[1] So these heavenly regions are first ensouled thence, and participate in soul first because they are better adapted to participate. But the body of earth is the last, and less naturally adapted to participate in soul and far from the bodiless nature. All souls then illuminate the heaven and give it the greatest and first part of themselves, but illuminate the rest of the world with their secondary parts; those which come down further throw their light lower, but it is not to their advantage to have gone on so far. For there is a kind of centre, and around this a circle shining out from it, and beyond these another, light from light [2]: but outside these there is no longer another circle of light but this next circle through lack of its own light needs illumination from another source. Let this be a wheel, or rather a sphere of a kind which from the third— for it borders upon it—obtains all the illumination which that third receives. So the great light abides and shines, and its radiance goes out through the world in rational order and proportion; the other lights join in illuminating, some staying in their places, but others are more attracted by the brightness of what is illuminated. Then as the things which are illuminated need more care, just as the steersmen of ships in a storm concentrate more and more on the care of their ships and are unaware that

to find exactly this phrase (φῶς ἐκ φωτός) which appears in Plotinus in strongly subordinationist contexts, occupying an important place in the first great credal affirmation of non-subordinationist Trinitarian theology, where the Fathers of Nicaea are trying to state with the utmost possible emphasis that the Son is *not* inferior to the Father as one Plotinian hypostasis is to that above it.

25 ἔλαθον, ὡς κινδυνεύειν συνεπισπασθῆναι πολλάκις
τῷ τῶν νεῶν ναυαγίῳ, ἔρρεψαν τὸ [1] πλέον καὶ
αὗται καὶ τοῖς ἑαυτῶν· ἔπειτα δὲ κατεσχέθησαν
πεδηθεῖσαι γοητείας δεσμοῖς, σχεθεῖσαι φύσεως
κηδεμονίᾳ. εἰ δ᾽ ἦν τοιοῦτον ἕκαστον ζῷον οἷον
καὶ τὸ πᾶν, τέλεον καὶ ἱκανὸν σῶμα καὶ ἀκίνδυνον
30 παθεῖν, καὶ παρεῖναι λεγομένη ψυχὴ οὐκ ἂν παρῆν
αὐτῷ, καὶ παρεῖχεν αὐτῷ ζωὴν μένουσα πάντη ἐν
τῷ ἄνω.

18. Πότερα δὲ λογισμῷ ψυχὴ χρῆται πρὶν ἐλθεῖν
καὶ πάλιν αὖ ἐξελθοῦσα; ἢ ἐνταῦθα ὁ λογισμὸς
ἐγγίγνεται ἐν ἀπόρῳ ἤδη οὔσης καὶ φροντίδος
πληρουμένης καὶ μᾶλλον ἀσθενούσης· ἐλάττωσις
5 γὰρ νοῦ εἰς αὐτάρκειαν τὸ λογισμοῦ δεῖσθαι·
ὥσπερ καὶ ἐν ταῖς τέχναις ὁ λογισμὸς ἀποροῦσι
τοῖς τεχνίταις, ὅταν δὲ μὴ χαλεπὸν ᾖ, κρατεῖ καὶ
ἐργάζεται ἡ τέχνη. ἀλλ᾽ εἰ ἐκεῖ ἄνευ λογισμῶν,
πῶς ἂν ἔτι λογικαὶ εἶεν; ἢ ὅτι δύνανται, εἴποι τις
ἄν, ὅταν περίστασις, εὐπορῆσαι διασκοποῦσαι.
10 δεῖ δὲ τὸν λογισμὸν λαβεῖν τὸν τοιοῦτον· ἐπεὶ εἴ
τις λογισμὸν λαμβάνει τὴν ἐκ νοῦ ἀεὶ γινομένην καὶ
οὖσαν ἐν αὐταῖς διάθεσιν, καὶ ἐνέργειαν ἑστῶσαν
καὶ οἷον ἔμφασιν οὖσαν, εἶεν ἂν κἀκεῖ λογισμῷ
χρώμεναι. οὐδὲ δὴ φωναῖς, οἶμαι, χρῆσθαι νομιστέον ἐν μὲν τῷ νοητῷ οὔσας καὶ πάμπαν, σώματα
15 δ᾽ ἐχούσας ἐν οὐρανῷ, ὅσα μὲν διὰ χρείας ἢ δι᾽

---

[1] Theiler: τε Enn.*, H–S[1].

[1] For the " magic " of the physical universe, the living power
of its organic unity on which the art of the magician depends,
see IV. 4. 40.

they are forgetting themselves, that they are in danger of being dragged down with the wreck of the ships, these souls incline downwards more with what is theirs. Then they are held fettered with bonds of magic,[1] held fast by their care for [bodily] nature. But if every living creature was like the All, a perfect and sufficient body and in no danger of suffering, then the soul which is said to be present would not be present in it, and would give it life while remaining altogether in the upper world.

18. Does the soul use discursive reasoning before it comes and again after it goes out of the body? No, discursive reasoning comes into it here below, when it is already in perplexity and full of care, and in a state of greater weakness; for feeling the need of reasoning is a lessening of the intellect in respect of its self-sufficiency; just as in the crafts reasoning occurs when the craftsmen are in perplexity, but, when there is no difficulty, the craft dominates and does its work. But if they are without reasoning processes there, how could they still be reasonable? Because they are capable, one might say, when the circumstances arise, of considering rationally with the greatest of ease. But one must understand reasoning in this sort of sense; because if one understands reasoning to be the state of mind which exists in them always proceeding from Intellect, and which is a static activity and a kind of reflection of Intellect, they would employ reasoning in that other world, too. Nor do I think that we should suppose that they use speech in the intelligible world, and altogether, even if they have bodies in heaven, there would be none of that talk there which they engage in here because of needs or over doubtful and dis-

ἀμφισβητήσεις διαλέγοντα ἐνταῦθα, ἐκεῖ οὐκ ἂν
εἴη· ποιοῦσαι δὲ ἐν τάξει καὶ κατὰ φύσιν ἕκαστα
οὐδ' ἂν ἐπιτάττοιεν οὐδ' ἂν συμβουλεύοιεν, γινώσ-
κοιεν δ' ἂν καὶ τὰ παρ' ἀλλήλων ἐν συνέσει. ἐπεὶ
20 καὶ ἐνταῦθα πολλὰ σιωπώντων γινώσκοιμεν δι'
ὀμμάτων· ἐκεῖ δὲ καθαρὸν πᾶν τὸ σῶμα καὶ οἷον
ὀφθαλμὸς ἕκαστος καὶ οὐδὲν δὲ κρυπτὸν οὐδὲ πε-
πλασμένον, ἀλλὰ πρὶν εἰπεῖν ἄλλῳ ἰδὼν ἐκεῖνος
ἔγνω. περὶ δὲ δαιμόνων καὶ ψυχῶν ἐν ἀέρι φωνῇ
χρῆσθαι οὐκ ἄτοπον· ζῷα γὰρ τοιάδε.

19. Πότερα δὲ ἐπὶ τοῦ αὐτοῦ τὸ ἀμέριστον καὶ
μεριστὸν ὥσπερ κραθέντων, ἢ ἄλλῃ μὲν καὶ
κατ' ἄλλο τὸ ἀμέριστον, τὸ δὲ μεριστὸν οἷον ἐφεξῆς
καὶ ἕτερον μέρος αὐτῆς, ὥσπερ τὸ μὲν λογιζόμενόν
5 φαμεν ἄλλο, τὸ δὲ ἄλογον; γνωσθείη δ' ἂν ληφ-
θέντος τί λέγομεν ἑκάτερον. ἀμέριστον μὲν οὖν
ἁπλῶς εἴρηται αὐτῷ, μεριστὸν δὲ οὐχ ἁπλῶς,
ἀλλὰ περὶ τὰ σώματά φησι γινομένην μερισ-
τὴν καὶ ταύτην οὐ γεγενημένην. τὴν δὴ σώματος
10 φύσιν ὁρᾶν δεῖ πρὸς τὸ ζῆν οἵας ψυχῆς προσδεῖται,
καὶ ὅ τι δεῖ τῆς ψυχῆς πανταχοῦ τῷ σώματι καὶ
ὅλῳ παρεῖναι. πᾶν μὲν δὴ τὸ αἰσθητικόν, εἴπερ
διὰ παντὸς αἰσθήσεται, ἀφικνεῖσθαι πρὸς τὸ μερί-
ζεσθαι· πανταχοῦ μὲν γὰρ ὂν μεμερίσθαι ἂν λέγοιτο·
ὅλον δὲ πανταχοῦ φαινόμενον οὐ μεμερίσθαι ἂν
15 παντελῶς λέγοιτο, περὶ δὲ τὰ σώματα γίγνεσθαι
μεριστόν. εἰ δέ τις λέγοι ἐν ταῖς ἄλλαις αἰσθήσεσι

puted points; but as they do everything they do in order and according to nature they would not give orders or advice and would know by intuition what passes from one to another. For here below, too, we can know many things by the look in people's eyes when they are silent; but there all their body is clear and pure and each is like an eye, and nothing is hidden or feigned, but before one speaks to another that other has seen and understood. But there is nothing absurd in spirits and souls in the air using voices; for they are [embodied] living creatures of a particular kind.

19. Are the " indivisible " and the " divisible " elements of the soul in the same place, as if they were mixed together, or is the " indivisible " in a different place and differently related, but the " divisible " so to speak following upon it and another part of soul, just as we say that the reasoning part is one thing and the unreasoning part another? This could be answered when it has been understood what we mean by each. The term " indivisible " is used without qualification, but " divisible " is not unqualified but Plato says that soul " becomes divisible in the sphere of bodies ", and not that it has already become so. One must then observe what kind of soul the nature of body requires in order to live, and what of soul must be present everywhere to body as a whole. Now the whole of the sense faculty, since it is going to operate throughout the whole body, comes to divide itself; for since it is everywhere it might be said to be divided; but since it appears everywhere as a whole, it could be said not to be absolutely and completely divided, but to become " divisible in the sphere of body ". But if anyone

93

μηδὲ μεμερίσθαι, ἀλλ' ἢ μόνον ἐν τῇ ἁφῇ, λεκτέον
ὅτι καὶ ἐν ταῖς ἄλλαις, εἴπερ σῶμά ἐστι τὸ μεταλαμ-
βάνον, ἀνάγκη οὕτω μερίζεσθαι, ἔλαττον δὲ ἢ
ἐν τῇ ἁφῇ. καὶ δὴ καὶ τὸ φυτικὸν αὐτῆς καὶ τὸ
20 αὐξητικὸν ὡσαύτως· καὶ εἰ περὶ τὸ ἧπαρ ἡ ἐπιθυμία, τὸ δὲ περὶ τὴν καρδίαν ὁ θυμός, ὁ αὐτὸς
λόγος καὶ ἐπὶ τούτων. ἀλλ' ἴσως ταῦτα οὐ παραλαμβάνει ἐν ἐκείνῳ τῷ μίγματι, ἴσως δὲ ἄλλον
τρόπον καὶ ἔκ τινος τῶν παραληφθέντων ταῦτα.
25 λογισμὸς δὲ καὶ νοῦς; οὐκέτι ταῦτα σώματι
δίδωσιν αὐτά· καὶ γὰρ τὸ ἔργον αὐτῶν οὐ δι' ὀργάνου
τελεῖται τοῦ σώματος· ἐμπόδιον γὰρ τοῦτο, εἴ τις
αὐτῷ ἐν ταῖς σκέψεσι προσχρῷτο. ἄλλο ἄρα
ἑκάτερον τὸ ἀμέριστον καὶ μεριστόν, καὶ οὐχ ὡς
ἐν κραθέντα, ἀλλ' ὡς ὅλον ἐκ μερῶν ἑκατέρου
30 καθαροῦ καὶ χωρὶς τῇ δυνάμει. εἰ μέντοι καὶ τὸ
περὶ τὰ σώματα γιγνόμενον μεριστὸν παρὰ
τῆς ἐπάνω δυνάμεως ἔχει τὸ ἀμέριστον, δύναται τὸ
αὐτὸ τοῦτο ἀμέριστον καὶ μεριστὸν εἶναι, οἷον
κραθὲν ἐξ αὐτοῦ τε καὶ τῆς εἰς αὐτὸ ἐλθούσης ἄνωθεν
δυνάμεως.

20. Εἰ δὲ καὶ ἐν τόπῳ ταῦτά τε καὶ τὰ ἄλλα τῆς
ψυχῆς λεγόμενα μέρη, ἢ ταῦτα μὲν ὅλως οὐκ ἐν
τόπῳ, τὰ δὲ ἄλλα ἐν τόπῳ καὶ ποῦ, ἢ ὅλως οὐδέν,
ἐπιστῆσαι προσήκει. εἴτε γὰρ μὴ ἀφοριοῦμεν

---

[1] With Theiler I take the subject of παραλαμβάνει here to
be " Plato ", not, as most editors (including Henry-Schwyzer),
" the body ". Plotinus in this chapter is trying to give a
coherent and philosophically satisfactory exposition of Plato's
account of human psychology in the *Timaeus*, based on the
often quoted text 35A1–3, to which he refers at the beginning

says that it is not divided at all in the other senses, but only in that of touch, we must reply that it must divide itself in the others too in this way, since it is body which participates in it, but less than in the sense of touch. And the plant principle in it, too, and the principle of growth are divided in the same way; and if desire is in the region of the liver and the spirited part in the region of the heart, the same argument will apply to them. But perhaps Plato does not admit that these sensations occur in the mixture of which we have been speaking: perhaps he considers that they arise in another way and as a result of some one of the things which have been already received.[1] But what about reasoning and intellect? These no longer give themselves to the body; for their work is not done through the instrument of the body: for this gets in the way if one uses it in rational investigations. So then the " indivisible " and the " divisible " are two different things, and not like one mingled thing but like a whole of parts, each of which is pure and separate in its power. If, however, that which is " divisible in the sphere of bodies " holds the " indivisible " from a higher power, this same thing can be both indivisible and divisible, as if it was mixed from itself and the power which comes into it from above.

20. It is proper that we should pay attention to the question whether these and the other so-called parts of the soul are in place, or whether these are

of the chapter. At this point he seems somewhat uneasy about Plato's firm attribution of different parts of the soul to different parts of the body in 70–71. In the next sentence he turns, perhaps with relief, to the clear-cut dualism of *Phaedo* 65.

5 ἑκάστοις τῶν τῆς ψυχῆς τόπον τινὰ οὐδαμοῦ οὐδὲν
θέντες, οὐ μᾶλλον εἴσω τοῦ σώματος ἢ ἔξω
ποιοῦντες, ἄψυχον αὐτὸ ποιήσομεν, τά τε δι᾽
ὀργάνων σωματικῶν ἔργα ὅπῃ γίγνεσθαι προσήκει
εἰπεῖν ἀπορήσομεν, εἴτε τοῖς μέν, τοῖς δ᾽ οὔ, οἷς
μὴ δίδομεν, οὐκ ἐν ἡμῖν αὐτὰ ποιεῖν δόξομεν, ὥστε
10 μὴ πᾶσαν ἡμῶν τὴν ψυχὴν ἐν ἡμῖν εἶναι. ὅλως
μὲν οὖν οὐδὲν τῶν τῆς ψυχῆς μερῶν οὐδὲ πᾶσαν
φατέον ὡς ἐν τόπῳ εἶναι τῷ σώματι· περιεκτικὸν
μὲν γὰρ ὁ τόπος καὶ περιεκτικὸν σώματος, καὶ
οὗ ἕκαστον μερισθέν ἐστιν, ἔστιν ἐκεῖ, ὡς μὴ ὅλον ἐν
ὁτῳοῦν εἶναι· ἡ δὲ ψυχὴ οὐ σῶμα, καὶ οὐ περι-
15 εχόμενον μᾶλλον ἢ περιέχον. οὐ μὴν οὐδ᾽ ὡς ἐν
ἀγγείῳ· ἄψυχον γὰρ ἂν γένοιτο τὸ σῶμα, εἴτε ὡς
ἀγγεῖον, εἴτε ὡς τόπος περιέχει· εἰ μὴ ἄρα
διαδόσει τινὶ αὐτῆς οὔσης πρὸς αὐτὴν συνηθροισ-
μένης, καὶ ἔσται, ὅσον μετέλαβε τὸ ἀγγεῖον, τοῦτο
ἀπολωλὸς αὐτῇ. ὁ δὲ τόπος ὁ κυρίως ἀσώματος
20 καὶ οὐ σῶμα· ὥστε τί ἂν δέοιτο ψυχῆς; καὶ τὸ
σῶμα τῷ πέρατι αὐτοῦ πλησιάσει τῇ ψυχῇ, οὐχ
αὐτῷ. πολλὰ δὲ καὶ ἄλλα ἐναντιοῖτο πρὸς τὸ ὡς

---

[1] The sense seems much better if, with Theiler, we omit the
comma between ψυχῆς and τόπον printed by Henry-Schwyzer.

[2] The denial that soul is in body as a place or a receptacle
is normal Aristotelian doctrine: cp. the long critical discussion
of ways in which the soul may be said to be " in " the body
by Alexander of Aphrodisias *De Anima* 13–15 Bruns, of which
Plotinus makes use here and in the next chapter. Plotinus

not in any way in place but the others are, and where
they are, or whether no part of the soul is in any way
in place. For either, if we do not allot a place to
each of the parts of the soul and put none of them
anywhere,[1] not making them any more inside the
body than outside, we shall make the body soulless,
and shall find it difficult to see how the works of the
soul which are done through bodily instruments ought
to come about; or, if we give a place to some of
them, but not to others, then it will appear that we
are not making those to which we do not give a
place work within us, so that the whole of our soul
is not in us. Now we must say in general that neither
any of the parts of the soul nor the whole soul are
in body as in a place. For place is something encompassing, and encompassing body, and where each
divided part is, there it is [and nowhere else] so that
the whole is not [as a whole] in any place; but soul
is not a body, and is no more encompassed than
encompassing. It is certainly not in the body as in
a receptacle either.[2] For the body would be soulless, whether it encompassed the soul as a receptacle
or as a place, unless perhaps [it was ensouled] by a
sort of transmission from the soul which remained
collected together in itself, and then the amount of
which the receptacle partakes will be lost to soul.
But place in the strict and proper sense is bodiless
and not a body: so what need would it have of
soul? And body would come near to soul with its
edge, not with itself. And many other objections
could be made to [soul's being in body] as in place.

thinks that, if one is to use spatial metaphors at all, it is
better to say that body is in soul than that soul is in body:
cp. e.g. lines 14–15 here and ch. 22. 8–9.

ἐν τόπῳ εἶναι. καὶ γὰρ συμφέροιτο ἂν ἀεὶ ὁ τόπος,
καὶ αὐτό τι ἔσται τὸν τόπον αὐτὸν περιφέρον.
25 ἀλλ’ οὐδ’ εἰ ὁ τόπος διάστημα εἴη, πολὺ μᾶλλον
οὐκ ἂν εἴη ὡς ἐν τόπῳ τῷ σώματι. τὸ γὰρ διάστημα
κενὸν εἶναι δεῖ· τὸ δὲ σῶμα οὐ κενόν, ἀλλ’ ἴσως
ἐν ᾧ τὸ σῶμα ἔσται, ὥστε ἐν τῷ κενῷ τὸ σῶμα.
ἀλλὰ μὴν οὐδ’ ὡς ἐν ὑποκειμένῳ ἔσται τῷ σώματι·
τὸ γὰρ ἐν ὑποκειμένῳ πάθος τοῦ ἐν ᾧ, ὡς χρῶμα
30 καὶ σχῆμα, καὶ χωριστὸν ἡ ψυχή. οὐ μὴν οὐδ’ ὡς
μέρος ἐν ὅλῳ· οὐ γὰρ μέρος ἡ ψυχὴ τοῦ σώματος.
εἰ δέ τις λέγοι, ὡς ἐν ὅλῳ μέρος τῷ ζῴῳ,
πρῶτον μὲν ἡ αὐτὴ ἂν μένοι ἀπορία, πῶς ἐν ὅλῳ·
οὐ γὰρ δὴ ὡς ἐν τῷ ἀμφορεῖ τοῦ οἴνου ὁ οἶνος, ἢ
ὡς ὁ ἀμφορεύς, οὐδ’ ᾗ καὶ αὐτό τι ἐν αὑτῷ ἔσται.
35 ἀλλ’ οὐδ’ ὡς ὅλον ἐν τοῖς μέρεσι· γελοῖον γὰρ τὴν
μὲν ψυχὴν ὅλον λέγειν, τὸ δὲ σῶμα μέρη. ἀλλ’
οὐδὲ ὡς εἶδος ἐν ὕλῃ· ἀχώριστον γὰρ τὸ ἐν ὕλῃ
εἶδος, καὶ ἤδη ὕλης οὔσης ὕστερον τὸ εἶδος. ἡ δέ
ψυχὴ τὸ εἶδος ποιεῖ ἐν τῇ ὕλῃ ἄλλη τοῦ εἴδους οὖσα.
40 εἰ δὲ οὐ τὸ γενόμενον εἶδος, ἀλλὰ τὸ χωριζόμενον
φήσουσι, πῶς τοῦτο τὸ εἶδος ἐν τῷ σώματι,
οὔπω φανερὸν [καὶ χωριστὸν ἡ ψυχή].[1] πῶς οὖν ἐν
τῷ σώματι ἡ ψυχὴ λέγεται πρὸς πάντων; ἢ
ἐπειδὴ οὐχ ὁρατὸν ἡ ψυχή, ἀλλὰ τὸ σῶμα. σῶμα
οὖν ὁρῶντες, ἔμψυχον δὲ συνιέντες, ὅτι κινεῖται
45 καὶ αἰσθάνεται, ἔχειν φαμὲν ψυχὴν αὐτό. ἐν αὐτῷ
ἄρα τῷ σώματι τὴν ψυχὴν εἶναι ἀκολούθως ἂν
λέγοιμεν. εἰ δέ γε ὁρατὸν ἡ ψυχὴ καὶ αἰσθητὸν ἦν

---

[1] del. Volkmann* ut iteratum e lin. 29–30.

For place would always be carried along with it, and body itself would be something carrying space itself about. But even if place is taken to mean interval, soul would still less be in body as in place. For an interval must be void; but body is not void; though that in which body is may be, so that body is in the void. But soul will certainly not be in body as in a substrate, either: for that which is in a substrate is an affection of that in which it is, colour and shape for instance, and soul is something separable. It is certainly not, either, like a part in the whole: for soul is not a part of body. If someone were to suggest that it was like a part in a whole living creature, first of all the same difficulty would remain about how it is in the whole: for it is not, presumably, as the wine is in the jar of wine, or the gallon in the gallon jar, or in the way in which some one thing is in itself. But it is not, either, in body as a whole is in its parts: for it would be absurd to say that the soul is a whole and the body its parts. But it is not, either, present like the form in matter: for the form in matter is inseparable, and it comes afterwards to the matter which is already there. But soul makes the form in matter and is other than the form [which it makes]. But if they assert that it is not the form which comes to be in the matter, but the separate form, it is not yet clear how this is the form in the body. How then is it that the soul is said by everyone to be in the body? It is because the soul is not visible, but the body is, so we see the body and are aware that it is ensouled because it moves and perceives, and so say that it has soul. It would then be a natural consequence for us to say that the soul is actually in the body. But if the soul was visible

99

περιειλημμένον πάντῃ τῇ ζωῇ καὶ μέχρις ἐσχάτων
οὖσα εἰς ἴσον, οὐκ ἂν ἔφαμεν τὴν ψυχὴν ἐν τῷ
σώματι εἶναι, ἀλλ' ἐν τῷ κυριωτέρῳ τὸ μὴ
50 τοιοῦτον, καὶ ἐν τῷ συνέχοντι τὸ συνεχόμενον,
καὶ ἐν τῷ μὴ ῥέοντι τὸ ῥέον.

21. Τί οὖν; πῶς πάρεστιν, εἴ τις ἐρωτῴη
μηδὲν αὐτὸς λέγων ὅπως, τί ἐροῦμεν; καὶ εἰ
ὁμοίως πᾶσα, ἢ ἄλλο μέρος ἄλλως, τὸ δ' ἄλλως;
ἐπεὶ τοίνυν τῶν νῦν λεγομένων τρόπων τοῦ ἔν τινι
5 οὐδεὶς φαίνεται ἐπὶ τῆς ψυχῆς πρὸς τὸ σῶμα
ἁρμόττων, λέγεται δὲ οὕτως ἐν τῷ σώματι εἶναι
ἡ ψυχή, ὡς ὁ κυβερνήτης ἐν τῇ νηί, πρὸς μὲν τὸ
χωριστὴν δύνασθαι εἶναι τὴν ψυχὴν καλῶς εἴρηται,
τὸν μέντοι τρόπον, ὡς νῦν ἡμεῖς ζητοῦμεν, οὐκ ἂν
πάνυ παραστήσειεν. ὡς μὲν γὰρ πλωτὴρ κατὰ
10 συμβεβηκὸς ἂν εἴη ἐν αὐτῇ ὁ κυβερνήτης, ὡς δὲ
κυβερνήτης πῶς; οὐδὲ γὰρ ἐν πάσῃ τῇ νηί,
ὥσπερ ἡ ψυχὴ ἐν τῷ σώματι. ἀλλὰ ἆρα οὕτω
φατέον, ὡς ἡ τέχνη ἐν τοῖς ὀργάνοις, οἷον ἐν τῷ
οἴακι, [οἷον] [1] εἰ ἔμψυχος ὁ οἴαξ ἦν, ὥστε κυβερνη-
τικὴν εἶναι ἔνδον τὴν κινοῦσαν τεχνικῶς; νῦν δὲ
15 τοῦτο διαλλάττειν, ὅτι ἔξωθεν ἡ τέχνη. εἰ οὖν κατὰ
τὸ παράδειγμα τὸ τοῦ κυβερνήτου τοῦ ἐνδύντος
πρὸς τὸν οἴακα θείμεθα τὴν ψυχὴν ἐν τῷ σώματι
εἶναι ὡς ἐν ὀργάνῳ φυσικῷ—κινεῖ γὰρ οὕτως αὐτὸ
ἐν οἷς ἂν ἐθέλῃ ποιεῖν—ἆρ' ἄν τι πλέον ἡμῖν πρὸς

[1] del. Volkmann*.

and perceptible, in every way surrounded by life and extending equally to all the extremities [of the body], we should not have said that the soul was in the body, but that the unimportant was in the more important, and what is held together in what holds it together, and that which flows away in that which does not.

21. Well then, how is it present? If someone asks the question and does not give any answer himself, what are we going to say? And is it all present in the same sort of way, or one part in one way and another in another? For indeed, none of the ways of a thing's being in anything which are currently spoken of fits the relationship of the soul to the body, but it is also said that the soul is in the body as the steersman is in the ship; this is a good comparison as far as the soul's ability to be separate from the body goes, but would not supply very satisfactorily the manner of its presence, which is what we ourselves are investigating. For the steersman as a voyager would be present incidentally in the ship, but how would he be present as steersman? Nor is he in the whole of the ship, as the soul is in the body. Are we then to say that it is present as the skill is in the tools, in the rudder for instance, so that if the rudder was ensouled the steersman's skill which moves it according to the rules of his art would be within it? But the difference is this, that the skill comes from outside. If then, according to the model of the steersman who has got into the rudder, we stated that the soul was in the body as in a natural tool—for this is how the soul moves the body in whatever it wants to do—should we gain any advantage from the next point of view of our investiga-

τὸ ζητούμενον γένοιτο; ἢ πάλιν ἀπορήσομεν πῶς
20 ἔστιν ἐν τῷ ὀργάνῳ, καίτοι τρόπος οὗτος ἕτερος
τῶν πρόσθεν· ἀλλ᾽ ὅμως ἔτι ποθοῦμεν ἐξευρεῖν καὶ
ἐγγυτέρω προσελθεῖν.

22. Ἆρ᾽ οὖν οὕτω φατέον, ὅταν ψυχὴ σώματι
παρῇ, παρεῖναι αὐτὴν ὡς τὸ πῦρ πάρεστι τῷ ἀέρι;
καὶ γὰρ αὖ καὶ τοῦτο παρὸν οὐ πάρεστι καὶ δι᾽
ὅλου παρὸν οὐδενὶ μίγνυται καὶ ἕστηκε μὲν αὐτό,
5 τὸ δὲ παραρρεῖ· καὶ ὅταν ἔξω γένηται τοῦ ἐν ᾧ τὸ
φῶς, ἀπῆλθεν οὐδὲν ἔχων, ἕως δέ ἐστιν ὑπὸ τὸ
φῶς, πεφώτισται, ὥστ᾽ ὀρθῶς ἔχειν καὶ ἐνταῦθα
λέγειν, ὡς ὁ ἀὴρ ἐν τῷ φωτί, ἤπερ τὸ φῶς ἐν τῷ
ἀέρι. διὸ καὶ Πλάτων καλῶς τὴν ψυχὴν οὐ θεὶς ἐν
τῷ σώματι ἐπὶ τοῦ παντός, ἀλλὰ τὸ σῶμα ἐν τῇ
10 ψυχῇ, καί[1] φησι τὸ μέν τι εἶναι τῆς ψυχῆς ἐν ᾧ τὸ
σῶμα, τὸ δὲ ἐν ᾧ σῶμα μηδέν, ὧν δηλονότι δυνάμεων
οὐ δεῖται τῆς ψυχῆς τὸ σῶμα. καὶ δὴ καὶ ἐπὶ τῶν
ἄλλων ψυχῶν ὁ αὐτὸς λόγος. τῶν μὲν ἄλλων δυνάμεων
οὐδὲ παρουσίαν τῷ σώματι λεκτέον τῆς ψυχῆς εἶναι,
15 ὧν δὲ δεῖται, ταῦτα παρεῖναι, καὶ παρεῖναι οὐκ
ἐνιδρυθέντα τοῖς μέρεσιν αὐτοῦ οὐδ᾽ αὖ τῷ ὅλῳ, καὶ
πρὸς μὲν αἴσθησιν παρεῖναι παντὶ τῷ αἰσθανομένῳ τὸ
αἰσθητικόν, πρὸς δὲ ἐνεργείας ἤδη ἄλλο ἄλλῳ.

23. Λέγω δὲ ὧδε· τοῦ σώματος πεφωτισμένου

---

[1] καί (etiam) Enn.: del. Vitringa, H–S².

tion? We shall again be in a difficulty about how it is in the tool, though this is a way of being in the body different from those mentioned before; all the same we are still anxious to discover it completely and approach nearer to the goal of our investigation.

22. Are we to say then that when soul is present to body it is present as fire is present to air? For this too like soul is present without being present, and is present throughout the whole and mixed with none of it, and stays still itself while the air flows past; and when the air goes outside the space where the light is, it departs without retaining anything of it, but while it is under the light it is illuminated, so that one can rightly say here too that the air is in the light rather than the light in the air. That is why Plato [1] rightly does not put the soul in the body when he is speaking of the universe, but the body in the soul, and says also that there is a part of the soul in which body is and part in which there is no body, clearly the powers of the soul of which the body has no need. And the same principle clearly applies to the other souls. We must not say that there is even a presence of the other powers of soul to the body, but that the powers which it needs are present, and present without being situated in its parts, or in the whole either, and the sense-faculty is present to the whole of the perceiving body for the purposes of sense-perception, but one part at one time to one and one to another according to the [particular] sense-activity [which is going on].

23. What I mean is this: when the ensouled body is illuminated by soul, one part of it participates in

---

[1] The reference is to *Timaeus* 36D9–E3: cp. ch. 20, n. 2.

τοῦ ἐμψύχου ὑπὸ τῆς ψυχῆς ἄλλο ἄλλως μεταλαμβάνειν αὐτοῦ μέρος· καὶ κατὰ τὴν τοῦ ὀργάνου
πρὸς τὸ ἔργον ἐπιτηδειότητα, δύναμιν τὴν προσ-
5 ήκουσαν εἰς τὸ ἔργον ἀποδιδοῦσαν, οὕτω τοι
λέγεσθαι τὴν μὲν ἐν ὀφθαλμοῖς δύναμιν τὴν ὁρα-
τικὴν εἶναι, τὴν δ' ἐν ὠσὶ τὴν ἀκουστικήν, καὶ
γευστικὴν ἐν γλώσσῃ, ὄσφρησιν ἐν ῥισί, τὴν δὲ
ἀπτικὴν ἐν παντὶ παρεῖναι· πρὸς γὰρ ταύτην τὴν
ἀντίληψιν πᾶν τὸ σῶμα ὄργανον τῇ ψυχῇ εἶναι.[1]
10 τῶν δὲ ἀπτικῶν ὀργάνων ἐν πρώτοις τοῖς νεύροις
ὄντων, ἃ δὴ καὶ πρὸς τὴν κίνησιν τοῦ ζῴου τὴν
δύναμιν ἔχει, ἐνταῦθα τῆς τοιαύτης δούσης ἑαυτήν,
ἀρχομένων δὲ ἀπὸ ἐγκεφάλου τῶν νεύρων, τὴν τῆς
αἰσθήσεως καὶ ὁρμῆς ἀρχὴν καὶ ὅλως παντὸς τοῦ
ζῴου ἐνταῦθα ἔθεσαν φέροντες, οὗ δηλονότι αἱ
15 ἀρχαὶ τῶν ὀργάνων, ἐκεῖ παρεῖναι τὸ χρησόμενον
τιθέμενοι—βέλτιον δὲ λέγειν τὴν ἀρχὴν τῆς
ἐνεργείας τῆς δυνάμεως ἐκεῖ—ὅθεν γὰρ ἔμελλε
κινεῖσθαι τὸ ὄργανον, ἐκεῖ ἔδει οἷον ἐναπερείδεσθαι
τὴν δύναμιν τοῦ τεχνίτου ἐκείνην τὴν τῷ ὀργάνῳ
πρόσφορον, μᾶλλον δὲ οὐ τὴν δύναμιν—πανταχοῦ
20 γὰρ ἡ δύναμις—ἐκεῖ δὲ τῆς ἐνεργείας ἡ ἀρχή, οὗ ἡ

---

[1] Beutler: παρεῖναι Enn.*

---

[1] The great doctor Herophilus of Chalcedon (first half of
the 3rd century B.C.) and his younger contemporary Erasi-
stratus of Ceos had discovered a great deal about the functions
of the nervous system and the importance of the brain as its

one way and one in another; and according to the
adaptation of [each] sense-organ to its task, as soul
gives [each] the appropriate power for its task, so
the power in the eyes is called that of sight, the
power in the ears that of hearing, and the power of
taste is said to be present in the tongue, that of smell
in the nostrils, and that of touch in the whole body:
for the whole body is sense-organ to the soul for this
perception. Since the organs of touch are in the
first nerves, which also have the power to set the
living being in motion because the appropriate soul-
power communicates itself at this point, and since
these nerves begin in the brain,[1] they established the
principle of perception and of impulse and in general
of the whole living being in the brain, assuming that
obviously that which was going to use the organs
would be there where their beginnings were—but it
would be better to say that the beginning of the
actualisation of the potency [of perception] is there.
For it was necessary that at the point from which
the organ [or tool] was going to be moved that the
power of the workman, as we may call it, which was
appropriate to the tool should be fixed: or rather
not the power—the power is everywhere—but the
beginning of its actualisation at the point where the

centre and seat of the intelligence. Their discoveries had
been used and developed by the great Galen (2nd century A.D.)
and were well known in the time of Plotinus. Platonists
welcomed these discoveries as confirmation of the view of
Plato that intelligence was located in the head (*Timaeus* 44D–
E: the reasons given are hardly scientific!) as against that of
Aristotle, the Stoics and the Epicureans, who located intelli-
gence in the heart—a view still defended by Alexander *De
Anima* 94, 7 ff. and 98. 24 ff. Bruns: cp. H. J. Blumenthal
Plotinus' Psychology (The Hague 1971) 75.

ἀρχὴ τοῦ ὀργάνου. ἐπεὶ οὖν ἡ τοῦ αἰσθάνεσθαι
δύναμις καὶ ἡ τοῦ ὁρμᾶν ψυχῆς οὖσα[1] αἰσθητικῆς
καὶ φανταστικῆς [φύσις][2] ἐπάνω ἑαυτῆς εἶχε τὸν
λόγον, ὡς ἂν ⟨φύσις⟩[2] γειτονοῦσα πρὸς τὸ κάτω
25 οὗ αὐτὴ ἐπάνω, ταύτῃ ἐτέθη τοῖς παλαιοῖς ἐν τοῖς
ἄκροις τοῦ ζῴου παντὸς ἐπὶ τῆς κεφαλῆς, ὡς οὖσα
οὐκ ἐν τῷ ἐγκεφάλῳ, ἀλλ' ὡς ἐν τούτῳ τῷ
αἰσθητικῷ, ὃ ἐν τῷ ἐγκεφάλῳ ἐκείνως ἵδρυτο.
τὸ μὲν γὰρ ἔδει σώματι διδόναι, καὶ τῷ σώματος
μάλιστα τῆς ἐνεργείας δεκτικῷ, τὸ δὲ σώματι
30 οὐδαμοῦ κοινωνοῦν πάντως ἐκείνῳ κοινωνεῖν ἔδει,
ὃ ψυχῆς εἶδος ἦν καὶ ψυχῆς δυναμένης τὰς παρὰ
τοῦ λόγου ἀντιλήψεις ποιεῖσθαι. αἰσθητικὸν γὰρ
κριτικόν πως, καὶ φανταστικὸν οἷον νοερόν, καὶ
ὁρμὴ καὶ ὄρεξις, φαντασίᾳ καὶ λόγῳ ἑπόμενα.
ἐκεῖ οὖν τὸ λογιζόμενον οὐχ ὡς ἐν τόπῳ, ἀλλ' ὅτι
35 τὸ ἐκεῖ ἀπολαύει αὐτοῦ. πῶς δὲ τὸ "ἐκεῖ" ἐπὶ
τοῦ αἰσθητικοῦ, εἴρηται. τοῦ δὲ φυτικοῦ αὖ καὶ
αὐξητικοῦ καὶ θρεπτικοῦ μηδενὸς ἀπολειπομένου,
τρέφοντος δὲ τῷ αἵματι, τοῦ δὲ αἵματος τοῦ
τρέφοντος ἐν φλεψὶν ὄντος, ἀρχῆς δὲ καὶ φλεβῶν
καὶ αἵματος ἐν ἥπατι, οἷον[3] ἐναπερειδομένης
40 ταύτης τῆς δυνάμεως ἐνταῦθα ἡ τοῦ ἐπιθυμητικοῦ
μοῖρα τῆς ψυχῆς οἰκεῖν ἀπεδόθη. ὃ γάρ τοι καὶ
γεννᾷ καὶ τρέφει καὶ αὔξει, τοῦτο καὶ τούτων

---

[1] Theiler: οὔσης Enn.
[2] transpos. Igal.
[3] Harder, H–S, cf. lin. 17: ὅθεν Enn.*

organ begins. Since, then, the power of sensation which is also that of impulsion, belonging to the soul which perceives and imagines, has reason above it, as it were a nature in close contact on its underside with that which this is above, the ancients thus put reason at the highest point of the whole living creature at the head, supposing it to be not in the brain but in this perceptive faculty which in the way described above was situated in the brain. For one part of the soul had to give itself to body, and to the part of body most receptive of its activity, but the other part, which had no communication with body, was under the absolute necessity of communicating with the first part, which was a form of soul, and of soul capable of apprehending what came from reason. For the perceptive part of the soul is in some way capable of judgement, and the imaging part has a sort of intelligence, and impulse and desire are there following the lead of the imaging faculty, and reason. The reasoning part therefore is there in the perceptive not as in a place but because that which is there draws upon it. We have already explained the sense in which we say that the perceptive part is "there". The part of the soul too which we have in common with plants, which is responsible for growth and nutrition, is not absent from any part of the body, and since it nourishes by means of the blood, and the nourishing blood is in the veins, and the starting point of veins and blood is in the liver, it is as if this [nutritive] power was fixed there, and so the appetitive part of the soul was assigned this place to dwell in. For that which generates and nourishes and produces growth must necessarily also have an appetite for generation, nourishment and

ἐπιθυμεῖν ἀνάγκη. τοῦ δὲ λεπτοῦ καὶ κούφου καὶ
ὀξέος καὶ καθαροῦ αἵματος, θυμῷ προσφόρου
⟨ὄντας⟩ [1] ὀργάνου, ἡ τούτου πηγή, ⟨ἡ καρδία⟩ [2]—
ἐνταῦθα γὰρ τὸ τοιοῦτον αἷμα ἀποκρίνεται—τῇ
45 τοῦ θυμοῦ ζέσει [καρδία] [3] πεποίηται οἴκησις
πρέπουσα. [ἔχουσαι δὲ τὸ σῶμα καὶ τὸ ἀντιλαμβάνεσθαι τῶν σωματικῶν κολάσεων ἔχουσιν.] [4]

24. Ἀλλὰ ποῦ ἐξελθοῦσα τοῦ σώματος γενήσε-
ται; ἢ ἐνταῦθα μὲν οὐκ ἔσται, οὗ οὐκ ἔστι τὸ
δεχόμενον ὁπωσοῦν, οὐδὲ δύναται παραμένειν τῷ
μὴ πεφυκότι αὐτὴν δέχεσθαι, εἰ μή τι ἔχοι αὐτοῦ ὃ
5 ἕλκει πρὸς αὐτὸ ἄφρονα οὖσαν. ἔστι δὲ ἐν
ἐκείνῳ, εἰ ἄλλο ἔχει, κἀκεῖ ἀκολουθεῖ, οὗ πέφυκε
τοῦτο εἶναι καὶ γίνεσθαι. ὄντος δὲ πολλοῦ καὶ
ἑκάστου τόπου, καὶ παρὰ τῆς διαθέσεως ἥκειν δεῖ
τὸ διάφορον, ἥκειν δὲ καὶ παρὰ τῆς ἐν τοῖς οὖσι
δίκης. οὐ γὰρ μή ποτέ τις ἐκφύγοι, ὃ παθεῖν ἐπ'
10 ἀδίκοις ἔργοις προσήκει· ἀναπόδραστος γὰρ ὁ
θεῖος νόμος ὁμοῦ ἔχων ἐν ἑαυτῷ τὸ ποιῆσαι τὸ κριθὲν
ἤδη. φέρεται δὲ καὶ αὐτὸς ὁ πάσχων ἀγνοῶν ἐφ'
ἃ παθεῖν προσήκει, ἀστάτῳ μὲν τῇ φορᾷ πανταχοῦ
αἰωρούμενος ταῖς πλάναις, τελευτῶν δὲ ὥσπερ
πολλὰ καμὼν οἷς ἀντέτεινεν εἰς τὸν προσήκοντα
15 αὐτῷ τόπον ἐνέπεσεν, ἑκουσίῳ τῇ φορᾷ τὸ
ἀκούσιον εἰς τὸ παθεῖν ἔχων. εἴρηται δὲ ἐν τῷ

---

[1] Kirchhoff*.
[2] Kleist.
[3] Kirchhoff*.
[4] del. Ficinus, Creuzer*, iterata ex 24, 20–21.

growth. But since the thin, light, quick, pure blood is the proper organ for the spirited part of the soul, the spring of this, the heart—for this is where blood of this kind is separated out—is made to be the appropriate dwelling place for the seething of the spirited part.[1]

24. But where will the soul be when it has left the body? It will not be here below, where there is nothing capable in any way of receiving it, and it cannot stay with that which is not naturally adapted to receive it, unless, because it is unreasonable, it still has something of body which draws it to it. If it has another body, it is in that, and accompanies it to the place naturally appropriate to its existence and development. But since there are many places for each as well [as many bodies], the difference between them must come from the disposition of the soul, and must come also from the justice in the nature of things. For no one can ever evade what he ought to suffer for his unrighteous doings: for the divine law is inescapable and has in itself together with the judgment already pronounced its execution. He too who is to suffer punishment is carried unknowing to what he has to suffer; on his unsteady course he is tossed about everywhere in his wanderings, and in the end, as if utterly weary, by his very efforts at resistance he falls into the place which suits him, having that which he did not will for his punish-

---

[1] I print and translate here the text and punctuation adopted by Beutler-Theiler: the minor alterations by Kirchhoff and Kleist which they accept, the insertion of ὄντος and the transposition of καρδία with their punctuation, seem to me to give a much better sense than the MSS text retained by Henry-Schwyzer.

νόμῳ καὶ ὅσον καὶ ἐφ' ὅσον δεῖ παθεῖν, καὶ πάλιν
αὖ ὁμοῦ συνέδραμεν ἡ ἄνεσις τῆς κολάσεως καὶ ἡ
δύναμις τοῦ ἀναφυγεῖν ἐξ ἐκείνων τῶν τόπων,
20 ἁρμονίας δυνάμει κατεχούσης τὰ πάντα. ἔχουσαι
δὲ σῶμα καὶ τὸ ἀντιλαμβάνεσθαι τῶν σωματικῶν
κολάσεων ἔχουσι· ταῖς δὲ τῶν ψυχῶν καθαραῖς
οὔσαις καὶ μηδὲν μηδαμῇ ἐφελκομέναις τοῦ
σώματος ἐξ ἀνάγκης ⟨καὶ⟩ [1] οὐδαμοῦ σώματος
ὑπάρξει εἶναι. εἰ οὖν εἰσι [καὶ] [1] μηδαμοῦ σώματος
25 —οὐδὲ γὰρ ἔχουσι σῶμα—οὗ ἐστιν ἡ οὐσία καὶ τὸ
ὂν καὶ τὸ θεῖον—ἐν τῷ θεῷ—ἐνταῦθα καὶ μετὰ
τούτων καὶ ἐν τούτῳ ἡ τοιαύτη ψυχὴ ἔσται. εἰ δ'
ἔτι ζητεῖς ποῦ, ζητητέον σοι ποῦ ἐκεῖνα· ζητῶν
δὲ ζήτει μὴ τοῖς ὄμμασι μηδ' ὡς ζητῶν σώματα.

25. Περὶ δὲ μνήμης, εἰ αὐταῖς ταῖς ψυχαῖς
τῶνδε τῶν τόπων ἐξελθούσαις μνημονεύειν
ὑπάρχει, ἢ ταῖς μέν, ταῖς δ' οὔ, καὶ πάντων ἢ
τινων, καὶ εἰ μνημονεύουσιν ἀεί, ἢ ἐπί τινα
5 χρόνον τὸν ἐγγὺς τῆς ἀφόδου, ζητεῖν ὁμοίως ἄξιον.
ἀλλ' εἰ μέλλομεν ὀρθῶς περὶ τούτων τὴν ζήτησιν
ποιεῖσθαι, ληπτέον τί ποτε τὸ μνημονεῦόν ἐστι.
λέγω δὲ οὐ τί μνήμη ἐστίν, ἀλλ' ἐν τίνι συνίστασθαι
πέφυκε τῶν ὄντων. τί μὲν γάρ ἐστι μνήμη,

---

[1] transpos. Beutler.

---

[1] It is not clear to what discussion of memory Plotinus is
here referring. His short treatise *On Sense-Perception and
Memory* (IV. 6) is, according to Porphyry, later than the
present one (No. 41 in the chronological order). In the
treatise III. 6 (26), written immediately before IV. 3–4, there
is a brief treatment of memory which again seems to presuppose
a previous discussion. In both these cases the references may
be to oral discussions; at any rate, no trace of any writing of

ment as a result of the course which he willed. But
it is stated in the law how much and how long he
must suffer, and again there come together the
release from punishment and the ability to escape
up from these regions by the power of the harmony
which holds the universe together. But if the souls
have bodies they have the capacity to be aware of
bodily punishments: but those souls which are pure
and do not in any way draw anything of body to them
will necessarily also have no place anywhere in body.
If then they are nowhere in body—for they have no
body—a soul of this kind will be where substance and
reality and the divine are—that is in god—there it
will be with them and in him. But if you are still
looking for the place where the soul is, you must
look for the place where they are; but in looking you
must not look for it with your eyes or in the way you
look for bodies.

25. It is likewise worth investigating the question
of memory, whether the souls themselves which have
left these regions have the power of remembering or
whether some of them have and others have not,
and whether they remember everything or only some
things, and if they always remember, or only for
the time close after their departure. But if we are
going to carry out our investigation of these questions correctly, we must understand what it is that
remembers, I do not mean what memory is, but in
what kind of realities it naturally exists. For what
memory is, we have discussed elsewhere and there
has been plenty of talk about it,[1] but we must

Plotinus on memory other than the long ch. 3 of IV. 6 and
the careful discussion of the subject and content of memory
which follows immediately here has survived.

εἴρηται ἐν ἄλλοις καὶ πολλάκις τεθρύλληται, τὸ δὲ
10 μνημονεύειν πεφυκὸς ὅ τί ποτέ ἐστιν ἀκρι-
βέστερον ληπτέον. εἰ δέ ἐστι τὸ τῆς· μνήμης
ἐπικτήτου τινὸς ἢ μαθήματος ἢ παθήματος, οὔτε
τοῖς ἀπαθέσι τῶν ὄντων οὔτε τοῖς ἐν ἀχρόνῳ[1]
ἐγγίνοιτο ἂν τὸ μνημονεύειν. μνήμην δὴ περὶ
θεὸν οὐδὲ περὶ τὸ ὂν καὶ νοῦν θετέον· οὐδὲν γὰρ
15 εἰς αὐτοὺς οὐδὲ χρόνος, ἀλλ' αἰὼν περὶ τὸ ὄν, καὶ
οὔτε τὸ πρότερον οὔτε τὸ ἐφεξῆς, ἀλλ' ἔστιν ἀεὶ
ὡς ἔχει ἐν τῷ αὐτῷ οὐ δεχόμενον παράλλαξιν.
τὸ δὲ ἐν τῷ αὐτῷ καὶ ὁμοίῳ πῶς ἂν ἐν μνήμῃ
γένοιτο, οὐκ ἔχον οὐδ' ἴσχον ἄλλην κατάστασιν
μεθ' ἣν εἶχε πρότερον, ἢ νόησιν ἄλλην μετ'
20 ἄλλην, ἵνα ἐν ἄλλῃ μὲν ᾖ,[2] ἄλλης δὲ μνημονεύῃ
ἣν εἶχε πρότερον; ἀλλὰ τί κωλύει τὰς ἄλλων μετα-
βολὰς εἰδέναι οὐ μεταβάλλοντα αὐτόν, οἷον κόσμου
τὰς περιόδους; ἢ ὅτι ἄλλο μὲν πρότερον, ἄλλο δὲ
ὕστερον νοήσει ἐπακολουθοῦν ταῖς τοῦ τρεπομένου
μεταβολαῖς, τό τε μνημονεύειν παρὰ τὸ νοεῖν ἄλλο.
25 τὰς δὲ αὐτοῦ νοήσεις οὐ μνημονεύειν λεκτέον· οὐ
γὰρ ἦλθον, ἵνα κατέχῃ μὴ ἀπέλθοιεν· ἢ οὕτω γε τὴν
οὐσίαν αὐτοῦ φοβοῖτο μὴ ἀπέλθοι ἀπ' αὐτοῦ. οὐ
τοίνυν οὐδὲ ψυχὴν φατέον μνημονεύειν τὸν αὐτὸν
τρόπον οἷον λέγομεν τὸ μνημονεύειν εἶναι ὧν ἔχει

---

[1] Igal: ἐν χρόνῳ Enn.: ⟨μὴ⟩ ἐν χρόνῳ Kirchhoff, H–S[1–2].
[2] H–S[2]: μὲν ᾖ A[ac]E, Kirchhoff*: μένῃ A[pc]xUC, Perna,
Creuzer, H–S[1].

understand more exactly what it is that has the natural capacity of remembering. If memory is something acquired, either learnt or experienced, then memory will not be present in those realities which are unaffected by experience or those which are in the timeless. We must certainly not attribute memory to God, or real being or Intellect; for nothing [external] comes to them and there is no time, but eternity in which real being is, and there is neither before nor after, but it is always as it is, in the same state not admitting of any change.[1] But how can that which stays in an identical and exactly similar state be in a condition of memory, when it neither has nor holds another way of being different from that which it had before, or one thought after another, so that it might stay in one and remember the other which it had before? But what prevents it from knowing the changes of other things without changing itself, the revolutions of the universe for instance? The reason is that it will think of one thing as before and another as after, following the changes of that which turns, and remembering is something different from thinking. One must not say that it remembers its own thoughts: for they did not come, so that it has to hold them fast to prevent them from going away; or in this way it would be afraid that its own essential nature might go away from it. In the same way, then, the soul must not be said to remember, either, in the sense in which we are speaking of remembering, the things

[1] The question whether divine beings (including higher souls and the World-Soul) have memory is fully treated and answered, as here, in the negative, in the latter part of the discussion which begins here (IV. 4. 16–17).

30 συμφύτων, ἀλλ' ἐπειδὴ ἐνταῦθά ἐστιν, ἔχειν καὶ
μὴ ἐνεργεῖν κατ' αὐτά, καὶ μάλιστα ἐνταῦθα
ἠκούσῃ. τὸ δὲ ἐνεργεῖν ἤδη—ταῖς ἐνεργούσαις
ἃ εἶχον μνήμην καὶ ἀνάμνησιν προστιθέναι ἐοίκα-
σιν οἱ παλαιοί. ὥσθ' ἕτερον εἶδος μνήμης τοῦτο·
διὸ καὶ χρόνος οὐ πρόσεστι τῇ οὕτω λεγομένῃ
35 μνήμῃ. ἀλλ' ἴσως εὐχερῶς περὶ τούτων ἔχομεν
καὶ οὐκ ἐξεταστικῶς. ἴσως γὰρ ἄν τις ἀπορήσειε,
μήποτε οὐ τῆς ψυχῆς ᾗ ἐκείνης ἡ λεγομένη τοιαύτη
ἀνάμνησις καὶ μνήμη, ἀλλὰ ἄλλης ἀμυδροτέρας,
ἢ τοῦ συναμφοτέρου τοῦ ζῴου. εἴτε γὰρ ἄλλης,
πότε ἢ πῶς λαμβανούσης; εἴτε τοῦ ζῴου, πότε ἢ
40 πῶς; διὸ ζητητέον τί ἐστι τῶν ἐν ἡμῖν τὸ τὴν
μνήμην ἴσχον, ὅπερ καὶ ἐξ ἀρχῆς ἐζητοῦμεν· καὶ
εἰ μὲν ἡ ψυχὴ ἡ μνημονεύουσα, τίς δύναμις ἢ τί
μέρος, εἰ δὲ τὸ ζῷον, ὥσπερ καὶ τὸ αἰσθανόμενον
ἔδοξέ τισι, τίς ὁ τρόπος, καὶ τί ποτε δεῖ φάναι τὸ
ζῷον, καὶ ἔτι εἰ τὸ αὐτὸ τῶν αἰσθημάτων δεῖ
45 τίθεσθαι ἀντιλαμβάνεσθαι καὶ τῶν νοημάτων, ἢ
ἄλλο τοῦ ἑτέρου.

26. Εἰ μὲν οὖν τὸ ζῷον τὸ συναμφότερόν ἐστιν
ἐν ταῖς αἰσθήσεσι ταῖς κατ' ἐνέργειαν, δεῖ τὸ
αἰσθάνεσθαι τοιοῦτον εἶναι—διὸ καὶ κοινὸν λέγεται

---

¹ The comparison of activities in which body and soul are
both involved to craft activities like weaving is taken from
Aristotle *De Anima* A 4, 408b13. But Plotinus has characteristically substituted the particular carpenter's operation τρυπᾶν
" boring holes " for Aristotle's vaguer and more general
οἰκοδομεῖν " building ", to make the picture more vivid.
κοινόν here means common to body and φύσις (nature or

which it possesses as part of its nature, but when it is here below it possesses them and does not act by them, particularly when it has just arrived here. But as for its activity, the ancients seem to apply the terms " memory " and " recollection " to the souls which bring into act what they possessed. So this is another kind of memory; and therefore time is not involved in memory understood in this sense. But perhaps we are being too easy-going about this, and not really examining it critically. For someone might perhaps raise the difficulty that perhaps what is called memory and recollection of this kind does not belong to that [higher] soul, but to another dimmer one, or to the composite, the living creature. Now if it belongs to another soul, when or how did it get it? And if it belongs to the living creature, when or how? So we must enquire what it is of the things within us which possesses memory, which is just what we were enquiring from the beginning. And if it is the soul which remembers, which power or what part of it; but if it is the living creature— just as the power of sense-perception has been thought by some to belong to this—how it works, and what one is to say that the living creature is, and, further, whether one must ascribe the apprehension of sense-perceptions and thoughts to the same thing, or a different one for each.

26. If then the composite living thing is involved in actual sense-perceptions, perception must be something like boring holes and weaving—that is why it is called " common " [1]—in order that the soul

lower soul), which is the other element in the " composite living thing ". See Blumenthal *Plotinus' Psychology* 61. There is no reference to anything like Aristotle's κοινὴ αἴσθησις.

—οἷον τὸ τρυπᾶν καὶ τὸ ὑφαίνειν, ἵνα κατὰ μὲν τὸν
5 τεχνίτην ἡ ψυχὴ ᾖ ἐν τῷ αἰσθάνεσθαι, κατὰ δὲ τὸ
ὄργανον τὸ σῶμα, τοῦ μὲν σώματος πάσχοντος καὶ
ὑπηρετοῦντος, τῆς δὲ ψυχῆς παραδεχομένης τὴν
τύπωσιν τὴν τοῦ σώματος, ἢ τὴν διὰ τοῦ σώματος,
ἢ τὴν κρίσιν, ἣν ἐποιήσατο ἐκ τοῦ παθήματος τοῦ
σώματος· οὗ δὴ ἡ μὲν αἴσθησις οὕτω κοινὸν
10 ἔργον λέγοιτο ἄν, ἡ δὲ μνήμη οὐκ ἀναγκάζοιτο τοῦ
κοινοῦ εἶναι τῆς ψυχῆς ἤδη παραδεξαμένης τὸν
τύπον καὶ ἢ φυλαξάσης ἢ ἀποβαλούσης αὐτήν· εἰ
μή τις τεκμαίροιτο κοινὸν καὶ τὸ μνημονεύειν εἶναι
ἐκ τοῦ ταῖς κράσεσι τῶν σωμάτων καὶ μνημονικοὺς
καὶ ἐπιλήσμονας ἡμᾶς γίγνεσθαι. ἀλλὰ καὶ ὡς
15 κωλυτικὸν ἂν ἢ οὐ κωλυτικὸν λέγοιτο τὸ σῶμα
γίνεσθαι, τῆς δὲ ψυχῆς τὸ μνημονεύειν οὐχ ἧττον
εἴη. τῶν δὲ δὴ μαθήσεων πῶς τὸ κοινόν, ἀλλ’
οὐχ ἡ ψυχὴ ἡ μνημονεύουσα ἔσται; εἰ δὲ τὸ ζῷον
τὸ συναμφότερον οὕτως, ὡς ἕτερον ἐξ ἀμφοῖν εἶναι,
20 πρῶτον μὲν ἄτοπον μήτε σῶμα μήτε ψυχὴν τὸ
ζῷον λέγειν· οὐ γὰρ δὴ μεταβαλόντων ἀμφοτέρων
ἕτερόν τι ἔσται τὸ ζῷον οὐδ’ αὖ κραθέντων, ὡς
δυνάμει τὴν ψυχὴν ἐν τῷ ζῴῳ εἶναι· ἔπειτα[1] καὶ
οὕτως οὐδὲν ἧττον τῆς ψυχῆς τὸ μνημονεύειν
ἔσται, ὥσπερ ἐν οἰνομέλιτος κράσει εἴ τι γλυκάζει,
25 παρὰ τοῦ μέλιτος τοῦτο ἔσται. τί οὖν, εἰ αὐτὴ
μὲν μνημονεύοι, τῷ δὲ ⟨τῷ⟩[2] ἐν σώματι εἶναι
[τῷ][2] μὴ καθαρὰ εἶναι, ἀλλ’ ὥσπερ ποιωθεῖσα,
ἀναμάττεσθαι δύναται τοὺς τῶν αἰσθητῶν τύπους

---

[1] Beutler: ἐπεὶ Enn.*
[2] transpos. Theiler.

may be in the position of the workman in perceiving and the body in that of the tool; the body experiences and serves, and the soul receives the impression made on the body, or the impression which comes through the body, or the judgment which it made as a result of the experience of the body: sense-perception would certainly have in this case to be called a common work, but memory would not have to belong to what was common, as the soul would have already received the impression and either kept it or thrown it away; unless one was going to conclude that remembering is a common activity from the fact that the mixture of bodily elements makes us have good or bad memories. But even so the body might be said to be obstructive or not obstructive, but remembering would none the less belong to the soul. And how can it be what is common, and not the soul, which is the principle which remembers what we study? But if the composite living thing is something of such a sort as to be different from both its components, first of all it is absurd to say that the living thing is neither body nor soul: for the living thing will not be something different as the result of both of them having changed, nor again as the result of their having been mixed, so that the soul is in the living thing potentially. And then even so remembering would belong just as much to the soul, as in a mixture of wine and honey any sweetness there is will be due to the honey. But suppose it itself remembers, but because it is not pure as a result of being in the body, but has a kind of special quality, it is able to receive the impressions made by the

καὶ τῷ οἷον ἕδραν ἐν τῷ σώματι πρὸς τὸ παρα-
δέχεσθαι καὶ μὴ ὥσπερ παραρρεῖν; ἀλλὰ πρῶτον μὲν
30 οἱ τύποι οὐ μεγέθη, οὐδ' ὥσπερ αἱ ἐνσφραγίσεις
οὐδ' ἀντερείσεις ἢ τυπώσεις, ὅτι μηδ' ὠθισμός,
μηδ' ὥσπερ ἐν κηρῷ, ἀλλ' ὁ τρόπος οἷον νόησις καὶ
ἐπὶ τῶν αἰσθητῶν. ἐπὶ δὲ τῶν νοήσεων τίς ἡ
ἀντέρεισις λέγοιτο ἄν; ἢ τί δεῖ σώματος ἢ
ποιότητος σωματικῆς μεθ' ἧς; ἀλλὰ μὴν καὶ τῶν
35 αὐτῆς κινημάτων ἀνάγκη μνήμην αὐτῇ γίγνεσθαι,
οἷον ὧν ἐπεθύμησε καὶ ὧν οὐκ ἀπέλαυσεν οὐδὲ
ἦλθεν εἰς σῶμα τὸ ἐπιθυμητόν. πῶς γὰρ ἂν εἴποι
τὸ σῶμα περὶ ὧν οὐκ ἦλθεν εἰς αὐτό; ἢ πῶς μετὰ
σώματος μνημονεύσει, ὃ μὴ πέφυκε γινώσκειν
ὅλως τὸ σῶμα; ἀλλὰ τὰ μὲν λεκτέον εἰς ψυχὴν
40 λήγειν, ὅσα διὰ σώματος, τὰ δὲ ψυχῆς εἶναι
μόνης, εἰ δεῖ τὴν ψυχὴν εἶναί τι καὶ φύσιν τινὰ
καὶ ἔργον τι αὐτῆς. εἰ δὲ τοῦτο, καὶ ἔφεσιν καὶ
μνήμην τῆς ἐφέσεως ἄρα καὶ τῆς τεύξεως καὶ τῆς
οὐ τεύξεως, ἐπείπερ καὶ ἡ φύσις αὐτῆς οὐ τῶν
45 ῥεόντων. εἰ γὰρ μὴ τοῦτο, οὐδὲ συναίσθησιν οὐδὲ
παρακολούθησιν δώσομεν οὐδέ τινα σύνθεσιν καὶ
οἷον σύνεσιν. οὐ γὰρ δὴ οὐδὲν ἔχουσα τούτων
ἐν τῇ φύσει αὐτῆς ταῦτα κομίζεται ἐν σώματι, ἀλλ'
ἐνεργείας μέν τινας ἴσχει ὧν ἔργων δεῖται ἡ
ἐπιτέλεσις ὀργάνων, τῶν δὲ τὰς δυνάμεις ἥκει

---

[1] An example of Plotinus's continually repeated attack on
the corporealist Stoic theory of sense-perception: cp. *SVF* I
484 and II 343 for the theory; Plotinus's fullest statement of
the Platonic case against Stoic psychology is IV. 7. 1–8[3] (ch. 6
deals with sense-impressions).

sense-objects [1] and is also able to do this because it
has a kind of standing-ground in the body for receiving them and does not, so to speak, flow away?
But to begin with, the impressions are not magnitudes;
nor are they like seal-impressions or counter-pressures
or stamps, because there is no pushing and it is not
like what happens in wax, but the way of it is like
thinking even in the case of sense-objects. But in
acts of thought what counter-pressure could there
be said to be? Or what need is there of a body or
bodily quality as an accompaniment? But surely,
too, the soul must have memory of its own movements,
of what it desired, for instance, and of what it did not
enjoy and the desired object did not enter the body.
For how could the body speak of what did not come
into it? Or how will it remember with the help of
the body something which the body has been in no
condition to know at all? But we must say that
some things, all that come through the body, reach
as far as the soul, and others belong to the soul
alone, if the soul must be something, and a distinct
nature, and have a work of its own. If this is so, it
will have aspiration, and memory of its aspiration,
and of attaining or not attaining it, since its nature
is not one of those which are in a state of flux.
For if this is not so, we shall not grant it self-aware-
ness or consciousness of its own activities or any
sort of power of combination and understanding.
For it certainly is not the case that it has none of
these in its own nature and acquired them in the
body, but it has some activities of the works required
for the completion of the bodily organs, and brings
the potentialities of some of them with it when it
comes, and the actualities of others. But as far as

50 φέρουσα, τῶν δὲ καὶ τὰς ἐνεργείας. τὸ δὲ τῆς
μνήμης καὶ τὸ σῶμα ἐμπόδιον ἔχει· ἐπεὶ καὶ νῦν
προστιθεμένων τινῶν λήθη, ἐν δ' ἀφαιρέσει καὶ
καθάρσει ἀνακύπτει πολλάκις ἡ μνήμη. μονῆς δὲ
οὔσης αὐτῆς ἀνάγκη τὴν τοῦ σώματος φύσιν
κινουμένην καὶ ῥέουσαν λήθης αἰτίαν, ἀλλ' οὐ
55 μνήμης εἶναι· διὸ καὶ ὁ τῆς Λήθης ποταμὸς
οὗτος ἂν ὑπονοοῖτο. ψυχῆς μὲν δὴ ἔστω τὸ
πάθημα τοῦτο.

27. Ἀλλὰ τίνος ψυχῆς, τῆς μὲν λεγομένης ὑφ'
ἡμῶν θειοτέρας, καθ' ἣν ἡμεῖς, τῆς δὲ ἄλλης τῆς
παρὰ τοῦ ὅλου; ἢ λεκτέον εἶναι μνήμας ἑκατέρας,
τὰς μὲν ἰδίας, τὰς δὲ κοινάς· καὶ ὅταν μὲν
5 συνῶσιν, ὁμοῦ πάσας, χωρὶς δὲ γενομένων, εἰ
ἄμφω εἶεν καὶ μένοιεν, ἑκατέραν ἐπιπλέον τὰ
ἑαυτῆς, ἐπ' ὀλίγον δὲ χρόνον τὰ τῆς ἑτέρας. τὸ
γοῦν εἴδωλον ἐν Ἅιδου Ἡρακλέους—τοῦτο γὰρ καὶ
τὸ εἴδωλον, οἶμαι, χρὴ νομίζειν ἡμᾶς—μνημονεύειν
τῶν πεπραγμένων πάντων κατὰ τὸν βίον, αὐτοῦ
10 γὰρ μάλιστα καὶ ὁ βίος ἦν. αἱ δὲ ἄλλαι τὸ
συναμφότερον ⟨γενόμεναι⟩ [οὖσαι][1] οὐδὲν πλέον
ὅμως εἶχον λέγειν· ἢ ἅ γε[2] τοῦ βίου τούτου, καὶ
αὐταὶ [τὸ συναμφότερον γενόμεναι][3] ταῦτα ᾔδεσαν·
ἢ εἴ τι δικαιοσύνης ἐχόμενον. ὁ δὲ Ἡρακλῆς

[1] γενόμεναι e lin. 12 transpos. H–S²: οὖσαι Enn.
[2] H–S²: ἅτε wBᵖᶜRJUC: ἀπὸ Bᵃᶜ: τὰ Kirchhoff, Volkmann*, B–T: ἐπὶ Dodds.
[3] del. H–S², ut correctionem ad lin. 10 falso loco insertam:
τὸ . . . ᾔδεσαν del. Theiler.

---

[1] An example of casual philosophical interpretation of a
Platonic myth: the "river of Lethe" is taken from the

memory is concerned, it has the body as an actual hindrance: since even as things are, some additions produce forgetfulness, and when they are removed and purged away the memory revives. And since memory is a stable condition, the body's nature, moving and flowing, must be a cause of forgetfulness, not of memory: this is why the "river of Lethe" might be understood in this sense.[1] So, then, let this experience [of memory] belong to the soul.

27. But to which soul, that which we shall call the more divine, by which we are ourselves, or the other which comes from the Whole? Perhaps we must say that there are memories of both kinds, some individual and some common; and when the two souls are together all their memories coincide; but if they become separated, if they were both to exist and persist in separation, each would have its own memories for a longer time and for a short time those of the other. At any rate the shade of Heracles in Hades [2]—this shade too, I think, we must

conclusion of the great myth which ends the *Republic* (621C).

[2] The reference is to *Odyssey* 11. 601ff., where the shade of Heracles in Hades is distinguished from Heracles himself, who is with the gods: cp. I, 1. 12. 31ff. The passage had been recognised since Aristarchus as a later interpolation, but Plotinus was not aware of this (he was not a scholar), or ignored it. His philosophical explanation had earlier forerunners, the ultimate source of which may be in the Old Academy or post-Platonic Pythagoreanism. See Plutarch *De facie in orbe lunae* 944F–945A with the note of H. Cherniss ad loc. (*Moralia*, Loeb edition vol. 12); F. Cumont *Lux Perpetua* (Paris 1949) 189–91: H. J. Blumenthal *op. cit.* 86; and the latest and most thorough examination by J. Pépin, "Héraclès et son reflet dans le Néoplatonisme " in *Le Néoplatonisme* (Paris 1971) 167–99.

αὐτὸς ὁ ἄνευ τοῦ εἰδώλου τί ἔλεγεν, οὐκ εἴρηται.

15 τί οὖν ἂν εἴποι ἡ ἑτέρα ψυχὴ ἀπαλλαγεῖσα μόνη;
ἢ γὰρ ἐφελκομένη ὅ τι κἂν, πάντα, ὅσα ἔπραξεν ἢ
ἔπαθεν ὁ ἄνθρωπος· χρόνου δὲ προϊόντος ἐπὶ τῷ
θανάτῳ καὶ ἄλλων μνῆμαι ἂν φανεῖεν ἐκ τῶν
πρόσθεν βίων, ὥστε τινὰ τούτων καὶ ἀτιμάσασαν
ἀφεῖναι. σώματος γὰρ καθαρωτέρα γενομένη καὶ

20 ἃ ἐνταῦθα οὐκ εἶχεν ἐν μνήμῃ ἀναπολήσει· εἰ δ᾽
ἐν σώματι γενομένη ἄλλῳ ἐξέλθοι, ἐρεῖ μὲν τὰ
τοῦ ἔξω βίου [καὶ ἐρεῖ εἶναι],[1] οἷ᾽ [2] ἄρτι ἀφῆκε
[ἐρεῖ δὲ] [3] καὶ πολλὰ τῶν πρόσθεν. χρόνοις δὲ
πολλῶν τῶν ἐπακτῶν ἀεὶ ἔσται ἐν λήθῃ. ἡ δὲ δὴ
μόνη γενομένη τί μνημονεύσει; ἢ πρότερον

25 σκεπτέον τίνι δυνάμει ψυχῆς τὸ μνημονεύειν
παραγίνεται.

28. Ἆρά γε ᾧ αἰσθανόμεθα καὶ ᾧ μανθάνομεν;
ἢ καὶ ᾧ ἐπιθυμοῦμεν τῶν ἐπιθυμητῶν, καὶ τῶν
ὀργιστῶν τῷ θυμοειδεῖ; οὐ γὰρ ἄλλο μὲν ἀπολαύσει,
φήσει τις, ἄλλο δὲ μνημονεύσει τῶν ἐκείνου. τὸ

---

[1] del. Theiler.
[2] Theiler: ὃ Enn.*
[3] del. H–S².

consider to be our self—remembers all that he did in his life, for the life particularly belonged to the shade. But the other souls which became composite entities [of higher and lower soul], all the same had nothing more to talk about than the things of this life, and they themselves knew them—except perhaps something concerned with righteousness. But Homer does not tell us what Heracles himself said, the Heracles without the shade. What then would the other soul say when it has been freed and is alone? The soul which drags after it anything at all [from the body] would speak of everything which the man had done or experienced. But as time goes on after death, memories of other things would appear from its former lives, so that it would even abandon with contempt some of these memories [of its immediately past life]. For since it has become freer from bodily contamination it will go over again in its memory also what it did not have in this life; but if when it goes out [of this body], it comes to exist in another, it will speak of the events of its outward life, of what it has just left and of many events of its former lives. But in time it will come to forgetfulness of many things which occurred to it from time to time. But when it comes to be alone what will it remember? First we must enquire what power of soul it is which remembering accompanies.

28. Is it that by which we perceive and by which we learn? Or does our remembrance of the things we desired accompany our power of desiring, and of the things which made us angry, our spirited power? For, someone will say, there will not be one thing which enjoys [the desired objects] and

5 γοῦν ἐπιθυμητικὸν ὧν ἀπέλαυσε τούτοις [1] κινεῖται
πάλιν ὀφθέντος τοῦ ἐπιθυμητοῦ δηλονότι τῇ
μνήμῃ. ἐπεὶ διὰ τί οὐκ ἄλλου, ἢ οὐχ οὕτως; τί
οὖν κωλύει καὶ αἴσθησιν τῶν τοιούτων διδόναι αὐτῷ
καὶ τῷ αἰσθητικῷ τοίνυν ἐπιθυμίαν καὶ πάντα
πᾶσιν ὥστε κατὰ τὸ ἐπικρατοῦν ἕκαστον λέγεσθαι;
10 ἢ αἴσθησιν ἄλλως ἑκάστῳ· οἷον εἶδε μὲν ἡ
ὅρασις, οὐ τὸ ἐπιθυμοῦν, ἐκινήθη δὲ παρὰ τῆς
αἰσθήσεως τὸ ἐπιθυμοῦν οἷον διαδόσει, οὐχ ὥστε
εἰπεῖν τὴν αἴσθησιν οἷα, ἀλλ' ὥστε ἀπαρακολου-
θήτως παθεῖν. καὶ ἐπὶ τοῦ θυμοῦ εἶδε τὸν
ἀδικήσαντα, ὁ δὲ θυμὸς ἀνέστη, οἷον εἰ ποιμένος
15 ἰδόντος ἐπὶ ποίμνῃ λύκον ὁ σκύλαξ τῇ ὀδμῇ ἢ τῷ
κτύπῳ αὐτὸς οὐκ ἰδὼν ὄμμασιν ὀρίνοιτο. καὶ
τοίνυν ἀπέλαυσε μὲν τὸ ἐπιθυμοῦν, καὶ ἔχει ἴχνος
τοῦ γενομένου ἐντεθὲν οὐχ ὡς μνήμην, ἀλλ' ὡς
διάθεσιν καὶ πάθος· ἄλλο δὲ τὸ ἑωρακὸς τὴν
ἀπόλαυσιν καὶ παρ' αὐτοῦ ἔχον τὴν μνήμην τοῦ
20 γεγενημένου. τεκμήριον δὲ τὸ μὴ ἡδεῖαν εἶναι τὴν
μνήμην πολλάκις ὧν μετέσχε τὸ ἐπιθυμοῦν,
καίτοι, εἰ ἐν αὐτῷ, ἦν ἄν.

29. Ἆρ' οὖν τῷ αἰσθητικῷ φέροντες ἀναθήσομεν

---

[1] suspic. Volkmann, scr. B–T: τοῦτο Enn.*

---

[1] The idea of "naming by predominance" goes back at least
to Anaxagoras (see Aristotle *Physics* A 4, 187b1 ff.) and was
used by Antiochus of Ascalon in discussing the question whether an incompletely happy life could be called "happy"
(Cicero *Tusculans* V 22). It became important in post-
Plotinian Neoplatonism: see P. Hadot, "Être, Vie, Pensée

another which remembers the objects enjoyed by the first. On this assumption the desiring power is moved by what it enjoyed when it sees the desired object again, obviously by means of the memory. For why [otherwise] should it not be moved when something else is seen, or seen in a different way? What then prevents us from giving the desiring power perception of desirable things and, again, the perceptive power desire, and giving everything to everything so that each is named by that which predominates in it [1]? Now perception can be attributed to each power in a different way. Sight, for instance, sees, not the desiring power, but the desiring power is moved by a sort of transmission from the perception, not so that it can say what sort of perception it is, but so that it is unconsciously affected by it. And in the case of anger, sight sees the wrongdoer and the anger arises; it is like when the shepherd sees the wolf by the flock and the sheepdog is excited by the scent or the noise, though he has not himself seen the wolf with his eyes. And the desiring power, certainly, enjoyed and has a trace of what happened implanted in it, not like a memory, but like an [unconscious] disposition and affection; but it is another power which has seen the enjoyment and of its own motion retains the memory of what happened. It is evidence of this that the memory of the desiring power's experiences is often not pleasant, though if it had been in it, it would have been.

29. Shall we then take the memory and put it in

chez Plotin et avant Plotin" in *Les Sources de Plotin* (*Entretiens Hardt* V, Vandoeuvres-Genève 1960), with the discussion, 107–57.

τὴν μνήμην, καὶ τὸ αὐτὸ ἡμῖν μνημονευτικὸν καὶ
αἰσθητικὸν ἔσται; ἀλλ᾽ εἰ καὶ τὸ εἴδωλον μνημονεύσει, ὡς ἐλέγετο, διττὸν τὸ αἰσθητικὸν ἔσται,
5 καὶ εἰ μὴ τὸ αἰσθητικὸν δὲ τὸ μνημονευτικόν, ἀλλ᾽
ὁτιοῦν ἄλλο, διττὸν τὸ μημονεῦον ἔσται. ἔτι εἰ
τὸ αἰσθητικόν, καὶ τῶν μαθημάτων ἔσται καὶ τῶν
διανοημάτων τὸ αἰσθητικόν. ἢ ἄλλο γε δεῖ ἑκατέρων.
ἆρ᾽ οὖν κοινὸν θέμενοι τὸ ἀντιληπτικὸν τούτῳ δώσομεν ἀμφοῖν τὴν μνήμην; ἀλλ᾽ εἰ μὲν ἓν καὶ ταὐτὸ
10 τὸ ἀντιλαμβανόμενον αἰσθητῶν τε καὶ νοητῶν,
τάχα ἄν τι λέγοιτο· εἰ δὲ διαιρεῖται διχῇ, οὐδὲν
ἧττον δύο ἂν εἴη. εἰ δὲ καὶ ἑκατέρᾳ τῇ ψυχῇ
δώσομεν ἄμφω, τέτταρα ἂν γένοιτο. ὅλως δὲ τίς
ἀνάγκη, ᾧ αἰσθανόμεθα, τούτῳ καὶ μνημονεύειν,
15 καὶ τῇ αὐτῇ δυνάμει γίνεσθαι ἄμφω, καὶ ᾧ
διανοούμεθα, τούτῳ τῶν διανοημάτων μνημονεύειν;
ἐπεὶ οὐδ᾽ οἱ αὐτοὶ διανοεῖσθαι κράτιστοι καὶ
μνημονεύειν, καὶ ἐπίσης αἰσθήσει χρησάμενοι οὐκ
ἐπίσης μνημονεύουσι, καὶ εὐαισθήτως ἔχουσιν
ἄλλοι, μνημονεύουσι δὲ ἄλλοι οὐκ ὀξέως ἐν αἰσθήσει
20 γεγενημένοι. ἀλλὰ πάλιν αὖ, εἰ ἄλλο ἑκάτερον
δεήσει εἶναι, καὶ ἄλλο μνημονεύσει ὧν ἡ αἴσθησις
ᾔσθετο πρότερον, κἀκεῖνο δεῖ αἰσθέσθαι οὗπερ
μελλήσει μνημονεύσειν; ἢ οὐδὲν κωλύσει τῷ μνη-
μονεύσοντι τὸ αἴσθημα φάντασμα εἶναι, καὶ τῷ
φανταστικῷ ἄλλῳ ὄντι τὴν μνήμην καὶ κατοχὴν

the perceptive power, and will what remembers and what perceives be the same thing for us? But if the shade, too, is going to remember, as was said, the perceptive power will be double, and even if it is not the perceptive power but something else which remembers, this remembering power will be double. Again, if it is the perceptive power which remembers, this will also perceive studies and thoughts [as well as sense-objects]. But there must be a different power for each of these. Shall we then assume that there is a common power of apprehension, and give to it the memory of both? But if that which apprehended the objects of both the senses and the intelligence was one and the same, perhaps there would be something in this statement; but if it is divided in two, there will all the same be two powers. But if we give both of them to each soul, then there will be four. But in general, what necessity is there for us to remember by that by which we perceive, and for both perceiving and remembering to come about by the same power, and for us to remember our thoughts by that by which we think? For the same people are not the best at thinking and at remembering, and those who are equally perceptive have not equally good memories, and some people have quick perceptions, but others whose perceptions are not keen remember well. But once more, if it is going to be necessary for each of the two to be different, and something else is going to remember what perception first perceived, will that something else have to perceive what it is going to remember? Now nothing will prevent a perception from being a mental image for that which is going to remember it, and the memory and the reten-

25 ὑπάρχειν· τοῦτο γάρ ἐστιν, εἰς ὃ λήγει ἡ αἴσθησις,
καὶ μηκέτι οὔσης τούτῳ πάρεστι τὸ ὅραμα. εἰ
οὖν παρὰ τούτῳ τοῦ ἀπόντος ἤδη ἡ φαντασία,
μνημονεύει ἤδη, κἂν ἐπ' ὀλίγον παρῇ. ᾧ δὴ εἰ
μὲν ἐπ' ὀλίγον παραμένοι, ὀλίγη ἡ μνήμη, ἐπὶ
πολὺ δέ, μᾶλλον μνημονικοὶ τῆς δυνάμεως ταύτης
30 οὔσης ἰσχυροτέρας, ὡς μὴ ῥᾳδίως τρεπομένης
ἀφεῖσθαι[1] ἀποσεισθεῖσαν τὴν μνήμην. τοῦ φανταστικοῦ ἄρα ἡ μνήμη, καὶ τὸ μνημονεύειν τῶν
τοιούτων ἔσται. διαφόρως δ' ἔχειν πρὸς μνήμας
φήσομεν ἢ ταῖς δυνάμεσιν αὐτῆς διαφόρως ἐχού-
σαις ἢ ταῖς προσέξεσιν ἢ μή, ἢ καὶ σωματικαῖς
35 κράσεσιν ἐνούσαις καὶ μή, καὶ ἀλλοιούσαις καὶ μή,
καὶ οἷον θορυβούσαις. ἀλλὰ ταῦτα μὲν ἑτέρωθι.

30. Τὸ δὲ τῶν διανοήσεων τί; ἆρά γε καὶ τούτων τὸ φανταστικόν; ἀλλ' εἰ μὲν πάσῃ νοήσει
παρακολουθεῖ φαντασία, τάχα ἂν ταύτης τῆς φαντασίας, οἷον εἰκόνος οὔσης τοῦ διανοήματος,
5 μενούσης οὕτως ἂν εἴη τοῦ γνωσθέντος ἡ μνήμη· εἰ
δὲ μή, ἄλλο τι ζητητέον. ἴσως δ' ἂν εἴη τοῦ λόγου
τοῦ τῷ νοήματι παρακολουθοῦντος ἡ παραδοχὴ εἰς
τὸ φανταστικόν. τὸ μὲν γὰρ νόημα ἀμερὲς καὶ

―――――――
[1] Creuzer*: ἐφεῖσθαι Enn., H–S.

tion of the object from belonging to the image-
making power, which is something different: for it
is in this that the perception arrives at its conclusion,
and what was seen is present in this when the perception is no longer there. If then the image of
what is absent is already present in this, it is already
remembering, even if the presence is only for a
short time.   The man with whom the image remains
for a short time will have a short memory, but
people with whom the images remain for a long time
have better memories; this power is stronger in
them, so that it does not easily change and let the
memory go, shaken out of it. Memory, then, will
belong to the image-making power, and remembering
will be of things of the mental image kind.   And we
shall say that the differences between men in respect
of memory are due to the fact that their image-
making powers are differently developed, or to the
degree to which they attend or do not attend to
them, or to the presence or absence of certain bodily
temperaments, and whether they change or not and,
so to speak, produce disturbances.   But this we shall
discuss elsewhere.[1]

30. But what is it that remembers thoughts?
Does the image-making power remember these too?
But if an image accompanies every intellectual act,
perhaps if this image remains, being a kind of picture
of the thought, in this way there would be memory
of what was known; but if not, we must look for
some other explanation.   Perhaps the reception into
the image-making power would be of the verbal
expression which accompanies the act of intelligence.

[1] These words seem to express the intention to write something like ch. 3 of the later treatise IV. 6.

οὔπω οἷον προεληλυθὸς εἰς τὸ ἔξω ἔνδον ὂν λανθάνει, ὁ
δὲ λόγος ἀναπτύξας καὶ ἐπάγων ἐκ τοῦ νοήματος εἰς
10 τὸ φανταστικὸν ἔδειξε τὸ νόημα οἷον ἐν κατόπτρῳ,
καὶ ἡ ἀντίληψις αὐτοῦ οὕτω καὶ ἡ μονὴ καὶ ἡ
μνήμη. διὸ καὶ ἀεὶ κινουμένης πρὸς νόησιν τῆς
ψυχῆς, ὅταν ἐν τούτῳ γένηται, ἡμῖν ἡ ἀντίληψις.
ἄλλο γὰρ ἡ νόησις, καὶ ἄλλο ἡ τῆς νοήσεως
15 ἀντίληψις, καὶ νοοῦμεν μὲν ἀεί, ἀντιλαμβανόμεθα
δὲ οὐκ ἀεί· τοῦτο δέ, ὅτι τὸ δεχόμενον οὐ μόνον
δέχεται νοήσεις, ἀλλὰ καὶ αἰσθήσεις κατὰ θάτερα.

31. Ἀλλ' εἰ τοῦ φανταστικοῦ ἡ μνήμη, ἑκατέρα
δὲ ἡ ψυχὴ μνημονεύειν εἴρηται, δύο τὰ φανταστικά.
χωρὶς μὲν οὖν οὖσαι ἐχέτωσαν ἑκάτερα, ἐν δὲ τῷ
αὐτῷ παρ' ἡμῖν πῶς τὰ δύο καὶ τίνι αὐτῶν
5 ἐγγίνεται; εἰ μὲν γὰρ ἀμφοτέροις, διτταὶ ἀεὶ αἱ
φαντασίαι· οὐ γὰρ δὴ τὸ μὲν τῆς ἑτέρας τῶν
νοητῶν, τὸ δὲ τῶν αἰσθητῶν· οὕτω γὰρ ἂν παντά-
πασι δύο ζῷα οὐδὲν ἔχοντα κοινὸν πρὸς ἄλληλα
ἔσται. εἰ οὖν ἀμφοτέραις, τίς ἡ διαφορά; εἶτα

---

[1] For this doctrine that the awareness of our own thinking
which makes memory possible can only take place when pure
thought is translated into images, cp. IV. 8. 8 and I. 4. 9–10;
these passages add that the translation into images depends
on the good health and freedom from disturbance of the body;
consciousness in the ordinary sense, with memory, is thus
secondary, dependent on our own physical condition, and

ON DIFFICULTIES ABOUT THE SOUL I

The intellectual act is without parts and has not, so to speak, come out into the open, but remains unobserved within, but the verbal expression unfolds its content and brings it out of the intellectual act into the image-making power, and so shows the intellectual act as if in a mirror, and this is how there is apprehension and persistence and memory of it. Therefore, even though the soul is always moved to intelligent activity, it is when it comes to be in the image-making power that we apprehend it. The intellectual act is one thing and the apprehension of it another, and we are always intellectually active but do not always apprehend our activity; and this is because that which receives it does not only receive acts of the intelligence, but also, on its other side, perceptions.[1]

31. But if memory belongs to the image-making power, and each of the two souls remembers, as has been said, there will be two image-making powers. Well, then, when the souls are separate we can grant that each of them will have an imaging power, but when they are together, in our earthly life, how are there two powers, and in which of them does memory reside? If it is in both of them, the images will always be double; for one certainly cannot suppose that the power of one soul has images [only] of intelligible things and the power of the other images [only] of perceptible things; for in this way there will be two living things with nothing at all in common with each other. If then [both kinds of images]

relatively unimportant. As it appears in an early, a middle-period, and a late treatise, Plotinus seems to have held this doctrine consistently throughout his writing period.

πῶς οὐ γινώσκομεν; ἢ ὅταν μὲν συμφωνῇ ἡ ἑτέρα
10 τῇ ἑτέρᾳ, οὐκ ὄντων οὐδὲ χωρὶς τῶν φανταστικῶν,
κρατοῦντός τε τοῦ τῆς κρείττονος, ἓν τὸ φάντασμα
γίνεται, οἷον παρακολουθούσης σκιᾶς τῷ ἑτέρῳ, καὶ
ὑποτρέχοντος οἷον σμικροῦ φωτὸς μείζονι· ὅταν
δὲ μάχη ᾖ καὶ διαφωνία, ἐκφανὴς ἐφ᾽ αὑτῆς καὶ ἡ
ἑτέρα γίνεται, λανθάνει δὲ ⟨ὅ τι⟩[1] ἐν ἑτέρῳ.
15 [ὅτι][1] καὶ ὅλως τὸ διττὸν τῶν ψυχῶν λανθάνει·
εἰς ἓν γὰρ ἦλθον ἄμφω καὶ ἐποχεῖται ἡ ἑτέρα.
ἑώρα οὖν ἡ ἑτέρα πάντα καὶ τὰ μὲν ἔχει ἐξελθοῦσα,
τὰ δ᾽ ἀφίησι τῶν τῆς ἑτέρας· οἷον ἑταίρων[2]
ὁμιλίας φαυλοτέρων λαβόντες ποτὲ ἄλλους ἀλλαξά-
20 μενοι ὀλίγα τῶν ἐκείνων μεμνήμεθα, χρηστοτέρων
δὲ γεγενημένων πλείω.

32. Τί δὲ δὴ φίλων καὶ παίδων καὶ γυναικός;
πατρίδος δὲ καὶ τῶν ὧν ἂν καὶ ἀστεῖος οὐκ ἄτοπος
μνημονεύων; ἢ τὸ μὲν μετὰ πάθους ἑκάστου, ὁ
δὲ ἀπαθῶς ἂν τὰς μνήμας τούτων ἔχοι· τὸ γὰρ
5 πάθος ἴσως καὶ ἐξ ἀρχῆς ἐν ἐκείνῳ καὶ τὰ ἀστεῖα
τῶν παθῶν τῇ σπουδαίᾳ, καθόσον τῇ ἑτέρᾳ τι
ἐκοίνωσε. πρέπει δὲ τὴν μὲν χείρονα καὶ τῶν τῆς
ἑτέρας ἐνεργημάτων ἐφίεσθαι τῆς μνήμης καὶ
μάλιστα, ὅταν ἀστεία ᾖ καὶ αὐτή· γένοιτο γὰρ ἂν
τις καὶ ἐξ ἀρχῆς ἀμείνων καὶ τῇ παιδεύσει τῇ παρὰ
10 τῆς κρείττονος. τὴν δὲ δεῖ ἀσμένως λήθην ἔχειν

---

[1] transpos. H–S[2], et sic verterat Bouillet: ⟨τὸ⟩ suspic. Creuzer, scr. Bréhier, B–T.
[2] Cpc, Creuzer* (sodalibus Ficinus): ἑτέρων wxCac: ἑκατέρων U.

are in both souls, what is the difference? And why do we not recognise it? Now when one soul is in tune with the other, and their image-making powers are not separate, and that of the better soul is dominant, the image becomes one, as if a shadow followed the other and as if a little light slipped in under the greater one; but when there is war and disharmony between them, the other image becomes manifest by itself, but we do not notice what is in the other power, and we do not notice in general the duality of the souls. For both have come together into one and the better soul is on top of the other. This other soul, then, sees everything, and takes some things with it which belong to the other when it goes out [of the body] but rejects others; as when we keep company with inferior people and then change to other companions, we remember little of the inferior ones but more of the better sort.

32. But what about the memories of our friends and children and wife? Of our country, and all the things it would not be absurd for a man of quality to remember? Now the image-making power remembers each of these with emotion, but the man of quality would have his memories of them without emotion; for the emotion, perhaps, was in the imaging power even from the beginning, and those of the emotions which have any good quality pass to the noble soul, in so far as it has any communication with the other one. It is proper for the whole soul to aspire to the activities of the memory of the higher soul, especially when it is of good quality itself: for a lower soul can be comparatively good from the beginning and can become so as a result of education by the higher soul. But the higher soul ought to

τῶν παρὰ τῆς χείρονος. εἴη γὰρ ἂν καὶ σπουδαίας
οὔσης τῆς ἑτέρας τὴν ἑτέραν τὴν φύσιν χείρονα
εἶναι κατεχομένην ὑπὸ τῆς ἑτέρας βίᾳ. ὅσῳ δὴ
σπεύδει πρὸς τὸ ἄνω, πλειόνων αὐτῇ ἡ λήθη, εἰ μή
που πᾶς ὁ βίος αὐτῇ καὶ ἐνταῦθα τοιοῦτος οἷος
15 μόνων τῶν κρειττόνων εἶναι τὰς μνήμας· ἐπεὶ καὶ
ἐνταῦθα καλῶς τὸ ἐξιστάμενον τῶν ἀνθρωπεί-
ων σπουδασμάτων. ἀνάγκη οὖν καὶ τῶν μνημο-
νευμάτων· ὥστε ἐπιλήσμονα ἄν τις λέγων τὴν
ἀγαθὴν ὀρθῶς ἂν λέγοι τρόπῳ τοιούτῳ. ἐπεὶ καὶ
20 φεύγει ἐκ τῶν πολλῶν, καὶ τὰ πολλὰ εἰς ἓν συνάγει
τὸ ἄπειρον ἀφιείς. οὕτω γὰρ καὶ οὐ μετὰ πολλῶν,
ἀλλὰ ἐλαφρὰ καὶ δι' αὐτῆς· ἐπεὶ καὶ ἐνταῦθα, ὅταν
ἐκεῖ ἐθέλῃ εἶναι, ἔτι οὖσα ἐνταῦθα ἀφίησι πάντα
ὅσα ἄλλα· ὀλίγα τοίνυν κἀκεῖ τὰ ἐντεῦθεν· καὶ ἐν
οὐρανῷ οὖσα πλείω. καὶ εἴποι ἂν ὁ Ἡρακλῆς ἐκεῖ-
25 νος ἀνδραγαθίας ἑαυτοῦ, ὁ δὲ καὶ ταῦτα σμικρὰ
ἡγούμενος καὶ μετατεθεὶς εἰς ἁγιώτερον τόπον καὶ
ἐν τῷ νοητῷ γεγενημένος καὶ ὑπὲρ τὸν Ἡρακλέα
ἰσχύσας τοῖς ἄθλοις, οἷα ἀθλεύουσι σοφοί,

be happy to forget what it has received from the worse soul. For it could be that even when the higher soul is noble, the other soul is naturally a rather bad one and is restrained forcibly by the higher soul. The more it presses on towards the heights the more it will forget, unless perhaps all its life, even here below, has been such that its memories are only of higher things; since here below too it is best to be detached from human concerns, and so necessarily from human memories; so that if anyone said that the good soul was forgetful, it would be correct to say so in this sort of sense. For the higher soul also flies from multiplicity, and gathers multiplicity into one and abandons the indefinite; because in this way it will not be [clogged] with multiplicity but light and alone by itself; for even here below, when it wants to be in that higher world, while it is still here below it abandons everything that is different [from that world]; and there are few things here that are also there; and when it is in heaven it will abandon still more. And Homer's Heracles might talk about his heroic deeds; but the man who thinks these of little account and has migrated to a holier place, and has been stronger than Heracles in the contexts in which the wise compete,[1]—

---

[1] Porphyry, oddly, divides the great treatise here in the middle of a sentence. This may seem rather less odd if we consider that the sentence is anacoluthic: that the point of division marks the transition from the man of middle virtue (symbolised by Heracles) to the contemplative sage; and that division here enables Porphyry to lay great emphasis on the important question which begins IV. 4 (cp. the way in which Porphyry divides the treatise *On Providence* (III. 2–3) and the exciting question with which Plotinus himself begins I. 1).

IV. 4. (28) ΠΕΡΙ ΨΥΧΗΣ ΑΠΟΡΙΩΝ ΔΕΥΤΕΡΟΝ

1. τί οὖν ἐρεῖ; καὶ τίνων τὴν μνήμην ἕξει ψυχὴ
ἐν τῷ νοητῷ καὶ ἐπὶ τῆς οὐσίας ἐκείνης γενομένη;
ἢ ἀκόλουθον εἰπεῖν ἐκεῖνα θεωρεῖν καὶ περὶ ἐκεῖνα
ἐνεργεῖν, ἐν οἷς ἔστιν, ἢ μηδὲ ἐκεῖ εἶναι. τῶν
5 οὖν ἐνταῦθα οὐδέν, οἷον ὅτι ἐφιλοσόφησε, καὶ δὴ
καὶ ὅτι ἐνταῦθα οὖσα ἐθεᾶτο τὰ ἐκεῖ; ἀλλ᾽ εἰ μὴ
ἔστιν, ὅτε τις ἐπιβάλλει τινὶ τῇ νοήσει, ἄλλο τι
ποιεῖν ἢ νοεῖν κἀκεῖνο θεωρεῖν—καὶ ἐν τῇ νοήσει
οὐκ ἔστιν ἐμπεριεχόμενον τὸ ''ἐνενοήκειν'', ἀλλ᾽
ὕστερον ἄν τις τοῦτ᾽, εἰ ἔτυχεν, εἴποι, τοῦτο δὲ
10 ἤδη μεταβάλλοντος—οὐκ ἂν εἴη ἐν τῷ νοητῷ
καθαρῶς ὄντα μνήμην ἔχειν τῶν τῇδέ ποτε
αὐτῷ τινι γεγενημένων.[1] εἰ δὲ καί, ὥσπερ δοκεῖ,
ἄχρονος πᾶσα νόησις, ἐν αἰῶνι, ἀλλ᾽ οὐκ ἐν χρόνῳ
ὄντων τῶν ἐκεῖ, ἀδύνατον μνήμην εἶναι ἐκεῖ οὐχ
15 ὅτι τῶν ἐνταῦθα, ἀλλὰ καὶ ὅλως ὁτουοῦν. ἀλλὰ
ἔστιν ἕκαστον παρόν· ἐπεὶ οὐδὲ διέξοδος οὐδὲ
μετάβασις ἀφ᾽ ἑτέρου ἐπ᾽ ἄλλο. τί οὖν; οὐκ

---

[1] τινι γεγενημένων Enn.*: ἐπιγεγενημένων Page, H–S[1]: co-
dices defendit Theiler, collato VI. 6. 13. 59.

IV. 4. ON DIFFICULTIES ABOUT THE SOUL II

1.—What will he say? And what will the soul remember when it has come to be in the intelligible world, and with that higher reality? It is consistent to say that it will contemplate those things among which it is, and its mental activity will be concerned with them, or else it will not be there at all. Will it not, then, remember any of its experiences here below, for instance that it engaged in philosophy, and even that while it was here it contemplated the things in that other world? But if it is not possible, when one has one's thought directed on something, to do anything else but think and contemplate that object—and the statement "I had thought [it before]" is not included in the thinking, but one would say it afterwards, if one said it at all, that is when an alteration in one's thinking has already taken place; it would not then be possible, when one is purely in the intelligible world, to remember the things which happened to one at any time when one was here. But if, as we believe, every act of intelligence is timeless, since the realities there are in eternity and not in time, it is impossible that there should be a memory there, not only of the things here below, but of anything at all. But each and every thing is present there; so there is no discursive thought or transition from one to the other. Well,

ἔσται διαίρεσις ἄνωθεν εἰς εἴδη, ἢ κάτωθεν ἐπὶ τὸ
καθόλου καὶ τὸ ἄνω; τῷ μὲν γὰρ νῷ[1] μὴ ἔστω
ἐνεργείᾳ ὁμοῦ ὄντι, τῇ δὲ ψυχῇ ἐκεῖ οὔσῃ διὰ τί
20 οὐκ ἔσται; τί οὖν κωλύει καὶ ταύτην τὴν ἐπιβολὴν
ἀθρόαν ἀθρόων γίγνεσθαι; ἆρ᾽ οὖν ὥς τινος ὁμοῦ;
ἢ ὡς πολλῶν ὁμοῦ πάσας νοήσεις. τοῦ γὰρ θεάμα-
τος ὄντος ποικίλου ποικίλην καὶ πολλὴν τὴν
νόησιν ἅμα γίγνεσθαι καὶ πολλὰς τὰς νοήσεις, οἷον
αἰσθήσεις πολλὰς προσώπου ὀφθαλμῶν[2] ἅμα
25 ὁρωμένων καὶ ῥινὸς καὶ τῶν ἄλλων. ἀλλ᾽ ὅταν ἕν
τι διαιρῇ καὶ ἀναπτύσσῃ; ἢ ἐν τῷ νῷ διῄρηται·
καὶ τὸ τοιοῦτον οἷον ἐναπέρεισις μᾶλλον. τὸ δὲ
πρότερον καὶ τὸ ὕστερον ἐν τοῖς εἴδεσιν οὐ χρόνῳ
ὂν οὐδὲ τὴν νόησιν τοῦ προτέρου καὶ ὑστέρου χρόνῳ
ποιήσει· ἔστι γὰρ καὶ τάξει, οἱονεὶ φυτοῦ ἡ τάξις
30 ἐκ ῥιζῶν ἀρξαμένη ἕως εἰς τὸ ἄνω τῷ θεωμένῳ
οὐκ ἔχει ἄλλως ἢ τάξει τὸ πρότερον καὶ τὸ ὕστερον
ἅμα τὸ πᾶν θεωμένῳ. ἀλλ᾽ ὅταν εἰς ἓν βλέπῃ,
εἶτα[3] πολλὰ καὶ πάντα ἔχῃ,[4] πῶς τὸ μὲν πρῶτον
ἔσχε, τὸ δὲ ἐφεξῆς; ἢ ἡ δύναμις ἡ μία οὕτως ἦν
μία, ὡς πολλὰ ἐν ἄλλῳ, καὶ οὐ κατὰ μίαν νόησιν
35 πάντα. αἱ γὰρ ἐνέργειαι [οὐ][5] καθ᾽ ἕνα, ἀλλ᾽ ἀεὶ

---

[1] Kleist, testatur Theologia II. 11: ἄνω Enn., H–S[1].
[2] Cpc, Kirchhoff* (*oculos* Ficinus): ὀφθαλμῷ wxUCac.
[3] xUC: εἶτα (sic) w: εἰ τὰ Perna, Creuzer, H–S[1].
[4] xUC: ἔχει w, Perna, Creuzer, H–S[1].
[5] del. Theiler, quod testatur Theologia II. 20.

then, will there be no division starting from above into species, or an ascent from below to the universal and the higher? Granted that the Intellect does not have this, since it is all together in one in its actuality, why should the soul when it is there not have it? What then prevents the soul too from having a unified intuition of all its objects in one? Can it really see them as one thing, all together? Rather, it is as if all its acts of intelligence, with their many objects, were all together. For since its object of contemplation is richly varied, the act of intelligence too is richly varied and multiple, and there are many acts of intelligence, as there are many acts of perception of a face when the eyes and the nose and the other features are all seen at once. But [what happens] when the soul divides and unfolds some one object? It is already divided in Intellect and an act of this kind is more like a concentration of attention. And, as the prior and the subsequent in the species-forms are not temporal, so neither will the soul make its acts of intelligence of the prior and the subsequent in temporal sequence. For there is also the prior and the subsequent in order, as in a plant the order which begins from the roots and extends to the topmost point does not have for the observer the prior and the subsequent in any other way than in order, since he observes the whole plant at once. But when the soul looks first at one [intelligible object], and then possesses the whole multiplicity of them, how does it possess one first and another next? The one power is one in such a way that it becomes many in something else, and does not comprehend all things by one act of intelligence. For its acts are individual, but always to-

πᾶσαι δυνάμει ἑστώσῃ· ἐν δὲ τοῖς ἄλλοις σχιζομέ-
νῃ.[1] ἤδη γὰρ ἐκεῖνο ὡς μὴ ἓν ὂν δυνηθῆναι τὴν
τῶν πολλῶν ἐν αὑτῷ φύσιν δέξασθαι πρότερον οὐκ
ὄντων.

2. Ἀλλὰ ταῦτα μὲν ταύτῃ. ἑαυτοῦ δὲ πῶς; ἢ
οὐδὲ ἑαυτοῦ ἕξει τὴν μνήμην, οὐδ' ὅτι αὐτὸς ὁ
θεωρῶν, οἷον Σωκράτης, ἢ ὅτι νοῦς ἢ ψυχή. πρὸς
δὴ ταῦτά τις ἀναμνησθήτω, ὡς ὅταν καὶ ἐνταῦθα
5 θεωρῇ καὶ μάλιστα ἐναργῶς, οὐκ ἐπιστρέφει πρὸς
ἑαυτὸν τότε τῇ νοήσει, ἀλλ' ἔχει μὲν ἑαυτόν, ἡ
δὲ ἐνέργεια πρὸς ἐκεῖνο, κἀκεῖνο γίνεται οἷον
ὕλην ἑαυτὸν παρασχών, εἰδοποιούμενος δὲ κατὰ τὸ
ὁρώμενον καὶ δυνάμει ὢν τότε αὐτός. τότε οὖν
αὐτός τί ἐστιν ἐνεργείᾳ, ὅταν μηδὲν νοῇ; ἤ, εἰ μὲν
10 αὐτός, κενός ἐστι παντός, ὅταν μηδὲν νοῇ. εἰ δέ
ἐστιν αὐτὸς τοιοῦτος οἷος πάντα εἶναι, ὅταν αὑτὸν
νοῇ, πάντα ὁμοῦ νοεῖ· ὥστε τῇ μὲν εἰς ἑαυτὸν ὁ
τοιοῦτος ἐπιβολῇ καὶ ἐνεργείᾳ ἑαυτὸν ὁρῶν τὰ
πάντα ἐμπεριεχόμενα ἔχει, τῇ δὲ πρὸς τὰ πάντα
ἐμπεριεχόμενον ἑαυτόν. ἀλλ' εἰ οὕτω ποιεῖ, μετα-
15 βάλλει τὰς νοήσεις, ὃ πρότερον αὐτοὶ οὐκ ἠξιοῦμεν.
ἢ λεκτέον ἐπὶ μὲν τοῦ νοῦ τὸ ὡσαύτως ἔχειν, ἐπὶ
δὲ τῆς ψυχῆς ἐν οἷον ἐσχάτοις τοῦ νοητοῦ κειμένης

---

[1] Theiler: γινομένων Enn., H–S[1]: †γινομένων† H–S[2]: ἐν
. . . γινομένων del. Kleist, Harder: ἄλλοις γινομένων ἤδη
⟨πολλῶν οὐκ ἀεὶ πᾶσαι· ἤδη⟩ Igal non male.

---

[1] I very tentatively adopt Theiler's σχιζομένη here to produce an intelligible text, though I think *locus nondum sanatus*
(H—S[2]) may well be right. Kleist and Harder delete ἐν . . .

gether in a power which remains unchanged, but is divided in other things.[1] For that intelligible object is able in virtue of its not being one to receive in itself the nature of the many which did not previously exist.

2. But enough about this. How does it remember itself? It will not even have the remembrance of itself, or that it is the man himself, Socrates for instance, who is contemplating, or that it is intellect or soul. Besides, one should certainly remember that even here below when one contemplates, especially when the contemplation is clear, one does not turn to oneself in the act of intelligence, but one possesses oneself; one's activity, however, is directed towards the object of contemplation, and one becomes this, offering oneself to it as a kind of matter, being formed according to what one sees, and being oneself then only potentially. Is a man then actually himself in any way when he is thinking nothing at all? Yes, if he is [merely] himself he is empty of everything, when he is thinking nothing at all. But if he is himself in such a way as to be everything, when he thinks himself, he thinks everything at once; so that a man in this state, by his intuition of himself, and when he actually sees himself, has everything included in this seeing, and by his intuition of everything has himself included. But if this is what he does, he changes his acts of intelligence, and we ourselves did not think it right to assert this before. Must we say then that unchangeability belongs to Intellect, but that in the case of Soul, which lies, so

γινομένων. It adds nothing to what has been said in the previous sentence, but Plotinus is frequently repetitive. Igal's suggestion is attractive, but not completely convincing.

γίνεσθαι τοῦτο δυνατὸν εἶναι, ἐπεὶ καὶ προσχωρεῖν
εἴσω; εἰ γάρ τι περὶ τὸ μένον γίνεται, δεῖ αὐτὸ
20 παραλλαγὴν πρὸς τὸ μένον ἔχειν μὴ ὁμοίως μένον.
ἢ οὐδὲ μεταβολὴν λεκτέον γίνεσθαι, ὅταν ἀπὸ τῶν
ἑαυτοῦ ἐφ’ ἑαυτόν, καὶ ὅταν ἀφ’ ἑαυτοῦ ἐπὶ τὰ
ἄλλα· πάντα γὰρ αὐτός ἐστι καὶ ἄμφω ἕν. ἀλλ’
ἡ ψυχὴ ἐν τῷ νοητῷ οὖσα τοῦτο πάσχει τὸ ἄλλο
καὶ ἄλλο πρὸς αὐτὴν καὶ τὰ ἐν αὐτῇ; ἢ καθαρῶς
25 ἐν τῷ νοητῷ οὖσα ἔχει τὸ ἀμετάβλητον καὶ αὐτή.
καὶ γὰρ αὐτή ἐστιν ἅ ἐστιν· ἐπεὶ καὶ ὅταν ἐν ἐκείνῳ
ᾖ τῷ τόπῳ, εἰς ἕνωσιν ἐλθεῖν τῷ νῷ ἀνάγκη,
εἴπερ ἐπεστράφη· στραφεῖσα γὰρ οὐδὲν μεταξὺ ἔχει,
εἴς τε νοῦν ἐλθοῦσα ἥρμοσται, καὶ ἁρμοσθεῖσα
ἥνωται οὐκ ἀπολλυμένη, ἀλλ’ ἕν ἐστιν ἄμφω καὶ
30 δύο. οὕτως οὖν ἔχουσα οὐκ ἂν μεταβάλλοι, ἀλλὰ
ἔχοι ἂν ἀτρέπτως πρὸς νόησιν ὁμοῦ ἔχουσα τὴν
συναίσθησιν αὐτῆς, ὡς ἓν ἅμα τῷ νοητῷ ταὐτὸν
γενομένη.

3. Ἐξελθοῦσα δὲ ἐκεῖθεν καὶ οὐκ ἀνασχομένη τὸ
ἕν, τὸ δὲ αὐτῆς ἀσπασαμένη καὶ ἕτερον ἐθελήσασα
εἶναι καὶ οἷον προκύψασα, μνήμην, ὡς ἔοικεν,
ἐφεξῆς λαμβάνει. μνήμη δὲ ἡ μὲν τῶν ἐκεῖ ἔτι
5 κατέχει μὴ πεσεῖν, ἡ δὲ τῶν ἐνταυθα ὡδὶ φέρει, ἡ
δὲ τῶν ἐν οὐρανῷ ἐκεῖ κατέχει, καὶ ὅλως, οὗ μνημονεύει, ἐκεῖνό ἐστι καὶ γίνεται. ἦν γὰρ τὸ μνημονεύ-

to speak, on the frontier of the intelligible, this change can happen, since it can also advance further into Intellect? For if something comes to be in the region of that which abides, it must be different from that which abides, and not abide in the same way. No, we must not even say that there is a change, when the soul moves from its own content to itself, and from itself to the rest of its content: for the self is all things, and both are one. But does the soul when it is in the intelligible world experience this " one thing after another " in relation to itself and its contents? No, when it is purely and simply in the intelligible world it has itself too the characteristic of unchangeability. For it is really all the things it is: since when it is in that region, it must come to unity with Intellect, by the fact that it has turned to it, for when it is turned, it has nothing between, but comes to Intellect and accords itself to it, and by that accord is united to it without being destroyed, but both of them are one and also two. When therefore it is in this state it could not change but would be unalterably disposed to intelligence while at the same time having a concurrent awareness of itself, as having become one and the same thing with its intelligible object.

3. But if it comes out of the intelligible world, and cannot endure unity, but embraces its own individuality and wants to be different and so to speak puts its head outside, it thereupon acquires memory. Its memory of what is in the intelligible world still holds it back from falling, but its memory of the things here below carries it down here; its memory

ειν ἢ νοεῖν ἢ φαντάζεσθαι, ἡ δὲ φαντασία αὐτῇ[1]
οὐ τῷ ἔχειν, ἀλλ' οἷα ὁρᾷ, καὶ [οἷα][2] διάκειται·
κἂν τὰ αἰσθητὰ ἴδῃ, ὁπόσον αὐτῶν ἂν ἴδῃ, τοσοῦτον
10 ἔχει τὸ βάθος. ὅτι γὰρ ἔχει πάντα δευτέρως καὶ
οὐχ οὕτω τελείως, πάντα γίνεται, καὶ μεθόριον
οὖσα καὶ ἐν τοιούτῳ κειμένη ἐπ' ἄμφω φέρεται.

4. Ἐκεῖ μὲν οὖν καὶ τἀγαθὸν διὰ νοῦ ὁρᾷ, οὐ γὰρ
στέγεται ἐκεῖνο, ὥστε μὴ διελθεῖν εἰς αὐτήν· ἐπεὶ
μὴ σῶμα τὸ μεταξὺ ὥστε ἐμποδίζειν· καίτοι καὶ
σωμάτων μεταξὺ πολλαχῇ εἰς τὰ τρίτα ἀπὸ τῶν
5 πρώτων ἡ ἄφιξις. εἰ δὲ πρὸς τὰ κάτω δοίη αὐτήν,
ἀναλόγως τῇ μνήμῃ καὶ τῇ φαντασίᾳ ἔχει ὃ
ἠθέλησε. διὸ ἡ μνήμη, καὶ ὅταν τῶν ἀρίστων ᾖ,
οὐκ ἄριστον. δεῖ δὲ τὴν μνήμην λαμβάνειν οὐ
μόνον ἐν τῷ οἷον αἰσθάνεσθαι ὅτι μνημονεύει, ἀλλὰ
καὶ ὅταν διακέηται κατὰ τὰ πρόσθεν παθήματα ἢ
10 θεάματα. γένοιτο γὰρ ἄν, καὶ μὴ παρακολουθοῦντα
ὅτι ἔχει, ἔχειν παρ' αὐτῷ ἰσχυροτέρως ἢ εἰ εἰδείη.
εἰδὼς μὲν γὰρ τάχα ἂν ὡς ἄλλο ἔχοι ἄλλος αὐτὸς
ὤν, ἀγνοῶν δὲ ὅτι ἔχει κινδυνεύει εἶναι ὃ ἔχει· ὃ
δὴ πάθημα μᾶλλον πεσεῖν ποιεῖ τὴν ψυχήν. ἀλλ'
15 εἰ ἀφισταμένη τοῦ ἐκεῖ τόπου ἀναφέρει τὰς μνήμας
ὁπωσοῦν, εἶχε κἀκεῖ. ἢ δυνάμει·[3] ἡ δὲ ἐνέργεια

___

[1] αὐτῇ (sc. τῇ ψυχῇ) Kirchhoff*: αὐτὴ xUC, Creuzer: αὕτη w, Perna.
[2] del. Beutler.
[3] Gollwitzer, Bréhier, Harder, Cilento, B–T: ἡ δύναμις Enn.: del. Kirchhoff, Müller, Volkmann.

of what is in heaven keeps it there, and in general it is and becomes what it remembers. For remembering is either thinking or imaging; and the image comes to the soul not by possession, but as it sees, so it is disposed; and if it sees sense-objects, it sinks low in proportion to the amount of them it sees. For because it possesses all things in a secondary way, and not so perfectly [as Intellect], it becomes all things, and since it is a thing belonging to the frontier between the worlds, and occupies a corresponding position, it moves in both directions.

4. Now in the intelligible world the soul also sees the Good through Intellect; for it is not excluded, so as not to come through to the soul, since what is between them is not a body which would obstruct it —yet even with bodies between there are many ways of arrival at the third level from the first. But if the soul gives itself to what is below it, it has what it wants in proportion to its memory and imaging power. Therefore memory, even when it is of the best, is not the best thing. But one must understand memory not only in the sense of a kind of perception that one is remembering, but as existing when the soul is disposed according to what it has previously experienced or contemplated. For it could happen that, even when one is not conscious that one has something, one holds it to oneself more strongly than if one knew. For perhaps if one knew one would have it as something else, being different oneself, but if one does not know that one has it one is liable to be what one has; and this is certainly the experience which makes the soul sink lower. But if when the soul leaves the intelligible region it recovers its memories, it had them somehow there

ἐκείνων ἠφάνιζε τὴν μνήμην. οὐ γὰρ ὡς κείμενοι
ἦσαν τύποι, ἵνα ἂν ᾖ ἴσως ἄτοπον τὸ συμβαῖνον,
ἀλλ' ἡ δύναμις ἦν ἡ ἀφεθεῖσα ὕστερον εἰς ἐνέργειαν.
παυσαμένης οὖν τῆς ἐν τῷ νοητῷ ἐνεργείας, εἶδεν ἃ
20 πρότερον ἡ ψυχή, πρὶν ἐκεῖ γενέσθαι, ἰδοῦσα ἦν.

5. Τί οὖν; κἀκεῖνα νῦν αὐτὴ ἡ δύναμις, καθ' ἣν
τὸ μνημονεύειν, εἰς ἐνέργειαν ἄγει; ἢ εἰ μὲν μὴ
αὐτὰ ἑωρῶμεν, μνήμῃ, εἰ δ' αὐτά, ᾧ κἀκεῖ ἑωρῶμεν.
ἐγείρεται γὰρ τοῦτο οἷς ἐγείρεται, καὶ τοῦτό ἐστι
5 τὸ ὁρῶν περὶ τῶν εἰρημένων. οὐ γὰρ εἰκασίᾳ δεῖ
χρώμενον ἀποφαίνεσθαι οὐδὲ συλλογισμῷ τὰς
ἀρχὰς ἄλλοθεν εἰληφότι, ἀλλ' ἔστι περὶ τῶν
νοητῶν, ὡς λέγεται, καὶ ἐνθάδε οὖσι τῷ αὐτῷ
λέγειν,[1] ὃ δύναμιν ἔχει τἀκεῖ θεωρεῖν. ταὐτὸ γὰρ
οἷον ἐγείραντας δεῖ ὁρᾶν τἀκεῖ, ὥστε καὶ ἐγεῖραι
10 ἐκεῖ· οἷον εἴ τις ἀνάγων αὐτοῦ τὸν ὀφθαλμὸν ἐπί
τινος ὑψηλῆς σκοπιᾶς ὁρῴη ἃ μηδεὶς τῶν οὐ σὺν
αὐτῷ ἀναβεβηκότων. ἡ τοίνυν μνήμη ἐκ τοῦ
λόγου φαίνεται ἄρχεσθαι ἀπ' οὐρανοῦ, ἤδη τῆς
ψυχῆς τοὺς ἐκεῖ τόπους καταλειπούσης. ἐντεῦθεν
μὲν οὖν ἐν οὐρανῷ γενομένη καὶ στᾶσα θαυμαστὸν
15 οὐδέν, εἰ τῶν ἐνθάδε μνήμην πολλῶν ἔχοι οἵων
εἴρηται, καὶ ἐπιγινώσκειν πολλὰς τῶν πρότερον

---

[1] Creuzer* (*dicere* Ficinus): λέγεται Enn.

too. Yes, it had them potentially, but the active actuality of the intelligible realities obscured the memory. For its memories were not like imprints left in it (a supposition which would possibly have absurd consequences), but the potentiality was there which was later let loose into actuality. So when the actuality in the intelligible world ceased to be active, the soul saw what it had been seeing before it came to be in that world.

5. Well, then, does this very potentiality by which we remember bring the intelligible realities also to actuality in us now? If we did not see them themselves, it is by memory [that they are actual], but if we did see them, it is by that with which we also saw them there. For this is awakened by that which awakens it, and this is the power which sees in the sphere of the realities we mentioned. For one must not, when one makes statements about the intelligible world, use analogy or syllogistic reasoning which takes its principles from elsewhere, but even when we are here below we can speak about the intelligible realities by that same power which is able to contemplate the higher world. For one must see the things in that world by a kind of awakening of the same power, so that one can awake it in the higher world also; as if one went up to some high viewpoint and raising one's eyes saw what no one saw who had not come up with one. From our discussion, then, it seems that memory begins in heaven, when the soul has already left the higher regions. Now if the soul has arrived in heaven from down here and stays there, it is in no way surprising if it remembers many things here below of the sort we have mentioned, and recognises many souls from

ἐγνωσμένων, εἴπερ καὶ σώματα ἔχειν περὶ αὐτὰς
ἀνάγκη ἐν σχήμασιν ὁμοίοις. καὶ εἰ τὰ σχήματα
δὲ ἀλλάξαιντο σφαιροειδῆ ποιησάμεναι, ἆρα διὰ
20 τῶν ἠθῶν καὶ τῆς τῶν τρόπων ἰδιότητος γνωρίζοιεν; οὐ γὰρ ἄτοπον. τὰ μὲν γὰρ πάθη ἔστωσαν
ἀποθέμεναι, τὰ δ᾽ ἤθη οὐ κωλύεται μένειν. εἰ δὲ
καὶ διαλέγεσθαι δύναιντο, καὶ οὕτως ἂν γνωρίζοιεν.
ἀλλ᾽ ὅταν ἐκ τοῦ νοητοῦ κατέλθωσι, πῶς; ἢ
ἀνακινήσουσι τὴν μνήμην, ἐλαττόνως μέντοι ἢ
25 ἐκεῖναι, τῶν αὐτῶν· ἄλλα τε γὰρ ἕξουσι μνημονεύειν, καὶ χρόνος πλείων λήθην παντελῆ πολλῶν
πεποιηκὼς ἔσται. ἀλλ᾽ εἰ τραπεῖσαι εἰς τὸν αἰσθητὸν κόσμον εἰς γένεσιν τῇδε πεσοῦνται, ποῖος
τρόπος [1] ἔσται τοῦ μνημονεύειν; ἢ οὐκ ἀνάγκη εἰς
πᾶν βάθος πεσεῖν. ἔστι γὰρ κινηθείσας καὶ στῆναι
30 ἐπί τι προελθούσας καὶ οὐδὲν δὲ κωλύει πάλιν
ἐκδῦναι, πρὶν γενέσεως ἐλθεῖν ἐπ᾽ ἔσχατον τόπον.

6. Τὰς μὲν οὖν μετιούσας καὶ μεταβαλλούσας
[τὰς ψυχὰς] [2] ἔχοι ἄν τις εἰπεῖν ὅτι καὶ μνημονεύ-
σουσι· τῶν γὰρ γεγενημένων καὶ παρεληλυθότων
ἡ μνήμη· αἷς δὲ ἐν τῷ αὐτῷ ὑπάρχει μένειν,
5 τίνων ἂν αὗται μνημονεύοιεν; ἄστρων δὲ περὶ
ψυχῆς τῶν γε ἄλλων ἁπάντων καὶ δὴ καὶ περὶ ἡλίου
καὶ σελήνης ἐπιζητεῖ ὁ λόγος τὰς μνήμας, καὶ τε-

[1] Kleist, Volkmann*: ποῖος χρόνος Enn.: πόσος χρόνος
Thillet.
[2] del. Kirchhoff, Müller, H–S.

148

among those it knew previously, especially if they must necessarily be clothed in bodies of similar forms [to their earthly ones]. And even if they have changed the forms of their bodies and adopted spherical ones, might they recognise [each other] by their characters and the individuality of their behaviour [1]? For this is not absurd. Granted that they have put away their passions, there is nothing to prevent their characters persisting. And if they were also able to talk, they could recognise [each other] in this way too. But when they come down from the intelligible world to heaven, how do they remember? They will arouse again their memories of the same things, but less than the souls which come from below; for they will have other things to remember, and the longer time which has elapsed will have produced complete forgetfulness of many things. But if they turn to the world of sense and fall to birth here, what will be the manner of their rememberings? It is not necessary to fall the whole way into the depths. For it is possible for souls in motion to halt when they have advanced a certain distance, and nothing prevents them from emerging again before they come to the lowest point of the process of generation.

6. One could say, then, that souls which migrate and change their state will also remember; for memory is of things which have happened and are past; but as for the souls to which it belongs to remain in the same state, what could they remember? The discussion is trying to find out about the memo-

---

[1] In view of the importance attached to spherical shape (and circular motion) as the most perfect in late antiquity, Plotinus's lack of interest in the shape of our heavenly bodies is striking.

λευτῶν εἰσι καὶ ἐπὶ τὴν τοῦ παντὸς ψυχήν, καὶ
ἐπιτολμήσει καὶ τοῦ Διὸς αὐτοῦ τὰς μνήμας πολυ-
πραγμονεῖν. ταῦτα δὲ ζητῶν καὶ τὰς διανοίας αὐ-
10 τῶν καὶ τοὺς λογισμοὺς τίνες εἰσὶ θεωρήσει, εἴπερ
εἰσίν. εἰ οὖν μήτε ζητοῦσι μήτε ἀποροῦσιν—οὐδενὸς γὰρ δέονται, οὐδὲ μανθάνουσιν, ἃ πρότερον οὐκ
ἦν αὐτοῖς ἐν γνώσει—τίνες ἂν λογισμοὶ ἢ τίνες συλ-
λογισμοὶ αὐτοῖς γίγνοιντο ἢ διανοήσεις; ἀλλ' οὐδὲ
περὶ τῶν ἀνθρωπίνων αὐτοῖς ἐπίνοιαι καὶ μηχαναί,
15 ἐξ ὧν διοικήσουσι τὰ ἡμέτερα ἢ ὅλως τὰ τῆς γῆς·
ἄλλος γὰρ τρόπος τῆς εἰς τὸ πᾶν παρ' αὐτῶν εὐθη-
μοσύνης.

7. Τί οὖν; ὅτι τὸν θεὸν εἶδον οὐ μνημονεύουσιν;
ἢ ἀεὶ ὁρῶσιν. ἕως δ' ἂν ὁρῶσιν, οὐκ ἔνι δήπου
φάναι αὐτοῖς ἑωρακέναι· παυσαμένων γὰρ τοῦτο
ἂν πάθος εἴη. τί δέ; οὐδ' ὅτι περιῆλθον χθὲς τὴν
5 γῆν καὶ [τὸ]¹ πέρυσιν, οὐδ' ὅτι ἔζων χθὲς καὶ
πάλαι καὶ ἐξ οὗ ζῶσιν; ἢ ζῶσιν ἀεί· τὸ δὲ ἀεὶ ταὐτὸν ἕν. τὸ δὲ χθὲς τῆς φορᾶς καὶ τὸ πέρυσι τοιοῦτον ἂν εἴη, οἷον ἂν εἴ τις τὴν ὁρμὴν τὴν κατὰ πόδα
ἕνα γενομένην μερίζοι εἰς πολλά, καὶ ἄλλην καὶ
ἄλλην καὶ πολλὰς ποιοῖ τὴν μίαν. καὶ γὰρ ἐνταῦθα
10 μία φορά, παρὰ δὲ ἡμῖν μετροῦνται πολλαὶ καὶ
ἡμέραι ἄλλαι, ὅτι καὶ νύκτες διαλαμβάνουσιν.
ἐκεῖ δὲ μιᾶς οὔσης ἡμέρας πῶς πολλαί; ὥστε
οὐδὲ τὸ πέρυσιν. ἀλλὰ τὸ διάστημα οὐ ταὐτόν,

¹ del. Buchwald.

ries of the soul of all the heavenly bodies in general,
and in particular about the sun and moon, and in the
end it will go as far as the soul of the All, and will
dare to be busy with the memories of Zeus himself.
And in looking for this it will observe what their
discursive reasonings and calculations are, if there
are any. If, then, they neither investigate nor are
perplexed—for they need nothing and learn nothing
which was not part of their knowledge before—
what could their calculations or logical deductions or
discursive reasonings be? They will not even have
designs and devices concerned with human affairs,
by which they will manage our business and that of
the earth in general: the right order which comes
from them to the All is of another kind.

7. Well, then, will they not remember that they
saw God? They always see him; and while they
see him it is surely not possible for them to say that
they have seen him: this would be something which
would happen to those who have ceased to see.
Well, will they not remember that they went round
the earth yesterday, and last year, and that they
lived yesterday and for a long time past and
from the beginning of their lives? They live for
ever: and "for ever" means an identical unity.
The "yesterday" of their transit and the "last
year" would be the same kind of thing as if one was
to divide the step taken by one foot into many parts,
and make the one step into many, one after another.
For up there there is one transit, but we measure
many, and different days, because nights intervene.
But there, since there is one [unbroken] day, how
can there be many? So there is not a last year
either. But the space traversed is not the same, but

ἀλλ' ἄλλο, καὶ τὸ ζῳδίου τμῆμα ἄλλο. διὰ τί οὖν
οὐκ ἐρεῖ "παρῆλθον τόδε, νῦν δὲ ἐν ἄλλῳ εἰμί"; εἰ
15 δὲ καὶ ἐφορᾷ τὰ ἀνθρώπων, πῶς οὐ καὶ τὰς μετα-
βολὰς τὰς περὶ αὐτούς, καὶ ὅτι νῦν ἄλλοι; εἰ δὲ
τοῦτο, καὶ ὅτι πρότερον ἕτεροι καὶ ἕτερα· ὥστε καὶ
μνήμη.

8. Ἢ οὐκ ἀνάγκη οὔτε ὅσα τις θεωρεῖ ἐν μνήμῃ
τίθεσθαι, οὔτε τῶν πάντη κατὰ συμβεβηκὸς
ἐπακολουθούντων ἐν φαντασίᾳ γίγνεσθαι, ὧν τε ἡ
νόησις καὶ ἡ γνῶσις ἐνεργεστέρα, εἰ ταῦτα αἰσθητῶς
5 γίγνοιτο, οὐκ ἀνάγκη παρέντα τὴν γνῶσιν αὐτῶν τῷ
κατὰ μέρος αἰσθητῷ τὴν ἐπιβολὴν ποιεῖσθαι, εἰ μή
τις ἔργῳ οἰκονομοῖτό τι, τῶν ἐν μέρει τῇ γνώσει
τοῦ ὅλου ἐμπεριεχομένων. λέγω δὲ ἕκαστον ὧδε·
πρῶτον μὲν τὸ μὴ ἀναγκαῖον εἶναι, ἅ τις ὁρᾷ,
παρατίθεσθαι παρ' αὐτῷ. ὅταν γὰρ μηδὲν[1] δια-
10 φέρῃ, ἢ μὴ πρὸς αὐτὸν ᾖ ὅλως ἡ αἴσθησις ἀπροαιρέτως τῇ διαφορᾷ τῶν ὁρωμένων κινηθεῖσα, τοῦτο
αὐτὴ ἔπαθε μόνη τῆς ψυχῆς οὐ δεξαμένης εἰς τὸ
εἴσω, ἅτε μήτε πρὸς χρείαν μήτε πρὸς ἄλλην
ὠφέλειαν αὐτῆς τῆς διαφορᾶς μέλον. ὅταν δὲ ἡ
15 ἐνέργεια αὐτὴ πρὸς ἄλλοις ᾖ καὶ παντελῶς, οὐκ ἂν
ἀνάσχοιτο τῶν τοιούτων παρελθόντων τὴν μνήμην,
ὅπου μηδὲ παρόντων γινώσκει τὴν αἴσθησιν. καὶ

---

[1] Beutler: μηδὲ Enn., H–S[1]: μὴ Kirchhoff*, Theiler.

---

[1] For the idea that we have sensations of which we are unconscious cp. IV. 9. 2; V. 1. 12; see E. R. Dodds " Tradition
and Personal Achievement in the Philosophy of Plotinus "
(*J.R.S.* 50, 1960, 5–6) for Plotinus's discovery of the unconscious. On the assimilation in these chapters of celestial

different, and the section of the Zodiac is different. Why, then, will not the star say, " I have passed through this section, and am now in another "? And if it keeps watch over human affairs, why does it not see the changes which take place among men, and that they are now different? And if this is so, it sees that men and their affairs were formerly otherwise: so that it also has memory.

8. Now it is not necessary to deposit in one's memory everything that one observes, or that altogether incidental consequences should come to be present in the imaging faculty; and further, in the case of things of which the thought and knowledge is more effective, it is not necessary, if these occur in the field of sense-perception, to let the knowledge of them go and pay attention to the particulars perceived by sense (unless one is engaged in the practical management of something), since the particulars are included in the knowledge of the whole. What I mean by each of these statements is as follows. First point: that it is not necessary to keep stored up in oneself what one sees. When what is perceived makes no difference, or the perception is not at all personally relevant, but is provoked involuntarily by the difference in the things seen, it is only the sense-perception which has this experience and the soul does not receive it into its interior, since the difference is not of concern to it either because it meets a need or is of benefit in some other way.[1] And when the

souls to the unchanging life of eternity, because they are not aware of and do not remember their embodied experience in so far as it is temporal and changing, see my " Eternity, Life and Movement in Plotinus' Accounts of Νοῦς " in *Le Néo-platonisme* (Paris 1971) 68–9.

μὴν ὅτι τῶν πάντη κατὰ συμβεβηκὸς γινομένων οὐκ
ἀνάγκη ἐν φαντασίᾳ γίνεσθαι, εἰ δὲ καὶ γίνοιτο,
οὐχ ὥστε καὶ φυλάξαι καὶ παρατηρῆσαι, ἀλλὰ καὶ
20 ὁ τύπος τοῦ τοιούτου οὐ δίδωσι συναίσθησιν, μάθοι
ἄν τις, εἰ τὸ λεγόμενον οὕτω λάβοι. λέγω δὲ ὧδε·
εἰ μηδέποτε προηγούμενον γίνεται τὸν ἀέρα τόνδε
εἶτα τόνδε τεμεῖν ἐν τῷ κατὰ τόπον κινεῖσθαι, ἢ
καὶ ἔτι μᾶλλον διελθεῖν, οὔτ' ἂν τήρησις αὐτοῦ οὔτ'
ἂν ἔννοια βαδίζουσι γένοιτο. ἐπεὶ καὶ τῆς ὁδοῦ εἰ
25 μὴ ἐγίνετο τὸ τόδε διανύσαι προηγούμενον, δι'
ἀέρος δὲ ἦν τὴν διέξοδον ποιήσασθαι, οὐκ ἂν
ἐγένετο ἡμῖν μέλειν τὸ ἐν ὅτῳ σταδίῳ γῆς ἐσμεν,
ἢ ὅσον ἠνύσαμεν· καὶ εἰ κινεῖσθαι δὲ ἔδει μὴ
τοσόνδε χρόνον, ἀλλὰ μόνον κινεῖσθαι, μηδ'
ἄλλην τινὰ πρᾶξιν εἰς χρόνον ἀνήγομεν, οὐκ ἂν ἐν
30 μνήμῃ ἄλλον ἂν καὶ ἄλλον χρόνον ἐποιησάμεθα.
γνώριμον δέ, ὅτι τῆς διανοίας ἐχούσης τὸ πραττόμενον ὅλον καὶ πιστευούσης οὕτω πάντως πραχθήσεσ-
θαι οὐκ ἂν ἔτι προσέχοι γιγνομένοις ἑκάστοις. καὶ
μὴν καὶ ὅταν τις ταὐτὸν ἀεὶ ποιῇ, μάτην ἂν ἔτι
35 παρατηροῖ ἕκαστα τοῦ ταὐτοῦ. εἰ οὖν τὰ ἄστρα
φερόμενα τὰ αὑτῶν πράττοντα φέρεται καὶ οὐχ ἵνα

soul's activity is directed to other things, and completely directed to them, it will not accept the memory of things like these when they have passed away, since it is not aware of the sense-impression produced by them when they are there. Then again, one might understand the point that things which happen altogether incidentally do not necessarily come to be present in the imaging faculty, and even if they did would not necessarily be there in such a way that it would guard and observe them, but the impression of a thing like this does not produce a conscious perception, if one took what was said in the following sense. This is what I mean: if it is never a primary consideration to us in local motion to cut through this piece of air and then that, or, even more, to pass through the air at all, we shall not observe the air or have an idea of it in our minds as we walk. For if it was not a primary consideration to us to complete a particular stretch of the road, but we could go on our way through the air, it would be no concern of ours at what milestone in the land we were, or how much of the way we had covered; and if we did not have to travel for a particular space of time, but only to travel, and referred no other activity to time, we should not remember successive periods of time. It is also well known that when our reason grasps what is being done as a whole, and has confidence that it will be completely carried out in this particular way, it will not any more attend to the details as they occur. Again, when someone is always doing the same thing, there would be no point in his observing the details of this same operation. If, then, the heavenly bodies in their courses move along concerned with their own affairs and not

παρέλθῃ ταῦτα ὅσα παρέρχεται, καὶ τὸ ἔργον
αὐτοῖς οὔτε ἡ θέα ὧν πάρεισιν, οὔτε τὸ παρελθεῖν,
κατὰ συμβεβηκός τε ἡ πάροδος, πρὸς ἄλλοις τε ἡ
γνώμη μείζοσι, τά τε αὐτὰ ἀεὶ δι' ὧν διέρχονται
40 ταῦτα, ὅ τε χρόνος οὐκ ἐν λογισμῷ ὁ ἐν τοσῷδε, εἰ
καὶ διῃρεῖτο, οὐκ ἀνάγκη οὔτε τόπων ὧν παρίασιν
οὔτε χρόνων εἶναι μνήμην· ζωήν [1] τε τὴν αὐτὴν
ἔχοντα, ὅπου καὶ τὸ τοπικὸν αὐτοῖς περὶ ταὐτόν, ὡς
μὴ τοπικόν, ἀλλὰ ζωτικὸν τὸ κίνημα εἶναι ζῴου
ἑνὸς εἰς αὐτὸ ἐνεργοῦντος ἐν στάσει μὲν ὡς πρὸς
45 τὸ ἔξω, κινήσει δὲ τῇ ἐν αὐτῷ ζωῇ ἀιδίῳ οὔσῃ—
καὶ μὴν εἰ καὶ χορείᾳ ἀπεικάσειέ τις τὴν κίνησιν
αὐτῶν, εἰ μὲν ἱσταμένη [2] ποτέ, ἡ πᾶσα ἂν εἴη
τελεία ἡ συντελεσθεῖσα ἐξ ἀρχῆς εἰς τέλος, ἀτελὴς
δὲ ἡ ἐν μέρει ἑκάστῃ· εἰ δὲ τοιαύτη [3] οἷα ἀεί,
50 τελεία ἀεί. εἰ δὲ ἀεὶ τελεία, οὐκ ἔχει χρόνον ἐν
ᾧ τελεσθήσεται οὐδὲ τόπον· ὥστε οὐδὲ ἔφεσιν ἂν
ἔχοι οὕτως· ὥστε οὔτε χρονικῶς οὔτε τοπικῶς
μετρήσει· ὥστε οὐδὲ μνήμη τούτων. εἰ μέντοι
αὐτοὶ μὲν ζωὴν ζῶσι μακαρίαν ταῖς αὐτῶν ψυχαῖς
τὸ ζῆν προσεμβλέποντες, ταύτῃ δὲ [4] τῶν ψυχῶν
55 αὐτῶν πρὸς ἓν [ταύτῃ] [5] τῇ νεύσει καὶ τῇ ἐξ αὐτῶι
εἰς τὸν σύμπαντα οὐρανὸν ἐλλάμψει—ὥσπερ χορδαν
ἐν λύρᾳ συμπαθῶς κινηθεῖσαι μέλος ἂν ᾄσειαν ἐν
φυσικῇ τινι ἁρμονίᾳ—εἰ οὕτω κινοῖτο ὁ σύμπας

[1] ApcCpc (=Schegk), Creuzer* (*vitam* Ficinus): ζώων Aac
ExUCac.
[2] Kirchhoff*: ἱσταμένη H-S1.
[3] Kirchhoff*: τοιαύτη H-S1.
[4] Volkmann*: τῇ δὲ wxC: τῆδε U.
[5] del. Volkmann*, ut correctionem ad τῇ falso loco insertam.

in order to cover the distance which they cover, and their business is not the sight of what they pass or the passing, and their passage is incidental and their mind is on other, greater things, and these things which they travel through are always the same, and the time taken on a particular stage of their course is not calculated (even if it were divided into stages): then there is no necessity for them to have any memory of the regions they have passed through or the periods of time; and they have the same life, in that their local movement also is around the same centre, so that it is not a local but a vital movement, the movement of a single living being with a self-directed activity, at rest in relation to what is outside it, but in motion by virtue of the everlasting life in it—even if one were to compare their motion to a dance, if it was a dance which at some time came to a stop, the whole would be perfect when it had been completed from beginning to end, but each figure which formed a part of it would be imperfect; but if it is the sort of dance which goes on for ever, it is for ever perfect. But if it is for ever perfect, it has no time or space within which it will be completed; so consequently it will have no aspiration [for completion]; and in consequence of this it will not measure either temporally or spatially; and consequently it will have no memory of this. If, of course, the heavenly bodies themselves live a blessed life, and contemplate this life besides with their souls, by this direction of their souls towards one object and by the illumination which extends from them to the whole heaven—like strings on a lyre plucked harmoniously they sing a song which is naturally in tune—if this is how the whole heaven

οὐρανὸς καὶ τὰ μέρη αὐτοῦ, πρὸς αὐτὸν φερόμενος
καὶ αὐτός, καὶ ἄλλα ἄλλως πρὸς τὸ αὐτὸ ἄλλης
60 αὐτοῖς καὶ τῆς θέσεως οὔσης, ἔτι ἂν μᾶλλον ὁ
λόγος ἡμῖν ὀρθοῖτο μιᾶς ζωῆς καὶ ὁμοίας τῆς
πάντων ἔτι μᾶλλον οὔσης.

9. Ὁ δὲ δὴ πάντα κοσμῶν Ζεὺς καὶ ἐπιτροπεύων
καὶ διατιθεὶς εἰσαεί, ψυχὴν βασιλικὴν καὶ
βασιλικὸν νοῦν ἔχων καὶ πρόνοιαν, ὅπως γίνοιτο,
καὶ γινομένων ἐπιστασίαν καὶ τάξει διοικῶν καὶ
5 περιόδους ἑλίττων πολλὰς ἤδη καὶ τελέσας, πῶς ἂν
ἐν τούτοις ἅπασι μνήμην οὐκ ἔχοι; ὁπόσαι τε
ἐγένοντο καὶ οἷαι αἱ περίοδοι, καὶ ὡς ἂν καὶ
ἔπειτα γένοιτο, μηχανώμενος καὶ συμβάλλων καὶ
λογιζόμενος μνημονικώτατος ἂν εἴη πάντων, ὅσῳ
καὶ δημιουργὸς σοφώτατος. τὸ μὲν οὖν τῶν
10 περιόδων τῆς μνήμης καὶ καθ' αὑτὸ ἂν ἔχοι πολλὴν ἀπορίαν, ὁπόσος ἀριθμὸς εἴη καὶ εἰ εἰδείη.
πεπερασμένος γὰρ ὢν ἀρχὴν τῷ παντὶ χρονικὴν
δώσει· εἰ δ' ἄπειρος, οὐκ εἰδήσει, ὁπόσα τὰ
αὐτοῦ ἔργα. ἢ ὅτι ἕν,[1] εἰδήσει, καὶ μία ζωὴ [2]
ἀεί—οὕτως [3] γὰρ ἄπειρος—καὶ τὸ ἓν οὐ γνώσει
15 ἔξωθεν, ἀλλ' ἔργῳ, συνόντος ἀεὶ τοῦ οὕτως ἀπείρου,
μᾶλλον δὲ παρεπομένου καὶ θεωρουμένου οὐκ
ἐπακτῷ γνώσει. ὡς γὰρ τὸ αὐτοῦ ἄπειρον τῆς

---

[1] Kirchhoff*: ἐν Enn., H–S¹.
[2] Theiler: μιᾷ ζωῇ Enn.*
[3] Kirchhoff, Volkmann*: οὗτος Enn., H–S¹.

---

[1] As Plotinus says at the beginning of the next chapter, it
was legitimate for a Platonist of his period to use " Zeus " as
a name either for Divine Intellect or for the Soul of the Universe: cp. III. 5. 8, where Zeus is Intellect. The general

and its parts move, the heaven itself being self-directed and the different parts having the same direction in different ways (since their positions are different), then our account will be still more correct, since the life of all the heavenly bodies is still more one and uniform.

9. But Zeus who sets all things in order and administers and directs them for ever, who has a "royal soul" and a "royal mind" and foresight of how things will happen and authority over them when they have happened, and arranges the heavens in order and sets their cycles turning and has already brought many cycles to completion, how could he not have memory when all this is going on[1]? In his devising and comparing and calculating how many cycles and of what kind there have been, and how thereafter they may come to be, he would have the best memory of all, just as he is the wisest craftsman. Now the matter of his memory of the cycles is in itself one of much difficulty; there is the question of how great the number is and whether he could know it. For if the number is limited it will give the All a temporal beginning; but if it is unlimited, he will not know how many his works are. Now he will know that his work is one and a single life for ever—this is how the number is unlimited—and will know the unity not externally, but in his work; the unlimited in this sense will always be with him, or rather follows upon him and is contemplated by a knowledge which has not come to him from something other than himself. For as he knows the

description of the activity of Zeus is inspired by Plato *Phaedrus* 246E4–6; his "royal soul" and "royal mind" are from *Philebus* 30D1–2.

ζωῆς οἶδεν, οὕτω καὶ τὴν ἐνέργειαν τὴν εἰς τὸ
πᾶν οὖσαν μίαν, οὐχ ὅτι εἰς τὸ πᾶν.

10. Ἀλλ' ἐπεὶ τὸ κοσμοῦν διττόν, τὸ μὲν ὡς τὸν
δημιουργὸν λέγομεν, τὸ δὲ ὡς τὴν τοῦ παντὸς
ψυχήν, καὶ τὸν Δία λέγοντες ὁτὲ μὲν ὡς ἐπὶ τὸν
δημιουργὸν φερόμεθα, ὁτὲ δὲ ἐπὶ τὸ ἡγεμονοῦν τοῦ
5 παντός. ἐπὶ μὲν τοῦ δημιουργοῦ ἀφαιρετέον
πάντη τὸ πρόσω καὶ ὀπίσω μίαν αὐτῷ ἄτρεπτον καὶ
ἄχρονον ζωὴν διδόντας. ἡ δὲ τοῦ κόσμου ζωὴ
τὸ ἡγούμενον ἐν αὐτῇ ἔχουσα ἔτι ἐπιζητεῖ λόγον, εἰ
οὖν καὶ αὕτη μὴ ἐν τῷ λογίζεσθαι ἔχει τὸ ζῆν, μηδ'
ἐν τῷ ζητεῖν ὅ τι δεῖ ποιεῖν. ἤδη γὰρ ἐξεύρηται
10 καὶ τέτακται ἃ δεῖ, οὐ ταχθέντα· τὰ γὰρ ταχθέντα
ἦν τὰ γινόμενα, τὸ δὲ ποιοῦν αὐτὰ ἡ τάξις· τοῦτο
δὲ ψυχῆς ἐνέργεια ἐξηρτημένης μενούσης [1] φρονήσεως, ἧς εἰκὼν ἡ ἐν αὐτῇ τάξις. οὐ τρεπομένης δὲ

---

[1] A^{ac}E, Creuzer*: μέσης οὔσης A^{pc}xUC, H–S^1.

---

[1] It seems to have been traditional in the Platonic school
to identify the Craftsman, the maker of the world in the
Timaeus, with Divine Intellect, and Plotinus maintains this
identification, though for him Universal Soul is the transcendent organising and directing principle of the material

unlimitedness of his own life, so he knows his activity exercised upon the All as being one single activity, but not that it is exercised upon the All.

10. But since the ordering principle is twofold, we speak of one form of it as the Craftsman and the other as the Soul of the All; and when we speak of Zeus we sometimes apply the name to the Craftsman [1] and sometimes to the ruling principle of the All. In the case of the Craftsman we must completely eliminate " before " and " after " and give him a single unchanging and timeless life. But the life of the universe which contains in itself the ruling principle still requires discussion [to determine] whether this too has a life which is not spent in calculation or in enquiring what it ought to do.[2] [It does], for the things it ought to do have already been discovered and ordered without being set in order; for the things set in order were the things that happened, and what made them was the order; and this is the activity of soul which depends on an abiding intellect of which the image is the order in soul. But if that intelligence does not change, it is

universe, its lower phase, Nature, being the immanent principle of life and bodily form. Soul's creative activity is for him real and important (cp. V. 1. 2; II. 9. 18) but instrumental and intermediary, entirely dependent on the creative energy of the living World of Forms which is Intellect: cp. V. 8. 15–16. So Intellect remains for him the " true Craftsman and maker of the universe " (V. 9. 3. 25–6).

[2] The spontaneous, unreasoning (though supremely intelligent) character of the creative activity of Intellect and higher soul is something on which Plotinus several times insists, against Jews, Christians and simple-minded Platonists who supposed that God thought out his plans for the world and then made it: cp. especially the chapter cited in the last note, V. 8. 7.

ἐκείνης ἀνάγκη μηδὲ ταύτην τρέπεσθαι· οὐ γὰρ ὁτὲ
15 μὲν βλέπει ἐκεῖ, ὁτὲ δὲ οὐ βλέπει· ἀπολειπομένη
γὰρ ἂν ἀποροῖ· μία γὰρ ψυχὴ καὶ ἓν ἔργον. τὸ
γὰρ ἡγεμονοῦν ἓν κρατοῦν ἀεί, καὶ οὐχ ὁτὲ μὲν
κρατοῦν, ὁτὲ δὲ κρατούμενον· πόθεν γὰρ τὰ
πλείω, ὥστε καὶ γενέσθαι μάχην ἢ ἀπορίαν; καὶ
τὸ διοικοῦν ἓν τὸ αὐτὸ ἀεὶ ἐθέλει· διὰ τί γὰρ ἂν
20 καὶ ἄλλο καὶ ἄλλο, ἵνα εἰς πλείω ἀπορῇ; καίτοι,
εἰ καὶ ἓν οὖσα μεταβάλλοι, οὐκ ἂν ἀποροῖ· οὐ γὰρ
ὅτι ἤδη πολλὰ τὸ πᾶν καὶ μέρη ἔχει καὶ ἐναντιώσεις
πρὸς τὰ μέρη, διὰ τοῦτο ἂν ἀποροῖ, ὅπως διαθεῖτο·
οὐ γὰρ ἀπὸ τῶν ἐσχάτων οὐδ᾽ ἀπὸ τῶν μερῶν
ἄρχεται, ἀλλ᾽ ἀπὸ τῶν πρώτων, καὶ ἀπὸ πρώτου
25 ἀρξαμένη ὁδῷ ἀνεμποδίστῳ ἐπὶ πάντα εἶσι καὶ
κοσμεῖ καὶ διὰ τοῦτο κρατεῖ, ὅτι ἐφ᾽ ἑνὸς ἔργου
μένει τοῦ αὐτοῦ καὶ ταὐτόν. εἰ δ᾽ ἄλλο καὶ ἄλλο
βούλοιτο, πόθεν τὸ ἄλλο; εἶθ᾽ ὅ τι χρὴ ποιεῖν
ἀπορήσει, καὶ ἀσθενήσει τὸ ἔργον αὐτῇ εἰς
ἀμφίβολον τοῦ πράττειν ἐν λογισμοῖς ἰούσῃ.

11. Ἔστι γὰρ ὥσπερ ἐφ᾽ ἑνὸς ζῴου ἡ διοίκησις, ἡ
μέν τις ἀπὸ τῶν ἔξωθεν καὶ μερῶν, ἡ δέ τις ἀπὸ
τῶν ἔνδον καὶ τῆς ἀρχῆς, καθάπερ ἰατρὸς μὲν
ἔξωθεν ἀρχόμενος καὶ κατὰ μέρος ἄπορος πολ-

necessary that this soul does not change either; for it does not sometimes look to Intellect and sometimes not; for if it left off looking it would be perplexed; for there is one soul and one work. For the ruling principle is one, always dominant, and not sometimes dominant and sometimes dominated: for from what source could come a multiplicity [of ruling principles] so that there would be strife between them and perplexity? And the one directing principle always wills the same thing: for why should it will now one thing and now another, so as to be perplexed about the multiple alternatives? Yet, even if, being one thing, it were to change, it would not be perplexed; for because the All is already many, and has parts, and oppositions between the parts, it is not for this reason in perplexity about how it shall arrange them; for it does not start from the last and lowest things, or from the parts, but from the primary things, and beginning from the first it proceeds by an unobstructed way to all things and arranges them in ordered beauty and dominates them for this reason, because it persists in one and the same work and is the same thing. But if it wishes for one thing after another, where would the other thing it wished for come from? Then it would be perplexed about what it ought to do, and its work would weaken as it advanced in its calculations to uncertainty about what to do.

11. The administration of the universe is like that of a single living being, where there is one kind which works from outside and deals with it part by part, and another kind which works from inside, from the principle of its life. So a doctor begins from outside and deals with particular parts and is often perplexed

5 λαχῇ καὶ βουλεύεται, ἡ δὲ φύσις ἀπὸ τῆς ἀρχῆς
ἀπροσδεὴς βουλεύσεως. καὶ δεῖ τοῦ παντὸς τὴν
διοίκησιν καὶ τὸν διοικοῦντα ἐν τῷ ἡγεῖσθαι οὐ
κατ' ἰατροῦ ἕξιν εἶναι, ἀλλ' ὡς ἡ φύσις. πολὺ δὲ
μᾶλλον ἐκεῖ τὸ ἁπλοῦν, ὅσῳ κατὰ πάντων ἐμπερι-
ειλημμένων ὡς μερῶν ζῴου ἑνός. πάσας γὰρ τὰς
10 φύσεις κρατεῖ μία, αἱ δὲ ἕπονται ἀνηρτημέναι καὶ
ἐξηρτημέναι καὶ οἷον ἐκφῦσαι, ὡς αἱ ἐν κλάδοις τῇ
τοῦ ὅλου φυτοῦ. τίς οὖν ὁ λογισμὸς ἢ τίς ἀρίθ-
μησις ἢ τίς ἡ μνήμη παρούσης ἀεὶ φρονήσεως καὶ
ἐνεργούσης καὶ κρατούσης καὶ κατὰ τὰ αὐτὰ
διοικούσης; οὐ γὰρ δὴ ὅτι ποικίλα καὶ διάφορα τὰ
15 γινόμενα, δεῖ συνεπόμενον ταῖς τοῦ γινομένου
μεταβολαῖς καὶ τὸ ποιοῦν ἡγεῖσθαι. ὅσῳ γὰρ
ποικίλα τὰ γινόμενα, τοσούτῳ τὸ ποιοῦν ὡσαύτως
μένον. πολλὰ γὰρ καὶ ἐφ' ἑνὸς ἑκάστου ζῴου τὰ
γινόμενα κατὰ φύσιν καὶ οὐχ ὁμοῦ πάντα, αἱ
ἡλικίαι, αἱ ἐκφύσεις ἐν χρόνοις, οἷον κεράτων,
20 γενείων, μαζῶν αὐξήσεις, ἀκμαί, γενέσεις ἄλλων,
οὐ τῶν πρόσθεν λόγων ἀπολλυμένων, ἐπιγιγνομένων
δὲ ἄλλων· δῆλον δὲ ἐκ τοῦ καὶ ἐν τῷ γεννωμένῳ
αὖ ζῴῳ τὸν αὐτὸν καὶ σύμπαντα λόγον εἶναι.
καὶ δὴ τὴν αὐτὴν φρόνησιν ἄξιον περιθεῖναι καὶ
καὶ ταύτην καθόλου εἶναι οἷον κόσμου φρόνησιν
25 ἑστῶσαν, πολλὴν μὲν καὶ ποικίλην καὶ αὖ ἁπλῆν
ζῴου ἑνὸς μεγίστου, οὐ τῷ πολλῷ ἀλλοιουμένην,

and considers what to do, but nature begins from the principle of life and has no need of consideration. And the administration and the administrator of the All must not behave like a doctor in its ruling, but like nature. But the administration of the universe is much simpler, in that all things with which it deals are included as parts of a single living being. For one nature rules all the natures, and they come after it, depending on and from it, growing out of it so to speak, as the natures in branches grow out of that of the whole plant. What calculation, then, can there be or counting or memory when intelligence is always present, active and ruling, ordering things in the same way? One certainly should not think that, because a great variety of different things comes to pass, that which produces them also conforms to the changes of the product. The unchanging stability of the producer is in proportion to the variety of products. For the things which happen according to nature in one single living being are many, and they do not all happen at once; there are the different ages and the growths which occur at particular times, for instance of the horns or the beard or the breasts; there is the prime of life and procreation of other living things; the previous rational forming principles are not destroyed, but others come into operation as well; this is clear from the fact that the same rational forming principle [which is in the parent], and the whole of it, is also in the offspring. So it is right to attribute the same [unchanging] intelligence [to the Soul of the All] and that this, as belonging to the universe, is a kind of static universal intelligence, manifold and varied, and yet at the same same time simple, belonging to a single mighty

ἀλλὰ ἕνα λόγον καὶ ὁμοῦ πάντα· εἰ γὰρ μὴ πάντα,
οὐκ ἐκείνη, ἀλλὰ τῶν ὑστέρων καὶ μερῶν ἡ φρόνησις.

12. Ἀλλ᾽ ἴσως τὸ μὲν τοιοῦτον ἔργον φύσεως
ἄν τις εἴποι, φρονήσεως δὲ ἐν τῷ παντὶ οὔσης καὶ
λογισμοὺς ἀνάγκη καὶ μνήμας εἶναι. ἔστι δὲ
τοῦτο ἀνθρώπων τὸ φρονεῖν ἐν τῷ μὴ φρονεῖν
5 τιθεμένων, καὶ τὸ ζητεῖν φρονεῖν τὸ αὐτὸ τῷ φρονεῖν
νενομικότων. τὸ γὰρ λογίζεσθαι τί ἄλλο ἂν εἴη ἢ
τὸ ἐφίεσθαι εὑρεῖν φρόνησιν[1] καὶ λόγον ἀληθῆ καὶ
τυγχάνοντα [νοῦ][2] τοῦ ὄντος; ὅμοιος γὰρ ὁ
λογιζόμενος κιθαρίζοντι εἰς κιθάρισιν καὶ μελετῶντι
εἰς ἕξιν καὶ ὅλως τῷ μανθάνοντι εἰς γνῶσιν.
10 ζητεῖ γὰρ μαθεῖν ὁ λογιζόμενος ὅπερ ὁ ἤδη ἔχων
φρόνιμος· ὥστε ἐν τῷ στάντι τὸ φρονεῖν. μαρτυρεῖ δὲ καὶ αὐτὸς ὁ λογισάμενος· ὅταν γὰρ εὕρῃ ὃ
δεῖ, πέπαυται λογιζόμενος· καὶ ἀνεπαύσατο ἐν τῷ
φρονῆσαι γενόμενος. εἰ μὲν οὖν κατὰ τοὺς
μανθάνοντας τὸ ἡγούμενον τοῦ παντὸς τάξομεν,
15 λογισμοὺς ἀποδοτέον καὶ ἀπορίας καὶ μνήμας
συμβάλλοντος τὰ παρεληλυθότα τοῖς παροῦσι καὶ
τοῖς μέλλουσιν. εἰ δὲ κατὰ τὸν εἰδότα, ἐν στάσει
ὅρον ἐχούσῃ νομιστέον αὐτοῦ εἶναι τὴν φρόνησιν.
εἶτα εἰ μὲν οἶδε τὰ μέλλοντα—τὸ γὰρ μὴ εἰδέναι
λέγειν ἄτοπον—διὰ τί οὐχὶ καὶ ὅπως ἔσται οὐκ
20 εἰδήσει; εἰ δὲ εἰδήσει καὶ ὅπως ἔσται, τί ἔτι δεῖ
τοῦ λογίζεσθαι καὶ τοῦ τὰ παρεληλυθότα πρὸς τὰ
παρόντα συμβάλλειν; καὶ ἡ γνῶσις δὲ τῶν

---

[1] AᵃᶜE, Perna*: φρονεῖν AᵖᶜxUC, H–S¹.
[2] del. Vitringa, Volkmann*.

living being, not subject to change because of the multiplicity of things, but a single rational principle and all things at once; for if it was not everything, it would not be that [universal] intelligence, but the intelligence of partial things.

12. But perhaps someone might say that a work of this kind belongs to nature, but it is necessary that the intelligence which is in the All should have calculations and memories. This is a statement of men who assume that unintelligence is intelligence, and have come to the conclusion that to seek to be intelligent is the same thing as being intelligent. For what else could calculation be but the effort to find intelligence and reason which is true and attains to the truly existent? For the man who calculates is like one who is playing the lyre to acquire the art of lyre-playing or who is practising to acquire habitual proficiency, or in general like one who is learning in order to know. For the man who is calculating seeks to learn that which if someone already possesses, he is intelligent: so that intelligence is in one who has come to rest. The man who has been calculating is himself a witness to this; for when he finds what is needed, he stops calculating; and he comes to rest because he has entered into intelligence. If then we are going to put the ruling principle of the universe into the class of learners, we should attribute to it calculations and perplexities and memories which are proper to one who compares the past with the present and the future. But if we are going to class it as the knower, we must consider that its knowing is in a repose which reached its term. Then if it knows future events—and it would be absurd to say that it did not—why will it not

μελλόντων, εἴπερ αὐτῷ συγχωρεῖται παρεῖναι, οὐ
τοιαύτη ἂν εἴη, οἷα τοῖς μάντεσι πάρεστιν, ἀλλ'
25 οἵα αὐτοῖς τοῖς ποιοῦσι τοῖς πεπιστευκόσιν ὅτι
ἔσται, τοῦτο δὲ ταὐτὸν τοῖς πάντα κυρίοις, οἷς
οὐδὲν ἀμφίβολον οὐδὲ ἀμφιγνοούμενον. οἷς ἄρα
ἄραρεν ἡ δόξα, τούτοις παραμένει. ἡ αὐτὴ ἄρα
καὶ περὶ μελλόντων φρόνησις, οἵα καὶ ἡ περὶ
παρόντων, κατὰ τὸ ἑστάναι· τοῦτο δὲ λογισμοῦ
30 ἔξω. ἀλλ' εἰ μὴ οἶδε τὰ μέλλοντα, ἃ αὐτὸς
ποιήσει, οὐδὲ εἰδήσει ποιήσει [1] οὐδὲ πρός τι
βλέπων [ποιήσει],[2] ἀλλὰ τὸ ἐπελθὸν ποιήσει·
τοῦτο δὲ ταὐτὸν τῷ εἰκῇ. μένει ἄρα καθὸ ποιήσει.
ἀλλ' εἰ μένει καθὸ ποιήσει, οὐκ ἄλλως ποιήσει, ἢ
ὡς οἷον τὸ ἐν αὐτῷ παράδειγμα ἔχει. μοναχῶς
35 ἄρα ποιήσει ὡσαύτως· οὐ γὰρ νῦν μὲν ἄλλως,
ὕστερον δὲ ἄλλως, ἢ τί κωλύει ἀποτυχεῖν; εἰ δὲ
τὸ ποιούμενον διαφόρως ἕξει, ἀλλ' ἔσχε γε
διαφόρως οὐ παρ' ἑαυτοῦ, ἀλλὰ δουλεῦον λόγοις·
οὗτοι δὲ παρὰ τοῦ ποιοῦντος· ὥστε ἠκολούθησε
τοῖς ἐφεξῆς λόγοις. ὥστε οὐδαμῇ τὸ ποιοῦν
40 ἀναγκάζεσθαι πλανᾶσθαι οὐδ' ἀπορεῖν οὐδ' ἔχειν
πράγματα, ὥσπερ τινὲς ᾠήθησαν δύσκολον εἶναι
τὴν τῶν ὅλων διοίκησιν. τὸ γὰρ ἔχειν πράγματα
ἦν, ὡς ἔοικε, τὸ ἐπιχειρεῖν ἔργοις ἀλλοτρίοις·

---

[1] Kirchhoff*: ποιῆσαι Enn., H–S[1].
[2] delevimus.

know how they will turn out? And if it knows how
they will turn out, why does it still need calculation
and comparison of past events with present? And
its knowledge of future events, granted that it has
it, will not be like that which diviners have, but like
that which those have who make things happen with
full confidence that they will do so; this is the same
as saying, those who are fully masters of the situation
to whom nothing is doubtful or disputable. Now
those who have a fixed opinion retain it permanently.
The intelligence of future things is, then, in its
stability, of the same kind as that of present things;
but this is outside the sphere of calculation. But if
it does not know the future things which it is going
to make, it will not make them with knowledge or
looking at any [model] but will make whatever comes
to it; but this is the same as saying, it will make at
random. [The model], then, according to which it
will make, abides. But if that according to which it
will make abides, it will not make otherwise than in
conformity with the pattern which it has in itself.
It will make, then, in one single unvarying way;
for it will not make now in one way and now in
another, or what is there to prevent its failing?
But if that which is being made is in different states,
these different states do not derive from itself, but
it is subservient to the rational forming principles;
and these come from the maker, so that it follows
upon the forming principles in their series. So the
maker is in no way compelled to be in doubt or
perplexity or to have difficulties, as some people
have thought who considered the administration of
the universe to be a burden. For to have difficulties
is a matter, so it seems, of undertaking tasks which

τοῦτο δὲ ὧν μὴ κρατεῖ. ὧν δέ τις κρατεῖ καὶ
μόνος, τίνος ἂν οὗτος δέοιτο ἢ αὑτοῦ καὶ τῆς
45 αὑτοῦ βουλήσεως; τοῦτο δὲ ταὐτὸν τῆς αὑτοῦ
φρονήσεως· τῷ γὰρ τοιούτῳ ἡ βούλησις φρόνησις.
οὐδενὸς ἄρα δεῖ τῷ τοιούτῳ εἰς τὸ ποιεῖν, ἐπειδὴ
οὐδ' ἡ φρόνησις ἀλλοτρία, ἀλλ' αὐτὸς οὐδενὶ
ἐπακτῷ χρώμενος. οὐδὲ λογισμῷ τοίνυν οὐδὲ
μνήμῃ· ἐπακτὰ γὰρ ταῦτα.

13. Ἀλλὰ τί διοίσει τῆς λεγομένης φύσεως ἡ
τοιαύτη φρόνησις; ἢ ὅτι ἡ μὲν φρόνησις πρῶτον,
ἡ δὲ φύσις ἔσχατον· ἴνδαλμα γὰρ φρονήσεως ἡ
φύσις καὶ ψυχῆς ἔσχατον ὂν ἔσχατον καὶ τὸν ἐν
5 αὐτῇ ἐλλαμπόμενον λόγον ἔχει, οἷον εἰ ἐν κηρῷ
βαθεῖ διικνοῖτο εἰς ἔσχατον ἐπὶ θάτερα ἐν τῇ
ἐπιφανείᾳ τύπος, ἐναργοῦς μὲν ὄντος τοῦ ἄνω,
ἴχνους δὲ ἀσθενοῦς ὄντος τοῦ κάτω. ὅθεν οὐδὲ
οἶδε, μόνον δὲ ποιεῖ· ὃ γὰρ ἔχει τῷ ἐφεξῆς
διδοῦσα ἀπροαιρέτως, τὴν δόσιν τῷ σωματικῷ καὶ
10 ὑλικῷ ποίησιν ἔχειν, οἷον καὶ τὸ θερμανθὲν τῷ
ἐφεξῆς ἁψαμένῳ δέδωκε τὸ αὑτοῦ εἶδος, θερμὸν
ἐλαττόνως ποιῆσαν. διὰ τοῦτό τοι ἡ φύσις οὐδὲ
φαντασίαν ἔχει· ἡ δὲ νόησις φαντασίας κρεῖττον·
φαντασία δὲ μεταξὺ φύσεως τύπου καὶ νοήσεως.
ἡ μέν γε οὐθενὸς ἀντίληψιν οὐδὲ σύνεσιν ἔχει, ἡ δὲ
15 φαντασία σύνεσιν ἐπακτοῦ· δίδωσι γὰρ τῷ

---

[1] Plotinus here recognises, but does not satisfactorily solve,
one of the great difficulties which his idea of unreasoning
intelligence brings with it in his hierarchical system. This is,
as he says here, how to explain in any intelligible way the
difference between the unreasoning intelligence of Intellect
and higher soul, which is above reason and imagination, and

do not belong to one, that is, of which one is not master. But in work of which someone is master, and sole master, what does he need except himself and his own will? But this is the same thing as his own intelligence; for in a being of this kind will is intelligence. So a being like this needs nothing for its making, since its intelligence does not belong to someone else but is itself, using nothing brought in from outside. So it does not use calculation or memory; for these come from outside.

13. But how will intelligence of this kind differ from what we call nature [1]? It differs in that intelligence is primary, but nature is last and lowest. For nature is an image of intelligence, and since it is the last and lowest part of soul has the last ray of the rational forming principle which shines in it, just as in a thick piece of wax a seal-stamp penetrates right through to the surface on the other side, and is clear on the upper side, but a faint trace on the lower. For this reason it does not know, but only makes; for since it gives what it has spontaneously to what comes after it, it has its giving to the corporeal and material as a making, just as a heated body gives its own form to that which is next in contact to it and makes it hot in a lesser degree. For this reason nature does not have an imaging faculty either; but intellect is higher than the power of imaging: the imaging faculty is between the impression of nature and intellect. Nature has no grasp or consciousness of anything, but the imaging faculty has consciousness of what comes from outside; for it gives to the

the unreasoning creativity of Nature, the soul-principle immanent in the physical world, which is below reason and imagination (for its unconscious activity see III. 8. 3–4).

φαντασθέντι εἰδέναι ἃ ἔπαθεν· ἡ δὲ γέννα αὐτὴ
καὶ ἐνέργεια ἐξ αὐτοῦ τοῦ ἐνεργήσαντος. νοῦς μὲν
οὖν ἔχει, ψυχὴ δὲ τοῦ παντὸς ἐκομίσατο εἰς ἀεὶ
καὶ ἐκεκόμιστο, καὶ τοῦτό ἐστιν αὐτῇ τὸ ζῆν, καὶ
τὸ φαινόμενον ἀεὶ σύνεσις νοούσης· τὸ δὲ ἐξ
20 αὐτῆς ἐμφαντασθὲν εἰς ὕλην φύσις, ἐν ᾗ ἵσταται τὰ
ὄντα, ἢ καὶ πρὸ τούτου, καὶ ἔστιν ἔσχατα ταῦτα
τοῦ νοητοῦ· ἤδη γὰρ τὸ ἐντεῦθεν τὰ μιμήματα.
ἀλλ' ἡ φύσις εἰς αὐτὴν ποιοῦσα καὶ πάσχουσα,
ἐκείνη δὲ ἡ πρὸ αὐτῆς καὶ πλησίον αὐτῆς ποιοῦσα
25 οὐ πάσχει, ἡ δ' ἔτι ἄνωθεν εἰς σώματα ἢ εἰς ὕλην
οὐ ποιεῖ.

14. Τὰ δὲ σώματα ὑπὸ φύσεως λεγόμενα
γίγνεσθαι τὰ μὲν στοιχεῖα αὐτὸ τοῦτο [τὰ σώματα],[1]
τὰ δὲ ζῷα καὶ τὰ φυτὰ ἆρα οὕτως, ὥστε τὴν
φύσιν οἷον παρακειμένην ἐν αὐτοῖς ἔχειν; οἷον
5 ἐπὶ φωτὸς ἔχει· ἀπελθόντος οὐδὲν ὁ ἀὴρ αὐτοῦ
ἔχει, ἀλλ' ἔστιν οἷον χωρὶς τὸ φῶς, χωρὶς δὲ ὁ ἀὴρ
οἷον οὐ[2] κιρνάμενος· ἢ οἷον ἐπὶ τοῦ πυρὸς καὶ τοῦ
θερμανθέντος, οὗ ἀπελθόντος μένει τις θερμότης
ἑτέρα οὖσα παρὰ τὴν οὖσαν ἐν τῷ πυρί, πάθος τι
τοῦ θερμανθέντος. τὴν μὲν γὰρ μορφήν, ἣν δίδωσι
10 τῷ πλασθέντι, ἕτερον εἶδος θετέον παρ' αὐτὴν τὴν
φύσιν. εἰ δέ τι ἄλλο παρὰ τοῦτο ἔχει, ὅ ἐστιν
οἷον μεταξὺ τούτου καὶ αὐτῆς τῆς φύσεως,
ζητητέον. καὶ ἥτις μὲν διαφορὰ φύσεως καὶ τῆς
εἰρημένης ἐν τῷ παντὶ φρονήσεως, εἴρηται.

---

[1] del. Kirchhoff.
[2] Creuzer, Volkmann* (*non* Ficinus), cf. IV. 3. 22. 3: ὁ Enn.,
H–S[1].

one who has the image the power to know what he has experienced; but intellect itself is origin and activity which comes from the active principle itself. Intellect, then, possesses, and the Soul of the All receives from it for ever and had always received, and this is its life, and what appears at each successive time is its consciousness as it thinks; and that which is reflected from it into matter is nature, in which, or indeed before it, the real beings come to a stop, and these are the last and lowest realities of the intelligible world: for what comes after at this point is imitation. But nature acts on matter and is affected by it, but that soul which is before nature and close to it acts without being affected, and that which is still higher does not act on bodies or matter.

14. As for the bodies which are said to be produced by nature, the elements are just precisely products of nature; but are the animals and plants so disposed as to have nature present in them? Their relationship to nature is like that of air to light: when light goes away air holds nothing of it, but the light is in a way separate and the air is separate and as if it did not mix with the light. Or it is like that of fire and the heated body, when if the fire goes away a heat remains which is distinct from the heat in the fire and is an affection of the heated body. In the same way the shape which nature gives to the formed body must be considered as another form, distinct from nature itself. But if the body has anything else besides this, which is somehow in between it and nature itself, we must investigate it. And so we have explained the difference between nature and the intelligence in the All about which we were speaking.

15. Ἐκεῖνο δὲ ἄπορον πρὸς [τὰ νῦν][1] ἅπαντα
τὰ ⟨νῦν⟩[1] εἰρημένα· εἰ γὰρ αἰὼν μὲν περὶ νοῦν,
χρόνος δὲ περὶ ψυχήν—ἔχειν γάρ φαμεν ⟨ἐν⟩[2] τῇ
ὑποστάσει[3] τὸν χρόνον περὶ τὴν τῆς ψυχῆς ἐν-
5 έργειαν καὶ ἐξ ἐκείνης—πῶς οὐ, μεριζομένου τοῦ χρόνου καὶ τὸ παρεληλυθὸς ἔχοντος, μερίζοιτο ἂν καὶ
ἡ ἐνέργεια, καὶ πρὸς τὸ παρεληλυθὸς ἐπιστρέφουσα
ποιήσει καὶ ἐν τῇ τοῦ παντὸς ψυχῇ τὴν μνήμην;
καὶ γὰρ αὖ ἐν μὲν τῷ αἰῶνι τὴν ταυτότητα, ἐν δὲ
τῷ χρόνῳ τὴν ἑτερότητα τίθεσθαι, ἢ ταὐτὸν αἰὼν
10 ἔσται καὶ χρόνος, εἰ καὶ ταῖς τῆς ψυχῆς ἐνεργείαις
τὸ μεταβάλλειν οὐ δώσομεν. ἆρ' οὖν τὰς μὲν
ἡμετέρας ψυχὰς μεταβολὴν δεχομένας τήν τε
ἄλλην καὶ τὴν ἔνδειαν οἷα ἐν χρόνῳ φήσομεν εἶναι,
τὴν δὲ τοῦ ὅλου γεννᾶν μὲν χρόνον, οὐ μὴν ἐν
χρόνῳ εἶναι; ἀλλ' ἔστω μὴ ἐν χρόνῳ· τί ἐστιν, ὃ
15 ποιεῖ γεννᾶν αὐτὴν χρόνον, ἀλλὰ μὴ αἰῶνα; ἢ ὅτι,
ἃ γεννᾷ, οὐκ ἀίδια, ἀλλὰ περιεχόμενα χρόνῳ.
ἐπεὶ οὐδ' αἱ ψυχαὶ ἐν χρόνῳ, ἀλλὰ τὰ πάθη αὐτῶν
ἄττα ἐστὶ καὶ τὰ ποιήματα. ἀίδιοι γὰρ αἱ ψυχαί,
καὶ ὁ χρόνος ὕστερος, καὶ τὸ ἐν χρόνῳ ἔλαττον
χρόνου· περιέχειν γὰρ δεῖ τὸν χρόνον τὸ ἐν χρόνῳ
20 ὥσπερ, φησί, τὸ ἐν τόπῳ καὶ ἐν ἀριθμῷ.

16. Ἀλλ' εἰ ἐν αὐτῇ τόδε μετὰ τόδε καὶ τὸ
πρότερον καὶ τὸ ὕστερον τῶν ποιουμένων, κἂν εἰ

---

[1] transpos. Theiler.
[2] Igal.
[3] Enn., H–S.: τὴν ὑπόστασιν Kirchhoff*.

ON DIFFICULTIES ABOUT THE SOUL II

15. But there is the following difficulty in relation to all that has just been said: for if eternity belongs to Intellect and time to Soul—for we maintain that we grasp time in its essential nature as around the activity of soul and deriving from it—how, if time is divided up, and has a past, will not the activity of soul be divided up, and when it turns towards the past will produce memory in the Soul of the All as well [as in our souls]? For, again, one must place sameness in eternity and otherness in time, or time and eternity will be the same, even if we do not attribute change to the activities of soul. Shall we then say that our souls, which are subject to other kinds of change and especially to deficiency, are somehow in time, but the soul of the universe generates time, but is not in time? But, granted that it is not in time, what makes it generate time, and not eternity? It is because the things which it generates are not eternal, but encompassed by time; since even the [individual] souls are not in time, but such affections as they have are, and the things they make. For the souls are eternal, and time is posterior to them, and that which is in time is less than time; for time must encompass what is in time, as is the case, Aristotle says, with what is in place and number.[1]

16. But if in soul one thing comes after another and if it itself makes some of its works earlier and some later, that is, if it makes them in time, it also

----

[1] φησί "he says" refers here, exceptionally, to Aristotle, not to Plato; cp. I. 1. 4. 26. The reference is to *Physics* Δ, 12, 221a18 and 28–30. This is the clearest assertion in Plotinus that individual human souls in their true, highest nature live, not in time, but in eternity.

ἐν χρόνῳ, αὐτὴ ποιεῖ, καὶ νεύει καὶ πρὸς τὸ
μέλλον· εἰ δὲ τοῦτο, καὶ πρὸς τὸ παρεληλυθός. ἢ
5 ἐν τοῖς ποιουμένοις τὸ πρότερον καὶ παρεληλυθός,
ἐν αὐτῇ δὲ οὐδὲν παρεληλυθός, ἀλλὰ πάντες οἱ
λόγοι ἅμα, ὥσπερ εἴρηται. ἐν δὲ τοῖς ποιουμένοις
τὸ οὐχ ἅμα, ἐπεὶ οὐδὲ τὸ ὁμοῦ, καίτοι ἐν τοῖς
λόγοις τὸ ὁμοῦ, οἷον χεῖρες καὶ πόδες οἱ ἐν λόγῳ·
ἐν δὲ τοῖς αἰσθητοῖς χωρίς. καίτοι κἀκεῖ ἄλλον
10 τρόπον τὸ χωρίς· ὥστε καὶ τὸ πρότερον ἄλλον
τρόπον. ἢ τὸ μὲν χωρὶς εἴποι ἄν τις ἑτερότητι· τὸ
δὲ πρότερον πῶς, εἰ μὴ ἐπιστατοῖ τὸ τάττον; ἐπιστατοῦν δὲ ἐρεῖ τὸ τόδε μετὰ τόδε· διὰ τί γὰρ οὐχ
ἅμα πάντα ἔσται; ἢ εἰ μὲν ἄλλο τὸ τάττον καὶ ἡ
τάξις, οὕτως ὡς οἷον λέγειν· εἰ δὲ τὸ ἐπιστατοῦν ἡ
15 πρώτη τάξις, οὐκέτι λέγει, ἀλλὰ ποιεῖ μόνον τόδε
μετὰ τόδε. εἰ γὰρ λέγει, εἰς τάξιν βλέπων λέγει·
ὥστε ἕτερον τῆς τάξεως ἔσται. πῶς οὖν ταὐτόν;
ὅτι μὴ ὕλη καὶ εἶδος τὸ τάττον, ἀλλ' εἶδος μόνον
καὶ δύναμις, καὶ ἐνέργεια δευτέρα μετὰ νοῦν ἐστι
20 ψυχή· τὸ δὲ τόδε μετὰ τόδε ἐν τοῖς πράγμασιν οὐ
δυναμένοις ἅμα πάντα. σεμνὸν γάρ τι καὶ ἡ ψυχὴ
ἡ τοιαύτη, οἷον κύκλος προσαρμόττων κέντρῳ εὐθὺς μετὰ κέντρον αὐξηθείς, διάστημα ἀδιάστατον·
οὕτω γὰρ ἔχει ἕκαστα. εἰ δὲ τἀγαθόν τις κατὰ
κέντρον τάξειε, τὸν νοῦν κατὰ κύκλον ἀκίνητον,
25 ψυχὴν δὲ κατὰ κύκλον κινούμενον ἂν τάξειε,

---

[1] The reference back is to the end of ch. 11.
[2] Cp. V. 8. 7. 23 ff.

directs itself to the future; and if so, also to the past. Now the earlier and the past are in the things it makes, but in it nothing is past, but all the rational forming principles are present at once, as has been said.[1] But in the things that are made there is no simultaneity, as there is no togetherness, though there is togetherness in the rational forming principles, as the hands and feet in the rational principle are together, but in the objects of sense they are separate. And yet there is separateness in another way in the intelligible world; so that there is also priority in another way. Now one could speak of separateness consisting in otherness; but how could one speak of priority unless the arranging principle gave orders? But if it gives orders it will say " this after that": for why will not all things exist at once? Now if the arranging principle is other than the arrangement, it will be of such a kind as to speak, in a way; but if that which gives orders is the primary arrangement, it no longer says, but only makes this after that.[2] For if it says it, it does so with its eye on the arrangement: so that it will be other than the arrangement. How then is it the same? Because the arranging principle is not form and matter, but only form and power, and Soul is the second active actuality after Intellect; but the " this after that " is in the [material] things which cannot all exist at once. For the soul of this kind is a noble thing, like a circle fitting itself round its centre, the first expansion after the centre, an unextended extension: for this is how each [of the intelligible realities] is. But if one ranks the Good as a centre one would rank Intellect as an unmoved circle and Soul as a moving circle; but moving by

κινούμενον δὲ τῇ ἐφέσει. νοῦς γὰρ εὐθὺς καὶ ἔχει
καὶ περιείληφεν, ἡ δὲ ψυχὴ τοῦ ἐπέκεινα ὄντος
ἐφίεται. ἡ δὲ τοῦ παντὸς σφαῖρα τὴν ψυχὴν
ἐκείνως ἐφιεμένην ἔχουσα ᾗ πέφυκεν ἐφίεσθαι
κινεῖται. πέφυκε δὲ ᾗ σῶμα τοῦ οὗ ἔστιν ἔξω
30 ἐφίεσθαι· τοῦτο δὲ περιπτύξασθαι καὶ περιελθεῖν
πάντῃ ἑαυτῷ. καὶ κύκλῳ ἄρα.

17. Ἀλλὰ πῶς οὐ καὶ ἐν ἡμῖν οὕτως αἱ νοήσεις
αἱ τῆς ψυχῆς καὶ οἱ λόγοι, ἀλλ᾿ ἐνταῦθα ἐν χρόνῳ
καὶ¹ τὸ ὕστερον καὶ αἱ ζητήσεις ὡδί; ἆρ᾿ ὅτι
πολλὰ ἃ ἄρχει καὶ κινεῖται, καὶ οὐχ ἓν κρατεῖ; ἢ
5 καὶ ὅτι ἄλλο καὶ ἄλλο πρὸς τὴν χρείαν καὶ πρὸς τὸ
παρὸν οὐχ ὡρισμένον ἐν αὐτῷ, ἀλλὰ πρὸς τὸ ἄλλο
ἀεὶ καὶ ἄλλο ἔξω. ὅθεν ἄλλο τὸ βούλευμα καὶ
πρὸς καιρόν, ὅτε ἡ χρεία πάρεστι καὶ συμβέβηκεν
ἔξωθεν τουτί, εἶτα τουτί. καὶ γὰρ τῷ πολλὰ
ἄρχειν ἀνάγκη πολλὰς καὶ τὰς φαντασίας εἶναι καὶ
10 ἐπικτήτους καὶ καινὰς ἄλλου ἄλλῳ καὶ ἐμποδίους
τοῖς αὐτοῦ ἑκάστου κινήμασι καὶ ἐνεργήμασιν.
ὅταν γὰρ τὸ ἐπιθυμητικὸν κινηθῇ, ἦλθεν ἡ φαντασία
τούτου οἷον αἴσθησις ἀπαγγελτικὴ καὶ μηνυτικὴ
τοῦ πάθους ἀπαιτοῦσα συνέπεσθαι καὶ ἐκπορίζειν
τὸ ἐπιθυμούμενον· τὸ δὲ ἐξ ἀνάγκης ἐν ἀπόρῳ
15 συνεπόμενον καὶ πορίζον ἢ καὶ ἀντιτεῖνον γίνεται.
καὶ ὁ θυμὸς δὲ εἰς ἄμυναν παρακαλῶν τὰ αὐτὰ
ποιεῖ κινηθείς, καὶ αἱ τοῦ σώματος χρεῖαι καὶ τὰ

---

¹ χρόνῳ καὶ Theiler: χρόνοις Enn.*

aspiration. For Intellect immediately possesses and encompasses the Good, but Soul aspires to [the Good] beyond being. But the sphere of the All, since it possesses the soul which aspires in that way, moves by its natural aspiration. But its natural aspiration as a body is to that which it is outside: that is, it is an enfolding and surrounding it on every side with itself, and so therefore [movement in] a circle.

17. But why are not the thoughts and reasonings of the soul of this kind in us too, but here below we are in time and there is succession and in this way investigations? Is it because there are many things which rule and are moved, and it is not one which has the power? Yes, and it is because there is one thing after another related to our needs and the present moment, not definite in itself but always related to one external thing after another; as a result our decisions are different and relevant to the occasion when the need arises, and now this and now that external incident occurs. For because there are many that rule it is necessary that there should be many mental images, and they must come in from outside and the images of one must be new to another, and they must get in the way of the movements and activities of each individual part. For when the desiring part of the soul is moved, the mental image of its object comes like a perception announcing and informing us of the experience, and demanding that we should follow along with it and obtain the desired object for it; but our other part necessarily falls into perplexity, whether it goes along and obtains the object or resists. And the spirited part when it summons us to repel something does the same when it is moved, and the needs of

πάθη ἄλλα ποιεῖ καὶ ἄλλα δοξάζειν· καὶ ἡ ἄγνοια
δὲ τῶν ἀγαθῶν, καὶ τὸ μὴ ἔχειν ὅ τι εἴπῃ πάντῃ
ἀγομένη, καὶ ἐκ τοῦ μίγματος τούτων ἄλλα.
20 ἀλλ’ εἰ καὶ τὸ βέλτιστον αὐτὸ ἄλλα δοξάζει; ἢ
τοῦ κοινοῦ ἡ ἀπορία καὶ ἡ ἀλλοδοξία· ἐκ δὲ τοῦ
βελτίστου ὁ λόγος ὁ ὀρθὸς εἰς τὸ κοινὸν δοθεὶς τῷ
[ἀσθενὴς] [1] εἶναι ἐν τῷ μίγματι, οὐ τῇ αὑτοῦ φύσει
ἀσθενής, ἀλλ’ οἷον ἐν πολλῷ θορύβῳ ἐκκλησίας ὁ
25 ἄριστος τῶν συμβούλων εἰπὼν οὐ κρατεῖ, ἀλλ’ οἱ
χείρονες τῶν θορυβούντων καὶ βοώντων, ὁ δὲ
κάθηται ἡσυχῇ οὐδὲν δυνηθείς, ἡττηθεὶς δὲ τῷ
θορύβῳ τῶν χειρόνων. καὶ ἔστιν ἐν μὲν τῷ
φαυλοτάτῳ ἀνδρὶ τὸ κοινὸν καὶ ἐκ πάντων ὁ
ἄνθρωπος κατὰ πολιτείαν τινὰ φαύλην· ἐν δὲ τῷ
μέσῳ ⟨ὡς⟩ [2] ἐν ᾗ πόλει κἂν χρηστόν τι κρατήσειε
30 δημοτικῆς πολιτείας οὐκ ἀκράτου οὔσης· ἐν δὲ
τῷ βελτίονι ἀριστοκρατικὸν τὸ τῆς ζωῆς φεύγοντος
ἤδη τὸ κοινὸν τοῦ ἀνθρώπου καὶ τοῖς ἀμείνοσι
διδόντος· ἐν δὲ τῷ ἀρίστῳ, τῷ χωρίζοντι, ἓν τὸ
ἄρχον, καὶ παρὰ τούτου εἰς τὰ ἄλλα ἡ τάξις· οἷον
35 διττῆς πόλεως οὔσης, τῆς μὲν ἄνω, τῆς δὲ τῶν
κάτω, κατὰ τὰ ἄνω κοσμουμένης. ἀλλ’ ὅτι γε ἐν

---

[1] del. Kirchhoff*.
[2] Theiler.

---

[1] Plotinus is not interested in politics. When, as here, he
expresses political opinions incidentally in the course of a
Platonic analogy between soul and state, they are taken from
Plato and Aristotle and have little relevance to the Roman
Empire in the 3rd century A.D.; though the belief in the
inferiority of democracy which he expresses here would have

the body and the passions make us have continually different opinions. Then there is ignorance of the [true] good, and the soul's not knowing what to say when it is dragged in every direction, and still other results from the mixture of all these. But is it actually our best part which has different opinions? No, perplexity and variety of opinions belong to the gathering [of our various parts and passions]: from our best part the right account of the matter is given to the common gathering, and is weak because it is in the mixture, not by its own nature. But it is as if in the great clamour of an assembly the best of the advisers does not prevail when he speaks, but the worse of those who clamour and shout, but he sits quietly unable to do anything, defeated by the clamour of the worse. And in the worst kind of man there is the common gathering and his human nature is composed of everything in the manner of a bad political constitution; in the middling man it is as it is in the city in which some good can prevail as the democratic constitution is not entirely out of control; but in the better kind of man the style of life is aristocratic; his human nature is already escaping from the common gathering and giving itself over to the better sort.[1] But in the best man, the man who separates himself, the ruling principle is one, and the order comes from this to the rest. It is as if there was a double city, one above and one composed of the lower elements set in order by the

been shared, not only by his friends of the Roman senatorial aristocracy but by everyone who wrote or spoke about politics in the later Roman Empire (Christians as well as pagans). For the sources of the opinions here see Plato *Republic* VIII 557 ff. and (for the μέσος and his state) Aristotle *Politics* IV 1295a25 ff.

τῇ τοῦ παντὸς ψυχῇ τὸ ἓν καὶ ταὐτὸν καὶ ὁμοίως,
ἐν δὲ τοῖς ἄλλοις ἄλλως, καὶ δι' ἅ, εἴρηται. ταῦτα
μὲν οὖν ταύτῃ.

18. Περὶ δὲ τοῦ εἰ ἐφ' ἑαυτοῦ τι ἔχει τὸ σῶμα
καὶ παρούσης ζῇ τῆς ψυχῆς ἔχον ἤδη τι ἴδιον, ἢ
ὃ ἔχει ἡ φύσις ἐστί, καὶ τοῦτό ἐστι τὸ προσομιλοῦν
τῷ σώματι ἡ φύσις. ἢ καὶ αὐτὸ τὸ σῶμα, ἐν ᾧ
5 καὶ ψυχὴ καὶ φύσις, οὐ τοιοῦτον εἶναι δεῖ, οἷον τὸ
ἄψυχον καὶ οἷον ὁ ἀὴρ ὁ πεφωτισμένος, ἀλλ' οἷον ὁ
τεθερμασμένος, καὶ ἔστι τὸ σῶμα τοῦ ζῴου καὶ
τοῦ φυτοῦ δὲ οἷον σκιὰν ψυχῆς ἔχοντα, καὶ τὸ
ἀλγεῖν καὶ τὸ ἥδεσθαι δὲ τὰς τοῦ σώματος ἡδονὰς
περὶ τὸ τοιόνδε σῶμά ἐστιν· ἡμῖν δὲ ἡ τούτου
10 ἀληδὼν καὶ ἡ τοιαύτη ἡδονὴ εἰς γνῶσιν ἀπαθῆ
ἔρχεται. λέγω δὲ ἡμῖν τῇ ἄλλῃ ψυχῇ, ἅτε καὶ τοῦ
τοιοῦδε σώματος οὐκ ἀλλοτρίου, ἀλλ' ἡμῶν ὄντος·
διὸ καὶ μέλει ἡμῖν αὐτοῦ ὡς ἡμῶν ὄντος. οὔτε
γὰρ τοῦτό ἐσμεν ἡμεῖς, οὔτε καθαροὶ τούτου
ἡμεῖς, ἀλλὰ ἐξήρτηται καὶ ἐκκρέμαται ἡμῶν,
15 ἡμεῖς δὲ κατὰ τὸ κύριον, ἡμῶν δὲ ἄλλως ὅμως
τοῦτο. διὸ καὶ ἡδομένου καὶ ἀλγοῦντος μέλει, καὶ
ὅσῳ ἀσθενέστεροι μᾶλλον, καὶ ὅσῳ ἑαυτοὺς μὴ
χωρίζομεν, ἀλλὰ τοῦτο ἡμῶν τὸ τιμιώτατον καὶ
τὸν ἄνθρωπον τιθέμεθα καὶ οἷον εἰσδυόμεθα εἰς
αὐτό. χρὴ γὰρ τὰ πάθη τὰ τοιαῦτα μὴ ψυχῆς
20 ὅλως εἶναι λέγειν, ἀλλὰ σώματος τοιοῦδε καί τινος
κοινοῦ καὶ συναμφοτέρου. ὅταν γὰρ ἕν τι ᾖ,
αὐτῷ οἷον αὔταρκές ἐστιν. οἷον σῶμα μόνον τί ἂν
πάθοι ἄψυχον ὄν; διαιρούμενόν τε γὰρ οὐκ αὐτό,

powers above. But now it has been explained that in the soul of the All there is unity, sameness and likeness, but in other souls things are different, and what the reasons for this are. So much, then, for that.

18. Now about whether the body has anything by itself, and possesses already something of its own in its life when soul is present, or whether what it has is nature, and this, nature, is what is in association with body. Now the body itself, in which are soul and nature, cannot be something of a soulless kind or like air which is illuminated, but it must be like air which is warmed; the body of an animal or a plant has a kind of shadow of soul, and pain and bodily pleasures affect a body which is so qualified; but the pain of this body and pleasure of this kind result for us in a dispassionate knowledge. When I say " for us " I am referring to the other soul, since the qualified body does not belong to someone else, but is ours, and so we are concerned with it because it belongs to us. We ourselves are not it, nor are we clear of it, but it depends upon and is attached to us. " We ourselves " refers to the dominant and essential part of us; this body is in a different way ours, but ours all the same. So we are concerned with its pains and pleasures, more in proportion as we are weaker and do not separate ourselves, but consider the body the most honourable part of ourselves and the real man, and, so to speak, sink ourselves in it. For we must say that experiences of this kind do not belong entirely to the soul, but to the qualified body and something common and composite. For when something is one, it is sufficient to itself; for example, what could happen to body by itself if it was lifeless?

ἀλλ' ἡ ἐν αὐτῷ ἕνωσις. ψυχή τε μόνη οὐδὲ τοῦτο
25 [οὐδὲ τὸ διαιρεῖσθαι],¹ καὶ οὕτως ἔχουσα ἐκφεύγει
πᾶν. ὅταν δὲ δύο ἐθέλῃ ἓν εἶναι, ἐπακτῷ χρη-
σάμενα τῷ ἓν ἐν τῷ οὐκ ἐᾶσθαι εἶναι ἓν τὴν
γένεσιν εἰκότως τοῦ ἀλγεῖν ἔχει. λέγω δὲ δύο
οὐκ, εἰ δύο σώματα· μία γὰρ φύσις· ἀλλ' ὅταν
ἄλλη φύσις ἄλλῃ ἐθέλῃ κοινωνεῖν καὶ γένει ἄλλῳ,
30 καί τι τὸ χεῖρον λάβῃ παρὰ τοῦ κρείττονος, καὶ
ἐκεῖνο μὲν μὴ δυνηθῇ λαβεῖν, ἐκείνου δέ τι ἴχνος,
καὶ οὕτω γένηται δύο καὶ ἓν μεταξὺ γενόμενον τοῦ
τε ὃ ἦν καὶ τοῦ ὃ μὴ ἐδυνήθη ἔχειν, ἀπορίαν
ἐγέννησεν αὐτῷ ἐπίκηρον κοινωνίαν καὶ οὐ
βεβαίαν εἰληχός, ἀλλ' εἰς τὰ ἐναντία ἀεὶ φερομένην.
35 κάτω τε οὖν καὶ ἄνω αἰωρούμενον φερόμενον μὲν
κάτω ἀπήγγειλε τὴν αὑτοῦ ἀλγηδόνα, πρὸς δὲ τὸν
ἄνω τὴν ἔφεσιν τῆς κοινωνίας.

19. Τοῦτο δὴ τὸ λεγόμενον ἡδονήν τε εἶναι καὶ
ἀλγηδόνα, εἶναι μὲν ἀλγηδόνα γνῶσιν ἀπαγωγῆς
σώματος ἰνδάλματος ψυχῆς στερισκομένου,
ἡδονὴν δὲ γνῶσιν ζῴου ἰνδάλματος ψυχῆς ἐν
5 σώματι ἐναρμοζομένου πάλιν αὖ. ἐκεῖ μὲν οὖν τὸ
πάθος, ἡ δὲ γνῶσις τῆς αἰσθητικῆς ψυχῆς ἐν τῇ
γειτονίᾳ αἰσθανομένης καὶ ἀπαγγειλάσης τῷ εἰς ὃ
λήγουσιν αἱ αἰσθήσεις. καὶ ἠλγύνθη μὲν ἐκεῖνο·

---

¹ del. Kirchhoff*, ut glossam ad οὐδὲ τοῦτο.

---

¹ For a clear and full explanation of Plotinus's doctrine of
the parts played by body and soul in experiencing pleasure
and pain see H. J. Blumenthal *Plotinus' Psychology* ch. 5,
" The Affections ". The essential point of it is that only body

ON DIFFICULTIES ABOUT THE SOUL II

For if it was divided the division would not affect it itself, but the unity in it. And soul by itself is not subject even to division, and when it is in this state escapes everything. But when two things aspire to unity, since the unity which they have is an extraneous one, the origin of pain, it is reasonable to expect, lies in their not being permitted to be one. I do not mean " two " as if there were two bodies, for they would have one and the same nature; but when one nature wants to share with another one, and a different kind, and the worse takes something from the better, and cannot take it itself but only a trace of it, and so there come to be two things, and one which has come to be in between what it was and what it could not grasp, this makes difficulties for itself by acquiring a communion with the other which is hazardous and insecure, always borne from one extreme to the other. So it swings up and down, and as it comes down it proclaims its pain, and as it goes up its longing for communion.

19. This is what people call pleasure and pain; pain is consciousness of withdrawal of a body which is being deprived of the image of soul, and pleasure is the knowledge of a living being that the image of soul is again fitting itself back in the body. The affection, then, is there, in the body, but the knowledge belongs to the perceptive soul, which perceives in the neighbourhood of the affection and reports to that in which the sense-perceptions terminate.[1] And it was the body which felt the pain—I mean by " felt

is genuinely affected: soul perceives the affection without being affected (on Plotinus's difficulties in maintaining this position see Blumenthal l.c.).

λέγω δὲ τὸ "ἠλγύνθη" τὸ "πέπονθεν ἐκεῖνο"·
οἷον ἐν τῇ τομῇ τεμνομένου τοῦ σώματος ἡ μὲν
10 διαίρεσις κατὰ τὸν ὄγκον, ἡ δ' ἀγανάκτησις κατὰ
τὸν ὄγκον τῷ μὴ μόνον ὄγκον, ἀλλὰ καὶ τοιόνδε
ὄγκον εἶναι· ἐκεῖ δὲ καὶ ἡ φλεγμονή· ᾔσθετο δὲ ἡ
ψυχὴ παραλαβοῦσα τῷ ἐφεξῆς οἷον κεῖσθαι.
πᾶσα δὲ ᾔσθετο τὸ ἐκεῖ πάθος οὐκ αὐτὴ παθοῦσα.
αἰσθανομένη γὰρ πᾶσα ἐκεῖ λέγει τὸ πάθος εἶναι,
15 οὗ ἡ πληγὴ καὶ ἡ ὀδύνη. εἰ δ' ἦν αὐτὴ παθοῦσα
ἐν παντὶ ὅλη τῷ σώματι οὖσα, οὐκ ἂν εἶπεν οὐδ'
ἂν ἐμήνυσεν ὅτι ἐκεῖ, ἀλλ' ἔπαθεν ἂν τὴν ὀδύνην
πᾶσα καὶ ὠδυνήθη ὅλη, καὶ οὐκ ἂν εἶπεν οὐδὲ
ἐδήλωσεν ὅτι ἐκεῖ, ἀλλὰ ὅπου ἐστὶν εἶπεν ἂν ἐκεῖ·
ἔστι δὲ πανταχοῦ. νῦν δὲ ὁ δάκτυλος ἀλγεῖ, καὶ ὁ
20 ἄνθρωπος ἀλγεῖ, ὅτι ὁ δάκτυλος ὁ τοῦ ἀνθρώπου.
τὸν δὲ δάκτυλον ὁ ἄνθρωπος λέγεται ἀλγεῖν,
ὥσπερ καὶ ὁ γλαυκὸς ἄνθρωπος κατὰ[1] τὸ ἐν
ὀφθαλμῷ γλαυκόν. ἐκεῖνο μὲν οὖν τὸ πεπονθὸς
ἀλγεῖ, εἰ μή τις τὸ "ἀλγεῖ" μετὰ τὸ ἐφεξῆς
αἰσθήσεως περιλαμβάνοι· περιλαμβάνων δὲ
25 δηλονότι τοῦτο σημαίνει, ὡς ὀδύνη μετὰ τοῦ μὴ
λαθεῖν τὴν ὀδύνην τὴν αἴσθησιν. ἀλλ' οὖν τὴν
αἴσθησιν αὐτὴν οὐκ ὀδύνην λεκτέον, ἀλλὰ γνῶσιν
ὀδύνης· γνῶσιν δὲ οὖσαν ἀπαθῆ εἶναι, ἵνα γνῷ
καὶ ὑγιῶς ἀπαγγείλῃ. πεπονθὼς γὰρ ἄγγελος
σχολάζων τῷ πάθει ἢ οὐκ ἀπαγγέλλει, ἢ οὐχ
ὑγιὴς ἄγγελος.

---

[1] suspic. Creuzer, scr. Kirchhoff*: καὶ Enn., H–S[1].

the pain " that the body was affected; as in a surgical operation when the body is cut the division is in its material mass, but the distress is felt in the mass because it is not only a mass, but a mass qualified in a particular way; it is there too that inflammation occurs. But the soul perceives it, taking it over because it is, so to speak, situated next to it. The whole soul perceives the affection in the body without being affected itself. For it perceives as a whole and says that the affection is there where the wound and the pain are. But if it was affected itself, being wholly present in every part of the body, it would not have said or indicated that the affection was there [in that particular place] but would all have been affected by the pain, and in pain as a whole, and would not have said or made clear that the pain was there [in that particular place] but would have said that it was there where the soul is; but the soul is everywhere. But as it is the finger has a pain, and the man has a pain, because the man's finger does. The man is said to have a pain in his finger in the same way as we speak of a bright-looking man, because of his bright eyes. So then that which is affected has the pain, unless one takes " has the pain " as including the immediately consequent perception: if one includes this obviously one is indicating that pain goes with sense-perception's awareness of the pain. But, then, the sense-perception itself is not to be called pain, but knowledge of pain; but since it is knowledge it is unaffected, so that it can know and give a sound report. For a messenger who is affected, if he gives himself over to the affection, either does not deliver his message or is not a sound and reliable messenger.

20. Καὶ τῶν σωματικῶν δὲ ἐπιθυμιῶν τὴν
ἀρχὴν ἐκ τοῦ οὕτω κοινοῦ καὶ τῆς τοιαύτης
σωματικῆς φύσεως ἀκόλουθον τίθεσθαι γίνεσθαι.
οὔτε γὰρ τῷ ὁπωσοῦν ἔχοντι σώματι δοτέον τὴν
5 ἀρχὴν τῆς ὀρέξεως καὶ προθυμίας, οὔτε τῇ ψυχῇ
αὐτῇ ἁλμυρῶν ἢ γλυκέων ζήτησιν, ἀλλὰ ὃ σῶμα
μέν ἐστιν, ἐθέλει δὲ μὴ μόνον σῶμα εἶναι, ἀλλὰ καὶ
κινήσεις ἐκτήσατο πλέον ἢ αὐτή, καὶ ἐπὶ πολλὰ διὰ
τὴν ἐπίκτησιν ἠνάγκασται τρέπεσθαι· διὸ οὑτωσὶ
μὲν ἔχον ἁλμυρῶν, οὑτωσὶ δὲ γλυκέων, καὶ
10 ὑγραίνεσθαι καὶ θερμαίνεσθαι οὐδὲν αὐτῷ μελῆσαν,
εἰ μόνον ἦν. ὥσπερ δὲ ἐκεῖ ἐκ τῆς ὀδύνης ἐγίνετο
ἡ γνῶσις, καὶ ἀπάγειν ἐκ τοῦ ποιοῦντος τὸ πάθος
ἡ ψυχὴ βουλομένη ἐποίει τὴν φυγήν, καὶ τοῦ
πρώτου παθόντος διδάσκοντος τοῦτο φεύγοντός
πως καὶ αὐτοῦ ἐν τῇ συστολῇ, οὕτω καὶ ἐνταῦθα ἡ
15 μὲν αἴσθησις μαθοῦσα καὶ ἡ ψυχὴ ἡ ἐγγύς, ἣν δὴ
φύσιν φαμὲν τὴν δοῦσαν τὸ ἴχνος, ἡ μὲν φύσις τὴν
τρανὴν ἐπιθυμίαν τέλος οὖσαν τῆς ἀρξαμένης ἐν
ἐκείνῳ, ἡ δ' αἴσθησις τὴν φαντασίαν, ἀφ' ἧς ἤδη ἢ
πορίζει ἡ ψυχή, ἧς τὸ πορίζειν, ἢ ἀντιτείνει καὶ
καρτερεῖ καὶ οὐ προσέχει οὔτε τῷ ἄρξαντι τῆς
20 ἐπιθυμίας, οὔτε τῷ μετὰ ταῦτα ἐπιτεθυμηκότι.
ἀλλὰ διὰ τί δύο ἐπιθυμίας, ἀλλ' οὐκ ἐκεῖνο εἶναι τὸ
ἐπιθυμοῦν μόνον τὸ σῶμα τὸ τοιόνδε; ἢ εἰ ἔστιν
ἕτερον ἡ φύσις, ἕτερον δὲ τὸ σῶμα τὸ τοιόνδε
παρὰ τῆς φύσεως γενόμενον—ἔστι γὰρ ἡ φύσις πρὸ
τοῦ τὸ τοιόνδε σῶμα γενέσθαι, αὕτη γὰρ ποιεῖ τὸ
25 τοιόνδε σῶμα πλάττουσα καὶ μορφοῦσα—ἀνάγκη

20. And it is consistent to attribute the origin of
the bodily desires to this kind of common entity and
bodily nature. For the origin of appetite and impulse is not to be attributed to the body in any sort
of state, nor the search for savoury or sweet to the
soul itself, but [the origin] is that which is body, but
wants to be not only body, but has acquired a greater
number of movements than the soul itself, and has
been compelled by this acquisition to turn in many
directions; so when it is in one state it desires savoury
things, in another sweet, and to be cooled, or warmed,
which would be of no concern of its if it was alone.
But just as in the case of pain it was from the pain
that the knowledge came, and the soul, wishing to
take the body away from that which produced the
affection, brought about flight—and the part which
was primarily affected taught it this by taking flight
itself in a way by its contraction—so in this case too
it is sense-perception which acquires knowledge and
the soul near by, which we call nature, which gives
the trace of soul to the body; nature knows the
explicit desire which is the final stage of that which
begins in the body, and sense-perception knows the
image, and the soul starts from the image, and
either provides what is desired—it is its function to
do so—or resists and holds out and pays no attention
either to what started the desire or to that which
desired afterwards. But why do we say that there
are two desires, but not that it is only that qualified
body which we have been discussing that desires?
Because, if nature is one thing and the qualified body
another which has come into being from nature (for
nature exists before the qualified body has come into
being, since it itself makes the qualified body, shap-

μήτε ἄρχειν αὐτὴν τῆς ἐπιθυμίας, ἀλλὰ τὸ τοιόνδε
σῶμα τὸ πεπονθὸς ταδὶ καὶ ἀλγυνόμενον τῶν
ἐναντίων ἢ πάσχει ἐφιέμενον, ἡδονῆς ἐκ τοῦ
πονεῖν καὶ πληρώσεως ἐκ τῆς ἐνδείας· τὴν δὲ
φύσιν ὡς μητέρα, ὥσπερ στοχαζομένην τῶν τοῦ
30 πεπονθότος βουλημάτων, διορθοῦν τε πειρᾶσθαι
καὶ ἐπανάγειν εἰς αὑτὴν καὶ ζήτησιν τοῦ ἀκεσο-
μένου ποιουμένην συνάψασθαι τῇ ζητήσει τῇ τοῦ
πεπονθότος ἐπιθυμίᾳ καὶ τὴν περάτωσιν ἀπ᾽
ἐκείνου πρὸς αὑτὴν ἥκειν. ὥστε τὸ μὲν ἐπιθυμεῖν
ἐξ αὐτοῦ—εἴποι ἄν τις προεπιθυμίαν ἴσως καὶ
35 προθυμίαν—τὴν δὲ ἐξ ἄλλου καὶ δι᾽ ἄλλου ἐπιθυμεῖν, τὴν δὲ ποριζομένην ἢ μὴ ἄλλην εἶναι.

21. Ὅτι δὲ τοῦτό ἐστι, περὶ ὃ ἡ ἀρχὴ τῆς
ἐπιθυμίας, καὶ αἱ ἡλικίαι μαρτυροῦσιν αἱ διάφοροι.
ἄλλαι γὰρ παίδων καὶ μειρακίων καὶ ἀνδρῶν αἱ
σωματικαὶ ὑγιαινόντων τε καὶ νοσούντων τοῦ
5 ἐπιθυμητικοῦ τοῦ αὐτοῦ ὄντος· δῆλον γὰρ ὅτι τῷ
σωματικὸν καὶ σῶμα τοιόνδε εἶναι τρεπόμενον
παντοίας τροπὰς παντοδαπὰς καὶ τὰς ἐπιθυμίας
ἴσχει. καὶ τὸ μὴ συνεγείρεσθαι δὲ πανταχοῦ ταῖς
λεγομέναις προθυμίαις τὴν πᾶσαν ἐπιθυμίαν, εἰς
τέλος τῆς σωματικῆς μενούσης, καὶ πρὸ τοῦ τὸν
10 λογισμὸν εἶναι μὴ βούλεσθαι ἢ φαγεῖν ἢ πιεῖν ἐπί
τι προελθοῦσαν τὴν ἐπιθυμίαν λέγει, ὅσον ἦν ἐν
τῷ τοιῷδε σώματι, τὴν δὲ φύσιν μὴ συνάψασθαι
αὐτὴν μηδὲ προσθέσθαι,[1] μηδὲ βούλεσθαι, ὥσπερ
οὐδὲ κατὰ φύσιν ἐχούσης, ἄγειν εἰς φύσιν, ὡς ἂν
αὐτὴν τῷ παρὰ φύσιν καὶ κατὰ φύσιν ἐπιστατοῦσαν.
15 εἰ δέ τις πρὸς τὸ πρότερον λέγοι ἀρκεῖν τὸ σῶμα

---

[1] Aᵃᶜ, Kirchhoff, Müller, Volkmann: προθέσθαι AᵖᶜExUC.

ing and forming it), then it is necessary that nature
should not begin desire; but it must be the qualified
body which is affected in particular ways and feels
pain in desiring the opposite of what it experiences,
pleasure instead of suffering and sufficiency instead
of want; but nature is like a mother, trying to make
out the wishes of the sufferer, and attempting to set
it right and bring it back to herself; and, searching
for the remedy, she attaches herself by her search
to the desire of the sufferer, and the consummation
of the desire passes from the body to nature. So
one might say, perhaps, that the desiring comes from
the body itself—one might call it preliminary desiring
and eagerness—but that nature desires from and
through something else, and it is another soul which
provides what is desired or does not.

21. The differences of age-groups show that it is
in this region that desire starts, for the bodily desires
of children and adolescents and men, and of healthy
men and sick men, are different though the desiring
faculty is the same: because it is bodily and a
qualified body it is subject to every sort of change
and has every variety of desire. And the whole
desire is not in all cases aroused by what we call
impulses and does not wish to eat or drink before
consideration though the bodily desire persists to
the end; this means that the desire reaches a certain
point, as far as it was in the qualified body, but
nature does not attach itself to the desire or associate
itself with it or wish, as the desire is not according to
nature, to bring it into nature, since it has to decide
itself what is against nature and according to nature.
But if someone answers this first argument by saying
that the body in its different states is sufficient to

διάφορον γινόμενον διαφόρους τῷ ἐπιθυμητικῷ τὰς
ἐπιθυμίας ποιεῖν, οὐκ αὔταρκες λέγει πρὸς τὸ
ἄλλου παθόντος ἄλλως αὐτὸ ὑπὲρ ἄλλου διαφόρους
ἐπιθυμίας ἔχειν, ὁπότε οὐδ' αὐτῷ γίνεται τὸ
πορίζόμενον. οὐ γὰρ δὴ τῷ ἐπιθυμητικῷ ἡ
20 τροφὴ ἢ θερμότης καὶ ὑγρότης [οὐδὲ κίνησις] [1]
οὐδὲ κούφισις κενουμένου οὐδὲ πλήρωσις μεστου-
μένου, ἀλλ' ἐκείνου πάντα.

22. Ἐπὶ δὲ τῶν φυτῶν ἆρα ἄλλο μὲν τὸ οἷον
ἐναπηχηθὲν τοῖς σώμασιν αὐτῶν, ἄλλο δὲ τὸ
χορηγῆσαν, ὃ δὴ ἐπιθυμητικὸν μὲν ἐν ἡμῖν, ἐν
ἐκείνοις δὲ φυτικόν, ἢ ἐν μὲν τῇ γῇ τοῦτο ψυχῆς ἐν
5 αὐτῇ οὔσης, ἐν δὲ τοῖς φυτοῖς τὸ ἀπὸ τούτου;
ζητήσειε δ' ἄν τις πρότερον, τίς ψυχὴ ἐν τῇ γῇ,
πότερα ἐκ τῆς σφαίρας τοῦ παντός, ἣν καὶ μόνην
δοκεῖ ψυχοῦν πρώτως Πλάτων, οἷον ἔλλαμψις [2]
εἰς τὴν γῆν, ἢ πάλιν αὖ λέγων πρώτην καὶ
πρεσβυτάτην θεῶν τῶν ἐντὸς οὐρανοῦ καὶ
10 αὐτῇ δίδωσι ψυχὴν οἵαν καὶ τοῖς ἄστροις· πῶς γὰρ
ἂν θεὸς εἴη, εἰ μὴ ἐκείνην ἔχοι; ὥστε συμβαίνει
καὶ τὸ πρᾶγμα ὅπως ἔχει ἐξευρεῖν δύσκολον, καὶ
μείζω ἀπορίαν ἢ οὐκ ἐλάττω ἐξ ὧν εἴρηκεν ὁ
Πλάτων γίνεσθαι. ἀλλὰ πρότερον, πῶς ἂν
εὐλόγως ἔχειν τὸ πρᾶγμα δόξειε. τὴν μὲν οὖν
φυτικὴν ψυχὴν ὡς ἔχει ἡ γῆ, ἐκ τῶν φυομένων

---

[1] del. Igal.
[2] Kirchhoff*: ἔλλαμψιν ARJUC, H–S: ἔλαμψιν EB.

---

[1] This passage illustrates the attitude of Plotinus to reason
and the traditional authority of Plato. He is primarily

make the desires in the desiring faculty different, he does not produce a sufficient reason to show why when one thing is affected in different ways the desiring faculty itself has various desires on behalf of this other, when what is provided to satisfy the desires is not for it. For certainly food, warmth, moisture, relief of what is emptied or satisfaction of what is filled, do not benefit the desiring faculty, but they all belong to the body.

22. But in the case of plants, is the kind of echo of soul in their bodies one thing and that which supplies it another, which is the desiring power in us, but the growth-power in them, or is this in the earth, as the earth has a soul in it, and is it what comes from this which is in plants? One might enquire first what soul there is in the earth. Is it a kind of illumination coming to the earth from the sphere of the All, which alone Plato seems to think primarily ensouled; or, on the other hand, when he says that the earth is " the first and oldest of the gods within heaven ", does he give it too a soul like that of the stars? For how could it be a god if it did not have a soul like that? So the consequence is that it is difficult to discover the real state of affairs, and what Plato has said makes the situation more, or at least not less, perplexing. But first of all we should consider what appears to be most probably the real state of affairs.[1] One might con-

concerned to arrive at a true, rationally defensible solution of the problem with which he is dealing; and, though Plato seems to him to be the safest guide to follow, his reverence for him is not so exaggerated as to prevent him here and elsewhere complaining of the difficulties raised by the obscurity or carelessness of the master's language: cp. III. 6. 12. 9–11.

15 ἐξ αὐτῆς ἄν τις τεκμαίροιτο· εἰ δὲ καὶ ζῷα πολλὰ
ἐκ γῆς γινόμενα ὁρᾶται, διὰ τί οὐ καὶ ζῷον ἄν τις
εἴποι αὐτὴν εἶναι; ζῷον δὲ τοσοῦτον οὖσαν καὶ
οὐ σμικρὰν μοῖραν τοῦ παντὸς διὰ τί οὐ καὶ νοῦν
ἔχειν φήσειε καὶ οὕτω θεὸν εἶναι; εἴπερ δὲ καὶ
20 τῶν ἄστρων ἕκαστον, διὰ τί οὐ καὶ τὴν γῆν ζῷον
μέρος τοῦ παντὸς ζῴου οὖσαν; οὐ γὰρ δὴ ἔξωθεν
μὲν συνέχεσθαι ὑπὸ ψυχῆς ἀλλοτρίας φατέον,
ἔνδον δὲ μὴ ἔχειν ὡς οὐ δυναμένης καὶ αὐτῆς ἔχειν
οἰκείαν. διὰ τί γὰρ τὰ μὲν πύρινα δύναται, τὸ δὲ
γήϊνον οὔ; σῶμα γὰρ ἑκάτερον καὶ οὐκ ἶνες
οὐδὲ ἐκεῖ οὐδὲ σάρκες οὐδ᾽ αἷμα οὐδὲ ὑγρόν·
25 καίτοι ἡ γῆ ποικιλώτερον καὶ ἐκ πάντων τῶν
σωμάτων. εἰ δ᾽ ὅτι δυσκίνητον, τοῦτο πρὸς
τὸ μὴ κινεῖσθαι ἐκ τόπου λέγοι τις ἄν. ἀλλὰ τὸ
αἰσθάνεσθαι πῶς; πῶς γὰρ καὶ τὰ ἄστρα; οὐ γὰρ
δὴ οὐδὲ σαρκῶν τὸ αἰσθάνεσθαι, οὐδ᾽ ὅλως
σῶμα δοτέον τῇ ψυχῇ, ἵνα αἰσθάνοιτο, ἀλλὰ τῷ
30 σώματι δοτέον ψυχήν, ἵνα ᾖ καὶ σῴζοιτο τὸ σῶμα·
κριτικῇ δὲ οὔσῃ τῇ ψυχῇ ὑπάρχει βλεπούσῃ εἰς
σῶμα καὶ τῶν τούτου παθημάτων τὴν κρίσιν
ποιεῖσθαι. τίνα οὖν ⟨τὰ⟩ [1] παθήματα γῆς, καὶ
τίνων αἱ κρίσεις; ἐπεὶ [2] καὶ τὰ φυτά, καθόσον
γῆς, οὐκ αἰσθάνεται. τίνων οὖν αἰσθήσεις καὶ διὰ
35 τίνων; ἢ οὐ τολμητέον καὶ ἄνευ ὀργάνων γίνεσθαι

[1] Theiler.
[2] Müller: ἔπειτα Enn., H–S[1] (τα correctio ad lin. 32 falso
loco inserta).

194

jecture from the things which grow out of it that the earth has a growth-soul; but if many animals are visibly produced by the earth, why should one not say also that it is an animal? But since it is so large an animal, and no small part of the All, why should not one say that it has intelligence also, and so is a god? For if each of the stars is a living thing, why should not the earth also be a living thing, since it is part of the universal living thing? For one must certainly not say that it is held together from outside by a soul which does not belong to it, but has no soul within it, as if it was not able to have a soul of its own as well as the stars. For why should the fiery bodies be able to have a soul, but not the body of earth? For both are bodies, and the stars do not have muscular fibres or flesh or blood or humours any more than the earth does; even though the earth is more varied in composition and made of all bodies. But if [it is objected] that it is not very mobile, one might say that this only refers to its not moving from its place. But how does it have sense-perception? Well, how do the stars? For perception does not belong to flesh, nor, in general, does a body have to be given to the soul so that it may perceive, but a soul to the body so that the body may exist and be kept in being; but since the soul has the power of making judgments it can look to the body and make a judgment also about the body's affections. What then are the affections of the earth, and about what are the judgments made? Plants, too, insofar as they belong to earth, have no perceptions. Of what, then, are the earth's perceptions, and through what organs do they come? It is surely not too rash to say that perceptions take place with-

αἰσθήσεις; καὶ εἰς τίνα δὲ χρείαν τὸ αἰσθάνεσθαι
αὐτῇ; οὐ γὰρ δὴ διὰ τὸ γινώσκειν· ἀρκεῖ γὰρ ἡ
τοῦ φρονεῖν ἴσως † γνῶσις, οἷς μὴ ἐκ τοῦ αἰσθάνεσθαι γίνεταί τις χρεία. ἢ τοῦτο μὲν οὐκ ἄν τις
συγχωρήσειεν. ἔστι γὰρ καὶ παρὰ τὴν χρείαν ἐν
40 τοῖς αἰσθητοῖς εἴδησίς τις οὐκ ἄμουσος, οἷον ἡλίου
καὶ τῶν ἄλλων καὶ οὐρανοῦ καὶ γῆς· αἱ γὰρ τούτων αἰσθήσεις καὶ παρ' αὐτῶν ἡδεῖαι. τοῦτο μὲν
οὖν σκεπτέον ὕστερον· νῦν δὲ πάλιν, εἰ αἱ αἰσθήσεις
τῇ γῇ, καὶ [ζῴων] [1] τίνων αἱ αἰσθήσεις, καὶ πῶς.
45 ἢ ἀναγκαῖον πρότερον ἀναλαβεῖν τὰ ἀπορηθέντα
καὶ καθόλου λαβεῖν, εἰ ἄνευ ὀργάνων ἔστιν αἰσθάνεσθαι, καὶ εἰ πρὸς χρείαν αἱ αἰσθήσεις, κἂν εἰ ἄλλο
τι παρὰ τὴν χρείαν γίγνοιτο.

23. Δεῖ δὴ θέσθαι, ὡς τὸ αἰσθάνεσθαι τῶν αἰσθητῶν ἐστι τῇ ψυχῇ ἢ τῷ ζῴῳ ἀντίληψις τὴν προσοῦ-
σαν τοῖς σώμασι ποιότητα συνιείσης καὶ τὰ εἴδη
αὐτῶν ἀποματτομένης. ἢ τοίνυν μόνη ἐφ' ἑαυτῆς
5 ἀντιλήψεται, ἢ μετ' ἄλλου. μόνη μὲν οὖν καὶ ἐφ'
ἑαυτῆς πῶς; ἐφ' ἑαυτῆς γὰρ τῶν ἐν αὐτῇ, καὶ
μόνον νόησις· εἰ δὲ καὶ ἄλλων, δεῖ πρότερον καὶ
ταῦτα ἐσχηκέναι ἤτοι ὁμοιωθεῖσαν ἢ τῷ ὁμοιωθέντι
συνοῦσαν. ὁμοιωθῆναι μὲν οὖν ἐφ' ἑαυτῆς μένουσαν

[1] del. Theiler.

---

[1] The most likely supposition seems to be that γνῶσις here
is a gloss on the whole phrase which has ousted some other
word now lost; as it is not possible to be quite certain what
that word was, I print the MSS text with Henry-Schwyzer
and translate δύναμις, a plausible suggestion of Cilento.

out organs. And what use would perception be to the earth? It would not need it for knowledge. For the power of thought [1] perhaps suffices for beings which have no need arising from sense-perception. One could not, however, accept this argument. For over and above need there is in the objects of perception a knowing which brings a not uncivilised pleasure, of the sun and the other heavenly bodies, and the sky and the earth, for instance: for the perception of these is pleasant in itself. This, then, we must consider later; now we must go back to the question whether the earth has perceptions, and of what it has perceptions, and how long it has them. First, we must take up again the difficulties which have been raised, and consider in general whether there can be perception without organs, and if perceptions are to meet a need, or if they have any other purpose independent of need.

23. We must suppose that the perception of sense-objects is for the soul or the living being an act of apprehension, in which the soul understands the quality attaching to bodies and takes the impression of their forms. Well, then, the soul will either apprehend alone by itself or in company with something else. But how can it do this when it is alone and by itself? For when it is by itself it apprehends what is in itself, and is pure thought; but if it also apprehends other things it must first have taken possession of them as well, either by becoming assimilated to them, or by keeping company with something which has been assimilated. But it cannot be

Henry-Schwyzer tentatively conjectured χρῆσις and Thillet (*Revue internationale de philosophie* 24, 1970, 206) now suggests δόσις.

οὐχ οἷόν τε. πῶς γὰρ ἂν ὁμοιωθείη σημεῖον
10 γραμμῇ; ἐπεὶ οὐδ᾽ ἡ νοητὴ τῇ αἰσθητῇ ἂν γραμμῇ
ἐφαρμόσειεν, οὐδὲ τὸ νοητὸν πῦρ ἢ ἄνθρωπος τῷ
αἰσθητῷ πυρὶ ἢ ἀνθρώπῳ. ἐπεὶ οὐδ᾽ ἡ φύσις ἡ
ποιοῦσα τὸν ἄνθρωπον τῷ γενομένῳ ἀνθρώπῳ εἰς
ταὐτόν. ἀλλὰ μόνη, κἂν εἰ οἷόν τε τῷ αἰσθητῷ
ἐπιβάλλειν, τελευτήσει εἰς νοητοῦ σύνεσιν, ἐκφυγόν-
15 τος τοῦ αἰσθητοῦ αὐτήν, οὐκ ἐχούσης ὅτῳ αὐτοῦ
λάβοιτο. ἐπεὶ καὶ τὸ ὁρατὸν ὅταν ψυχὴ πόρρωθεν
ὁρᾷ, κἂν ὅτι μάλιστα εἶδος εἰς αὐτὴν ἥκῃ, ἀρχόμενον τὸ πρὸς αὐτὴν οἷον ἀμερὲς ὂν λήγει εἰς τὸ
ὑποκείμενον χρῶμα καὶ σχῆμα, ὅσον ἐστὶν ἐκεῖ
ὁρώσης. οὐ τοίνυν δεῖ μόνα ταῦτα εἶναι, τὸ ἔξω
20 καὶ τὴν ψυχήν· ἐπεὶ οὐδ᾽ ἂν πάθοι· ἀλλὰ δεῖ τὸ
πεισόμενον τρίτον εἶναι, τοῦτο δέ ἐστι τὸ τὴν
μορφὴν δεξόμενον. συμπαθὲς ἄρα καὶ ὁμοιοπαθὲς
δεῖ εἶναι καὶ ὕλης μιᾶς καὶ τὸ μὲν παθεῖν, τὸ δὲ
γνῶναι, καὶ τοιοῦτον γενέσθαι τὸ πάθος, οἷον
σῴζειν μέν τι τοῦ πεποιηκότος, μὴ μέντοι ταὐτὸν
25 εἶναι, ἀλλὰ ἅτε μεταξὺ τοῦ πεποιηκότος καὶ ψυχῆς
ὄν, τὸ πάθος ἔχειν μεταξὺ αἰσθητοῦ καὶ νοητοῦ
κείμενον μέσον ἀνάλογον, συνάπτον πως τὰ ἄκρα
198

assimilated while it remains by itself. For how could a point be assimilated to a line? For even the intelligible line would not assimilate to the sensible one, nor would the intelligible fire or man assimilate to the sense-perceived fire or man (since even the nature which makes the man does not identify itself with the man who comes into being). But when the soul is alone, even if it is possible for it to direct its attention to the world of sense, it will end with an understanding of the intelligible; what is perceived by sense will escape it, as it has nothing with which to grasp it. Since also when the soul sees the visible object from a distance, however much it is a form which comes to it, that which reaches it, though it starts by being in a way without parts, ends in the substrate of the form as colour and shape, when the soul sees all that is there outside. There cannot, then, be nothing but these two things, the external object and the soul: since then the soul would not be affected; but there must be a third thing which will be affected, and this is that which will receive the form. This must be jointly subject to like affections and of one matter with the sense-object, and it must be this which is affected and the other principle [the soul] which knows; and its affection must be of such a kind that it retains something of that which produced it, but is not the same as it, but as it is between the producer of the affection and the soul, it must have an affection which lies between the sensible and the intelligible, a proportional mean somehow linking the extremes to each other, with

ἀλλήλοις, δεκτικὸν ἅμα καὶ ἀπαγγελτικὸν ὑπάρχον,
ἐπιτήδειον ὁμοιωθῆναι ἑκατέρῳ. ὄργανον γὰρ ὂν
30 γνώσεώς τινος οὔτε ταὐτὸν δεῖ τῷ γινώσκοντι
εἶναι οὔτε τῷ γνωσθησομένῳ, ἐπιτήδειον δὲ ἑκατέρῳ ὁμοιωθῆναι, τῷ μὲν ἔξω διὰ τοῦ παθεῖν, τῷ
δὲ εἴσω διὰ τοῦ τὸ πάθος αὐτοῦ εἶδος γενέσθαι.
εἰ δή τι νῦν[1] ὑγιὲς λέγομεν, δι' ὀργάνων δεῖ
σωματικῶν τὰς αἰσθήσεις γίνεσθαι. καὶ γὰρ τοῦτο
35 ἀκόλουθον τῷ τὴν ψυχὴν πάντη σώματος ἔξω
γενομένην μηδενὸς ἀντιλαμβάνεσθαι αἰσθητοῦ. τὸ
δὲ ὄργανον δεῖ ἢ πᾶν τὸ σῶμα, ἢ μέρος τι πρὸς
ἔργον τι ἀφωρισμένον εἶναι, οἷον ἐπὶ ἁφῆς καὶ
ὄψεως. καὶ τὰ τεχνητὰ δὲ τῶν ὀργάνων ἴδοι τις
ἂν μεταξὺ τῶν κρινόντων καὶ τῶν κρινομένων
40 γινόμενα καὶ ἀπαγγέλλοντα τῷ κρίνοντι τὴν τῶν
ὑποκειμένων ἰδιότητα· ὁ γὰρ κανὼν τῷ εὐθεῖ τῷ
ἐν τῇ ψυχῇ καὶ τῷ ἐν τῷ ξύλῳ συναψάμενος ἐν τῷ
μεταξὺ τεθεὶς τὸ κρίνειν τῷ τεχνίτῃ τὸ τεχνητὸν
ἔδωκεν. εἰ δὲ συνάπτειν δεῖ τὸ κριθησόμενον τῷ
ὀργάνῳ, ἢ καὶ διά τινος μεταξὺ διεστηκότος πόρρω
45 τοῦ αἰσθητοῦ, οἷον εἰ πόρρω τὸ πῦρ τῆς σαρκός,
⟨ἢ καὶ⟩[2] τοῦ μεταξὺ μηδὲν παθόντος, [ἢ][2] οἷον
εἰ κενόν τι εἴη μεταξὺ ὄψεως καὶ χρώματος, δυνατὸν ὁρᾶν τοῦ ὀργάνου τῇ δυνάμει παρόντος, ἑτέρου
λόγου. ἀλλ' ὅτι ψυχῆς ἐν σώματι καὶ διὰ σώματος
ἡ αἴσθησις, δῆλον.

[1] νῦν Theiler: τοίνυν Enn.*
[2] Kleist.

the capacity both of receiving and of transmitting information, suitable to be assimilated to each of the extremes. For since it is the organ of a kind of knowledge it must not be the same either as the knower or what is going to be known, but suitable to be assimilated to each, to the external object by being affected, and to the internal knower by the fact that its affection becomes form. If, certainly, what we are going to say now is sound, sense-perceptions must take place through bodily organs. This is consistent as well with the fact that the soul when it is altogether outside the body does not apprehend anything perceived by the senses. The organ must be either the body as a whole or some member of it set apart for a particular work; an example of the first is touch, of the second, sight. And one can see how the artificial kind of organs [or tools] are intermediaries between those who judge and what they are judging, and inform the judger of the characteristics of the object under consideration: for the ruler acts as link between the straightness in the soul and that in the wood; it has its place between them and enables the craftsman to judge that on which he is working. But it belongs to another discussion to determine whether what is to be judged must be immediately linked to the organ, or can affect it through a space between when it is at a distance from the sense-object, as when the fire is at a distance from the flesh, or if the medium is not affected, as if there was a void between the seeing and the colour, the possibility of seeing being due to the potential presence of the organ. But it is clear that sense-perception belongs to the soul in the body and working through the body.

24. Τὸ δὲ εἰ τῆς χρείας μόνον ἡ αἴσθησις, ὧδε
σκεπτέον. εἰ δὴ ψυχῇ μὲν μόνῃ οὐκ ἂν αἴσθησις
γίνοιτο, μετὰ δὲ σώματος αἱ αἰσθήσεις, διὰ σῶμα
ἂν εἴη, ἐξ οὗπερ καὶ αἱ αἰσθήσεις, καὶ διὰ τὴν
5 σώματος κοινωνίαν δοθεῖσα, καὶ ἤτοι ἐξ ἀνάγκης
ἐπακολουθοῦσα—ὅ τι γὰρ πάσχει τὸ σῶμα, καὶ
φθάνει τὸ πάθος μεῖζον ὂν μέχρι ψυχῆς—ἢ καὶ
μεμηχάνηται, ὅπως καὶ πρὶν μεῖζον γενέσθαι τὸ
ποιοῦν, ὥστε καὶ φθεῖραι, ἢ καὶ πρὶν πλησίον
γενέσθαι, φυλάξασθαι. εἰ δὴ τοῦτο, πρὸς χρείαν ἂν
10 εἶεν αἱ αἰσθήσεις. καὶ γὰρ εἰ καὶ πρὸς γνῶσιν, τῷ
μὴ ἐν γνώσει ὄντι ἀλλ' ἀμαθαίνοντι διὰ συμφοράν,
καὶ ἵνα ἀναμνησθῇ διὰ λήθην, οὐ τῷ μήτε ἐν
χρείᾳ μήτε ἐν λήθῃ. ἀλλ' εἰ τοῦτο, οὐ περὶ τῆς
γῆς ἂν μόνον εἴη σκοπεῖσθαι, ἀλλὰ καὶ περὶ ἄστρων
ἁπάντων καὶ μάλιστα περὶ παντὸς τοῦ οὐρανοῦ
15 καὶ τοῦ κόσμου. μέρεσι μὲν γὰρ πρὸς μέρη, οἷς
καὶ τὸ παθεῖν ὑπάρχει, γένοιτο ἂν αἴσθησις κατὰ
τὸν παρόντα λόγον, ὅλῳ δὲ πρὸς αὐτὸ τίς ἂν εἴη
ἀπαθῶς ἔχοντι πανταχῇ ἑαυτοῦ πρὸς ἑαυτόν; καὶ
γὰρ εἰ δεῖ τὸ μὲν ὄργανον τοῦ αἰσθανομένου εἶναι,
ἕτερον δὲ παρὰ τὸ ὄργανον τὸ οὗ αἰσθάνεται
20 ὑπάρχειν, τὸ δὲ πᾶν ὅλον ἐστίν, οὐκ ἂν εἴη αὐτῷ
τὸ μὲν δι' οὗ, τὸ δὲ οὗ ἡ αἴσθησις· ἀλλὰ συναίσ-

24. But the question whether perception is only concerned with need must be considered in this way. If the soul when it is alone could not have sense-perception, but its perceptions are with the body, then perception would be for the sake of the body, from which the perceptions also come, and would be given to the soul because of its communion with the body; and either it would be a necessary conse-quence—for every affection of the body, if it is one of the stronger ones, also reaches as far as the soul— or it has been devised so that we can take steps to guard ourselves against what is acting on the body before it becomes so strong as to destroy us, or before it comes too near. If this is so, perceptions would be intended for need. For even if they are also intended for knowledge, this would be for a being which is not in knowledge but is ignorant because of its misfortune, and so that it might remember again because of its forgetfulness, not for a being which is not in a state of need or forgetfulness. But if this is so, our investigation will not be confined to the earth, but must be about all the heavenly bodies and particularly the whole heaven and uni-verse. For according to the present argument parts which are subject to being affected will have sensation directed to other parts, but what sensation directed to itself could the whole have, when it is in every way incapable of being affected; what sensation of itself directed to itself could the universe have? Again, if the organ of perception must belong to that which perceives, and that which it perceives must be something different from the organ, but the All is one whole, it would not have an organ through which the perception comes distinct from the object

θησιν μὲν αὑτοῦ, ὥσπερ καὶ ἡμεῖς ἡμῶν συναισ-
θανόμεθα, δοτέον, αἴσθησιν δὲ ἀεὶ ἑτέρου οὖσαν
οὐ δοτέον· ἐπεὶ καὶ ὅταν ἡμεῖς παρὰ τὸ καθεστὼς
ἀεί τινος τῶν ἐν τῷ σώματι ἀντιλαμβανώμεθα,
25 ἔξωθεν προσελθόντος ἀντιλαμβανόμεθα. ἀλλ' ὥσπερ ἐφ' ἡμῶν οὐ μόνον τῶν ἔξωθεν ἡ ἀντίληψις,
ἀλλὰ καὶ μέρει μέρους, τί κωλύει καὶ τὸ πᾶν τῇ
ἀπλανεῖ τὴν πλανωμένην ὁρᾶν, καὶ ταύτῃ τὴν γῆν
καὶ τὰ ἐν αὐτῇ βλέπειν; καὶ εἰ μὴ ἀπαθῆ ταῦτα
τῶν ἄλλων παθῶν, καὶ ἄλλας αἰσθήσεις ἔχειν καὶ
30 τὴν ὅρασιν μὴ μόνον ὡς καθ' αὑτὴν τῆς ἀπλανοῦς
εἶναι, ἀλλ' ὡς ὀφθαλμοῦ ἀπαγγέλλοντος τῇ τοῦ
παντὸς ψυχῇ ἃ εἶδε; καὶ γὰρ εἰ τῶν ἄλλων ἀπαθής,
διὰ τί ὡς ὄμμα οὐκ ὄψεται φωτοειδὲς ἔμψυχον ὄν;
ἀλλ' ὀμμάτων, φησίν, οὐκ ἐπεδεῖτο. ἀλλ' εἰ
35 ὅτι μηδὲν ἔξωθεν ὑπελέλειπτο ὁρατόν, ἀλλ' ἔνδον
γε ἦν καὶ ἑαυτὸν ὁρᾶν οὐδὲν ἐκώλυσεν· εἰ δ'
ὅτι μάτην ἂν ἦν αὐτὸν ὁρᾶν, ἔστω μὴ προηγου-
μένως μὲν οὕτως ἕνεκα τοῦ ὁρᾶν γεγονέναι, ἀκο-
λουθεῖν δὲ τῷ οὕτως ἔχειν ἐξ ἀνάγκης. διὰ τί οὐκ
ἂν εἴη τοιούτῳ ὄντι σώματι διαφανεῖ τὸ ὁρᾶν;

25. Ἢ οὐκ ἀρκεῖ εἶναι τὸ δι' οὗ, ἵνα ὁρᾷ καὶ

which it perceives; but we must grant it self-perception, just as we are aware of ourselves, but not perception of a continual succession of different objects; since we too, when we apprehend something in our body which differs from its permanent state, apprehend it as something coming from outside. But just as with us there is not only apprehension of things outside, but apprehension of part by part, what prevents the All from seeing the sphere of the planets with that of the fixed stars, and looking at the earth and the things in it with the planetary sphere? And, if these [parts of the universe] are not free from the other affections, why should they not have other sense-perception, and particularly why should not sight not only belong to the sphere of the fixed stars as its own by itself, but as an eye announcing to the soul of the All what it sees? And even if it is not subject to the other affections, why should it not see as an eye when it is luminous and ensouled? But, Plato says, " it had no need of eyes ".[1] But if this was because there was nothing visible left outside, there were things to see within it, and nothing prevented it looking at itself; but if it was because it would be pointless for it to look at itself, let us assume that it was not brought into being as it is with the main purpose of seeing, but that seeing is a necessary consequence of its being as it is. Why should not a translucent body of this kind have the power of seeing?

25. [The answer is that] the existence of the medium is not a sufficient cause for sight, and in

---

[1] The reference is to *Timaeus* 33C1-2. As always, what Plato says is accepted as in some sense true, but very firmly interpreted to fit in with Plotinus's present line of argument.

ὅλως αἰσθάνηται, ἀλλὰ δεῖ τὴν ψυχὴν οὕτως ἔχειν,
ὡς νεύειν πρὸς τὰ αἰσθητά. ᾗ [1] δὲ ψυχῇ ὑπάρχει
ἀεὶ πρὸς τοῖς νοητοῖς εἶναι, κἂν οἷόν τε ᾖ αὐτῇ αἰσ-
5 θάνεσθαι, οὐκ ἂν γένοιτο τοῦτο τῷ πρὸς κρείττοσιν
εἶναι, ὁπότε καὶ ἡμῖν σφόδρα πρὸς τοῖς νοητοῖς
οὖσιν, ὅτε ἐσμέν, λανθάνουσι καὶ ὄψεις καὶ αἰσθήσει
ἄλλαι· κἂν πρὸς ἑτέρῳ δὲ ὅλως, τὰ ἕτερα λανθάνει.
ἐπεὶ καὶ τὸ μέρει τινὶ μέρους ἀντιλαμβάνεσθαι
θέλειν, οἷον ἑαυτὸν εἰ καταβλέποι, περίεργον καὶ
10 ἐφ' ἡμῶν, καὶ εἰ μὴ ἕνεκά τινος, μάτην. ἄλλου τε
ὄψιν ὡς καλοῦ ὁρᾶν, πεπονθότος καὶ ἐνδεοῦς.
ὀσφραίνεσθαι δὲ [καὶ ἀκούειν] [2] καὶ γεύεσθαι
χυμῶν περιστάσεις ἄν τις καὶ περιελκυσμοὺς τῆς
ψυχῆς θεῖτο· ἥλιον δὲ καὶ τὰ ἄλλα ἄστρα κατὰ
συμβεβηκὸς ὁρᾶν καὶ ἀκούειν δέ. εἰ δὲ δὴ καὶ
15 ἐπιστρέφεσθαι δι' ἄμφω, οὐκ ἄλογος ἡ θέσις.
ἀλλ' εἰ ἐπιστρέφοιτο, καὶ μνημονεύσει· ἢ ἄτοπον,
ὧν εὐεργετεῖ, μὴ μνημονεύειν. πῶς οὖν εὐεργετεῖ,
εἰ μὴ μνημονεύει;

26. Γίνονται δὲ εὐχῶν γνώσεις κατὰ οἷον
σύναψιν καὶ κατὰ τοιάνδε σχέσιν ἐναρμοζομένων,
καὶ αἱ ποιήσεις οὕτως· καὶ ἐν ταῖς μάγων τέχναις
εἰς τὸ συναφὲς πᾶν· ταῦτα δὲ δυνάμεσιν ἑπομέναις
συμπαθῶς.

5 Εἰ δὲ τοῦτο, διὰ τί οὐ καὶ τὴν γῆν αἰσθάνεσθαι

---

[1] Theiler: τῇ Enn., H–S[1].
[2] del. Kleist.

general for perception, but the soul must be so disposed as to incline towards sense-objects. But for the soul [of the universe], to which it is natural to be always directed towards the objects of intellect, even if it can perceive, this could not happen because it is always directed towards higher things; so with us too, when we are strongly concentrating on the objects of intellect, as long as we are in this state, sights and other perceptions pass unnoticed; and in general, when one is concentrating entirely on one thing, all the others are unnoticed. And then, too, it is mere inquisitiveness to want to apprehend a part by a part, as if a man were to look at himself, and if it is not for some purpose, it is futile. And to see the sight of something else as beautiful is the mark of someone who is suffering or in need. But smelling and tasting flavours one would consider as mere externalities and distractions of the soul; but one would suppose that the sun and the other heavenly bodies see and hear incidentally. Certainly if one supposes that they pay attention [to the world below] by means of both these senses, the supposition would not be unreasonable. But if they pay attention, they will remember: it is absurd not to remember the benefits one confers. How then will they confer benefits, if they do not remember?

26. Their knowledge of prayers is the result of a sort of linking and a particular disposition of things fitted into the whole, and the same applies to their accomplishment of what we pray for; and in the arts of the magicians everything is directed to this linking: this means that magic works by powers which follow on sympathetically.

But if this is so, why should we not give perception

δώσομεν; ἀλλὰ ποίας αἰσθήσεις; ἢ διὰ τί οὐ
πρῶτον ἀφὴν καὶ μέρει μέρους ἀναπεμπομένης ἐπὶ
τὸ ἡγούμενον τῆς αἰσθήσεως καὶ τῷ ὅλῳ πυρὸς καὶ
τῶν ἄλλων; καὶ γὰρ εἰ τὸ σῶμα δυσκίνητον, οὔτι
10 γε ἀκίνητον. ἀλλ' ἔσονται αἱ αἰσθήσεις οὐ τῶν
μικρῶν, ἀλλὰ τῶν μεγάλων. ἀλλὰ διὰ τί; ἢ ὅτι
ἀνάγκη ψυχῆς ἐνούσης τὰς κινήσεις τὰς μεγίστας
μὴ λανθάνειν. κωλύει δ' οὐδὲν καὶ διὰ τοῦτο τὸ
αἰσθάνεσθαι γίνεσθαι, ἵνα εὖ τίθοιτο τὰ πρὸς
ἀνθρώπους, ὅσον εἰς αὐτὴν τὰ ἀνθρώπων ἀνάκειται
15 —εὖ τίθοιτο δὲ οἷον συμπαθῶς—καὶ ἀκούειν δὲ
εὐχομένων καὶ ἐπινεύειν εὐχαῖς οὐχ ὃν ἡμεῖς τρόπον, καὶ ταῖς ἄλλαις αἰσθήσεσι παθητὴν εἶναι πρὸς
αὐτήν. καὶ τἆλλα, οἷον ὀσμῶν πέρι καὶ τῶν γευσ-
τῶν; ἀλλ' ἤ,[1] ὅσα ὀσφραντὰ κατὰ τὰς τῶν χυλῶν
ὀσμάς, πρὸς ζῴων πρόνοιαν καὶ κατασκευὴν καὶ
20 ἐπισκευὴν τοῦ σωματικοῦ αὐτῆς. καὶ οὐκ ἀπαιτητέον ἃ ἐφ' ἡμῶν ὄργανα· οὐδὲ γὰρ πᾶσι ζῴοις
ταὐτά· οἷον ὦτα οὐ πᾶσι, καὶ οἷς μὴ ἔστιν, ἀντί-
ληψίς ἐστι ψόφων. περὶ δὲ ὄψεως, εἰ φωτὸς δεῖ,
πῶς; οὐ γὰρ δὴ ἀπαιτητέον ὄμματα. εἰ οὖν τοῦ
φυτικοῦ συγχωρουμένου ἦν συγχωρεῖν, ἢ ἐν πνεύ-
25 ματι ὄντος τοῦ φυτικοῦ πρώτως, οὕτως ἔχειν,
⟨ἢ⟩[2] ὄντος πνεύματος, τί χρὴ ἀπιστεῖν καὶ διαφανὲς εἶναι; μᾶλλον δ' εἴπερ πνεῦμα, καὶ διαφανὲς

---

[1] coniecimus: ἄλλοις ἢ Enn.: ἄλλως ἢ Theiler: ἄλλων καὶ
Blumenthal: del. Kirchhoff*.
[2] suspic. Cilento, add. Harder.

to the earth? But what sort of perceptions? Why not first touch, both touching of part by part (with sense-perception reporting this to the governing principle) and touching of fire and the other elements by the whole? For even if the earth's body is difficult to move, it is certainly not immovable. But the earth's perceptions will not be of small things, but of great ones. But why? Because it is necessary, since there is a soul in it, that it should not be unaware of the greatest movements. And there is nothing to prevent the earth having perceptions for this reason, too, that it may make good arrangements for men, as far as the affairs of men concern it—it will make good arrangements by a kind of sympathy —and hearing those who pray to it, and answering their prayers, not in the way we do, and being subject to affection by the other senses in relation to itself. And what about other things, for instance concerning scents and flavours? But [it will perceive] the scents which come from the juices of plants in order to provide for living things and for the construction and repair of its own bodily parts. And we must not require it to have the organs which we have: for these are not the same in all living creatures; for instance, not all have ears, and those which do not have them are able to apprehend sounds. But how about sight, if light is necessary? For we certainly must not require eyes. If, then, accepting that the earth has a power of growth, we could agree that this was so either because the power of growth was primarily in the breath of life, or because it was the breath of life, why should we disbelieve that this is also translucent? But rather, if it is the breath of life, it must also be translucent, and, when it is

καί, ἐλλαμπόμενον παρὰ τοῦ κύκλου, ἐνεργείᾳ δια-
φανές· ὥστε οὐδὲν ἄτοπον οὐδ' ἀδύνατον ὁρᾶν τὴν
ἐν τῇ γῇ ψυχήν. καὶ δεῖ [1] καὶ νοεῖν ψυχὴν οὐ
30 φαύλου σώματος εἶναι, ὥστε καὶ θεὸν εἶναι·
πάντως γὰρ καὶ ἀγαθὴν δεῖ ἀεὶ τὴν ψυχὴν εἶναι.

27. Εἰ οὖν τοῖς φυτοῖς δίδωσι τὴν γεννητικήν—
ἢ αὐτὴν τὴν γεννητικήν, ἢ ἐν αὐτῇ μὲν ἡ γεν-
νητική, ταύτης δὲ ἴχνος ἡ ἐν τοῖς φυτοῖς—καὶ οὕτως
ἂν εἴη ὡς ἡ σὰρξ ἔμψυχος ἤδη καὶ ἐκομίσατο, εἰ
5 ἔχει, καὶ τὴν γεννητικὴν ἐν αὐτοῖς τὰ φυτά.
ἐνοῦσα δὲ δίδωσι τῷ σώματι τοῦ φυτοῦ ὅπερ
βέλτιον, ᾧ διαφέρει τοῦ κοπέντος καὶ οὐκέτι
φυτοῦ, ἀλλὰ μόνον ξύλου. ἀλλ' αὐτῷ γε τῷ
σώματι τῆς γῆς τί δίδωσιν ἡ ψυχή; οὐ ταὐτὸν δεῖ
νομίζειν σῶμα εἶναι γήινον ἀποτμηθέν τε τῆς γῆς
10 καὶ μένον συνεχές, οἷα λίθοι δεικνύουσιν αὐξόμενοι
μέν, ἕως εἰσὶ συνηρτημένοι, μένοντες δὲ ὅσον
ἐτμήθησαν ἀφῃρημένοι. ἕκαστον μὲν οὖν μέρος
ἴχνος ἔχειν δεῖ νομίζειν, ἐπιθεῖν δὲ ἐπὶ τούτῳ τὸ
πᾶν φυτικόν, ὃ οὐκέτι τοῦδέ ἐστιν ἢ τοῦδε, ἀλλὰ

[1] w, Perna*: δὴ xUC.

illuminated by the heavenly circuit, actively translucent; so that there is nothing absurd or impossible in the earth's soul seeing. And we must certainly consider that it is the soul of no inferior body, so that it is even a god: for this soul must also be always good in every way.

27. If, then, the earth gives the generative soul to plants—either the generative soul itself, or the generative soul is in the earth itself and a trace of it is the generative principle in plants—in this latter case too, plants would be like flesh which is already ensouled and have acquired, if they possess it, the generative soul in themselves. And this generative soul, being present in the body of the plant, gives it what is better in it, that by which it differs from the piece which has been cut off and is no longer a plant, but only a stick. But what does the soul give to the body of the earth itself? One should not consider an earthy body the same when it is cut off from the earth and when it remains connected with it, as stones show, which grow as long as they are attached to the earth but remain the size they were cut when they are taken away from it.[1] One must therefore consider that each part has a trace of the generative soul, and the whole power of growth is diffused over this, and belongs no more to this part or that, but

---

[1] This remarkable doctrine that stones grow as long as they remain parts of the living body of the earth (cp. VI. 7. 11. 24–5) is a striking illustration of the strength of the conviction that the great parts of the universe, the earth and the heavenly bodies, and the universe as a whole are living organisms. The idea that minerals and stones in the earth grow is to be found in Strabo V. 2. 6 and VII. 5. 8 and may well go back to the great Stoic geographer and philosopher Posidonius: see W. Theiler *Vorbereitung d. Neuplatonismus* (Berlin 1930) 74.

τῆς ὅλης· εἶτα τὴν τοῦ αἰσθητικοῦ φύσιν οὐκέτι
15 τῷ σώματι συμπεφυρμένην, ἐποχουμένην δέ·
εἶτα τὴν ἄλλην ψυχὴν καὶ νοῦν, ἣν δὴ Ἑστίαν καὶ
Δήμητραν ἐπονομάζουσιν ἄνθρωποι θείᾳ φήμῃ καὶ
φύσει ἀπομαντευομένῃ τὰ τοιαῦτα χρώμενοι.

28. Καὶ ταῦτα μὲν ταύτῃ. ἐπανιτέον δὲ πάλιν
καὶ περὶ τοῦ θυμοειδοῦς ζητητέον, εἰ, ὥσπερ τῶν
ἐπιθυμιῶν τὴν ἀρχὴν καὶ ἀλγηδόνας καὶ ἡδονάς—
τὰ πάθη, οὐ τὰς αἰσθήσεις—ἐν τῷ οὕτως ἔχοντι
5 σώματι ἐτίθεμεν τῷ οἷον ζωωθέντι, οὕτω καὶ τοῦ
θυμοῦ τὴν ἀρχὴν ἢ καὶ πάντα τὸν θυμὸν τοῦ οὕτως
ἔχοντος σώματος θησόμεθα ἢ μέρους τινὸς σώματος, οἷον καρδίας οὕτως ἐχούσης ἢ χολῆς οὐ νεκροῦ
σώματος· καὶ εἰ, ἄλλου ὄντος τοῦ διδόντος, τὸ
ἴχνος τὸ ψυχικόν, ἢ ἐνταῦθα ἔν τι τοῦτο ὁ θυμός,
10 οὐκέτι παρὰ φυτικοῦ[1] ἢ αἰσθητικοῦ. ἐκεῖ μὲν οὖν
καθ' ὅλον τὸ σῶμα τὸ φυτικὸν ὂν παντὶ ἐδίδου τῷ
σώματι τὸ ἴχνος, καὶ τὸ ἀλγεῖν ἦν ἐν παντὶ καὶ τὸ
ἥδεσθαι, καὶ ἡ ἀρχὴ τῆς ἐπιθυμίας ἐν παντὶ τοῦ
πληροῦσθαι· ἡ δὲ τῶν ἀφροδισίων οὐκ εἴρητο, ἀλλ'
15 ἔστω περὶ τὰ μόρια τῶν τοιούτων τελεστικά. ἔστω
δὲ ὁ περὶ τὸ ἧπαρ τόπος τῆς ἐπιθυμίας ἀρχή, ὅτι τὸ
φυτικὸν ἐκεῖ ἐνεργεῖ μάλιστα, ὃ τὸ ἴχνος τὸ ψυχικὸν τῷ ἥπατι καὶ τῷ σώματι παρέχει· ἐκεῖ δέ, ὅτι
ἐκεῖ ἄρχεται ἡ ἐνέργεια. ἀλλὰ περὶ τοῦ θυμικοῦ[2]

---

[1] Sleeman (C.Q. 20, 1926, 53): θυμικοῦ Enn.*
[2] Theiler: θυμοῦ Enn.*

to the whole earth: then comes the nature of sense-perception which is no longer " mixed up with the body "[1] but in contact with it from above; then the rest of the soul and its intelligence, which men, making use of divine revelation and a nature which divines such things, call Hestia and Demeter.

28. So much, then, for this. But we must go back again and enquire about the passionate power, whether, just as we placed the origin of desires, and pains and pleasures—the feelings, not the perceptions—in the body in a particular state, the body, that is, somehow given life, so we shall attribute the origin of the passionate spirit, or the passionate spirit as a whole, to the body in a particular state, or some part of the body, for instance to the heart in a particular state or the bile in a body which is not dead; and also whether, if it is something else which gives it, the passionate power is the trace of soul, or whether here the passionate spirit is this one particular thing, no longer derived from a power of growth or perception. Now in the case of desires the power of growth, which is in the whole body, gave the trace of soul to all the body, and pain and pleasure were in it all, and the origin of desire was in all the body, the desire, that is, of being satisfied; the desire of sexual pleasures was not mentioned, but let us assume that it concerns the parts which bring them to fruition. Let us grant, too, that the region around the liver is the origin of desire, because the power of growth is most active there which gives the trace of soul to the liver and to the body: it is there because its activity begins there. But about the passionate

---

[1] Plato *Phaedo* 66B5.

τί τε αὐτὸ καὶ τίς ψυχή, καὶ εἰ ἀπ᾽ αὐτοῦ ἴχνος περὶ
20 τὴν καρδίαν ἢ ἄλλο τι τὴν κίνησιν εἰς συναμφότερον
τελοῦν παρέχεται, ἢ ἐνταῦθα οὐκ ἴχνος, ἀλλ᾽ αὐτὸ
τὸ ὀργίζεσθαι παρέχεται. πρῶτον οὖν σκεπτέον, τί
αὐτό. ὅτι μὲν οὖν οὐχ ὑπὲρ ὧν ἂν πάσχῃ τὸ σῶμα
μόνον, ἀλλὰ καὶ ὑπὲρ ὧν ἂν καὶ ἕτερός τις τῶν
προσηκόντων, καὶ ὅλως ὑπὲρ ὧν ἄν τις παρὰ τὸ
25 προσῆκον ποιῇ, ὀργιζόμεθα, δῆλόν που· ὅθεν καὶ
αἰσθήσεως δεῖ καὶ συνέσεώς τινος ἐν τῷ ὀργίζεσθαι.
διὸ καὶ εἰς ταῦτά τις ὁρῶν οὐκ ἐκ τοῦ φυτικοῦ
ὡρμῆσθαι, ἀλλ᾽ ἐξ ἄλλου ἂν ζητοῖ τὸν θυμὸν τὴν
γένεσιν ἴσχειν. ἀλλ᾽ ὅταν ταῖς σωματικαῖς δια-
30 θέσεσιν ἕπηται τὸ τῆς ὀργῆς πρόχειρον, καὶ ὅταν
οἱ μὲν ζέοντες αἵματι καὶ χολῇ ἕτοιμοι εἰς τὸ
ὀργίζεσθαι ὦσιν, ἀνειμένοι δὲ πρὸς ὀργὰς οἱ
ἄχολοι λεγόμενοι καὶ κατεψυγμένοι, τά τε θηρία
πρὸς τὰς κράσεις ἀλλ᾽ οὐ[1] πρὸς τὸ δοκηθὲν

---

[1] κράσεις ἀλλ᾽ οὐ Bréhier: κράσεις οὐδενὸς ἄλλου ἀλλὰ Enn.:
βράσεις οὐδενὸς ἄλλου ἀλλὰ H–S.

---

[1] With the utmost regret I find myself compelled (with
Theiler and B. S. Page in his latest (1969) revision of Mac-
Kenna's translation) to reject Professor H.-R. Schwyzer's
emendation βράσεις—printed in the Henry-Schwyzer text—
and fall back on the best of Bréhier's usually unacceptable
critical suggestions. All that can be said in favour of βράσεις
is excellently said by Schwyzer in his "Sieben ἅπαξ εἰρημένα
bei Plotin" in *Mus. Helv.* 20 (1963) 193–5. My reason for
rejecting it is not the unprecedented sense given to the rare
word βράσις ("boiling"). Schwyzer makes a reasonable case
for this, and is also of course right in saying that the substi-
tution of κράσεις for βράσεις is paleographically easy to explain.

power [we must enquire] what it is itself and what kind of a soul it is, and whether a trace derived from it causes movement around the heart or something else which is classed as part of the composite being, or whether here it is not a trace, but the passionate power of soul itself which causes anger. First of all, then, we must consider what it is itself. It is obvious, I think, that we are angry not only over whatever our bodies suffer, but over the sufferings of anyone closely connected with us, and in general over anyone's improper behaviour. So there is need of perception and some kind of understanding in being angry. For this reason anyone looking at these facts would not think that passion arose from the power of growth, but would try to find that it had its source in some other power of soul. But when a propensity to anger follows bodily dispositions, and when those whose blood and bile are boiling are prompt to fly into a rage, and those who are said to be " without bile " and " chilly " are easy-going and slow to anger, and animals are angry because of their temperaments,[1] but not because it appears to them that

But the sense given by this emendation—that animals are not made angry by the " boiling up " of anger in another animal, but only by their supposition that they are being ill-treated—seems to me inconsistent with the whole argument of the sentence, which is that the causes of anger should be looked for in the constitution and state of the body, not in the soul. Bréhier's emendation gives exactly the necessary sense here and does not seem to me an intolerably violent change. I append Schwyzer's latest note on the passage (on a postcard to me), in which he makes clear with force and elegance in both ancient languages that he maintains his original position: " In IV 4, 28, 32 (quamvis ab omnibus nec non ab infideli Page despectus repulsus derelictus) βράσεις (κἀγὼ τὰς ὀργὰς ἔχω πρὸς τὸ δοκηθὲν λυμήνασθαι)."

λυμήνασθαι τὰς ὀργὰς ἔχωσι, πρὸς τὸ σωμα-
35 τικώτερον πάλιν αὖ καὶ πρὸς τὸ συνέχον τὴν τοῦ
ζῴου σύστασιν τὰς ὀργὰς ἄν τις ἀνοίσειε. καὶ ὅταν
οἱ αὐτοὶ νοσοῦντες μὲν ὀργιλώτεροι ἢ ὑγιαίνοντες,
ἄγευστοι δὲ σιτίων ἢ λαβόντες, σώματος τοιοῦδε
μηνύουσι τὰς ὀργὰς ἢ τὰς ἀρχὰς τῆς ὀργῆς εἶναι,
καὶ τὴν χολὴν ἢ τὸ αἷμα οἷον ψυχοῦντα παρ-
40 έχεσθαι τὰς τοιάσδε κινήσεις, ὥστε παθόντος τοῦ
τοιοῦδε σώματος εὐθέως κινεῖσθαι τὸ αἷμα ἢ τὴν
χολήν, αἰσθήσεως δὲ γενομένης τὴν φαντασίαν
κοινώσασαν τὴν ψυχὴν τῇ τοιοῦδε σώματος δια-
θέσει ἤδη πρὸς τὸ ποιοῦν τὴν ἀλγηδόνα ἵεσθαι·
ἄνωθεν δὲ αὖ τὴν ψυχὴν τὴν λογισμῷ χρωμένην
45 φανέντος ἀδικήματος—κἂν [1] μὴ περὶ τὸ σῶμα—
ἔχουσαν ἕτοιμον τὸ ἐκείνως θυμούμενον ἅτε πεφυκὸς τῷ ἀποδειχθέντι ἐναντίῳ μάχεσθαι σύμ-
μαχον τοῦτο ποιεῖσθαι. καὶ εἶναι τὸ μὲν ἐγειρόμε-
νον ἀλόγως καὶ ἐφέλκεσθαι τῇ φαντασίᾳ τὸν
λόγον, τὸ δὲ ἀρχόμενον ἀπὸ λόγου καὶ λῆγον εἰς
50 τὸ πεφυκὸς χολοῦσθαι· καὶ παρὰ τοῦ φυτικοῦ καὶ
γεννητικοῦ ἄμφω γίγνεσθαι κατασκευάζοντος τὸ
σῶμα οἷον ἀντιληπτικὸν ἡδέων καὶ λυπηρῶν, τὸ δὲ
πεποιηκέναι χολῶδες καὶ πικρόν. καὶ ⟨τῷ⟩ [2] ἐν
τοιούτῳ ⟨εἶναι⟩ [2] ψυχῆς ἴχνος [τῷ ἐν τοιούτῳ
εἶναι] [2] τοιάδε κινεῖσθαι δυσχεραντικὰ καὶ ὀργίλα
55 καὶ τῷ κεκακῶσθαι πρῶτον αὐτὸ κακοῦν πως
ζητεῖν καὶ τὰ ἄλλα καὶ οἷον ὁμοιοῦν ἑαυτῷ.

[1] Igal: καὶ Enn.
[2] transposuimus.

they have been ill-treated, one would be inclined to attribute anger again to the more bodily part and to that which keeps the living organism together. And when the same people are more prone to anger when they are ill than when they are healthy, and when they have not tasted food than when they have eaten, they indicate that fits of anger, or the origins of anger, belong to the qualified body, and that the bile or the blood, as a kind of animating principle, produce these movements of such a kind that, when the qualified body suffers, the blood or the bile are immediately set in motion, and a perception occurs, and the mental image puts the soul in touch with the state of the qualified body, and the soul launches itself against what has caused the pain; but on the other hand, the process can start from above: the reasoning soul, when a wrong appears, even if it is not a wrong which concerns the body, has that impassioned thing just described ready to hand and makes an ally of it, as it is naturally adapted to fight against the enemy which has been shown to it. And there are two kinds of angry passion, one which is irrationally awakened and drags the reason over to its side by means of the mental image, and one which begins in the reason and comes to its conclusion in that which is naturally adapted to be angry; and both of these derive from the power of growth and generation which constructs the body so as to be receptive of pleasures and pains, and it is this which makes the body bilious and bitter. And by being in a body of this kind the trace of soul is moved in this way by displeasure and anger, and, because wrong has been done to it itself first, it tries in a way to wrong the others too and, so to speak, make them

μαρτύριον δὲ τοῦ ὁμοούσιον εἶναι τοῦτο τῷ ἑτέρῳ
ἴχνει ψυχῆς τὸ τοὺς ἧττον τῶν σωματικῶν ἡδέων
ἐφιεμένους καὶ ὅλως σώματος καταφρονοῦντας
ἧττον κινεῖσθαι πρὸς ὀργὰς [καὶ ἀλόγῳ ἀπαθείᾳ].[1]
60 τὸ δὲ τὰ δένδρα μὴ ἔχειν θυμὸν καίπερ τὸ φυτικὸν
ἔχοντα οὐ δεῖ θαυμάζειν· ἐπεὶ οὐδ' αἵματος οὐδὲ
χολῆς αὐτοῖς μέτεστιν. ἐγγενομένων μὲν γὰρ
τούτων ἄνευ αἰσθήσεως ζέσις ἂν ἐγένετο μόνον καὶ
οἷον ἀγανάκτησις, αἰσθήσεως δὲ ἐγγενομένης καὶ
πρὸς τὸ ἀδικοῦν ἂν ἤδη, ὥστε καὶ ἀμύνεσθαι,
65 ὁρμή. ἀλλ' εἰ τὸ ἄλογον τῆς ψυχῆς διαιροῖτο εἰς τὸ
ἐπιθυμητικὸν καὶ θυμοειδὲς καὶ τὸ μὲν εἴη τὸ
φυτικόν, τὸ δὲ θυμοειδὲς ἐξ αὐτοῦ ἴχνος περὶ αἷμα
ἢ χολὴν ἢ τὸ συναμφότερον, οὐκ ἂν ὀρθὴ ἡ
ἀντιδιαίρεσις γίνοιτο, τοῦ μὲν προτέρου, τοῦ δὲ
ὑστέρου ὄντος. ἢ οὐδὲν κωλύει ἄμφω ὕστερα καὶ
70 τῶν ἐπιγενομένων ἐκ τοῦ αὐτοῦ τὴν διαίρεσιν
εἶναι· ὀρεκτικῶν γὰρ ἡ διαίρεσις, ᾗ ὀρεκτικά, οὐ
τῆς οὐσίας, ὅθεν ἐλήλυθεν. ἐκείνη δὲ ἡ οὐσία καθ'
αὑτὴν οὐκ ὄρεξις, ἀλλ' ἴσως τελειοῦσα τὴν ὄρεξιν
συνάψασα αὐτῇ τὴν παρ' αὑτῆς ἐνέργειαν. καὶ τὸ
ἐκπεσὸν δὲ εἰς θυμὸν ἴχνος περὶ τὴν καρδίαν λέγειν
75 οὐκ ἄτοπον· οὐ γὰρ τὴν ψυχὴν ἐνταῦθα, ἀλλὰ τὴν
τοῦ αἵματος ἀρχὴν τοῦ τοιοῦδε ἐνταῦθα λεγέσθω
εἶναι.

[1] del. Harder.

like itself. The fact that those who are less desirous of bodily pleasures and in general despise the body are less moved to anger is evidence that this trace of soul is consubstantial [1] with the other. But there is no need to be surprised that trees do not have a passionate spirit although they have the power of growth, since they have no share of blood or bile. For if these were present in them without sense-perception there would only be a seething and a kind of irritation, but if sense-perception was present as well there would then be a drive against the cause of the wrong, resulting also in a movement of self-defence. But if the irrational part of the soul was divided into the desiring and the passionate, and the first was taken to be the power of growth, and the passionate a trace of it in the blood or the gall or the composite being, the dichotomy would not be a correct one, as one would be prior and one posterior. There is however nothing to prevent both being posterior, and the division being one between two things which are derived from a common source: for the division is one of impulses in so far as they are impulses, not of the substance from which they have come. But that substance in itself is not an impulse, but perhaps it brings the impulse to its goal by taking to itself the activity which comes from it. And it is not absurd to say that the trace of soul which is expressed in passion is in the region of the heart; for this is not to say that the soul is there, but the starting point of the blood which has this qualification.

[1] The occurrence of the word ὁμοούσιος, so theologically important later, as an ordinary philosophical term here should be noted.

29. Πῶς οὖν, εἴπερ τῷ θερμανθέντι τὸ σῶμα
ἔοικεν ἀλλ' οὐ τῷ φωτισθέντι, ἐξελθούσης τῆς
ἄλλης ψυχῆς οὐδέν τι ζωτικὸν ἔχει; ἢ ἔχει ἐπ'
ὀλίγον, ἀπομαραίνεται δὲ θᾶττον, ὥσπερ καὶ ἐπὶ
5 τῶν θερμανθέντων ἀποστάντων τοῦ πυρός. μαρτυροῦσι δὲ καὶ τρίχες φυόμεναι ἐπὶ τῶν νεκρῶν
σωμάτων καὶ ὄνυχες αὐξόμενοι καὶ ζῷα διαιρούμενα
ἐπὶ πολὺ κινούμενα· τοῦτο γὰρ τὸ ἔτι ἐγκείμενον
ἴσως. καὶ εἰ συναπέρχεται δὲ τῇ ἄλλῃ ψυχῇ, οὐ
τεκμήριον τοῦτο τοῦ μὴ ἕτερον εἶναι. καὶ γὰρ
10 ἀπελθόντος ἡλίου οὐ μόνον τὸ ἐφεξῆς φῶς καὶ κατ'
αὐτὸν καὶ ἐξηρτημένον ἀπέρχεται, ἀλλὰ καὶ τὸ ἀπὸ
τούτου εἰς τὸ ἔξω τούτου ὁρώμενον ἐν τοῖς παρακει-
μένοις ἕτερον ὂν ἐκείνου συναπέρχεται. ἆρ' οὖν συναπέρχεται, ἢ φθείρεται; τοῦτο δὲ καὶ ἐπὶ τοῦ
φωτὸς τοῦ τοιούτου ζητητέον καὶ ἐπὶ τῆς ζωῆς τῆς
15 ἐν τῷ σώματι, ἣν δή φαμεν οἰκείαν τοῦ σώματος
εἶναι. ὅτι μὲν γὰρ οὐδέν ἐστιν τοῦ φωτὸς λειπόμενον
ἐν τοῖς πεφωτισμένοις, δῆλον· ἀλλ' εἰ μεταπίπτει εἰς
τὸ πεποιηκὸς ἢ οὐκ ἔστιν ἁπλῶς, ζητεῖ ὁ λόγος.
πῶς οὖν οὐκ ἔστιν ἁπλῶς ὄν γέ τι πρότερον; ἀλλὰ
20 τί ἦν ὅλως; ὅτι μὲν αὐτῶν τῶν σωμάτων, ἀφ'
ὧν τὸ φῶς, ἡ λεγομένη χρόα, [καὶ]¹ ὅταν φθαρτὰ
ᾖ τὰ σώματα, μεταβαλόντων² οὐκ ἔστι, [καὶ]³
οὐδεὶς ζητεῖ, ⟨οἷον⟩⁴ ὅπου τὸ χρῶμα τοῦ πυρὸς
φθαρέντος, ὥσπερ οὐδ' ὅπου τὸ σχῆμα; ἢ

---

¹ del. Theiler.
² Theiler: μεταβαλλόντων Enn., H–S.
³ del. Kleist.
⁴ Theiler.

ON DIFFICULTIES ABOUT THE SOUL II

29. Why, then, supposing that the body is like something warmed, but not like something illuminated, does it not have any trace of life when the other soul has gone out of it? It does have it for a short time, but it fades quickly, just as with things which are warmed when they go away from the fire. There is evidence for this in the growth of hair on corpses, and the growth of their nails, and the living creatures which move for a long time after they have been cut in two; for this is probably the trace of life still present in them. And if it goes away with the other soul, this is not a sign that it is not different from it. For when the sun goes away it is not only the light which is continuous with it and depends on it and is attached to it which goes, but the light which passes from this to that which is outside it and is seen in the things near by it, which is different from that first light, goes away too. Does it then really go away too, or does it perish? This is a question we must ask both about light of this kind and about the life in the body, which we say belongs to the body as its own. It is obvious that there is nothing of the light left in the things illuminated; but our discussion is enquiring whether it changes back into that which produced it or does not exist at all. How then can it not exist at all when it was certainly something before? But what, anyhow, was it? That in the case of corrupt bodies, when the bodies from which the light (which we call colour) comes have changed, the light does not exist is something into which nobody enquires, for instance where the colour of a burnt-out fire is, just as no one enquires where its shape is. But still, shape is a disposition, like clench-

τὸ μὲν σχῆμα σχέσις τις, ὥσπερ συστολὴ τῆς
χειρὸς καὶ ἡ ἔκτασις, χρῶμα δὲ οὐχ οὕτως, ἀλλ᾽
25 ὥσπερ γλυκύτης. τί γὰρ κωλύει φθαρέντος τοῦ
σώματος τοῦ γλυκέος τὴν γλυκύτητα μὴ ἀπολωλέναι καὶ τοῦ εὐώδους τὴν εὐωδίαν, ἐν ἄλλῳ δὲ
σώματι γίνεσθαι, οὐκ αἰσθητὰ δὲ εἶναι διὰ τὸ μὴ
τοιαῦτα εἶναι τὰ σώματα τὰ μετειληφότα, ὥστε
ἀντερείδειν τὰς ἐπ᾽ αὐτῶν γενομένας ποιότητας τῇ
30 αἰσθήσει; οὕτως οὖν καὶ τὸ φῶς τῶν φθαρέντων
σωμάτων μένειν, τὴν δὲ ἀντιτυπίαν τὸ ἐκ πάντων
οὖσαν μὴ μένειν. εἰ μή τις λέγοι νόμῳ ὁρᾶν, καὶ
τὰς λεγομένας ποιότητας μὴ ἐν τοῖς ὑποκειμένοις
εἶναι. ἀλλ᾽ εἰ τοῦτο, ἀφθάρτους ποιήσομεν καὶ οὐ
35 γινομένας ἐν ταῖς τῶν σωμάτων συστάσεσι τὰς
ποιότητας, καὶ οὐδὲ τοὺς λόγους τοὺς ἐν τοῖς
σπέρμασι ποιεῖν τὰς χρόας, οἷον καὶ ἐπὶ τῶν ποικί-
λων ὀρνίθων, ἀλλ᾽ οὔσας συνάγειν ἢ ποιεῖν μέν,
προσχρῆσθαι δὲ καὶ ταῖς ἐν τῷ ἀέρι πλήρει ὄντι
τῶν τοιούτων· καὶ γὰρ καὶ εἶναι ἐν τῷ ἀέρι οὐ
40 τοιαῦτα, οἷα, ὅταν γένηται, ἐν τοῖς σώμασι φαίνεται.
ἀλλ᾽ αὕτη μὲν ἔστω ἡ ἀπορία ἐνθαδὶ κειμένη·
μενόντων δὲ τῶν σωμάτων εἰ συνήρτηται καὶ οὐκ
ἀποτέτμηται, τί κωλύει τὸ φῶς μετακινουμένου
τοῦ σώματος συμμετακινεῖσθαι τό τε προσεχὲς
καὶ εἴ τι τῷ προσεχεῖ συνήρτηται, κἂν μὴ ὁρᾶται
45 ἀπιόν, ὥσπερ οὐδὲ προσιὸν φαίνεται; ἀλλ᾽ ἐπὶ τῆς
ψυχῆς, εἰ συνέπεται τὰ δεύτερα τοῖς προτέροις καὶ

---

[1] The reference is to the doctrine of Democritus the Atomist
that " secondary qualities " exist only " by convention ",

ing and opening the hand, but colour is not like this, but like sweetness. What then prevents sweetness and sweet scent from not perishing with the destruction of the sweet or sweet-scented body, but passing into another body, but not being perceptible because the bodies which have received something of them are not of such a kind that the qualities in them make an impact on sense-perception? So then the light of bodies which have perished would remain, but the repercussion, which is the result of all the [visible] qualities, would not remain. One might of course say that one sees by convention, and that the so-called qualities are not in their substrates.[1] But if this is so, we shall make the qualities indestructible and not originating in the structure of bodies, and [we shall maintain] that it is not the forming principles in the seeds which make the colours, in the case of many-coloured birds, for instance, but they bring existing colours together, or produce them but make use in doing so also of the colours in the air, which is full of things of this kind; for in the air they are not as they appear in bodies when they come to exist in them. But let us leave this difficult question here. When, however, the [luminous] bodies remain unchanged, if the light is continuous with them and not cut off, what prevents it, when the luminous body moves to another place, from moving along with it? [This would apply both to] the light immediately adjacent to the luminous body and to any light which is continuous with that adjacent to it, even if it is not seen to move away, just as it does not appear to approach. But in the case of soul, we have discussed

and really there are only atoms and void: see fr. B 125 Diels-Kranz.

PLOTINUS: ENNEAD IV. 4.

τὰ ἐφεξῆς ἀεὶ τοῖς πρὸ αὐτῶν, ἢ ἐφ᾽ ἑαυτῶν ἕκαστα
καὶ ἐστερημένα τῶν πρὸ αὐτῶν καὶ δυνάμενα ἐφ᾽
ἑαυτῶν μένειν ἢ ὅλως οὐδὲν ἀποτέτμηται τῆς ψυχῆς
μέρος, ἀλλὰ πᾶσαι μία καὶ πολλαί, καὶ ὅστις ὁ
50 τρόπος, ἐν ἄλλοις. ἀλλὰ τί τὸ ἤδη ˙ σώματος
γενόμενον ἴχνος τῆς ψυχῆς ὄν; ἢ εἰ μὲν ψυχή,
συνέψεται, εἴπερ μὴ ἀποτέτμηται, τῷ ψυχῆς
λόγῳ· εἰ δὲ οἷον ζωὴ τοῦ σώματος, ὁ αὐτὸς λόγος
ἐκεῖ, ὃς περὶ φωτὸς ἰνδάλματος ἠπορεῖτο, καὶ εἰ
δυνατὸν ζωὴν ἄνευ ψυχῆς εἶναι, εἰ μὴ ἄρα τῷ
55 παρακεῖσθαι τὴν ψυχὴν ἐνεργοῦσαν εἰς ἄλλο, ταῦτα
σκεπτέον.

30. Νῦν δ᾽ ἐπειδὴ μνήμας μὲν ἐν τοῖς ἄστροις
περιττὰς εἶναι ἐθέμεθα, αἰσθήσεις δὲ ἔδομεν καὶ
ἀκούσεις πρὸς ταῖς ὁράσεσι καὶ εὐχῶν δὴ κλύοντας
ἔφαμεν, ἃς πρὸς ἥλιον ποιούμεθα καὶ δὴ καὶ πρὸς

---

[1] The reference back is to the earlier treatise IV. 9 (8) *If All Souls are One.*

[2] At this point the MSS preserve a note which tells us that in the edition of Eustochius the second book on the soul ended here and the third book began with the next chapter. This is the only evidence for the existence of another edition of the works of Plotinus by his physician Eustochius (see *Life* chs. 2 and 7 and my *Preface* to Vol I, ix). Whether this was the edition from which Eusebius took his quotations in the *Praeparatio Evangelica*, as Henry and Schwyzer, with some probability, still maintain, or whether, as a number of other good Plotinian scholars suppose, Eusebius was using Porphyry's edition, is a much disputed but not very important question: in either case the evidence of the Eusebius quotations confirms the soundness of the textual tradition (see Henry and Schwyzer *Plotini Opera* II (1959) *Praefatio* X–XI). If, of course, we could be certain that Eusebius was using the Eustochius edition, we should have some confirmation of the general belief of Plotinian scholars that Porphyry did not as editor tamper with the text of Plotinus.

elsewhere [1] whether the secondary parts follow along
with the prior ones, and those in successive order go
along always with those before them, or whether all
the individual parts are on their own and separated
from those before them and able to remain permanently on their own, or whether in general no part
of soul is cut off, but all are one and many, and in
what way this is so. But what is that which already
belongs to the body and is a trace of soul? Now if
it is soul, it will, if it is not cut off, go along with the
rational principle of soul. But if it is a kind of life
of the body, the same problem arises which arose
about the vestige of light, and we must also enquire
whether it is possible to have life without soul, except
perhaps by the close presence of soul working on
something else.[2]

30. But now, since we established that memory in
the heavenly bodies was unnecessary, but gave them
perceptions, and hearing as well as sight, and said
that they heard the prayers which we make to the
sun, and other men to the stars,[3] and since it is

[3] The cult of the sun was rare, but not unknown, in the
ancient Greek world: it flourished particularly at Rhodes,
where Helios was the most important god. Socrates prayed
to the sun, and this was not considered unusual (Plato *Symposium* 220D4–5). Everyone admitted that the sun was a god,
even if he was not much worshipped. In Plotinus's own time
the cult of the sun was gaining in importance, and shortly
after his death, in 274, the Emperor Aurelian established the
cult of the Sun Lord of the Empire at Rome, with a college of
senatorial *pontifices*. For devout pagans of the first Christian
centuries the sun was often of central religious importance:
see Julian *Oration* IV (Hymn to King Helios) and Macrobius
Saturnalia I. 17 ff. But the cult of the star-gods was always
rightly regarded in the Greek world as Oriental (especially
Chaldean) and not belonging to the ancient Greek religious
tradition.

PLOTINUS: ENNEAD IV. 4.

5 ἄστρα ἄλλοι τινὲς ἄνθρωποι, καὶ πεπίστευται, ὡς
δι' αὐτῶν αὐτοῖς πολλὰ καὶ τελεῖται καὶ δὴ καὶ
οὕτω ῥᾶστα, ὡς μὴ μόνον πρὸς τὰ δίκαια τῶν
ἔργων συλλήπτορας εἶναι, ἀλλὰ καὶ πρὸς τὰ πολλὰ
τῶν ἀδίκων, τούτων τε πέρι παραπεπτωκότων
ζητητέον—ἔχει γὰρ καὶ καθ' ἑαυτὰ μεγίστας καὶ
10 πολυθρυλλήτους παρὰ τοῖς δυσχεραίνουσιν ἀπορίας,
θεοὺς συνεργοὺς καὶ αἰτίους γίγνεσθαι ἀτόπων
ἔργων, τῶν τε ἄλλων καὶ δὴ καὶ πρὸς ἔρωτας καὶ
ἀκολάστους συλλήψεις—τούτων τε οὖν εἵνεκα καὶ
μάλιστα περὶ οὗ ἐξ ἀρχῆς ὁ λόγος, τῆς μνήμης
αὐτῶν. δῆλον γὰρ ὅτι, εἰ εὐξαμένων ποιοῦσι καὶ
15 οὐ παραχρῆμα δρῶσιν αὐτά, ἀλλ' εἰς ὕστερον καὶ
πάνυ πολλάκις εἰς χρόνους, μνήμην ὧν εὔχονται
ἄνθρωποι πρὸς αὐτοὺς ἔχουσιν. ὁ δὲ πρόσθεν λόγος
ὁ παρ' ἡμῶν λεγόμενος οὐκ ἐδίδου τοῦτο. ἀλλὰ καὶ
πρὸς τὰς εἰς ἀνθρώπους εὐεργεσίας ἦν ἂν τοιοῦτον,
20 οἷον Δήμητρος καὶ Ἑστίας γῆς γε οὔσης εἰ μή τις
τῇ γῇ μόνον τὸ εὖ ποιεῖν τὰ ἀνθρώπεια λέγοι.
ἀμφότερα οὖν πειρατέον δεικνύναι, πῶς τε τὰ τῆς
μνήμης θησόμεθα ἐν τούτοις—ὃ δὴ πρὸς ἡμᾶς ἔχει,
οὐ πρὸς τὰ δοκοῦντα τοῖς ἄλλοις, οἳ οὐ κωλύονται
μνήμας διδόναι—καὶ περὶ τῶν ἀλλοκότως δοκούν-
25 των γίγνεσθαι, ὃ φιλοσοφίας ἔργον ἐπισκέψασθαι,
εἴ πῃ ἔστιν ἀπολογήσασθαι πρὸς τὰ κατὰ θεῶν τῶν

believed that the heavenly bodies accomplish many
things for men, and do so in such a casual way that
they are not only helpers in right actions, but in
many wrong actions too, we must enquire into these
incidental questions—for there are very great difficulties about them in themselves and these are much
talked about by those who dislike the idea that gods
should be culpable accomplices in improper behaviour, especially in love-affairs and wanton couplings
—for these reasons, and particularly about what we
were discussing at the beginning, their memory.
For it is obvious that if when we pray they act, and
do not do it at once, but afterwards, and very often
after a long delay, they have memory of the prayers
which mortals offer to them.   But the argument
which we expounded earlier did not allow this.   But
there would also be some such need of memory for
the conferring of benefits on mortals as with Demeter
and Hestia—earth after all [1]—unless one were to
attribute to the earth alone a beneficent influence on
human life.   We must therefore try to explain both
how we are going to understand the phenomena of
memory in these beings—this is something which
concerns us, not the opinions of others, who are not
prevented from giving [the heavenly bodies] memory—and also about these strange and unpleasant
things which seem to happen, which it is the task of
philosophy to investigate and see if there is any
defence to be found to the charges brought against

[1] Demeter was, naturally, always closely connected (though
not originally identified) with the earth in Greek religious
tradition. The identification of Hestia with earth is to be
found in the 5th century B.C. (Euripides frs. 938 and 944
Nauck) and cp. Plato *Phaedrus* 247A1.

ἐν οὐρανῷ· καὶ δὴ καὶ περὶ αὐτοῦ παντὸς τοῦ
κόσμου—ὡς καὶ εἰς τοῦτον εἰσιν ἡ αἰτία ἡ τοιαύτη—
εἰ πιστοὶ οἱ λέγοντες, οἳ καὶ αὐτόν φασι τὸν
σύμπαντα οὐρανὸν γοητεύεσθαι ὑπὸ ἀνθρώπων τόλ-
30 μης καὶ τέχνης. καὶ περὶ δαιμόνων δὲ ἐπιζητήσει
ὁ λόγος, ὅπως τὰ τοιαῦτα ὑπουργεῖν λέγονται, εἰ μὴ
διὰ τῶν προτέρων λύσιν καὶ τὰ τούτων λαμβάνοι.

31. Καθόλου τοίνυν τὰς ποιήσεις ληπτέον ἁπάσας
καὶ τὰς πείσεις, ὅσαι γίγνονται ἐν τῷ παντὶ κόσμῳ,
τάς τε λεγομένας φύσει, καὶ ὅσαι τέχνῃ γίνονται·
καὶ τῶν φύσει τὰς μὲν φατέον ἐκ τοῦ παντὸς
5 γίνεσθαι εἰς τὰ μέρη καὶ ἐκ τῶν μερῶν εἰς τὸ πᾶν
ἢ μερῶν εἰς μέρη, τὰς δὲ τέχνῃ γινομένας ἢ τῆς
τέχνης, ὥσπερ ἤρξατο, ἐν τοῖς τεχνητοῖς τελευτώ-
σης, ἢ προσχρωμένης δυνάμεσι φυσικαῖς εἰς ἔργων
φυσικῶν ποιήσεις τε καὶ πείσεις. τὰς μὲν οὖν τοῦ
10 ὅλου λέγω, ὅσα τε ἡ φορὰ ἡ πᾶσα ποιεῖ εἰς αὑτὴν
καὶ εἰς τὰ μέρη—κινουμένη γὰρ καὶ αὐτὴ διατί-
θησί πως καὶ τὰ μέρη αὑτῆς—τά τε ἐν αὐτῇ τῇ
φορᾷ καὶ ὅσα δίδωσι τοῖς ἐπὶ γῆς· μερῶν δὲ
πρὸς μέρη πείσεις ⟨καὶ ποιήσεις⟩[1] εὔδηλοί που
παντί, ἡλίου τε πρός τε τὰ ἄλλα σχέσεις [καὶ ποι-
ήσεις][1] καὶ πρὸς τὰ ἐπὶ γῆς καὶ τὰ ἐν τοῖς ἄλλοις
15 στοιχείοις αὐτοῦ τε καὶ τῶν ἄλλων καὶ τῶν ἐπὶ γῆς
καὶ ἐν τοῖς ἄλλοις—περὶ ὧν ἑκάστου ἐξεταστέον.
τέχναι δὲ αἱ μὲν οἰκίαν ποιοῦσαι καὶ τὰ ἄλλα

---

[1] Theiler post Bréhier in versione.

the gods in the sky; and we must also try to explain about the whole universe itself—since this kind of charge is directed against it too—and see if those people are to be believed who say that the whole heavenly system is subject to spells put upon it by the presumption and skill of men. And our discussion will also enquire about spirits, in what way they are said to serve magical purposes, unless the problems of spirits are also solved by the previous discussion.

31. We must, then, take a general view of all actions and experiences which occur in the whole universe, both the ones which are called natural and those which come about by art: we must say that some of the natural ones are effects of the All on its parts and [some] of the parts on the All or of the parts on the parts; and that in those which come about by art the art either ends as it began, in the products of art, or brings in natural powers to help in producing acts and experiences which belong to the works of nature. By the acts of the whole universe I mean those which the whole heavenly circuit does to itself and its parts—for as it moves it disposes both itself and its parts in a certain way—both those within the circuit itself and all the effects which it produces on the things on earth. The effects and actions of parts on parts are obvious, presumably, to everyone, the positions of the sun in relation to the other heavenly bodies and the things on earth, and in the other elements, and not only the actions of the sun but those of the other heavenly bodies and of the things on the earth and in the other elements —each of these requires separate investigation. As for the arts, those which produce a house and the

τεχνητὰ εἰς τοιοῦτον ἔληξαν· ἰατρικὴ δὲ καὶ
γεωργία καὶ αἱ τοιαῦται ὑπηρετικαὶ καὶ βοήθειαν
εἰς τὰ φύσει εἰσφερόμεναι, ὡς κατὰ φύσιν ἔχειν·
20 ῥητορείαν δὲ καὶ μουσικὴν καὶ πᾶσαν ψυχαγωγίαν
ἢ πρὸς τὸ βέλτιον ἢ πρὸς τὸ χεῖρον ἄγειν ἀλλοιού-
σας, ἐν αἷς ζητητέον, ὅσαι αἱ τέχναι καὶ τίνα τὴν
δύναμιν ἔχουσι· καί, εἴπερ οἷόν τε, ἐν τούτοις
ἅπασι τοῖς πρὸς τὴν παροῦσαν χρείαν ἡμῖν καὶ τὸ
25 διατί ἐφ᾽ ὅσον δυνατὸν πραγματευτέον. ὅτι μὲν
οὖν ἡ φορὰ ποιεῖ, αὐτὴν μὲν πρῶτον διαφόρως
διατιθεῖσα καὶ τὰ ἐντὸς αὐτῆς, ἀναμφισβητήτως
μὲν τὰ ἐπίγεια οὐ μόνον τοῖς σώμασιν, ἀλλὰ καὶ
ταῖς τῆς ψυχῆς διαθέσεσι, καὶ τῶν μερῶν ἕκαστον
εἰς τὰ ἐπίγεια καὶ ὅλως τὰ κάτω ποιεῖ, πολλαχῇ
30 δῆλον. εἰ δὲ καὶ ταῦτα εἰς ἐκεῖνα, ὕστερον· νῦν
δὲ τὰ πᾶσιν ἢ τοῖς πλείστοις συγχωρούμενα ἐάσαν-
τες οὕτως ἔχειν, ὅσα διὰ λόγου φανεῖται, πειρατέον
λέγειν τὸν τρόπον ἐξ ἀρχῆς τῆς ποιήσεως λαβόντας.
οὐ γὰρ μόνον θερμὰ καὶ ψυχρὰ καὶ τὰ τοιαῦτα, ἃ δὴ
ποιότητες πρῶται τῶν στοιχείων λέγονται, οὐδ᾽
35 ὅσαι ἐκ τῆς τούτων μίξεως ποιεῖν λεκτέον οὐδὲ
πάντα τὸν ἥλιον θερμότητι, ψύξει δὲ ἄλλον τινά—τί
γὰρ ἂν ψυχρὸν εἴη ἐν οὐρανίῳ [1] καὶ πυρίνῳ σώματι;
—οὐδ᾽ ἄλλον ὑγρῷ πυρί. οὕτω τε γὰρ οὐδὲ τὴν διαφορὰν αὐτῶν λαβεῖν οἷόν τε. πολλὰ δὲ καὶ τῶν
40 γινομένων εἰς τούτων τι οὐχ οἷόν τε ἀναγαγεῖν.
οὐδὲ γὰρ εἴ τις τὰς τῶν ἠθῶν διαφορὰς δοίη αὐτοῖς

---

[1] Harder: οὐρανῷ Enn.*

other products of art terminate in these; but the
arts of medicine and agriculture and others of this
kind are ancillary and help natural things to be in a
natural state; but rhetoric and music and all the
class of arts which influence the soul must be said
to lead men to be better or worse by changing them;
in these we must enquire how many they are and
what is the power they have; and in all these which
are relevant to our present purpose we must, as far
as is possible, concern ourselves with the reason why.
Now it is abundantly clear that the heavenly circuit
acts, first of all disposing itself and the bodies within
it in different ways, and indisputably acting on the
things of earth, not only in their bodies but in the
dispositions of their souls, and that each of the parts
of the circuit acts on the things of earth and in
general on what is below it. But we shall discuss
later whether the things of earth also act on the
heavenly bodies; but for the present, we grant that
what is agreed by all, or by most people, is so, in so
far as rational discussion will show it to be so, and
we must try to explain the way in which the heavenly
bodies act, starting from the beginning. For we
must not simply assert that it is hot and cold and
things of this kind which act, the things which are
called the primary qualities of the elements, nor
that the sun does everything by its heat, and some
other heavenly body by its cold—for what cold
could there be in a fiery body in the heavens?—and
another by its humid fire. In this way it is not
possible to understand the difference between them,
and there are many things which happen which
cannot be referred to one of these qualities as its
cause. For even if one were to attribute differences

κατὰ τὰς τῶν σωμάτων κράσεις διὰ ψυχρότητα
ἐπικρατοῦσαν ἢ διὰ θερμότητα τοιαύτας—πῶς
ἂν φθόνους ἢ ζηλοτυπίας ἢ πανουργίας εἰς ταῦτα
ἀνάγοι; ἀλλ' εἰ καὶ ταῦτα, τύχας γοῦν πῶς, χεί-
45 ρους τε καὶ βελτίους, πλουσίους καὶ πένητας, καὶ
πατέρων εὐγενείας ἢ αὐτῶν, θησαυρῶν τε εὑρέσεις;
μυρία ἄν τις ἔχοι λέγειν πόρρω ἄγων σωματικῆς
ποιότητος τῆς ἐκ τῶν στοιχείων εἰς τὰ τῶν ζῴων
σώματα καὶ ψυχὰς ἰούσης. οὐ μὴν οὐδὲ προαιρέσει
50 ἀναθετέον τῶν ἄστρων καὶ τῇ τοῦ παντὸς γνώμῃ καὶ
τοῖς τούτων λογισμοῖς τὰ συμπίπτοντα περὶ
ἕκαστα τῶν ὑπ' αὐτά. ἄτοπον γὰρ ἐκείνους
μηχανᾶσθαι περὶ τὰ τῶν ἀνθρώπων, ὅπως οἱ μὲν
γένοιντο κλέπται, οἱ δὲ ἀνδραποδισταὶ τοι-
χωρύχοι τε καὶ ἱερόσυλοι, ἄνανδροί τε ἄλλοι
55 καὶ θήλεις τὰ ἔργα καὶ τὰ πάθη καὶ τὰ αἰσχρὰ
δρῶντες. οὐ γὰρ ὅτι θεῶν, ἀλλ' οὐδὲ ἀνθρώπων
μετρίων, τάχα δὲ οὐδὲ ὡντινωνοῦν τὰ τοιαῦτα
ἐργάζεσθαι καὶ καταμηχανᾶσθαι, ἐξ ὧν αὐτοῖς
οὐδ' ἡτισοῦν ὠφέλεια ἂν γίγνοιτο.

32. Εἰ οὖν μήτε σωματικαῖς αἰτίαις ἀναθήσομεν
μήτε προαιρέσεσιν, ὅσα ἔξωθεν εἰς ἡμᾶς τε καὶ τὰ
ἄλλα ζῷα καὶ ὅλως ἐπὶ γῆς ἀφικνεῖται ἐξ οὐρανοῦ,
τίς ἂν εἴη λοιπὴ καὶ εὔλογος αἰτία; πρῶτον τοίνυν

of character to these qualities [and say that] they
were as they were according to the bodily temperaments,[1] because of the predominance of cold or heat
—how could one refer envy or jealousy or wickedness
to these causes? But even if one could, how could
one anyhow make them responsible for fortunes, for
men being good and bad, rich and poor, for the
nobility of their families or themselves, and for the
finding of treasures? One could mention a vast
number of things, leading the discussion very far
from the bodily quality which comes from the elements to the bodies and souls of living creatures.
We must certainly not, either, attribute to the deliberate choice of stars and the decision of the All,
and to their rational calculations, what happens to
the individuals subject to them. For it would be
inappropriate for those divinities to plan human
affairs so that some men became thieves, and other
kidnappers, housebreakers and temple-robbers, others
again effeminate, womanish in their doings and feelings and committing indecencies. So far from being
appropriate behaviour for gods, it would not even be
appropriate for respectable men, or perhaps any kind
of men, to do and plan things like this, from which
they would get not the slightest benefit.

32. If, then, we are not to attribute all that comes
from the sky to us and the other living creatures,
and in general upon the earth, to bodily causes or
the deliberate choices of the heavenly bodies, what
reasonable explanation is left? First of all we must

---

[1] The " bodily temperaments " are those of men, not of the
stars. Plotinus follows a long Greek tradition in attributing
differences in emotional character and strength of the desires
to the varying proportions of the elements mixed in the body.

5 θετέον ζῷον ἓν πάντα τὰ ζῷα τὰ ἐντὸς αὐτοῦ
περιέχον τόδε τὸ πᾶν εἶναι, ψυχὴν μίαν ἔχον εἰς
πάντα αὐτοῦ μέρη, καθόσον ἐστὶν ἕκαστον αὐτοῦ
μέρος· μέρος δὲ ἕκαστόν ἐστι τὸ ἐν τῷ παντὶ
αἰσθητῷ, κατὰ μὲν τὸ σῶμα καὶ πάντη, ὅσον δὲ
καὶ ψυχῆς τοῦ παντὸς μετέχει, κατὰ τοσοῦτον καὶ
10 ταύτῃ· καὶ τὰ μὲν μόνης ταύτης μετέχοντα κατὰ
πᾶν ἐστι μέρη, ὅσα δὲ καὶ ἄλλης, ταύτῃ ἔχει τὸ μὴ
μέρη πάντῃ εἶναι, πάσχει δὲ οὐδὲν ἧττον παρὰ τῶν
ἄλλων, καθόσον αὐτοῦ τι ἔχει, καὶ κατ' ἐκεῖνα, ἃ
ἔχει. συμπαθὲς δὴ πᾶν τοῦτο τὸ ἕν, καὶ ὡς ζῷον
15 ἕν, καὶ τὸ πόρρω δὴ ἐγγύς, ὥσπερ ἐφ' ἑνὸς τῶν
καθέκαστα ὄνυξ καὶ κέρας καὶ δάκτυλος καὶ ἄλλο
τι τῶν οὐκ ἐφεξῆς ἀλλὰ διαλείποντος τοῦ μεταξὺ
καὶ παθόντος οὐδὲν ἔπαθε τὸ οὐκ ἐγγύς. οὐ γὰρ
ἐφεξῆς τῶν ὁμοίων κειμένων, διειλημμένων δὲ
ἑτέροις μεταξύ, τῇ δὲ ὁμοιότητι συμπασχόντων,
20 καὶ εἰς τὸ πόρρω ἀφικνεῖσθαι ἀνάγκη τὸ παρὰ τοῦ
μὴ παρακειμένου δρώμενον· ζῴου τε ὄντος καὶ εἰς
ἓν τελοῦντος οὐδὲν οὕτω πόρρω τόπῳ, ὡς μὴ ἐγγὺς
εἶναι τῇ τοῦ ἑνὸς ζῴου πρὸς τὸ συμπαθεῖν φύσει.

posit that this All is a " single living being which encompasses all the living beings that are within it "; it has one soul which extends to all its parts, in so far as each individual thing is a part of it; and each thing in the perceptible All is a part of it, and completely a part of it as regards its body; and in so far as it participates in the soul of the All, it is to this extent a part of it in this way too; and those things which participate in the soul of the All alone are altogether parts, but all those which also participate in another soul are in this way not altogether parts, but none the less are affected by the other parts in so far as they have something of the All, and in a way corresponding to what they have.[1] This one universe is all bound together in shared experience and is like one living creature, and that which is far is really near, just as, in one of the individual living things, a nail or horn or finger or one of the other limbs which is not contiguous: the intermediate part leaves a gap in the experience and is not affected, but that which is not near is affected. For the like parts are not situated next to each other, but are separated by others between, but share their experiences because of their likeness, and it is necessary that something which is done by a part not situated beside it should reach the distant part; and since it is a living thing and all belongs to a unity nothing is so distant in space that it is not close enough to the

---

[1] The quotation which introduces this sentence is Plato *Timaeus* 30D3–31A1. The doctrine indicated here, that men are truly parts of the all but not only parts—there is something in them which transcends the organic unity of the cosmos in which their lower natures share—is of great importance to Plotinus: see the *Introduction* to this treatise, p. 27.

τὸ μὲν οὖν ὁμοιότητα πρὸς τὸ ποιοῦν ἔχον πεῖσιν
ἔχει οὐκ ἀλλοτρίαν, ἀνομοίου δὲ ὄντος τοῦ ποιοῦν-
25 τος ἀλλότριον τὸ πάθημα καὶ οὐ προσηνὲς τὸ πάσχον ἴσχει. βλαβερὰν δὲ ποίησιν ἄλλου πρὸς ἄλλου ἑνὸς ὄντος ζῴου οὐ δεῖ τεθαυμακέναι· ἐπεὶ καὶ
ἐφ' ἡμῶν ἐν ταῖς ἐνεργείαις ταῖς ἡμετέραις βλάπτοι
ἂν ἄλλο πρὸς ἄλλου μέρος, ἐπεὶ καὶ χολὴ καὶ ὁ
θυμὸς ἄλλο, ὡς δοκεῖ, πιέζει καὶ κεντεῖ. καὶ δὴ
30 καὶ ἐν τῷ παντὶ ἔστι τι θυμῷ καὶ χολῇ ἀνάλογον
καὶ ἄλλο ἄλλῳ· καὶ ἐν τοῖς φυτοῖς δὲ ἐμπόδιον
ἔσται ἄλλο ἄλλῳ, ὥστε καὶ ἀφαυᾶναι. τοῦτο δὲ
οὐ μόνον ἓν ζῷον, ἀλλὰ καὶ πολλὰ ὂν ὁρᾶται·
ὥστε καθόσον μὲν ἕν, ἕκαστον τῷ ὅλῳ σῴζεται,
καὶ καθόσον δὲ καὶ πολλά, πρὸς ἄλληλα συνιόντα
35 πολλαχῇ τῷ διαφόρῳ ἔβλαψε· καὶ πρὸς τὴν
αὑτοῦ χρείαν ἄλλο ἕτερον ἔβλαψε, καὶ δὴ καὶ
τροφὴν ἐποιήσατο συγγενὲς ἅμα καὶ διάφορον
ὑπάρχον· καὶ σπεῦδον ἕκαστον ἑαυτῷ κατὰ φύσιν,
ὅσον τε οἰκεῖον τοῦ ἑτέρου, λαμβάνει εἰς αὑτό, καὶ
ὅσον ἀλλότριον ἐγίνετο, ἀφανίζει εὐνοίᾳ τῇ ἑαυτοῦ.
40 ἔργον τε τὸ αὑτοῦ ποιοῦν ἕκαστον τὸ μὲν δυνηθὲν
ἀπολαῦσαί τι τῶν αὑτοῦ ἔργων ὠφέλησεν, ὃ δ'
ἀδύνατον ἦν ὑπομεῖναι τὴν ὁρμὴν τοῦ ἔργου,
ἠφάνισεν ἢ ἔβλαψεν, ὥσπερ ὅσα αὐανθείη ἂν
παριόντος πυρός, ἢ ζῷα ἐλάττω ὑπὸ μειζόνων
δρόμου παρασυρείη ἢ καί που πατηθείη. πάντων
45 δὲ τούτων ἡ γένεσις ἥ τε φθορὰ ἀλλοίωσίς τε
πρὸς τὸ χεῖρον ἢ βέλτιον τὴν τοῦ ἑνὸς ζῴου

nature of the one living thing to share experience. So, then, that part which has a likeness to that which is acting upon it has an experience which is not alien to it, but if that which is acting is unlike, that which is affected has an experience which is alien and unpleasant. But one should not be surprised if the action of one part on another is harmful when it is one living creature: for in ourselves too in our activities one part can harm another, since bile and the passionate spirit, so it seems, oppress and sting another part. And there is certainly something in the All which corresponds to bile and the passionate spirit, and other things which correspond to others [in our bodies]; and in plants one part gets in the way of another, so as even to make it wither. This All is visibly not only one living creature, but many; so that in so far as it is one, each individual part is preserved by the whole, but in so far as it is many, when the many encounter each other they often injure each other because they are different; and one injures another to supply its own need, and even makes a meal of another which is at the same time related to and different from it; and each one, naturally striving to do the best for itself, takes to itself that part of the other which is akin to it, and makes away with all that is alien to itself because of its self-love. Each as it does its own work benefits that which can profit in any way from its workings, but makes away with or injures that which cannot endure the impact of its activity, like the things which are withered when fire comes near them, or the smaller animals which are swept aside or even trampled underfoot by the rush of larger ones. The coming into being and destruction and alteration for

ἐκείνου ἀνεμπόδιστον καὶ κατὰ φύσιν ἔχουσαν ζωὴν
ἀποτελεῖ, ἐπείπερ οὐχ οἷόν τε ἦν ἕκαστα οὕτως
ἔχειν, ὡς μόνα ὄντα, οὐδὲ πρὸς αὑτὰ τὸ τέλος
εἶναι καὶ βλέπειν μέρη ὄντα, ἀλλὰ πρὸς ἐκεῖνο,
50 οὗπερ καὶ μέρη, διάφορά τε ὄντα μὴ πάντα τὸ
αὑτῶν ἐν μιᾷ ζωῇ ὄντα ἀεὶ ἔχειν· οὐκ ἦν τε
μένειν οὐδὲν πάντῃ ὡσαύτως, εἴπερ ἔμελλε τὸ
πᾶν μένειν ἐν τῷ κινεῖσθαι τὸ μένειν ἔχον.

33. Τῆς δὴ φορᾶς τὸ εἰκῆ οὐκ ἐχούσης, ἀλλὰ
λόγῳ τῷ κατὰ τὸ ζῷον φερομένης, ἔδει καὶ
συμφωνίαν τοῦ ποιοῦντος πρὸς τὸ πάσχον εἶναι
καί τινα τάξιν εἰς ἄλληλα καὶ πρὸς ἄλληλα
5 συντάσσουσαν, ὥστε καθ' ἑκάστην σχέσιν τῆς
φορᾶς καὶ τῶν αὖ ὑπὸ τὴν φορὰν ἄλλην καὶ ἄλλην
τὴν διάθεσιν εἶναι, οἷον μίαν ὄρχησιν ἐν ποικίλῃ
χορείᾳ ποιούντων· ἐπεὶ καὶ ἐν ταῖς παρ' ἡμῖν
ὀρχήσεσι τὰ μὲν ἔξω [πρὸς τὴν ὄρχησιν]¹ καθ'
ἕκαστον τῶν κινημάτων, ὡς ἑτέρως μεταβαλλόντων
10 τῶν συντελούντων πρὸς τὴν ὄρχησιν, αὐλῶν τε καὶ
ᾠδῶν καὶ τῶν ἄλλων τῶν συνηρτημένων, τί ἄν τις
λέγοι φανερῶν ὄντων; ἀλλὰ τὰ μέρη τοῦ τὴν
ὄρχησιν παρεχομένου καθ' ἕκαστον σχῆμα ἐξ
ἀνάγκης οὐκ ἂν ὡσαύτως δύναιτο ἔχειν, τῶν μελῶν
τοῦ σώματος ταύτῃ συνεπομένου καὶ καμπτομένου
15 καταπιεζομένου² μὲν ἑτέρου, ἀνιεμένου δὲ ἄλλου,
καὶ τοῦ μὲν πονοῦντος, τοῦ δὲ ἀναπνοήν τινα ἐν τῷ
διαφόρῳ σχηματισμῷ δεχομένου. καὶ ἡ μὲν
προαίρεσις τοῦ ὀρχουμένου πρὸς ἄλλο βλέπει, τὰ
δὲ πάσχει τῇ ὀρχήσει ἑπομένως καὶ ὑπουργεῖ τῇ

¹ del. Theiler ut iteratum e lin. 9–10.
² Igal: καὶ πιεζομένου Enn.: καὶ ⟨τῶν μελῶν⟩ πιεζομένου
Theiler.

worse or better of all these individual things brings
to its fulness the unhindered life according to nature
of that one [universal] living creature; since it was
not possible for all the individual things to be as if
they were alone nor for the final purpose to be
directed and look towards them when they are
[only] parts, but it must be directed to that of
which they are parts, and since they are different,
they cannot all have their own for ever in a single
life; it was not possible for anything to persist altogether the same, if the All was going to persist,
which has its persistence in its movement.

33. The heavenly circuit has nothing casual in it,
but goes according to the rational principle of its
living organism; there must therefore be a harmony
of action and experience and an order which arranged
things together, adapting them and bringing them
into due relation with each other, so that according
to every figure of the heavenly circuit there is a
different disposition of the things which it governs,
as if they were performing a single ballet in a rich
variety of dance-movements. In our ballets, too,
there is no need to mention, since they are obvious,
the external elements, the way in which piping and
singing and everything else which joins in contributing to the total effect of the performance change
variously at every movement. But the parts of the
dancer's body, too, cannot possibly keep the same
position in every figure: as his body follows the
pattern of the dance and bends with it, one of his
limbs is pressed hard down, another relaxed, one
works hard and painfully, another is given a rest as
the figuring changes. The dancer's intention looks
elsewhere; his limbs are affected in accordance with

ὀρχήσει καὶ συναποτελεῖ τὴν πᾶσαν, ὥστε τὸν
20 ἔμπειρον ὀρχήσεως εἰπεῖν ἄν, ὡς τῷ τοιούτῳ
σχηματισμῷ αἴρεται μὲν ὑψοῦ τοδὶ μέλος τοῦ
σώματος, συγκάμπτεται δὲ τοδί, τοδὶ δὲ ἀπο-
κρύπτεται, ταπεινὸν δὲ ἄλλο γίνεται, οὐκ ἄλλως τοῦ
ὀρχηστοῦ προελομένου τοῦτο ποιεῖν, ἀλλ' ἐν τῇ
τοῦ ὅλου σώματος ὀρχήσει θέσιν ταύτην ἀναγκαίαν
25 ἴσχοντος τοῦδε τοῦ μέρους τοῦ τὴν ὄρχησιν
διαπεραίνοντος. τοῦτον τοίνυν τὸν τρόπον καὶ τὰ
ἐν οὐρανῷ φατέον ποιεῖν, ὅσα ποιεῖ, τὰ δὲ καὶ
σημαίνειν, μᾶλλον δὲ τὸν μὲν ὅλον κόσμον τὴν
ὅλην αὑτοῦ ζωὴν ἐνεργεῖν κινοῦντα ἐν αὑτῷ τὰ
μέρη τὰ μεγάλα καὶ μετασχηματίζοντα ἀεί, τὰς δὲ
30 σχέσεις τῶν μερῶν πρὸς ἄλληλα καὶ πρὸς τὸ ὅλον
καὶ τὰς διαφόρους αὐτῶν θέσεις ἑπόμενα καὶ τὰ
ἄλλα, ὡς ζῴου ἑνὸς κινουμένου, παρέχεσθαι, ὡδὶ
μὲν ἴσχοντα κατὰ τὰς ὡδὶ σχέσεις καὶ θέσεις καὶ
σχηματισμούς, ὡδὶ δὲ κατὰ τὰς ὡδί, ὡς μὴ τοὺς
σχηματιζομένους τοὺς ποιοῦντας εἶναι, ἀλλὰ τὸν
35 σχηματίζοντα, μηδ' αὖ τὸν σχηματίζοντα ἄλλο
ποιοῦντα ἄλλο ποιεῖν—οὐ γὰρ εἰς ἄλλο—ἀλλὰ
αὐτὸν πάντα τὰ γινόμενα εἶναι, ἐκεῖ μὲν τὰ
σχήματα, ἐνθαδὶ δὲ τὰ συνεπόμενα τοῖς σχήμασιν
ἀναγκαῖα παθήματα περὶ τὸ οὑτωσὶ κινούμενον
40 ζῷον εἶναι, καὶ αὖ περὶ τὸ οὑτωσὶ συγκείμενον καὶ
συνεστὼς φύσει καὶ πάσχον καὶ δρῶν εἰς αὑτὸ
ἀνάγκαις.

---

[1] The dancer here, as in III. 2. 16, is one of the great solo
ballet artists of the Empire, the *pantomimi*, who danced whole
mythological stories by themselves to a choral and orchestral
accompaniment. These excellent descriptions, and the choice

the dance and serve the dance, and help to make it perfect and complete; and the connoisseur of ballet can say that to fit a particular figure one limb is raised, another bent together, one is hidden, another degraded; the dancer does not choose to make these movements for no reason, but each part of him as he performs the dance has its necessary position in the dancing of the whole body.[1] It is in this way, then, that we must say that the beings in the sky do what they do (but some things they only indicate); or, better, we should say that the whole universe actively lives its own complete life, moving its great parts within itself, and continually rearranging them, and, as when a single living thing moves, the relations of the parts to each other and to the whole and their different positions make everything else follow, being disposed in one way according to one set of relationships, positions, and arrangements and another way according to another, so that it is not the arranged parts which do what is done, but the arranger; but the arranger is not a doer distinct from what he does —for he is not acting on something different from himself—but he is himself all the things he does, the arrangements up in the sky and their consequences here below, which are experiences necessarily affecting the living being when it moves in this particular way, the living being, that is, which is composed in this particular way and naturally conjoined, and necessarily both acts upon itself and experiences its own action.

of the *pantomimus* to symbolise the living and moving harmony of the cosmos, suggest that Plotinus may at some period of his life have attended and enjoyed performances by *pantomimi*. The coincidence of symbolism with the (much later) bronze figures of the dancing Shiva from India is striking.

34. Ἡμᾶς δὲ διδόντας τὸ μέρος αὐτῶν εἰς τὸ
πάσχειν, ὅσον ἦν ἡμέτερον ἐκείνου τοῦ σώματος,
μὴ τὸ πᾶν ἐκείνου νομίζοντας, μέτρια παρ᾽ αὐτοῦ
πάσχειν· ὥσπερ οἱ ἔμφρονες τῶν θητευόντων τὸ
5 μέν τι τοῖς δεσπόζουσιν ὑπηρετοῦντες, τὸ δ᾽
αὐτῶν ὄντες, μετριωτέρων τῶν παρὰ τοῦ δεσπότου
ἐπιταγμάτων διὰ τοῦτο τυγχάνοντες, ἅτε μὴ
ἀνδράποδα ὄντες μηδὲ τὸ πᾶν ἄλλου. τὸ δὲ τῶν
σχηματισμῶν διάφορον τῶν θεόντων μὴ ἰσοταχῶν
ὄντων ἀναγκαῖον ἦν γίνεσθαι, ὡς νῦν γίνεται.
10 λόγῳ δὲ φερομένων καὶ διαφόρων τῶν σχέσεων
τοῦ ζῴου γινομένων, εἶτα καὶ ἐνταῦθα τούτων τῶν
παρ᾽ ἡμῖν συμπαθῶν πρὸς τὰ ἐκεῖ γινομένων,
εὔλογον ζητεῖν, πότερα συνέπεσθαι φατέον ταῦτα
συμφωνοῦντα ἐκείνοις, ἢ τὰ σχήματα τὰς δυνάμεις
τῶν ποιουμένων ἔχειν, καὶ τὰ σχήματα ἁπλῶς
15 ἢ τὰ τούτων. οὐ γὰρ ὁ αὐτὸς σχηματισμὸς
ταὐτοῦ ἐπ᾽ ἄλλου καὶ αὖ ἄλλων τὴν αὐτὴν σημ-
ασίαν ἢ ποίησιν ἐργάζεται· ἐπεὶ καὶ καθ᾽ αὑτὸν
ἕκαστος διάφορον ἔχειν τὴν φύσιν δοκεῖ. ἢ ὀρθῶς
ἔχει λέγειν τὴν τούτων σχημάτισιν ταδὶ καὶ
τοιάνδε διάθεσιν εἶναι, τὴν δὲ ἄλλων τὴν αὐτὴν
20 οὖσαν ἐν σχηματισμῷ ἄλλην; ἀλλ᾽ εἰ τοῦτο,
οὐκέτι τοῖς σχήμασιν, ἀλλ᾽ αὐτοῖς τοῖς σχηματι-
ζομένοις δώσομεν. ἢ συναμφοτέροις; τοῖς γοῦν
αὐτοῖς διάφορον σχέσιν λαβοῦσιν, ἀλλὰ καὶ τῷ

34. But we, by yielding that part of ourselves to experience which was our share of the body of the All, and not considering the whole of ourselves to belong to it, are subject to experience only within reasonable limits: just as sensible serfs with one part of themselves serve their master, but with another belong to themselves, and therefore receive more reasonably limited orders from their master since they are not slaves and do not totally belong to another. But it was necessary that the arrangements of the heavenly bodies should vary as they now do, since the heavenly bodies do not run their courses at equal speeds. But since the heavenly bodies move according to reason and their relationships within the [universal] living being vary, and then here below these events occur in our own sphere in sympathy with those above, it is reasonable to en-quire whether we should assert that these earthly occurrences follow on those above by correspondence, or whether the figures have the powers which bring about what is done, and whether it is simply the figures or the figures made by particular heavenly bodies. For the same arrangement of the same body in relation to another body and then again to others does not produce the same signification or action: since even by itself each appears to have a different nature. Or is it right to say that the configuration of these particular heavenly bodies is of a particular kind and this specific disposition, but the configura-tion of other heavenly bodies which is the same in arrangement is another? But if this is so, we shall give the power no more to the figures but to the actual bodies which are arranged. Should we give it to both? For we shall certainly give different

αὐτῷ μόνῳ διάφορον τόπον ἄλλα. ἀλλὰ τί;
ποιήσεις ἢ σημασίας; ἢ τῷ συναμφοτέρῳ τῷ
25 σχηματισμῷ τῷ τούτων ἄμφω καὶ ποιήσεις καὶ
σημασίας ἐν πολλοῖς, ἀλλαχοῦ δὲ σημασίας μόνον.
οὗτος τοίνυν ὁ λόγος δυνάμεις μὲν δίδωσι τοῖς
σχήμασι, δυνάμεις δὲ καὶ τοῖς σχηματιζομένοις·
ἐπεὶ καὶ τῶν ὀρχουμένων ἔχει μὲν δύναμίν τινα καὶ
χεὶρ ἑκατέρα καὶ τὰ ἄλλα μέλη, ἔχει δὲ καὶ τὰ
30 σχήματα πολλήν, τρίτα δέ ἐστι τὰ συνεπόμενα,
αὐτῶν τε τῶν εἰς τὴν ὄρχησιν παραλαμβανομένων
τὰ μέρη καὶ ἐξ ὧν ταῦτα, οἷον χειρὸς τὰ συνθλι-
βόμενα καὶ νεῦρα καὶ φλέβες συμπαθοῦντα.

35. Πῶς δὴ οὖν αὗται αἱ δυνάμεις; σαφέστερον
γὰρ πάλιν λεκτέον, τί τὸ τρίγωνον παρὰ τὸ
τρίγωνον διάφορον ἔχει, τί δὲ ὁδὶ πρὸς τονδί, καὶ
κατὰ τί τοδὶ ἐργάζεται καὶ μέχρι τίνος. ἐπειδὴ
5 οὔτε τοῖς σώμασιν αὐτῶν οὔτε ταῖς προαιρέσεσιν
ἀπέδομεν τὰς ποιήσεις· τοῖς μὲν σώμασιν, ὅτι μὴ
μόνον σώματος ἦν ποιήματα τὰ γινόμενα, ταῖς δὲ
προαιρέσεσιν, ὅτι ἄτοπον ἦν προαιρέσεσι θεοὺς
ποιεῖν ἄτοπα. εἰ δὲ μνημονεύοιμεν, ὅτι ζῷον ἓν
ὑπεθέμεθα εἶναι, καὶ ὅτι οὕτως ἔχον συμπαθὲς
10 αὐτὸ ἑαυτῷ, ἐξανάγκης ἔδει εἶναι, καὶ δὴ καὶ ὅτι

---

[1] " Triangles " are among the important " configurations "
or " aspects " of the apparent patterns of the signs of the
Zodiac at various seasons on which a great deal of astrological

powers to the same heavenly bodies when they take up different relative positions, and even to the same single one when it occupies a different place. But what powers are we giving them? Powers of action or of signification? To the combination, the arrangement of these particular stars, both, and in many cases there is both action and signification, but elsewhere there are only significations. This argument, then, gives powers to the figures and powers to the bodies arranged: since with dancers each hand has a distinct power and so have the other limbs, but the figures also have great power, and then there is a third group of consequentially effective things, the parts of the limbs which are brought into the dance and their constituents, for instance the clenched fingers of the hand and the muscles and veins which are affected along with them.

35. How, then, should we understand these powers? We need to explain again more clearly what is the difference between triangle and triangle,[1] in what way this heavenly body differs from that, and why and up to what point it acts in this particular way. For we did not attribute their activities either to their bodies or to their deliberate choices: not to their bodies, because the things which happened were not the works of body alone, and not to their choices, because it would be inappropriate for gods to choose to do inappropriate things. But if we remember that we posited that the universe is a single living thing, and that since it is so it was absolutely necessary for it to have an internal self-communication of its experiences; and if we remember further that the

calculation was based: cp. II. 3. 4, where Plotinus shows himself much more hostile to the astrologers than here.

κατὰ λόγον ἡ διέξοδος τῆς ζωῆς σύμφωνος ἑαυτῇ
ἅπασα, καὶ ὅτι τὸ εἰκῆ οὐκ ἔστιν ἐν τῇ ζωῇ, ἀλλὰ
μία ἁρμονία καὶ τάξις, καὶ οἱ σχηματισμοὶ κατὰ
λόγον, καὶ κατ' ἀριθμοὺς δὲ ἕκαστα καὶ τὰ
χορεύοντα ζῴου μέρη, ἄμφω ἀνάγκη ὁμολογεῖν
15 τὴν ἐνέργειαν τοῦ παντὸς εἶναι, τά τε ἐν αὐτῷ
γινόμενα σχήματα καὶ τὰ σχηματιζόμενα μέρη
αὐτοῦ, καὶ τὰ τούτοις ἑπόμενα καὶ οὕτω, καὶ
τοῦτον τὸν τρόπον ζῆν τὸ πᾶν, καὶ τὰς δυνάμεις
εἰς τοῦτο συμβάλλειν, ἅσπερ [1] καὶ ἔχοντες ἐγένοντο
ὑπὸ τοῦ ἐν λόγοις [2] πεποιηκότος. καὶ τὰ μὲν
20 σχήματα οἷον λόγους εἶναι ἢ διαστάσεις ζῴου
καὶ ῥυθμοὺς καὶ σχέσεις ζῴου κατὰ λόγον, τὰ δὲ
διεστηκότα καὶ ἐσχηματισμένα μέλη· ἀλλὰ [3] καὶ
εἶναι τοῦ ζῴου δυνάμεις χωρὶς [τῆς] [4] προαιρέσεως
ἄλλας τὰς ὡς ζῴου μέρη, ἐπεὶ τὸ τῆς προαιρέσεως
αὐτοῖς ἔξω καὶ οὐ συντελοῦν πρὸς τοῦ ζῴου τοῦδε
25 τὴν φύσιν. μία γὰρ ἡ προαίρεσις ἑνὸς ζῴου, αἱ δὲ
δυνάμεις αἱ ἄλλαι αὐτοῦ πρὸς αὐτὸ πολλαί. ὅσαι δ'
ἐν αὐτῷ προαιρέσεις, πρὸς τὸ αὐτό, πρὸς ὃ καὶ ἡ
τοῦ παντὸς ἡ μία. ἐπιθυμία μὲν γὰρ ἄλλου πρὸς
ἄλλο τῶν ἐν αὐτῷ· λαβεῖν γάρ τι τῶν ἑτέρων ἐθέλει
μέρος τὸ ἄλλο μέρος ἐνδεὲς ὂν αὐτό· καὶ θυμὸς
30 πρὸς ἕτερον, ὅταν τι παραλυπῇ, καὶ ἡ αὔξησις
παρ' ἄλλου καὶ ἡ γένεσις εἰς ἄλλο τῶν μερῶν.
τὸ δ' ὅλον καὶ ἐν τούτοις μὲν ταῦτα ποιεῖ, αὐτὸ
δὲ τὸ ἀγαθὸν ζητεῖ, μᾶλλον δὲ βλέπει. τοῦτο
τοίνυν καὶ ἡ ὀρθὴ προαίρεσις ἡ ὑπὲρ τὰ πάθη

---

[1] Theiler: ὥσπερ Enn.*
[2] Enn., H–S[1] recte: εὐλόγως H–S[2].
[3] Dodds, Cilento: ἄλλα Enn.*
[4] del. Theiler.

process of its life must be rational and all in tune
with itself, and that there is nothing casual in its life
but a single melody and order, and that the celestial
arrangements are rational, and each individual part
moves by numbers, as do the dancing parts of the
living being, we must admit that both are the activity
of the All, the figures in it and the parts of it which
are arranged in figures (and the consequences of
these and how they follow), and that this is the way
in which the All lives, and the powers contribute to
this, which they were brought into existence possessing by him who made them in their rational principles. And the figures are like the proportions and
intervals of the living being and its rational rhythms
and relationships, and the bodies which are set at
intervals and arranged in figures are its limbs; but
there are other powers of the living being, which are,
apart from deliberate choice, like parts of the living
being, since what belongs to deliberate choice in these
beings is outside [the universal organism] and does
not contribute to the nature of this living being. For
the deliberate choice of the one living being is one,
but the other powers which it has directed towards
itself are many. But all the choices which occur in
it are directed to the same end to which that one
choice of the All is directed. For the desire of one
thing in it is directed towards another thing in it;
for one part wants to take a part of the others since
it is itself in need; and anger is felt against another
part, when it is annoying in some way, and growth
derives from another of the parts and coming into
being results in another. But the Whole does these
things in these parts, but itself seeks the Good, or
rather gazes upon it. This too is what the right

ζητεῖ καὶ εἰς τὸ αὐτὸ ταύτῃ συμβάλλει· ἐπεὶ καὶ
35 τῶν παρ' ἄλλῳ θητευόντων πολλὰ μὲν τῶν ἔργων
αὐτοῖς βλέπει πρὸς τὰ ἐπιταχθέντα ὑπὸ τοῦ δεσπότου, ἡ δὲ τοῦ ἀγαθοῦ ὄρεξις πρὸς τὸ αὐτό, πρὸς
ὃ καὶ ὁ δεσπότης. εἰ δὴ δρᾷ τι ἥλιος καὶ τὰ ἄλλα
ἄστρα εἰς τὰ τῇδε, χρὴ νομίζειν αὐτὸν μὲν ἄνω
βλέποντα εἶναι—ἐφ' ἑνὸς γὰρ τὸν λόγον ποιητέον
40 —ποιεῖσθαι δὲ παρ' αὐτοῦ, ὥσπερ τὸ θερμαίνεσθαι
τοῖς ἐπὶ γῆς, οὕτω καὶ εἴ τι μετὰ τοῦτο, ψυχῆς
διαδόσει, ὅσον ἐν αὐτῷ, φυτικῆς [1] ψυχῆς πολλῆς
οὔσης. καὶ ἄλλο δὲ ὁμοίως οἷον ἐλλάμπον
δύναμιν παρ' αὐτοῦ ἀπροαίρετον διδόναι. καὶ
45 πάντας [2] δὴ ἕν τι οὕτως ἐσχηματισμένον γενομένους τὴν διάθεσιν ἄλλην καὶ ἄλλην αὖ διδόναι·
ὥστε καὶ τὰ σχήματα δυνάμεις ἔχει—παρὰ γὰρ τὸ
οὕτως ἢ οὕτως ἄλλως καὶ ἄλλως—καὶ δι' αὐτῶν
τῶν ἐσχηματισμένων γίνεσθαί τι—παρὰ γὰρ [τὸ] [3]
τούτους ἄλλο καὶ ἄλλο αὖ παρ' ἄλλους. ἐπεὶ καὶ
50 καθ' αὑτὰ τὰ σχήματα, ὡς δυνάμεις ἔχει, καὶ
ἐπὶ τῶν τῇδε ἄν τις ἴδοι. διατί γὰρ τὰ μὲν
φοβερὰ τοῖς ὁρῶσι τῶν σχημάτων μηδέν τι
προπεπονθότων τῶν φοβουμένων, τὰ δὲ οὐ φοβεῖ
ὀφθέντα; καὶ ἄλλους μὲν ταδί, ἄλλους δὲ ταδί;
ἢ ὅτι εἰς μὲν τὸν [4] τοιόνδε ταδὶ ἐργάζεται, εἰς δὲ

---

[1] Kirchhoff*: φυσικῆς Enn., H–S[1].
[2] πάντας (sc. ἀστέρας, masc. sicut 47–8 ἐσχηματισμένων) et
τούτους suspic. Theiler: πάντα Enn.*
[3] del. Creuzer.
[4] Kirchhoff*: τὸ Enn., H–S.

choice which transcends the emotions seeks and in this way it contributes to the achievement of the same purpose: since when serfs work for another man many of the things they do are directed to fulfilling the commands of their master, but their aspiration to the Good is directed to the same end to which their master also aspires. If then the sun and the other heavenly bodies act in any way on the things here below, one must think that the sun—it is best to speak of one body only—remains looking above, but just as its warming of the things on earth proceeds from it, so do any subsequent actions upon them, by a dissemination of soul, as far as is in its power, since there is plenty of the growth-soul in it. And in the same way any other heavenly body, without choosing to do so, gives off a kind of irradiation from itself. And all the heavenly bodies when they have been unified in this or that particular configuration produce now one and now another disposition of things: so that the figures have power —for according to this or that figure different consequences follow—and something is due to the actual heavenly bodies arranged in the figures—for one consequence follows if these particular heavenly bodies are in the figure, and another if others are. As regards the figures themselves, one can see from what happens here below that they have powers. For why are some figures terrifying to those who see them though those who are terrified have had no experience of evil from them before, but others when they are seen do not terrify? And why do these particular figures terrify some people and different ones others? It is because these particular ones work on a man of a particular kind and

55 τοῦτον ἄλλα, οὐκ ἂν μὴ δυναμένων εἰς τὸ πεφυκὸς
ποιεῖν. καὶ οὑτωσὶ μὲν σχηματισθὲν ἐκίνησε τὴν
ὄψιν, οὑτωσὶ δὲ οὐ τὸν αὐτόν. καὶ γὰρ εἴ τις
λέγοι τὸ κάλλος εἶναι τὸ κινοῦν, διατί τὸν μὲν
τοῦτο, τὸν δὲ ἄλλο ἐκίνησε, μὴ τῆς κατὰ τὸ
σχῆμα διαφορᾶς τὴν δύναμιν ἐχούσης; διατί γὰρ
60 τὰς μὲν χρόας φήσομεν δύναμιν ἔχειν καὶ ποιεῖν,
τὰ δὲ σχήματα οὐ φήσομεν; ἐπεὶ καὶ ὅλως
ἄτοπον εἶναι μέν τι ἐν τοῖς οὖσι, μὴ μέντοι ἔχειν τι
ὃ δύναται. τὸ γὰρ ὂν τοιοῦτον, οἷον ἢ ποιεῖν ἢ
πάσχειν· καὶ ἐν μὲν τοῖς δοτέον τὸ ποιεῖν, ἐπὶ δὲ
τῶν ἄλλων ἄμφω. καὶ ἐν τοῖς ὑποκειμένοις δὲ
65 δυνάμεις καὶ παρὰ τὰ σχήματα· καὶ ἐν τοῖς παρ᾽
ἡμῖν εἰσι πολλαί, ἃς οὐ θερμὰ ἢ ψυχρὰ παρέχεται,
ἀλλὰ γενόμενα ποιότησι διαφόροις καὶ λόγοις
εἰδοποιηθέντα καὶ φύσεως δυνάμεως μεταλαβόντα,
οἷον καὶ λίθων φύσεις καὶ βοτανῶν ἐνέργειαι
θαυμαστὰ πολλὰ παρέχονται.

36. Ποικιλώτατον γὰρ τὸ πᾶν καὶ λόγοι πάντες
ἐν αὐτῷ καὶ δυνάμεις ἄπειροι καὶ ποικίλαι· οἷον
δέ φασι καὶ ἐπ᾽ ἀνθρώπου ἄλλην μὲν δύναμιν
ἔχειν [ὀφθαλμὸν καὶ] [1] ὀστοῦν τόδε, τοδὶ δ᾽ ἄλλην,
5 χειρὸς μὲν τοδὶ καὶ δακτύλου τοῦ ποδός, καὶ
οὐδὲν μέρος εἶναι ὃ μὴ ἔχει καὶ οὐ τὴν αὐτὴν δὲ
ἔχει—ἀγνοοῦμεν δὲ ἡμεῖς, εἰ μή τις τὰ τοιαῦτα
μεμάθηκεν—οὕτω καὶ πολὺ μᾶλλον· μᾶλλον δὲ

---

[1] del. Theiler, Harder.

others on this other man, since they cannot fail to act on that which corresponds to their nature. And something with one kind of figure stimulates one to look at it, but another kind does not stimulate the same man. And if someone were to say that it is the beauty which stimulates, why does one stimulate one man and another another, if it is not the difference in figure which has the power? For why should we assert that colours have power and act, but not assert that figures do? It would be absolutely absurd for something to exist in reality but not to have any power which it could exercise. For anything which exists is of such a kind that it can either act or be acted upon [1]: in some cases we should attribute action, in other cases both. But besides the figures there are also powers in the bodies subject to configuration; and in the bodies in our world there are many powers which are not produced by hot or cold things but by things which have come into existence as the result of different qualities and been formed by rational principles and have a share in the power of nature, as the natures of stones and the active powers of herbs produce many astonishing results.

36. The All is full of the richest variety: all rational formative principles are present in it, and an unbounded store of varied powers. It is like what they say about man, that each of the bones has its own distinctive powers, the bones of the hand one power and the toe-bone another, and there is no part which has not a power, and one different from every other—but we know nothing about it, unless one of us has studied this sort of subject. The

[1] This philosophical commonplace goes back to Plato *Sophist* 247D–E and 248C.

ἴχνος ταῦτα ἐκείνων· ἐν τῷ παντὶ ἀδιήγητον δὲ
καὶ θαυμαστὴν ποικιλίαν εἶναι δυνάμεων, καὶ δὴ
10 καὶ ἐν τοῖς κατ' οὐρανὸν φερομένοις. οὐ γὰρ δή,
ὥσπερ ἄψυχον οἰκίαν μεγάλην ἄλλως καὶ πολλὴν
ἔκ τινων εὐαριθμήτων κατ' εἶδος, οἷον λίθων καὶ
ξύλων, εἰ δὲ βούλει, καὶ ἄλλων τινῶν, εἰς κόσμον
ἔδει αὐτὸ γεγονέναι, ἀλλ' εἶναι αὐτὸ ἐγρηγορὸς
πανταχῇ καὶ ζῶν ἄλλο ἄλλως καὶ μηδὲν δύνασθαι
15 εἶναι, ὃ μὴ ἔστιν αὐτῷ. διὸ καὶ ἐνταῦθα λύοιτο
ἂν ἡ ἀπορία ἡ πῶς ἐν ζῴῳ ἐμψύχῳ ἄψυχον·
οὕτως γὰρ ὁ λόγος φησὶν ἄλλο ἄλλως ζῆν ἐν τῷ
ὅλῳ, ἡμᾶς δὲ τὸ μὴ αἰσθητῶς παρ' αὐτοῦ
κινούμενον ζῆν μὴ λέγειν· τὸ δέ ἐστιν ἕκαστον
ζῶν λανθάνον, καὶ τὸ αἰσθητῶς ζῶν συγκείμενον
20 ἐκ τῶν μὴ αἰσθητῶς μὲν ζώντων, θαυμαστὰς δὲ
δυνάμεις εἰς τὸ ζῆν τῷ τοιούτῳ ζῴῳ παρεχο-
μένων. μὴ γὰρ ἂν κινηθῆναι ἐπὶ τοσαῦτα ἄνθρωπον
ἐκ πάντῃ ἀψύχων τῶν αὐτῷ δυνάμεων κινούμενον,
μηδ' αὖ τὸ πᾶν οὕτω ζῆν μὴ ἑκάστου τῶν ἐν αὐτῷ
25 ζώντων τὴν οἰκείαν ζωήν, κἂν προαίρεσις αὐτῷ
μὴ παρῇ· ποιεῖ γὰρ καὶ προαιρέσεως οὐ δεηθέν,
ἅτε προαιρέσεως ὂν προγενέστερον· διὸ καὶ πολλὰ
δουλεύει αὐτῷ [1] ταῖς δυνάμεσιν.

37. Οὐδὲν οὖν τῷ παντὶ ἀπόβλητον αὐτοῦ·
ἐπεὶ καὶ πῦρ καὶ ὅσα τῶν τοιούτων λέγομεν
ποιεῖν, εἴ τις τὸ ποιεῖν αὐτῶν ζητήσειε τί ποτ'

[1] Theiler: αὐτῶν wxUC: αὐτοῦ z.

252

All is like this, but even more so: or rather the parts of our bodies with their powers are only traces of the parts and powers of the universe. In the All there is an indescribably wonderful variety of powers, especially in the bodies which move through the heavens. For it did not have to come to be an ordered universe like a soulless house, even if a large and complex one, made of materials easy to reckon up according to kind, stones and timber, perhaps, and other things of the sort; but it exists, all awake and alive differently in different parts, and nothing can exist which does not belong to it. This then solves the difficulty of how there can be anything without soul in an ensouled living being; for in this way the account explains that different things in the Whole live in different ways, but we do not say that anything is alive which does not move itself perceptibly; but each thing of this sort has a hidden life; and the thing which is perceptibly alive is composed of parts which are not perceptibly alive but contribute wonderful powers to the life of a living thing of this kind. Man would not have been moved to such great achievements if the powers in himself from which he started had been without soul, nor would the All live as it does if each particular thing in it did not live its own life—even if the All does not exercise deliberate choice. For it acts without need of deliberate choice, since it is of older birth than choice; and therefore many things serve it with their powers.

37. Nothing, therefore, which belongs to the All can be discarded by it; since with fire and all the other things of the kind which we say are active, if any one of the people who have the reputation of experts tried to find out what their activity was, he

PLOTINUS: ENNEAD IV. 4.

ἐστὶ τῶν νῦν δοκούντων εἰδέναι, ἀπορήσειεν ἄν,
5 εἰ μὴ δύναμιν ταύτην ἀποδοίη αὐτῷ ⟨τῷ⟩[1] ἐν τῷ
παντὶ εἶναι, καὶ τοῖς ἄλλοις δὲ τὸ τοιοῦτον τοῖς ἐν
χρήσει λέγοι. ἀλλ' ἡμεῖς τὰ μὲν συνήθη οὔτ'
ἀξιοῦμεν ζητεῖν οὔτ' ἀπιστοῦμεν, περὶ δὲ τῶν
ἄλλων τῶν ἔξω τοῦ συνήθους δυνάμεων ἀπισ-
τοῦμέν τε ὡς ἔχει ἕκαστον, καὶ τῷ ἀσυνήθει τὸ
10 θαυμάζειν προστίθεμεν θαυμάσαντες ἂν καὶ ταῦτα,
εἰ ἀπείροις αὐτῶν οὖσιν ἕκαστόν τις προσφέρων
ἐξηγεῖτο αὐτῶν τὰς δυνάμεις. ἔχειν μὲν οὖν
ἕκαστον δύναμίν τινα ἄλογον φατέον ἐν τῷ παντὶ
πλασθὲν καὶ μορφωθὲν καὶ μετειληφός πως ψυχῆς παρὰ τοῦ ὅλου ὄντος ἐμψύχου καὶ περιειλημ-
15 μένον ὑπὸ τοιούτου καὶ μόριον ὂν ἐμψύχου—
οὐδὲν γὰρ ἐν αὐτῷ ὅ τι μὴ μέρος—ἄλλα δὲ ἄλλων
πρὸς τὸ δρᾶν δυνατώτερα καὶ τῶν ἐπὶ γῆς καὶ τῶν
οὐρανίων μᾶλλον, ἅτε ἐναργεστέρᾳ φύσει χρώμενα·
καὶ γίνεσθαι πολλὰ κατὰ τὰς δυνάμεις ταύτας, οὐ
τῇ προαιρέσει ἀφ' ὧν δοκεῖ ἰέναι τὸ δρώμενον—
20 ἔστι γὰρ καὶ ἐν τοῖς προαίρεσιν οὐκ ἔχουσιν—
οὐδὲ ἐπιστραφέντων τῇ δόσει τῆς δυνάμεως, κἂν
ψυχῆς τι ἀπ' αὐτῶν ἴῃ. γένοιτο γὰρ ἂν καὶ ζῷα
ἐκ ζῴου οὐ τῆς προαιρέσεως ποιούσης οὐδ' αὖ
ἐλαττουμένου οὐδ' αὖ παρακολουθοῦντος· ἀργὸς[2]

---

[1] Bréhier.
[2] Theiler: αὐτὸς Enn., H–S[1]: αὐτὸ Kirchhoff*.

---

[1] A philosophical commonplace, probably of Stoic origin,

would get into difficulties if he did not attribute this power to their actually being in the All, and did not say the same sort of thing about everything else which is in daily use. But we do not think it proper to investigate ordinary things, nor do we disbelieve in them, but we disbelieve in the detailed working of the other powers which are out of the ordinary, and encounter the extraordinary with astonishment,[1] though we should be astonished at these ordinary things too if we were unfamiliar with them and someone presented a detailed account of them to us and explained their powers. We must admit, then, that each particular thing has an unreasoned power, since it is moulded and shaped in the All and in some way has a share of soul from the Whole which is ensouled, and is surrounded by a universe of this kind and is part of an ensouled being—for there is nothing in it which is not a part—but some things are more powerfully effective than others, both among the things on earth and still more among those in the heavens, since these have a clearer nature; and many things happen according to these powers, not by deliberate choice of the beings from which the action appears to proceed—for the powers exist also in beings which have no choice—nor with any direction of attention to the giving of the power, even if there is some transmission of soul from them. For living beings could be generated from a living being without any act of deliberate choice, nor any diminution of the original living being, nor any consciousness of what is happening: for the act of choice would be inactive, if he had it, or it would not be the choice

rhetorically amplified by Seneca *Naturales Quaestiones* VII 1. 1.

γὰρ ἦν ἡ προαίρεσις, εἰ ἔχοι, ἢ οὐκ ἦν ἡ ποιοῦσα.
25 εἰ δὲ μὴ ἔχοι τι προαίρεσιν ζῷον, ἔτι μᾶλλον τὸ μὴ
παρακολουθεῖν.

38. Ἅ τε [1] οὖν ἐξ αὐτοῦ μηδενὸς κινήσαντος ἐκ
τῆς ἄλλης αὐτοῦ ζωῆς γίνεται [καὶ ὅλως ὅσα ἐξ
αὐτοῦ],[2] ὅσα τε κινήσαντος ἄλλου, οἷον εὐχαῖς ἢ
ἁπλαῖς ἢ τέχνῃ ᾀδομέναις, ταῦτα οὐκ εἰς ἐκεῖνον
5 ἕκαστον, ἀλλ᾽ εἰς τὴν τοῦ δρωμένου φύσιν ἀνενεκτέον. καὶ ὅσα μὲν χρηστὰ [3] πρὸς ζωὴν ἤ τινα
ἄλλην χρείαν συμβάλλεται, τῇ δόσει ἀνενεκτέον,
ἐξ ἄλλου μέρους μείζονος εἰς ἄλλο ἔλαττον ἰόν·
ὅ τι δ᾽ ἂν δυσχερὲς ἐξ αὐτῶν λέγηται εἰς τὰς
γενέσεις τῶν ζῴων ἰέναι, ἢ τῷ μὴ δύνασθαι τὸ
10 εὔχρηστον δέξασθαι τὸ ὑποκείμενον—οὐ γὰρ
ἁπλῶς γίνεται τὸ γινόμενον, ἀλλ᾽ εἰς τοδὶ καὶ ὡδί·
καὶ δὴ καὶ τὸ πάσχον καὶ τὸ πεισόμενον ὑποκειμένην τινὰ καὶ τοιάνδε φύσιν ἔχειν—πολλὰ δὲ καὶ
αἱ μίξεις ποιοῦσιν, ἑκάστου τι εὔχρηστον εἰς τὸ ζῆν
διδόντος. γίνοιτο δ᾽ ἄν τῳ καὶ μὴ συμφερόντων
15 τῶν λυσιτελῶν τὴν φύσιν, καὶ ἡ σύνταξις ἡ τῶν
ὅλων οὐ δίδωσιν ἑκάστῳ ἀεὶ ὃ βούλεται· πολλὰ δὲ
καὶ προστίθεμεν αὐτοὶ τοῖς δοθεῖσι. πάντα δ᾽
ὅμως εἰς ἓν συμπλέκεται καὶ θαυμαστὴν τὴν
συμφωνίαν ἔχει καὶ ἀπ᾽ ἄλλων ἄλλα, κἂν ἀπ᾽
ἐναντίων ἴῃ· πάντα γὰρ ἑνός. καὶ εἴ τι δὲ

---

[1] Kirchhoff*: ἅτε Perna, Creuzer, H–S[1]: ὅσα τε Harder:
ὅσα B–T.

[2] del. Bouillet, Harder, B–T, ut glossam complectentem lin.
1–2 ἅ τε et ὅσα τε.

[3] Kirchhoff* (utilia Ficinus): χρὴ τὰ Enn.

which would be operative. But if a living being had no choice, still more would there be an absence of consciousness.

38. The effects, then, which come from the heavenly body from its other kind of life without anything stimulating it, and all which are produced by the stimulation of another, for instance by prayers, either plain or sung according to art, all these are to be attributed, not to each individual heavenly body, but to the nature of what is done. And all the effects which are beneficial for the preservation of life or some other useful purpose are to be attributed to the gift [of the heavenly body] and are something which comes from the greater part of the universe to another lesser one; but whatever bad influence is said to come from the heavenly bodies upon the births of living creatures is to be attributed to the inability of the substrate to receive the favourable influence—for what happens does not simply happen, but happens to this specific thing and in this specific way; and that which is affected, and that which is going to be affected, has a specific kind of underlying nature—but also the mixtures of influences produce many effects, though each individual heavenly body gives something beneficial to life. And a bad effect on something may occur also because the naturally favourable forces are not operating to help it, and the concatenation of universal forces does not always give each individual what it wants; and we too add a great deal to what we are given. But all the same, all things are woven into one, and are marvellously in tune, and things come from other things, even if they come from opposites: for all belong to one [universe]. And if anything among the things

20 ἐλλεῖπον πρὸς τὸ βέλτιον τῶν γινομένων μὴ
εἰδοποιηθὲν εἰς τέλος μὴ κρατηθείσης τῆς ὕλης,
οἷον ἐλλεῖπον τῷ γενναίῳ, οὗ στερηθὲν πίπτει εἰς
αἰσχρότητα. ὥστε τὰ μὲν ποιεῖσθαι ὑπ' ἐκείνων,
τὰ δὲ τὴν ὑποκειμένην φύσιν εἰσφέρεσθαι, τὰ δὲ
παρ' αὐτῶν προστιθέναι.

39. Συνταττομένων δὲ ἀεὶ πάντων καὶ εἰς ἓν
συντελούντων πάντων, σημαίνεσθαι πάντα.
ἀρετὴ δὲ ἀδέσποτον· συνυφαίνεσθαι δὲ καὶ τὰ
αὐτῆς ἔργα τῇ συντάξει, ἅτε καὶ τῶν τῇδε ἐκεῖθεν
5 ἐξηρτημένων, τῶν ἐν τῷδε τῷ παντὶ τοῖς θειοτέροις,
καὶ μετέχοντος καὶ τοῦδε ἐκείνων. γίνεται τοίνυν
τὰ ἐν τῷ παντὶ οὐ κατὰ σπερματικούς, ἀλλὰ κατὰ
λόγους περιληπτικοὺς καὶ τῶν προτέρων ἢ κατὰ
τοὺς τῶν σπερμάτων λόγους· οὐ γὰρ ἐν σπερματι-
κοῖς λόγοις ἔνι τι τῶν γινομένων παρὰ τοὺς
10 σπερματικοὺς αὐτοὺς λόγους οὐδὲ τῶν παρὰ τῆς
ὕλης εἰς τὸ ὅλον συντελούντων οὐδὲ τῶν δρωμένων
εἰς ἄλληλα παρὰ τῶν γενομένων. ἀλλὰ μᾶλλον
ἂν ἐοίκοι ὁ λόγος τοῦ παντὸς κατὰ λόγον τιθέντα
κόσμον πόλεως καὶ νόμον, ἤδη εἰδότα ἃ πράξουσιν
οἱ πολῖται καὶ δι' ἃ πρᾳξουσι, καὶ πρὸς ταῦτα
15 πάντα νομοθετοῦντος καὶ συνυφαίνοντος τοῖς
νόμοις τὰ πάθη πάντα αὐτῶν καὶ τὰ ἔργα καὶ τὰς
ἐπὶ τοῖς ἔργοις τιμὰς καὶ ἀτιμίας, πάντων ὁδῷ
οἷον αὐτομάτῃ εἰς συμφωνίαν χωρούντων. ἡ δὲ

which come into being is at all lacking in excellence, since it is not completely formed because the matter has not been mastered, it is, so to speak, lacking in nobility of birth, and since it is deprived of this falls into ugliness. Some things, then, are done by the heavenly bodies, some the underlying nature introduces, and some are additions due to ourselves.

39. But since all things are for ever brought together into order and all are directed to a single end, all are signified. " But virtue has no master ",[1] yet its works, too, are woven into the common order, since the things here below depend on the world above, the things in this world on diviner beings, and this universe has a share, also, in those higher realities. What comes to be in the All, then, does not come to be according to seminal formative principles but according to formative principles which include powers which are prior to the principles in the seeds; for in the seminal principles there is nothing of what happens outside the sphere of the seminal principles themselves, or of the contributions which come from matter to the whole, or of the interactions on each other of the things which have come to be. But the rational formative principle of the All is more like the formative thought which establishes the order and law of a state, which knows already what the citizens are going to do and why they are going to do it, and legislates with regard to all this, and weaves together by the laws all their experiences and arts and the honour or dishonour that their acts merit, so that all that happens in the state moves as if spontaneously into a harmonious order. But the

---

[1] This Platonic phrase, from *Republic* X 617E3, is more than once quoted by Plotinus: cp. II. 3. 9. 17; VI. 8. 5. 31.

σημασία οὐ τούτου χάριν, ἵνα σημαίνῃ προηγου-
μένως, ἀλλ᾽ οὕτω γιγνομένων σημαίνεται ἐξ
20 ἄλλων ἄλλα· ὅτι γὰρ ἓν καὶ ἑνός, καὶ ἀπ᾽ ἄλλου
ἄλλο γινώσκοιτ᾽ ἄν, καὶ ἀπὸ αἰτιατοῦ δὲ τὸ αἴτιον,
καὶ τὸ ἑπόμενον ἐκ τοῦ προηγησαμένου, καὶ
τὸ σύνθετον ἀπὸ θατέρου, ὅτι θάτερον καὶ θάτερον
ὁμοῦ ποιῶν. εἰ δὴ ταῦτα ὀρθῶς λέγεται, λύοιντο
ἂν ἤδη αἱ ἀπορίαι, ἥ τε πρὸς τὸ κακῶν δόσιν
25 παρὰ θεῶν γίνεσθαι τῷ μήτε προαιρέσεις εἶναι
τὰς ποιούσας, φυσικαῖς δὲ ἀνάγκαις γίνεσθαι,
ὅσα ἐκεῖθεν, ὡς μερῶν πρὸς μέρη, καὶ ἑπόμενα
ἑνὸς ζωῇ, καὶ τῷ πολλὰ παρ᾽ αὐτῶν τοῖς γινομένοις
προστιθέναι, καὶ τῷ τῶν διδομένων παρ᾽ ἑκάστων
οὐ κακῶν ὄντων ἐν τῇ μίξει γίγνεσθαι ἄλλο τι, καὶ
30 τῷ μὴ ἕνεκα ἑκάστου ἀλλ᾽ ἕνεκα τοῦ ὅλου τὴν
ζωήν, καὶ τὴν ὑποκειμένην δὲ φύσιν ἄλλο λαβοῦσαν
ἄλλο πάσχειν καὶ μηδὲ δύνασθαι κρατῆσαι τοῦ
δοθέντος.

40. Τὰς δὲ γοητείας πῶς; ἢ τῇ συμπαθείᾳ, καὶ
τῷ πεφυκέναι συμφωνίαν εἶναι ὁμοίων καὶ ἐναντίωσιν ἀνομοίων, καὶ τῇ τῶν δυνάμεων τῶν πολλῶν
ποικιλίᾳ εἰς ἓν ζῷον συντελούντων. καὶ γὰρ
5 μηδενὸς μηχανωμένου ἄλλου πολλὰ ἕλκεται καὶ
γοητεύεται· καὶ ἡ ἀληθινὴ μαγεία ἡ ἐν τῷ παντὶ
φιλία καὶ τὸ νεῖκος αὖ. καὶ ὁ γόης ὁ πρῶτος

---

[1] The reference is to Empedocles: cp. e.g. fr. B 17, 19–20.
This and the following chapters make clear that magic was
for Plotinus a manipulation of natural forces, attractions and
sympathies resulting from the living organic unity of the
physical universe. His interest in it was philosophical rather
than practical (see further n. 1 on ch. 43). An idea of the
sort of magic of which Plotinus is thinking can be obtained

signification is not designed for the sake of indicating what is going to happen before it does, but since things happen as they do some are indicated by others; for since all is one and belongs to one, one thing can be known from another, the cause from what is caused and the consequence from the antecedent, and the composite from one of its parts, because the rational principle of the universe composes one part and another together. If this argument is correct, the difficulties would be solved, that about the gift of evils coming from the gods by the consideration that it is not their deliberate choices which are effective but all that comes from above happens by natural necessity, as actions of parts on parts, and as consequences of the life of the one universe; and that we by ourselves contribute much to what happens, and that, though the gifts of the individual heavenly bodies are not evil, something else comes about in their mixture, and that the life of the universe does not serve the purposes of each individual but of the whole, and that the underlying nature receives one thing but experiences another, and is unable to master what it is given.

40. But how do magic spells work? By sympathy and by the fact that there is a natural concord of things that are alike and opposition of things that are different, and by the rich variety of the many powers which go to make up the life of the one living creature. For many things are drawn and enchanted without anyone else's magical contrivance: and the true magic is the " Love " and also the " Strife " in the All.[1] And this is the primary wizard and enchan-

from the spells published in the *Papyri Graecae Magicae* ed. and tr. K. Preisendanz (2 vols., Berlin and Leipzig 1928, 1931).

καὶ φαρμακεὺς οὗτός ἐστιν, ὃν κατανοήσαντες
ἄνθρωποι ἐπ' ἀλλήλοις χρῶνται αὐτοῦ τοῖς
φαρμάκοις καὶ τοῖς γοητεύμασι. καὶ γάρ, ὅτι
10 ἐρᾶν πεφύκασι καὶ τὰ ἐρᾶν ποιοῦντα ἕλκει πρὸς
ἄλληλα, ἀλκὴ [1] ἐρωτικῆς διὰ γοητείας τέχνης
γεγένηται, προστιθέντων ἐπαφαῖς φύσεις ἄλλας
ἄλλοις συναγωγοὺς καὶ ἐγκείμενον ἐχούσας ἔρωτα·
καὶ συνάπτουσι δὲ ἄλλην ψυχὴν ἄλλῃ, ὥσπερ ἂν εἰ
φυτὰ διεστηκότα ἐξαψάμενοι πρὸς ἄλληλα. καὶ
15 τοῖς σχήμασι δὲ προσχρῶνται δυνάμεις ἔχουσι,
καὶ αὐτοὺς σχηματίζοντες ὡδὶ ἐπάγουσιν ἐπ'
αὐτούς ἀψοφητὶ δυνάμεις ἐν ἑνὶ ὄντες εἰς ἕν.
ἐπεὶ ἔξω γε τοῦ παντὸς εἴ τις ὑποθοῖτο τὸν
τοιοῦτον, οὔτ' ἂν ἕλξειεν οὔτ' ἂν καταγάγοι
ἐπαγωγαῖς ἢ καταδέσμοις· ἀλλὰ νῦν, ὅτι μὴ οἷον
20 ἀλλαχοῦ ἄγει, ἔχει ἄγειν εἰδὼς ὅπη τι ἐν τῷ ζῴῳ
πρὸς ἄλλο ἄγεται. πέφυκε δὲ καὶ ἐπῳδαῖς τῷ
μέλει καὶ τῇ τοιᾷδε ἠχῇ καὶ τῷ σχήματι τοῦ
δρῶντος· ἕλκει γὰρ τὰ τοιαῦτα, οἷον τὰ ἐλεεινὰ
σχήματα καὶ φθέγματα. [ἀλλ' ἡ ψυχὴ] [2] οὐδὲ γὰρ
ἡ προαίρεσις οὐδ' ὁ λόγος ὑπὸ μουσικῆς θέλγεται
25 ἀλλ' ἡ ἄλογος ψυχή, καὶ οὐ θαυμάζεται ἡ γοητεία
ἡ τοιαύτη· καίτοι φιλοῦσι κηλούμενοι, κἂν μὴ τοῦτο
αἰτῶνται παρὰ τῶν τῇ μουσικῇ χρωμένων. καὶ
τὰς ἄλλας δὲ εὐχὰς οὐ τῆς προαιρέσεως ἀκουούσης
οἰητέον· οὐδὲ γὰρ οἱ θελγόμενοι ταῖς ἐπῳδαῖς

---

[1] E, Creuzer, Cilento (*efficacia* nominativus Ficinus): ἀλκῇ
ARJUCz, Perna, H–S: ἀλκῆς B.
[2] om. z: delendum ut e glossa ad 24–5 ἀλλ' ἡ . . . ψυχὴ
ortum.

ter, from observing whom men came to use his philtres and spells on each other. For, because love is natural to men and the things that cause love have a force of attraction to each other, there has come into existence the helpful power of a magical art of love, used by those who apply by contact to different people different magical substances designed to draw them together and with a love-force implanted in them; they join one soul to another, as if they were training together plants set at intervals. They use as well figures with power in them, and by putting themselves into the right postures they quietly bring powers upon themselves, since they are within one universe and work upon one universe. For if anyone put a magician outside the All, he could not draw or bring down by attractive or binding spells. But now, because he does not operate as if he were somewhere else, he can work on his subjects knowing by what way one thing is drawn to another in the living being. And there is a natural drawing power in spells wrought by the tune and the particular intonation and posture of the magician—for these things attract, as pitiable figures and voices attract; for it is the irrational soul—not the power of choice or the reason—which is charmed by music, and this kind of magic causes no surprise: people even like being enchanted, even if this is not exactly what they demand from the musicians. And we must not think that other kinds of prayers either are freely and deliberately answered: for people charmed by spells do not act with free deliberation, nor, when

οὕτως, οὐδ' ὅταν γοητεύῃ ὄφις ἀνθρώπους, σύνεσιν
30 ὁ γοητευόμενος ἔχει, οὐδ' αἰσθάνεται, ἀλλὰ
γινώσκει, ἤδη παθών, ὅτι πέπονθεν, ἀπαθὲς δ'
αὐτῷ τὸ ἡγούμενόν ἐστιν. ᾧ δ' ηὔξατο, ἦλθέ τι
πρὸς αὐτὸν ἐξ ἐκείνου ἢ πρὸς ἄλλον.

41. Ὁ δὲ ἥλιος ἢ ἄλλο ἄστρον οὐκ ἐπαΐει. καὶ
γίνεται τὸ κατὰ τὴν εὐχὴν συμπαθοῦς μέρους
μέρει γενομένου, ὥσπερ ἐν μιᾷ νευρᾷ τεταμένῃ·
κινηθεῖσα γὰρ ἐκ τοῦ κάτω καὶ ἄνω ἔχει τὴν κίνησιν.
5 πολλάκις δὲ καὶ ἄλλης κινηθείσης ἄλλη οἷον
αἴσθησιν ἔχει κατὰ συμφωνίαν καὶ τῷ ὑπὸ μιᾷ
ἡρμόσθαι ἁρμονίᾳ. εἰ δὲ καὶ ἐν ἄλλῃ λύρᾳ ἡ
κίνησις ἀπ' ἄλλης ἔρχεται, ὅσον τὸ συμπαθές, καὶ
ἐν τῷ παντὶ τοίνυν μία ἁρμονία, κἂν ἐξ ἐναντίων
ᾖ· καὶ ἐξ ὁμοίων δέ ἐστι καὶ πάντων συγγενῶν
10 καὶ τῶν ἐναντίων. καὶ ὅσα λωβᾶται ἀνθρώπους,
οἷον τὸ θυμοειδὲς ἑλχθὲν μετὰ χολῆς εἰς ἥπατος
φύσιν ἦλθεν, οὐχ ὡς λωβησόμενα· οἷον εἰ πῦρ τις
ἐκ πυρὸς λαβὼν ἔβλαψεν ἄλλον † ὁ μηχανησάμενος
ἢ ἐλθεῖν ἢ ὁ λαβών† [1] ἐκεῖνος ποιεῖ τῷ [2] δεδωκέναι
γοῦν τι [3] οἷον μετατιθέν τι [4] ἐξ ἄλλου εἰς ἄλλο·
15 καὶ τὸ ἐληλυθὸς [5] δέ, εἰ μὴ οἷός τε ἐγένετο
δέξασθαι εἰς ὃν μετηνέχθη.

[1] locus nondum sanatus.　　[2] wUz: τὸ xC.
[3] γοῦν τι Enn., H–S: ἀγνοοῦντι Theiler.
[4] τῷ δεδωκέναι . . . μετατιθέν τι quoniam aliquid (sc. ignem)
praebuit quod quasi traderet quiddam (sc. alterum ignem):
μετατιθέν τι Enn.: μετατεθὲν Creuzer (translatum Ficinus):
μετατεθέν τι Theiler.　　[5] τὸ ἐληλυθὸς (i.e. τὸ πῦρ) sc. λωβᾶται.

---

[1] The text here is very uncertain. H–S's critical note,
printed under the Greek text, gives the principal suggestions

a snake fascinates men, does the one who is fascinated understand or perceive what is happening, but he knows only afterwards that he has had the experience; his ruling intellect, however, remains unaffected. But, when a man prays to a heavenly body, some influence comes from it upon him or upon another person.

41. But the sun, or another heavenly body, does not hear his prayers. And that which he prays for comes about because one part is in sympathetic connection with another, just as in one tense string; for if the string is plucked at the lower end, it has a vibration at the upper. But often, too, when one string is plucked another has a kind of sense of this by its concord and the fact that it is tuned to the same scale. But if the vibration can even pass from one lyre to another in so far as a sympathy exists, then there is also one single harmony in the All, even if it is composed of opposites; and it is in fact composed of parts which are alike and all akin, even when they are opposites. And all the things which harm men do not come with the intention of harming, but as when the passionate spirit is drawn down with the bile and enters the nature of the liver; just as if someone, taking a light from a fire, hurts someone else—either the person who has made arrangements to go or that one who took it does the damage by having given some fire to someone who, in a way, moves it about from one place to another; and the fire which has come hurts if the person to whom it was transferred was unable to take hold of it.[1]

for improvement. I, very hesitantly, follow Cilento's suggestion (see his commentary ad loc.) in my translation, as it gives some sort of sense without too violent alteration.

42. Ὥστε οὔτε μνήμης διὰ τοῦτο δεήσει τοῖς
ἄστροις, οὗπερ χάριν καὶ ταῦτα πεπραγμάτευται,
οὔτε αἰσθήσεων ἀναπεμπομένων· οὔτε ἐπινεύσεις
τοῦτον τὸν τρόπον εὐχαῖς, ὡς οἴονταί τινες,
5 προαιρετικάς τινας, ἀλλὰ καὶ μετ' εὐχῆς γίνεσθαί
τι δοτέον καὶ εὐχῆς ἄνευ παρ' αὐτῶν, ᾗ μέρη καὶ
ἑνός· καὶ ὅτι δυνάμεις καὶ χωρὶς προαιρέσεως
πολλαὶ καὶ αὗται καὶ ἄνευ μηχανῆς καὶ μετὰ
τέχνης, ὡς ἐν ζῴῳ ἑνί· καὶ ἀπολαύει ἄλλο ἄλλον
10 καὶ βλάπτεται τῷ οὕτω πεφυκέναι, καὶ τέχναις
ἰατρῶν καὶ ἐπαοιδῶν ἄλλο ἄλλῳ ἠναγκάσθη
παρασχεῖν τι τῆς δυνάμεως τῆς αὑτοῦ. καὶ τὸ
πᾶν δὲ ὡσαύτως εἰς τὰ μέρη δίδωσι καὶ παρ'
αὑτοῦ καὶ ἑλκύσαντος ἄλλου εἰς μέρος τι αὑτοῦ,
κείμενον τοῖς αὑτοῦ μέρεσι τῷ αὑτοῦ φυσικῷ, ὡς
μηδενὸς ἀλλοτρίου τοῦ αἰτοῦντος ὄντος. εἰ δὲ
15 κακὸς ὁ αἰτῶν, θαυμάζειν οὐ δεῖ· καὶ γὰρ ἐκ
ποταμῶν ἀρύονται οἱ κακοί, καὶ τὸ διδὸν αὐτὸ[1]
οὐκ οἶδεν ᾧ[2] δίδωσιν, ἀλλὰ δίδωσι μόνον· ἀλλ'
ὅμως συντέτακται καὶ ⟨ὃ⟩[3] δέδοται τῇ φύσει τοῦ
παντός· ὥστε, εἴ τις ἔλαβεν ἐκ τῶν πᾶσι κειμένων,
οὐ δέον, ἕπεσθαι αὐτῷ ἀναγκαίῳ νόμῳ τὴν δίκην.
20 οὔκουν δοτέον τὸ πᾶν πάσχειν· ἢ τὸ μὲν ἡγεμονοῦν
αὐτοῦ ἀπαθὲς δοτέον πάντῃ εἶναι, γιγνομένων δὲ
παθῶν ἐν μέρεσιν αὐτοῦ ἐκείνοις μὲν ἥκειν τὸ

---

[1] z, Creuzer, Müller*: αὐτοῦ wxC: αὑτοῦ U.
[2] Harder, B–T, et testatur Theologia VI. 41: ὃ Enn.* (ὃ
correctio ad lin. 17).
[3] καὶ ὃ Theiler: καὶ Enn.* : ὃ Kleist (Programm 19).

42. So there will be no need for the heavenly
bodies to have memory, either, for this purpose [of
answering prayers]—this was the reason why this
investigation was undertaken—or sense-perceptions
arising from the lower world; nor, if we look at it
in this way, do they deliberately choose to attend
to prayers, but we must admit that some influence
comes from them both with and without prayer in so
far as they are parts, and parts of one whole; and
that there are many powers which work even without
deliberate choice, both without contrivance and with
[magic] art, as in a single living being; and one thing
is benefited and harmed by another because it is
naturally so disposed, and by the arts of physicians
and magicians one thing is compelled to give something of its power to another. And in the same
way the All gives to its parts, both spontaneously
and if someone else magically attracts [its power]
to a part of it; for it lies at the disposal of its parts
by its own natural disposition, and so the one who
makes the prayer is no alien. But if the man who
prays is evil, there is no need to be surprised; for
the wicked draw water from the streams and that
which gives does not know itself to what it gives,
but only gives; but all the same that which is given
is also co-ordinated with the nature of the All; so
that if someone takes what he ought not from what
lies at the disposal of all, justice pursues him by an
inevitable law. We must not therefore assume that
the All can be affected; or we must grant that its
ruling principle is altogether impassible, and when
the parts come to be affected, the affection pene-

πάθος, παρὰ φύσιν δὲ μηδενὸς αὐτῷ ὄντος ἀπαθὲς
[τὸ γενόμενον] ¹ ὡς πρὸς αὐτὸ εἶναι. ἐπεὶ καὶ
τοῖς ἄστροις, καθόσον μὲν μέρη, τὰ πάθη, ἀπαθῆ
25 μέντοι αὐτὰ εἶναι τῷ τε τὰς προαιρέσεις καὶ
αὐτοῖς ἀπαθεῖς εἶναι καὶ τὰ σώματα αὐτῶν καὶ τὰς
φύσεις ἀβλαβεῖς ὑπάρχειν καὶ τῷ, καὶ εἰ διὰ τῆς
ψυχῆς τι διδόασι, μὴ ἐλαττοῦσθαι αὐτοῖς τὴν
ψυχὴν καὶ τὰ σώματα αὐτοῖς τὰ αὐτὰ μένειν καί,
εἴ τι ὑπεκρεῖ, ἀναισθήτως ἀπιόντος καὶ τοῦ
30 προσιόντος, εἰ πρόσεισι, λανθάνοντος.

43. Ὁ δὲ σπουδαῖος πῶς ὑπὸ γοητείας καὶ
φαρμάκων; ἢ τῇ μὲν ψυχῇ ἀπαθὴς εἰς γοήτευσιν,
καὶ οὐκ ἂν τὸ λογικὸν αὐτοῦ πάθοι, οὐδ' ἂν
μεταδοξάσειε· τὸ δὲ ὅσον τοῦ παντὸς ἐν αὐτῷ
5 ἄλογον, κατὰ τοῦτο πάθοι ἄν, μᾶλλον δὲ τοῦτο
πάθοι ἄν· ἀλλ' οὐκ ἔρωτας ἐκ φαρμάκων, εἴπερ τὸ
ἐρᾶν ἐπινευούσης καὶ τῆς ψυχῆς τῆς ἄλλης τῷ τῆς
ἄλλης παθήματι. ὥσπερ δὲ ἐπῳδαῖς τὸ ἄλογον
πάσχει, οὕτω καὶ αὐτὸς ἀντᾴδων καὶ ἀντεπᾴδων
τὰς ἐκεῖ δυνάμεις ἀναλύσει. θάνατον δὲ ἐκ
10 τοιούτων ἢ νόσους ἢ ὅσα σωματικὰ πάθοι ἄν· τὸ
γὰρ μέρος τοῦ παντὸς ὑπὸ μέρους ἄλλου ἢ τοῦ
παντὸς πάθοι ἄν, αὐτὸς δὲ ἀβλαβής. τὸ δὲ μὴ
εὐθύς, ἀλλ' ὕστερον, οὐκ ἀποστατεῖ φύσεως.

---

¹ delevimus: ⟨εἰς⟩ τὸ γενόμενον Seidel, B–T.

---

¹ I still think it probable that, although ἐπῳδαῖς in this
sentence means ordinary magic spells, when Plotinus speaks
of the σπουδαῖος as ἀντᾴδων καὶ ἀντεπᾴδων he is thinking of
Plato's metaphorical use of ἐπῳδή for salutary philosophical
exhortation in *Charmides* 156–7. He uses the word himself
in this way, of the highest sort of philosophy, in V. 3. 17.
18–20. For a further discussion of this passage, and in general

trates to them, but since there is nothing there which is contrary to the nature of the All, it is unaffected, directed as it is towards itself. For the heavenly bodies, too, in so far as they are parts, are subject to affections; they are however impassible in themselves, because their powers of choice, as well [as that of the All], cannot be affected and their bodies and natures remain unharmed, and if they give something by means of their soul, their soul is not diminished and their bodies remain the same, and if anything flows from them, it goes imperceptibly, and if anything is added to them, it is unnoticed.

43. But how is the good man affected by magic and drugs? He is incapable of being affected in his soul by enchantment, and his rational part would not be affected, nor would he change his mind; but he would be affected in whatever part of the irrational in the All there is in him, or rather this part would be affected; but he will feel no passionate loves provoked by drugs, if falling in love happens when one soul assents to the affection of the other. But, just as the irrational part of him is affected by incantations, so he himself by counter-chants and counter-incantations will dissolve the powers on the other side.[1] But he might suffer death or illnesses or anything bodily from such incantations; for the part of the All [in him] would be affected by another part or by the All, but he himself would be unharmed. (That the effects of magic do not follow immediately, but later, is not out of line with nature.) But spirits

of the attitude of Plotinus to magic, see my contribution to the *Cambridge History of Later Greek and Early Mediaeval Philosophy* 207–8 and the literature there referred to.

PLOTINUS: ENNEAD IV. 4.

δαίμονες δὲ οὐκ ἀπαθεῖς οὐδ' αὐτοὶ τῷ ἀλόγῳ·
μνήμας δὲ καὶ αἰσθήσεις τούτοις οὐκ ἄτοπον
διδόναι καὶ θέλγεσθαι φυσικῶς ἀγομένους καὶ
15 κατακούειν καλούντων τοὺς αὐτῶν ἐγγυτέρω τῶν
τῇδε καὶ ὅσῳ πρὸς τὰ τῇδε. πᾶν γὰρ τὸ πρὸς ἄλλο
γοητεύεται ὑπ' ἄλλου· πρὸς ὃ γὰρ ἐστιν, ἐκεῖνο
γοητεύει καὶ ἄγει αὐτό· μόνον δὲ τὸ πρὸς αὐτὸ
ἀγοήτευτον. διὸ καὶ πᾶσα πρᾶξις γεγοήτευται
20 καὶ πᾶς ὁ τοῦ πρακτικοῦ βίος· κινεῖται γὰρ πρὸς
ταῦτα, ἃ θέλγει αὐτόν. ὅθεν καὶ τὸ εὐπρόσωπος
γὰρ ὁ τοῦ μεγαλήτορος Ἐρεχθέως δῆμος.
τί γὰρ μαθών τις πρὸς ἄλλο ἔχει; ἢ ἑλκόμενος οὐ
μάγων τέχναις, ἀλλὰ τῆς φύσεως, τὴν ἀπάτην[1]
δούσης καὶ συναψάσης ἄλλο πρὸς ἄλλο οὐ τοῖς
τόποις, ἀλλ' οἷς ἔδωκε φίλτροις.

44. Μόνη δὲ λείπεται ἡ θεωρία ἀγοήτευτος εἶναι,
ὅτι μηδεὶς πρὸς αὑτὸν γεγοήτευται· εἷς γάρ ἐστι,
καὶ τὸ θεωρούμενον αὐτός ἐστι, καὶ ὁ λόγος οὐκ
ἠπατημένος, ἀλλ' ὃ δεῖ ποιεῖ, καὶ τὴν αὑτοῦ
5 ζωὴν καὶ τὸ ἔργον ποιεῖ. ἐκεῖ δὲ οὐ τὸ αὑτοῦ, καὶ
οὐχ ὁ λόγος τὴν ὁρμήν, ἀλλ' ἀρχὴ καὶ τοῦ ἀλόγου,
αἱ τοῦ πάθους προτάσεις. τέκνων μὲν γὰρ ἐπιμέ-
λειαι καὶ πρὸς γάμον[2] σπουδαὶ φανερὰν τὴν ὁλκὴν

---

[1] Kirchhoff*: τῆς ἀπάτης Enn., H–S.
[2] wz, Perna*: γάμων xUC, H–S[1].

---

[1] This is a reference to Plato *Alcibiades* I 132A5, where
Plato is adapting *Iliad* 2. 547 to his own purposes. Plato adds
"but you ought to see it undressed", and the context is the
attempt by Socrates to prevent Alcibiades from being cor-
rupted by falling in love with the Athenian *demos*. This
serves Plotinus as a good Platonic illustration of the charms

themselves, also, are not incapable of being affected in their irrational part; it is not out of place to ascribe memory and sense-perceptions to them and to grant that they are charmed by attractions appropriate to their nature and that those of them who are nearer to the things here below hear the prayers of those who call upon them according to the degree of their concern with things here below. For everything which is directed to something else is enchanted by something else; for that to which it is directed enchants and draws it; but only that which is self-directed is free from enchantment. For this reason all practical action is under enchantment, and the whole life of the practical man: for he is moved to that which charms him. This is the reason for saying " The citizen body of great-hearted Erectheus looks attractive ".[1] For why does a man direct himself to something else? He is drawn not by the arts of wizards but of nature, which brings illusion and links one thing to another not spatially but by the magic draughts which it gives.

44. Contemplation alone remains incapable of enchantment because no one who is self-directed is subject to enchantment: for he is one, and that which he contemplates is himself, and his reason is not deluded, but he makes what he ought and makes his own life and work. But in practical life there is no self-possession, and the reason does not produce the impulse, but the irrational also has an origin in the premises derived from the affection. For the care of children and concern for marriage have a manifest drawing power, and so do all the things

of the lower world, which are always illusory, whether political or sexual.

ἔχουσιν, ὅσα τε ἀνθρώπους δελεάζει ἡδέα γινόμενα
ταῖς ἐπιθυμίαις. πράξεις δὲ αἱ μὲν διὰ θυμὸν
10 ἀλόγως κινοῦνται, αἱ δὲ δι' ἐπιθυμίας ὡσαύτως,
πολιτεῖαι δὲ καὶ ἀρχῶν ὀρέξεις τὸ φίλαρχον τὸ ἐν
ἡμῖν ἔχουσι προκαλούμενον. καὶ αἱ μὲν γινόμεναι
ὑπὲρ τοῦ μὴ παθεῖν ἀρχὴν ἔχουσι τὸν φόβον, αἱ δ'
ὑπὲρ τοῦ πλείονος τὴν ἐπιθυμίαν. αἱ δὲ τῶν χρει-
15 ωδῶν χάριν τὴν τῆς φύσεως ἔνδειαν ζητοῦσαι ἀπο-
πληροῦν φανερῶς ἔχουσι τὴν τῆς φύσεως βίαν πρὸς
τὸ ζῆν οἰκειώσασαν. εἰ δέ τις λέγοι τὰς πράξεις
τῶν καλῶν ἀγοητεύτους εἶναι ἢ καὶ τὴν θεωρίαν
καλῶν οὖσαν γοητεύεσθαι λεκτέον, εἰ μὲν ὡς
ἀναγκαίας καὶ τὰς καλὰς λεγομένας πράξεις
20 πράττοι ἄλλο τὸ ὄντως καλὸν ἔχων, οὐ γεγοήτευται
—οἶδε γὰρ τὴν ἀνάγκην καὶ οὐ πρὸς τὸ τῇδε
βλέπει, οὐδὲ πρὸς ἄλλα ὁ βίος—ἀλλὰ τῇ τῆς
φύσεως τῆς ἀνθρωπίνης βίᾳ καὶ τῇ πρὸς τὸ ζῆν
τῶν ἄλλων ἢ καὶ αὑτοῦ οἰκειώσει—δοκεῖ γὰρ
εὔλογον ἴσως μὴ ἐξάγειν ἑαυτὸν διὰ τὴν οἰκείωσιν
25 —[ὅτι]¹ οὕτως ἐγοητεύθη. εἰ δὲ τὸ ἐν ταῖς
πράξεσιν ἀγαπήσας καλὸν τὰς πράξεις αἱρεῖται
ἀπατηθεὶς τοῖς ἴχνεσι τοῦ καλοῦ, γεγοήτευται τὸ
περὶ τὰ κάτω καλὸν διώκων· ὅλως γὰρ ἡ περὶ τὸ
ἐοικὸς τῷ ἀληθεῖ πραγματεία καὶ ὁλκὴ εἰς αὐτὸ
πᾶσα ἠπατημένου ἐξ ἐκείνων τῶν ἐπ' αὐτὰ

¹ del. Theiler.

which entice men since they give pleasure to their carnal desires. And the practical actions which are caused by our passionate spirit are the result of an irrational impulse, as are in the same way those caused by our carnal desires; political activity and the pursuit of office have the desire of power in us provoking them. And the activities which are undertaken to avoid suffering have fear as their origin, and those for the sake of getting more, carnal desire. Those undertaken because of necessary requirements, since they seek to satisfy a need of nature, obviously have the force of nature behind them making survival our own essential concern. But if someone says that noble practical activities are free from enchantment, or, if they are not, contemplation also, which is of noble objects, is under enchantment, [the answer is] that if one carries out the so-called noble activities as necessary ones, and grasps that what is really noble is something else, one has not been enchanted —for one knows the necessity, and does not look to this world, and one's life is not directed to other things—but one has been enchanted in this way by the force of human nature and by the essential concern for the survival of others, or indeed of oneself—for it seems, perhaps, reasonable not to take oneself out of this world on account of this essential concern. But if one is content with the nobility in practical activities, and chooses activity because one is deluded by its vestiges of nobility, one has been enchanted in one's pursuit of the nobility in the lower world; for, in general, to be actively occupied with the semblance of truth and drawn towards it in any way is characteristic of someone who has been deluded by the forces which draw one to the lower

30 ἑλκόντων· τοῦτο δὲ ἡ τῆς φύσεως γοητεία ποιεῖ·
τὸ γὰρ οὐκ ἀγαθὸν ὡς ἀγαθὸν διώκειν ἐλχθέντα τῷ
ἐκείνου εἴδει ἀλόγοις ὁρμαῖς, τοῦτό ἐστιν ἀγομένου
ὅπου μὴ ἤθελεν οὐκ εἰδότος. τοῦτο δὲ τί ἄν τις
ἄλλο ἢ γοητείαν εἴποι; μόνος οὖν ἀγοήτευτος, ὃς
ἑλκόμενος τοῖς ἄλλοις αὑτοῦ μέρεσι τούτων οὐδὲν
35 ἀγαθὸν λέγει εἶναι ὧν ἐκεῖνα λέγει, ἀλλὰ μόνον ὃ
οἶδεν αὐτὸς οὐκ ἠπατημένος οὐδὲ διώκων, ἀλλ᾽
ἔχων. οὐκ ἂν οὖν ἕλκοιτο οὐδαμοῦ.

45. Ἐκ δὴ τῶν εἰρημένων ἁπάντων ἐκεῖνο
φανερόν, ὅτι, ὡς ἕκαστον τῶν ἐν τῷ παντὶ ἔχει
φύσεως καὶ διαθέσεως, οὕτω τοι συντελεῖ εἰς τὸ
πᾶν καὶ πάσχει καὶ ποιεῖ, καθάπερ ἐφ᾽ ἑκάστου
5 ζῴου ἕκαστον τῶν μερῶν, ὡς ἔχει φύσεως καὶ
κατασκευῆς, οὕτω πρὸς τὸ ὅλον συντελεῖ καὶ
ὑπουργεῖ καὶ τάξεως καὶ χρείας ἠξίωται· δίδωσί
τε τὸ παρ᾽ αὑτοῦ καὶ δέχεται τὰ παρὰ τῶν ἄλλων,
ὅσων αὐτῷ δεκτικὴ ἡ φύσις· καὶ οἷον συναίσθησις
παντὸς πρὸς πᾶν· καὶ εἰ ἕκαστον δὲ τῶν μερῶν
10 καὶ ζῷον ἦν, εἶχεν ἂν καὶ ζῴου ἔργα ἕτερα ὄντα
τῶν τοῦ μέρους. καὶ δὴ κἀκεῖνο ἀναφαίνεται,
ὅπως τὸ καθ᾽ ἡμᾶς ἔχει, ὡς ποιοῦντές τι καὶ ἡμεῖς
ἐν τῷ παντί, οὐ μόνον ὅσα σῶμα πρὸς σῶμα καὶ
πάσχον αὖ τὰ τοιαῦτα, ἔτι καὶ τὴν ἄλλην αὐτῶν
φύσιν εἰσφερόμεθα συναφθέντες τοῖς συγγενέσιν
15 οἷς ἔχομεν πρὸς τὰ συγγενῆ τῶν ἔξω· καὶ δὴ καὶ
ψυχαῖς ἡμῶν καὶ διαθέσεσι συναφεῖς γινόμενοι,
μᾶλλον δὲ ὄντες, πρός τε τὰ ἐφεξῆς ἐν τῷ δαιμονίῳ

world: this is what the magic of nature does; for to pursue what is not good as if it was good, drawn by the appearance of good by irrational impulses, belongs to one who is being ignorantly led where he does not want to go. And what would anyone call this other than magical enchantment? The man, then, is alone free from enchantment who when his other parts are trying to draw him says that none of the things are good which they declare to be so, but only that which he knows himself, not deluded or pursuing, but possessing it. So he would not be drawn in any direction.

45. From everything which has been said this is perfectly clear, that each thing in the All, according to how it is in nature and disposition, contributes to the All and is acted upon and acts, just as in each individual living thing each of the parts, according to how it is in nature and condition, contributes to the whole and serves its purposes and has its own proper rank and utility; it gives what comes from it and receives as much of what comes from the others as its nature is capable of receiving; and all has a kind of common awareness of all ; and if each of the parts was a living being, it would have functions as a living being different from its functions as a part. And this too has become obvious, how it is with us, that we too do something in the All, not only all that body does to body, and the kind of ways in which body is affected in return, but we also introduce the other nature which we have, in that we are connected by what we have that is akin to us in things outside us: we have certainly become connected, or rather we are connected, by our souls and dispositions both to what is next to us in the region of

τόπῳ καὶ τὰ ἐπέκεινα αὐτῶν οὐκ ἔστιν ὅπως λαν-
θάνομεν ὁποῖοί τινες ἐσμέν. οὐ τοίνυν οὐδὲ τὰ
αὐτὰ πάντες δίδομεν οὐδὲ ταὐτὸν δεχόμεθα· ὃ γὰρ
20 μὴ ἔχομεν πῶς ἂν μεταδοίημεν ἄλλῳ, οἷον ἀγαθόν;
οὐδ' αὖ τῷ μὴ δεκτικῷ ἀγαθοῦ ἀγαθόν τι κομιού-
μεθα. τὴν οὖν αὐτοῦ τις κακίαν συνάψας ἐγνώσθη
τε ὅς ἐστι καὶ κατὰ τὴν αὐτοῦ φύσιν ὤσθη εἰς ὃ
ἔχει καὶ ἐνταῦθα καὶ ἐντεῦθεν ἀπαλλαγεὶς εἰς
25 ἄλλον τοιοῦτον τόπον φύσεως ὁλκαῖς. τῷ δὲ
ἀγαθῷ αἵ τε λήψεις αἵ τε δόσεις καὶ αἱ μεταθέσεις
ἄλλαι, ὥσπερ ἐκ μηρίνθων ὁλκαῖς τισι φύσεως
μετατιθεμένων. οὕτω θαυμαστῶς ἔχει δυνάμεως
καὶ τάξεως τόδε τὸ πᾶν γινομένων ἁπάντων
ἀψόφῳ κελεύθῳ κατὰ δίκην, ἣν οὐκ ἔστι
φυγεῖν οὐδενί, ἧς ἐπαΐει μὲν ὁ φαῦλος οὐδέν,
30 ἄγεται δὲ οὐκ εἰδὼς οἷ δεῖ ἐν τῷ παντὶ φέρεσθαι·
ὁ δ' ἀγαθὸς καὶ οἶδε, καὶ οὗ δεῖ ἄπεισι, καὶ
γινώσκει πρὶν ἀπιέναι οὗ ἀνάγκη αὐτῷ ἐλθόντι
οἰκεῖν, καὶ εὔελπίς ἐστιν, ὡς μετὰ θεῶν ἔσοιτο.
ἐν μὲν γὰρ ὀλίγῳ ζῴῳ σμικραὶ τῶν μερῶν αἱ
μεταβολαὶ καὶ συναισθήσεις καὶ οὐκ ἔστιν ἐν
35 αὐτῷ τὰ μέρη ζῷα εἶναι, εἰ μή που ἐπὶ βραχὺ

---

[1] As in IV. 3. 15–17 (see notes there) some influence of the
"cosmic religiosity" of the period can be detected here. The
"region of the spirits" is the air, "what lies beyond them"
is the Upper Cosmos of the heavenly bodies.

[2] Plotinus is here summarising the doctrine of Plato *Laws*
X 903E ff., with a reminiscence of the passage about men as

the spirits and to what lies beyond them and it is impossible that it should be unknown what sort of people we are.[1] But of course we do not all give the same things, or receive the same: for how could we give to another what we have not got—for instance, good? Nor, again, could we get any good if we have an incapacity to receive it. Anyone, therefore, who connects up his wickedness is recognised for what he is, and according to his own nature is thrust into that which holds him here in this world, and, when he escapes from here, into another region of the same kind by the pull of nature. But for the good man his acts of taking and giving and his transferences are different, since [all things] are transferred by pulls of nature as if they were drawn by lines.[2] So wonderfully is this All possessed of power and order; all things go their quiet way according to a justice which nobody can escape; the bad man understands nothing of it, but is taken without knowing it to the place in the All to which he is destined to be carried; but the good man both knows and departs where he must, and knows before he departs where it is necessary for him to come and dwell, and has the good hope that he will be with gods.[3] For in a small living being the changes of the parts and their mutual perceptions of each other are little ones, and it is not possible for the parts in it to be living beings— ᴇxcept perhaps for a short time in some things [4]; but

puppets of the gods moved by strings in I 644D–E (σμήρινθοι 644E2). The " quiet way " is from Euripides *Troades* 887–8.

[3] Cp. Plato *Phaedo* 63B–C.

[4] Plotinus may possibly be thinking here of Aristotle's reflections on the psychology of cut-up insects in *De Anima* A 5, 411b19–22 and B 2, 413b19–24.

ἔν τισιν· ἐν δὲ τῷ ἐν ᾧ διαστάσεις τε τοσαῦται
καὶ ἕκαστον τῶν ἐν αὐτῷ χάλασιν ἔχει καὶ ζῷά
ἐστι πολλά, τὰς κινήσεις δεῖ καὶ τὰς μεταστάσεις
μείζους εἶναι. ὁρῶμεν δὲ καὶ ἥλιον καὶ σελήνην
καὶ τὰ ἄλλα ἄστρα ἐν τάξει μετατιθέμενα καὶ
40 μετακινούμενα. οὐ τοίνυν ἄλογον οὐδὲ τὰς ψυχὰς
μετατίθεσθαι μὴ τὸ αὐτὸ ἀεὶ ἦθος σῳζομένας, τατ-
τομένας δὲ ἀνάλογον ὧν ἔπαθον καὶ ποιοῦσι, τάξιν
οἷον κεφαλῆς, τὰς δὲ οἷον ποδῶν λαβούσας, πρὸς τὸ
πᾶν σύμφωνον. ἔχει γὰρ καὶ αὐτὸ διαφορὰς πρὸς τὸ
45 ἄμεινόν τε καὶ χεῖρον. ἢ δ' ἂν μήτε τὸ ἄμεινον τὸ
ἐνταῦθα αἱρῆται μήτε τοῦ χείρονος μετέχουσα ᾖ,
ἄλλον τόπον καὶ καθαρὸν ἠλλάξατο τοῦτον, ὃν
εἵλετο, λαβοῦσα. αἱ δὲ κολάσεις ὥσπερ νενοσηκότων
μερῶν, τῶν μὲν ἐπιστύψεις φαρμάκοις, τῶν δὲ
ἐξαιρέσεις ἢ καὶ ἀλλοιώσεις, ἵνα ὑγιαίνοι τὸ πᾶν
50 ἑκάστου διατιθεμένου οὗ δεῖ· τὸ δ' ὑγιεινὸν τοῦ
παντὸς ἀλλοιουμένου, τοῦ δὲ ἐξαιρουμένου ἐντεῦθεν,
ὡς ἐνθαδὶ νοσοῦντος, οὗ δὲ μὴ νοσήσει, τιθεμένου.

in that in which the distances are so great and each of the things in it has freedom of movement, and there are many living beings, the movements and transitions must be greater. And we see that the sun and moon and the other heavenly bodies make their transits and move from place to place in order. It is not then unreasonable either for souls to change their places, since they do not always keep the same character, and are ranked in accordance with their experiences and actions, some receiving a rank like that of the head, others like that of the feet, in tune with the All: for the All itself has differences of better and worse. But the soul which neither chooses what is better here below, nor has any part in what is worse, changes to another place, a pure one, and has the position which it chose. But the punishments are like [the medical treatment] of diseased parts; some have caustics applied to them, others are extracted or modified, so that the All may be healthy when every part is disposed where it should be; but the healthy state of the All comes about when one part is modified, and another extracted from the place where it is diseased and placed where it will not be diseased.

IV. 5. (29) ΠΕΡΙ ΨΥΧΗΣ ΑΠΟΡΙΩΝ ΤΡΙΤΟΝ Η ΠΕΡΙ ΟΨΕΩΣ

1. Ἐπεὶ δὲ ὑπερεθέμεθα σκέψασθαι, εἰ μηδενὸς ὄντος μεταξὺ ἔστιν ὁρᾶν οἷον ἀέρος ἢ ἄλλου τινὸς τοῦ λεγομένου διαφανοῦς σώματος, νῦν σκεπτέον. ὅτι μὲν οὖν διὰ σώματός τινος δεῖ τὸ ὁρᾶν καὶ 5 ὅλως τὸ αἰσθάνεσθαι γίνεσθαι, εἴρηται· ἄνευ μὲν γὰρ σώματος πάντῃ ἐν τῷ νοητῷ τὴν ψυχὴν εἶναι. τοῦ δὲ αἰσθάνεσθαι ὄντος ἀντιλήψεως οὐ νοητῶν, ἀλλὰ αἰσθητῶν μόνον, δεῖ πως τὴν ψυχὴν συναφῆ γενομένην τοῖς αἰσθητοῖς διὰ τῶν προσομοίων κοινωνίαν τινὰ πρὸς αὐτὰ γνώσεως ἢ παθήματος 10 ποιεῖσθαι. διὸ καὶ δι' ὀργάνων σωματικῶν ἡ γνῶσις· διὰ γὰρ τούτων οἷον συμφυῶν ἢ συνεχῶν ὄντων οἷον εἰς ἕν πως πρὸς αὐτὰ τὰ αἰσθητὰ ἰέναι, ὁμοπαθείας τινὸς οὕτω πρὸς αὐτὰ γινομένης. εἰ οὖν δεῖ συναφήν τινα πρὸς τὰ γινωσκόμενα γίνεσθαι, 15 περὶ μὲν τῶν ὅσα ἁφῇ τινι γινώσκεται, τί ἄν τις ζητοῖ; περὶ δὲ τῆς ὁράσεως—εἰ δὲ καὶ περὶ τῆς ἀκοῆς, ὕστερον—ἀλλὰ περὶ τοῦ ὁρᾶν, εἰ δεῖ τι

IV. 5. ON DIFFICULTIES ABOUT THE SOUL III, OR ON SIGHT

1. Since we undertook [1] to investigate whether it is possible to see without any medium, like air or some other body of the kind called transparent, we must now carry out the investigation. Now we have said that seeing, and in general sense-perception, must take place by means of some body; for without body the soul is wholly in the intelligible world. Since sense-perception is an apprehension, not of intelligible objects, but of sense-objects alone, the soul must somehow be connected with sense-objects through things which are very much like them and establish a sort of communion of knowledge or affection with them. This is why this knowledge comes through bodily organs; for through these, which are in a way naturally united to or continuous with sense-objects, the soul must somehow in some way come to a unity with the sense-objects themselves, and so a sort of common affection with them must arise. If then there must be a connection with the objects which are being known, why should one investigate all the things which are known by some kind of touch? But about seeing—we shall discuss later if we also ought to include hearing—but about sight, we must enquire whether there must be

[1] In IV. 4. 23. 42 ff. The reference back in the next sentence is to the same chapter.

μεταξὺ εἶναι σῶμα τῆς ὄψεως καὶ τοῦ χρώματος.
ἢ νύττοι κατὰ συμβεβηκὸς ἂν τὸ μεταξὺ σῶμα,
συμβάλλεται δὲ οὐδὲν πρὸς ὅρασιν τοῖς ὁρῶσιν;
20 ἀλλ' εἰ πυκνὰ μὲν ὄντα τὰ σώματα, ὥσπερ τὰ
γεηρά, κωλύει ὁρᾶν, ὅσῳ δὲ λεπτότερα ἀεὶ τὰ
μεταξύ, μᾶλλον ὁρῶμεν, συνεργὰ ἄν τις τοῦ ὁρᾶν τὰ
μεταξὺ θείη. ἤ, εἰ οὐ συνεργά, οὐ κωλυτικά· ταῦτα
δὲ κωλυτικὰ ἄν τις εἴποι. ἀλλ' εἰ τὸ πάθος πρότερον τὸ μεταξὺ παραδέχεται καὶ οἷον τυποῦται—
25 σημεῖον δὲ τό, εἰ καὶ ἔμπροσθέν τις ἡμῶν ἔστη [1]
πρὸς τὸ χρῶμα βλέπων, κἀκεῖνον ὁρᾶν—πάθους ἐν
τῷ μεταξὺ μὴ γενομένου οὐδ' ἂν εἰς ἡμᾶς τοῦτο
ἀφικνοῖτο. ἢ οὐκ ἀνάγκη τὸ μεταξὺ πάσχειν, εἰ τὸ
πεφυκὸς πάσχειν—ὁ ὀφθαλμός—πάσχει· ἤ, εἰ
30 πάσχοι, ἄλλο πάσχει· ἐπεὶ οὐδ' ὁ κάλαμος ὁ
μεταξὺ τῆς νάρκης καὶ τῆς χειρός, ὃ πάσχει ἡ χείρ·
καὶ μὴν κἀκεῖ, εἰ μὴ μεταξὺ ὁ κάλαμος εἴη καὶ ἡ
θρίξ, οὐκ ἂν πάθοι ἡ χείρ. ἢ τοῦτο μὲν καὶ αὐτὸ
ἀμφισβητοῖτο ἄν· καὶ γάρ, εἰ ἐντὸς δικτύου γένοιτο,
ὁ θηρευτὴς πάσχειν λέγεται τὸ ναρκᾶν. ἀλλὰ γὰρ
35 κινδυνεύει ὁ λόγος ἐπὶ τὰς λεγομένας συμπαθείας
ἰέναι. εἰ δὲ τοδὶ ὑπὸ τουδὶ πέφυκε πάσχειν συμπα-

---

[1] Beutler: ἔσται ἢ Enn.: ἔσται ᾗ H–S[1]: ἔσται Kirchhoff,
Volkmann*.

some body between the eye and the colour. Or does the body in between impinge [1] incidentally on the sight, but contribute nothing to the seeing for those who see? But if when the bodies in between are dense, earthy for instance, they prevent us seeing, but we see better in proportion as the intervening bodies are subtler, one might maintain that the intermediaries are a help to sight. Otherwise, if they cannot be a help, they cannot be a hindrance: but one would say that earthy bodies are a hindrance. But if the body in between receives the affection first, and is in a way stamped by it—an indication that this is so is the fact that if someone is standing in front of us, in so far as he is looking at the colour, he sees it too—then, if there was no affection in the intermediary, this would not reach us either. But on the other hand it is not necessary that the intermediary should be affected if that which is naturally disposed to be affected—the eye—is affected; or if it is affected, it is affected in a different way: for the rod which is between the torpedo-fish and the hand is not affected at all in the same way as the hand; and certainly there too, if the rod and the line were not in between, the hand would not be affected.[2] Or even this might be disputed: for if the torpedo-fish gets into a net, the fisherman is said to receive a shock. But really the discussion seems to be moving in the direction of the sympathies we

[1] The word νύττοι was used in this context by the Stoics; cp. Alexander of Aphrodisias *Mantissa* p. 130, 15 Bruns (=*SVF* II. 864).

[2] The example of the torpedo-fish is probably drawn from ordinary observation; but the comparison of Socrates to the fish in Plato *Meno* 80A may have suggested it to Plotinus.

θῶς τῷ τινα ὁμοιότητα ἔχειν πρὸς αὐτό, οὐκ ἂν τὸ
μεταξὺ ἀνόμοιον ὂν πάθοι, ἢ τὸ αὐτὸ οὐκ ἂν πάθοι.
εἰ τοῦτο, πολλῷ μᾶλλον μηδενὸς ὄντος μεταξὺ
πάθοι ἂν τὸ πεφυκὸς πάσχειν, κἂν τὸ μεταξὺ
40 τοιοῦτον ᾖ, οἷον αὐτὸ καὶ παθεῖν τι.

2. Εἰ μὲν οὖν τοιοῦτόν ἐστι τὸ ὁρᾶν, οἷον τὸ τῆς
ὄψεως φῶς συνάπτειν πρὸς τὸ μεταξὺ [φῶς] [1] μέχρι
τοῦ αἰσθητοῦ, δεῖ μεταξὺ τοῦτο εἶναι τὸ φῶς, καὶ
ἡ ὑπόθεσις αὕτη τὸ μεταξὺ τοῦτο ζητεῖ· εἰ δὲ
5 τροπὴν ἐργάζεται τὸ ὑποκείμενον σῶμα κεχρωσμένον, τί κωλύει τὴν τροπὴν εὐθὺς πρὸς τὸ ὄμμα
ἰέναι μηδενὸς ὄντος μεταξύ; εἰ καὶ νῦν ἐξ ἀνάγκης,
ὅτε ἐστί, τρέπεταί πως τὸ τῶν ὀμμάτων πρόσθεν
κείμενον. καὶ οἱ ἐκχέοντες δὲ τὰς ὄψεις οὐκ ἂν
10 ἔχοιεν ἀκολουθοῦν τὸ πάντως μεταξύ τι εἶναι, εἰ
μὴ φοβοῖντο, μὴ πέσῃ ἡ ἀκτίς· ἀλλὰ φωτός ἐστι,
καὶ τὸ φῶς εὐθυπορῶν. οἱ δὲ τὴν ἔνστασιν αἰτιώ-
μενοι δέοιντο ἂν πάντως τοῦ μεταξύ. οἱ δὲ τῶν
εἰδώλων προστάται διὰ τοῦ κενοῦ λέγοντες διέναι
χώραν ζητοῦσιν, ἵνα μὴ κωλυθῇ· ὥστε, εἰ ἔτι
μᾶλλον οὐ κωλύσει τὸ μηδὲν εἶναι μεταξύ, οὐκ
15 ἀμφισβητοῦσι τῇ ὑποθέσει. ὅσοι δὲ συμπαθείᾳ τὸ

[1] delevimus.

---

[1] This very summary sketch of the doctrines of earlier
philosophers, which introduces Plotinus's own view that
seeing is by sympathy, seems to depend on earlier brief collec-
tions and summary refutations of philosophical theories of
vision: cp. especially Alexander of Aphrodisias op. cit. pp. 127,
17 ff. Bruns; also Pseudo-Plutarch *De Placitis Philosophorum*

talk about. But if one thing is naturally disposed to be sympathetically affected by another because it has some kind of likeness to it, then the intermediary between them, being unlike, would not be affected, or would not be affected in the same way. If this is so, then that which is naturally disposed to be affected would be so much more if there was nothing in between them, even if the intermediary was of such a kind as to be affected also in some way itself.

2. If then seeing is an activity of such a kind that the light of the eye connects with the intermediary which extends as far as the seen object, the light must be this intermediary, and this supposition requires this intermediary; but if the coloured body which is the object brings about an alteration [in the eye], what prevents the alteration getting to the eye immediately without any intermediary? This is all the more likely if, even as things are, that which is situated immediately in front of the eyes, when it is there, is necessarily altered in some way. Those who regard seeing as an efflux [of light from the eye] would not in consequence have to maintain that there was any intermediary at all, unless they were afraid that the ray might fall down, but it is a ray of light, and light goes straight. Those who regard resistance as the cause of sight would have every reason for requiring an intermediary. The advocates of images, who say that these pass through the void, require space to prevent obstruction; so that, if the absence of an intermediary will result in even less obstruction, they have no quarrel with the supposition.[1]

IV. 13, 901A–C; other references in the notes of the Harder–Beutler–Theiler edition II b, p. 548.

ὁρᾶν λέγουσιν, ἧττον μὲν ὁρᾶν φήσουσιν, εἴ τι
μεταξὺ εἴη, ἢ κωλύοι καὶ ἐμποδίζοι καὶ ἀμυδρὰν
ποιοῖ τὴν συμπάθειαν· μᾶλλον δὲ ἀκόλουθον λέγειν
ποιεῖν πάντως ἀμυδρὰν καὶ τὸ συγγενές, ᾗ καὶ
20 αὐτὸ πάσχον. καὶ γὰρ εἰ σῶμα συνεχὲς ἐν βάθει
ἐκ προσβολῆς πυρὸς καίοιτο, ἀλλὰ τὸ ἐν βάθει
αὐτοῦ τῇ προσβολῇ τοῦ πρόσθεν ἧττον ἂν πάσχοι.
ἀλλ᾽ εἰ ζῴου ἑνὸς μόρια εἴη συμπαθῆ, ἆρ᾽ ἂν
ἧττον πάθοι, ὅτι μεταξύ τί ἐστιν; ἢ ἧττον μὲν ἂν
πάθοι, σύμμετρον δ᾽ ἂν εἴη τὸ πάθος, ὅσον ἐβούλετο
25 ἡ φύσις, κωλύοντος τὸ ἄγαν τοῦ μεταξύ· εἰ μή
που τοιοῦτον εἴη τὸ διδόμενον, ὥστε ὅλως τὸ
μεταξὺ μὴ πάσχειν. ἀλλ᾽ εἰ συμπαθὲς τῷ ἓν ζῷον
εἶναι, καὶ ἡμεῖς πάσχομεν ὅτι ἐν ἑνὶ καὶ ἑνός, πῶς
οὐ δεῖ, ὅταν τοῦ πόρρω αἴσθησις ᾖ, συνέχειαν εἶναι;
ἢ τὴν συνέχειαν καὶ τὸ μεταξὺ διὰ τὸ τὸ ζῷον δεῖν
30 συνεχὲς εἶναι, τὸ δὲ πάθος κατὰ συμβεβηκὸς
συνεχοῦς, ἢ πᾶν ὑπὸ παντὸς φήσομεν πάσχειν. εἰ
δὲ τόδε μὲν ὑπὸ τοῦδε, ἄλλο δὲ ὑπ᾽ ἄλλου οὐ τὸ
αὐτό, οὐκ ἂν δέοιτό τις τοῦ μεταξὺ πανταχοῦ. εἰ
οὖν ἐπὶ ὄψεως λέγοι τις δεῖσθαι, διὰ τί φατέον·
ἐπεὶ οὐδὲ πανταχοῦ φαίνεται τὸ δι᾽ ἀέρος ἰὸν
35 πάσχειν ποιοῦν τὸν ἀέρα, ἀλλ᾽ ἢ μόνον διαιρεῖν·
οἷον λίθος εἰ ἄνωθεν πίπτοι, τί ἄλλο ἢ οὐχ ὑπομένει
286

But all those who say that seeing takes place by sympathy will assert that one would see less well if there was any intermediary, in that it would obstruct and hinder and weaken the sympathy; but it would be more consistent to say that even that which is akin in all circumstances weakens the sympathy, in so far as it is itself affected. Certainly, if a body continuous to the bottom is set alight by the application of fire, all the same the bottom of it will be less affected by the fire applied to it than the part before it. But if the parts of one living being are in sympathy will they be less affected because there is something between them? Yes, perhaps they might be less affected, but the affection would be in the proportion which nature willed, and the intermediary would prevent excess: unless what is conceded amounts to this, that the intermediary is not affected at all. But if sympathy depends on being one living thing, and we are affected because we are in one and belong to one, how is continuity not needed when there is perception of something far off? The answer is that continuity and the intermediary are there because the living being must be continuous, but the affection is only incidentally of something continuous, or we shall have to say that everything is affected by everything. But if one thing is affected by one thing and another by another, not in the same way, one would have no need at all of an intermediary. If then someone says that an intermediary is needed in the case of sight, he must say why; since it does not seem to be even generally true that what goes through the air produces any effect on the air, apart from simply dividing it: for instance, if a stone falls from above, does anything

ὁ ἀήρ; ἐπεὶ οὐδὲ τῇ ἀντιπεριστάσει εὔλογον κατὰ
φύσιν οὔσης τῆς φορᾶς· ἐπεὶ οὕτω καὶ τὸ πῦρ ἄνω
τῇ ἀντιπεριστάσει· ἀλλ’ ἄτοπον· φθάνει γὰρ τὸ πῦρ
40 τῇ αὑτοῦ κινήσει ταχείᾳ οὔσῃ τὴν ἀντιπερίστασιν
τοῦ ἀέρος. εἰ δ’ ὑπὸ τοῦ τάχους ταχύνεσθαί τις
τὴν ἀντιπερίστασίν φησιν, ἀλλὰ κατὰ συμβεβηκὸς
ἂν γίνοιτο, οὐκ εἰς τὸ ἄνωθεν· ἐπεὶ καὶ ἀπὸ τῶν
ξύλων ἡ ὁρμὴ πρὸς τὸ ἄνω οὐκ ὠθούντων· καὶ
45 ἡμεῖς δὲ κινούμενοι τέμνομεν τὸν ἀέρα, καὶ οὐχ ἡ
ἀντιπερίστασις ὠθεῖ, πληροῖ δὲ μόνον ἐφεπόμενος
τὸ παρ’ ἡμῶν κενούμενον. εἰ οὖν τοῖς σώμασι
διίσταται τοῖς τοιούτοις μηδὲν παθών, τί κωλύει καὶ
ἄνευ διαστάσεως συγχωρεῖν παριέναι τοῖς εἰς
ὄψιν εἴδεσιν; εἰ δὲ μηδὲ πάρεισιν ὡς ἐν ῥοῇ τὰ
εἴδη, τίς πάσχειν ἀνάγκη καὶ δι’ αὐτοῦ τὸ πάθος
50 πρὸς ἡμᾶς τῷ προπαθεῖν ἰέναι; εἰ γὰρ τῷ προπαθεῖν τὸν ἀέρα ἡ αἴσθησις ἡμῖν, οὐκ ἂν πρὸς αὐτὸ
βλέποντες τὸ ὁρώμενον εἴδομεν, ἀλλ’ ἐκ τοῦ παρακειμένου ἔσχομεν ἂν τὴν αἴσθησιν, ὥσπερ ἐπὶ τοῦ
θερμαίνεσθαι. ἐκεῖ γὰρ οὐ τὸ πόρρωθεν πῦρ, ἀλλὰ
55 ὁ ἀὴρ ὁ παρακείμενος θερμανθεὶς θερμαίνειν δοκεῖ·
ἀφῇ γὰρ τοῦτο, ἐν δὲ τοῖς ὁράμασιν οὐχ ἁφή· ὅθεν
οὐδ’ ἐπιτεθὲν τῷ ὄμματι τὸ αἰσθητὸν ὁρᾶν ποιεῖ,
ἀλλὰ φωτισθῆναι δεῖ τὸ μεταξύ· ἢ ὅτι σκοτεινὸν ὁ

---

[1] Cp. again Alexander of Aphrodisias op. cit. 129, 1 Bruns.
[2] Cp. IV. 6. 1. 32–3; Aristotle De Anima B 7, 419a12–13.

else happen except that the air does not stay as it is? For it is unreasonable to say [that the stone falls] as the result of the reciprocal thrust[1] of bodies, when its fall is natural, since if this was so fire would go upwards by reciprocal thrust: but this is absurd, for the fire by the speed of its movement gets ahead of the reciprocal thrust of air. But if anyone says that the reciprocal thrust is speeded up by the speed of the movement of fire, this would all the same happen incidentally, and would not cause the upward movement; for in trees also the impulse to grow upwards comes from themselves, without anything pushing them; and we when we are in motion cut through the air, and the reciprocal thrust does not push us on, but only follows us and fills up the place we have left empty. If then the air parts to make way for bodies like these without being affected, what prevents it from allowing passage, even without parting, for the forms which come to our sight? But if the forms do not even pass through the air as if in a stream, what need is there for the air to be affected and for the affection to reach us through it as the result of its previous affection? For if our perception resulted from the air being previously affected, when we looked at the object of sight we should not see it, but we should get our perception from the air which lay close to us, just as when we are warmed. For in this case it is not considered to be the distant fire, but the warmed air lying close, that warms us; for warming is by contact, but in acts of seeing there is no contact; this is the reason why the sense-object does not produce sight when it is placed on the eye,[2] but the intermediary space must be illu-

ἀήρ. μὴ ὄντος δὲ τούτου σκοτεινοῦ οὐδ' ἂν ἐδέησε
φωτὸς ἴσως. τὸ γὰρ σκοτεινὸν ἐμπόδιον ὂν τοῦ
60 ὁρᾶν δεῖ κρατηθῆναι τῷ φωτί. τάχα δὲ ἂν καὶ
προσαχθὲν τῇ ὄψει οὐχ ὁρᾶται, ὅτι σκιὰν φέρει
τὴν τοῦ ἀέρος καὶ τὴν αὑτοῦ.

3. Μέγιστον δὲ μαρτύριον τοῦ μὴ διὰ τοῦ ἀέρος
παθόντος τὸ εἶδος τοῦ αἰσθητοῦ ὁρᾶν [καὶ τὰς τούτων μορφὰς]¹ ὥσπερ διαδόσει τὸ νύκτωρ ἐν σκότῳ
πῦρ τε καὶ τὰ ἄστρα ὁρᾶσθαι καὶ τὰς τούτων μορ-
5 φάς. οὐ γὰρ δὴ φήσει τις ἐν τῷ σκοτεινῷ τὰ εἴδη
γενόμενα οὕτω συνάψασθαι· ἢ οὐκ ἂν ἦν σκότος
τοῦ πυρὸς ἐλλάμψαντος τὸ αὑτοῦ εἶδος. ἐπεὶ καὶ
πάνυ πολλοῦ σκότου ὄντος καὶ κεκρυμμένων καὶ
τῶν ἄστρων [καὶ τοῦ πυρὸς]² καὶ τοῦ φωτὸς τοῦ
παρ' αὐτῶν μὴ ἐλλάμποντος ἐκ τῶν φρυκτωριῶν
10 ὁρᾶται τὸ πῦρ, καὶ ἐκ τῶν πύργων τῶν ταῖς ναυσὶ
σημαινόντων. εἰ δὲ καὶ διιέναι τις λέγοι καὶ ἐν
τούτοις τὸ πῦρ ἐναντιούμενος τῇ αἰσθήσει, ἐχρῆν
τὴν ὄψιν τοῦ ἀμυδροῦ τοῦ ἐν τῷ ἀέρι ποιεῖσθαι τὴν
ἀντίληψιν, οὐκ ἐκείνου αὐτοῦ, οἷόν ἐστιν ἐναργές.
εἰ δὲ μεταξὺ σκότου ὄντος ὁρᾶται τὸ ἐπέκεινα,
15 πολλῷ μᾶλλον μηδενός. ἀλλ' ἐκείνῳ ἄν τις ἐπιστή-
σειε, μὴ τῷ μεταξὺ μηδὲν οὐκ ἔσται ὁρᾶν, οὐχ ὅτι
μηδέν ἐστι μεταξύ, ἀλλ' ὅτι ἡ συμπάθεια τοῦ ζῴου
ἀναιρεῖται πρὸς αὑτὸ καὶ ἡ πρὸς ἄλληλα τῶν μερῶν
τῷ ἓν εἶναι. τούτῳ γὰρ ἔοικε καὶ τὸ αἰσθάνεσθαι

¹ del. Kirchhoff, ut iteratum e lin. 4.
² del. Volkmann*.

minated—or this may be because the air is [naturally] dark. If it was not dark, it would not perhaps need light. For the darkness which hinders seeing needs to be mastered by the light. But perhaps when the object is applied to the eye it is not seen because it brings with it the shadow of the air and its own shadow.

3. The most important evidence that we do not see the form of the sense-object by a kind of transmission through the medium of the air which has been affected is that fire and the heavenly bodies and their shapes are seen by night. For certainly nobody will assert that the forms come to be present in the darkness and so make connection with the eye: or there would not be a darkness, as the fire would radiate its own form. For even when it is very dark indeed and the stars are hidden and the light from them does not shine, the fire from beacons and lighthouses is seen. But if someone, contradicting the evidence of the senses, says that even in these cases the fire passes through the air, then the eye would have to apprehend the dimness in the air, not that original fire in all its brightness. But if when darkness intervenes what lies beyond is seen, it would be all the more visible with nothing intervening. But one might pause to consider this further point, whether it is not possible to see in the absence of an intermediary, not because there is no intermediary but because the sympathy of the living being with itself and of its parts with each other, which depends on being one thing, will be done away with. For it

20 ὁπωσοῦν εἶναι, ὅτι συμπαθὲς τὸ ζῷον—τόδε τὸ πᾶν
—ἑαυτῷ. εἰ γὰρ μὴ τοῦτο, πῶς ἂν ἄλλο ἄλλου τῆς
δυνάμεως μετελάμβανε καὶ μάλιστα τῆς πόρρω;
τοῦτο δὴ ἐπισκεπτέον, εἰ ἄλλος κόσμος ἦν καὶ ἄλλο
ζῷον μὴ συντελοῦν πρὸς τοῦτο καὶ ὄψις ἦν ἐπὶ
τοῖς νώτοις τοῦ οὐρανοῦ, εἰ ἐθεάσατο ἐκεῖνον
25 ἐκ διαστήματος συμμέτρου· ἢ οὐδὲν ἂν εἴη πρὸς
ἐκεῖνον τούτῳ. ἀλλὰ τοῦτο μὲν ὕστερον. νῦν δὲ
κἀκεῖνο ἄν τις μαρτύραιτο εἰς τὸ μὴ τῷ πάσχειν τὸ
μεταξὺ τούτῳ τὸ ὁρᾶν γίνεσθαι. εἰ γὰρ δὴ πάσχοι
τὸ τοῦ ἀέρος, σωματικῶς δήπουθεν ἀνάγκη πάσ-
χειν· τοῦτο δέ ἐστιν οἷον ἐν κηρῷ τύπον γενέσθαι.
30 μέρος δὴ δεῖ τοῦ ὁρατοῦ καθ' ἕκαστον μόριον τυ-
ποῦσθαι· ὥστε καὶ τὸ συναφὲς τῇ ὄψει μόριον τοσοῦτον, ὅσον καὶ ἡ κόρη τὸ καθ' αὑτὸ μόριον τοῦ
ὁρατοῦ δέχοιτο ἄν. νῦν δὲ πᾶν τε ὁρᾶται, καὶ ὅσοι
ἐν τῷ ἀέρι κατά γε τὸ καταντικρὺ ἔκ τε πλαγίων
ἐπὶ πολὺ ὁρῶσιν ἐγγύς τε καὶ κατόπιν οὐκ ἐπιπροσ-
35 θούμενοι· ὥστε ἕκαστον μόριον τοῦ ἀέρος ὅλον
οἷον τὸ πρόσωπον τὸ ὁρώμενον ἔχειν· τοῦτο δὲ οὐ
κατὰ σώματος πάθημα, ἀλλὰ κατὰ μείζους καὶ
ψυχικὰς καὶ ζῴου ἑνὸς συμπαθοῦς ἀνάγκας.

4. Ἀλλὰ τὸ συναφὲς τῆς ὄψεως φῶς πρὸς τὸ περὶ

looks as if any kind of perception depends on this, that the living being—this All—is in sympathy with itself. For if this were not so, how would one thing share in the power of another, and especially in power from a distance? But we should consider this problem: if there was another universe, that is another living being making no contribution to the life of this one, and there was an eye " on the back of the sky ", would it see that other universe at a proportionate distance [1]? This universe would have nothing to do with that one. But we will discuss this later. But now one might produce this additional evidence to show that seeing does not happen through the intermediary being affected. For if the intermediary air was affected, the affection would presumably have to be a bodily one; but this means there would have to be an impression, as in wax. Then a part of the seen object would have to be stamped on each part of the air; so that the part of the air in contact with the eye would receive a part of the seen object just as large as the part which the pupil of the eye would receive according to its own size. But as it is, the whole object is seen, and all those who are in the air see it, from the front and sideways, from far and near, and from the back, as long as their line of sight is not blocked; so that each part of the air contains the whole seen object, the face for instance; but this is not a bodily affection, but is brought about by higher necessities of the soul belonging to a single living being in sympathy with itself.

4. But what is the situation with the light of the

---

[1] The phrase " on the back of the sky " is taken from Plato *Phaedrus* 247B7–C1. This interesting speculation is pursued further in ch. 8: see note there.

τὴν ὄψιν καὶ μέχρι τοῦ αἰσθητοῦ πῶς; ἢ πρῶτον
μὲν τοῦ μεταξὺ ἀέρος οὐ δεῖται, εἰ μὴ ἄρα τὸ φῶς
οὐκ ἂν ἀέρος ἄνευ λέγοιτο. οὕτω δὲ τοῦτο μεταξὺ
5 κατὰ συμβεβηκός, αὐτὸ δὲ φῶς ἂν εἴη μεταξὺ οὐ
πάσχον· οὐδ' ὅλως πάθους ἐνταῦθα δεῖ, ἀλλ'
ὅμως τοῦ μεταξύ· εἰ δὲ τὸ φῶς οὐ σῶμα, οὐ
σώματος. καὶ δὴ οὐ πρὸς τὸ ὁρᾶν ἁπλῶς δέοιτο ἂν
τοῦ φωτὸς τοῦ ἀλλοτρίου καὶ μεταξὺ ἡ ὄψις, ἀλλὰ
πρὸς τὸ πόρρω ὁρᾶν. τὸ μὲν οὖν εἰ τὸ φῶς γένοιτο
10 ἄνευ τοῦ ἀέρος, ὕστερον· νῦν δὲ ἐκεῖνο σκεπτέον.
εἰ μὲν γὰρ τὸ φῶς τοῦτο τὸ συναφὲς ἔμψυχον
γίνεται, καὶ ἡ ψυχὴ δι' αὐτοῦ φερομένη καὶ ἐν
αὐτῷ γιγνομένη, ὥσπερ καὶ ἐπὶ τοῦ ἔνδον, ἐν τῷ
ἀντιλαμβάνεσθαι δήπουθεν, ὅπερ ἐστὶν ὁρᾶν, οὐδὲν
15 ἂν δέοιτο τοῦ μεταξὺ φωτός, ἀλλ' ἁφῇ ἔσται ἐοικὸς
τὸ ὁρᾶν τῆς ὁρατικῆς δυνάμεως ἐν φωτὶ ἀντιλαμ-
βανομένης πάσχοντος οὐδὲν τοῦ μεταξύ, ἀλλὰ
γίνεται τῆς ὄψεως φορὰ ἐκεῖ. οὗ δὴ ζητητέον,
πότερα τῷ διάστημά τι εἶναι ἐκεῖ δεῖ πορευθῆναι
τὴν ὄψιν ἢ τῷ σῶμά τι εἶναι ἐν τῷ διαστήματι.
20 καὶ εἰ μὲν τῷ σῶμα ἐν τῷ διαστήματι εἶναι τὸ
διεῖργον, εἰ ἀφαιρεθείη τοῦτο, ὄψεται· εἰ δ' ὅτι
διάστημα ἁπλῶς, ἀργὴν δεῖ ὑποθέσθαι τὴν τοῦ
ὁρατοῦ φύσιν καὶ οὐδὲν δρῶσαν ὅλως. ἀλλ' οὐχ
οἷόν τε· οὐ γὰρ μόνον ἡ ἁφὴ ὅτι ἐγγύς τι

eye which is connected to the light around the eye
and as far as the object? Now first of all the intermediate air is not needed—unless it might be said
that the light could not be there without air. In this
way the air would be incidentally intermediate, but
the light itself would be intermediate without being
affected; and in general there is no need of an
affection here, but there is, all the same, need for an
intermediary; but if the light is not a body, there is
no need for a body. And, further, the eye would
not need this intermediate light, which is not its
own, just for seeing, but only for seeing at a distance.
The question then whether light could occur without
air will be discussed later [1]; but now we must consider our first question. If, then, this connecting
light is ensouled, and the soul moves through it and
is present in it, as it is also the case with the light
within the eye, then of course in the apprehension
of the object, which is what seeing is, there would
be no need of the intermediate light, but seeing will
be like touch; the power of sight will apprehend its
object in the light and the intermediary will not be
affected but the sight moves to its object. At this
point one must enquire whether the sight must move
there because there is a space between or because
there is a body in the space. And if it is because it
is a body in the intervening space which separates
sight and object, if this was removed, the sight would
see; but if it is simply because there is a space
between, one must assume that the nature of the
seen object is inert and does nothing at all. But
this is not possible: for touch does not only tell us

[1] In ch. 6.

λέγει καὶ ἅπτεται, ἀλλὰ τὰς τοῦ ἁπτοῦ πάσχουσα
25 ἀπαγγέλλει διαφοράς, καὶ εἰ μὴ διείργοι τι, κἂν
τοῦτο πόρρω, ᾔσθετο. ἅμα γὰρ ὁ ἀὴρ ὁ μεταξὺ
καὶ ἡμεῖς πυρὸς αἰσθανόμεθα οὐκ ἀναμείναντες
θερμανθῆναι ἐκεῖνον. μᾶλλον γοῦν τὸ σῶμα
θερμαίνεται τὸ στερεὸν ἢ ὁ ἀήρ· ὥστε δι᾽ αὐτοῦ
μᾶλλον, ἀλλ᾽ οὐ δι᾽ αὐτό. εἰ οὖν ἔχει δύναμιν
30 εἰς τὸ δρᾶν, τὸ δὲ εἰς τὸ πάσχειν, ἢ καὶ ὁπωσοῦν ἡ
ὄψις, διὰ τί ἄλλου δεῖται μέσου εἰς ὃ δύναται πρὸς
τὸ ποιῆσαι; τοῦτο γὰρ ἐμποδίου ἐστὶ δεῖσθαι.
ἐπεὶ καὶ ὅταν τὸ φῶς προσίῃ τὸ τοῦ ἡλίου, οὐ
πρότερον δεῖ τὸν ἀέρα εἶτα καὶ ἡμᾶς, ἀλλ᾽ ἅμα,
καὶ πρὶν ἐγγὺς τῆς ὄψεως γενέσθαι πολλάκις
ὄντος ἀλλαχοῦ, ὡς μὴ παθόντος τοῦ ἀέρος ἡμᾶς
35 ὁρᾶν, μεταξὺ ὄντος τοῦ μὴ πεπονθότος καὶ τοῦ
φωτὸς μήπω ἐληλυθότος, πρὸς ὃ δεῖ τὴν ὄψιν
συνάψαι. ἐπεὶ καὶ τὸ τῆς νυκτὸς ὁρᾶν τὰ ἄστρα
ἢ ὅλως πῦρ χαλεπὸν ταύτῃ τῇ ὑποθέσει ἀπευθῦναι.
εἰ δὲ μένει μὲν ἡ ψυχὴ ἐφ᾽ ἑαυτῆς, φωτὸς δὲ δεῖται
40 ὥσπερ βακτηρίας πρὸς τὸ φθάσαι, ἔδει τὴν ἀντίληψιν βίαιον καὶ ἀντερείδοντος εἶναι καὶ τεταμένου
τοῦ φωτός, καὶ τὸ αἰσθητόν, τὸ χρῶμα, ᾗ χρῶμα,
ἀντιτυποῦν καὶ αὐτὸ εἶναι· οὕτω γὰρ διὰ μέσου αἱ

that something is near and that it is touching it, but it is affected by and reports the distinctive characteristics of the object, and if there was nothing to separate it, it would perceive the object even if it was a long way off. For the intermediate air and we ourselves perceive a fire at the same time; we do not wait for the air to be warmed. Certainly the solid body [1] is more warmed than the air: so that [the perception of warmth] comes through the air but is not caused by the air. If then the object has the capacity to act, and the recipient of the perception, or in any way the sight, has the capacity to be affected, why does it need another medium to act on what it is capable of acting on? This is to need a hindrance. For when the light of the sun approaches, it does not have to reach the air first and then us, but it reaches both at the same time, and we often perceive it when it is elsewhere, before it comes near our eyes; so we see without the air being affected, with that which has not been affected in between and when the light with which our sight must connect has not yet arrived. Also it would be difficult on this hypothesis to explain correctly how we see the stars, or any kind of fire, at night. But if the soul stays in its own place, but needs light like a stick to reach the object with,[2] then the apprehension would be a violent business, with the light stretched out and pushing against the object and the object of perception, the colour as colour, itself pressing back: for this is how sensations of touch occur through a medium. And [on this hypothesis] the object was

---

[1] I.e. our body.

[2] Again the Stoic theory according to Alexander of Aphrodisias, op. cit. 130, 17 Bruns ($=SVF$ II 867).

ἀφαί. εἶτα καὶ πρότερον ἐγγὺς γέγονε μηδενὸς
μεταξὺ ὄντος τότε· οὕτω γὰρ ὕστερον τὸ διὰ
45 μέσου ἅπτεσθαι ποιεῖ τὴν γνῶσιν, οἷον τῇ μνήμῃ
καὶ ἔτι μᾶλλον συλλογισμῷ· νῦν δὲ οὐχ οὕτως.
ἀλλ᾽ εἰ παθεῖν δεῖ τὸ πρὸς τὸ αἰσθητὸν φῶς, εἶτα
διαδοῦναι μέχρι ὄψεως, ἡ αὐτὴ γίνεται ὑπόθεσις τῇ
ἀπὸ τοῦ αἰσθητοῦ τὸ μεταξὺ πρότερον τρεπούσῃ,
πρὸς ἣν ἤδη καὶ ἐν ἄλλοις ἠπόρηται.

5. Περὶ δὲ τοῦ ἀκούειν ἆρα ἐνταῦθα συγχωρητέον,
πάσχοντος τοῦ ἀέρος τὴν κίνησιν τὴν πρώτην τοῦ
παρακειμένου [1] ὑπὸ τοῦ τὸν ψόφον ποιοῦντος, τῷ
τὸν μέχρι ἀκοῆς ἀέρα πάσχειν τὸ αὐτό, οὕτως εἰς
5 αἴσθησιν ἀφικνεῖσθαι; ἢ κατὰ συμβεβηκὸς μὲν τὸ
μεταξὺ τῷ παρεῖναι ἐν μέσῳ ἀναιρεθέντος δὲ τοῦ
μεταξύ, ἅπαξ δὲ γενομένου τοῦ ψόφου, οἷον
συμβαλλόντων δύο σωμάτων, εὐθέως ἀπαντᾶν
πρὸς ἡμᾶς τὴν αἴσθησιν; ἢ καὶ δεῖ μὲν ἀέρος τὴν
πρώτην τοῦ πληττομένου, τὸ δὲ ἐντεῦθεν ἤδη
10 ἄλλως τὸ μεταξύ; ἐνταῦθα μὲν γὰρ δοκεῖ κύριος
εἶναι ὁ ἀὴρ τοῦ ψόφου· μὴ γὰρ ἂν μηδὲ τὴν
ἀρχὴν γενέσθαι ψόφον δύο σωμάτων συρραγέντων,
εἰ μὴ ὁ ἀὴρ πληγεὶς ἐν τῇ ταχείᾳ συνόδῳ αὐτῶν
καὶ ἐξωσθεὶς πλήξας ἔδωκε τῷ ἐφεξῆς μέχρις
15 ὤτων καὶ ἀκοῆς. ἀλλ᾽ εἰ ὁ ἀὴρ κύριος τοῦ ψόφου
καὶ τούτου κινηθέντος ἡ πληγή, παρὰ τί ἂν εἶεν αἱ

[1] Harder: τὸν παρακείμενον Enn.*: del. Beutler.

formerly close to the eye, and there was nothing then between them: for this is the way in which touching through a medium causes knowledge, as if by memory and, still more, by a process of reasoning: but as things are [seeing] is not like this. But if the light near the sense-object has to be affected first, and the affection then transmitted to the eye, this hypothesis becomes the same as that which first brings about an alteration in the intermediary which originates from the sense-object, against which we have raised objections elsewhere.[1]

5. But as far as hearing is concerned, must we agree that the neighbouring air is given the first movement by that which makes the sound, and that by the air as far as the ear being affected in the same way the movement reaches our perception? Or is the intermediary affected incidentally because it is in between, and if the intermediary was taken away would the sound, once it had occurred, for instance when two bodies collide, encounter our perception immediately? Or must there be air, that which is set vibrating by the first movement, and will the intermediary air from that point onwards have a different degree of importance? It does seem that there air is responsible for sound: for there would be no sound at all to begin with when two bodies clash together unless the air, struck by their quick coming together and pushed out, struck the air next to it and so transmitted the vibration to our ears and hearing. But if the air is responsible for sound and the vibration is of air in motion, what

---

[1] It is not clear to what Plotinus is referring here. The passage suggested by Henry–Schwyzer, IV. 4. 23. 20 ff. is, as Theiler points out, not very relevant.

διαφοραὶ τῶν φωνῶν καὶ τῶν ψόφων; ἄλλο γὰρ
ἠχεῖ χαλκὸς πρὸς χαλκὸν ἢ πρὸς ἄλλο, ἄλλο δὲ
ἄλλο· ὁ δὲ ἀὴρ εἷς καὶ ἡ ἐν αὐτῷ πληγή· οὐ γὰρ
μόνον τῷ μεγάλῳ καὶ τῷ μικρῷ διαφοραί. εἰ δ'
20 ὅτι πρὸς ἀέρα γενομένη πληγὴ ψόφον ἐποίησεν,
οὐχ ᾗ ἀὴρ φατέον· τότε γὰρ φωνεῖ, ὅταν στάσιν
λάβῃ στερεοῦ σώματος, πρὶν χυθῆναι μένων ὥσπερ
στερεόν τι· ὥστε ἀρκεῖ τὰ συγκρούοντα, καὶ τὴν
σύρρηξιν καὶ ταύτην τὴν πληγὴν εἶναι τὸν ψόφον
εἰς αἴσθησιν ἐλθοῦσαν· μαρτυρεῖν δὲ καὶ τοὺς
25 ἔνδον ἤχους τῶν ζῴων οὐκ ἐν ἀέρι, ἀλλὰ συγκρού-
σαντος καὶ πλήξαντος ἄλλο ἄλλου· οἷον καὶ
ὀστῶν κάμψεις καὶ πρὸς ἄλληλα παρατριβομένων
ἀέρος μὴ ὄντος μεταξὺ [καὶ][1] πρίσεις. ἀλλὰ περὶ
μὲν τούτου ἠπορήσθω ὁμοίου ἤδη καὶ ἐνταῦθα τοῦ
ζητήματος γενομένου, ὅπερ ἐλέγετο ἐπὶ τῆς
30 ὄψεως εἶναι, συναισθήσεώς τινος ὡς ἐν ζῴῳ καὶ
τοῦ κατὰ τὴν ἀκοὴν πάθους ὄντος.

6. Εἰ δὲ καὶ τὸ φῶς γένοιτο ἂν μὴ ὄντος ἀέρος,
οἷον ἡλίου [ὄντος][2] ἐν ἐπιφανείᾳ τῶν σωμάτων
ἐπιλάμποντος, τοῦ μεταξὺ ὄντος κενοῦ καὶ νῦν κατὰ
συμβεβηκός, ὅτι πάρεστι, φωτιζομένου; ἀλλ' εἰ
5 δι' αὐτὸν παθόντα καὶ τὰ ἄλλα, καὶ τὴν ὑπόστασιν
εἶναι τῷ φωτὶ διὰ τὸν ἀέρα—πάθημα γὰρ αὐτοῦ
εἶναι—μὴ ἂν οὖν ἔσεσθαι τὸ πάθημα μὴ ὄντος τοῦ
πεισομένου. ἢ πρῶτον μὲν οὐκ αὐτοῦ πρώτως
οὐδ' ᾗ αὐτός. ἔστι γὰρ καὶ αὐτοῦ ἑκάστου

[1] del. Theiler.
[2] del. Müller*.

would account for the differences between voices and between other sounds? For bronze when it strikes bronze has a different ring from when it strikes something else, and other things striking others make different noises; but the air is one and so is the vibration in it; the differences of sounds are not just differences of loud and soft. But if a stroke produces sound because it strikes air, it must be admitted that it is not in so far as it is air: for air speaks when it has the static quality of a solid body, when it stays still like something solid before it is set flowing; so that the colliding bodies and their clash are enough [to produce sound] and their impact is the sound which comes to our perception; the sounds inside living beings are evidence of this, which are not in air, but are produced by one part knocking and striking another: bending of joints, for instance, and the grinding of one bone against another with no air between them. But enough of our problems [about hearing]! The line of enquiry has been much the same here too as in the case of sight, since the experience of hearing is a kind of common awareness of the sort which occurs in a living being.

6. But could light also occur if there was no air, as when the sun shines upon the surfaces of bodies, if the intermediary was void—and even as things are the intermediary is illuminated incidentally, because it is there? But if light resulted from an affection of air and the other [translucent bodies], and light had its substantial existence through the air—for it would be an affection of it—the affection could not exist without something to be affected. Now, first of all light does not belong primarily to air, nor to air in virtue of its intrinsic character; for it belongs

σώματος πυρίνου καὶ λαμπροῦ· καὶ δὴ καὶ λίθων
10 τοιούτων φωτεινὴ χρόα. ἀλλὰ τὸ εἰς ἄλλο ἀπὸ τοῦ
ἔχοντος χρόαν τοιαύτην ἰὸν ἆρα ἂν εἴη μὴ ὄντος
ἐκείνου; ἀλλ' εἰ μὲν ποιότης μόνον καί τινος
ποιότης, ἐν ὑποκειμένῳ οὔσης πάσης ποιότητος,
ἀνάγκη καὶ τὸ φῶς ζητεῖν ἐν ᾧ ἔσται σώματι. εἰ
15 δὲ ἐνέργεια ἀπ' ἄλλου, διὰ τί οὐκ ὄντος ἐφεξῆς
σώματος, ἀλλὰ οἷον κενοῦ μεταξύ, εἴπερ οἷόν τε,
οὐκ ἔσται καὶ ἐπιβαλεῖ καὶ εἰς τὸ ἐπέκεινα; ἀτενὲς
γὰρ ὂν διὰ τί οὐ περάσει οὐκ ἐποχούμενον; εἰ δὲ
δὴ καὶ τοιοῦτον οἷον πεσεῖν, καταφερόμενον ἔσται.
20 οὐ γὰρ δὴ ὁ ἀὴρ οὐδ' ὅλως τὸ φωτιζόμενον ἔσται
τόδε ἕλκον ἀπὸ τοῦ φωτίζοντος καὶ βιαζόμενον
προελθεῖν· ἐπεὶ οὐδὲ συμβεβηκός, ὥστε πάντως
ἐπ' ἄλλῳ, ἢ πάθημα ἄλλου, ὥστε δεῖ εἶναι τὸ
πεισόμενον· ἢ ἔδει μένειν ἐληλυθότος· νῦν δὲ
ἄπεισιν· ὥστε καὶ ἔλθοι ἄν· ποῦ οὖν; ἢ τόπον
δεῖ μόνον εἶναι. ἢ οὕτω γε ἀπολεῖ τὴν ἐνέργειαν
25 [αὐτοῦ][1] τὴν ἐξ αὐτοῦ τὸ τοῦ ἡλίου σῶμα· τοῦτο
δὲ ἦν τὸ φῶς. εἰ δὲ τοῦτο, οὐδὲ τὸ φῶς τινος
ἔσται. ἔστι δὲ ἡ ἐνέργεια ἔκ τινος ὑποκειμένου,
οὐκ εἰς ὑποκείμενον δέ· πάθοι δ' ἄν τι τὸ ὑποκείμενον, εἰ παρείη. ἀλλ' ὥσπερ ζωὴ ἐνέργεια οὖσα
ψυχῆς ἐστιν ἐνέργεια παθόντος ἄν τινος, οἷον τοῦ
30 σώματος, εἰ παρείη, καὶ μὴ παρόντος δέ ἐστι, τί
ἂν κωλύοι καὶ ἐπὶ φωτὸς οὕτως, εἴπερ ἐνέργειά τις
[τὸ φωτεινὸν][2] εἴη; οὐδὲ γὰρ νῦν τὸ φωτεινὸν[3]

---

[1] del. Volkmann*.
[2] del. Theiler, ut correctionem ad τὸ σκοτεινὸν falso loco
insertam: τοῦ φωτεινοῦ suspic. Creuzer, scr. Kirchhoff*.
[3] Kleist (Studien 136), B–T: σκοτεινὸν Enn.*

also to each and every bright and fiery body: there
are even stones of this kind with a shining surface.
But could that which passes to something else from
a thing which has a surface of this kind exist if air
did not? But if it is only a quality, and a quality
of something, since every quality is in a substrate,
one must look for a body in which light will be.
But if it is an activity from something else, why should
it not exist and travel to what lies beyond without
the existence of an adjoining body, but with a kind
of void in between (if that is possible)? For since
it is stretched out straight, why should it not get
across without support? But if it is of such a kind
as to fall, it will move downwards. For it will
certainly not be the air (or in general what is illuminated) which pulls it out of the luminary and compels it to proceed: since it is not something which
occurs incidentally, so that it is completely dependent on something else, nor is it an affection of
something else, so that there must be something
which is affected; or it would have to stay when it
arrived; but now it goes away, so that it could also
come. But where is it then? All it needs is a
place. If this is so, the body of the sun will lose
the activity which comes from it. But this was the
light. If this is so the light will not belong to anything else. But activity comes from a substrate,
but does not pass into a substrate; but the substrate,
if it was there, would be affected in some way. But,
just as life, being an activity, is activity of the soul,
and if something, body for instance, is there, it is
affected, but life also exists if this something is not
there, what would prevent this being so also in the
case of light, if it is a kind of activity? For as things

τοῦ ἀέρος γεννᾷ τὸ φῶς, ἀλλὰ γῇ συμμιγνύμενος[1]
σκοτεινὸν ποιεῖ καὶ οὐ καθαρὸν ὄντως· ὥστε
ὅμοιον εἶναι λέγειν τὸ γλυκὺ εἶναι, εἰ πικρῷ
35 μιγείη. εἰ δέ τις τροπὴν λέγοι τοῦ ἀέρος τὸ φῶς,
λεκτέον ὡς ἐχρῆν αὐτὸν τρέπεσθαι τὸν ἀέρα τῇ
τροπῇ, καὶ τὸ σκοτεινὸν αὐτοῦ μὴ σκοτεινὸν
γεγονέναι ἠλλοιωμένον. νῦν δὲ ὁ ἀὴρ οἷός ἐστι
μένει, ὡς ἂν οὐδὲν παθών. τὸ δὲ πάθημα ἐκείνου
δεῖ εἶναι, οὗ πάθημα· οὐ τοίνυν οὐδὲ χρῶμα αὐτοῦ,
40 ἀλλ' αὐτὸ ἐφ' αὑτοῦ· πάρεστι δὲ ὁ ἀήρ. καὶ
τοῦτο μὲν οὑτωσὶ ἐπεσκέφθω.

7. Πότερα δὲ ἀπόλλυται ἢ ἀνατρέχει; τάχα γὰρ
ἄν τι καὶ ἐκ τούτου λάβοιμεν εἰς τὸ πρόσθεν. ἢ
εἰ μὲν ἦν ἔνδοθεν, ὥστε τὸ μετειληφὸς ἔχειν
οἰκεῖον ἤδη, τάχα ἄν τις εἶπεν ἀπόλλυσθαι· εἰ δέ
5 ἐστιν ἐνέργεια οὐ ῥέουσα—περιέρρεε γὰρ ἂν καὶ
ἐχεῖτο εἴσω πλέον ἢ ὅσον τὸ παρὰ τοῦ ἐνεργοῦντος
ἐπεβάλλετο—οὐκ ἂν ἀπολλύοιτο μένοντος ἐν
ὑποστάσει τοῦ φωτίζοντος. μετακινουμένου δὲ ἐν
ἄλλῳ ἐστὶ τόπῳ οὐχ ὡς παλιρροίας ἢ μεταρροίας
γενομένης, ἀλλ' ὡς τῆς ἐνεργείας ἐκείνου οὔσης
10 καὶ παραγινομένης, εἰς ὅσον κωλύει οὐδέν. ἐπεὶ
καὶ εἰ πολλαπλασία ἡ ἀπόστασις ἦν ἢ νῦν ἐστι
πρὸς ἡμᾶς τοῦ ἡλίου, ἦν ἂν καὶ μέχρι ἐκεῖ φῶς
μηδενὸς κωλύοντος μηδὲ ἐμποδὼν ἐν τῷ μεταξὺ
ἱσταμένου. ἔστι δὲ ἡ μὲν ἐν αὐτῷ ἐνέργεια καὶ οἷον

_____
[1] Kleist (loc. cit.), B–T: συμμιγνύμενον Enn.*

are it is not the luminosity of air which generates the light, but air, being mixed with earth, makes it dark and not genuinely pure; so that it is like saying that something sweet exists if it is mixed with something bitter. But if someone says that light is a modification of air, one must reply that the actual air would have to be modified by the modification, and its darkness would be altered and cease to be dark. But now the air stays as it is, as if it was not affected at all. But an affection must belong to that of which it is an affection; light therefore is not the colour of air either, but exists independently. Air is [simply] present. And so let us conclude this enquiry.

7. But does light perish or return to its source? For perhaps from this too we could gain something which would contribute to the solution of our previous problem. Now if it entered into what participated in it, so that this possessed it as its own, perhaps one would have said that it perished; but if it is an activity which does not flow away—for if it was, more of it would overflow all round and pour into the interior of the recipient than reached the recipient from the source of activity—it would not perish as long as the luminary remained in existence. But if the luminary moves, the light is in another place, not as if it flowed back or changed the course of its flow, but because the activity belongs to the luminary and becomes present in so far as there is no obstacle. For even if the distance between us and the sun was many times greater than it is, light would extend over that further distance if there was no obstacle or obstruction standing in between. But the activity within the luminous body, which is

ζωὴ τοῦ σώματος τοῦ φωτεινοῦ πλείων καὶ οἷον
15 ἀρχὴ τῆς ἐνεργείας καὶ πηγή· ἡ δὲ μετὰ τὸ πέρας
τοῦ σώματος, εἴδωλον τοῦ ἐντός, ἐνέργεια δευτέρα
οὐκ ἀφισταμένη τῆς προτέρας. ἔχει γὰρ ἕκαστον
τῶν ὄντων ἐνέργειαν, ἥ ἐστιν ὁμοίωμα αὐτοῦ,
ὥστε αὐτοῦ ὄντος κἀκεῖνο εἶναι καὶ μένοντος
20 φθάνειν εἰς τὸ πόρρω, τὸ μὲν ἐπιπλέον, τὸ δὲ εἰς
ἔλαττον· καὶ αἱ μὲν ἀσθενεῖς καὶ ἀμυδραί, αἱ δὲ
καὶ λανθάνουσαι, τῶν δ' εἰσὶ μείζους καὶ εἰς τὸ
πόρρω· καὶ ὅταν εἰς τὸ πόρρω, ἐκεῖ δεῖ νομίζειν
εἶναι, ὅπου τὸ ἐνεργοῦν καὶ δυνάμενον, καὶ αὖ οὗ
φθάνει. ἔστι δὲ καὶ ἐπὶ ὀφθαλμῶν ἰδεῖν ζῴων
25 λαμπόντων τοῖς ὄμμασι, γινομένου αὐτοῖς φωτὸς
καὶ ἔξω τῶν ὀμμάτων· καὶ δὴ καὶ ἐπὶ ζῴων, ἃ
ἔνδον συνεστραμμένον πῦρ ἔχοντα ταῖς ἀνοι-
δάνσεσιν ἐν σκότῳ ἐκλάμπει εἰς τὸ ἔξω, καὶ ἐν
ταῖς συστολαῖς αὐτῶν οὐδέν ἐστι φῶς ἔξω, οὐδ' αὖ
ἐφθάρη, ἀλλ' ἢ ἔστιν ἢ οὐκ ἔστιν ἔξω. τί οὖν;
30 εἰσελήλυθεν; ἢ οὐκ ἔστιν ἔξω, ὅτι μηδὲ τὸ πῦρ
πρὸς τὸ ἔξω, ἀλλ' ἔδυ εἰς τὸ εἴσω. τὸ οὖν φῶς
ἔδυ καὶ αὐτό; ἢ οὔ, ἀλλ' ἐκεῖνο μόνον· δύντος δὲ
ἐπίπροσθέν ἐστι τὸ ἄλλο σῶμα, ὡς μὴ ἐνεργεῖν
ἐκεῖνο πρὸς τὸ ἔξω. ἔστιν οὖν τὸ ἀπὸ τῶν
σωμάτων φῶς ἐνέργεια φωτεινοῦ σώματος πρὸς τὸ

---

¹ Plotinus speaks of the light within the eyes, which sometimes flashes out from them, in V. 5. 7. 24 ff. (a comparison
for the internal contemplation of Intellect). Aristotle speaks
briefly of the phenomenon of phosphorescence (mentioning
luminous fish and fungi and eyes which shine in the dark) in

like its life, is greater and is a kind of source and origin of its [outward] activity; that which is outside the limits of the body, an image of that within, is a second activity which is not separated from the first. For each thing that exists has an activity, which is a likeness of itself, so that while it exists that likeness exists, and while it stays in its place the likeness goes far out, sometimes a longer, sometimes a lesser distance; and some activities are weak and dim, and some even indiscernible, but other things have greater activities which go far; and when an activity goes far, one must think that it is there where the active and powerful thing is, and again there at the point it reaches. As for eyes, one can see what happens when animals have luminous eyes, and their light is also outside the eyes; and with animals which have compressed fire within them, and when they expand, in the darkness, the fire shines outside them, and when they contract there is no light outside, neither has it perished, but it either is outside or is not outside.[1] What then? Has it gone in? Now, it is not outside because the fire is not reaching to the outside, but has gone into the inside. Has the light itself, then, gone in too? No, but only the fire; but when it has gone in the rest of the body is in front of it, so that its activity does not reach the outside. The light from bodies, therefore, is the external activity of a luminous body; but the light

De Anima B 7 419a2–6; Plotinus may be using this passage here or a Peripatetic commentary on it.

35 ἔξω· αὐτὸ δὲ ὅλως [φῶς]¹ τὸ ἐν τοῖς τοιούτοις
σώμασιν, ἃ δὴ πρώτως ἐστὶ τοιαῦτα, οὐσία ἡ κατὰ
τὸ εἶδος τοῦ φωτεινοῦ πρώτως σώματος. ὅταν
δὲ μετὰ τῆς ὕλης τὸ τοιοῦτον σῶμα ἀναμιχθῇ,
χρόαν ἔδωκε· μόνη δὲ ἡ ἐνέργεια οὐ δίδωσιν,
ἀλλ' οἷον ἐπιχρώννυσιν, ἅτε οὖσα ἄλλου κἀκείνου
40 οἷον ἐξηρτημένη, οὗ τὸ ἀποστὰν κἀκείνου τῆς
ἐνεργείας ἄπεστιν. ἀσώματον δὲ πάντως δεῖ
τιθέναι, κἂν σώματος ᾖ. διὸ οὐδὲ τὸ "ἀπελήλυθε"
κυρίως οὐδὲ τὸ "πάρεστιν", ἀλλὰ τρόπον ἕτερον
ταῦτα, καὶ ἔστιν ὑπόστασις αὐτοῦ ὡς ἐνέργεια.
ἐπεὶ καὶ τὸ ἐν τῷ κατόπτρῳ εἴδωλον ἐνέργεια
45 λεκτέον τοῦ ἐνορωμένου ποιοῦντος εἰς τὸ πάσχειν
δυνάμενον οὐ ῥέοντος· ἀλλ' εἰ πάρεστι, κἀκεῖνο
ἐκεῖ φαίνεται καὶ ἔστιν οὕτως ὡς εἴδωλον χρόας
ἐσχηματισμένης ὡδί· κἂν ἀπέλθῃ, οὐκέτι τὸ
διαφανὲς ἔχει, ὃ ἔσχε πρότερον, ὅτε παρεῖχεν εἰς
50 αὐτὸ ἐνεργεῖν τὸ ὁρώμενον. ἀλλὰ καὶ ἐπὶ τῆς
ψυχῆς, ὅσον ἐνέργεια ἄλλης προτέρας, μενούσης
τῆς προτέρας μένει καὶ ἡ ἐφεξῆς ἐνέργεια. εἴ τις
δὲ μὴ ἐνέργεια, ἀλλ' ἐξ ἐνεργείας, οἵαν ἐλέγομεν
τὴν τοῦ σώματος οἰκείαν ἤδη ζωήν, ὥσπερ τὸ φῶς

¹ del. Kirchhoff*.

---

¹ For the incorporeality of light in Plotinus cp. I. 6. 3. 18–19;
II. 1. 7. 26–8. The background of the doctrine is Aristotelian
(cp. *De Anima* B 7 418b3 ff.); but for Plotinus it means, as
it did not for Aristotle, that light is, as here (cp. lines 49–51),
closely parallel to the life which is the incorporeal activity of
soul, and is itself, as he says in I. 6. 3, formative principle and

in bodies of this kind, bodies, that is, which are primarily and originally of this kind, is altogether substance, corresponding to the form of the primarily luminous body. When a body of this kind together with its matter enters into a mixture, it gives colour; but the activity by itself does not give colour, but only, so to speak, tints the surface, since it belongs to something else and is, one might say, dependent on it, and what separates itself from this something else separates itself from its activity. But one must consider light as altogether incorporeal, even if it belongs to a body.[1] Therefore " it has gone away " or " it is present " are not used of it in their proper sense, but in a different way, and its real existence is as an activity. For the image in a mirror must also be called an activity: that which is reflected in it acts on what is capable of being affected without flowing into it; but if the object reflected is there, the reflection too appears in the mirror and it exists as an image of a coloured surface shaped in a particular way; and if the object goes away, the mirror-surface no longer has what it had before, when the object seen in it offered itself to it for its activity. But with soul also, in so far as it is an activity of another prior soul, as long as the prior soul remains, so does the dependent activity. But suppose someone says that it is not an activity, but the product of an activity, as we said that the life was which belongs to the body already, just like the light which has

form. The doctrine of the incorporeality of light is not very much stressed by Plotinus, and seems to have been of only moderate importance to him; but it did provide a justification (if he felt he needed one) for his very free use of the symbolic language of light when speaking of spiritual activity.

τὸ ἀναμεμιγμένον ἤδη τοῖς σώμασιν; ἢ ἐνταῦθα
55 τῷ καὶ συμμεμίχθαι τὸ ποιοῦν τὸ χρῶμα. ἐπὶ δὲ
τῆς ζωῆς τῆς τοῦ σώματος τί; ἢ παρακειμένης
ψυχῆς ἄλλης ἔχει. ὅταν οὖν τὸ σῶμα φθαρῇ—οὐ γὰρ
δὴ ψυχῆς τι ἄμοιρον δύναται εἶναι—φθειρομένου
οὖν τοῦ σώματος καὶ οὐκ ἐπαρκούσης αὐτῷ οὔτε
60 τῆς δούσης οὔτ' εἴ τις παράκειται, πῶς ἂν ἔτι ζωὴ
μένοι; τί οὖν; ἐφθάρη αὕτη; ἢ οὐδὲ αὕτη·
εἴδωλον γὰρ ἐκλάμψεως καὶ τοῦτο· οὐκέτι δέ
ἐστιν ἐκεῖ μόνον.

8. Εἰ δ' εἴη σῶμα ἔξω τοῦ οὐρανοῦ, καὶ ὄψις τις
ἐντεῦθεν μηδενὸς κωλύοντος εἰς τὸ ἰδεῖν, ἆρ' ἂν
θεάσαιτο ὅ τι μὴ συμπαθὲς πρὸς ἐκεῖνο, εἰ τὸ
συμπαθὲς νῦν διὰ τὴν ζῴου ἑνὸς φύσιν; ἢ εἰ τὸ
5 συμπαθὲς διὰ τὸ ἑνὸς ζῴου τὰ αἰσθανόμενα καὶ τὰ
αἰσθητά, καὶ αἱ αἰσθήσεις οὕτως οὐκ ἄν, εἰ μὴ τὸ
σῶμα τοῦτο τὸ ἔξω μέρος τοῦδε τοῦ ζῴου· εἰ γὰρ
εἴη, τάχα ἄν. εἰ μέντοι μὴ μέρος εἴη, σῶμα δὲ
κεχρωσμένον καὶ τὰς ἄλλας ποιότητας ἔχον, οἷον
τὸ ἐνταῦθα, ὁμοειδὲς ὂν τῷ ὀργάνῳ; ἢ οὐδ'
10 οὕτως, εἰ ὀρθὴ ἡ ὑπόθεσις· εἰ μή τις τούτῳ γε
αὐτῷ τὴν ὑπόθεσιν ἀνελεῖν πειρῷτο ἄτοπον εἶναι
λέγων, εἰ μὴ χρῶμα ὄψεται ἡ ὄψις παρόν, καὶ αἱ
ἄλλαι αἰσθήσεις τῶν αἰσθητῶν παρόντων αὐταῖς
οὐκ ἐνεργήσουσι πρὸς αὐτά. ἀλλὰ τὸ ἄτοπον
τοῦτο, πόθεν δὴ φαίνεται, φήσομεν. ἢ ὅτι ἐνταῦθα

already been mixed with bodies? Now in this case there is colour because that which produces it has been mixed with the bodies. But what about the life of the body? It has it because there is another soul close by it. When, therefore, the body perishes —for nothing can exist without a share of soul—when the body, then, is perishing and neither the soul which gave it life nor any neighbouring soul is sufficient [to avert its destruction] how could the life still remain? Well, then, has this life perished? No, certainly not; for this too is the image of an irradiation: it is simply no longer there.

8. But if there was a body outside the heavenly sphere and there was an eye looking from our universe with nothing to obstruct its vision, would it see what would not be sympathetically connected with our universe, if as things are sympathetic connection is due to the nature of a single living being? Now if sympathetic connection is due to the fact that perceiving subjects and perceived objects belong to a single living thing, there would be no perception, unless this outside body was part of our [universal] living being: for if it was, there would perhaps be perceptions of it. But suppose it was not a part, but a body which was coloured and had the other qualities like those of a body in this world, and so had the appropriate form for the organ of vision? No, it would not be perceived even so, if our hypo-thesis is correct: unless someone were to try to destroy the hypothesis by saying that it will be absurd if the sight does not see a colour when it is present, and if the other senses, when their objects are presented to them, do not exercise their activities in relation to them. But we shall state the origin

15 ἐν ἑνὶ ὄντες καὶ ἑνὸς ταῦτα ποιοῦμεν καὶ πάσχομεν.
τοῦτο οὖν σκεπτέον, εἰ παρὰ τοῦτο. καὶ εἰ μὲν
αὐτάρκως δέδεικται· εἰ δὲ μή, καὶ δι' ἄλλων
δεικτέον. τὸ μὲν οὖν ζῷον ὅτι συμπαθὲς αὑτῷ,
δῆλον· καὶ εἰ εἴη ζῷον, ἀρκεῖ· ὥστε καὶ τὰ μέρη,
ᾗ ἑνὸς ζῴου. ἀλλ' εἰ δι' ὁμοιότητά τις λέγοι;
20 ἀλλ' ἡ ἀντίληψις κατὰ τὸ ζῷον καὶ ἡ αἴσθησις,
ὅτι τοῦ ὁμοίου μετέχει τὸ αὐτό· τὸ γὰρ ὄργανον
ὅμοιον αὐτοῦ· ὥστε ἡ αἴσθησις ψυχῆς ἀντίληψις
ἔσται δι' ὀργάνων ὁμοίων τοῖς ἀντιληπτοῖς. ἐὰν
οὖν ζῷον ὂν αἰσθάνηται μὲν μὴ τῶν ἐν αὐτῷ, τῶν δὲ
25 ὁμοίων τοῖς ἐν αὐτῷ, ᾗ μὲν ζῷον, ἀντιλήψεται·
ᾗ [1] μέντοι τὰ ἀντιληπτὰ ⟨ἀντιληπτὰ⟩ [2] ἔσται οὐχ ᾗ
αὐτοῦ, ἀλλ' ᾗ ὅμοια τοῖς ἐν αὐτῷ. ἢ καὶ τὰ
ἀντιληπτὰ οὕτως ἀντιληπτὰ ὅμοια ὄντα, ὅτι αὕτη
αὐτὰ ὅμοια πεποίηκεν, ὥστε μὴ οὐ προσήκοντα
εἶναι· ὥστε εἰ τὸ ποιοῦν ἐκεῖ εἴη [3] ψυχὴ πάντη
30 ἑτέρα, καὶ τὰ ἐκεῖ ὑποτεθέντα ὅμοια οὐδὲν πρὸς
αὑτήν. ἀλλὰ γὰρ ἡ ἀτοπία τὸ μαχόμενον ἐν τῇ
ὑποθέσει δείκνυσιν ὡς αἴτιόν ἐστιν αὐτῆς· ἅμα γὰρ
ψυχὴν λέγει καὶ οὐ ψυχήν, καὶ συγγενῆ καὶ οὐ
συγγενῆ, καὶ ὅμοια ταῦτα [4] καὶ ἀνόμοια· ὥστε

---

[1] A¹JUC: ᾗ BR, H–S¹.
[2] Igal.
[3] Igal: ἡ Enn.
[4] Kirchhoff*: ταῦτα Enn., H—S¹.

312

of this apparent absurdity. It is that here, being in one and belonging to one, we act and are affected in this way. We must therefore investigate whether this is the reason why we do so. And if this has already been sufficiently shown, our demonstration is complete; if not, we must demonstrate it by other arguments as well. Now it is clear that a living being is sympathetically aware of itself; and if the universe is a living being, this is enough; so that the parts also will be sympathetically aware of each other in that they belong to one living being. But suppose someone were to say that this [sympathy] is because of their likeness? But apprehension and perception take place in the living being because one and the same thing participates in likeness; for its organ is like itself; so that perception is the soul's apprehension through organs like the objects apprehended. If then the universe, being a living being, perceives, not the things in itself but things like those in itself, will it perceive them by virtue of being a living thing? In so far as the objects apprehended are apprehended, they will be so not by virtue of their belonging to itself, but in virtue of their being like the things in itself. Now the objects apprehended are apprehended in this way by being like, because this soul [of the universe] has made them like, so that they are not incongruous; so that if the active principle out there is the altogether different soul [of that other universe], the objects assumed to exist there would be in no way like the soul of our universe. Certainly, then, the absurdity shows that the contradiction in the hypothesis was its cause: for it says at once " soul " and " not soul " and " akin " and " not akin ", and that the objects apprehended

ἔχουσα τὰ ἀντικείμενα ἐν αὑτῇ οὐδ' ἂν ὑπόθεσις
35 εἴη. καὶ γάρ, ὡς ἡ ψυχὴ ἐν τούτῳ· ὥστε πᾶν καὶ
οὐ πᾶν τίθησι, καὶ ἄλλο καὶ οὐκ ἄλλο, καὶ τὸ
μηδὲν καὶ οὐ τὸ μηδέν, καὶ τέλεον καὶ οὐ τέλεον.
ὥστε ἀφετέον τὴν ὑπόθεσιν, ὡς οὐκ ὂν ζητεῖν τὸ
ἀκόλουθον τῷ αὐτὸ τὸ ὑποτεθὲν ἐν αὑτῷ ἀναιρεῖν.

are " like " and " unlike "; so that since it has these oppositions in itself it is no hypothesis at all. For, besides, it asserts that the soul is in this other universe, so that it postulates something which is " all " and " not-all " and " other " and " not-other ", and " nothing " and " not-nothing " and " perfect " and " not-perfect ". So the hypothesis must be dismissed, as it is not possible to investigate the consequence of it by destroying its foundation in the very investigation.[1]

[1] Plotinus in this chapter draws an extreme logical conclusion from his doctrine that perception is due to the sympathy which unites the parts of the great living organism which is the physical universe. Taking up the (to him completely fantastic) suggestion made in ch. 3 that there might be another universe outside this one, he argues that, even if our universe had an eye on its outside, it could not see the other one because it would be outside the universal sympathy which causes perception: the two universes would be distinct organisms with different and unconnected souls. Plotinus does not seem to advert here to his discussion in IV. 3. 1–5, of which the conclusion is that the hypostasis Soul, of which all souls are parts, is not identical with the Soul of the universe, which is a partial soul, like our souls (though of greater power and dignity). If he had done so, he would have had to consider the possibility that there might be two (or more) such partial souls of distinct universes, united by sympathy as being parts in some sense of the hypostasis Soul. But the unity and uniqueness of the physical universe was a dogma so firmly held and passionately defended in late antiquity that this line of thought probably never occurred to him.

ENNEAD IV. 6

IV. 6. ON SENSE-PERCEPTION AND MEMORY

Introductory Note

THIS little treatise is a later supplement to the great treatise on the soul which it immediately follows in the Ennead arrangement. Plotinus is, as always, concerned to show that perceiving and remembering are activities of the soul, and that soul is not a quasi-corporeal thing which passively receives stamps or impressions from sense-objects and then stores them up in its memory.

Synopsis

The expression theory of sense-perception fails to correspond with the facts of sense-experience (ch. 1). The soul is active, not passive, exercising its power of knowing in its acts of sense-perception, as it does to a higher degree in its knowledge of intelligible reality (ch. 2). Memory again is the exercise of a power, which can be strengthened by training and varies in different people (ch. 3).

IV. 6. (41) ΠΕΡΙ ΑΙΣΘΗΣΕΩΣ ΚΑΙ ΜΝΗΜΗΣ

1. Τὰς αἰσθήσεις οὐ τυπώσεις οὐδ' ἐνσφραγίσεις λέγοντες ἐν ψυχῇ γίγνεσθαι, οὐδὲ τὰς μνήμας πάντως τε καὶ ἀκολούθως ἐροῦμεν κατοχὰς μαθημάτων καὶ αἰσθήσεων εἶναι τοῦ τύπου
5 μείναντος ἐν τῇ ψυχῇ, ὃς μηδὲ τὸ πρῶτον ἐγένετο. διὸ τοῦ αὐτοῦ λόγου ἂν εἴη ἄμφω, ἢ ἐγγίγνεσθαί τε ἐν τῇ ψυχῇ καὶ μένειν, εἰ μνημονεύοιτο, ἢ τὸ ἕτερον ὁποτερονοῦν μὴ διδόντα μὴ διδόναι μηδὲ θάτερον. ὅσοι δὴ λέγομεν μηδέτερον, ἀναγκαίως
ζητήσομεν, τίς τρόπος ἑκατέρου, ἐπειδὴ οὔτε τὸν
10 τύπον τοῦ αἰσθητοῦ ἐγγίγνεσθαί φαμεν τῇ ψυχῇ καὶ τυποῦν αὐτήν, οὔτε τὴν μνήμην λέγομεν εἶναι τοῦ τύπου ἐμμείναντος. εἰ δ' ἐπὶ τῆς ἐναργεστάτης αἰσθήσεως θεωροῦμεν τὸ συμβαῖνον, τάχ' ἂν καὶ ἐπὶ τῶν ἄλλων αἰσθήσεων μεταφέροντες τὸ αὐτὸ ἐξεύροιμεν ἂν τὸ ζητούμενον. δῆλον δὲ
15 δήπου ἐν παντί, ὡς αἴσθησιν ὁτουοῦν λαμβάνοντες δι' ὁράσεως ἐκεῖ ὁρῶμεν καὶ τῇ ὄψει προσβάλλομεν, οὗ τὸ ὁρατόν ἐστιν ἐπ' εὐθείας κείμενον, ὡς ἐκεῖ δηλονότι τῆς ἀντιλήψεως γινομένης καὶ πρὸς τὸ ἔξω τῆς ψυχῆς βλεπούσης, ἅτε μηδενός, οἶμαι,

---

[1] Cp. Aristotle De Memoria I. 450a30–32 for the doctrine here rejected.

[2] The phrase comes from Plato Phaedrus 250D2.

IV. 6. ON SENSE-PERCEPTION
AND MEMORY

1. Since we say that sense-perceptions are not impressions or seal-stamps on the soul, we cannot say either with any sort of consistency that memories are retentions of what we have learnt or perceived while the impression remains on the soul which was not there to begin with.[1] Both would be a part of the same argument; either one must maintain that an impression enters the soul and remains if there is memory, or, if one does not grant one or the other of these propositions, one must not grant the other either. Those of us who do not say either will necessarily enquire how we perceive and how we remember, since we do not assert that the impression of the sense-object enters the soul and stamps it, nor do we say that memory exists because the impression remains. But if we observe what happens in the case of the " clearest sense ",[2] perhaps we could apply the same also to the other senses and find what we are looking for. It is clear presumably in every case that when we have a perception of anything through the sense of sight, we look there where it is and direct our gaze where the visible object is situated in a straight line from us; obviously it is there that the apprehension takes place and the soul looks outwards, since, I think, no impression has

τύπου ἐν αὐτῇ γενομένου ἢ γιγνομένου, οὐδέπω [1]
20 σφραγῖδα [λαμβανούσης] [2] ὥσπερ ἐν κηρῷ
δακτυλίου λαμβανούσης.[3] οὐδὲν γὰρ ἂν ἐδεήθη τοῦ
ἔξω βλέπειν, ἤδη ἔχουσα παρ' ἑαυτῆς εἶδος τοῦ
ὁρωμένου τούτῳ τῷ ἐκεῖ εἰσελθεῖν τὸν τύπον
βλέπουσα. τὸ δὲ δὴ διάστημα προστιθεῖσα τῷ ὁρά-
ματι καὶ ἐξ ὅσου ἡ θέα ἡ ψυχὴ λέγουσα οὕτως ἂν
25 τὸ ἐν αὐτῇ οὐδὲν ἀφεστηκὸς ἀφ' αὑτῆς ὡς πόρρω
ὂν βλέποι; τό τε μέγεθος αὐτοῦ, ὅσον ἐστὶν ἔξω,
πῶς ἂν ὅσον ἐστὶ λέγοι, ἢ ὅτι μέγα, οἷον τὸ τοῦ
οὐρανοῦ, τοῦ ἐν αὐτῇ τύπον τοσοῦδε εἶναι οὐ
δυναμένου; τὸ δὲ μέγιστον ἁπάντων· εἰ γὰρ
30 τύπους λαμβάνοιμεν ὧν ὁρῶμεν, οὐκ ἔσται βλέπειν
αὐτὰ ἃ ὁρῶμεν, ἰνδάλματα δὲ ὁραμάτων καὶ σκιάς,
ὥστε ἄλλα μὲν εἶναι αὐτὰ τὰ πράγματα, ἄλλα δὲ
τὰ ἡμῖν ὁρώμενα. ὅλως δέ, ὥσπερ λέγεται, ὡς
οὐκ ἔστιν ἐπιθέντα τῇ κόρῃ τὸ ὁρατὸν θεάσασθαι,
ἀποστήσαντα δὲ δεῖ οὕτως ὁρᾶν, τοῦτο χρὴ καὶ
35 πολὺ μᾶλλον ἐπὶ τὴν ψυχὴν μεταφέρειν. εἰ γὰρ
τὸν τύπον τοῦ ὁρατοῦ θείμεθα ἐν αὐτῇ, ἐκεῖνο μέν,
ᾧ ἐνεσφράγισται, οὐκ ἂν ὅραμα ἴδοι· δεῖ γὰρ καὶ [4]
δύο γενέσθαι τό τε ὁρῶν καὶ τὸ ὁρώμενον. ἄλλο
ἄρα δεῖ εἶναι τὸ ὁρῶν ἀλλαχοῦ [5] κείμενον τὸν

---

[1] Igal: οὐδὲ τῷ A¹BJUC: οὐδὲ τὴν R.
[2] del. Igal.
[3] Igal: βλεπούσης Enn.
[4] καὶ defendit Igal, collato V. 5. 11. 4: del. Kirchhoff, H–S.
[5] ὁρῶν ⟨καὶ⟩ ἀλλαχοῦ H–S¹, sed τὸν τύπον obiectum ad τὸ
ὁρῶν.

been or is being imprinted on it, nor has it yet received a seal-stamp, like the mark of a seal-ring on wax. For there would have been no need for it to look outwards, if it already had in it the form of the visible object since it saw by this entrance into it of the impression. And when the soul adds the distance to what it sees and says how far it is looking at it from, could it in this way be seeing as distant what was in it and not separated from it by any interval? And how would it be able to state the size as it is outside or say that it is large, to state for instance the size of the sky, when it would be impossible for as large an impression to be inside it? Most important of all: if we received impressions of what we see, there will be no possibility of looking at the actual things we see, but we shall look at images and shadows of the objects of sight, so that the objects themselves will be different from the things we see.[1] But in general, just as it is said that it is not possible to look at a visible object if one puts it on the pupil of the eye, but one must move it away to see it,[2] so, much more, one should transfer this to the soul. For if we placed in it the impression of the visible object, that in which the impression was stamped could not see the sight: for that which sees and that which is seen must be two [distinct things]. That which sees, then, must be a distinct thing seeing the impression situated else-

---

[1] In V. 5. 1. 17–18, where Plotinus is contrasting sense-perception with the immediate intuition of Intellect, he says that in sense-perception we do only see an image of the thing, not the thing itself.

[2] Cp. Aristotle *De Anima* B 7, 419a12–13.

τύπον, ἀλλ᾽ οὐκ ἐν ᾧ ἐστι [1] κείμενον. δεῖ ἄρα
40 τὴν ὅρασιν οὐ κειμένου εἶναι, ἀλλὰ μὴ κειμένου
εἶναι, ἵνα ᾖ ὅρασις.

2. Εἰ οὖν μὴ οὕτως, τίς ὁ τρόπος; ἢ λέγει περὶ
ὧν οὐκ ἔχει· τοῦτο γὰρ δυνάμεως, οὐ τὸ παθεῖν τι,
ἀλλὰ τὸ δυνηθῆναι καὶ ἐφ᾽ ᾧ τέτακται ἐργάσασθαι.
οὕτως γὰρ ἄν, οἶμαι, καὶ διακριθείη τῇ ψυχῇ καὶ τὸ
5 ὁρατὸν καὶ τὸ ἀκουστόν, οὐκ εἰ τύποι ἄμφω, ἀλλ᾽
εἰ μὴ τύποι μηδὲ πείσεις, ἀλλ᾽ ἐνέργειαι περὶ ὃ
ἔπεισι πεφύκασιν. ἡμεῖς δὲ ἀπιστοῦντες, μὴ οὐ
δύνηται, ἐὰν μὴ πληγῇ, τὸ αὐτῆς γινώσκειν δύναμις
ἑκάστη, πάσχειν, ἀλλ᾽ οὐ γινώσκειν τὸ ἐγγὺς
ποιοῦμεν, οὗ κρατεῖν δέδοται, ἀλλ᾽ οὐ κρατεῖσθαι.
10 τὸν αὐτὸν δὴ τρόπον καὶ ἐπὶ ἀκοῆς δεῖ νομίζειν
γίνεσθαι· τὸν μὲν τύπον εἶναι ἐν τῷ ἀέρι πληγήν τινα
οὖσαν διηρθρωμένην, οἷον γραμμάτων ἐγγεγραμ-
μένων ὑπὸ τοῦ τὴν φωνὴν πεποιηκότος, τὴν μέντοι δύναμιν καὶ τὴν τῆς ψυχῆς οὐσίαν οἷον ἀναγνῶναι
15 τοὺς τύπους ἐν τῷ ἀέρι γεγραμμένους ἐλθόντας πλησίον, εἰς ὃ ἐλθόντες πεφύκασιν ὁρᾶσθαι. γεύσεως
δὲ καὶ ὀσφρήσεως τὰ μὲν πάθη, τὰ δ᾽ ὅσα αἰσθήσεις
αὐτῶν καὶ κρίσεις, τῶν παθῶν εἰσι γνώσεις ἄλλαι
τῶν παθῶν οὖσαι. τῶν δὲ νοητῶν ἡ γνῶσις

---

[1] ad ἐστι subiectum τὸ ὁρῶν.

where, but not in that in which that which sees it is. The seeing, then, cannot be of an object situated where the seeing is, but of something not situated there.

2. If, then, it is not like this, how does it work? [The soul] speaks about things which it does not possess: this is a matter of power, not of being affected in some way but of being capable of and doing the work to which it has been assigned. This is the way, I think, in which a distinction is made by the soul between what is seen and what is heard, not if both are impressions, but if they are not by nature impressions or affections, but activities concerned with that which approaches [the soul]. But we men do not believe that each particular power [of perception] can come to know its object unless it is struck by it, and make it be affected by the object near it instead of coming to know it, though it has been appointed to master it, not to be mastered by it. One should suppose that the same kind of process takes place in the case of hearing: the impression is in the air, and is a sort of articulated stroke, like letters written on the air by the maker of the sound; but the power and the substance of the soul does something like reading the impressions written on the air when they come near and reach the point at which they can be seen.[1] And where taste and smell are concerned, there are some affections, but all [tastings and smellings] that are perceptions of them and judgments are acts of knowledge of the affections distinct from the affections themselves. But the

---

[1] The pre-eminence of sight, the " clearest sense " (cp. p. 321, n. 2), in Greek psychological thought is well illustrated by this casual use of sight-language to describe hearing.

ἀπαθὴς καὶ ἀτύπωτός ἐστι μᾶλλον· ἀνάπαλιν γὰρ
20 ἔσωθεν οἷον προπίπτει, τὰ δὲ ἔξωθεν θεωρεῖται·
καὶ ἔστιν ἐκεῖνα μᾶλλον ἐνέργειαι καὶ κυριώτεραι·
αὑτῆς γάρ, καὶ ἔστιν αὐτὴ ἐνεργοῦσα ἕκαστον.
πότερα δὲ αὑτὴν μὲν ἡ ψυχὴ δύο καὶ ὡς ἕτερον
ὁρᾷ, νοῦν δὲ ἓν καὶ ἄμφω τὰ δύο ἕν, ἐν ἄλλοις.

3. Νῦν δὲ τούτων εἰρημένων περὶ μνήμης ἐφεξῆς
λεκτέον εἰποῦσι πρότερον, ὡς οὐ θαυμαστόν—μᾶλλον δὲ θαυμαστὸν μέν, ἀπιστεῖν δὲ οὐ δεῖ τῇ
τοιαύτῃ δυνάμει τῆς ψυχῆς—εἰ μηδὲν λαβοῦσα εἰς
5 αὑτὴν ἀντίληψιν ὧν οὐκ ἔσχε ποιεῖται. λόγος γάρ
ἐστι πάντων, καὶ λόγος ἔσχατος μὲν τῶν νοητῶν
καὶ τῶν ἐν τῷ νοητῷ ἡ ψυχῆς φύσις, πρῶτος δὲ
τῶν ἐν τῷ αἰσθητῷ παντί. διὸ δὴ καὶ πρὸς
ἄμφω ἔχει, ὑπὸ μὲν τῶν εὐπαθοῦσα καὶ ἀναβιωσ-
κομένη, ὑπὸ δὲ τῶν τῇ ὁμοιότητι ἀπατωμένη καὶ
10 κατιοῦσα ὥσπερ θελγομένη. ἐν μέσῳ δὲ οὖσα
αἰσθάνεται ἀμφοῖν, καὶ τὰ μὲν νοεῖν λέγεται εἰς
μνήμην ἐλθοῦσα, εἰ πρὸς αὐτοῖς γίγνοιτο· γινώσκει γὰρ τῷ αὐτά πως εἶναι· γινώσκει γὰρ οὐ τῷ
ἐνιζάνειν αὐτά, ἀλλὰ τῷ πως ἔχειν αὐτὰ καὶ ὁρᾶν
αὐτὰ καὶ εἶναι αὐτὰ ἀμυδρότερον καὶ γίνεσθαι ἐκ
15 τοῦ ἀμυδροῦ τῷ οἷον ἐγείρεσθαι ἐναργεστέρα καὶ

---

[1] The reference is probably to V. 6. 1–2.

[2] The idea of Soul as the intermediary logos, the lowest
principle in the intelligible world which is first in the world of
sense because it expresses the intelligible there as far as it
can, is frequent in Plotinus (and in general in the Platonist or
Platonically-influenced thought of late antiquity): cp. in this
Ennead, for Soul as in the lowest region of the intelligible

knowledge of intelligible objects is much freer from affections and impressions; sense-objects are observed from outside, but the intelligibles in reverse come out, one can say, from within; and they are activities in a higher degree and more authentically: for the object belongs to the knowledge, and the knowledge in its active exercise is each of its objects. But we discuss elsewhere [1] whether the soul sees itself as two and as another, but Intellect is one, or whether both the dualities are one.

3. But now that we have said this [about sense-perception] we must next speak about memory; first we must say that it is not astonishing, or rather it is astonishing, but we should not disbelieve that the soul has a power of this kind, if it receives nothing itself and contrives an apprehension of what it does not have. For it is the rational principle of all things, and the nature of soul is the last and lowest rational principle of the intelligibles and the beings in the intelligible world, but first of those in the whole world perceived by the senses.[2] Therefore it is certainly in relation with both; by the power of the one it flourishes and gains new life, by the power of the others it is deceived because of their likeness and comes down as if charmed. But, being in the middle, it perceives both, and is said to think the intelligibles when it arrives at memory of them, if it comes to be near them; for it knows them by being them in a way: for it knows, not because they settle in it, but because it has them in some way and sees them and is them in a rather dim way, and becomes them more clearly out of the dimness by

IV. 4. 2. 17, and for Soul as the link between the two worlds IV. 8. 7.

ἐκ δυνάμεως εἰς ἐνέργειαν ἰέναι. τὰ δ' αἰσθητὰ
τὸν αὐτὸν τρόπον οἷον συναψάμενα καὶ ταῦτα παρ'
αὑτῆς οἷον ἐκλάμπειν ποιεῖ καὶ πρὸ ὀμμάτων εἶναι
ἐργάζεται ἑτοίμης οὔσης καὶ πρὸ οἷον ὠδινούσης
πρὸς αὐτὰ τῆς δυνάμεως. ὅταν τοίνυν ῥωσθῇ
20 πρὸς ὁτιοῦν τῶν φανέντων, ὥσπερ πρὸς παρὸν διάκειται ἐπὶ πολὺν χρόνον καὶ ὅσῳ μᾶλλον, τόσῳ ἀεί.
διὸ καὶ τὰ παιδία μνημονεύειν λέγεται μᾶλλον, ὅτι
μὴ ἀφίστανται, ἀλλὰ κεῖται αὐτοῖς πρὸ ὀμμάτων
ὡς ἂν ὁρῶσιν οὔπω εἰς πλῆθος, ἀλλὰ πρὸς ὀλίγα·
25 οἷς δὲ ἐπὶ πολλὰ ἡ διάνοια καὶ ἡ δύναμις, ὥσπερ
παραθέουσι καὶ οὐ μένουσιν. εἰ δέ γε ἔμενον οἱ
τύποι, οὐκ ἂν ἐποίησε τὸ πλῆθος ἧττον μνήμας.
ἔτι, εἰ τύποι μένοντες, οὐδὲν ἔδει σκοπεῖν, ἵνα
ἀναμνησθῶμεν, οὐδὲ πρότερον ἐπιλαθομένους ὕστερον ἀναμιμνήσκεσθαι κειμένων. καὶ αἱ εἰς ἀνά-
30 ληψιν δὲ μελέται δηλοῦσι δυνάμωσιν ψυχῆς τὸ
γινόμενον ὑπάρχον, ὥσπερ χειρῶν ἢ ποδῶν τὰ
γυμνάσια εἰς τὸ ποιεῖν ῥᾳδίως, ἃ μὴ ἐν ταῖς χερσὶν
ἢ ποσὶ κεῖται, ἀλλὰ πρὸς ἃ τῇ συνεχείᾳ ἠτοίμασται.
διὰ τί γὰρ ἅπαξ μὲν ἀκούσας ἢ δεύτερον οὐ μέμνηται, ὅταν δὲ πολλάκις, καὶ ὃ πρότερον ἀκούσας οὐκ
35 ἔσχε, πολλῷ ὕστερον χρόνῳ μέμνηται ἤδη; οὐ γὰρ
δὴ τῷ μέρη ἐσχηκέναι πρότερον τοῦ τύπου· ἔδει
γὰρ τούτων μεμνῆσθαι· ἀλλ' οἷον ἐξαίφνης γίγνε-

a kind of awakening, and passes from potentiality to actuality. In the same way [the soul] makes the objects of sense which are, so to speak, connected with it, shine out, one might say, by its own power, and brings them before its eyes, since its power [of sense-perception] is ready for them and, in a way, in travail towards them. When, therefore, the soul is strongly moved to anything that appears to it, it is for a long time in a state as if the object was present to it, and the more strongly it is moved, the more lasting the presence. This is why children are said to be better at remembering, because they do not go away from things, but they remain before their eyes, since they do not look at a multiplicity of things, but at few; but those whose thought and soul-power are directed to many things, as it were, rush past them and do not linger on them. But if the impressions remained, their multiplicity would not make memories less. Further, if impressions remained, there would be no need for us to consider in order to remember, nor should we forget before and remember afterwards if the impressions were lying ready to hand. And exercises to improve our mental grasp show that what is going on is an empowering of the soul, just like physical training of our arms and legs to make them do easily what does not lie in the arms or legs, but what they are made ready for by continuous exercise. For why, when one has heard something once or twice, does one not remember it, but [only] when one has heard it many times, and, when one has heard something before and not retained it, why does one remember it long afterwards? It is certainly not because one previously had the parts of the impression; for then one would

ται τοῦτο ἔκ τινος [τῆς]¹ ὑστέρας ἀκροάσεως ἢ
μελέτης. ταῦτα γὰρ μαρτυρεῖ πρόκλησιν τῆς δυνά-
40 μεως καθ' ἣν μνημονεύομεν τῆς ψυχῆς ὡς ῥωσθεῖσαν ἢ ἁπλῶς ἢ πρὸς τοῦτο. ὅταν δὲ μὴ μόνον
πρὸς ἃ ἐμελετήσαμεν τὸ τῆς μνήμης ἡμῖν παρῇ,
ἀλλ' οἵπερ πολλὰ ἀνειλήφασιν ἐκ τοῦ εἰθίσθαι
ἀπαγγελίαις χρῆσθαι, ῥᾳδίας ἤδη καὶ τῶν ἄλλων
τὰς λεγομένας ἀναλήψεις ποιῶνται, τί ἄν τις ἐπαιτι-
45 ῷτο τῆς μνήμης ἢ τὴν δύναμιν τὴν ῥωσθεῖσαν εἶναι;
οἱ μὲν γὰρ τύποι μένοντες ἀσθένειαν μᾶλλον ἢ
δύναμιν κατηγοροῖεν· τὸ γὰρ ἐντυπώτατον τῷ
εἴκειν ἐστὶ τοιοῦτον, καὶ πάθους ὄντος τοῦ τύπου τὸ
μᾶλλον πεπονθὸς τοῦτό ἐστι τὸ μνημονεῦον μᾶλλον.
50 τούτου δὲ τοὐναντίον φαίνεται συμβαῖνον· οὐδαμοῦ γὰρ ἡ πρὸς ὁτιοῦν γυμνασία εὐπαθὲς τὸ γυμνα-
σάμενον ποιεῖ· ἐπεὶ καὶ ἐπὶ τῶν αἰσθήσεων οὐ τὸ
ἀσθενὲς ὁρᾷ οἷον ὀφθαλμός, ἀλλ' ὅτῳ δύναμίς ἐστιν
εἰς ἐνέργειαν πλείων. διὸ καὶ οἱ γεγηρακότες καὶ
πρὸς τὰς αἰσθήσεις ἀσθενέστεροι καὶ πρὸς τὰς
55 μνήμας ὡσαύτως. ἰσχὺς ἄρα τις καὶ ἡ αἴσθησις
καὶ ἡ μνήμη. ἔτι τῶν αἰσθήσεων τυπώσεων οὐκ
οὐσῶν, πῶς οἷόν τε τὰς μνήμας κατοχὰς τῶν οὐκ
ἐντεθέντων οὐδὲ τὴν ἀρχὴν εἶναι; ἀλλ' εἰ δύναμίς
τις καὶ παρασκευὴ πρὸς τὸ ἕτοιμον, πῶς οὐχ ἅμα,
ἀλλ' ὕστερον εἰς ἀναπόλησιν τῶν αὐτῶν ἐρχόμεθα;
60 ἢ ὅτι τὴν δύναμιν δεῖ οἷον ἐπιστῆσαι καὶ ἑτοιμάσασ-

----
¹ om. RJ: delendum suspic. Volkmann: del. Theiler.

have to remember these; but this happens with a kind of suddenness, as the result of some later hearing or exercise. This is evidence of a calling out of the power of soul by which we remember, in that this is strengthened, either in a general way or for the specific art of remembering. But when the power of memory is present to us not only for what we have trained ourselves [to remember], but men who have acquired a great deal of knowledge through being accustomed to use reports come to a point where they easily apprehend (as people say)[1] other information, what could one say was the cause of memory if not the strengthened power? For the persistence of impressions would tell of weakness rather than power; for that which is most impressible is so by giving way, and, since the impression is an affection, that which is more affected must remember more. But what actually occurs appears to be the opposite of this; for nowhere does exercise for any purpose make what is exercised easily affected; since with the senses also it is not what is weak, an eye for instance, which sees, but that organ which has greater power for its activity. This is why those who have grown old are weaker in perception, and in just the same way in memory. So both perception and memory are a kind of strength. Further, when sense-perceptions are not impressions, how could memories be retentions of imprints which were never made [in the soul] at all? But if memory is a power and a preparation for readiness, why do we not come to recall the same things at once, but only later? Because one needs to set up the power, so to speak,

---

[1] Cp. Aristotle *De Memoria* 2. 451a20.

θαι. τοῦτο γὰρ καὶ ἐπὶ τῶν ἄλλων δυνάμεων
ὁρῶμεν εἰς τὸ ποιῆσαι ὃ δύνανται ἑτοιμαζομένων
καὶ τὰ μὲν εὐθύς, τὰ δέ, εἰ συλλέξαιντο ἑαυτάς,
ἐργαζομένων. γίγνονται δὲ ὡς ἐπὶ τὸ πολὺ οὐχ οἱ
65 αὐτοὶ μνήμονες καὶ ἀγχίνοι [πολλάκις],[1] ὅτι οὐχ ἡ
αὐτὴ δύναμις ἑκατέρου, ὥσπερ οὐδ' ὁ αὐτὸς
πυκτικὸς καὶ δρομικός· ἐπικρατοῦσι γὰρ ἄλλαι
ἐν ἄλλῳ ἰδέαι. καίτοι οὐκ ἐκώλυε τὸν ἀστινασοῦν
ἔχοντα πλεονεξίας ψυχῆς ἀναγινώσκειν τὰ κείμενα,
οὐδὲ τὸν ταύτῃ ῥυέντα τὴν τοῦ πάσχειν καὶ ἔχειν
70 τὸ πάθος ἀδυναμίαν κεκτῆσθαι. καὶ τὸ τῆς
ψυχῆς δὲ ἀμέγεθες [καὶ ὅλως][2] ψυχὴν μαρτυρεῖ
δύναμιν εἶναι. καὶ ὅλως τὰ περὶ ψυχὴν πάντ' οὐ[3]
θαυμαστὸν ἄλλον τρόπον ἔχειν, ἢ ὡς ὑπειλήφασιν
ὑπὸ τοῦ μὴ ἐξετάζειν ἄνθρωποι, ἢ ὡς πρόχειροι
αὐτοῖς ἐπιβολαὶ ἐξ αἰσθητῶν ἐγγίνονται δι' ὁμοιο-
75 τήτων ἀπατῶσαι. οἷον γὰρ ἐν πίναξιν ἢ δέλτοις
γεγραμμένων γραμμάτων, οὕτως περὶ τῶν αἰσθήσεων καὶ τοῦ μνημονεύειν διάκεινται, καὶ οὔτε οἱ
σῶμα αὐτὴν τιθέμενοι ὁρῶσιν, ὅσα ἀδύνατα τῇ
ὑποθέσει αὐτῶν συμβαίνει, οὔτε οἱ ἀσώματον.

---

[1] del. Müller.
[2] del. Müller, ut iteratum e lin. 71.
[3] Theiler (πάντα ⟨οὐ⟩ Kirchhoff*): πάντα Enn.

and get it ready. For we see this with the other powers, which are made ready to do what they are able to do, and effect some things at once and some if they collect themselves. But the same people do not as a general rule have both good memories and quick minds,[1] because it is not the same power in each case, just as the same man is not a good boxer and a good runner: for different characteristics dominate in different people. And yet there would be nothing to prevent a man who had any kind of superiority of soul from reading off the deposited impressions, nor would a man who had a strong inclination this way have to possess an inability to be affected and to retain the affection. And the sizelessness of soul is also evidence that soul is a power. And in general it is not surprising that anything about the soul is different from what men have supposed because they have not examined it, or from the hasty notions derived from sense-objects which occur to them and deceive them by likenesses. For they think about perception and memory as they do about letters written on tablets or pages, and neither do those who assume that the soul is a body see all the impossibilities which their hypothesis involves, nor do those who assume it to be bodiless.

[1] Cp. Aristotle *De Memoria* 1. 449b7–8.

ENNEAD IV. 7

IV. 7. ON THE IMMORTALITY OF
THE SOUL

Introductory Note

THIS very early treatise is more " scholastic " than any
other writing of Plotinus. The greater part of it is occupied by refutations of school-positions opposed to the
Platonic doctrine of the immateriality and immortality of
the soul by standard arguments taken from any convenient
source; and the positive exposition of Platonic doctrine
has little that is originally Plotinian. Bréhier's *Notice*
introducing the treatise gives an excellent short account
of the origins of the various arguments. Those against
Stoic corporealism (to the refutation of which most of the
controversial part of the treatise is devoted) are Peripatetic
in origin, probably derived from the *De Anima* of Plotinus's favourite Aristotelian author, Alexander of Aphrodisias; those against a misinterpretation (so Plotinus
thinks) of the Pythagorean soul-harmony doctrine derive
from Aristotle's *De Anima* as well as Plato's *Phaedo*;
those against Aristotle's own entelechy-doctrine are of
course Platonic (and perhaps original), but sometimes
intelligently exploit difficulties raised by Aristotle himself
in the *De Anima*. The Epicurean position is, as usual,
very summarily dismissed (at the beginning of ch. 3)
with an objection of Stoic origin.

Considerable portions of the treatise were missing from
the archetype of our MSS of the *Enneads*, but were preserved in the excerpts made by Eusebius (*Praeparatio
Evangelica* XV, 22 and 10). Henry and Schwyzer give
precise details in *Plotini Opera* II, *Praefatio* xviii–xxii.
The awkward double numbering of chs. 8^1–8^5 is due to

ON THE IMMORTALITY OF THE SOUL

the fact that these chapters, preserved by Eusebius, were not included in the Latin translation of Ficino, from which our chapter-numbering derives; the first printed edition to insert them was that of F. Creuzer.

Chapter 15 is an odd little appendix to the treatise, indicating cursorily the support for belief in the immortality of the soul which those who feel they need this sort of thing can find in traditional religious beliefs and practices. There is no reason to doubt that it is really by Plotinus: it is quite in accordance with his normal respectfully detached attitude to traditional Hellenic religion.

Synopsis

Man is not a simple thing, but a composite of soul and body; the body perishes, but the soul, which is the real self, survives (ch. 1). The soul is not a body: refutation of the Stoic corporealist position (and, incidentally and in passing, the Epicurean) in detail (chs. 2–8³). Refutation of the soul-harmony theory supposed to be held by the Pythagoreans (ch. 8⁴). Refutation of Aristotle's theory that the soul is the body's " entelechy " or inseparable form (ch. 8⁵). Exposition and defence of the Platonic doctrine (chs. 9–14). Those who need this sort of evidence can find support for the doctrine of immortality in oracles and the cult of the dead (ch. 15).

IV. 7. (2) ΠΕΡΙ ΑΘΑΝΑΣΙΑΣ ΨΥΧΗΣ

1. Εἰ δέ ἐστιν ἀθάνατος ἕκαστος ἡμῶν, ἢ φθείρεται πᾶς, ἢ τὰ μὲν αὐτοῦ ἄπεισιν εἰς σκέδασιν καὶ φθοράν, τὰ δὲ μένει εἰς ἀεί, ἅπερ ἐστὶν αὐτός, ὧδ' ἄν τις μάθοι κατὰ φύσιν ἐπισκοπούμενος. ἁπλοῦν
5 μὲν δή τι οὐκ ἂν εἴη ἄνθρωπος, ἀλλ' ἔστιν ἐν αὐτῷ ψυχή, ἔχει δὲ καὶ σῶμα εἴτ' οὖν ὄργανον ὂν ἡμῖν, εἴτ' οὖν ἕτερον τρόπον προσηρτημένον. ἀλλ' οὖν διῃρήσθω τε ταύτῃ καὶ ἑκατέρου τὴν φύσιν τε καὶ οὐσίαν καταθεατέον. τὸ μὲν δὴ σῶμα καὶ αὐτὸ
10 συγκείμενον οὔτε παρὰ τοῦ λόγου δύναται μένειν, ἥ τε αἴσθησις ὁρᾷ λυόμενόν τε καὶ τηκόμενον καὶ παντοίους ὀλέθρους δεχόμενον, ἑκάστου τε τῶν ἐνόντων πρὸς τὸ αὑτοῦ φερομένου, φθείροντός τε ἄλλου ἕτερον καὶ μεταβάλλοντος εἰς ἄλλο καὶ ἀπολλύντος, καὶ μάλιστα ὅταν ψυχὴ ἡ φίλα ποιοῦσα μὴ παρῇ
15 τοῖς ὄγκοις. κἂν μονωθῇ δὲ ἕκαστον γενόμενον ἕν, οὐκ ἔστι, λύσιν δεχόμενον εἴς τε μορφὴν καὶ ὕλην, ἐξ ὧν ἀνάγκη καὶ τὰ ἁπλᾶ τῶν σωμάτων τὰς συστάσεις ἔχειν. καὶ μὴν καὶ μέγεθος ἔχοντα, ἅτε σώματα ὄντα, τεμνόμενά τε καὶ εἰς μικρὰ θραυό-

IV. 7. ON THE IMMORTALITY
OF THE SOUL

1. One might discover as follows, by an investigation according to the nature of the subject, whether each individual one of us human beings is immortal, or whether the whole human being is destroyed, or whether some of it goes away to dispersion and destruction but some of it, the part which is the self, abides for ever. Man could not be a simple thing, but there is in him a soul, and he has a body as well, whether it is our tool or attached to us in some other way. But let us divide man like this, and consider the essential nature of each part of him. The body, certainly, is also itself a composite thing and so cannot reasonably be supposed to last, and, besides, our senses perceive it dissolving and wasting away and undergoing all sorts of destructions, when each one of its component parts moves to its own place, and one destroys another, and changes into another and does away with it, especially when soul, which reconciles the parts, is not present to their material masses. And even if one part is isolated when it has become one, it is not really [one], since it admits dissolution into form and matter, from which it is necessary that even the elementary bodies should have their composition. And besides this, since they have size, because they are bodies, they can be divided and broken up into little pieces and so under-

20 μενα καὶ ταύτῃ φθορὰν ἂν ὑπομένοι. ὥστ᾽ εἰ μὲν
μέρος ἡμῶν τοῦτο, οὐ τὸ πᾶν ἀθάνατοι, εἰ δὲ
ὄργανον, ἔδει γε αὐτὸ εἰς χρόνον τινὰ δοθὲν τοιοῦτον
τὴν φύσιν εἶναι. τὸ δὲ κυριώτατον καὶ αὐτὸς ὁ
ἄνθρωπος, εἴπερ τοῦτο, κατὰ τὸ εἶδος ὡς πρὸς ὕλην
τὸ σῶμα ἢ κατὰ τὸ χρώμενον ὡς πρὸς ὄργανον·
25 ἑκατέρως δὲ ἡ ψυχὴ αὐτός.

2. Τοῦτο οὖν τίνα φύσιν ἔχει; ἢ σῶμα μὲν ὂν
πάντως ἀναλυτέον· σύνθετον γὰρ πᾶν γε σῶμα.
εἰ δὲ μὴ σῶμα εἴη, ἀλλὰ φύσεως ἄλλης, κἀκείνην ἢ
τὸν αὐτὸν τρόπον ἢ κατ᾽ ἄλλον σκεπτέον. πρῶτον
5 δὲ σκεπτέον, εἰ ὅ τι δεῖ τοῦτο τὸ σῶμα, ὃ λέγουσι
ψυχήν, ἀναλύειν. ἐπεὶ γὰρ ζωὴ ψυχῇ πάρεστιν
ἐξανάγκης, ἀνάγκη τοῦτο τὸ σῶμα, τὴν ψυχήν, εἰ
μὲν ἐκ δύο σωμάτων ἢ πλειόνων εἴη, ἤτοι ἑκάτερον
αὐτῶν ἢ ἕκαστον ζωὴν σύμφυτον ἔχειν, ἢ τὸ μὲν
ἔχειν, τὸ δὲ μή, ἢ μηδέτερον ἢ μηδὲν ἔχειν. εἰ μὲν
10 δὴ ἑνὶ αὐτῶν προσείη τὸ ζῆν, αὐτὸ τοῦτο ἂν εἴη
ψυχή. τί ἂν οὖν εἴη σῶμα ζωὴν παρ᾽ αὑτοῦ ἔχον;
πῦρ γὰρ καὶ ἀὴρ καὶ ὕδωρ καὶ γῆ ἄψυχα παρ᾽
αὐτῶν· καὶ ὅτῳ πάρεστι τούτων ψυχή, τοῦτο
ἐπακτῷ κέχρηται τῇ ζωῇ, ἄλλα δὲ παρὰ ταῦτα
σώματα οὐκ ἔστι. καὶ οἷς γε δοκεῖ εἶναι καὶ στοι-
15 χεῖα τούτων ἕτερα, σώματα, οὐ ψυχαί, ἐλέχθησαν
εἶναι οὐδὲ ζωὴν ἔχοντα. εἰ δὲ μηδενὸς αὐτῶν ζωὴν
ἔχοντος ἡ σύνοδος πεποίηκε ζωήν, ἄτοπον—εἰ δὲ
ἕκαστον ζωὴν ἔχοι, καὶ ἓν ἀρκεῖ—μᾶλλον δὲ ἀδύνατον συμφόρησιν σωμάτων ζωὴν ἐργάζεσθαι καὶ νοῦν

go destruction also in this way. So, if this body of
ours is a part of us, the whole of us is not immortal,
but if it is a tool, it must, since it was given us for a
certain time, be of a nature to last for that time.
But the other part is the most important and the
man himself; if it is this, then it is related to the
body as form to matter or user to tool; in either way,
the soul is the self.

2. What nature, then, does this have? If it is a
body, it must be completely separable into its parts,
for every body is a composite. But if it was not a
body, but of another nature, then that nature also
would have to be investigated either by the same
[analytic] method or by another. But first we must
enquire into what [constituent parts] we are to
analyse this body which they call soul. For since
life is necessarily present in soul, then of necessity
if this body, the soul, was composed of two or more
bodies, either both or all of them will have a con-
natural life, or one of them will have it and another
not, or neither or none of them will have it. Now if
life was a property of one of them, this one would
actually be the soul. What body, then, could there
be which has life of itself? For fire and air and
water and earth are lifeless of themselves; and when
soul is present to any one of them this makes use of
a borrowed life—but there are no other bodies besides these. And those who hold that there are
elements other than these have maintained that
they were bodies, not souls, and that they did not
have life. But if, when no single one of them had
life, their coming together produced life, it would
be absurd (but if each one of them has life, one is
enough) or rather impossible for a drawing together

γεννᾶν τὰ ἀνόητα. καὶ δὴ καὶ οὐχ ὁπωσοῦν
20 κραθέντα ταῦτα φήσουσι γίγνεσθαι. δεῖ ἄρα
εἶναι τὸ τάξον καὶ τὸ τῆς κράσεως αἴτιον· ὥστε
τοῦτο τάξιν ἂν ἔχοι ψυχῆς. οὐ γὰρ ὅτι [1] σύνθετον,
ἀλλ᾽ οὐδὲ ἁπλοῦν ἂν εἴη σῶμα ἐν τοῖς οὖσιν ἄνευ
ψυχῆς οὔσης ἐν τῷ παντί, εἴπερ λόγος προσελθὼν τῇ
25 ὕλῃ σῶμα ποιεῖ, οὐδαμόθεν δ᾽ ἂν προσέλθοι λόγος
ἢ παρὰ ψυχῆς.

3. Εἰ δέ τις μὴ οὕτως, ἀλλὰ ἀτόμους ἢ ἀμερῆ
συνελθόντα ψυχὴν ποιεῖν τῇ ἑνώσει λέγοι καὶ
ὁμοπαθείᾳ, ἐλέγχοιτ᾽ ἂν καὶ τῇ παραθέσει μὴ δι᾽
ὅλου δέ, οὐ γιγνομένου ἑνὸς οὐδὲ συμπαθοῦς ἐξ
5 ἀπαθῶν καὶ μὴ ἑνοῦσθαι δυναμένων σωμάτων·
ψυχὴ δὲ αὑτῇ συμπαθής. ἐκ δὲ ἀμερῶν σῶμα οὐδὲ
μέγεθος ἂν γένοιτο. καὶ μὴν εἰ ἁπλοῦ ὄντος τοῦ
σώματος τὸ μὲν ὅσον ὑλικὸν παρ᾽ αὑτοῦ ζωὴν
ἔχειν οὐ φήσουσιν—ὕλην γὰρ ἄποιον—τὸ δὲ κατὰ
τὸ εἶδος τεταγμένον ἐπιφέρειν τὴν ζωήν, εἰ μὲν
10 οὐσίαν φήσουσι τὸ εἶδος τοῦτο εἶναι, οὐ τὸ συναμφότερον, θάτερον δὲ τούτων ἔσται ἡ ψυχή· ὃ

[1] ὅτι H–S.

342

of bodies to produce life and for mindless things to generate mind. [The holders of this theory] will not themselves assert that their elements come alive when mixed at random. There is need, therefore, of an ordering principle and a cause of the mixture; so that this would rank as soul. This is not only because body is composite, but not even a simple body could be in existence without soul being in the universe, if it is the coming of a formative principle to matter which makes body, but a formative principle could not come from anywhere except from soul.

3. But if someone says that it is not so, but that atoms or things without parts make the soul when they come together by unity and community of feeling, he could be refuted by their [mere] juxtaposition, and that not a complete one, since nothing which is one and united with itself in community of feeling can come from bodies which are without feeling and unable to be united, but soul is united with itself in community of feeling.[1] But no body or magnitude could be produced from partless constituents. Further, if the body is simple and they [2] are not going to assert that what is material in it has life of itself, but that what holds the rank of form brings the life, then if they are going to say that this form is a substance, it will not be the composite body but one of these constituents which will

[1] The true sense of this difficult passage was seen and clearly explained by Dr. H-R. Schwyzer in his review of Harder, *Gnomon* 32 (1960) 34–5.
[2] After a very summary dismissal of the Epicurean position in the first six lines of the chapter, Plotinus returns here to his main corporealist opponents, the Stoics.

οὐκέτ᾽ ἂν σῶμα· οὐ γὰρ ἐξ ὕλης καὶ τοῦτο, ἢ
πάλιν τὸν αὐτὸν τρόπον ἀναλύσομεν. εἰ δὲ πάθημα
τῆς ὕλης, ἀλλ᾽ οὐκ οὐσίαν φήσουσιν εἶναι, ἀφ᾽ οὗ
τὸ πάθημα καὶ ἡ ζωὴ εἰς τὴν ὕλην ἐλήλυθε, λεκτέον
15 αὐτοῖς. οὐ γὰρ δὴ ἡ ὕλη αὑτὴν μορφοῖ οὐδὲ αὑτῇ
ψυχὴν ἐντίθησι. δεῖ ἄρα τι εἶναι τὸ χορηγὸν τῆς
ζωῆς, εἴτε τῇ ὕλῃ ἡ χορηγία, εἴθ᾽ ὁτῳοῦν τῶν
σωμάτων, ἔξω ὂν καὶ ἐπέκεινα σωματικῆς φύσεως
ἁπάσης. ἐπεὶ οὐδ᾽ ἂν εἴη σῶμα οὐδὲν ψυχικῆς
δυνάμεως οὐκ οὔσης. ῥεῖ γάρ, καὶ ἐν φορᾷ αὐτοῦ
20 ἡ φύσις, καὶ ἀπόλοιτο ἂν ὡς τάχιστα, εἰ πάντα
σώματα εἴη, κἂν εἰ ὄνομα ἑνὶ αὐτῶν ψυχήν τις
θεῖτο. ταὐτὰ γὰρ ἂν πάθοι τοῖς ἄλλοις σώμασιν
ὕλης μιᾶς οὔσης αὐτοῖς. μᾶλλον δὲ οὐδ᾽ ἂν γένοιτο, ἀλλὰ στήσεται ἐν ὕλῃ τὰ πάντα, μὴ ὄντος τοῦ
μορφοῦντος αὐτήν. τάχα δ᾽ ἂν οὐδ᾽ ἂν ἡ ὕλη τὸ
25 παράπαν εἴη. λυθήσεταί τε καὶ τόδε τὸ ξύμπαν, εἴ
τις αὐτὸ πιστεύσειε σώματος συνέρξει, διδοὺς αὐτῷ
ψυχῆς τάξιν μέχρι τῶν ὀνομάτων, ἀέρι καὶ πνεύματι
σκεδαστοτάτῳ καὶ τὸ ἑνὶ εἶναι ἔχοντι οὐ παρ᾽
αὐτοῦ. πῶς γὰρ τεμνομένων τῶν πάντων σωμάτων
30 ὡτινιοῦν τις ἀναθεὶς τόδε τὸ πᾶν οὐκ ἀνόητόν τε καὶ
φερόμενον εἰκῇ ποιήσει; τίς γὰρ τάξις ἐν πνεύματι
δεομένῳ παρὰ ψυχῆς τάξεως ἢ λόγος ἢ νοῦς;
ἀλλὰ ψυχῆς μὲν οὔσης ὑπουργὰ ταῦτα πάντα
αὐτῇ εἰς σύστασιν κόσμου καὶ ζῴου ἑκάστου,

be the soul, and this one would no longer be body: for this cannot also be made of matter, or we shall separate it again [into matter and form] in the same way; but if they are going to assert that it is an affection of matter, but not a substance, they must say where the affection and the life came from into matter. For certainly matter does not shape itself or implant soul in itself. There must, then, be something which supplies life, whether it is to matter that it supplies it or to any one of the bodies, and it must be outside and transcend all bodily nature. For there would not even be any body if the power of soul did not exist. For it flows away, and its nature is transitory, and it would perish very quickly if all things were bodies, even if somebody gave one of them the name of soul. For [the body called soul] would be affected in the same way as the other bodies if they had one and the same matter. Or rather it would not even come into existence, but all things would stick [undeveloped] in matter, if there was nothing to shape it. But perhaps there would not even be any matter at all. And this universe of ours would be dissolved if one entrusted it to the conjoining power of a body, giving the rank of soul as far as names go to this body, to air and breath which is extremely liable to dispersion and does not have its unity of itself. For how, since all bodies are in process of division, if one attributed the origin of this universe to any one of them, would one not make it a mindless thing, moving at random? For what order could there be in a breath, which needs order from soul, or what reason or intelligence? But, if soul exists, all these bodies serve it for the maintenance of the world and of each individual

ἄλλης παρ' ἄλλου δυνάμεως εἰς τὸ ὅλον συντε-
35 λούσης· ταύτης δὲ μὴ παρούσης ἐν τοῖς ὅλοις
οὐδὲν ἂν εἴη ταῦτα, οὐχ ὅτι ἐν τάξει.

4. Μαρτυροῦσι δὲ καὶ αὐτοὶ ὑπὸ τῆς ἀληθείας
ἀγόμενοι, ὡς δεῖ τι πρὸ τῶν σωμάτων εἶναι κρεῖττον αὐτῶν ψυχῆς εἶδος, ἔννουν τὸ πνεῦμα καὶ πῦρ
νοερὸν τιθέμενοι, ὥσπερ ἄνευ πυρὸς καὶ πνεύματος
5 οὐ δυναμένης τῆς κρείττονος μοίρας ἐν τοῖς οὖσιν
εἶναι, τόπον δὲ ζητούσης εἰς τὸ ἱδρυθῆναι, δέον
ζητεῖν, ὅπου τὰ σώματα ἱδρύσουσιν, ὡς ἄρα δεῖ
ταῦτα ἐν ψυχῆς δυνάμεσιν ἱδρῦσθαι. εἰ δὲ μηδὲν
παρὰ τὸ πνεῦμα τὴν ζωὴν καὶ τὴν ψυχὴν τίθενται,
τί τὸ πολυθρύλλητον αὐτοῖς "πὼς ἔχον" εἰς ὃ
10 καταφεύγουσιν ἀναγκαζόμενοι τίθεσθαι ἄλλην παρὰ
τὰ σώματα φύσιν δραστήριον; εἰ οὖν οὐ πᾶν μὲν
πνεῦμα ψυχή, ὅτι μυρία πνεύματα ἄψυχα, τὸ δέ
πως ἔχον πνεῦμα φήσουσι, τό πως ἔχον τοῦτο καὶ
ταύτην τὴν σχέσιν ἢ τῶν ὄντων τι φήσουσιν ἢ
15 μηδέν. ἀλλ' εἰ μὲν μηδέν, πνεῦμα ἂν εἴη μόνον, τὸ
δέ πως ἔχον ὄνομα. καὶ οὕτω συμβήσεται αὐτοῖς
οὐδὲ ἄλλο οὐδὲν εἶναι λέγειν ἢ τὴν ὕλην καὶ ψυχὴν
καὶ θεόν, καὶ ὀνόματα πάντα, ἐκεῖνο δὲ μόνον. εἰ
δὲ τῶν ὄντων ἡ σχέσις καὶ ἄλλο παρὰ τὸ ὑποκείμενον καὶ τὴν ὕλην, ἐν ὕλη μέν, ἄυλον δὲ αὐτὸ τῷ
20 μὴ πάλιν αὖ συγκεῖσθαι ἐξ ὕλης, λόγος ἂν εἴη τις

346

living thing, with different powers from different bodies contributing to the whole; but if soul was not present in the Whole these bodies would be nothing, and certainly not in order.

4. But they themselves are driven by the truth to bear witness that there must be a form of soul prior to bodies and stronger than they are, when they state that the breath has a mind in it and the fire is intelligent, as if without fire and breath the higher part of reality could not be in existence, and as if this higher part was looking for a place to establish itself in; when what they ought to be looking for is a place where they will establish body, as bodies must be established in the powers of soul. But if they hold that life and soul are nothing but the breath, what is this " character " which they are always talking about, in which they take refuge when they are compelled to posit another working principle besides bodies? If, then, not every breath is soul, because there are innumerable soulless breaths, but they are going to assert that the breath " with a certain character " is soul, they will either say that this character and this condition belongs to the class of real beings or that it does not. But if it does not, then soul would be only breath and the character would be a mere word. And so it will happen to them that they will not be saying that soul and God are anything but matter, and these will all be mere names—only that [material breath] will exist. But if the condition belongs to the class of real beings and is something else over and above the substrate and the matter, in matter but immaterial itself— because it is not again composed of matter and form —then it would be a rational principle, and not a

καὶ οὐ σῶμα καὶ φύσις ἑτέρα. ἔτι δὲ καὶ ἐκ τῶνδε
οὐχ ἧττον φαίνεται ἀδύνατον ὂν τὴν ψυχὴν εἶναι
σῶμα ὁτιοῦν. ἢ γὰρ θερμόν ἐστιν ἢ ψυχρόν, ἢ
σκληρὸν ἢ μαλακόν, ὑγρόν τε ἢ πεπηγός, μέλαν τε
25 ἢ λευκόν, καὶ πάντα ὅσα ποιότητες σωμάτων ἄλλαι
ἐν ἄλλοις. καὶ εἰ μὲν θερμὸν μόνον, θερμαίνει, ψυχρὸν δὲ μόνον, ψύξει· καὶ κοῦφα ποιήσει τὸ κοῦφον
προσγενόμενον καὶ παρόν, καὶ βαρυνεῖ τὸ βαρύ· καὶ
μελανεῖ τὸ μέλαν, καὶ τὸ λευκὸν λευκὸν ποιήσει.
οὐ γὰρ πυρὸς τὸ ψύχειν, οὐδὲ τοῦ ψυχροῦ θερμὰ
30 ποιεῖν. ἀλλ' ἤ γε ψυχὴ καὶ ἐν ἄλλοις μὲν ζῴοις
ἄλλα, τὰ δ' ἄλλα ποιεῖ, καὶ ἐν τῷ δὲ αὐτῷ τὰ
ἐναντία, τὰ μὲν πηγνῦσα, τὰ δὲ χέουσα, καὶ τὰ μὲν
πυκνά, τὰ δὲ ἀραιά, μέλανα λευκά, κοῦφα βαρέα.
καίτοι ἓν δεῖ ποιεῖν κατὰ τὴν τοῦ σώματος ποιότητά
τε τὴν ἄλλην καὶ δὴ καὶ χρόαν· νῦν δὲ πολλά.

5. Τὰς δὲ δὴ κινήσεις πῶς διαφόρους, ἀλλ' οὐ
μίαν, μιᾶς οὔσης παντὸς σώματος κινήσεως; εἰ δὲ
τῶν μὲν προαιρέσεις, τῶν δὲ λόγους αἰτιάσονται,
ὀρθῶς μὲν τοῦτο· ἀλλ' οὐ σώματος ἡ προαίρεσις
5 οὐδὲ οἱ λόγοι διάφοροί γε ὄντες, ἑνὸς ὄντος καὶ
ἁπλοῦ τοῦ σώματος καὶ οὐ μετὸν αὐτῷ τοιούτου
γε λόγου, ἢ ὅσος δέδοται αὐτῷ παρὰ τοῦ ποιήσαν-
τος θερμὸν αὐτὸ ἢ ψυχρὸν εἶναι. τὸ δὲ καὶ ἐν
χρόνοις αὔξειν, καὶ μέχρι τοσούτου μέτρου, πόθεν
ἂν τῷ σώματι αὐτῷ γένοιτο, ᾧ προσήκει ἐναύξεσ-
10 θαι, αὐτῷ δὲ ἀμοίρῳ τοῦ αὔξειν εἶναι, ἢ ὅσον παρα-
ληφθείη ἂν ἐν ὕλης ὄγκῳ ὑπηρετοῦν τῷ δι' αὐτοῦ

body, and so a different kind of nature. And besides, it is equally obvious for the following reasons that it is impossible for soul to be any kind of body. For [if it is], it is hot or cold, hard or soft, fluid or solid, black or white, and [one could mention] all the other qualities of bodies which are different in different ones. And if it is only hot, it heats, but if it is only cold, it will cool, and the light when it is present makes things light and the heavy makes them heavy; and the black will blacken, and the white will make things white. For it does not belong to fire to cool things, nor to the cold to make them hot. But the soul does different things in different living beings, and even opposite things in the same one, solidifying some and liquefying others, and making some things dense and others rarefied, making things black and white, light and heavy. But [if it was a body] it ought to produce one effect according to the body's qualities, all of them including its colour; but as it is it produces many effects.

5. But why, I ask, are the movements different, and not one, when every body has one movement? If they make choices responsible for some and rational principles for others, that is correct; but choice does not belong to body and neither do rational principles which are various, while body is one and simple and has no share in rational principle of this kind, but only as much rational principle as is given to it by what made it hot or cold. But from where could the body get the power to cause growth in season and up to a certain measure? It is proper to body to grow, but to be without the power of causing growth except as much as may be received in the mass of matter for the service of that which

τὴν αὔξην ἐργαζομένῳ; καὶ γὰρ εἰ ἡ ψυχὴ σῶμα
οὖσα αὔξοι, ἀνάγκη καὶ αὐτὴν αὔξεσθαι, προσθήκῃ
δηλονότι ὁμοίου σώματος, εἰ μέλλει εἰς ἴσον ἰέναι
15 τῷ αὐξομένῳ ὑπ᾿ αὐτῆς. καὶ ἢ ψυχὴ ἔσται τὸ
προστιθέμενον ἢ ἄψυχον σῶμα. καὶ εἰ μὲν ψυχή,
πόθεν καὶ πῶς εἰσιούσης, καὶ πῶς προστιθεμένης;
εἰ δὲ ἄψυχον τὸ προστιθέμενον, πῶς τοῦτο ψυχώσε-
ται καὶ τῷ πρόσθεν ὁμογνωμονήσει καὶ ἓν ἔσται
καὶ τῶν αὐτῶν δοξῶν τῇ πρόσθεν μεταλήψεται,
20 ἀλλ᾿ οὐχ ὥσπερ ξένη ψυχὴ αὕτη ἐν ἀγνοίᾳ ἔσται ὧν
ἡ ἑτέρα; εἰ δὲ καί, ὥσπερ ὁ ἄλλος ὄγκος ἡμῶν, τὸ
μέν τι ἀπορρεύσεται αὐτοῦ, τὸ δέ τι προσελεύ-
σεται, οὐδὲν δὲ ἔσται τὸ αὐτό, πῶς οὖν ἡμῖν αἱ
μνῆμαι, πῶς δὲ ἡ γνώρισις οἰκείων οὐδέποτε τῇ
αὐτῇ ψυχῇ χρωμένων; καὶ μὴν εἰ σῶμά ἐστι,
25 φύσις δὲ σώματος μεριζόμενον εἰς πλείω ἕκαστον
μὴ τὸ αὐτὸ εἶναι τῶν μερῶν τῷ ὅλῳ, εἰ τὸ τοσόνδε
μέγεθος ψυχή, ὃ ἐὰν ἔλαττον ᾖ ψυχὴ οὐκ ἔσται,
ὥσπερ πᾶν ποσὸν ἀφαιρέσει τὸ εἶναι τὸ πρόσθεν
ἠλλάξατο—εἰ δέ τι τῶν μέγεθος ἐχόντων τὸν
ὄγκον ἐλαττωθὲν τῇ ποιότητι ταὐτὸν μένοι, ᾗ μὲν
30 σῶμα ἕτερόν ἐστι, καὶ ᾗ ποσόν, τῇ δὲ ποιότητι
ἑτέρᾳ τῆς ποσότητος οὔσῃ τὸ ταὐτὸν ἀποσῴζειν
δύναται—τί τοίνυν φήσουσιν οἱ τὴν ψυχὴν σῶμα
εἶναι λέγοντες; πρῶτον μὲν περὶ ἑκάστου μέρους
τῆς ψυχῆς τῆς ἐν τῷ αὐτῷ σώματι πότερον ἕκαστον ψυχήν, οἷα ἐστὶ καὶ ἡ ὅλη; καὶ πάλιν τοῦ
35 μέρους τὸ μέρος; οὐδὲν ἄρα τὸ μέγεθος συνε-

brings about growth by means of it. For if soul, being a body, was to cause growth, it would have to grow itself, obviously by the addition of similar body, if it was going to keep pace with the body it was causing to grow. And what is added will be either soul or soulless body. And if it is soul, where will it come from, and how will it get in and how is it added? But if what is added is soulless, how will this become soul and how will it come to agreement with what was there before, and be one with it and share the same thoughts with the soul which was there before, but not be like a strange soul which will be ignorant of what the other soul knows? But if, just like the rest of our [bodily] mass, some of its substance will flow away, and some of it will come from outside, and nothing will be the same, how then do we have memories, and how do friends and relations recognise each other when they never have the same souls? Then again, if soul is a body, and when the nature of body is divided into several parts each part is not the same as the whole, if soul is a particular definite size of body, which is not soul if it is smaller, as every quantity changes from its former existence by subtraction—but if one of the things which have size remains the same in quality when its mass is diminished, it is different in so far as it is body, and in so far as it is a particular size, but can retain its identity by its quality which is different from its quantity—what then are the people who assert that soul is a body going to say about this? First of all about each individual part of the soul which is in the same body: is each of them a soul in the same way as the whole is? And again, is the part of the part? If this is so, the size contri-

βάλλετο τῇ οὐσίᾳ αὐτῆς· καίτοι ἔδει γε ποσοῦ τινος
ὄντος· καὶ ὅλον πολλαχῇ ὅπερ σώματι παρεῖναι
ἀδύνατον ἐν πλείοσι τὸ αὐτὸ ὅλον εἶναι καὶ τὸ
μέρος ὅπερ τὸ ὅλον ὑπάρχειν. εἰ δὲ ἕκαστον τῶν
μερῶν οὐ ψυχὴν φήσουσιν, ἐξ ἀψύχων ψυχὴ αὐτοῖς
40 ὑπάρξει. καὶ προσέτι ψυχῆς ἑκάστης τὸ μέγεθος
ὡρισμένον ἔσται [οὐδὲ] [1] ἐφ᾽ ἑκάτερα, ἡ [2] ἐπὶ τὸ
ἔλαττόν γε [ἢ ἐπὶ τὸ μεῖζον] [3] ψυχὴ οὐκ ἔσται.
ὅταν τοίνυν ἐκ συνόδου μιᾶς καὶ ἑνὸς σπέρματος
δίδυμα γένηται γεννήματα, ἢ καί, ὥσπερ καὶ ἐν τοῖς
45 ἄλλοις ζῴοις, πλεῖστα τοῦ σπέρματος εἰς πολλοὺς
τόπους μεριζομένου, οὗ δὴ ἕκαστον ὅλον ἐστί, πῶς
οὐ διδάσκει τοῦτο τοὺς βουλομένους μανθάνειν,
ὡς, ὅπου τὸ μέρος τὸ αὐτό ἐστι τῷ ὅλῳ, τοῦτο ἐν τῇ
αὑτοῦ οὐσίᾳ τὸ ποσὸν εἶναι ὑπερβέβηκεν, ἄποσον δὲ
αὐτὸ εἶναι δεῖ ἐξ ἀνάγκης; οὕτω γὰρ ἂν μένοι τὸ
50 αὐτὸ τοῦ ποσοῦ κλεπτομένου, ἅτε μὴ μέλον αὐτῷ
ποσότητος καὶ ὄγκου, ὡς ἂν τῆς οὐσίας αὐτοῦ
ἕτερόν τι οὔσης. ἄποσον ἄρα· ἡ ψυχὴ καὶ οἱ λόγοι.

6. Ὅτι δέ, εἰ σῶμα εἴη ἡ ψυχή, οὔτε τὸ αἰσθάνεσθαι οὔτε τὸ νοεῖν οὔτε τὸ ἐπίστασθαι οὔτε ἀρετὴ οὔτε
τι τῶν καλῶν ἔσται, ἐκ τῶνδε δῆλον. εἴ τι μέλλει
αἰσθάνεσθαί τινος, ἓν αὐτὸ δεῖ εἶναι καὶ τῷ αὐτῷ
5 παντὸς ἀντιλαμβάνεσθαι, καὶ εἰ διὰ πολλῶν
αἰσθητηρίων πλείω τὰ εἰσιόντα εἴη ἢ πολλαὶ περὶ
ἓν ποιότητες, κἂν δι᾽ ἑνὸς ποικίλον οἷον πρόσωπον.
οὐ γὰρ ἄλλο μὲν ῥινός, ἄλλο δὲ ὀφθαλμῶν, ἀλλὰ

---

[1] om. Eusebius*.
[2] Eus.: ἢ Enn.
[3] om. Eus.

butes nothing to its essential being; and yet it ought to, if the soul is a particular size, and it is as a whole in many places; this is something of which a body cannot possibly be capable, for the same body to be as a whole in more than one place and for the part to be what the whole is. But if they are going to say that each of the parts is not a soul, their soul will consist of soulless parts. And besides, if the size of each soul is limited in both directions, that at any rate which is less [than the minimum size] will not be soul; when, therefore, from one act of intercourse and one seed twin offspring are produced or, as in other living things a great many, the seed being distributed to many parts [of the womb], and each is a complete whole, why does this not teach those who are willing to learn that, where the part is the same as the whole, this thing transcends quantity in its own essential being, and must necessarily itself be non-quantitative? For thus it would remain the same when robbed of quantity since it would not care about quantity and mass, because its own nature would be something else. The soul and rational principles, then, are without quantity.

6. But it is clear from the following arguments that if soul is a body, neither perception nor thinking nor knowing nor virtue nor anything of value will exist. If anything is going to perceive anything, it must itself be one and perceive every object by one and the same means, both if a number of impressions are received through many sense-organs, or many qualities are perceived in one thing, or if through one sense-organ a complex thing, for example a face, is perceived. For there is not one perception of the nose and another of the eyes, but one and the

ταὐτὸν ὁμοῦ πάντων. καὶ εἰ τὸ μὲν δι' ὀμμάτων,
10 τὸ δὲ δι' ἀκοῆς, ἕν τι δεῖ εἶναι, εἰς ὃ ἄμφω. ἢ
πῶς ἂν εἴποι, ὅτι ἕτερα ταῦτα, μὴ εἰ τὸ αὐτὸ ὁμοῦ
τῶν αἰσθημάτων ἐλθόντων; δεῖ τοίνυν τοῦτο
ὥσπερ κέντρον εἶναι, γραμμὰς δὲ συμβαλλούσας ἐκ
περιφερείας κύκλου τὰς πανταχόθεν αἰσθήσεις
πρὸς τοῦτο περαίνειν, καὶ τοιοῦτον τὸ ἀντιλαμ-
15 βανόμενον εἶναι, ἓν ὂν ὄντως. εἰ δὲ διεστὼς τοῦτο
γένοιτο, καὶ οἷον γραμμῆς ἐπ' ἄμφω τὰ πέρατα αἱ
αἰσθήσεις προσβάλλοιεν, ἢ συνδραμεῖται εἰς ἓν
καὶ τὸ αὐτὸ πάλιν, οἷον τὸ μέσον, ἢ ἄλλο, τὸ δὲ
ἄλλο, ἑκάτερον ἑκατέρου αἴσθησιν ἕξει· ὥσπερ ἂν
εἰ ἐγὼ μὲν ἄλλου, σὺ δὲ ἄλλου αἴσθοιο. καὶ εἰ
20 ἓν εἴη τὸ αἴσθημα, οἷον πρόσωπον, ἢ εἰς ἓν
συναιρεθήσεται—ὅπερ καὶ φαίνεται· συναιρεῖται
γὰρ καὶ ἐν αὐταῖς ταῖς κόραις· ἢ πῶς ἂν τὰ
μέγιστα διὰ ταύτης ὁρῷτο; ὥστε ἔτι μᾶλλον εἰς
τὸ ἡγεμονοῦν ἰόντα οἷον ἱμερῆ νοήματα γίγνεσθαι
—καὶ ἔσται ἀμερὲς τοῦτο· ἢ μεγέθει ὄντι τούτῳ
25 συμμερίζοιτο ἄν, ὥστε ἄλλο ἄλλου μέρος καὶ
μηδένα ἡμῶν ὅλου τοῦ αἰσθητοῦ τὴν ἀντίληψιν
ἴσχειν. ἀλλὰ γὰρ ἕν ἐστι τὸ πᾶν· πῶς γὰρ ἂν καὶ

same perception of all together. And if one perception comes through the eyes and another through hearing, there must be some one thing to which both come. Or how could one say that these sense-perceptions are different, if they did not all come together to one and the same [recipient]? This then must be like a centre, and the sense-perceptions from every quarter, lines coming together from the circumference of the circle, must reach it, and that which apprehends them must be of this kind, really one.[1] But if this were extended, and the sense-perceptions arrived at something like the terminal points at both ends of a line, either they will run together again at one and the same point, like the middle of the line, or the two different terminal points will each have a perception of something different (as if I perceived one thing and you another).[2] And if the object of perception was one, a face for instance, either it will be gathered together into a unity—which is what does obviously happen; for it is gathered together in the pupils of the eyes themselves: or how could the largest things be seen through the pupil of our eye? So still more when they reach the ruling principle they will become like partless thoughts—and this ruling principle will be partless; or if this is a size the sense-objects would be divided up along with it, so that each part would perceive a different part of the object and none of us would apprehend the perceptible thing as a whole. But the whole is one: for how could it be divided?

---

[1] This is a Peripatetic comparison: cp. Alexander of Aphrodisias *De Anima* p. 63, 8–13 Bruns.

[2] Again Peripatetic language: cp. Aristotle *De Anima* 2, 426b19 and Alexander *De Anima* p. 61, 1–3 Bruns.

διαιροῖτο; οὐ γὰρ δὴ τὸ ἴσον τῷ ἴσῳ ἐφαρμόσει,
ὅτι οὐκ ἴσον τὸ ἡγεμονοῦν παντὶ αἰσθητῷ. κατὰ
30 πηλίκα οὖν ἡ διαίρεσις; ἢ εἰς τοσαῦτα διαιρε-
θήσεται, καθόσον ἂν ἀριθμοῦ ἔχοι εἰς ποικιλίαν τὸ
εἰσιὸν αἴσθημα; καὶ ἕκαστον δὴ ἐκείνων τῶν
μερῶν τῆς ψυχῆς ἆρα καὶ τοῖς μορίοις αὐτοῦ
αἰσθήσεται. ἢ ἀναίσθητα τὰ μέρη τῶν μορίων
ἔσται; ἀλλὰ ἀδύνατον. εἰ δὲ ὁτιοῦν παντὸς
35 αἰσθήσεται, εἰς ἄπειρα διαιρεῖσθαι τοῦ μεγέθους
πεφυκότος ἀπείρους καὶ αἰσθήσεις καθ᾽ ἕκαστον
αἰσθητὸν συμβήσεται γίγνεσθαι ἑκάστῳ οἷον τοῦ
αὐτοῦ ἀπείρους ἐν τῷ ἡγεμονοῦντι ἡμῶν εἰκόνας.
καὶ μὴν σώματος ὄντος τοῦ αἰσθανομένου οὐκ ἂν
ἄλλον τρόπον γένοιτο τὸ αἰσθάνεσθαι ἢ οἷον ἐν
40 κηρῷ ἐνσημανθεῖσαι ἀπὸ δακτυλίων σφραγῖδες,
εἴτ᾽ οὖν εἰς αἷμα, εἴτ᾽ οὖν εἰς ἀέρα τῶν αἰσθητῶν
ἐνσημαινομένων. καὶ εἰ μὲν ὡς ἐν σώμασιν
ὑγροῖς, ὅπερ καὶ εὔλογον, ὥσπερ εἰς ὕδωρ συγχυ-
θήσεται, καὶ οὐκ ἔσται μνήμη· εἰ δὲ μένουσιν οἱ
τύποι, ἢ οὐκ ἔστιν ἄλλους ἐνσημαίνεσθαι ἐκείνων
45 κατεχόντων, ὥστε ἄλλαι αἰσθήσεις οὐκ ἔσονται, ἢ
γινομένων ἄλλων ἐκεῖνοι οἱ πρότεροι ἀπολοῦνται·
ὥστε οὐδὲν ἔσται μνημονεύειν. εἰ δὲ ἔστι τὸ
μνημονεύειν καὶ ἄλλων αἰσθάνεσθαι ἐπ᾽ ἄλλοις
οὐκ ἐμποδιζόντων τῶν πρόσθεν, ἀδύνατον τὴν
ψυχὴν σῶμα εἶναι.

7. Ἴδοι δ᾽ ἄν τις καὶ ἐκ τοῦ ἀλγεῖν καὶ ἐκ τῆς
τοῦ ἀλγεῖν αἰσθήσεως τὸ αὐτὸ τοῦτο. ὅταν
δάκτυλον λέγηται ἀλγεῖν ἄνθρωπος, ἡ μὲν ὀδύνη
περὶ τὸν δάκτυλον δήπουθεν, ἡ δ᾽ αἴσθησις τοῦ

So equal will certainly not fit equal, because the ruling principle is not equal to every perceptible object. Into how many parts, then, will its division be? Will it be divided into a number of parts corresponding to the varied complexity of the entering sense-object? And of course each of those parts of the soul will perceive with its own subdivisions. Or will the parts of the parts be without perception? But this is impossible. But if any and every part perceives the whole, since a size is naturally capable of division to infinity, there will come to be an infinity of perceptions for each observer regarding the sense-object, like an infinite number of images of the same thing in our ruling principle. Again, since the object being perceived is a body, perception could not occur in any other way than that in which seal-impressions are imprinted in wax from seal-rings, whether the sense-objects are imprinted on blood or on air. And if this happens as it does in fluid bodies, which is probable, the impression will be obliterated as if it was on water, and there will be no memory. But if the impressions persist, either it will not be possible for others to be imprinted because the first will prevent them, so that there will be no other sense-impressions, or if others are made, those former impressions will be destroyed: so that there will be no possibility of remembering. But if it is possible to remember and to perceive one set of things after another without the previous ones hindering, it is impossible for the soul to be a body.

7. One might see this very same thing also from pain and from the perception of pain. When a man is said to have a pain in his toe, the pain is presumably in the region of the toe, but they will obviously

5 ἀλγεῖν δῆλον ὅτι ὁμολογήσουσιν, ὡς περὶ τὸ
ἡγεμονοῦν γίγνεται. ἄλλου δὴ ὄντος τοῦ πονοῦντος
μέρους τοῦ παθήματος [1] τὸ ἡγεμονοῦν αἰσθάνεται,
καὶ ὅλη ἡ ψυχὴ τὸ αὐτὸ πάσχει. πῶς οὖν τοῦτο
συμβαίνει; διαδόσει, φήσουσι, παθόντος μὲν
πρώτως τοῦ περὶ τὸν δάκτυλον ψυχικοῦ πνεύματος,
10 μεταδόντος δὲ τῷ ἐφεξῆς καὶ τούτου ἄλλῳ, ἕως
πρὸς τὸ ἡγεμονοῦν ἀφίκοιτο. ἀνάγκη τοίνυν, εἰ τὸ
πρῶτον πονοῦν ᾔσθετο, ἄλλην τὴν αἴσθησιν τοῦ
δευτέρου εἶναι, εἰ κατὰ διάδοσιν ἡ αἴσθησις, καὶ
τοῦ τρίτου ἄλλην, καὶ πολλὰς αἰσθήσεις καὶ
ἀπείρους περὶ ἑνὸς ἀλγήματος γίγνεσθαι, καὶ
15 τούτων ἁπασῶν ὕστερον τὸ ἡγεμονοῦν αἴσθεσθαι
καὶ τῆς ἑαυτοῦ παρὰ ταύτας. τὸ δὲ ἀληθὲς
ἑκάστην ἐκείνων μὴ τοῦ ἐν τῷ δακτύλῳ ἀλγήματος,
ἀλλὰ τὴν μὲν ἐφεξῆς τῷ δακτύλῳ, ὅτι ὁ ταρσὸς
ἀλγεῖ, τὴν δὲ τρίτην, ὅτι ἄλλο τὸ πρὸς τῷ ἄνωθεν,
καὶ πολλὰς εἶναι ἀλγηδόνας, τό τε ἡγεμονοῦν μὴ
20 τοῦ πρὸς τῷ δακτύλῳ ἀλγήματος αἰσθάνεσθαι,
ἀλλὰ τοῦ πρὸς αὑτῷ, καὶ τοῦτο γινώσκειν μόνον,
τὰ δ' ἄλλα χαίρειν ἐᾶν μὴ ἐπιστάμενον, ὅτι ἀλγεῖ ὁ
δάκτυλος. εἰ τοίνυν κατὰ διάδοσιν οὐχ οἷόν τε
τὴν αἴσθησιν τοῦ τοιούτου γίγνεσθαι μηδὲ σώματος,
25 ὄγκου ὄντος, ἄλλου παθόντος ἄλλου γνῶσιν εἶναι—
παντὸς γὰρ μεγέθους τὸ μὲν ἄλλο, τὸ δὲ ἄλλο ἐστί—
δεῖ τοιοῦτον τίθεσθαι τὸ αἰσθανόμενον, οἷον

---

[1] Vitringa: πνεύματος Enn., Eus., H–S.

agree that the perception of pain is in the region of the ruling principle.[1] Well then, though the breath or life is different from the suffering part, the ruling principle perceives that it is affected, and the whole soul is affected in the same way. How then does this happen? They will assert that it is by transmission[2]: first of all the soul-breath in the region of the toe is affected, and passes the affection to the part situated next to it, and this to another, until it arrives at the ruling principle. It is necessary then, if the first part when it suffered perceived the suffering, that the second part's perception should be different, if the perception is by transmission, and the third part's different again, and there would be many perceptions, even an infinite number, of one pain, and the ruling principle would perceive after all these and have its own perception over and above all these. But the truth would be that each of those perceptions would not be of the pain in the toe, but the perception next to the toe would be that the sole of the foot was suffering, and the third perception that another part higher up was, and there would be many feelings of pain, and the ruling principle would not perceive the pain in the toe but the pain in the part next to itself, and would know this alone and let the other pains go, and not understand that the toe had a pain. If, then, it is not possible for the perception of this kind of thing to come about by transmission, nor for one body to have knowledge when another is affected, since body is mass—for every size has one part different from another—one must suppose that the perceiving principle is of such

[1] Cp. *SVF* II 854.
[2] This Stoic doctrine is attacked again at IV. 2. 2. 13.

πανταχοῦ αὐτὸ ἑαυτῷ τὸ αὐτὸ εἶναι. τοῦτο δὲ
ἄλλῳ τινὶ τῶν ὄντων ἢ σώματι ποιεῖν προσήκει.

8. Ὅτι δὲ οὐδὲ νοεῖν οἷόν τε, εἰ σῶμα ἡ ψυχὴ
ὁτιοῦν εἴη, δεικτέον ἐκ τῶνδε. εἰ γὰρ τὸ αἰσθάνεσθαί ἐστι τὸ σώματι προσχρωμένην τὴν ψυχὴν
ἀντιλαμβάνεσθαι τῶν αἰσθητῶν, οὐκ ἂν εἴη καὶ τὸ
5 νοεῖν τὲ διὰ σώματος καταλαμβάνειν, ἢ ταὐτὸν
ἔσται τῷ αἰσθάνεσθαι. εἰ οὖν τὸ νοεῖν ἐστι τὸ
ἄνευ σώματος ἀντιλαμβάνεσθαι, πολὺ πρότερον δεῖ
μὴ σῶμα αὐτὸ τὸ νοῆσον εἶναι. ἔτι εἰ αἰσθητῶν
μὲν ἡ αἴσθησις, νοητῶν δὲ ἡ νόησις—εἰ δὲ μὴ
βούλονται, ἀλλ’ οὖν ἔσονταί γε καὶ νοητῶν τινων
10 νοήσεις καὶ ἀμεγέθων ἀντιλήψεις—πῶς οὖν
μέγεθος ὂν τὸ μὴ μέγεθος νοήσει καὶ τῷ μεριστῷ
τὸ μὴ μεριστὸν νοήσει; ἢ μέρει τινὶ ἀμερεῖ
αὑτοῦ. εἰ δὲ τοῦτο, οὐ σῶμα ἔσται τὸ νοῆσον·
οὐ γὰρ δὴ τοῦ ὅλου χρεία πρὸς τὸ θίγειν· ἀρκεῖ
γὰρ καθ’ ἕν τι. εἰ μὲν οὖν συγχωρήσονται
15 τὰς πρώτας νοήσεις, ὅπερ ἀληθές ἐστιν, εἶναι
τῶν πάντη σώματος καθαρωτάτων αὐτοεκάστου,
ἀνάγκη καὶ τὸ νοοῦν σώματος καθαρὸν ὂν ἢ
γιγνόμενον γινώσκειν. εἰ δὲ τῶν ἐν ὕλῃ εἰδῶν
τὰς νοήσεις φήσουσιν εἶναι, ἀλλὰ χωριζομένων γε
τῶν σωμάτων γίγνονται τοῦ νοῦ χωρίζοντος. οὐ

360

a kind that it is everywhere identical with itself. But this action is characteristic of some other kind of reality than body.

8. It can be shown by the following arguments that it would not even be possible to think if soul was any kind of body. For if sense-perception is the soul's apprehension of the objects of sense by making use of the body, thinking cannot be comprehension through the body, or it will be the same as sense-perception. If then thinking is apprehension without the body, it is much more necessary that what is going to do the thinking should not be body. Again, if sense-perception is of sense-objects, and thinking is of objects of thought—even if they do not like it, yet all the same there will be thoughts at least of some objects of thought and apprehensions of things without size—how then will something which is a size think what is not a size and think what is partless with something which has parts? Perhaps [it will do so] with a partless part of itself. But if what is going to do the thinking is this, it will not be a body; for there is no need of the whole for touching: contact at one point is enough.[1] If then they are going to agree that the primary thoughts, as is true, are of the objects most completely free from body, of absolute individual reality, then what thinks must know these objects by being or becoming free of body. But if they are going to say that thoughts are of the forms in matter, yet these thoughts come to be by the separation from them of the bodies,

[1] This is again an argument of Aristotle: cp. *De Anima* A 407a15–22. Plotinus does not appear to have noticed that it is directed against Plato (against a literal interpretation of the "soul-circles" of *Timaeus* 35A–37C).

20 γὰρ δὴ μετὰ σαρκῶν ἢ ὅλως ὕλης ὁ χωρισμὸς
κύκλου καὶ τριγώνου καὶ γραμμῆς καὶ σημείου.
δεῖ ἄρα καὶ τὴν ψυχὴν σώματος αὐτὴν ἐν τῷ
τοιούτῳ χωρίσαι. δεῖ ἄρα μηδὲ αὐτὴν σῶμα εἶναι.

  Ἀμέγεθες δέ, οἶμαι, καὶ τὸ καλὸν καὶ τὸ
25 δίκαιον· καὶ ἡ τούτων ἄρα νόησις. ὥστε καὶ
προσιόντα ἀμερεῖ αὐτῆς ὑποδέξεται καὶ ἐν αὐτῇ ἐν
ἀμερεῖ κείσεται. πῶς δ' ἂν καὶ σώματος ὄντος
τῆς ψυχῆς ἀρεταὶ αὐτῆς, σωφροσύνη καὶ δικαιο-
σύνη ἀνδρία τε καὶ αἱ ἄλλαι; πνεῦμά τι γὰρ ἢ
αἷμά τι ἂν τὸ σωφρονεῖν εἴη ἢ δικαιότης ἢ ἀνδρία,
30 εἰ μὴ ἄρα ἡ ἀνδρία τὸ δυσπαθὲς τοῦ πνεύματος εἴη,
καὶ ἡ σωφροσύνη ἡ εὐκρασία, τὸ δὲ κάλλος
εὐμορφία τις ἐν τύποις, καθ' ἣν λέγομεν ἰδόντες
ὡραίους καὶ καλοὺς τὰ σώματα. ἰσχυρῷ μὲν οὖν
καὶ καλῷ ἐν τύποις πνεύματι εἶναι προσήκοι ἄν·
σωφρονεῖν δὲ τί δεῖ πνεύματι; ἀλλ' οὐ τοὐναντίον
35 ἐν περιπτύξεσι καὶ ἀφαῖς εὐπαθεῖν, ὅπου ἢ
θερμανθήσεται ἢ συμμέτρως ψύχεος ἱμείροι
ἢ μαλακοῖς τισι καὶ ἁπαλοῖς καὶ λείοις πελάσει; τὸ
δὲ κατ' ἀξίαν νεῖμαι τί ἂν αὐτῷ μέλοι; πότερον
δὲ ἀιδίων ὄντων τῶν τῆς ἀρετῆς θεωρημάτων καὶ
40 τῶν ἄλλων νοητῶν ἡ ψυχὴ ἐφάπτεται, ἢ γίνεταί
τῳ ἡ ἀρετή, ὠφελεῖ καὶ πάλιν φθείρεται; ἀλλὰ
τίς ὁ ποιῶν καὶ πόθεν; οὕτω γὰρ ἂν ἐκεῖνο πάλιν

and it is mind which separates them. For the separation of " circle " and " triangle " and " line " and " point " is certainly not carried out with the help of flesh, or in general of matter. The soul, then, must separate itself from body in this kind of [abstractive] thinking.

But nobility and justice are also, I think, without size; so, then, is thinking about them. So that when they come to it, our thought will receive them in its partlessness and they will remain in it as partless. But how, if the soul is a body, could its virtues exist, self-control and justice and courage and the rest? For self-control or justice or courage would be a kind of breath or blood, unless courage was the breath's lack of susceptibility to affection, and self-control the well-balanced mixture of its elements, and beauty a kind of shapeliness in impressions, by which we say when we see them that people are fresh and young and beautiful in body. Now it might be appropriate to strength and beauty to consist in impressions on the breath: but what does breath need self-control for? Would it not rather find its comfort in embracing and touching, where it will be warmed or have a moderated desire to be cool,[1] or come close to soft, delicate, smooth things? But what would it care about distribution according to worth? But does the soul attain the objects of its contemplation of the virtues and other intelligible things as eternal, or does virtue just happen to someone, benefit them and perish again? But who is it who makes it happen, and where does it come from? For if there is something which

---

[1] An allusion to *Odyssey* 10. 555.

μένοι. δεῖ ἄρα ἀιδίων εἶναι καὶ μενόντων, οἷα καὶ
τὰ ἐν γεωμετρίᾳ. εἰ δὲ ἀιδίων καὶ μενόντων, οὐ
σωμάτων. δεῖ ἄρα καὶ ἐν ᾧ ἔσται τοιοῦτον εἶναι·
45 δεῖ ἄρα μὴ σῶμα εἶναι. οὐ γὰρ μένει, ἀλλὰ ῥεῖ ἡ
σώματος φύσις πᾶσα.

8[1]. Εἰ δὲ τὰς τῶν σωμάτων ποιήσεις ὁρῶντες
θερμαινούσας καὶ ψυχούσας καὶ ὠθούσας καὶ
βαρυνούσας ἐνταῦθα τάττουσι τὴν ψυχὴν οἷον ἐν
δραστηρίῳ τόπῳ ἱδρύοντες αὐτήν, πρῶτον μὲν
5 ἀγνοοῦσιν, ὡς καὶ αὐτὰ [1] τὰ σώματα δυνάμεσι ταῖς
ἐν αὑτοῖς ἀσωμάτοις ταῦτα ἐργάζεται· ἔπειτα, ὅτι
οὐ ταύτας τὰς δυνάμεις περὶ ψυχὴν εἶναι ἀξιοῦμεν,
ἀλλὰ τὸ νοεῖν, τὸ αἰσθάνεσθαι, λογίζεσθαι, ἐπιθυμεῖν,
ἐπιμελεῖσθαι ἐμφρόνως καλῶς,[2] ἃ πάντα ἄλλην
οὐσίαν ζητεῖ. τὰς οὖν δυνάμεις τῶν ἀσωμάτων
10 μεταβιβάσαντες εἰς τὰ σώματα οὐδεμίαν ἐκείνοις
καταλείπουσιν. ὅτι δὲ καὶ τὰ σώματα ἀσωμάτοις
δυνάμεσι δύναται ἃ δύναται, ἐκ τῶνδε δῆλον.
ὁμολογήσουσι γὰρ ἕτερον ποιότητα καὶ ποσότητα
εἶναι, καὶ πᾶν σῶμα ποσὸν εἶναι, καὶ ἔτι οὐ πᾶν
15 σῶμα ποιὸν [3] εἶναι, ὥσπερ τὴν ὕλην. ταῦτα δὲ
ὁμολογοῦντες τὴν ποιότητα ὁμολογήσουσιν ἕτερον
οὖσαν ποσοῦ ἕτερον σώματος εἶναι. πῶς γὰρ μὴ

---

[1] Kirchhoff*: ταῦτα Eus., H–S[1].
[2] Eus., Schwyzer (*Mus. Helv.* 26, 1969, 254): ἐμφρόνως καὶ
καλῶς *Vigier**, Creuzer*: ἐμφρόνως κακῶς H–S[1]: an coniciendum
[ἐμφρόνως] καλῶς (cf. ἐπιμελεῖσθαι καλῶς Plat. Leg. 766A7)?
[3] suspic. *Vigier*, scr. Volkmann*, *Gifford*: ποσὸν Eus.,
Stephanus, *Gaisford*, Creuzer, Kirchhoff, Cilento.

makes it happen, that again would abide. The virtues, then, are required to be eternal and abiding, like the objects of geometry. But if they are eternal and abiding they are not bodies. That, therefore, in which they are must be of the same kind: therefore it cannot be a body. For the whole nature of body does not abide, but flows away.

8[1]. But if when they see the actions of bodies heating and cooling and pushing and weighing down they rank the soul with them and in a kind of way establish it in a field of action, first of all they are ignorant that bodies themselves do these things by the bodiless powers in them; and then that these are not the powers which we consider to belong to the soul, but thinking, perceiving, reasoning, desiring, supervising, intelligently and well,[1] which all require another kind of being. By transferring, therefore, the powers of bodiless realities to bodies, they leave nothing for the bodiless. But that bodies are able to do what they can do by bodiless powers is obvious for the following reasons. They will agree that quality is different from quantity, and that every body is of a certain quantity, and also that not every body is of a certain quality, as matter is not. But in admitting this they will also admit that quality in being different from quantity is different from body. For how without being of a

---

[1] This list of powers of soul may be influenced by the list of soul-movements in Plato *Laws* X 897A1–4, but the resemblance is not very close. Plato's list is neutral and comprehensive: bad as well as good soul-movements are included. In Plotinus's more conventional list there are only good powers, if the reading of the MSS of Eusebius καλῶς in line 8 is accepted, as it is now by Henry and Schwyzer, and has generally been by editors of Eusebius and Plotinus.

ποσὸν οὖσα σῶμα ἔσται, εἴπερ πᾶν σῶμα ποσόν;
καὶ μήν, ὅπερ καὶ ἄνω που ἐλέγετο, εἰ πᾶν σῶμα
μεριζόμενον καὶ ὄγκος πᾶς ἀφαιρεῖται ὅπερ ἦν,
20 κερματιζομένου δὲ τοῦ σώματος ἐφ᾽ ἑκάστῳ μέρει
ἡ αὐτὴ ὅλη ποιότης μένει, οἷον γλυκύτης ἡ τοῦ
μέλιτος οὐδὲν ἔλαττον γλυκύτης ἐστὶν ἡ ἐφ᾽
ἑκάστῳ, οὐκ ἂν εἴη σῶμα ἡ γλυκύτης. ὁμοίως καὶ
αἱ ἄλλαι. ἔπειτα, εἰ σώματα ἦσαν αἱ δυνάμεις,
ἀναγκαῖον ἦν τὰς μὲν ἰσχυρὰς τῶν δυνάμεων
25 μεγάλους ὄγκους, τὰς δὲ ὀλίγον δρᾶν δυναμένας
ὄγκους μικροὺς εἶναι. εἰ δὲ μεγάλων μὲν ὄγκων
μικραί, ὀλίγοι δὲ καὶ μικρότατοι τῶν ὄγκων
μεγίστας ἔχουσι τὰς δυνάμεις, ἄλλῳ τινὶ ἢ μεγέθει
τὸ ποιεῖν ἀναθετέον· ἀμεγέθει ἄρα. τὸ δὲ ὕλην
μὲν τὴν αὐτὴν εἶναι σῶμα, ὥς φασιν, οὖσαν,
30 διάφορα δὲ ποιεῖν ποιότητας προσλαβοῦσαν, πῶς
οὐ δῆλον ποιεῖ τὰ προσγενόμενα λόγους ἀύλους [1]
καὶ ἀσωμάτους εἶναι; μή, διότι πνεύματος ἢ
αἵματος ἀποστάντων ἀποθνήσκει τὰ ζῷα, λεγόντων.
οὐ γὰρ ἔστιν ἄνευ τούτων εἶναι, οὐδ᾽ ἄνευ πολλῶν
35 ἄλλων, ὧν οὐδὲν ἂν ἡ ψυχὴ εἴη. καὶ μὴν οὔτε
πνεῦμα διὰ πάντων οὔτε αἷμα, ψυχὴ δέ.

8[2]. Ἔτι εἰ σῶμα οὖσα ἡ ψυχὴ διῆλθε διὰ παντός,
κἂν κραθεῖσα εἴη, ὃν τρόπον τοῖς ἄλλοις σώμασιν ἡ
κρᾶσις. εἰ δὲ ἡ τῶν σωμάτων κρᾶσις οὐδὲν
ἐνεργείᾳ ἐᾷ εἶναι τῶν κραθέντων, οὐδ᾽ ἂν ἡ ψυχὴ
5 ἔτι ἐνεργείᾳ ἐνείη τοῖς σώμασιν, ἀλλὰ δυνάμει
μόνον ἀπολέσασα τὸ εἶναι ψυχή· ὥσπερ, εἰ γλυκὺ
καὶ πικρὸν κραθείη, τὸ γλυκὺ οὐκ ἔστιν· οὐκ ἄρα

---

[1] Arnim (*SVF* II. 375), Theologia III. 14: αὐτοὺς Eus.,
Stephanus*.

certain quantity could it be a body, if every body is of a certain quantity? And further, as I think was said above, if every body and every mass ceases to be what it was before when divided, but when a body is broken up the same quality remains complete in every piece, as for instance the sweetness of the honey is no less sweetness in every fragment, sweetness could not be a body, and the same is true of the other qualities. Then again, if the powers were bodies, it would be necessary for the strong powers to be large masses, and the ones which could do little, small masses. But if the powers of large masses are small, but even the smallest masses have great powers, action must be attributed to something other than size: to something sizeless, therefore. And the fact that matter remains the same, being, as they say, a body, but does different things when it acquires qualities, surely makes clear that what it acquires are immaterial and bodiless rational principles. And they must not say that [soul is a body because] living things die when breath or blood leaves them. For it is not possible for living things to exist without them, or without a great many other things, none of which is soul. And further, neither does breath pervade the whole body nor does blood, but soul does.

8². Again, if soul was a body and permeated the whole body, it would be mixed with it in the way in which other bodies are intermixed. But if the mixture of bodies allows none of the bodies which are mixed to exist in actuality, the soul would not be actually present in bodies either, but only potentially, and would lose its existence as soul, just as, if sweet and bitter are mixed, the sweet does not

ἔχομεν ψυχήν. τὸ δὲ δὴ σῶμα ὂν σώματι κεκρᾶσθαι
ὅλον δι' ὅλων, ὡς ὅπου ἂν ᾖ θάτερον, καὶ θάτερον
εἶναι, ἴσον ὄγκων ἀμφοτέρων καὶ τόπον [1] κατεχόν-
10 των, καὶ μηδεμίαν αὔξην γεγονέναι ἐπεμβληθέν-
τος τοῦ ἑτέρου, οὐδὲν ἀπολείψει ὃ μὴ τέμῃ. οὐ
γὰρ κατὰ μεγάλα μέρη παραλλὰξ ἡ κρᾶσις—οὕτω
γάρ φησι παράθεσιν ἔσεσθαι—διεληλυθὸς δὲ διὰ
παντὸς τὸ ἐπεμβληθέν, ἔτι εἰ [2] σμικρότερον—
ὅπερ ἀδύνατον, τὸ ἔλαττον ἴσον γενέσθαι τῷ
15 μείζονι—ἀλλ' οὖν διεληλυθὸς πᾶν τέμοι [3] κατὰ πᾶν·
ἀνάγκη τοίνυν, εἰ καθ' ὁτιοῦν σημεῖον καὶ μὴ
μεταξὺ σῶμα ἔσται ὃ μὴ τέτμηται, εἰς σημεῖα τὴν
διαίρεσιν τοῦ σώματος γεγονέναι, ὅπερ ἀδύνατον.
εἰ δέ, ἀπείρου τῆς τομῆς οὔσης—ὃ γὰρ ἂν λάβῃς
20 σῶμα, διαιρετόν ἐστιν—οὐ δυνάμει μόνον, ἐνεργείᾳ
δὲ τὰ ἄπειρα ἔσται. οὐ τοίνυν ὅλον δι' ὅλου
χωρεῖν δυνατὸν τὸ σῶμα· ἡ δὲ ψυχὴ δι' ὅλων·
ἀσώματος ἄρα.

8[3]. Τὸ δὲ καὶ φύσιν μὲν προτέραν τὸ αὐτὸ
πνεῦμα λέγειν, ἐν δὲ ψυχρῷ γενομένην καὶ
στομωθεῖσαν ψυχὴν γίνεσθαι λεπτοτέραν ἐν ψυχρῷ
γιγνομένην—ὃ δὴ καὶ αὐτὸ ἄτοπον· πολλὰ γὰρ
5 ζῷα ἐν θερμῷ γίγνεται καὶ ψυχὴν ἔχει οὐ ψυχθεῖσαν
—ἀλλ' οὖν φασί γε προτέραν φύσιν ψυχῆς εἶναι

---

[1] Schwyzer (*Gnomon* 15, 1939, 10): τὸ πᾶν Eus.
[2] ἔτι εἰ (*etiam si*) Schwyzer (*Rh. Mus.* 88, 1939, 377 §16):
ἐπεὶ *TJMV*: ἐπὶ *ONDPQ*, *Stephanus**, Creuzer*: εἰ καὶ Harder:
del. Arnim (*SVF* II. 799).
[3] Henry (Etats 13), Mras: τέμῃ *ONPTJM*: τέμει *DQV*:
τεμεῖ Harder: τέμνει *Stephanus-Gifford*, Creuzer*.

ON THE IMMORTALITY OF THE SOUL

exist; we shall not then have a soul. But if it is a body and is mixed with the body " whole through whole " so that wherever the one is, the other is also, with both bodily masses also occupying an equal amount of space, and if no increase takes place when the other one is inserted, this will leave nothing undivided. For mixture is not by large parts placed side by side—for in this way [the Stoic] says it will be juxtaposition [not mixture]—but what is inserted penetrates through every part, even if it is smaller—this is impossible, for the less to be equal to the greater—but, anyhow, in penetrating it all it divides it everywhere; it is necessary therefore, if it divides it at every geometrical point, and there is no body in between which is not divided, that the division of the body must be into geometrical points, which is impossible. But if this is so, since the division is infinite—for whatever body you take is divisible—the infinity of parts will exist not only potentially but actually. It is impossible therefore for one body to penetrate another " whole through whole "[1]: but soul penetrates through whole bodies, therefore it is immaterial.

8[3]. But as for saying that the same breath was growth-principle before, but when it got into the cold and was tempered became soul, since it becomes rarefied in the cold—this is absurd to start with; for many animals come into existence in heat and have a soul which has not been cooled—but anyhow

---

[1] For the curious Stoic doctrine of " complete transfusion " see e.g. *SVF* I. 102, II. 467 and 471. For a fuller refutation of it by Plotinus, based on Peripatetic arguments from Alexander of Aphrodisias critically used, see *Enneads* II. 7.

κατὰ συντυχίας τὰς ἔξω γιγνομένης.[1] συμβαίνει
οὖν αὐτοῖς τὸ χεῖρον πρῶτον ποιεῖν καὶ πρὸ τούτου
ἄλλο ἔλαττον, ἣν λέγουσιν ἕξιν, ὁ δὲ νοῦς ὕστατος
ἀπὸ τῆς ψυχῆς δηλονότι γενόμενος. ἢ εἰ πρὸ
10 πάντων νοῦς, ἐφεξῆς ἔδει ψυχὴν ποιεῖν, εἶτα φύσιν,
καὶ αἰεὶ τὸ ὕστερον χεῖρον, ᾗπερ πέφυκεν. εἰ οὖν
καὶ ὁ θεὸς αὐτοῖς κατὰ τὸν νοῦν ὕστερος καὶ
γεννητὸς καὶ ἐπακτὸν τὸ νοεῖν ἔχων, ἐνδέχοιτο ἂν
μηδὲ ψυχὴν μηδὲ νοῦν μηδὲ θεὸν εἶναι. εἰ τὸ
δυνάμει, μὴ ὄντος πρότερον τοῦ ἐνεργείᾳ καὶ νοῦ,
15 γένοιτο, οὐδὲ ἥξει εἰς ἐνέργειαν. τί γὰρ ἔσται τὸ
ἄγον μὴ ὄντος ἑτέρου παρ’ αὐτὸ προτέρου; εἰ δ’
αὐτὸ ἄξει εἰς ἐνέργειαν, ὅπερ ἄτοπον, ἀλλὰ
βλέπον γε πρός τι ἄξει, ὃ οὐ δυνάμει, ἐνεργείᾳ δὲ
ἔσται. καίτοι τὸ ἀεὶ μένειν τὸ αὐτὸ εἴπερ τὸ
δυνάμει ἕξει, καθ’ ἑαυτὸ εἰς ἐνέργειαν ἄξει, καὶ
20 τοῦτο κρεῖττον ἔσται τοῦ δυναμένου οἷον ὀρεκτὸν
ὂν ἐκείνου. πρότερον ἄρα τὸ κρεῖττον καὶ ἑτέραν
φύσιν ἔχον σώματος καὶ ἐνεργείᾳ ὂν ἀεί· πρότερον
ἄρα καὶ νοῦς καὶ ψυχὴ φύσεως. οὐκ ἄρα οὕτως
ψυχὴ ὡς πνεῦμα οὐδ’ ὡς σῶμα. ἀλλ’ ὅτι μὲν μὴ
σῶμα λέγοιτ’ ἄν, καὶ εἴρηται καὶ ἄλλοις ἕτερα,
25 ἱκανὰ δὲ καὶ ταῦτα.

8[4]. Ἐπεὶ δὲ ἄλλης φύσεως, δεῖ ζητεῖν, τίς αὕτη.

---

[1] Kirchhoff*, cf. Theol. III. 37: γι(γ)νομένην Eus.

they assert that growth-principle is prior to soul which comes into existence because of external happenings. So they find themselves making the worse first, and before this another of less good quality, which they call " character ", and intellect last, obviously originating from the soul. Now if Intellect is before all things, then they ought to have made soul come next to it, then growth-principle, and have made what comes after always worse, as is the natural state of affairs. If then God (conceived as Intellect) is for them posterior and generated and has his intelligence as something brought in from outside, it would be possible for neither soul nor intellect nor God to exist. If the potential, without the prior existence of what is actual and of Intellect, were to come into existence it could not attain to actuality. For what will be the principle which will bring it there if there is not one different from and prior to itself? But if it is going to bring itself to actuality, which is absurd, all the same it will bring itself by looking to something, which will exist not potentially, but actually; though, if the potential is to have the property of always remaining the same, it will bring itself to an actuality corresponding to itself, and this will be better than that which is potential, as it is the potential's desired objective. The better, which has a nature different from body, and always exists in actuality, is therefore prior: so intellect and soul are prior to growth-principle. Soul, then, is not like breath or like body. But that soul should not be called a body has been proved by others with different arguments, but these too are sufficient.

8⁴. But since it is of another nature, we must

ἆρ᾽ οὖν ἕτερον μὲν σώματος, σώματος δέ τι, οἷον
ἁρμονία; τοῦτο γὰρ ἁρμονίαν τῶν ἀμφὶ Πυθαγόραν
λεγόντων ἕτερον τρόπον ᾠήθησαν αὐτὸ τοιοῦτόν τι
5 εἶναι οἷον καὶ ἡ περὶ χορδὰς ἁρμονία. ὡς γὰρ
ἐνταῦθα ἐντεταμένων τῶν χορδῶν ἐπιγίνεταί τι
οἷον πάθημα ἐπ᾽ αὐταῖς, ὃ λέγεται ἁρμονία, τὸν
αὐτὸν τρόπον καὶ τοῦ ἡμετέρου σώματος ἐν κράσει
ἀνομοίων γινομένου τὴν ποιὰν κρᾶσιν ζωήν τε
ἐργάζεσθαι καὶ ψυχὴν οὖσαν τὸ ἐπὶ τῇ κράσει
10 πάθημα. ὅτι δὲ ἀδύνατον, πολλὰ ἤδη πρὸς ταύτην
τὴν δόξαν εἴρηται· καὶ γάρ, ὅτι τὸ μὲν πρότερον ἡ
ψυχή, ἡ δ᾽ ἁρμονία ὕστερον, καὶ ὡς τὸ μὲν ἄρχει
τε καὶ ἐπιστατεῖ τῷ σώματι καὶ μάχεται πολλαχῇ,
ἁρμονία δὲ οὐκ ἂν οὖσα ταῦτα ποιοῖ, καὶ ὡς τὸ
μὲν οὐσία, ἡ δ᾽ ἁρμονία οὐκ οὐσία, καὶ ὅτι ἡ
15 κρᾶσις τῶν σωμάτων, ἐξ ὧν συνέσταμεν, ἐν λόγῳ
οὖσα ὑγεία ἂν εἴη, καὶ ὅτι καθ᾽ ἕκαστον μέρος
ἄλλως κραθὲν εἴη ἂν ψυχὴ ἑτέρα, ὥστε πολλὰς
εἶναι, καὶ τὸ δὴ μέγιστον, ὡς ἀνάγκη πρὸ τῆς
ψυχῆς ταύτης ἄλλην ψυχὴν εἶναι τὴν ποιοῦσαν τὴν
ἁρμονίαν ταύτην, οἷον ἐπὶ τῶν ὀργάνων τὸν
20 μουσικὸν τὸν ἐντιθέντα ταῖς χορδαῖς τὴν ἁρμονίαν
λόγον ἔχοντα παρ᾽ αὑτῷ, καθ᾽ ὃν ἁρμόσει. οὔτε
γὰρ ἐκεῖ αἱ χορδαὶ παρ᾽ αὑτῶν οὔτ᾽ ἐνταῦθα τὰ
σώματα ἑαυτὰ εἰς ἁρμονίαν ἄγειν δυνήσεται.
ὅλως δὲ καὶ οὗτοι ἐξ ἀψύχου ἔμψυχα ποιοῦσι καὶ
25 [τὰ] [1] ἐξ ἀτάκτων κατὰ συντυχίαν τεταγμένα, καὶ
τὴν τάξιν οὐκ ἐκ τῆς ψυχῆς, ἀλλ᾽ αὐτὴν ἐκ τῆς

[1] del. Stephanus, Creuzer*.

enquire what this nature is. Is it, then, something different from body, but belonging to body, like its tuning? For, though the Pythagoreans meant this term, tuning, in another sense, people thought it was something like the tuning of strings. For just as here, when the strings are stretched, they come to be affected in a kind of way, and this being affected is called being in tune, in the same way, since our body also consists of a mixture of dissimilar parts, the mixture of a particular kind produces life and soul, which is the way of being affected which comes upon the mixture. But many arguments have already been brought against this view to show that it is impossible: they are, that the soul is the prior and the tuning subsequent to it; and that this prior reality rules and directs the body and fights it in many ways, but the soul would not do this if it was a being in tune; and that the prior reality is a substance, but being in tune is not a substance, and that the mixture of bodies of which we consist, when it was in proportion, would be health [not soul]; and that in each part, which is mixed in a different way, there would be a different soul, so that there would be many; and what is certainly the greatest difficulty of all, that it is necessary that there should be another soul before this soul producing this being in tune, as with musical instruments there is the player who brings the strings into tune and has a proportion in himself according to which he will tune them. For neither can the strings nor the bodies here bring themselves into tune by themselves. And in general these people also make ensouled things out of soulless, and things casually arranged out of things in disorder, and do not make order arise from

αὐτομάτου τάξεως τὴν ὑπόστασιν εἰληφέναι.
τοῦτο δὲ οὔτε ἐν τοῖς κατὰ μέρος οὔτε ἐν τοῖς
ἄλλοις δυνατὸν γενέσθαι. οὐκ ἄρα ἡ ψυχὴ ἁρμονία.

8⁵. Τὸ δὲ τῆς ἐντελεχείας ὧδ' ἄν τις ἐπισκέψαιτο,
πῶς περὶ ψυχῆς λέγεται· τὴν ψυχήν φασιν ἐν τῷ
συνθέτῳ εἴδους τάξιν ὡς πρὸς ὕλην τὸ σῶμα
ἔμψυχον ⟨ὂν⟩ ¹ ἔχειν, σώματος δὲ οὐ παντὸς εἶδος
5 οὐδὲ ἧ σῶμα, ἀλλὰ φυσικοῦ ² ὀργανικοῦ
δυνάμει ζωὴν ἔχοντος. εἰ μὲν οὖν ἧ παρα-
βέβληται ὡμοίωται, ὡς μορφὴ ἀνδριάντος πρὸς
χαλκόν, καὶ διαιρουμένου τοῦ σώματος συμμε-
ρίζεσθαι τὴν ψυχήν, καὶ ἀποκοπτομένου τινὸς
μέρους μετὰ τοῦ ἀποκοπέντος ψυχῆς μόριον εἶναι,
10 τήν τε ἐν τοῖς ὕπνοις ἀναχώρησιν μὴ γίνεσθαι,
εἴπερ δεῖ προσφυᾶ τὴν ἐντελέχειαν οὗ ἐστιν εἶναι,
τὸ δ' ἀληθές, μηδὲ ὕπνον γίνεσθαι· καὶ μὴν
ἐντελεχείας οὔσης οὐδὲ ἐναντίωσιν λόγου πρὸς
ἐπιθυμίας, ἓν δὲ καὶ ταὐτὸν δι' ὅλου πεπονθέναι τὸ
πᾶν οὐ διαφωνοῦν ἑαυτῷ. αἰσθήσεις δὲ μόνον
15 δυνατὸν ἴσως γίνεσθαι, τὰς δὲ νοήσεις ἀδύνατον.
διὸ καὶ αὐτοὶ ἄλλην ψυχὴν ἢ νοῦν εἰσάγουσιν, ὃν
ἀθάνατον τίθενται. τὴν οὖν λογιζομένην ψυχὴν
ἄλλως ἐντελέχειαν ἢ τοῦτον τὸν τρόπον ἀνάγκη
εἶναι, εἰ δεῖ τῷ ὀνόματι τούτῳ χρῆσθαι. οὐδ' ἡ
αἰσθητική, εἴπερ καὶ αὕτη τῶν αἰσθητῶν ἀπόντων

---

¹ Dodds.
² Stephanus, Creuzer*: ψυχικοῦ Eus.

¹ This is a slightly paraphrased version of Aristotle De
Anima B 1, 412a27–b1. The MSS of Eusebius here read ψυχικοῦ for Aristotle's φυσικοῦ and Schwyzer suggests that this
could just possibly be a slip of Plotinus himself (who, if we

the soul, but say that the soul has received its existence from a chance arrangement. But this cannot happen either in parts or wholes. The soul, then, is not being in tune.

8[5]. One might investigate the question of how the term " entelechy " could be applied to the soul in the following way: [the Peripatetics] assert that the soul in the composite being holds the rank of form in relation to the ensouled body as matter, but is not the form of every kind of body, and not of body simply as body, but of a " natural organic body which has life potentially."[1] If then it is assimilated to the body by being applied to it, as the form of the statue is to the bronze, then when the body was divided the soul would be separated into parts along with it, and when a part was cut off there would be a bit of soul with the cut-off piece of body, and the withdrawal in sleep would not take place, if the entelechy must be firmly fixed where it is—but in fact there could not even be sleep; further, if the soul was an entelechy there could be no opposition of reason to desire, but the whole would be affected throughout in one and the same way without disagreeing with itself. But perhaps it would only be possible for sense-perceptions to occur, but thoughts would be impossible. For this reason [the Peripatetics] themselves introduce another soul or intelligence, which they assume to be immortal. The reasoning soul, therefore, must be an entelechy in some sense other than this, if one really ought to use the name. And the perceiving soul, if this also possesses the impressions of absent sense-objects,

keep the MSS text, rather illogically qualified the body, which is matter to the soul as form, as ἔμψυχον in line 3).

20 τοὺς τύπους ἔχει, αὐτοὺς οὐ μετὰ τοῦ σώματος ἄρα
ἕξει· εἰ δὲ μὴ οὕτως, ἐνέσονται ὡς μορφαὶ καὶ
εἰκόνες· ἀλλ' ἀδύνατον ἄλλους δέχεσθαι, εἰ οὕτως
ἐνεῖεν. οὐκ ἄρα ὡς ἀχώριστος ἐντελέχεια. καὶ
μὴν οὐδὲ τὸ ἐπιθυμοῦν, μὴ σιτίων μηδὲ ποτῶν
25 ἀλλ' ἄλλων παρὰ τὰ τοῦ σώματος, οὐδ' αὐτὸ
ἀχώριστος ἐντελέχεια. λοιπὸν δὲ τὸ φυτικὸν ἂν
εἴη, ὃ ἀμφισβήτησιν ἂν δόξειεν ἔχειν, μὴ τοῦτον
τὸν τρόπον ἐντελέχεια ἀχώριστος ᾖ. ἀλλ' οὐδὲ
τοῦτο φαίνεται οὕτως ἔχον. εἰ γὰρ ἡ ἀρχὴ παντὸς
φυτοῦ περὶ τὴν ῥίζαν καὶ αὐαινομένου τοῦ ἄλλου
30 σώματος περὶ τὴν ῥίζαν καὶ τὰ κάτω ἐν πολλοῖς
τῶν φυτῶν ἡ ψυχή, δῆλον ὅτι[1] ἀπολιποῦσα τὰ
ἄλλα μέρη εἰς ἕν τι συνεστάλη· οὐκ ἄρα ἦν ἐν τῷ
ὅλῳ ὡς ἀχώριστος ἐντελέχεια. καὶ γὰρ αὖ ἐστι
πρὶν αὐξηθῆναι τὸ φυτὸν ἐν τῷ ὀλίγῳ ὄγκῳ. εἰ
οὖν καὶ εἰς ὀλίγον ἔρχεται ἐκ μείζονος φυτοῦ καὶ
35 ἐξ ὀλίγου ἐπὶ πᾶν, τί κωλύει καὶ ὅλως χωρίζεσθαι·
πῶς δ' ἂν καὶ ἀμερὴς οὖσα μεριστοῦ τοῦ σώματος
ἐντελέχεια γένοιτο; ἥ τε αὐτὴ ψυχὴ ἐξ ἄλλου
ζῴου ἄλλον γίνεται· πῶς οὖν ἡ τοῦ προτέρου τοῦ
ἐφεξῆς ἂν γένοιτο, εἰ ἦν ἐντελέχεια ἑνός; φαίνεται
δὲ τοῦτο ἐκ τῶν μεταβαλλόντων ζῴων εἰς ἄλλα
40 ζῷα. οὐκ ἄρα τῷ εἶδος εἶναί τινος τὸ εἶναι ἔχει,
ἀλλ' ἔστιν οὐσία οὐ παρὰ τὸ ἐν σώματι ἱδρῦσθαι τὸ
εἶναι λαμβάνουσα, ἀλλ' οὖσα πρὶν καὶ τοῦδε
γενέσθαι [οἷον ζῴου οὐ τὸ σῶμα τὴν ψυχὴν

----

[1] Gifford, Mras, Harder: φυτῶν, ἡ ψυχὴ δηλονότι H–S[1].

376

will therefore hold them without the assistance of the body; but if this is not so, they will be present in it as shapes and images; but it would be impossible for it to receive other impressions if they were in it in this way. It is therefore not [in the body] as an inseparable entelechy. Furthermore, not even that which desires, not food and drink but other things besides those of body, can be an inseparable entelechy. There would remain the growth-principle, and there might seem to be some possibility of questioning whether this might not be an inseparable entelechy in this sense. But even this is clearly not so. For if the principle of every plant is in the region of the root, and when the rest of the body of the plant withers up, in many plants the soul [remains] in the region of the root and the lower parts, it is obvious that it has left the other parts and gathered itself together into one: it was not, then, in the whole as an inseparable entelechy. And again, before the plant grows, the soul is in the small bulk [of the root]. If then the soul passes into a small root from a larger plant and from a small root to the whole plant, what prevents it from being completely separated? But also, how when it is without parts could it become the entelechy of a body with parts? And the same soul belongs to one living thing after another: how then could the soul of the first become the soul of that which comes next, if it was the entelechy of one? (This is obvious from the change of living things into other living things.) The soul, therefore, does not have its existence by being the form of something, but it is a substance which does not derive its existence from its foundation in body, but exists before belonging to this particular body. What then is its

γεννήσει].[1] τίς οὖν οὐσία αὐτῆς; εἰ δὲ μήτε
σῶμα, μήτε πάθος σώματος, πρᾶξις δὲ καὶ
45 ποίησις, καὶ πολλὰ καὶ ἐν αὐτῇ καὶ ἐξ αὐτῆς,
οὐσία παρὰ τὰ σώματα οὖσα ποία τίς ἐστιν; ἢ
δῆλον ὅτι ἣν φαμεν ὄντως οὐσίαν εἶναι. τὸ μὲν
γὰρ γένεσις, ἀλλ' οὐκ οὐσία, πᾶν τὸ σωματικὸν
εἶναι λέγοιτ' ἄν, γινόμενον καὶ ἀπολλύμενον,
ὄντως δὲ οὐδέποτε ὄν, μεταλήψει δὲ τοῦ ὄντος
50 σωζόμενον, καθόσον ἂν αὐτοῦ μεταλαμβάνῃ.

9. Ἡ δὲ ἑτέρα φύσις, ἡ παρ' αὐτῆς ἔχουσα τὸ
εἶναι, πᾶν τὸ ὄντως ὄν, ὃ οὔτε γίνεται οὔτε
ἀπόλλυται· ἢ τὰ ἄλλα πάντα οἰχήσεται, καὶ οὐκ
ἂν ὕστερον γένοιτο τούτου ἀπολωλότος, ὃ παρέχει
5 αὐτοῖς σωτηρίαν, τοῖς τε ἄλλοις καὶ τῷδε τῷ
παντὶ διὰ ψυχῆς σωζομένῳ καὶ κεκοσμημένῳ.
ἀρχὴ γὰρ κινήσεως ἥδε χορηγοῦσα τοῖς ἄλλοις
κίνησιν, αὐτὴ δὲ ἐξ ἑαυτῆς κινουμένη, καὶ ζωὴν
τῷ ἐμψύχῳ σώματι διδοῦσα, αὐτὴ δὲ παρ'
ἑαυτῆς ἔχουσα, ἣν οὔποτε ἀπόλλυσιν, ἅτε παρ'
10 ἑαυτῆς ἔχουσα. οὐ γὰρ δὴ πάντα ἐπακτῷ ζωῇ
χρῆται· ἢ εἰς ἄπειρον εἶσιν· ἀλλὰ δεῖ τινα φύσιν
πρώτως ζῶσαν εἶναι, ἣν ἀνώλεθρον καὶ ἀθάνατον
εἶναι δεῖ ἐξ ἀνάγκης, ἅτε ἀρχὴν ζωῆς καὶ τοῖς
ἄλλοις οὖσαν. ἔνθα δὴ καὶ τὸ θεῖον ἅπαν καὶ τὸ
μακάριον ἱδρῦσθαι δεῖ ζῶν παρ' αὐτοῦ καὶ ὂν παρ'
15 αὐτοῦ, πρώτως ὂν καὶ ζῶν πρώτως, μεταβολῆς
κατ' οὐσίαν ἄμοιρον, οὔτε γινόμενον οὔτε ἀπολλύμενον. πόθεν γὰρ ἂν καὶ γένοιτο, ἢ εἰς τί
ἀπόλοιτο; καὶ εἰ δεῖ ἐπαληθεύειν τὴν τοῦ ὄντος

---

[1] del. Page, ut glossam.

substance? If it is not a body or an affection of body, but action and making and many things are in it and come from it, then since it is a substance distinct from bodies, of what kind is it? It is obviously what we call real substance. For everything bodily should be called becoming, not substance; it " comes to be and passes away, but never really is ", but is preserved by participation in being, in so far as it does participate in it.

9. But the other nature, which has being of itself, is all that really exists, which does not come into being or perish: or everything else will pass away, and could not come into being afterwards if this real existence had perished which preserves all other things and especially this All, which is preserved and given its universal order and beauty by soul. For soul is the " origin of motion "[1] and is responsible for the motion of other things, and it is moved by itself, and gives life to the ensouled body, but has it of itself, and never loses it because it has it of itself. For certainly all things cannot have a borrowed life: or it will go on to infinity; but there must be some nature which is primarily alive, which must be indestructible and immortal of necessity since it is also the origin of life to the others. Here, assuredly, all that is divine and blessed must be situated, living of itself and existing of itself, existing primarily and living primarily, without any part in essential change, neither coming to be nor perishing. For where could it come into being from, or into what could it change when it perished? And if we are to apply the name " being " to it truly, then being itself ought not to

---

[1] Plato *Phaedrus* 245C9.

προσηγορίαν, αὐτὸ οὐ ποτὲ μὲν εἶναι, ποτὲ δὲ οὐκ
εἶναι δεήσει. ὡς καὶ τὸ λευκόν, αὐτὸ τὸ χρῶμα,
20 οὐ ποτὲ μὲν λευκόν, ποτὲ δὲ οὐ λευκόν· εἰ δὲ καὶ
ὂν ἦν τὸ λευκὸν μετὰ τοῦ λευκὸν εἶναι, ἦν ἂν
ἀεί· ἀλλὰ μόνον ἔχει τὸ λευκόν. ᾧ δ' ἂν τὸ ὂν ᾖ
παρὸν παρ' αὑτοῦ καὶ πρώτως, ὂν ἀεὶ ἔσται.
τοῦτο τοίνυν τὸ ὂν πρώτως καὶ ἀεὶ ὂν οὐχὶ νεκρόν,
25 ὥσπερ λίθον ἢ ξύλον, ἀλλὰ ζῶν εἶναι δεῖ, καὶ ζωῇ
καθαρᾷ κεχρῆσθαι, ὅσον ἂν αὐτοῦ μένῃ μόνον· ὃ
δ' ἂν συμμιχθῇ χείρονι, ἐμπόδιον μὲν ἔχειν πρὸς τὰ
ἄριστα—οὔτι γε μὴν τὴν αὑτοῦ φύσιν ἀπολωλέναι—
ἀναλαβεῖν δὲ τὴν ἀρχαίαν κατάστασιν ἐπὶ τὰ
αὑτοῦ ἀναδραμόν.

10. Ὅτι δὲ τῇ θειοτέρᾳ φύσει συγγενὴς ἡ ψυχὴ
καὶ τῇ ἀιδίῳ, δῆλον μὲν ποιεῖ καὶ τὸ μὴ σῶμα
αὐτὴν δεδεῖχθαι. καὶ μὴν οὐδὲ σχῆμα ἔχει οὐδὲ
χρῶμα ἀναφής τε. οὐ μὴν ἀλλὰ καὶ ἐκ τῶνδε
5 ἔστι δεικνύναι. ὁμολογουμένου δὴ ἡμῖν παντὸς τοῦ
θείου καὶ τοῦ ὄντως ὄντος ζωῇ ἀγαθῇ κεχρῆσθαι καὶ
ἔμφρονι, σκοπεῖν δεῖ τὸ μετὰ τοῦτο ἀπὸ τῆς
ἡμετέρας ψυχῆς, οἷόν ἐστι τὴν φύσιν. λάβωμεν δὲ
ψυχὴν μὴ τὴν ἐν σώματι ἐπιθυμίας ἀλόγους καὶ
θυμοὺς προσλαβοῦσαν καὶ πάθη ἄλλα ἀναδεξαμένην,
10 ἀλλὰ τὴν ταῦτα ἀποτριψαμένην καὶ καθόσον οἷόν
τε μὴ κοινωνοῦσαν τῷ σώματι. ἥτις καὶ δῆλον
ποιεῖ, ὡς προσθῆκαι τὰ κακὰ τῇ ψυχῇ καὶ ἄλλοθεν,
καθηραμένῃ δὲ αὐτῇ ἐνυπάρχει τὰ ἄριστα, φρόνησις
καὶ ἡ ἄλλη ἀρετή, οἰκεῖα ὄντα. εἰ οὖν τοιοῦτον ἡ
15 ψυχή, ὅταν ἐφ' ἑαυτὴν ἀνέλθῃ, πῶς οὐ τῆς φύσεως

exist at one time, but not at another; as for instance
white, the colour itself, is not white at one time and
not-white another; but if white was being as well
as being white, it would exist for ever; but [as it is]
it only has the white [not being]. But that with
which being is from itself, and primarily, will always
be existent. This, then, which is primarily and
always existent cannot be dead, like a stone or wood,
but must be alive, and have a pure life, as much of it
as remains alone; but whatever is mixed with what
is worse has an impeded relationship to the best—
yet it certainly cannot lose its own nature—but recovers its " ancient state "[1] when it runs up to its own.

10. Our demonstration that the soul is not a body
makes it clear that it is akin to the diviner and to
the eternal nature. It certainly does not have a
shape or a colour, and it is intangible. But we can
also demonstrate its kinship in the following way.
We agree of course that all the divine and really
existent has a good, intelligent life; now we must
investigate what comes next, starting from our own
soul and finding out what sort of nature it has. Let
us take soul, not the soul in body which has acquired
irrational desires and passions and admitted other
affection, but the soul which has wiped these away
and which, as far as possible, has no communion
with the body. This soul does make it clear that
its evils are external accretions to the soul and come
from elsewhere, but that when it is purified the best
things are present in it, wisdom and all the rest of
virtue, and are its own. If, then, the soul is something of this kind when it goes up again to itself,

---

[1] Plato *Republic* 547B6–7.

ἐκείνης, οἵαν φαμὲν τὴν τοῦ θείου καὶ ἀιδίου
παντὸς εἶναι; φρόνησις γὰρ καὶ ἀρετὴ ἀληθὴς
θεῖα ὄντα οὐκ ἂν ἐγγένοιτο φαύλῳ τινὶ καὶ θνητῷ
πράγματι, ἀλλ᾽ ἀνάγκη θεῖον τὸ τοιοῦτον εἶναι,
ἅτε θείων μετὸν αὐτῷ διὰ συγγένειαν καὶ τὸ
20 ὁμοούσιον. διὸ καὶ ὅστις τοιοῦτος ἡμῶν ὀλίγον
ἂν παραλλάττοι τῶν ἄνω τῇ ψυχῇ αὐτῇ μόνον
τοῦτο, ὅσον ἐστὶν ἐν σώματι, ἐλαττούμενος. διὸ
καί, εἰ πᾶς ἄνθρωπος τοιοῦτος ἦν, ἢ πλῆθός τι
τοιαύταις ψυχαῖς κεχρημένον, οὐδεὶς οὕτως ἦν
ἄπιστος, ὡς μὴ πιστεύειν τὸ τῆς ψυχῆς αὐτοῖς
25 πάντη ἀθάνατον εἶναι. νῦν δὲ πολλαχοῦ λελωβη-
μένην τὴν ἐν τοῖς πλείστοις ψυχὴν ὁρῶντες οὔτε ὡς
περὶ θείου οὔτε ὡς περὶ ἀθανάτου χρήματος
διανοοῦνται. δεῖ δὲ τὴν φύσιν ἑκάστου σκοπεῖσθαι
εἰς τὸ καθαρὸν αὐτοῦ ἀφορῶντα, ἐπείπερ τὸ
προστεθὲν ἐμπόδιον ἀεὶ πρὸς γνῶσιν τοῦ ᾧ
30 προσετέθη γίγνεται. σκόπει δὴ ἀφελών, μᾶλλον
δὲ ὁ ἀφελὼν ἑαυτὸν ἰδέτω καὶ πιστεύσει ἀθάνατος
εἶναι, ὅταν ἑαυτὸν θεάσηται ἐν τῷ νοητῷ καὶ ἐν τῷ
καθαρῷ γεγενημένον. ὄψεται γὰρ νοῦν ὁρῶντα οὐκ
αἰσθητόν τι οὐδὲ τῶν θνητῶν τούτων, ἀλλὰ ἀιδίῳ
35 τὸ ἀίδιον κατανοοῦντα, πάντα τὰ ἐν τῷ νοητῷ, κόσμον καὶ αὐτὸν νοητὸν καὶ φωτεινὸν γεγενημένον,
ἀληθείᾳ καταλαμπόμενον τῇ παρὰ τοῦ ἀγαθοῦ, ὃ
πᾶσιν ἐπιλάμπει τοῖς νοητοῖς ἀλήθειαν· ὡς
πολλάκις αὐτῷ δόξαι τοῦτο δὴ καλῶς εἰρῆσθαι·
χαίρετ᾽, ἐγὼ δ᾽ ὑμῖν θεὸς ἄμβροτος πρὸς τὸ
40 θεῖον ἀναβὰς καὶ[1] τὴν πρὸς αὐτὸ ὁμοιότητα

---

[1] Enn., defendit Seidel: καὶ ⟨εἰς⟩ Kirchhoff*: εἰς H–S[1].

it must surely belong to that nature which we assert is that of all the divine and eternal. For wisdom and true virtue are divine things, and could not occur in some trivial mortal being, but something of such a kind [as to possess them] must be divine, since it has a share in divine things through its kinship and consubstantiality. For this reason any one of us who is like this would deviate very little from the beings above as far as his soul itself was concerned and would only be inferior by that part which is in body. For this reason, if every man was like this, or there were a great number who had souls like this, no one would be so unbelieving as not to believe that what is soul in men is altogether immortal. But, as it is, they see the soul in the great majority of people damaged in many ways, and do not think of it as if it was divine or immortal. But when one considers the nature of any particular thing one must concentrate on its pure form, since what is added is always a hindrance to the knowledge of that to which it has been added. Consider it by stripping, or rather let the man who has stripped look at himself and believe himself to be immortal, when he looks at himself as he has come to be in the intelligible and the pure. For he will see an intellect which sees nothing perceived by the senses, none of these mortal things, but apprehends the eternal by its eternity, and all the things in the intelligible world, having become itself an intelligible universe full of light, illuminated by the truth from the Good, which radiates truth over all the intelligibles; so he will often think that this was very well said: " Greetings, I am for you an immortal god "[1] having ascended

---

[1] Empedocles fr. B 112 Diels-Kranz 4.

ἀτενίσας. εἰ δ' ἡ κάθαρσις ποιεῖ ἐν γνώσει τῶν
ἀρίστων εἶναι, καὶ αἱ ἐπιστῆμαι ἔνδον οὖσαι
ἀναφαίνονται, αἳ δὴ καὶ ὄντως ἐπιστῆμαί εἰσιν.
οὐ γὰρ δὴ ἔξω που δραμοῦσα ἡ ψυχὴ σωφροσύνην
καθορᾷ καὶ δικαιοσύνην, ἀλλ' αὐτὴ παρ' αὑτῇ
45 ἐν τῇ κατανοήσει ἑαυτῆς καὶ τοῦ ὃ πρότερον ἦν
ὥσπερ ἀγάλματα ἐν αὐτῇ ἱδρυμένα ὁρῶσα οἷα
ὑπὸ χρόνου ἰοῦ πεπληρωμένα καθαρὰ ποιησαμένη·
οἷον εἰ χρυσὸς ἔμψυχος εἴη, εἶτα ἀποκρουσάμενος
ὅσον γεηρὸν ἐν αὐτῷ, ἐν ἀγνοίᾳ πρότερον ἑαυτοῦ
ὤν, ὅτι μὴ χρυσὸν ἑώρα, τότε δὴ αὐτὸν ἤδη τοῦ
50 χρήματος θαυμάσειεν ὁρῶν μεμονωμένον, καὶ ὡς
οὐδὲν ἄρα ἔδει αὐτῷ κάλλους ἐπακτοῦ ἐνθυμοῖτο,
αὐτὸς κρατιστεύων, εἴ τις αὐτὸν ἐφ' ἑαυτοῦ ἐῴη εἶναι.

11. Περὶ τοιούτου χρήματος τίς ἂν ἀμφισβητοίη
νοῦν ἔχων, ὡς οὐκ ἀθάνατον; ᾧ πάρεστι μὲν ἐξ
ἑαυτοῦ ζωή, ἣν οὐχ οἷόν τε ἀπολέσθαι· πῶς γὰρ
οὐκ ἐπίκτητόν γε οὖσαν οὐδ' αὖ οὕτως ἔχουσαν,
5 ὡς τῷ πυρὶ ἡ θερμότης πάρεστι; λέγω δὲ οὐχ ὡς
ἐπακτὸν ἡ θερμότης τῷ πυρί, ἀλλ' ὅτι, εἰ καὶ μὴ
τῷ πυρί, ἀλλὰ τῇ ὑποκειμένῃ τῷ πυρὶ ὕλῃ. ταύτῃ
γὰρ καὶ διαλύεται τὸ πῦρ. ἡ δὲ ψυχὴ οὐχ οὕτω
τὴν ζωὴν ἔχει, ὡς ὕλην μὲν οὖσαν ὑποκεῖσθαι,
ζωὴν δὲ ἐπ' αὐτῇ γενομένην τὴν ψυχὴν ἀποδεῖξαι.
10 ἢ γὰρ οὐσία ἐστὶν ἡ ζωή, καὶ ἔστιν οὐσία ἡ
τοιαύτη παρ' αὑτῆς ζῶσα, ὅπερ ἐστὶν ὃ ζητοῦμεν,

---

[1] Again the *Phaedrus* myth (247D5 ff.), but remarkably
transformed. The moral forms stand, not as in Plato in the
" place above the heavens ", but within the soul itself, and
the soul sees them not as transcendent realities, but as included in its self-vision when it has in the course of its self-

to the divine and concentrating totally on likeness to it. But if purification causes us to be in a state of knowledge of the best, then the sciences which lie within become apparent, the ones which really are sciences. For it is certainly not by running around outside that the soul " sees self-control and justice ", but itself by itself in its understanding of itself and what it formerly was, seeing them standing in itself like splendid statues all rusted with time which it has cleaned [1]: as if gold had a soul, and knocked off all that was earthy in it; it was before in ignorance of itself, because it did not see the gold, but then, seeing itself isolated, it wondered at its worth, and thought that it needed no beauty brought in from outside, being supreme itself, if only one would leave it alone by itself.

11. Who with any sense could doubt that a thing of this kind is immortal? It has life of itself, which cannot perish: for how could it, since it is not brought in from outside, nor again does soul have it in the way in which heat is present to fire. I do not mean, of course, that heat in relation to fire is something brought in from outside, but that, even if it is not so for fire, it is for the matter which underlies fire; for it is by this that fire comes to an end. But soul does not have life in this way, as if it was underlying matter and life came upon it and made it soul. For life is rather a substance, and soul is a substance of this kind, living of itself—which is the thing we are looking for—and they will admit that this is

purification " cleansed the rust of time " off them and returned to a true self-understanding. The image of the " living gold " hammering away its own dross which follows is one of Plotinus's most original dynamic images.

ἡ ψυχή, καὶ τοῦτο ἀθάνατον ὁμολογοῦσιν, ἢ ἀναλύ-
σουσιν ὡς σύνθετον καὶ τοῦτο πάλιν, ἕως ἂν εἰς
ἀθάνατον ἔλθωσι παρ' αὐτοῦ κινούμενον, ᾧ μὴ
θέμις θανάτου μοῖραν δέχεσθαι. ἢ πάθος ἐπακτὸν
15 τῇ ὕλῃ λέγοντες τὴν ζωήν, παρ' ὅτου τοῦτο τὸ
πάθος ἐλήλυθεν εἰς τὴν ὕλην, αὐτὸ ἐκεῖνο ἀναγκα-
σθήσονται ὁμολογεῖν ἀθάνατον εἶναι, ἄδεκτον ὂν
τοῦ ἐναντίου ᾧ ἐπιφέρει. ἀλλὰ γάρ ἐστι μία φύσις
ἐνεργείᾳ ζῶσα.

12. Ἔτι εἰ πᾶσαν φήσουσι φθαρτήν, πάλαι ἂν
ἔδει πάντα ἀπολωλέναι· εἰ δὲ τὴν μέν, τὴν δ' οὔ,
οἷον τὴν τοῦ παντὸς ἀθάνατον εἶναι, τὴν δ' ἡμετέραν μή, λεκτέον αὐτοῖς τὴν αἰτίαν. ἀρχή τε γὰρ
5 κινήσεως ἑκατέρα, καὶ ζῇ παρ' αὑτῆς ἑκατέρα,
καὶ τῶν αὐτῶν τῷ αὐτῷ ἐφάπτεται νοοῦσα τά τε ἐν
τῷ οὐρανῷ τά τε οὐρανοῦ ἐπέκεινα καὶ πᾶν ὅ ἐστι
κατ' οὐσίαν ζητοῦσα καὶ μέχρι τῆς πρώτης ἀρχῆς
ἀναβαίνουσα. ἥ τε δὲ παρ' αὑτῆς ἐκ τῶν ἐν αὑτῇ
θεαμάτων κατανόησις αὐτοεκάστου καὶ ἐξ ἀναμνή-
10 σεως γιγνομένη πρὸ σώματός τε αὐτῇ δίδωσι τὸ
εἶναι καὶ ἀιδίοις ἐπιστήμαις κεχρημένην ἀΐδιον καὶ
αὐτὴν εἶναι. πᾶν τε τὸ λυόμενον σύνθεσιν εἰς τὸ
εἶναι εἰληφὸς ταύτῃ διαλύεσθαι πέφυκεν, ᾗ συνε-
τέθη. ψυχὴ δὲ μία καὶ ἁπλῆ ἐνεργείᾳ οὖσα ἐν τῷ
15 ζῆν φύσις· οὐ τοίνυν ταύτῃ φθαρήσεται. ἀλλ' ἄρα
μερισθεῖσα κερματιζομένη ἀπόλοιτο ἄν. ἀλλ' οὐκ
ὄγκος τις οὐδὲ ποσόν, ὡς ἐδείχθη, ἡ ψυχή. ἀλλ'

immortal, or they will treat it also as a composite and separate its parts until they come to an immortal thing moved by itself; it is against the divine law for this to accept the fate of death. Or if they say that life is an external affection of matter, they will be compelled to admit that the very thing from which this affection came into matter is immortal, unable to receive the opposite of the life it brings. But there really is one single nature which is actually alive.

12. Besides, if they are going to assert that every soul is destructible, everything ought to have perished long ago; but if they say that one soul is destructible and another is not, for instance that the soul of the All is immortal, but ours is not, they must explain why. For each of them is a principle of movement, and each of them lives of itself, and each of them apprehends the same things by the same means, thinking the things in heaven and the things beyond heaven and searching out everything which has substantial existence, and ascending to the first principle. And the intellection of the authentic reality of each thing which the soul derives from itself, from the contemplations within it, and from recollection, gives it an existence prior to body and makes it everlasting because it has everlasting knowledge. Again, everything which is dissoluble has come into existence by being put together and is naturally liable to be disintegrated in the same way in which it was put together. But the soul is a single and simple nature which has actual existence in its living; it cannot, then, be destroyed in this way. " But then if it was divided into parts it would be chopped up and so perish." But the soul, as has been demonstrated, is not a mass or a quantity.

PLOTINUS: ENNEAD IV. 7.

ἀλλοιωθεῖσα ἥξει εἰς φθοράν. ἀλλ' ἡ ἀλλοίωσις
φθείρουσα τὸ εἶδος ἀφαιρεῖ, τὴν δὲ ὕλην ἐᾷ· τοῦτο
δὲ συνθέτου πάθος. εἰ οὖν κατὰ μηδὲν τούτων
20 οἷόν τε φθείρεσθαι, ἄφθαρτον εἶναι ἀνάγκη.

13. Πῶς οὖν τοῦ νοητοῦ χωριστοῦ ὄντος ἥδε εἰς
σῶμα ἔρχεται; ὅτι, ὅσος μὲν νοῦς μόνος, ἀπαθὴς
ἐν τοῖς νοητοῖς ζωὴν μόνον νοερὰν ἔχων ἐκεῖ ἀεὶ
μένει—οὐ γὰρ ἔνι ὁρμὴ οὐδ' ὄρεξις—ὃ δ' ἂν ὄρεξιν
5 προσλάβῃ ἐφεξῆς ἐκείνῳ τῷ νῷ ὄν, τῇ προσθήκῃ
τῆς ὀρέξεως οἷον πρόεισιν ἤδη ἐπὶ πλέον καὶ
κοσμεῖν ὀρεγόμενον καθὰ ἐν νῷ εἶδεν, ὥσπερ κυοῦν
ἀπ' αὐτῶν καὶ ὠδῖνον γεννῆσαι, ποιεῖν σπεύδει καὶ
δημιουργεῖ. καὶ τῇ σπουδῇ ταύτῃ περὶ τὸ αἰσθητὸν τεταμένη, μετὰ μὲν πάσης τῆς τῶν ὅλων
10 ψυχῆς ὑπερέχουσα τοῦ διοικουμένου εἰς τὸ ἔξω καὶ
τοῦ παντὸς συνεπιμελουμένη, μέρος δὲ διοικεῖν βου-
ληθεῖσα μονουμένη καὶ ἐν ἐκείνῳ γιγνομένη, ἐν ᾧ
ἐστιν, οὐχ ὅλη οὐδὲ πᾶσα τοῦ σώματος γενομένη,
ἀλλά τι καὶ ἔξω σώματος ἔχουσα. οὔκουν οὐδὲ ὁ
15 ταύτης νοῦς ἐμπαθής· αὕτη δὲ ὁτὲ μὲν ἐν σώματι,
ὁτὲ δὲ σώματος ἔξω, ὁρμηθεῖσα μὲν ἀπὸ τῶν πρώτων, εἰς δὲ τὰ τρίτα προελθοῦσα εἰς τὰ ἐπὶ τάδε,
νοῦ ἐνεργείᾳ τοῦ[1] μένοντος ἐν τῷ αὐτῷ καὶ διὰ
ψυχῆς πάντα καλῶν πληροῦντος καὶ διακοσμοῦντος,
ἀθανάτου δι' ἀθανάτου, εἴπερ ἀεὶ καὶ αὐτὸς ὢν
20 ἔσται δι' ἐνεργείας ἀπαύστου.

[1] Harder: ἐνεργείᾳ νοῦ A^pc: ἐνέργεια νοῦ A^acEUCD:
ἐνέργειαν οὐ x.

388

ON THE IMMORTALITY OF THE SOUL

" But it will come to destruction by qualitative change." But a qualitative change which destroys anything takes away its form, but leaves its matter; but this is something which happens to a compound. If then soul cannot be destroyed in any of these ways, it must be indestructible.

13. How then, since the intelligible is separate, does soul come into body? It is in this way: as much of it as is only intellect has a purely intellectual life in the intelligible and stays there for ever without being affected; but that which acquires desire, which follows immediately on that intellect, goes out further in a way by its acquisition of desire, and, desiring to impart order and beauty according to the pattern which it sees in Intellect, is as if pregnant by the intelligibles and labouring to give birth, and so is eager to make, and constructs the world. And, straining towards the sense-world by its eagerness, along with the whole of the soul of the universe it transcends what it directs and shares in the care of the All, but when it wants to direct a part it is isolated and comes to be in that part in which it is; it does not come to belong wholly and altogether to the body, but has some part as well outside the body. And not even the intellect of this [individual] soul is subject to affection; but this soul is sometimes in the body and sometimes out of the body; it starts from the first realities and goes out to the third, the things down here, by the activity of the Intellect which remains the same and fills all things through soul with beauties and sets them in order, immortal through immortal, since Intellect will be existent for ever through its in-exhaustible activity.

14. Περὶ δὲ τῆς τῶν ἄλλων ζῴων ψυχῆς, ὅσαι μὲν αὐτῶν σφαλεῖσαι καὶ μέχρι θηρίων ἧκον σωμάτων, ἀνάγκη καὶ ταύτας ἀθανάτους εἶναι. εἰ δὲ ἔστιν ἄλλο τι εἶδος ψυχῆς, οὐκ ἄλλοθεν ἢ ἀπὸ τῆς ζώσης
5 φύσεως δεῖ καὶ ταύτην εἶναι καὶ αὐτὴν οὖσαν ζωῆς τοῖς ζῴοις αἰτίαν, καὶ δὴ καὶ τὴν ἐν τοῖς φυτοῖς· ἅπασαι γὰρ ὡρμήθησαν ἀπὸ τῆς αὐτῆς ἀρχῆς ζωὴν ἔχουσαι οἰκείαν ἀσώματοί τε καὶ αὖται καὶ ἀμερεῖς καὶ οὐσίαι. εἰ δὲ τὴν ἀνθρώπου ψυχὴν τριμερῆ οὖσαν τῷ συνθέτῳ λυθήσεσθαι [1] ⟨λέγεται⟩,[2]
10 καὶ ἡμεῖς φήσομεν τὰς μὲν καθαρὰς ἀπαλλαττομένας τὸ προσπλασθὲν ἐν τῇ γενέσει ἀφήσειν, τὰς δὲ τούτῳ συνέσεσθαι ἐπὶ πλεῖστον· ἀφειμένον δὲ τὸ χεῖρον οὐδὲ αὐτὸ ἀπολεῖσθαι, ἕως ἂν ᾖ, ὅθεν ἔχει τὴν ἀρχήν. οὐδὲν γὰρ ἐκ τοῦ ὄντος ἀπολεῖται.

15. Ἃ μὲν οὖν πρὸς τοὺς ἀποδείξεως δεομένους ἐχρῆν λέγεσθαι, εἴρηται. ἃ δὲ καὶ πρὸς δεομένους πίστεως αἰσθήσει κεκρατημένης, ἐκ τῆς ἱστορίας τῆς περὶ τὰ τοιαῦτα πολλῆς οὔσης ἐκλεκτέον, ἔκ
5 τε ὧν θεοὶ ἀνεῖλον κελεύοντες μῆνιν ψυχῶν ἠδικημένων ἱλάσκεσθαι τιμάς τε νέμειν τεθνηκόσιν ὡς ἐν αἰσθήσει οὖσι, καθὰ καὶ πάντες ἄνθρωποι ποιοῦσιν εἰς τοὺς ἀπεληλυθότας. πολλαὶ δὲ ψυχαὶ πρότερον ἐν ἀνθρώποις οὖσαι σωμάτων ἔξω γενόμεναι οὐκ ἀπέστησαν τοῦ εὐεργετεῖν ἀνθρώπους· αἳ δὴ καὶ
10 μαντεῖα ἀποδειξάμεναι εἴς τε τὰ ἄλλα χρῶσαι ὠφελοῦσι καὶ δεικνύουσι δι᾽ αὐτῶν καὶ περὶ τῶν ἄλλων ψυχῶν, ὅτι μή εἰσιν ἀπολωλυῖαι.

[1] wD: λυθήσεται xUC.
[2] coniecimus: ⟨λεχθήσεται⟩ Igal.

ON THE IMMORTALITY OF THE SOUL

14. As for the souls of other living things, those of them which have been failures and come into animal bodies must also be immortal. But if there is another [non-human] kind of soul, it cannot come from anywhere else than from the nature which lives, and this too must really exist and be the cause of life in living things, and the same is certainly true of the soul in plants: for they all started from the same origin and have their own life and they too are bodiless and without parts and substances. But if it is said that the human soul, since it is tripartite, will be dissolved because of its composition, we too shall say that pure souls when they are set free abandon what was plastered on to them at their birth, but the others remain with it for a very long time; but when the worse part is abandoned, even it does not perish, as long as that from which it has its origin exists. For nothing of real being perishes.

15. Well, then, we have said what needed to be said to those who require proof. But what needs to be said to those who require confidence supported by the evidence of the senses is to be selected from the body of information about such things, which is extensive; from the oracles of the gods commanding appeasement of the wrath of souls which have been wronged, and the giving of honours to the dead (which supposes that they are conscious of them), just as all men do to those who have passed away. And many souls which were formerly in human beings did not cease to benefit mankind when they were out of the body: they have established oracular shrines and give help by their prophecies in other ways and demonstrate through themselves that the other souls have also not perished.

ENNEAD IV. 8

IV. 8. ON THE DESCENT OF THE
SOUL INTO BODIES

Introductory Note

THIS early treatise, written in a style which suggests that
it was intended for a comparatively wide circle of readers,
is particularly interesting in a number of ways. It shows
more clearly than any other work of Plotinus how conscious he was of the tension between the two sides of
Plato's thought about the material world and the human
body, the pessimistic dualism most strikingly apparent in
the *Phaedo* and the optimistic view of the physical universe
as the good product of ungrudging divine goodness which
all later Platonists found in the *Timaeus*; and it shows
how hard (even if never entirely successfully) he tried to
reconcile them. The movement of his thought in the
treatise is worth noticing, from the pessimistic and dualistic
beginning to a view (in chapters 6 and 7) of the material
world and of soul's descent into body as positive and
optimistic as anything in the *Enneads*. Read as a whole,
the treatise is strong evidence against the view that
there is a development in the thought of Plotinus from
a pessimism about the material world with Gnostic affini-
ties to a sane positive Hellenic view. The tension, and
some never fully reconciled inconsistency, between the
two sides of Platonism appears in his latest works as it
does in this early one. The extremely positive attitude to
matter in chapter 6 should be noted. Whether it is to be
regarded as an independent reality or as derived from
higher principles is a question he here leaves open (in fact
he adopted the second alternative; cp. III. 4. [15] 1;
II. 3. [52] 17; I. 8. [51] 7). But in either case he sees it

THE DESCENT OF THE SOUL INTO BODIES

here as a capacity for good rather than, as he does in later treatises, as the principle of evil (see II. 4 [12]; I. 8 [51]). The passage points forward to the abandonment of the doctrine of matter as the principle of evil and its positive valuation as an expression of the infinity immediately derived from the Good by the later Neoplatonists. The ten lines of spiritual autobiography at the beginning of chapter 1 say more about the personal experience of Plotinus than any other passage in the *Enneads*, and justify the belief generally held by his readers that very much of what he says in the *Enneads* about divine reality is in some way based on his own religious experience.

Synopsis

The experience of " waking up from the body "; how is the fact that we are in the body to be explained? What Heraclitus, Empedocles, Pythagoras and Plato have to say about Universal Soul in the physical universe (chs. 1–2); and about the human soul and its descent to and life in the body (chs. 3–4). Reconciliation of the apparent contradiction in Plato's thought between the idea of a " fall " and the idea of a " mission " of the soul (ch. 5). The necessity of the material world as the term of the divine outgoing, and its closeness to the intelligible of which it is an image (ch. 6). Our souls need not be harmed, and may even be benefited by their necessary descent into this lower world (ch. 7). And we do not altogether descend. Our highest part remains in the intelligible, though we are not always conscious of it (ch. 8).

IV. 8. (6) ΠΕΡΙ ΤΗΣ ΕΙΣ ΤΑ ΣΩΜΑΤΑ ΚΑΘΟΔΟΥ ΤΗΣ ΨΥΧΗΣ

1. Πολλάκις ἐγειρόμενος εἰς ἐμαυτὸν ἐκ τοῦ
σώματος καὶ γινόμενος τῶν μὲν ἄλλων ἔξω, ἐμαυ-
τοῦ δὲ εἴσω, θαυμαστὸν ἡλίκον ὁρῶν κάλλος, καὶ
τῆς κρείττονος μοίρας πιστεύσας τότε μάλιστα
5 εἶναι, ζωήν τε ἀρίστην ἐνεργήσας καὶ τῷ θείῳ εἰς
ταὐτὸν γεγενημένος καὶ ἐν αὐτῷ ἱδρυθεὶς εἰς
ἐνέργειαν ἐλθὼν ἐκείνην ὑπὲρ πᾶν τὸ ἄλλο νοητὸν
ἐμαυτὸν ἱδρύσας, μετὰ ταύτην τὴν ἐν τῷ θείῳ στάσιν
εἰς λογισμὸν ἐκ νοῦ καταβὰς ἀπορῶ, πῶς ποτε καὶ
10 νῦν καταβαίνω, καὶ ὅπως ποτέ μοι ἔνδον ἡ ψυχὴ
γεγένηται τοῦ σώματος τοῦτο οὖσα, οἷον ἐφάνη καθ᾽
ἑαυτήν, καίπερ οὖσα ἐν σώματι. ὁ μὲν γὰρ
Ἡράκλειτος, ὃς ἡμῖν παρακελεύεται ζητεῖν τοῦτο,
ἀμοιβάς τε ἀναγκαίας τιθέμενος ἐκ τῶν ἐναντίων,
ὁδόν τε ἄνω κάτω εἰπὼν καὶ μεταβάλλον
15 ἀναπαύεται καὶ κάματός ἐστι τοῖς αὐτοῖς
μοχθεῖν καὶ ἄρχεσθαι εἰκάζειν ἔδωκεν ἀμελή-
σας σαφῆ ἡμῖν ποιῆσαι τὸν λόγον, ὡς δέον ἴσως
παρ᾽ αὐτῷ ζητεῖν, ὥσπερ καὶ αὐτὸς ζητήσας εὗρεν.
Ἐμπεδοκλῆς τε εἰπὼν ἁμαρτανούσαις νόμον εἶναι
ταῖς ψυχαῖς πεσεῖν ἐνταῦθα καὶ αὐτὸς φυγὰς
20 θεόθεν γενόμενος ἥκειν πίσυνος μαινομένῳ
νείκει τοσοῦτον παρεγύμνου, ὅσον καὶ Πυθαγόρας,

396

IV. 8. ON THE DESCENT OF THE SOUL INTO BODIES

1. Often I have woken up out of the body to my self and have entered into myself, going out from all other things; I have seen a beauty wonderfully great and felt assurance that then most of all I belonged to the better part; I have actually lived the best life and come to identity with the divine; and set firm in it I have come to that supreme actuality, setting myself above all else in the realm of Intellect. Then after that rest in the divine, when I have come down from Intellect to discursive reasoning, I am puzzled how I ever came down, and how my soul has come to be in the body when it is what it has shown itself to be by itself, even when it is in the body. Heraclitus, who urges us to investigate this, positing " necessary changes " from opposite to opposite, and saying " way up and down " and " changing it is at rest ", and " weariness to toil at and be subjected to the same things ", has left us guessing, since he has neglected to make clear to us what he is saying, perhaps because we ought to seek by ourselves, as he himself sought and found. And Empedocles, when he said that it is a law that sinful souls should fall into this world, and that he himself has come here as " an exile from the country of the gods " who " put his trust in raving strife ", revealed just as much as the riddling statements of Pythagoras

οἶμαι, καὶ οἱ ἀπ' ἐκείνου ἠνίττοντο περί τε τούτου
περί τε πολλῶν ἄλλων. τῷ δὲ παρῆν καὶ διὰ ποίησιν οὐ σαφεῖ εἶναι. λείπεται δὴ ἡμῖν ὁ θεῖος
Πλάτων, ὃς πολλά τε καὶ καλὰ περὶ ψυχῆς εἶπε
25 περί τε ἀφίξεως αὐτῆς πολλαχῇ εἴρηκεν ἐν τοῖς
αὐτοῦ λόγοις, ὥστε ἐλπίδα ἡμῖν εἶναι λαβεῖν παρ'
αὐτοῦ σαφές τι. τί οὖν λέγει ὁ φιλόσοφος οὗτος;
οὐ ταὐτὸν λέγων πανταχῇ φανεῖται, ἵνα ἄν τις ἐκ
ῥαδίας τὸ τοῦ ἀνδρὸς βούλημα εἶδεν, ἀλλὰ τὸ
αἰσθητὸν πᾶν πανταχοῦ ἀτιμάσας καὶ τὴν πρὸς τὸ
30 σῶμα κοινωνίαν τῆς ψυχῆς μεμψάμενος ἐν δεσμῷ τε
εἶναι καὶ τεθάφθαι ἐν αὐτῷ τὴν ψυχὴν λέγει, καὶ
τὸν ἐν ἀπορρήτοις λεγόμενον λόγον μέγαν
εἶναι, ὃς ἐν φρουρᾷ τὴν ψυχήν φησιν εἶναι· καὶ
τὸ σπήλαιον αὐτῷ, ὥσπερ Ἐμπεδοκλεῖ τὸ
35 ἄντρον, τόδε τὸ πᾶν—δοκῶ μοι—λέγειν, ὅπου γε
λύσιν τῶν δεσμῶν καὶ ἄνοδον ἐκ τοῦ σπηλαίου
τῇ ψυχῇ φησιν εἶναι τὴν πρὸς τὸ νοητὸν πορείαν.
ἐν δὲ Φαίδρῳ πτερορρύησιν αἰτίαν τῆς ἐνταῦθα
ἀφίξεως· καὶ περίοδοι αὐτῷ ἀνελθοῦσαν πάλιν
φέρουσι τῇδε, καὶ κρίσεις δὲ καταπέμπουσιν ἄλλας
40 ἐνταῦθα καὶ κλῆροι καὶ τύχαι καὶ ἀνάγκαι. καὶ
ἐν τούτοις ἅπασι μεμψάμενος τὴν τῆς ψυχῆς
ἄφιξιν πρὸς σῶμα, ἐν Τιμαίῳ περὶ τοῦδε τοῦ

---

[1] Plotinus here starts from an account of his own personal
experience unique in the *Enneads*, and then turns to tradition
to help him to explain that experience. As always, he spends
little time in considering the Pre-Socratics and does not seem
to find them very helpful. " Necessary changes " is a phrase
attributed to Heraclitus by both Iamblichus (cp. Stobaeus

THE DESCENT OF THE SOUL INTO BODIES

and his followers about this, and many other matters
(and, besides, he is unclear because he writes poetry).[1] We are left with the godlike Plato, who said
many fine things about the soul and about its coming
[into this world] in his writings, so that we hope we
can get something clear from him. What, then,
does this philosopher say? He is obviously not
saying the same thing everywhere, so that one can
easily know what his intention is; but he everywhere
speaks with contempt of the whole world of sense
and disapproves of the soul's fellowship with body
and says that soul is fettered and buried in it, and
that " the esoteric saying is a great one ", which
asserts that the soul is " in custody "; and his cave,
like the den of Empedocles, means, I think, this
universe, where he says that the soul's journey to the
intelligible world is a " release from fetters " and an
" ascent from the cave ". And in the *Phaedrus* he
makes " moulting " the cause of coming here; and
he has cycles which bring here again the soul which
has ascended, and judgments send others down here,
and lots and chances and necessities. And, though
in all these passages he disapproves of the soul's
coming to body, in the *Timaeus* when speaking about

Anth. I 49 p. 378, 21–5) and Stobaeus; the other Heraclitus
quotations are fr. B 60, B 84a, and B 84b DK (the last two
known from Plotinus alone). The Empedocles quotation is
from B 115 DK, lines 13–14. The impatience with which
Pythagoras and his followers are dismissed is noteworthy:
for Numenius and other Neopythagoreans before Plotinus,
and for the later Neoplatonists after him, Pythagoras was a
traditional authority if anything more venerable than Plato.
The attitude of Plotinus to Pythagoras is here closer to that of
Aristotle than to that which was normal in his own school-
tradition.

παντὸς λέγων τόν τε κόσμον ἐπαινεῖ καὶ θεὸν λέγει
εἶναι εὐδαίμονα τήν τε ψυχὴν παρὰ ἀγαθοῦ τοῦ
δημιουργοῦ πρὸς τὸ ἔννουν τόδε τὸ πᾶν εἶναι
45 δεδόσθαι, ἐπειδὴ ἔννουν μὲν αὐτὸ ἔδει εἶναι, ἄνευ δὲ
ψυχῆς οὐχ οἷόν τε ἦν τοῦτο γενέσθαι. ἥ τε οὖν
ψυχὴ ἡ τοῦ παντὸς τούτου χάριν εἰς αὐτὸ παρὰ τοῦ
θεοῦ ἐπέμφθη, ἥ τε ἑκάστου ἡμῶν, πρὸς τὸ τέλεον
αὐτὸ εἶναι· ἐπειδὴ ἔδει, ὅσα ἐν νοητῷ κόσμῳ, τὰ
50 αὐτὰ ταῦτα γένη ζῴων καὶ ἐν τῷ αἰσθητῷ ὑπάρχειν.

2. Ὥστε ἡμῖν συμβαίνει περὶ τῆς ἡμετέρας
ψυχῆς παρ᾽ αὐτοῦ μαθεῖν ζητήσασιν ἐξ ἀνάγκης
ἐφάπτεσθαι καὶ περὶ ψυχῆς ὅλως ζητῆσαι, πῶς ποτε
κοινωνεῖν σώματι πέφυκε, καὶ περὶ κόσμου φύσεως
5 οἷόν τινα δεῖ αὐτὸν τίθεσθαι, ἐν ᾧ ψυχὴ ἐνδιαιτᾶται
ἑκοῦσα εἴτε ἀναγκασθεῖσα εἴτε τις ἄλλος τρόπος·
καὶ περὶ ποιητοῦ δέ, εἴτε ὀρθῶς εἴτε ὡς ἡμέτεραι,
ψυχαὶ ἴσως, ἃς ἔδει σώματα διοικούσας χείρω δι᾽
αὐτῶν εἴσω πολὺ δῦναι, εἴπερ ἔμελλον κρατήσειν,
10 σκεδασθέντος μὲν ἂν ἑκάστου καὶ πρὸς τὸ οἰκεῖον
τόπον φερομένου—ἐν δὲ τῷ παντὶ πάντα ἐν οἰκείῳ
κατὰ φύσιν κεῖται—πολλῆς δὲ καὶ ὀχλώδους προ-
νοίας δεομένων, ἅτε πολλῶν τῶν ἀλλοτρίων αὐτοῖς
προσπιπτόντων ἀεί τε ἐνδείᾳ συνεχομένων καὶ

---

[1] As always, Plotinus thinks that Plato will be our best guide
to the truth if we take the trouble to interpret him rightly and
to reconcile his apparent contradictions. The passages in
Plato's dialogues quoted or alluded to here are *Phaedo* 67D1;
Cratylus 400C2; *Phaedo* 62B2–5; *Republic* 514A5; 515C4;
517B4–5; *Phaedrus* 246C2; 247D4–5; 249A6; *Republic*
619D7; *Timaeus* 34B8. The *Phaedo*, the image of the cave
in the *Republic*, and the *Phaedrus* myth are for Plotinus the

this All he praises the universe and calls it a blessed god, and says that the soul was given by the goodness of the Craftsman, so that this All might be intelligent, because it had to be intelligent, and this could not be without soul. The Soul of the All, then, was sent into it for this reason by the god, and the soul of each one of us was sent that the All might be perfect: since it was necessary that all the very same kinds of living things which were in the intelligible world should also exist in the world perceived by the senses.[1]

2. So that what happens to us when we seek to learn from Plato about our own soul is that we have also to undertake a general enquiry about soul, about how it has ever become naturally adapted to fellowship with body, and about what kind of a universe we ought to suppose that it is in which soul dwells, willingly or under compulsion or in any other way; and about its maker, whether [he has done his work] rightly, or whether perhaps [the Soul of the All] is in the same state as our souls, which, since they direct worse bodies, had to sink deep into the world because of them, if they were going to control them, as otherwise each [element of the individual bodies] would be dispersed and carried to its appropriate place—but in the All all parts are naturally set in their appropriate place—and our individual bodies need a great deal of troublesome thought, since many alien forces assail them and they are continually in the grip of poverty, and require every

principal Platonic authorities for the negative view of the soul's descent into the world, the *Timaeus* the principal authority for the positive view.

πάσης βοηθείας ὡς ἐν πολλῇ δυσχερείᾳ δεομένων.
15 τὸ δὲ τέλεόν τε ὂν καὶ ἱκανὸν καὶ αὔταρκες καὶ
οὐδὲν ἔχον αὐτῷ παρὰ φύσιν βραχέος οἷον κελεύσ-
ματος δεῖται· καὶ ὡς πέφυκε ψυχὴ ἐθέλειν,
ταύτῃ καὶ ἀεὶ ἔχει οὔτ᾽ ἐπιθυμίας ἔχουσα οὔτε
πάσχουσα· οὐδὲν γὰρ ἄπεισιν οὐδὲ πρόσεισι.
διὸ καί φησι καὶ τὴν ἡμετέραν, εἰ μετ᾽ ἐκείνης
20 γένοιτο τελέας, τελεωθεῖσαν καὶ αὐτὴν μετεωρο-
πορεῖν καὶ πάντα τὸν κόσμον διοικεῖν,
ὅτε ἀφίσταται εἰς τὸ μὴ ἐντὸς εἶναι τῶν σωμάτων
μηδέ τινος εἶναι, τότε καὶ αὐτὴν ὥσπερ τὴν τοῦ
παντὸς συνδιοικήσειν ῥᾳδίως τὸ πᾶν, ὡς οὐ
κακὸν ὂν ψυχῇ ὁπωσοῦν σώματι παρέχειν τὴν
25 τοῦ εὖ δύναμιν καὶ τοῦ εἶναι, ὅτι μὴ πᾶσα πρόνοια
τοῦ χείρονος ἀφαιρεῖ τὸ ἐν τῷ ἀρίστῳ τὸ προνοοῦν
μένειν. διττὴ γὰρ ἐπιμέλεια παντός, τὸ[1] μὲν
καθόλου κελεύσει κοσμοῦντος ἀπράγμονι ἐπιστασίᾳ
βασιλικῇ, τὸ δὲ καθέκαστα ἤδη αὐτουργῷ τινι
30 ποιήσει συναφῇ τῇ πρὸς τὸ πραττόμενον τὸ πρᾶτ-
τον τοῦ πραττομένου τῆς φύσεως ἀναπιμπλᾶσα.
τῆς δὲ θείας ψυχῆς τοῦτον τὸν τρόπον τὸν οὐρανὸν
ἅπαντα διοικεῖν ἀεὶ λεγομένης, ὑπερεχούσης μὲν
τῷ κρείττονι, δύναμιν δὲ τὴν ἐσχάτην εἰς τὸ εἴσω
πεμπούσης, αἰτίαν μὲν ὁ θεὸς οὐκ ἂν ἔτι λέγοιτο
35 ἔχειν τὴν τοῦ τὴν ψυχὴν τοῦ παντὸς ἐν χείρονι
πεποιηκέναι, ἥ τε ψυχὴ οὐκ ἀπεστέρηται τοῦ κατὰ
φύσιν ἐξ ἀιδίου τοῦτ᾽ ἔχουσα καὶ ἕξουσα ἀεί, ὃ μὴ
οἷόν τε παρὰ φύσιν αὐτῇ εἶναι, ὅπερ διηνεκῶς αὐτῇ
ἀεὶ ὑπάρχει οὔποτε ἀρξάμενον. τάς τε τῶν ἀστέ-

[1] Igal: τοῦ Enn.

sort of help as being in great trouble. But since [the body of the universe] is perfect and adequate and self-sufficient and there is nothing in it contrary to its nature it needs only a kind of brief command; and its soul is always as it naturally wants to be; it has no desires and is not affected: for [the world's body] " loses nothing and gains nothing ".[1] For this reason Plato says that our soul as well, if it comes to be with that perfect soul, is perfected itself and " walks on high and directs the whole universe "[2]; when it departs to be no longer within bodies and not to belong to any of them, then it also like the Soul of the All will share with ease in the direction of the All, since it is not evil in every way for soul to give body the ability to flourish and to exist, because not every kind of provident care for the inferior deprives the being exercising it of its ability to remain in the highest. For there are two kinds of care of everything, the general, by the inactive command of one setting it in order with royal authority, and the particular, which involves actually doing something oneself and by contact with what is being done infects the doer with the nature of what is being done. Now, since the divine soul is always said to direct the whole heaven in the first way, transcendent in its higher part but sending its last and lowest power into the interior of the world, God could not still be blamed for making the soul of the All exist in something worse, and the soul would not be deprived of its natural due, which it has from eternity and will have for ever, which cannot be against its nature in that it belongs to it continually and without beginning.

<hr />

[1] *Timaeus* 33C6–7.
[2] *Phaedrus* 246C1–2.

ρων ψυχὰς τὸν αὐτὸν τρόπον πρὸς τὸ σῶμα ἔχειν
40 λέγων, ὥσπερ τὸ πᾶν—ἐντίθησι γὰρ καὶ τούτων
τὰ σώματα εἰς τὰς τῆς ψυχῆς περιφοράς—
ἀποσῴζοι ἂν καὶ τὴν περὶ τούτους πρέπουσαν
εὐδαιμονίαν. δύο γὰρ ὄντων δι' ἃ δυσχεραίνεται ἡ
ψυχῆς πρὸς σῶμα κοινωνία, ὅτι τε ἐμπόδιον
πρὸς τὰς νοήσεις γίγνεται, καὶ ὅτι ἡδονῶν καὶ
45 ἐπιθυμιῶν καὶ λυπῶν πίμπλησιν αὐτήν, οὐδέτε-
ρον τούτων ἂν γένοιτο ψυχῇ, ἥτις μὴ εἰς τὸ εἴσω
ἔδυ τοῦ σώματος, μηδέ τινός ἐστι, μηδὲ ἐκείνου
ἐγένετο, ἀλλ' ἐκεῖνο αὐτῆς, ἔστι τε τοιοῦτον, οἷον
μήτε τινὸς δεῖσθαι μήτε τινὶ ἐλλείπειν· ὥστε μηδὲ
50 τὴν ψυχὴν ἐπιθυμιῶν πίμπλασθαι ἢ φόβων· οὐδὲν
γὰρ δεινὸν μήποτε περὶ σώματος προσδοκήσῃ
τοιούτου, οὔτε τις ἀσχολία νεῦσιν ποιοῦσα κάτω
ἀπάγει τῆς κρείττονος καὶ μακαρίας θέας, ἀλλ'
ἔστιν ἀεὶ πρὸς ἐκείνοις ἀπράγμονι δυνάμει τόδε τὸ
πᾶν κοσμοῦσα.

3. Περὶ δὲ τῆς ἀνθρωπείας ψυχῆς, ἣ ἐν σώματι
πάντα λέγεται κακοπαθεῖν καὶ ταλαιπωρεῖν
ἐν ἀνοίαις καὶ ἐπιθυμίαις καὶ φόβοις καὶ τοῖς
ἄλλοις κακοῖς γιγνομένη, ᾗ καὶ δεσμὸς τὸ σῶμα
5 καὶ τάφος, καὶ ὁ κόσμος αὐτῇ σπήλαιον καὶ
ἄντρον, ἥντινα γνώμην οὐ διάφωνον ἔχει ἐκ τῶν
αἰτιῶν οὐ τῶν αὐτῶν τῆς καθόδου, νῦν λέγωμεν.
ὄντος τοίνυν παντὸς νοῦ ἐν τῷ τῆς νοήσεως τόπῳ
ὅλου τε καὶ παντός, ὃν δὴ κόσμον νοητὸν τιθέμεθα,
ὄντων δὲ καὶ τῶν ἐν τούτῳ περιεχομένων νοερῶν

THE DESCENT OF THE SOUL INTO BODIES

And when Plato says that the souls of the stars are related to their bodies in the same way as the All—for he inserts their bodies also into the circles of the soul[1]—he keeps safe for them also their appropriate state of well-being. For, as there are two reasons why the soul's fellowship with body is displeasing, that body becomes a hindrance to thought and that it fills the soul with pleasures, desires and griefs,[2] neither of these things could happen to a soul which has not sunk into the interior of its body, and is not anyone's property, and does not belong to the body, but the body belongs to it, and is of such a kind as to want nothing and be defective in nothing; so that the soul will not be filled with desires or fears; for it will never have any frightening expectations about a body of this kind, nor does any business make it turn to what is below and take it away from the better, blessed vision, but it is always directed to those higher realities and sets this world in order with a power which requires no active effort.

3. As for what Plato says about the human soul, which is said to suffer all kinds of evils and to be in misery because it comes to exist among stupidities and desires and fears and all other evils, in that the body is its chain and tomb and the universe its cave and den, let us now state his thought about it, not inconsistent because the reasons [which he gives] for its descent are different. Now since universal Intellect exists in the realm of thought as a universal whole, which we call the intelligible universe, and since there also exist the intellectual powers con-

---

[1] *Timaeus* 38C7–8.
[2] *Phaedo* 65A10 and 66C2–3.

PLOTINUS: ENNEAD IV. 8.

10 δυνάμεων καὶ νόων τῶν καθέκαστα—οὐ γὰρ εἷς
μόνος, ἀλλ' εἷς καὶ πολλοί—πολλὰς ἔδει καὶ ψυχὰς
καὶ μίαν εἶναι, καὶ ἐκ τῆς μιᾶς τὰς πολλὰς διαφόρους, ὥσπερ ἐκ γένους ἑνὸς εἴδη τὰ μὲν ἀμείνω, τὰ
δὲ χείρω, νοερώτερα, τὰ δ' ἧττον ἐνεργείᾳ τοιαῦτα.
καὶ γὰρ ἐκεῖ ἐν τῷ νῷ τὸ μὲν νοῦς περιέχων δυνά-
15 μει τἆλλα οἷον ζῷον μέγα, τὰ δὲ ἐνεργείᾳ ἕκαστον,
ἃ δυνάμει περιεῖχε θάτερον· οἷον εἰ πόλις ἔμψυχος
ἦν περιεκτικὴ ἐμψύχων ἄλλων, τελειοτέρα μὲν ⟨ἡ⟩[1]
πόλεως καὶ δυνατωτέρα, οὐδὲν μὴν ἐκώλυε τῆς
αὐτῆς φύσεως εἶναι καὶ τὰς ἄλλας. ἢ ὡς ἐκ τοῦ
20 παντὸς πυρὸς τὸ μὲν μέγα, τὸ δὲ μικρὰ πυρὰ εἴη·
ἔστι δὲ ἡ πᾶσα οὐσία ἡ τοῦ παντὸς πυρός, μᾶλλον
δὲ ἀφ' ἧς καὶ τοῦ παντός. ψυχῆς δὲ ἔργον τῆς
λογικωτέρας νοεῖν μέν, οὐ τὸ νοεῖν δὲ μόνον· τί γὰρ
ἂν καὶ νοῦ διαφέροι; προσλαβοῦσα γὰρ τῷ νοερὰ
εἶναι καὶ ἄλλο, καθὸ νοῦς οὐκ ἔμεινεν· ἔχει τε
25 ἔργον καὶ αὐτή, εἴπερ πᾶν, ὃ ἐὰν ᾖ τῶν νοητῶν.
βλέπουσα δὲ πρὸς μὲν τὸ πρὸ ἑαυτῆς νοεῖ, εἰς δὲ
ἑαυτὴν τὸ μετ' αὐτὴν [ὃ][2] κοσμεῖ τε καὶ διοικεῖ
καὶ ἄρχει αὐτοῦ· ὅτι μηδὲ οἷόν τε ἦν στῆναι τὰ
πάντα ἐν τῷ νοητῷ, δυναμένου ἐφεξῆς καὶ ἄλλου
γενέσθαι ἐλάττονος μέν, ἀναγκαίου δὲ εἶναι, εἴπερ
30 καὶ τὸ πρὸ αὐτοῦ.

4. Τὰς δὴ καθέκαστα ψυχὰς ὀρέξει μὲν νοερᾷ

[1] Kirchhoff*.
[2] del. Kirchhoff*.

406

tained in this and the individual intellects—for Intellect is not only one, but one and many—there had to be many souls and one soul, and the many different souls springing from the one, like the species of one genus, some better and others worse, some more intelligent, and some whose intelligence is less actualized. For There, in Intellect, we have on the one hand Intellect potentially including the others like a great living creature, and on the other the individual intellects, each of which actualizes a potentiality which the other [universal] intellect includes; as if, supposing that a city had a soul and included other beings with souls, the soul of the city would be more complete and more powerful, but there would certainly be nothing to prevent the others from being the same kind of thing. Or it is like universal fire, from which comes the great fire and the little ones; but the universal substance is that of the universal fire, or rather that from which the substance of the universal fire comes. The work, then, of the more rational kind of soul is intellection, but not only intellection; for [if it was] why would it be different from Intellect? For by adding to its being intelligent something else, according to which it did not remain intelligence, it itself also has a work to do, like any other intelligible reality which exists. But when it looks to what comes before it it exercises its intelligence, when it looks to itself it sets in order what comes after it and directs and rules it; because everything could not be stationary in the intelligible, when it was possible for something else as well to exist next in order to it, something less, but something which must exist if that before it exists.

4. The individual souls, certainly, have an intelli-

χρωμένας ἐν τῇ ἐξ οὗ ἐγένοντο πρὸς αὐτὸ ἐπιστροφῇ, δύναμιν δὲ καὶ εἰς τὸ ἐπίταδε ἐχούσας, οἷά περ
φῶς ἐξηρτημένον μὲν κατὰ τὰ ἄνω ἡλίου, τῷ δὲ
5 μετ' αὐτὸ οὐ φθονοῦν τῆς χορηγίας, ἀπήμονας μὲν
εἶναι μετὰ τῆς ὅλης μενούσας ἐν τῷ νοητῷ, ἐν
οὐρανῷ δὲ μετὰ τῆς ὅλης συνδιοικεῖν ἐκείνῃ, οἷα οἱ
βασιλεῖ τῶν πάντων κρατοῦντι συνόντες συνδιοικοῦ-
σιν ἐκείνῳ οὐ καταβαίνοντες οὐδ' αὐτοὶ ἀπὸ τῶν
βασιλείων τόπων· καὶ γάρ εἰσιν ὁμοῦ ἐν τῷ αὐτῷ
10 τότε. μεταβάλλουσαι δὲ ἐκ τοῦ ὅλου εἰς τὸ μέρος
τε εἶναι καὶ ἑαυτῶν καὶ οἷον κάμνουσαι τὸ σὺν
ἄλλῳ εἶναι ἀναχωροῦσιν εἰς τὸ ἑαυτῶν ἑκάστη.
ὅταν δὴ τοῦτο διὰ χρόνων ποιῇ φεύγουσα τὸ πᾶν καὶ
τῇ διακρίσει ἀποστᾶσα καὶ μὴ πρὸς τὸ νοητὸν
15 βλέπῃ, μέρος γενομένη μονοῦταί τε καὶ ἀσθενεῖ καὶ
πολυπραγμονεῖ καὶ πρὸς μέρος βλέπει καὶ τῷ ἀπὸ
τοῦ ὅλου χωρισμῷ ἑνός τινος ἐπιβᾶσα καὶ τὸ ἄλλο
πᾶν φυγοῦσα, ἐλθοῦσα καὶ στραφεῖσα εἰς τὸ ἓν
ἐκεῖνο πληττόμενον ὑπὸ τῶν ὅλων κατὰ πᾶν, τοῦ
τε ὅλου ἀπέστη καὶ τὸ καθέκαστον μετὰ περιστά-
20 σεως διοικεῖ ἐφαπτομένη ἤδη καὶ θεραπεύουσα τὰ
ἔξωθεν καὶ παροῦσα καὶ δῦσα αὐτοῦ πολὺ εἰς τὸ
εἴσω. ἔνθα καὶ συμβαίνει αὐτῇ τὸ λεγόμενον πτε-
ρορρυῆσαι καὶ ἐν δεσμοῖς τοῖς τοῦ σώματος γενέσθαι ἁμαρτούσῃ τοῦ ἀβλαβοῦς τοῦ ἐν τῇ διοικήσει

---

[1] This is a particularly clear expression of Plotinus's con-
stant conviction that the sin of the soul is self-isolation,
individualism, a turning away (never quite complete) from

gent desire consisting in the impulse to return to itself springing from the principle from which they came into being, but they also possess a power directed to the world here below, like a light which depends from the sun in the upper world but does not grudge of its abundance to what comes after it, and they are free from sorrow if they remain with universal soul in the intelligible, but in heaven with the universal soul they can share in its government, like those who live with a universal monarch and share in the government of his empire; these also do not come down from the abode of royalty: for they are then all together in the same [place]. But they change from the whole to being a part and belonging to themselves, and, as if they were tired of being together, they each go to their own. Now when a soul does this for a long time, flying from the All and standing apart in distinctness, and does not look towards the intelligible, it has become a part and is isolated and weak and fusses and looks towards a part and in its separation from the whole it embarks on one single thing and flies from everything else; it comes to and turns to that one thing battered by the totality of things in every way, and has left the whole and directs the individual part with great difficulty; it is by now applying itself to and caring for things outside and is present and sinks deep into the individual part.[1] Here the " moulting ", as it is called, happens to it, and the being in the fetters of the body, since it has missed the immunity which it had when it was with the universal soul directing

the free universality of its higher state to bind itself to the particular. This for him provides the key to the understanding of the Platonic passages referred to in ch. 1.

25 τοῦ κρείττονος, ὃ ἦν παρὰ τῇ ψυχῇ τῇ ὅλῃ· τὸ δὲ
πρὸ τοῦ ἦν παντελῶς ἄμεινον ἀναδραμούσῃ·
εἴληπται οὖν πεσοῦσα καὶ πρὸς τῷ δεσμῷ οὖσα καὶ
τῇ αἰσθήσει ἐνεργοῦσα διὰ τὸ κωλύεσθαι τῷ νῷ
ἐνεργεῖν καταρχάς, τεθάφθαι τε λέγεται καὶ ἐν
σπηλαίῳ εἶναι, ἐπιστραφεῖσα δὲ πρὸς νόησιν λύεσθαί
30 τε ἐκ τῶν δεσμῶν καὶ ἀναβαίνειν, ὅταν ἀρχὴν λάβῃ
ἐξ ἀναμνήσεως θεᾶσθαι τὰ ὄντα· ἔχει γάρ τι
ἀεὶ οὐδὲν ἧττον ὑπερέχον τι. γίγνονται οὖν οἷον
ἀμφίβιοι ἐξ ἀνάγκης τόν τε ἐκεῖ βίον τόν τε ἐνταῦθα
παρὰ μέρος βιοῦσαι, πλεῖον μὲν τὸν ἐκεῖ, αἳ
δύνανται πλεῖον τῷ νῷ συνεῖναι, τὸν δὲ ἐνθάδε
35 πλεῖον, αἷς τὸ ἐναντίον ἢ φύσει ἢ τύχαις ὑπῆρξεν.
ἃ δὴ ὑποδεικνὺς ὁ Πλάτων ἠρέμα, ὅτε διαιρεῖ αὖ
τὰ[1] ἐκ τοῦ ὑστέρου κρατῆρος καὶ μέρη ποιεῖ, τότε
καὶ φησιν ἀναγκαῖον εἶναι εἰς γένεσιν ἐλθεῖν,
ἐπείπερ ἐγένοντο μέρη τοιαῦτα. εἰ δὲ λέγει σπεῖραι
τὸν θεὸν αὐτάς, οὕτως ἀκουστέον, ὥσπερ ὅταν καὶ
40 λέγοντα καὶ οἷον δημηγοροῦντα ποιῇ· ἃ γὰρ ἐν
φύσει ἐστὶ τῶν ὅλων, ταῦτα ἡ ὑπόθεσις γεννᾷ τε
καὶ ποιεῖ εἰς δεῖξιν προάγουσα ἐφεξῆς τὰ ἀεὶ οὕτω
γιγνόμενά τε καὶ ὄντα.

5. Οὐ τοίνυν διαφωνεῖ ἀλλήλοις ἥ τε εἰς γένεσιν

[1] Igal: αὐτὰ Enn.: αὐτὰς Kirchhoff.

the better part [of the universe]; it was altogether
better for it before when it was running upwards;
it is fallen, therefore, and is caught, and is engaged
with its fetter, and acts by sense because its new
beginning prevents it from acting by intellect, and
it is said to be buried and in a cave, but, when it
turns to intelligence, to be freed from its fetters and
to ascend, when it is started on the contemplation of
reality by recollection: for, in spite of everything,
it always possesses something transcendent in some
way. Souls, then, become, one might say, amphi-
bious, compelled to live by turns the life There, and
the life here: those which are able to be more in the
company of Intellect live the life There more, but
those whose normal condition is, by nature or chance,
the opposite, live more the life here below. Plato
indicates this unobtrusively when he distinguishes
again the products of the second mixing-bowl and
makes parts of them; then he says also that they
must enter into becoming, since they became parts
of this kind.[1] But if he says that God " sowed "
them, this must be understood in the same way as
when he makes God talk, and even deliver a kind of
public speech; for the plan of his exposition generates
and makes the things which exist in the nature of
the Whole, bringing out in succession for purposes of
demonstration what are always coming into being
and always existing there.

5. There is then no contradiction between the

---

[1] Cp. Plato *Timaeus* 41D5–8. There is in fact only one
" mixing-bowl " in Plato, though there are two mixtures.
But Atticus before Plotinus and Theodore of Asine after him
read two mixing-bowls into the Platonic text, as Proclus notes
with disapproval (*In Tim.* III 246–7 Diehl).

σπορὰ ἥ τε εἰς τελείωσιν κάθοδος τοῦ παντός, ἥ τε
δίκη τό τε σπήλαιον, ἥ τε ἀνάγκη τό τε ἑκούσιον,
ἐπείπερ ἔχει τὸ ἑκούσιον ἡ ἀνάγκη, καὶ τὸ ἐν κακῷ
5 τῷ σώματι εἶναι· οὐδ' ἡ Ἐμπεδοκλέους φυγὴ ἀπὸ
τοῦ θεοῦ καὶ πλάνη οὐδ' ἡ ἁμαρτία, ἐφ' ᾗ ἡ δίκη,
οὐδ' ἡ Ἡρακλείτου ἀνάπαυλα ἐν τῇ φυγῇ, οὐδ'
ὅλως τὸ ἑκούσιον τῆς καθόδου καὶ τὸ ἀκούσιον
αὖ. πᾶν μὲν γὰρ ἰὸν ἐπὶ τὸ χεῖρον ἀκούσιον, φορᾷ
γε μὴν οἰκείᾳ ἰὸν πάσχον τὰ χείρω ἔχειν λέγεται
10 τὴν ἐφ' οἷς ἔπραξε δίκην. ὅταν δὲ ταῦτα πάσχειν
καὶ ποιεῖν ᾖ ἀναγκαῖον ἀιδίως φύσεως νόμῳ, τὸ δὲ
συμβαῖνον εἰς ἄλλου του χρείαν ἐν τῇ προσόδῳ
ἀπαντᾷ καταβαῖνον ἀπὸ τοῦ ὑπὲρ αὐτόν, θεὸν εἴ τις
λέγοι καταπέμψαι, οὐκ ἂν ἀσύμφωνος οὔτε τῇ
15 ἀληθείᾳ οὔτε ἑαυτῷ ἂν εἴη. καὶ γὰρ ἀφ' ἧς ἀρχῆς
ἕκαστα, εἰ καὶ τὰ μεταξὺ πολλά, καὶ τὰ ἔσχατα
εἰς αὐτὴν ἀναφέρεται. διττῆς δὲ τῆς ἁμαρτίας
οὔσης, τῆς μὲν ἐπὶ τῇ τοῦ κατελθεῖν αἰτίᾳ, τῆς δὲ
ἐπὶ τῷ ἐνθάδε γενομένην κακὰ δρᾶσαι, ⟨δίκη⟩ [1] ἡ
20 μέν ἐστιν αὐτὸ τοῦτο, ὃ πέπονθε κατελθοῦσα, τῆς
δὲ τὸ ἔλαττον εἰς σώματα ἄλλα δῦναι καὶ θᾶττον
ἐκ κρίσεως τῆς κατ' ἀξίαν—ὃ δὴ θεσμῷ θείῳ
γιγνόμενον διὰ τοῦ τῆς κρίσεως ὀνόματος δηλοῦται
—τὸ δὲ τῆς κακίας ἄμετρον εἶδος μείζονος καὶ τῆς
δίκης ἠξίωται ἐπιστασίᾳ τιννυμένων δαιμόνων.
25 οὕτω τοι καίπερ οὖσα θεῖον καὶ ἐκ τῶν τόπων τῶν
ἄνω ἐντὸς γίνεται τοῦ σώματος καὶ θεὸς οὖσα ὁ
ὕστερος ῥοπῇ αὐτεξουσίῳ καὶ αἰτίᾳ δυνάμεως καὶ

---

[1] Theiler.

sowing to birth and the descent for the perfection of the All, and the judgment and the cave, and necessity and free-will (since necessity contains the free-will) and the being in the body as an evil; nor [is there anything inconsistent about] Empedocles' flight from God and wandering nor the sin upon which judgment comes, nor Heraclitus' rest on the flight, nor in general the willingness and also the unwillingness of the descent. For everything which goes to the worse does so unwillingly, but, since it goes by its own motion, when it experiences the worse it is said to be punished for what it did. But when it is eternally necessary by the law of nature that it should do and experience these things, and, descending from that which is above it, it meets the need of something else in its encounter with it, if anyone said that a god sent it down he would not be out of accord with the truth or with himself. For final results are referred to the principle from which they spring, even if there are many intervening stages. And since the sin of the soul can refer to two things, either to the course of the descent or to doing evil when the soul has arrived here below, the punishment of the first is the very experience of descent, and of the lesser degree of the second the entrance, and a very quick one, into other bodies according to the judgment passed on its deserts—the word " judgment " indicates what happens by divine decree—but the boundless kind of wickedness is judged to deserve greater punishment in charge of chastising spirits. So then the soul, though it is divine and comes from above, enters into the body and, though it is a god of the lowest rank, comes to this world by a spontaneous inclination, its own power and the

τοῦ μετ' αὐτὴν κοσμήσει ὡδὶ ἔρχεται· κἂν μὲν
θᾶττον φύγῃ, οὐδὲν βέβλαπται γνῶσιν κακοῦ
προσλαβοῦσα καὶ φύσιν κακίας γνοῦσα τάς τε
30 δυνάμεις ἄγουσα αὐτῆς εἰς τὸ φανερὸν καὶ δείξασα
ἔργα τε καὶ ποιήσεις, ἃ ἐν τῷ ἀσωμάτῳ ἠρεμοῦντα
μάτην τε ἂν ἦν εἰς τὸ ἐνεργεῖν ἀεὶ οὐκ ἰόντα, τήν
τε ψυχὴν αὐτὴν ἔλαθεν ἂν ἃ εἶχεν οὐκ ἐκφανέντα
οὐδὲ πρόοδον λαβόντα· εἴπερ πανταχοῦ ἡ ἐνέργεια τὴν δύναμιν ἔδειξε κρυφθεῖσαν ἂν ἀπάντη καὶ
35 οἷον ἀφανισθεῖσαν καὶ οὐκ οὖσαν μηδέποτε ὄντως
οὖσαν. νῦν μὲν γὰρ θαῦμα ἔχει τῶν ἔνδον ἕκαστος
διὰ τῆς ποικιλίας τῶν ἔξω, οἷόν ἐστιν ἐκ τοῦ τὰ
γλαφυρὰ ταῦτα δρᾶσαι.

6. Εἴπερ οὖν δεῖ μὴ ἓν μόνον εἶναι—ἐκέκρυπτο
γὰρ ἂν πάντα μορφὴν ἐν ἐκείνῳ οὐκ ἔχοντα, οὐδ'
ἂν ὑπῆρχέ τι τῶν ὄντων στάντος ἐν αὐτῷ ἐκείνου,
οὐδ' ἂν τὸ πλῆθος ἦν ἂν τῶν ὄντων τούτων τῶν ἀπὸ
5 τοῦ ἑνὸς γεννηθέντων μὴ τῶν μετ' αὐτὰ τὴν πρόοδον λαβόντων, ἃ ψυχῶν εἴληχε τάξιν—τὸν αὐτὸν
τρόπον οὐδὲ ψυχὰς ἔδει μόνον εἶναι μὴ τῶν δι'
αὐτὰς γενομένων φανέντων, εἴπερ ἑκάστῃ φύσει
τοῦτο ἔνεστι τὸ μετ' αὐτὴν ποιεῖν καὶ ἐξελίττεσ-
θαι οἷον σπέρματος ἔκ τινος ἀμεροῦς ἀρχῆς εἰς τέλος
10 τὸ αἰσθητὸν ἰούσης, μένοντος μὲν ἀεὶ τοῦ προτέρου

---

[1] The same image of the seed is used in III. 7. 11. 23–7, but
with a significant difference of tone: here the emphasis is on
the both necessary and generous self-expansion and self-

setting in order of what comes after it being the cause of its descent. If it escapes quickly it takes no harm by acquiring a knowledge of evil and coming to know the nature of wickedness, and manifesting its powers, making apparent works and activities which if they had remained quiescent in the spiritual world would have been of no use because they would never have come into actuality; and the soul itself would not have known the powers it had if they had not come out and been revealed. Actuality everywhere reveals completely hidden potency, in a way obliterated and non-existent because it does not yet truly exist. As things are, everyone wonders at what is within because of the varied splendour of the outside and admires what the doer is because it does these fine things.

6. If, then, there must not be just one alone—for then all things would have been hidden, shapeless within that one, and not a single real being would have existed if that one had stayed still in itself, nor would there have been the multiplicity of these real beings which are generated from the One, if the things after them had not taken their way out which have received the rank of souls—in the same way there must not be just souls alone either, without the manifestation of the things produced through them, if this is in every nature, to produce what comes after it and to unfold itself as a seed does,[1] from a partless beginning which proceeds to the final stage perceived by the senses, with what comes before abiding for ever in its own proper

communication of the One, there on the degeneration and weakening which is the inevitable result of the passage from unity to multiplicity.

ἐν τῇ οἰκείᾳ ἕδρᾳ, τοῦ δὲ μετ᾽ αὐτὸ οἷον γεννωμένου
ἐκ δυνάμεως ἀφάτου, ὅση ἐν ἐκείνοις, ἣν οὐκ ἔδει
στῆσαι οἷον περιγράψαντα φθόνῳ, χωρεῖν δὲ ἀεί,
ἕως εἰς ἔσχατον μέχρι τοῦ δυνατοῦ τὰ πάντα ἥκῃ
15 αἰτίᾳ δυνάμεως ἀπλέτου ἐπὶ πάντα παρ᾽ αὐτῆς
πεμπούσης καὶ οὐδὲν περιδεῖν ἄμοιρον αὐτῆς
δυναμένης. οὐ γὰρ δὴ ἦν ὃ ἐκώλυεν ὁτιοῦν ἄμοιρον
εἶναι φύσεως ἀγαθοῦ, καθόσον ἕκαστον οἷόν τ᾽ ἦν
μεταλαμβάνειν. εἴτ᾽ οὖν ἦν ἀεὶ ἡ τῆς ὕλης φύσις,
οὐχ οἷόν τε ἦν αὐτὴν μὴ μετασχεῖν οὖσαν τοῦ πᾶσι
20 τὸ ἀγαθὸν καθόσον δύναται ἕκαστον χορηγοῦντος·
εἴτ᾽ ἠκολούθησεν ἐξ ἀνάγκης ἡ γένεσις αὐτῆς
τοῖς πρὸ αὐτῆς αἰτίοις, οὐδ᾽ ὡς ἔδει χωρὶς εἶναι,
ἀδυναμίᾳ πρὶν εἰς αὐτὴν ἐλθεῖν στάντος τοῦ καὶ τὸ
εἶναι οἷον ἐν χάριτι δόντος. δεῖξις οὖν τῶν ἀρίστων
ἐν νοητοῖς τὸ ἐν αἰσθητῷ κάλλιστον, τῆς τε
25 δυνάμεως τῆς τε ἀγαθότητος αὐτῶν, καὶ συνέχεται
πάντα εἰσαεὶ τά τε νοητῶς τά τε αἰσθητῶς ὄντα,
τὰ μὲν παρ᾽ αὐτῶν ὄντα, τὰ δὲ μετοχῇ τούτων
τὸ εἶναι εἰσαεὶ λαβόντα, μιμούμενα τὴν νοητὴν
καθόσον δύναται φύσιν.

7. Διττῆς δὲ φύσεως ταύτης οὔσης, νοητῆς, τῆς
δὲ αἰσθητῆς, ἄμεινον μὲν ψυχῇ ἐν τῷ νοητῷ εἶναι,
ἀνάγκη γε μὴν ἔχειν καὶ τοῦ αἰσθητοῦ μεταλαμβάνειν τοιαύτην φύσιν ἐχούσῃ, καὶ οὐκ ἀγανακτη-

dwelling-place, but, in a way, bringing to birth what comes after it from a power unspeakably great, all the power which was in those higher beings, which could not stand still as if it had drawn a line round itself in selfish jealousy, but had to go on for ever, until all things have reached the ultimate possible limit [impelled] by the power itself, which sends them out and cannot leave anything without a share of itself. For there was certainly nothing which hindered anything whatever from having a share in the nature of good, as far as each thing was able to participate in it. The nature of matter, then, either existed for ever, and it was impossible for it, since it existed, not to participate in that which grants all things as much good as each one of them can take; or else its coming into being was a necessary consequence of the causes before it, and not even so was it required to be separate because that which gave it existence as a kind of gracious gift became stationary through lack of power before it came to it. The greatest beauty in the world of sense, therefore, is a manifestation of the noblest among the intelligibles, of their power and of their goodness, and all things are held together for ever, those which exist intelligibly and those which exist perceptibly, the intelligibles existing of themselves and the things perceived by the senses receiving their existence for ever by participation in them, imitating the intelligible nature as far as they can.

7. Since this nature is twofold, partly intelligible and partly perceptible, it is better for the soul to be in the intelligible, but all the same, since it has this kind of nature, it is necessarily bound to be able to participate in the perceptible, and it should not

5 τέον αὐτὴν ἑαυτῇ, εἰ μὴ πάντα ἐστὶ τὸ κρεῖττον,
μέσην τάξιν ἐν τοῖς οὖσιν ἐπισχοῦσαν, θείας μὲν
μοίρας οὖσαν, ἐν ἐσχάτῳ δὲ τοῦ νοητοῦ οὖσαν,
ὡς ὅμορον οὖσαν τῇ αἰσθητῇ φύσει διδόναι μέν τι
τούτῳ τῶν παρ' αὐτῆς, ἀντιλαμβάνειν δὲ καὶ παρ'
αὐτοῦ, εἰ μὴ μετὰ τοῦ αὐτῆς ἀσφαλοῦς διακοσμοῖ,
10 προθυμίᾳ δὲ πλείονι εἰς τὸ εἴσω δύοιτο μὴ μείνασα
ὅλη μεθ' ὅλης, ἄλλως τε καὶ δυνατὸν αὐτῇ πάλιν
ἐξαναδῦναι, ἱστορίαν ὧν ἐνταῦθα εἶδέ τε καὶ ἔπαθε
προσλαβούσῃ καὶ μαθούσῃ, οἷον ἄρα ἐστὶν ἐκεῖ
εἶναι, καὶ τῇ παραθέσει τῶν οἷον ἐναντίων οἷον
15 σαφέστερον τὰ ἀμείνω μαθούσῃ. γνῶσις γὰρ
ἐναργεστέρα τἀγαθοῦ ἡ τοῦ κακοῦ πεῖρα οἷς ἡ
δύναμις ἀσθενεστέρα, ἢ ὥστε ἐπιστήμῃ τὸ κακὸν
πρὸ πείρας γνῶναι. ὥσπερ δὲ ἡ νοερὰ διέξοδος
κατάβασίς ἐστιν εἰς ἔσχατον τὸ χεῖρον—οὐ γὰρ ἔνι
20 εἰς τὸ ἐπέκεινα ἀναβῆναι, ἀλλ' ἀνάγκη ἐνεργήσασαν
ἐξ ἑαυτῆς καὶ μὴ δυνηθεῖσαν μεῖναι ἐφ' ἑαυτῆς
φύσεως δὲ [1] ἀνάγκη καὶ νόμῳ μέχρι ψυχῆς ἐλθεῖν·
τέλος γὰρ αὐτῇ τοῦτο· ταύτῃ δὲ τὸ ἐφεξῆς παρα-
δοῦναι αὐτὴν πάλιν ἀναδραμοῦσαν—οὕτως καὶ
ψυχῆς ἐνέργεια· τὸ μὲν μετ' αὐτὴν τὰ τῇδε, τὸ δὲ
πρὸ αὐτῆς ἡ θέα τῶν ὄντων, ταῖς μὲν παρὰ μέρος
25 καὶ χρόνῳ γιγνομένου τοῦ τοιούτου καὶ ἐν τῷ
χείρονι γιγνομένης ἐπιστροφῆς πρὸς τὰ ἀμείνω, τῇ
δὲ λεγομένῃ τοῦ παντὸς εἶναι τὸ μηδ' ἐν τῷ χείρονι
ἔργῳ γεγονέναι, ἀπαθεῖ δὲ κακῶν οὔσῃ θεωρίᾳ τε
περινοεῖν τὰ ὑπ' αὐτὴν ἐξηρτῆσθαί τε τῶν πρὸ

---

[1] Enn., defendit Igal (*Helmantica* 28, 1977, 252): δὴ Creuzer.

be annoyed with itself because, granted that all
things are not the best, it occupies a middle rank
among realities, belonging to that divine part but
being on the lowest edge of the intelligible, and,
having a common boundary with the perceptible
nature, gives something to it of what it has in itself
and receives something from it in return, if it does
not use only its safe part in governing the universe,
but with greater eagerness plunges into the interior
and does not stay whole with whole; especially as
it is possible for it to emerge again having acquired
the whole story of what it saw and experienced
here and learnt what it is like to be There, and, by
the comparison of things which are, in a way, opposite, learning, in a way more clearly, the better
things. For the experience of evil is a clearer
knowledge of the Good for those whose power is too
weak to know evil with clear intellectual certainty
before experiencing it. And just as the intellectual
way of outgoing is a descent to the lower limit of
that which is worse [than Intellect]—for it is not
possible for it to go up to that which transcends it;
but it must, acting outwards from itself and unable to
remain on its own, by the necessity and law of
nature arrive at soul; for this is its goal, and it must
hand over what comes after to soul and run up again
itself—so is the activity of soul; what comes after
it is this world and what is before it is the contemplation of real being; this kind of experience comes
slowly to partial souls, when they are in the worse
and a turn takes place to the better, but that which
is called the Soul of the All has not become engaged
in the worse kind of work and, having no experience
of evils, considers what lies below it contemplatively

419

30 αὐτῆς ἀεί· ἢ ἅμα δυνατὸν καὶ ἄμφω, λαμβανούσῃ
μὲν ἐκεῖθεν, χορηγούσῃ δὲ ἅμα ἐνταῦθα, ἐπείπερ
ἀμήχανον ἦν μὴ καὶ τούτων ἐφάπτεσθαι ψυχῇ
οὔσῃ.

8. Καὶ εἰ χρὴ παρὰ δόξαν τῶν ἄλλων τολμῆσαι
τὸ φαινόμενον λέγειν σαφέστερον, οὐ πᾶσα οὐδ' ἡ
ἡμετέρα ψυχὴ ἔδυ, ἀλλ' ἔστι τι αὐτῆς ἐν τῷ νοητῷ
ἀεί· τὸ δὲ ἐν τῷ αἰσθητῷ εἰ κρατοῖ, μᾶλλον δὲ εἰ
5 κρατοῖτο καὶ θορυβοῖτο, οὐκ ἐᾷ αἴσθησιν ἡμῖν εἶναι
ὧν θεᾶται τὸ τῆς ψυχῆς ἄνω. τότε γὰρ ἔρχεται εἰς
ἡμᾶς τὸ νοηθέν, ὅταν εἰς αἴσθησιν ἥκῃ καταβαῖνον·
οὐ γὰρ πᾶν, ὃ γίγνεται περὶ ὁτιοῦν μέρος ψυχῆς,
γινώσκομεν, πρὶν ἂν εἰς ὅλην τὴν ψυχὴν ἥκῃ· οἷον
10 καὶ ἐπιθυμία ἐν τῷ ἐπιθυμητικῷ μένουσα γιγνώσ-
κεται ἡμῖν, ἀλλ' ὅταν τῇ αἰσθητικῇ τῇ ἔνδον δυνάμει
ἢ καὶ διανοητικῇ ἀντιλαβώμεθα ἢ ἄμφω. πᾶσα
γὰρ ψυχὴ ἔχει τι καὶ τοῦ κάτω πρὸς σῶμα καὶ τοῦ
ἄνω πρὸς νοῦν. καὶ ἡ μὲν ὅλη καὶ ὅλου τῷ αὑτῆς
μέρει τῷ πρὸς τὸ σῶμα τὸ ὅλον κοσμεῖ ὑπερέχου-
15 σα ἀπόνως, ὅτι μηδ' ἐκ λογισμοῦ, ὡς ἡμεῖς, ἀλλὰ
νῷ ὡς ἡ τέχνη οὐ βουλεύεται,[1] †τὸ κάτω

---

[1] R²ᵐᵍ (*consultare* Ficinus): βούλεται Enn.

---

[1] For this doctrine, that our consciousness of what goes on
in the soul is limited and dependent on our bodily condition,
cp. IV. 3. (27) 30 and I. 4. (46) 10.

[2] " Art does not deliberate " is a quotation from Aristotle
Physics B 199b28–9: " Art in fact does not deliberate either,
and if the ship building art were incorporate in the timber,
it would proceed by nature in the same way in which it now
proceeds by art " (tr. Wicksteed-Cornford). This passage
seems to be the starting-point for the development of the
doctrine that the activity of Soul and Nature in forming and

and remains attached to the realities before it for ever; both are certainly possible; it can receive from There and at the same time distribute here, since it was impracticable for it as soul not to be in contact with this world.

8. And, if one ought to dare to express one's own view more clearly, contradicting the opinion of others, even our soul does not altogether come down, but there is always something of it in the intelligible; but if the part which is in the world of sense-perception gets control, or rather if it is itself brought under control, and thrown into confusion [by the body], it prevents us from perceiving the things which the upper part of the soul contemplates.[1] For what is grasped by the intellect reaches us when it arrives at perception in its descent, for we do not know everything which happens in any part of the soul before it reaches the whole soul; for instance desire which remains in the desiring part is known by us, but [only] when we apprehend it by the power of inner sense or discursive reason, or both. For every soul has something of what is below, in the direction of the body, and of what is above, in the direction of Intellect. And the soul which is a whole and is the soul of the whole, by its part which is directed to body, maintains the beauty and order of the whole in effortless transcendence because it does not do so by calculating and considering, as we do, but by intellect, as art does not deliberate. . . .[2] But the

directing the physical world is non-deliberative, on which Plotinus always insists strongly. It seems impossible to make any tolerable sense of the words which follow, and no convincing emendations have been suggested; so I follow Harder in leaving them untranslated.

αὐτῆς κοσμοῦντος ὅ τι ὅλου †. αἱ δ᾽ ἐν μέρει
γινόμεναι καὶ μέρους ἔχουσι μὲν καὶ αὗται τὸ
ὑπερέχον, ἄσχολοι δὲ τῇ αἰσθήσει καὶ ἀντιλήψει
πολλῶν ἀντιλαμβανόμεναι τῶν παρὰ φύσιν καὶ
20 λυπούντων καὶ ταραττόντων, ἅτε οὗ ἐπιμέλονται
μέρους καὶ ἐλλειποῦς καὶ πολλὰ ἔχοντος τὰ ἀλ-
λότρια κύκλῳ, πολλὰ δὲ ὧν ἐφίεται· καὶ ἥδεται δὲ
καὶ ἡδονὴ ἠπάτησε. τὸ δέ ἐστι καὶ ἀνήδονον ὂν
τὰς προσκαίρους ἡδονάς, ἡ δὲ διαγωγὴ ὁμοία.

souls which are partial and of a part have also the transcendent element, but they are occupied with sense-perception, and by their [lower] faculty of conscious apprehension they apprehend many things which are contrary to their nature and grieve and trouble them, since what they care for is a part, and defective, and has a great many alien and hostile things around it, and a great many which it desires; and it has pleasures, and pleasure deceives it; but there is a higher part which the transitory pleasures do not please, and its life is conformable [to its nature].

ENNEAD IV. 9

IV. 9. IF ALL SOULS ARE ONE

Introductory Note

THIS short early treatise takes up and carries forward the discussion of the same subject in the shorter and earlier IV. 2 (4) and anticipates the much more careful and elaborate discussions of the unity-in-multiplicity of Intellect and of Soul in VI. 4–5 (22–3) and of the relationship of our souls to the Soul of the Universe in IV. 3. (27) 1–8. The subject was one of much concern to Plotinus, to which he often returns in his writings; and he shows clearly by his defensive and argumentative tone in this treatise that he is aware that his characteristic doctrine of the unity-in-diversity of immaterial beings would seem paradoxical and objectionable to some Platonists.

Synopsis

Are all souls one? Objections from differences of perception, virtue, desire, experience and rationality between souls (ch. 1). Answers to these objections; bodily differences affect our perceptions etc. and the unity of soul does not completely exclude diversity (ch. 2). The argument for unity of souls from universal sympathy; and soul is no less a unity because it has many powers, of reason, perception, growth etc. (ch. 3). The one immanent soul in the many bodies derives from a prior, transcendent one which is not many (ch. 4). Soul both gives itself and does not give itself to the multiplicity of individuals; the analogy (often tacit and unnoticed) of the whole of a body of knowledge in each of its parts (ch. 5).

IV. 9. (8) ΠΕΡΙ ΤΟΥ ΕΙ ΠΑΣΑΙ ΑΙ ΨΥΧΑΙ ΜΙΑ

1. Ἀρ' ὥσπερ ψυχὴν ἑκάστου μίαν φαμὲν εἶναι,
ὅτι πανταχοῦ τοῦ σώματος ὅλη πάρεστι, καὶ ἔστιν
ὄντως τὸν τρόπον τοῦτον μία, οὐκ ἄλλο μέν τι
αὐτῆς ὡδί, ἄλλο δὲ ὡδὶ τοῦ σώματος ἔχουσα, ἔν τε
5 τοῖς αἰσθητικοῖς οὕτως ἡ αἰσθητική, καὶ ἐν τοῖς
φυτοῖς δὲ ὅλη πανταχοῦ ἐν ἑκάστῳ μέρει, οὕτως
καὶ ἡ ἐμὴ καὶ ἡ σὴ μία καὶ πᾶσαι μία; καὶ ἐπὶ
τοῦ παντὸς ἡ ἐν πᾶσι μία οὐχ ὡς ὄγκῳ μεμερισμένη,
ἀλλὰ πανταχοῦ ταὐτόν; διὰ τί γὰρ ἡ ἐν ἐμοὶ μία,
10 ἡ δ' ἐν τῷ παντὶ οὐ μία; οὐ γὰρ ὄγκος οὐδὲ ἐκεῖ
οὐδὲ σῶμα. εἰ μὲν οὖν ἐκ τῆς τοῦ παντὸς καὶ ἡ
ἐμὴ καὶ ἡ σή, μία δὲ ἐκείνη, καὶ ταύτας δεῖ εἶναι
μίαν. εἰ δὲ καὶ ἡ τοῦ παντὸς καὶ ἡ ἐμὴ ἐκ ψυχῆς
μιᾶς, πάλιν αὖ πᾶσαι μία. αὕτη τοίνυν τίς ἡ μία;
15 ἀλλὰ πρότερον λεκτέον, εἰ ὀρθῶς λέγεται τὸ μίαν
τὰς πάσας, ὥσπερ ἡ ἑνὸς ἑκάστου. ἄτοπον γάρ, εἰ
μία ἡ ἐμὴ καὶ ἡ ὁτουοῦν ἄλλου· ἐχρῆν γὰρ ἐμοῦ
αἰσθανομένου καὶ ἄλλον αἰσθάνεσθαι, καὶ ἀγαθοῦ
ὄντος ἀγαθὸν ἐκεῖνον εἶναι καὶ ἐπιθυμοῦντος ἐπιθυμεῖν, καὶ ὅλως ὁμοπαθεῖν ἡμᾶς τε πρὸς ἀλλήλους

428

IV. 9. IF ALL SOULS ARE ONE

1. Is it true that, just as we maintain that the soul of each individual is one because it is present as a whole at every point of the body, and is really one in this way, not having one part of it here and another there in the body, and in beings which have sense-perception the perceptive soul is there in this way, and in plants [the growth-soul] is present as a whole everywhere in each part; so in the same way my soul and your soul are one, and all the souls are one? And in the All is the soul in all things one, not as divided into parts by its mass, but one and the same thing everywhere? For why should my soul be one, but the soul in the universe not one? For there is no mass or body there either. Now if my soul and your soul come from the soul of the All, and that soul is one, these souls also must be one. But if the soul of the All and my soul come from one soul, again all souls are one. Well, then, what is this one soul? But, before this, we must discuss whether it is correct to say that all the souls are one soul, like the soul of each individual. For it would be absurd if my soul and anyone else's were one soul: for if I perceived anything another would have to perceive it too, and if I was good he would have to be good, and if I desired anything he would have to desire it, and in general we should have to have the same experiences as each other and as the All, so

καὶ πρὸς τὸ πᾶν, ὥστε ἐμοῦ παθόντος συναισθάνεσ-
20 θαι τὸ πᾶν. πῶς δὲ καὶ μιᾶς οὔσης ἡ μὲν λογική, ἡ
δὲ ἄλογος, καὶ ἡ μὲν ἐν ζῴοις, ἡ δὲ ἐν φυτοῖς ἄλλη;
πάλιν δὲ εἰ μὴ θησόμεθα ἐκείνως, τό τε πᾶν ἓν οὐκ
ἔσται, μία τε ἀρχὴ ψυχῶν οὐχ εὑρεθήσεται.

2. Πρῶτον μὲν οὖν οὐκ, εἰ ἡ ψυχὴ μία ἡ ἐμὴ καὶ
ἡ ἄλλου, ἤδη καὶ τὸ συναμφότερον τῷ συναμφοτέρῳ
ταὐτόν. ἐν ἄλλῳ γὰρ καὶ ἐν ἄλλῳ ταὐτὸν ὂν οὐ τὰ
αὐτὰ πάθη ἕξει ἐν ἑκατέρῳ, ὡς ἄνθρωπος ὁ ἐν ἐμοὶ
5 κινουμένῳ· ἐν ἐμοὶ γὰρ κινουμένῳ καὶ ἐν σοὶ μὴ
κινουμένῳ ἐν ἐμοὶ μὲν κινούμενος, ἐν σοὶ δὲ ἑστὼς
ἔσται· καὶ οὐκ ἄτοπον οὐδὲ παραδοξότερον τὸ ἐν
ἐμοὶ καὶ σοὶ ταὐτὸν εἶναι· οὐ δὴ ἀνάγκη αἰσθανομένου ἐμοῦ καὶ ἄλλον πάντη τὸ αὐτὸ πάθος ἔχειν.
οὐδὲ γὰρ ἐπὶ τοῦ ἑνὸς σώματος τὸ τῆς ἑτέρας χειρὸς
10 πάθημα ἡ ἑτέρα ᾔσθετο, ἀλλ' ἡ ἐν τῷ ὅλῳ. εἰ δὴ
ἔδει τὸ ἐμὸν γινώσκειν καὶ σέ, ἔν τι ἐξ ἀμφοῖν ὄν,
συνημμένον σῶμα ἐχρῆν εἶναι· οὕτω γὰρ συναφθεῖ-
σαι ἑκατέρα ᾔσθετο ταὐτόν. ἐνθυμεῖσθαι δὲ προσήκει τὸ καὶ πολλὰ λανθάνειν τὸ ὅλον καὶ τῶν ἐν
15 ἑνὶ καὶ τῷ αὐτῷ σώματι γιγνομένων, καὶ τοσούτῳ,
ὅσῳ ἂν μέγεθος ἔχῃ τὸ σῶμα πολύ, ὥσπερ ἐπὶ κη-
τῶν λέγεται μεγάλων, ἐφ' ὧν παθήματός τινος
περὶ τὸ μέρος ὄντος τῷ ὅλῳ αἴσθησις διὰ
μικρότητα τοῦ κινήματος οὐδεμία προσέρχεται·

that if I had an experience the All would share in the perception of it. And how, if there is [only] one soul, is one soul rational and another irrational, and one in animals but a different one in plants? But on the other hand, if we are not going to make that assumption, the All will not be one, and we shall not discover one principle of souls.

2. First of all, then, it is not true that, if my soul and someone else's are one soul, just for that reason my composite [of body and soul] is the same as his composite. For when something which is the same is both in one thing and in another it will not have the same experiences in each of them, as for instance the [form of] the human being in me when I am in motion: the form in me in motion and in you not in motion will be in motion in me and stationary in you; and there is nothing absurd, nothing really disconcerting about the same thing being in me and in you: it is certainly not necessary that when I have a perception the other also should have exactly the same experience. For even in one body one hand does not perceive what happens to the other, but the soul in the whole body. If you really had to know what happened to me because there was some one thing composed of both of us, it would have to be a joint body; for if they were joined together in this way each soul would have the same perceptions. But one ought to consider also that there are a great many things which the whole being does not notice, even among those which happen in one and the same body, and this is all the more so when the body is of great size, as they say happens with great sea-beasts, with whom, when a part is affected, no perception of it reaches the whole because of the

ὥστε οὐκ ἀνάγκη διάδηλον τύπῳ τὴν αἴσθησιν τῷ
20 ὅλῳ καὶ παντὶ εἰσαφικνεῖσθαι ἑνός τινος παθόντος.
ἀλλὰ συμπάσχειν μὲν οὐκ ἄτοπον οὐδὲ ἀπογνω-
στέον, τύπωσιν δὲ αἰσθητικὴν οὐκ ἀναγκαῖον
γίγνεσθαι. ἀρετὴν δὲ ἐν ἐμοὶ ἔχειν, κακίαν δὲ ἐν
ἑτέρῳ, οὐκ ἄτοπον, εἴπερ καὶ κινεῖσθαι ἐν ἄλλῳ
καὶ ἐν ἄλλῳ ἑστάναι ταὐτὸν οὐκ ἀδύνατον. οὐδὲ
25 γὰρ οὕτως μίαν λέγομεν, ὡς πάντη πλήθους
ἄμοιρον—τοῦτο γὰρ τῇ κρείττονι φύσει δοτέον—
ἀλλὰ μίαν καὶ πλῆθος λέγομεν καὶ μετέχειν τῆς
φύσεως τῆς περὶ τὰ σώματα μεριστῆς γινομένης καὶ τῆς ἀμερίστου αὖ, ὥστε πάλιν
εἶναι μίαν. ὥσπερ δὲ ἐπ' ἐμοῦ τὸ γενόμενον περὶ
30 τὸ μέρος πάθος οὐκ ἀνάγκη κρατεῖν τοῦ ὅλου, ὃ δ'
ἂν περὶ τὸ κυριώτερον γένηται φέρει τι εἰς τὸ
μέρος, οὕτω τὰ μὲν ἐκ τοῦ παντὸς εἰς ἕκαστον
σαφέστερα μᾶλλον ὁμοπαθούντων πολλαχοῦ τῷ
ὅλῳ, τὰ δὲ παρ' ἡμῶν ἄδηλον εἰ συντελεῖ πρὸς τὸ
ὅλον.

3. Καὶ μὴν ἐκ τῶν ἐναντίων φησὶν ὁ λόγος καὶ
συμπαθεῖν ἀλλήλοις ἡμᾶς καὶ συναλγοῦντας ἐκ
τοῦ ὁρᾶν καὶ διαχεομένους καὶ εἰς τὸ φιλεῖν

smallness of the disturbance; so that it is not necessary, when one part is affected, for a clearly impressed
perception to reach the total whole. But it is not
absurd, and we do not have to abandon the idea,
that the whole is jointly affected, but there is no
need for there to be a perceptible impression. And
it is not absurd that [the one soul] should possess
virtue in me, but vice in another man, since it is not
impossible for the same thing to be in motion in one
and at rest in another. For we do not say, either,
that it is one in such a way as to be altogether
without a share in multiplicity—this must be attributed to a higher nature—but we say that it is one
and a multiplicity, and participates in " that nature
which is divisible in the sphere of bodies ", and also
in the " indivisible nature ",[1] so that again it is one.
But just as in me the experience of a part need not
dominate the whole, but what happens to what is
more essential has an influence on the part, in the
same way the influences which come from the All
to the individual are more obvious, and we are often
affected in the same way as the whole, but it is not
clear whether what comes from us contributes anything to the whole.

3. Indeed, the argument deriving from facts opposed [to the assumption of complete separation of
souls] asserts that we do share each other's experiences
when we suffer with others from seeing their pain
and feel happy and relaxed [in their company] and

---

[1] The phrases from Plato's *Timaeus* 35A1-3 which provide
the starting-point for the earlier discussion in IV. 2 (4), the
much more careful and thorough discussion of the unity of
souls in IV. 3. (27) 1-8, and for many later Neoplatonic
discussions of the same subject.

ἑλκομένους κατὰ φύσιν· μήποτε γὰρ τὸ φιλεῖν
5 διὰ τοῦτο. εἰ δὲ καὶ ἐπῳδαὶ καὶ ὅλως μαγεῖαι
συνάγουσι καὶ συμπαθεῖς πόρρωθεν ποιοῦσι, πάντως
τοι διὰ ψυχῆς μιᾶς. καὶ λόγος δὲ ἠρέμα λεχθείς
διέθηκε τὸ πόρρω, καὶ κατακούειν πεποίηκε τὸ
διεστὼς ἀμήχανον ὅσον τόπον· ἐξ ὧν ἐστι τὴν
ἑνότητα μαθεῖν ἁπάντων τῆς ψυχῆς μιᾶς οὔσης.

10 Πῶς οὖν, εἰ ψυχὴ μία, ἡ μὲν λογική, ἡ δὲ
ἄλογος, καί τις καὶ φυτική; ἢ ὅτι τὸ μὲν ἀμέριστον
αὐτῆς κατὰ τὸ λογικὸν τακτέον οὐ μεριζόμενον
ἐν τοῖς σώμασι, τὸ δὲ μεριζόμενον περὶ σώματα
ἓν μὲν ὂν καὶ αὐτό, περὶ δὲ τὰ σώματα μεριζόμενον παρεχόμενον τὴν αἴσθησιν πανταχοῦ
15 ἄλλην δύναμιν αὐτῆς θετέον, τό τε πλαστικὸν
αὐτῆς καὶ ποιητικὸν σωμάτων δύναμιν ἄλλην.
οὐχ ὅτι δὲ πλείους αἱ δυνάμεις, οὐ μία· καὶ γὰρ
ἐν τῷ σπέρματι πλείους αἱ δυνάμεις καὶ ἕν· καὶ ἐξ
ἑνὸς τούτου πολλὰ ἕν. διὰ τί οὖν οὐ πανταχοῦ
20 πᾶσαι; καὶ γὰρ ἐπὶ τῆς μιᾶς ψυχῆς πανταχοῦ
λεγομένης εἶναι ἡ αἴσθησις οὐκ ἐν πᾶσι τοῖς
μέρεσιν ὁμοία, ὅ τε λόγος οὐκ ἐν ὅλῳ, τό τε
φυτικὸν καὶ ἐν οἷς μὴ αἴσθησις· καὶ ὅμως εἰς
ἓν ἀνατρέχει ἀποστάντα τοῦ σώματος. τὸ δὲ
θρεπτικόν, εἰ ἐκ τοῦ ὅλου, ἔχει καὶ ἐκείνης. διὰ
τί οὖν οὐ καὶ παρὰ τῆς ἡμετέρας ψυχῆς τὸ
25 θρεπτικόν; ὅτι τὸ τρεφόμενον μέρος τοῦ ὅλου, ὃ
καὶ παθητικῶς αἰσθητικόν, ἡ δὲ αἴσθησις ἡ

are naturally drawn to love them: for without a sharing of experience there could not be love for this reason. And if spells and magical acts in general draw men together and make them share experiences at a distance, this must be altogether due to the one soul. And a word spoken quietly acts on what is far off, and makes something separated by an enormous distance listen; from this one can learn the unity of all because their soul is one.

How then, if the soul is one, is one soul rational and another irrational, and one a mere principle of growth? It is because the indivisible part of it must be put on the rational level, and is not divided in bodies, but the part which is divided in the sphere of bodies is also itself one, but since it is divided in the sphere of bodies, when it supplies sense-perception in every part of the body this is to be counted as one of its powers, and its ability to shape and make bodies as another. Not because it has many powers is it not one: for in the seed there are many powers and it is one; and from this one come many units. Why then are not all souls everywhere? Well, in the case of the one soul which is said to be everywhere in the body, the sense-perception is not alike in all the parts, and the reason is not in the whole, and the growth-principle is also in the parts where there is no perception; and all the same it runs up into one when it leaves the body. But the nutritive power, if it comes from the whole, has also something from that [universal] soul. But why does not the nutritive power also come from our soul? Because what is nourished is a part of the whole, that which also is passively perceptive, but the perception which judges with intelligence belongs to the

κρίνουσα μετὰ νοῦ ἑκάστου, ᾗ οὐδὲν ἔδει πλάττειν
τὸ ὑπὸ τοῦ ὅλου τὴν πλάσιν ἔχον. ἐπεὶ κἂν
ἐποίησεν αὐτήν, εἰ μὴ ἐν τῷ ὅλῳ τούτῳ ἔδει
αὐτὴν εἶναι.

4. Ταῦτα μὲν οὖν εἴρηται ὡς μὴ θαυμάζειν τὴν
εἰς ἓν ἀναγωγήν. ἀλλὰ γὰρ ζητεῖ ὁ λόγος, πῶς
μία; ἆρα γὰρ ὡς ἀπὸ μιᾶς ἢ μία αἱ πᾶσαι; καὶ εἰ
ἀπὸ μιᾶς, μεριζομένης ταύτης ἢ μενούσης μὲν
5 ὅλης, ποιούσης δὲ παρ' αὑτῆς οὐδὲν ἧττον πολλάς;
καὶ πῶς ἂν μένουσα οὐσία πολλὰς ποιοῖ ἐξ αὑτῆς;
λέγωμεν οὖν θεὸν συλλήπτορα ἡμῖν γενέσθαι
παρακαλέσαντες, ὡς δεῖ μὲν εἶναι μίαν πρότερον,
εἴπερ πολλαί, καὶ ἐκ ταύτης τὰς πολλὰς εἶναι. εἰ
μὲν οὖν σῶμα εἴη, ἀνάγκη μεριζομένου τούτου τὰς
10 πολλὰς γίγνεσθαι, ἄλλην πάντη οὐσίαν, τὴν δὲ
ἄλλην γινομένην· καὶ ὁμοιομεροῦς οὔσης ὁμοειδεῖς
πάσας γενέσθαι εἶδος ἓν ταὐτὸν φερούσας ὅλον,
τοῖς δὲ ὄγκοις ἑτέρας· καὶ εἰ μὲν κατὰ τοὺς ὄγκους
εἶχον τοὺς ὑποκειμένους τὸ ψυχαὶ εἶναι, ἄλλας
15 ἀλλήλων εἶναι, εἰ δὲ κατὰ τὸ εἶδος, μίαν τῷ εἴδει
ψυχὰς εἶναι. τοῦτο δέ ἐστι τὸ μίαν καὶ τὴν αὐτὴν
ἐν πολλοῖς σώμασι ψυχὴν ὑπάρχειν καὶ πρὸ ταύτης
τῆς μιᾶς τῆς ἐν πολλοῖς ἄλλην αὖ εἶναι μὴ ἐν
πολλοῖς, ἀφ' ἧς ἡ ἐν πολλοῖς μία, ὥσπερ εἴδωλον
οὖσα πολλαχοῦ φερόμενον τῆς ἐν ἑνὶ μιᾶς, οἷον εἰ
20 ἐκ δακτυλίου ἑνὸς πολλοὶ κηροὶ τὸν αὐτὸν τύπον
ἀπομαξάμενοι φέροιεν. ἐκείνως μὲν οὖν ἀνηλίσκετο
ἂν εἰς πολλὰς ἡ μία, ὡς δὲ τὸ δεύτερον ἀσώματον

individual, and there was no need for this to shape
that which had its shaping from the All. It would
also have made this shaping, if it had not been
necessary for it to be in this All.

4. We have said this, then, to prevent astonishment at the bringing back of all souls to one. But
our discussion still wants to find out how they are
one. Is it because they all come from one or because
they all are one? And if they all come from one,
is this one divided or does it remain whole, but
none the less make many from itself? And how
could it continue to exist as a substance and make
many souls out of itself? Let us then call upon God
to be our helper and say that there must be one
which is prior, if there are many, and the many must
come from this. If then it was a body, it would be
necessary for the many to come into existence by
the division of this, each one becoming an entirely
different substance; and if the one soul was uniform
in all its parts, all the souls would be formally the
same, bearing one and the same complete form, but
would differ in their [corporeal] masses; and if
their soulness was due to their underlying masses,
they would be different from each other, but if it
was due to the form, the souls would be formally
the same. But this means that there is one and the
same soul in many bodies, and, before this one in
the many bodies, another again exists which is not
in many bodies, from which derives the one in the
many, which is like an image of the one in one pro-
jected in many places, as if many pieces of wax took
and bore the impression of one seal-ring. Now in the
former way the one soul would be used up in making
the many, but in the second way the soul would be

μὲν ἡ ψυχὴ ἐγίνετο. καὶ πάθημα μὲν ὂν θαυμαστὸν
οὐδὲν εἶχε μίαν ποιότητα γενομένην ἐξ ἑνός τινος
25 ἐν πολλοῖς εἶναι· καὶ εἰ κατὰ τὸ συναμφότερον δὲ
ἡ ψυχή, θαυμαστὸν οὐδέν. νῦν δὲ ἀσώματόν τε
αὐτὸ τιθέμεθα καὶ οὐσίαν.

5. Πῶς οὖν οὐσία μία ἐν πολλαῖς; ἢ γὰρ ἡ μία
ἐν πᾶσιν ὅλη, ἢ ἀπὸ ὅλης καὶ μιᾶς αἱ πολλαὶ
ἐκείνης μενούσης. ἐκείνη μὲν οὖν μία, αἱ δὲ
πολλαὶ εἰς ταύτην ὡς μίαν δοῦσαν ἑαυτὴν εἰς
5 πλῆθος καὶ οὐ δοῦσαν· ἱκανὴ γὰρ πᾶσι παρασχεῖν
ἑαυτὴν καὶ μένειν μία· δύναται γὰρ εἰς πάντα
ἅμα καὶ ἑκάστου οὐκ ἀποτέτμηται πάντη· τὸ αὐτὸ
οὖν ἐν πολλοῖς. μὴ δή τις ἀπιστείτω· καὶ γὰρ ἡ
ἐπιστήμη ὅλη, καὶ τὰ μέρη αὐτῆς ὡς μένειν τὴν
ὅλην καὶ ἀπ᾽ αὐτῆς τὰ μέρη. καὶ τὸ σπέρμα ὅλον
10 καὶ ἀπ᾽ αὐτοῦ τὰ μέρη, ἐν οἷς πέφυκε μερίζεσθαι,
καὶ ἕκαστον ὅλον καὶ μένει ὅλον οὐκ ἠλαττωμένον
τὸ ὅλον—ἡ δ᾽ ὕλη ἐμέρισε—καὶ πάντα ἕν. ἀλλ᾽
ἐν τῇ ἐπιστήμῃ, εἴποι τις ἄν, τὸ μέρος οὐχ ὅλον.
ἢ κἀκεῖ ἐνεργείᾳ μὲν μέρος τὸ προχειρισθὲν οὗ
χρεία, καὶ τοῦτο προτέτακται, ἕπεται μέντοι καὶ
15 τὰ ἄλλα δυνάμει λανθάνοντα καὶ ἔστι πάντα ἐν
τῷ μέρει. καὶ ἴσως ταύτῃ ἡ ὅλη λέγεται, τὸ δὲ
μέρος· ἐκεῖ μὲν οἷον ἐνεργείᾳ ἅμα πάντα· ἕτοιμον
οὖν ἕκαστον, ὃ προχειρίσασθαι θέλεις· ἐν δὲ τῷ

incorporeal. And, even if it was an affection, there would be nothing surprising in one quality being produced in many things from some one thing; and if the soul existed as a composition [of affection and substance] there would be nothing surprising. But as it is we suppose it to be incorporeal and a substance.

5. How, then, is there one substance in many souls? Either the one is present as a whole in them all, or the many come from the whole and one while it abides [unchanged]. That soul, then, is one, but the many [go back] to it as one which gives itself to multiplicity and does not give itself; for it is adequate to supply itself to all and to remain one; for it has power extending to all things, and is not at all cut off from each individual thing; it is the same, therefore, in all. Certainly, no one should disbelieve this; for knowledge is a whole, and its parts are such that the whole remains and the parts derive from it. And the seed is a whole and the parts into which it naturally divides derive from it, and each part is a whole and the whole remains an undiminished whole—but matter divides it—and all the parts are one. But someone might say that in knowledge the part is not a whole. Now there too that which has been brought into readiness because it is needed is an actualised part, and this part is put in front, but the other parts follow as unnoticed possibilities, and all are in the part [which is brought forward]. And perhaps this is the meaning of " whole " and " part " here: there [in the whole body of knowledge] all the parts are in a way actual at once; so each one which you wish to bring forward for use is ready; but in the part only that which is

μέρει τὸ ἕτοιμον, ἐνδυναμοῦται δὲ οἷον πλησιάσαν
20 τῷ ὅλῳ. ἔρημον δὲ τῶν ἄλλων θεωρημάτων οὐ
δεῖ νομίζειν· εἰ δὲ μή, ἔσται οὐκέτι τεχνικὸν οὐδὲ
ἐπιστημονικόν, ἀλλ᾿ ὥσπερ ἂν καὶ εἰ παῖς λέγοι.
εἰ οὖν ἐπιστημονικόν, ἔχει δυνάμει καὶ τὰ πάντα.
ἐπιστήσας γοῦν ὁ ἐπιστήμων ἐπάγει τὰ ἄλλα οἷον
ἀκολουθίᾳ· καὶ ὁ γεωμέτρης δὲ ἐν τῇ ἀναλύσει
25 δηλοῖ, ὡς τὸ ἓν ἔχει τὰ πρὸ αὐτοῦ πάντα, δι᾿ ὧν ἡ
ἀνάλυσις, καὶ τὰ ἐφεξῆς δέ, ἃ ἐξ αὐτοῦ γεννᾶται.
ἀλλὰ ταῦτα διὰ τὴν ἡμετέραν ἀσθένειαν ἀπιστεῖται,
καὶ διὰ τὸ σῶμα ἐπισκοτεῖται· ἐκεῖ δὲ φανὰ πάντα
καὶ ἕκαστον.

ready for use is actual; but it is given power by a
kind of approach to the whole. But one must not
think of it as isolated from all other rational specu-
lations; if one does, it will no longer be according to
art or knowledge, but just as if a child was talking.
If then it is according to knowledge, it contains also
all the other parts potentially. So then the knower
in knowing [one part] brings in all the others by a
kind of sequence; and the geometer in his analysis
makes clear that the one proposition contains all the
prior propositions by means of which the analysis is
made and the subsequent propositions which are
generated from it. But we do not believe all this
because of our weakness, and it is obscured by the
body; but There [in the intelligible world] all and
each shine out.

THE LOEB CLASSICAL LIBRARY

VOLUMES ALREADY PUBLISHED

Latin Authors

AMMIANUS MARCELLINUS. Translated by J. C. Rolfe. 3 Vols.

APULEIUS: THE GOLDEN ASS (METAMORPHOSES). W. Adlington (1566). Revised by S. Gaselee.

ST. AUGUSTINE: CITY OF GOD. 7 Vols. Vol. I. G. E. McCracken. Vols. II and VII. W. M. Green. Vol. III. D. Wiesen. Vol. IV. P. Levine. Vol. V. E. M. Sanford and W. M. Green. Vol. VI. W. C. Greene.

ST. AUGUSTINE, CONFESSIONS OF. W. Watts (1631). 2 Vols.

ST. AUGUSTINE, SELECT LETTERS. J. H. Baxter.

AUSONIUS. H. G. Evelyn White. 2 Vols.

BEDE. J. E. King. 2 Vols.

BOETHIUS: TRACTS and DE CONSOLATIONE PHILOSOPHIAE. Rev. H. F. Stewart and E. K. Rand. Revised by S. J. Tester.

CAESAR: ALEXANDRIAN, AFRICAN and SPANISH WARS. A. G. Way.

CAESAR: CIVIL WARS. A. G. Peskett.

CAESAR: GALLIC WAR. H. J. Edwards.

CATO: DE RE RUSTICA. VARRO: DE RE RUSTICA. H. B. Ash and W. D. Hooper.

CATULLUS. F. W. Cornish. TIBULLUS. J. B. Postgate. PERVIGILIUM VENERIS. J. W. Mackail.

CELSUS: DE MEDICINA. W. G. Spencer. 3 Vols.

CICERO: BRUTUS and ORATOR. G. L. Hendrickson and H. M. Hubbell.

[CICERO]: AD HERENNIUM. H. Caplan.

CICERO: DE ORATORE, etc. 2 Vols. Vol. I. DE ORATORE, Books I and II. E. W. Sutton and H. Rackham. Vol. II. DE ORATORE, Book III. DE FATO; PARADOXA STOICORUM; DE PARTITIONE ORATORIA. H. Rackham.

CICERO: DE FINIBUS. H. Rackham.

CICERO: DE INVENTIONE, etc. H. M. Hubbell.

CICERO: DE NATURA DEORUM and ACADEMICA. H. Rackham.

CICERO: DE OFFICIIS. Walter Miller.

CICERO: DE REPUBLICA and DE LEGIBUS. Clinton W. Keyes.

CICERO: DE SENECTUTE, DE AMICITIA, DE DIVINATIONE. W. A. Falconer.

CICERO: IN CATILINAM, PRO FLACCO, PRO MURENA, PRO SULLA. New version by C. Macdonald.

CICERO: LETTERS TO ATTICUS. E. O. Winstedt. 3 Vols.

CICERO: LETTERS TO HIS FRIENDS. W. Glynn Williams, M. Cary, M. Henderson. 4 Vols.

CICERO: PHILIPPICS. W. C. A. Ker.

CICERO: PRO ARCHIA, POST REDITUM, DE DOMO, DE HARUS-PICUM RESPONSIS, PRO PLANCIO. N. H. Watts.

CICERO: PRO CAECINA, PRO LEGE MANILIA, PRO CLUENTIO, PRO RABIRIO. H. Grose Hodge.

CICERO: PRO CAELIO, DE PROVINCIIS CONSULARIBUS, PRO BALBO. R. Gardner.

CICERO: PRO MILONE, IN PISONEM, PRO SCAURO, PRO FONTEIO, PRO RABIRIO POSTUMO, PRO MARCELLO, PRO LIGARIO, PRO REGE DEIOTARO. N. H. Watts.

CICERO: PRO QUINCTIO, PRO ROSCIO AMERINO, PRO ROSCIO COMOEDO, CONTRA RULLUM. J. H. Freese.

CICERO: PRO SESTIO, IN VATINIUM. R. Gardner.

CICERO: TUSCULAN DISPUTATIONS. J. E. King.

CICERO: VERRINE ORATIONS. L. H. G. Greenwood. 2 Vols.

CLAUDIAN. M. Platnauer. 2 Vols.

COLUMELLA: DE RE RUSTICA. DE ARBORIBUS. H. B. Ash, E. S. Forster and E. Heffner. 3 Vols.

CURTIUS, Q.: HISTORY OF ALEXANDER. J. C. Rolfe. 2 Vols.

FLORUS. E. S. Forster.

FRONTINUS: STRATAGEMS and AQUEDUCTS. C. E. Bennett and M. B. McElwain.

FRONTO: CORRESPONDENCE. C. R. Haines. 2 Vols.

GELLIUS. J. C. Rolfe. 3 Vols.

HORACE: ODES and EPODES. C. E. Bennett.

HORACE: SATIRES, EPISTLES, ARS POETICA. H. R. Fairclough.

JEROME: SELECTED LETTERS. F. A. Wright.

JUVENAL and PERSIUS. G. G. Ramsay.

LIVY. B. O. Foster, F. G. Moore, Evan T. Sage, and A. C. Schlesinger and R. M. Geer (General Index). 14 Vols.

LUCAN. J. D. Duff.

LUCRETIUS. W. H. D. Rouse. Revised by M. F. Smith.

MANILIUS. G. P. Goold.

MARTIAL. W. C. A. Ker. 2 Vols. Revised by E. H. Warmington.

MINOR LATIN POETS: from PUBLILIUS SYRUS to RUTILIUS NAMATIANUS, including GRATTIUS, CALPURNIUS SICULUS, NEMESIANUS, AVIANUS and others, with "Aetna" and the "Phoenix." J. Wight Duff and Arnold M. Duff. 2 Vols.

MINUCIUS FELIX. Cf. TERTULLIAN.
NEPOS CORNELIUS. J. C. Rolfe.
OVID: THE ART OF LOVE and OTHER POEMS. J. H. Mosley.
Revised by G. P. Goold.
OVID: FASTI. Sir James G. Frazer
OVID: HEROIDES and AMORES. Grant Showerman. Revised
by G. P. Goold
OVID: METAMORPHOSES. F. J. Miller. 2 Vols. Vol. 1 revised
by G. P. Goold.
OVID: TRISTIA and EX PONTO. A. L. Wheeler.
PERSIUS. Cf. JUVENAL.
PERVIGILIUM VENERIS. Cf. CATULLUS.
PETRONIUS. M. Heseltine. SENECA: APOCOLOCYNTOSIS.
W. H. D. Rouse. Revised by E. H. Warmington.
PHAEDRUS and BABRIUS (Greek). B. E. Perry.
PLAUTUS. Paul Nixon. 5 Vols.
PLINY: LETTERS, PANEGYRICUS. Betty Radice. 2 Vols.
PLINY: NATURAL HISTORY. 10 Vols. Vols. I–V and IX. H.
Rackham. VI.–VIII. W. H. S. Jones. X. D. E. Eichholz.
PROPERTIUS. H. E. Butler.
PRUDENTIUS. H. J. Thomson. 2 Vols.
QUINTILIAN. H. E. Butler. 4 Vols.
REMAINS OF OLD LATIN. E. H. Warmington. 4 Vols. Vol. I.
(ENNIUS AND CAECILIUS) Vol. II. (LIVIUS, NAEVIUS
PACUVIUS, ACCIUS) Vol. III. (LUCILIUS and LAWS OF XII
TABLES) Vol. IV. (ARCHAIC INSCRIPTIONS)
RES GESTAE DIVI AUGUSTI. Cf. VELLEIUS PATERCULUS.
SALLUST. J. C. Rolfe.
SCRIPTORES HISTORIAE AUGUSTAE. D. Magie. 3 Vols.
SENECA, THE ELDER: CONTROVERSIAE, SUASORIAE. M.
Winterbottom. 2 Vols.
SENECA: APOCOLOCYNTOSIS. Cf. PETRONIUS.
SENECA: EPISTULAE MORALES. R. M. Gummere. 3 Vols.
SENECA: MORAL ESSAYS. J. W. Basore. 3 Vols.
SENECA: TRAGEDIES. F. J. Miller. 2 Vols.
SENECA: NATURALES QUAESTIONES. T. H. Corcoran. 2 Vols.
SIDONIUS: POEMS and LETTERS. W. B. Anderson. 2 Vols.
SILIUS ITALICUS. J. D. Duff. 2 Vols.
STATIUS. J. H. Mozley. 2 Vols.
SUETONIUS. J. C. Rolfe. 2 Vols.
TACITUS: DIALOGUS. Sir Wm. Peterson. AGRICOLA and
GERMANIA. Maurice Hutton. Revised by M. Winterbottom,
R. M. Ogilvie, E. H. Warmington.
TACITUS: HISTORIES and ANNALS. C. H. Moore and J. Jackson.
4 Vols.

3

TERENCE. John Sargeaunt. 2 Vols.

TERTULLIAN: APOLOGIA and DE SPECTACULIS. T. R. Glover. MINUCIUS FELIX. G. H. Rendall.

TIBULLUS. Cf. CATULLUS.

VALERIUS FLACCUS. J. H. Mozley.

VARRO: DE LINGUA LATINA. R. G. Kent. 2 Vols.

VELLEIUS PATERCULUS and RES GESTAE DIVI AUGUSTI. F. W. Shipley.

VIRGIL. H. R. Fairclough. 2 Vols.

VITRUVIUS: DE ARCHITECTURA. F. Granger. 2 Vols.

Greek Authors

ACHILLES TATIUS. S. Gaselee.

AELIAN: ON THE NATURE OF ANIMALS. A. F. Scholfield. 3 Vols.

AENEAS TACTICUS. ASCLEPIODOTUS and ONASANDER. The Illinois Greek Club.

AESCHINES. C. D. Adams.

AESCHYLUS. H. Weir Smyth. 2 Vols.

ALCIPHRON, AELIAN, PHILOSTRATUS: LETTERS. A. R. Benner and F. H. Fobes.

ANDOCIDES, ANTIPHON. Cf. MINOR ATTIC ORATORS.

APOLLODORUS. Sir James G. Frazer. 2 Vols.

APOLLONIUS RHODIUS. R. C. Seaton.

APOSTOLIC FATHERS. Kirsopp Lake. 2 Vols.

APPIAN: ROMAN HISTORY. Horace White. 4 Vols.

ARATUS. Cf. CALLIMACHUS.

ARISTIDES: ORATIONS. C. A. Behr. Vol. I.

ARISTOPHANES. Benjamin Bickley Rogers. 3 Vols. Verse trans.

ARISTOTLE: ART OF RHETORIC. J. H. Freese.

ARISTOTLE: ATHENIAN CONSTITUTION, EUDEMIAN ETHICS, VICES AND VIRTUES. H. Rackham.

ARISTOTLE: GENERATION OF ANIMALS. A. L. Peck.

ARISTOTLE: HISTORIA ANIMALIUM. A. L. Peck. Vols. I.–II.

ARISTOTLE: METAPHYSICS. H. Tredennick. 2 Vols.

ARISTOTLE: METEOROLOGICA. H. D. P. Lee.

ARISTOTLE: MINOR WORKS. W. S. Hett. On Colours, On Things Heard, On Physiognomies, On Plants, On Marvellous Things Heard, Mechanical Problems, On Indivisible Lines, On Situations and Names of Winds, On Melissus, Xenophanes, and Gorgias.

ARISTOTLE: NICOMACHEAN ETHICS. H. Rackham.

ARISTOTLE: OECONOMICA and MAGNA MORALIA. G. C. Armstrong (with METAPHYSICS, Vol. II).

ARISTOTLE: ON THE HEAVENS. W. K. C. Guthrie.

ARISTOTLE: ON THE SOUL, PARVA NATURALIA, ON BREATH. W. S. Hett.

ARISTOTLE: CATEGORIES, ON INTERPRETATION, PRIOR ANALYTICS. H. P. Cooke and H. Tredennick.

ARISTOTLE: POSTERIOR ANALYTICS, TOPICS. H. Tredennick and E. S. Forster.

ARISTOTLE: ON SOPHISTICAL REFUTATIONS.
On Coming to be and Passing Away, On the Cosmos. E. S. Forster and D. J. Furley.

ARISTOTLE: PARTS OF ANIMALS. A. L. Peck; MOTION AND PROGRESSION OF ANIMALS. E. S. Forster.

ARISTOTLE: PHYSICS. Rev. P. Wicksteed and F. M. Cornford. 2 Vols.

ARISTOTLE: POETICS and LONGINUS. W. Hamilton Fyfe; DEMETRIUS ON STYLE. W. Rhys Roberts.

ARISTOTLE: POLITICS. H. Rackham.

ARISTOTLE: PROBLEMS. W. S. Hett. 2 Vols.

ARISTOTLE: RHETORICA AD ALEXANDRUM (with PROBLEMS. Vol. II). H. Rackham.

ARRIAN: HISTORY OF ALEXANDER and INDICA. Rev. E. Iliffe Robson. 2 Vols. New version P. Brunt.

ATHENAEUS: DEIPNOSOPHISTAE. C. B. Gulick. 7 Vols.

BABRIUS AND PHAEDRUS (Latin). B. E. Perry.

ST. BASIL: LETTERS. R. J. Deferrari. 4 Vols.

CALLIMACHUS: FRAGMENTS. C. A. Trypanis. MUSAEUS: HERO AND LEANDER. T. Gelzer and C. Whitman.

CALLIMACHUS, Hymns and Epigrams, and LYCOPHRON. A. W. Mair; ARATUS. G. R. Mair.

CLEMENT OF ALEXANDRIA. Rev. G. W. Butterworth.

COLLUTHUS. Cf. OPPIAN.

DAPHNIS AND CHLOE. Thornley's Translation revised by J. M. Edmonds: and PARTHENIUS. S. Gaselee.

DEMOSTHENES I.: OLYNTHIACS, PHILIPPICS and MINOR ORATIONS I.–XVII. AND XX. J. H. Vince.

DEMOSTHENES II.: DE CORONA and DE FALSA LEGATIONE. C. A. Vince and J. H. Vince.

DEMOSTHENES III.: MEIDIAS, ANDROTION, ARISTOCRATES, TIMOCRATES and ARISTOGEITON I. and II. J. H. Vince.

DEMOSTHENES IV.–VI: PRIVATE ORATIONS and IN NEAERAM. A. T. Murray.

DEMOSTHENES VII: FUNERAL SPEECH, EROTIC ESSAY, EXORDIA and LETTERS. N. W. and N. J. DeWitt.

DIO CASSIUS: ROMAN HISTORY. E. Cary. 9 Vols.

DIO CHRYSOSTOM. J. W. Cohoon and H. Lamar Crosby. 5 Vols.

DIODORUS SICULUS. 12 Vols. Vols. I.–VI. C. H. Oldfather. Vol. VII. C. L. Sherman. Vol. VIII. C. B. Welles. Vols. IX. and X. R. M. Geer. Vol. XI. F. Walton. Vol. XII. F. Walton. General Index. R. M. Geer.

DIOGENES LAERTIUS. R. D. Hicks. 2 Vols. New Introduction by H. S. Long.

DIONYSIUS OF HALICARNASSUS: ROMAN ANTIQUITIES. Spelman's translation revised by E. Cary. 7 Vols.

DIONYSIUS OF HALICARNASSUS: CRITICAL ESSAYS. S. Usher. 2 Vols. Vol. I.

EPICTETUS. W. A. Oldfather. 2 Vols.

EURIPIDES. A. S. Way. 4 Vols. Verse trans.

EUSEBIUS: ECCLESIASTICAL HISTORY. Kirsopp Lake and J. E. L. Oulton. 2 Vols.

GALEN: ON THE NATURAL FACULTIES. A. J. Brock.

GREEK ANTHOLOGY. W. R. Paton. 5 Vols.

GREEK BUCOLIC POETS (THEOCRITUS, BION, MOSCHUS). J. M. Edmonds.

GREEK ELEGY AND IAMBUS with the ANACREONTEA. J. M. Edmonds. 2 Vols.

GREEK LYRIC. D. A. Campbell. 4 Vols. Vol. I.

GREEK MATHEMATICAL WORKS. Ivor Thomas. 2 Vols.

HERODES. Cf. THEOPHRASTUS: CHARACTERS.

HERODIAN. C. R. Whittaker. 2 Vols.

HERODOTUS. A. D. Godley. 4 Vols.

HESIOD AND THE HOMERIC HYMNS. H. G. Evelyn White.

HIPPOCRATES and the FRAGMENTS OF HERACLEITUS. W. H. S. Jones and E. T. Withington. 4 Vols.

HOMER: ILIAD. A. T. Murray. 2 Vols.

HOMER: ODYSSEY. A. T. Murray. 2 Vols.

ISAEUS. E. W. Forster.

ISOCRATES. George Norlin and LaRue Van Hook. 3 Vols.

[ST. JOHN DAMASCENE]: BARLAAM AND IOASAPH. Rev. G. R. Woodward, Harold Mattingly and D. M. Lang.

JOSEPHUS. 10 Vols. Vols. I.–IV. H. Thackeray. Vol. V. H. Thackeray and R. Marcus. Vols. VI.–VII. R. Marcus. Vol. VIII. R. Marcus and Allen Wikgren. Vols. IX.–X. L. H. Feldman.

JULIAN. Wilmer Cave Wright. 3 Vols.

LIBANIUS. A. F. Norman. 3 Vols. Vols. I.–II.

LUCIAN. 8 Vols. Vols. I.–V. A. M. Harmon. Vol. VI. K. Kilburn. Vols. VII.–VIII. M. D. Macleod.

LYCOPHRON. Cf. CALLIMACHUS.

LYRA GRAECA, J. M. Edmonds. 2 Vols.

LYSIAS. W. R. M. Lamb.

MANETHO. W. G. Waddell.

MARCUS AURELIUS. C. R. Haines.

MENANDER. W. G. Arnott. 3 Vols. Vol. I.

MINOR ATTIC ORATORS (ANTIPHON, ANDOCIDES, LYCURGUS, DEMADES, DINARCHUS, HYPERIDES). K. J. Maidment and J. O. Burtt. 2 Vols.

MUSAEUS: HERO AND LEANDER. Cf. CALLIMACHUS.

NONNOS: DIONYSIACA. W. H. D. Rouse. 3 Vols.

OPPIAN, COLLUTHUS, TRYPHIODORUS. A. W. Mair.

PAPYRI. NON-LITERARY SELECTIONS. A. S. Hunt and C. C. Edgar. 2 Vols. LITERARY SELECTIONS (Poetry). D. L. Page.

PARTHENIUS. Cf. DAPHNIS and CHLOE.

PAUSANIAS: DESCRIPTION OF GREECE. W. H. S. Jones. 4 Vols. and Companion Vol. arranged by R. E. Wycherley.

PHILO. 10 Vols. Vols. I.–V. F. H. Colson and Rev. G. H. Whitaker. Vols. VI.–IX. F. H. Colson. Vol. X. F. H. Colson and the Rev. J. W. Earp.

PHILO: two supplementary Vols. (*Translation only.*) Ralph Marcus.

PHILOSTRATUS: THE LIFE OF APOLLONIUS OF TYANA. F. C. Conybeare. 2 Vols.

PHILOSTRATUS: IMAGINES; CALLISTRATUS: DESCRIPTIONS. A. Fairbanks.

PHILOSTRATUS and EUNAPIUS: LIVES OF THE SOPHISTS. Wilmer Cave Wright.

PINDAR. Sir J. E. Sandys.

PLATO: CHARMIDES, ALCIBIADES, HIPPARCHUS, THE LOVERS, THEAGES, MINOS and EPINOMIS. W. R. M. Lamb.

PLATO: CRATYLUS, PARMENIDES, GREATER HIPPIAS, LESSER HIPPIAS. H. N. Fowler.

PLATO: EUTHYPHRO, APOLOGY, CRITO, PHAEDO, PHAEDRUS, H. N. Fowler.

PLATO: LACHES, PROTAGORAS, MENO, EUTHYDEMUS. W. R. M. Lamb.

PLATO: LAWS. Rev. R. G. Bury. 2 Vols.

PLATO: LYSIS, SYMPOSIUM, GORGIAS. W. R. M. Lamb.

PLATO: Republic. Paul Shorey. 2 Vols.

PLATO: STATESMAN, PHILEBUS. H. N. Fowler; ION. W. R. M. Lamb.

PLATO: THEAETETUS and SOPHIST. H. N. Fowler.

PLATO: TIMAEUS, CRITIAS, CLITOPHO, MENEXENUS, EPISTULAE. Rev. R. G. Bury.

PLOTINUS: A. H. Armstrong. 7 Vols. Vols. I.–V.

PLUTARCH: MORALIA. 16 Vols. Vols I.–V. F. C. Babbitt.
Vol. VI. W. C. Helmbold. Vols. VII. and XIV. P. H. De
Lacy and B. Einarson. Vol. VIII. P. A. Clement and H. B.
Hoffleit. Vol. IX. E. L. Minar, Jr., F. H. Sandbach, W. C.
Helmbold. Vol. X. H. N. Fowler. Vol. XI. L. Pearson
and F. H. Sandbach. Vol. XII. H. Cherniss and W. C.
Helmbold. Vol. XIII 1–2. H. Cherniss. Vol. XV. F. H.
Sandbach.

PLUTARCH: THE PARALLEL LIVES. B. Perrin. 11 Vols.

POLYBIUS. W. R. Paton. 6 Vols.

PROCOPIUS. H. B. Dewing. 7 Vols.

PTOLEMY: TETRABIBLOS. F. E. Robbins.

QUINTUS SMYRNAEUS. A. S. Way. Verse trans.

SEXTUS EMPIRICUS. Rev. R. G. Bury. 4 Vols.

SOPHOCLES. F. Storr. 2 Vols. Verse trans.

STRABO: GEOGRAPHY. Horace L. Jones. 8 Vols.

THEOCRITUS. Cf. GREEK BUCOLIC POETS.

THEOPHRASTUS: CHARACTERS. J. M. Edmonds. HERODES,
etc. A. D. Knox.

THEOPHRASTUS: ENQUIRY INTO PLANTS. Sir Arthur Hort,
Bart. 2 Vols.

THEOPHRASTUS: DE CAUSIS PLANTARUM. G. K. K. Link and
B. Einarson. 3 Vols. Vol. I.

THUCYDIDES. C. F. Smith. 4 Vols.

TRYPHIODORUS. Cf. OPPIAN.

XENOPHON: CYROPAEDIA. Walter Miller. 2 Vols.

XENOPHON: HELLENCIA. C. L. Brownson. 2 Vols.

XENOPHON: ANABASIS. C. L. Brownson.

XENOPHON: MEMORABILIA AND OECONOMICUS. E. C. Marchant.
SYMPOSIUM AND APOLOGY. O. J. Todd.

XENOPHON: SCRIPTA MINORA. E. C. Marchant. CONSTITU-
TION OF THE ATHENIANS. G. W. Bowersock.